RUSSIAN MUSIC STUDIES

Malcolm Hamrick Brown, founding editor

Musical Cultures in Seventeenth-Century Russia

Claudia R. Jensen

Indiana University Press

Bloomington & Indianapolis

This book is a publication of

Indiana University Press
601 North Morton Street
Bloomington, IN 47404-3797 USA

www.iupress.indiana.edu

Telephone orders	800-842-6796
Fax orders	812-855-7931
Orders by e-mail	iuporder@indiana.edu

♾ The paper used in this publication meets the
minimum requirements of the American National
Standard for Information Sciences—Permanence of
Paper for Printed Library Materials,
ANSI Z39.48-1992.

Manufactured in the United States of America

Library of Congress Cataloging-in-Publication Data

Jensen, Claudia Rae.
Musical cultures in seventeenth-century Russia / Claudia R. Jensen.
p. cm. — (Russian music studies)
Includes bibliographical references and index.
ISBN 978-0-253-35354-2 (cloth : alk. paper)
1. Music—Social aspects—Russia—History—17th century.
2. Music—Russia—17th century—History and criticism. I. Title.
ML3917.R8J46 2009
780.947′09032—dc22
2009017095

1 2 3 4 5   14 13 12 11 10 09

To Dan—teacher, mentor, and friend—with many thanks.

Contents

Acknowledgments · *ix*

List of Abbreviations · *xi*

Introduction: The New Patriarch · *1*

ONE

The True False Dmitrii and the Death of Music in Moscow · *10*

TWO

"Wondrous singers and exceptional voices": Singers and
Singing in Muscovy · *25*

THREE

"Sweet and harmonious singing": Domestic Singers and
Domestic Singing · *57*

FOUR

Tavern and Wedding: The Instrumental Traditions at the
Muscovite Court · *77*

FIVE

Nikolai Diletskii: Language and Imagery in
Muscovite Music Theory · *105*

SIX

The Muscovite Court Theater · *163*

Epilogue. Reversing Our Gaze: A Case Study · *212*

Appendix · *225*

Notes · *229*

Bibliography · *311*

Index · *343*

Acknowledgments

It is truly a pleasure to acknowledge the many people who have helped, explained, encouraged, and read these chapters in many forms over many years. Daniel Waugh has been a teacher, an advisor, and a very patient friend for more than twenty years; any insights that have found their way into this book are largely due to his efforts. Elena Dubinets read every word of this book more than once, explained more Russian than I care to admit, and sustained my momentum when it was most needed; Deborah Pierce was an equally tireless reader and supporter. Gregory Myers and the late Miloš Velimirović shared their expertise on liturgical matters with extraordinary generosity and patience—I am profoundly sorry that I will not be able to put a copy of this book into Mish's hands. We all miss him tremendously. Evgenii Vorob'ev's expertise in the mysteries of Muscovite music theory was shared with graciousness and abundance; this work would have been far poorer without his advice. Bob Fradkin, linguist extraordinaire, put up with endless "final" e-mails covering a multitude of languages, and Russell Martin shared his knowledge of Muscovite source material and wedding practices. Hans Rothe generously provided a copy of the earliest Muscovite *kant* source (RGB, f. 178, No. 10944), and Martha Lahana was equally generous with her important source discoveries, sending me a copy of the crucial Swedish material describing the Orpheus production in Moscow and supplying the Latin text of the important account by Jacob Reutenfels. Ruth Petersky and David Williamson both gave vital help in deciphering the difficult German describing this event—Ruth's ingenious solutions contributed greatly to chapter 6. Michael Biggins, at the University of Washington's Suzzallo Library, was able to find any source at any time, and he added to this a linguistic expertise that I exploited mercilessly. George-Julius Papadopoulos, Wanda Griffiths, and Ben Albritton all gave advice and support, reading documents and clarifying sources whenever I asked. I am most grateful to the University of Washington's Department of Slavic Languages and Literatures, which gave me crucial support at a crucial time (especially Galya Diment, James Augerot, Barbara Henry, and Katarzyna Dziwirek), and to the ever-willing staff of the Inter-Library Borrowing services. I am grateful to Valerie Kivelson for her insights into the hymn text discussed in chapter 6, and to John Hall for sharing his expertise in *skomorokhi*. My evolving thinking on Muscovite music has certainly been influenced by my work on Nikolai Findeizen's monumental study of Russian music, and I am grateful to Malcolm Brown's tireless efforts in that context to sharpen my thinking and my prose, and for his many important suggestions for this monograph. My thanks also go to Vladimir Morosan for his gracious generosity in allowing me to use musical examples issued by his Musica Russica Press, and to the wonderfully meticulous work by copy editor Maureen Epp. I was fortunate to have studied with the late Vladimir Protopopov at the Moscow Conservatory under the auspices of a grant provided by the International Research and Exchanges Board. Finally, this work would not have been completed without the generous support of the National Endowment for the Humanities during the 2004–2005 academic year. My family—Brad, Anna, and Becky—offered unending patience and support, as they always do.

Abbreviations

AAE	*Akty, sobrannye v bibliotekakh i arkhivakh Rossiiskoi imperii Arkheograficheskoi ekspeditsiei Akademii nauk,* 4 vols. (St. Petersburg: V Tip. II-go otdeleniia Sobstvennoi E. I. V. kantseliarii, 1841–42)
ChOIDR	*Chteniia v Imperatorskom obshchestve istorii i drevnostei rossiiskikh pri Moskovskom universitete*
DAI	*Dopolneniia k Aktam istoricheskim,* vol. 5 (St. Petersburg: Arkheograficheskaia komissiia, 1842)
DLB	*Oxford Dictionary of Literary Biography*
DNB	*Dictionary of National Biography*
DR	*Dvortsovye razriady,* 4 vols. (St. Petersburg: V Tip. II-go otdeleniia Sobstvennoi E. I. V. kantseliarii, 1850–55)
DRV	*Drevniaia rossiiskaia vivliofika,* ed. N. I. Novikov, 2nd ed. (Moscow: Tip. Kompanii tipograficheskoi, 1788–91)
IRM	*Istoriia russkoi muzyki v desiati tomakh,* ed. Iu. V. Keldysh and others, vols. 1 and 2 (Moscow: Muzyka, 1983 and 1984)
MERSH	*Modern Encyclopedia of Russian and Soviet History*
MP	*Muzykal'nyi Peterburg: Entsiklopedicheskii slovar',* ed. A. L. Porfir'eva and others (St. Petersburg: Kompozitor, 1996–)

NG2	*New Grove Dictionary of Music and Musicians,* 2nd ed., 2001; available online at www.grovemusic.com
OLDP	*Obshchestvo liubitelei drevnei pis'mennosti;* various series, as listed
PDS	*Pamiatniki diplomaticheskikh snoshenii Drevnei Rossii s derzhavami inostrannymi,* 10 vols. (St. Petersburg: V Tip. II-go otdeleniia Sobstvennoi E. I. V. kantseliarii, 1851–71)
PKNO	*Pamiatniki kul'tury. Novye otkrytiia*
PLDR	*Pamiatniki literatury Drevnei Rusi*
PRMI	*Pamiatniki russkogo muzykal'nogo iskusstva*
RBS	*Russkii biograficheskii slovar',* 25 vols. (St. Petersburg: Izdanie Imperatorskogo Russkogo istoricheskogo obshchestva, 1896–1918)
RIB	*Russkaia istoricheskaia biblioteka,* 39 vols. (St. Petersburg: Arkheograficheskaia komissiia, 1872–1927)
RRD	*Ranniaia russkaia dramaturgiia XVII–pervaia polovina XVIII v.,* ed. A. N. Robinson and others, 5 vols. (Moscow: Nauka, 1972–76)
SEER	*Slavonic and East European Review*
SGGD	*Sobranie gosudarstvennykh gramot i dogovorov,* 5 vols. (Moscow: Tip. N. S. Vsevolozhskogo, 1813–94)
SKK	*Slovar' knizhnikov i knizhnosti Drevnei Rusi*
SM	*Sovetskaia muzyka.* Moscow, 1933–91; continued by *Muzykal'naia akademiia,* 1992–
TKDA	*Trudy Kievskoi dukhovnoi akademii*
TODRL	*Trudy Otdela drevnerusskoi literatury Instituta russkoi literatury*
V-K 1642–1644 gg.	*Vesti-kuranty 1642–1644 gg.,* ed. N. I. Tarabasova, V. G. Dem'ianov, and A. I. Sumkina (Moscow: Nauka, 1976)
V-K 1645–1646, 1648 gg.	*Vesti-kuranty 1645–1646, 1648 gg.,* ed. N. I. Tarabasova and V. G. Dem'ianov (Moscow: Nauka, 1980)
V-K 1648–1650 gg.	*Vesti-kuranty 1648–1650 gg.,* ed. V. G. Dem'ianov and R. V. Bakhturina (Moscow: Nauka, 1983)
ZhMNP	*Zhurnal Ministerstva narodnogo prosveshcheniia*

Musical Cultures in Seventeenth-Century Russia

Introduction

The New Patriarch

Early in 1589, in a procession glittering with gold and gemstones and perfumed with incense, the first Russian patriarch was installed by the highest-ranking dignitary of the Eastern Church, Hieremias, Patriarch of Constantinople. It was a glorious moment for the Muscovite church. Although by the late sixteenth century Muscovite Russia was the wealthiest and most powerful state in the Orthodox world, it had no patriarchal seat of its own, and its leaders, secular and spiritual alike, were growing increasingly dissatisfied with this second-rate status. The new patriarchate was thus an important acknowledgment of both Russian piety and Russian power. The ceremonies surrounding the creation of this new office were described vividly by one of the foreign participants, Arsenios of Elasson (1550–1626), a Greek cleric who had already spent several years in Muscovy and Ukraine.[1] His observations show that this momentous event was replete with music, encapsulating the most important styles, trends, and performers in late sixteenth-century Muscovite liturgical practice.

There was singing at nearly every step of the celebrations. Each of the principals, Tsar Fedor Ivanovich (r. 1584–98), Patriarch Hieremias of Constantinople, and the new Patriarch Iov, was accompanied by a special singing ensemble, and there were additional singers associated with other important hierarchs, for example the newly elevated Aleksandr, Metropolitan of Novgorod.[2] At the installation ceremony itself, held at the Uspenskii (Dormition) Cathedral in the Kremlin, the Divine Liturgy was celebrated by both patriarchs and by both of their singing ensembles. The Greek singers took the lead on several occasions, headed by a specialist, the great *domestikos* Paschales from Constantinople, who was part of the visiting delegation.[3] Russian and Greek singers from all three choirs sang together at the special ceremony of enthronement, during which the new patriarch was seated and then raised from his seat three times by participating clergy. The text they sang was the "Ispolaeti despota," a loose transliteration of the Greek benediction "Eís pollá étē, déspota" that appears frequently in Russian sources; in Russian this is called a *mnogoletie*, or Many Years. Here and elsewhere, the Russian accounts specify that the first or great rank (*bol'shaia stanitsa*) of the new patriarch's choir performed. The large Russian choral ensembles were divided into hierarchical units or ranks called *stanitsy*, each with several singers, and this ordering was preserved for the new patriarchal ensemble (comprising, presumably, the former Metropolitan Iov's singers).

The Russian and Greek singers also performed together outside the church, particularly at the several banquets that were held after the ceremony. These were sumptuous affairs, and Arsenios describes in loving detail the quantities of gold plate and the endless presentation of food and drink supplied by the Russian hosts. The proceedings were further enlivened by performances of various hymns in both languages. At times, these performances amounted to a kind of elaborate sacred *Tafelmusik*. At one of the banquets, for example, Patriarch Iov's great *stanitsa* began by performing the hymn of praise for the Dormition of the Virgin, followed by the second rank of his singers performing a hymn for the Eve of the Dormition. Next, the Greek singers were requested to perform: "The Patriarchs consulted with one another and had Patriarch Hieremias's singer Dmitrii [Demetrios] and his companions sing in Greek." Finally, singers associated with the new Metropolitan of Novgorod performed, appropriately, a hymn to Novgorod's Ivan the Miracle Worker.[4]

The banquets concluded with the traditional and elaborate Muscovite toasts (called *chashi*, cups), each accompanied by a *mnogoletie* as well as by special hymns. The toasts formed yet another suite of musical performances. The Tuesday banquet, for instance, included a toast to the Virgin and one to Peter the Miracle Worker, followed by a hymn. A toast was then offered to Tsar Fedor, which included a special hymn and a "great *mnogoletie*" performed by the sovereign's singers, and the same two types of pieces were performed at the final toast, to the tsar's wife, Tsaritsa Irina.[5]

The installation ceremony also provided an important occasion for singers from outside the capital city, for instance the Metropolitan of Novgorod's ensemble, to hear the Moscow singers and the visiting Greek performers. After about a week in Moscow, the Greek party went to the nearby Trinity-St. Sergius Monastery for several days, where there would have been a similar musical exchange. The Greek party took a singer with them to the monastery, and their brief stay there was marked by the normal and extensive rounds of liturgical singing.[6]

All the important musical elements of late sixteenth-century Muscovite liturgical life were thus in place at this 1589 ceremony. The daily worship cycle was filled with music—vocal music only, as the Orthodox Church did not, and does not, employ instruments in worship—performed by large organized ensembles of specialist singers, generally around twenty-five to thirty strong, attached to the leaders of state and church. Important local singing traditions had been forced to bow, at least to a certain degree, to the centralizing authority of Moscow by this date. Ivan IV ("the Terrible," r. 1533–84) had shipped many singers to his capital in Moscow, especially from the formerly independent city of Novgorod, which had its own intensely cultivated singing tradition.[7]

The repertoire of these ensembles was undergoing explosive growth, particularly in the second half of the sixteenth century, with new monophonic and polyphonic genres recorded in ever more precise notation and preserved in hundreds of manuscripts. New and existing musical settings were (for the most part) written to fit the eight-fold modal cycle, and theoretical works, mostly listings of neumes called *azbuki* (alphabets), focused on notation. New, named chant styles emerged throughout this period. The most important addition to the traditional chant repertoire (called *znamennyi* singing, from *znamia,* sign) was the virtuosic *demestvennyi* chant, preserved in monophonic and polyphonic settings that stand outside the eight-fold modal system.[8] Another type, the so-called Kazan' chant, seems to have been associated with Ivan IV and the group of composers assembled at his court, as was *bol'shoi raspev* (great or elaborate singing, another highly melismatic style). These and other new chant dialects and singing styles were not uniformly accepted, and polemical works particularly decried what their authors considered to be uselessly ornate performances preferred by the specialist singers, whose virtuosity obscured the sacred texts. As the monk Evfrosin wrote in the mid-seventeenth century: "We only fill the air with shouting and chirping . . . In our singing we only decorate the voice . . . while thoroughly crippling the sacred words . . .ʺ⁹ The issue of the relationship between words, especially the sacred words of liturgical texts, and music was to echo throughout the seventeenth century.

Arsenios's experiences in Russia also foreshadow the tumultuous liturgical reforms that would take place in the mid-seventeenth century. Arsenios remained in Russia after the 1589 ceremony, and one of his continuing functions was to act as mediator, explaining the differences that had evolved among the various Orthodox practices. This was his role in 1619, when Theophanes, Patriarch of Jerusalem, visited Russia for the familiar purpose of collecting alms. The foreign party celebrated the Divine Liturgy along with some Russian clerics, singing in Greek and following what were to the Russian observers unfamiliar and disturbing liturgical practices. The Russian hosts promptly summoned Arsenios, who was able to provide appropriate translation and guidance for the visitors.[10] These differences in musical practice set the stage for some of the modest theological investigations and emendations directed by the Russian Patriarch Filaret in the 1620s, and hint at the more extensive and, ultimately, divisive reforms undertaken three decades later by Patriarch Nikon, who instituted wide-ranging changes based on observation of just such divergent practices.[11]

Liturgical singing, however, was not the only music to sound out at the Muscovite court during Arsenios's stay there. Arsenios himself mentions military-style fanfare or processional music, as do many other visitors. The English trade representative Giles Fletcher, who gave his readers a brief (and somewhat confused) account of Iov's elevation to the newly created patriarchal seat, reported that Tsar Fedor also enjoyed other kinds of musical entertainment, particularly singing "after the Ruse manner" by the court dwarves and tumblers. Another English agent, Jerome Horsey, brought a collection of keyboard instruments to Fedor's court. The tsar and his wife marveled at their beauty, and performances by members of the English party, at least according to Horsey's notoriously self-serving account, were immensely popular.[12]

Judging from pervasive complaints enumerated at the Stoglav Council (a mid-sixteenth-century church conference whose resolutions were produced in a book of one hundred chapters, or *sto glav*), far less savory music also echoed throughout the Russian countryside, in cities, and at the court itself. This music, both vocal and instrumental, is generally associated in contemporary documents with the *skomorokhi*, itinerant *jongleur*-type entertainers whose pervasive presence forms a continuing theme in denunciations from church hierarchs throughout the sixteenth and seventeenth centuries. Not only were the *skomorokhi* guilty of inappropriate and suggestive games, dances, and songs, but their use of musical instruments, forbidden in church, made their activities even more suspect. They had been active at Tsar Ivan's court; indeed, Ivan collected not only church singers from Novgorod but also *skomorokhi*, who had been particularly concentrated in that northern city. Their music frequently formed part of Ivan's entertainment. Prince Andrei Kurbskii, a former advisor to Tsar Ivan, for example, accused the ruler of favoring "*skomorokhi* who played the *dudka* [a pipe] and sang ungodly songs."[13]

Skomorokh antics were especially offensive to the authorities because they focused on (although were certainly not limited to) some of the landmark events the church considered its domain: weddings, funerals, and important church holidays.[14] Even foreign observers were aware of *skomorokh* participation. An account of a 1557 voyage made by Anthony Jenkinson, one of the early English representatives of the Russia Company, describes the raucous celebration of a Russian wedding following the official church ceremony: "When they come home, the wife is set at the upper end of the table, and the husband next unto her: they fall then to drinking till they bee all drunke, they perchance have a minstrell or two, and two naked men, which led her from the Church daunce naked a long time before all the companie."[15] Funerals were not exempt from such ancient and obviously non-Orthodox associations. At the end of his trip to Russia, Patriarch Theophanes of Jerusalem issued an edict that appears to summarize his experiences in both Muscovy and Ukraine, laying out several specific objections to practices he had observed, including one relating to memorial services. He had taken note of the presence of music—apparently instrumental music—and food at gravesite services for the dead; such services, he says, should involve only prayers in church and alms.[16]

The glittering ceremonies Arsenios witnessed in the late sixteenth century were mirrored decades later when, in the mid-1660s, an English diplomatic party arrived for their audience with Tsar Aleksei Mikhailovich (r. 1645–76). Entering the royal reception hall, the English account recalls, was like moving from night into day, and the visitors' eyes were "dazled with the brightnes of the Sun" and the "splendor of their jewels."[17] Such splendor was a very real part of the rich musical lives—public as well as private—of the tsars and the highest society, and reflected the wealth of musical experiences ordinary Muscovites enjoyed both inside and outside the church. My goal in this study is to examine the ways in which many types of music found expression in this rich culture, particularly the official, literate culture of the court, in the second half of the seventeenth century. My focus is thus on a rather small slice of Muscovite music—generally secular and non-liturgical—and a small slice of Muscovy itself—the upper reaches of society. Even so, there is enormous variety, and by exploring this aspect of Muscovy, I hope that this study will complement the more numerous investigations into its liturgical music, sources, and personnel. My focus takes a different approach to some (relatively) familiar subjects. In chapter 1, I consider the role of music and musical associations in the well-studied events surrounding the rise and fall of the False Dmitrii at the beginning of the seventeenth century, in particular raising two related questions: Why was music such a significant image during these events, and why were the invited Polish musicians such obvious targets for the enraged Muscovites who killed Dmitrii a week after his wedding? As this chapter suggests, the story reveals the deeply ambivalent nature of Russian views of music and serves as an introduction to a larger consideration of ways of thinking about music, particularly instrumental music, in Muscovy.

The following two chapters explore the singing styles characteristic of the Muscovite court and religious institutions throughout the seventeenth century. Although I discuss the professional liturgical singing ensembles, I do not focus on their liturgical roles (which were, of course, their primary duties) but rather on their musical presence within Muscovite society. Other scholars have addressed admirably the development and cultivation of musical styles and genres in Muscovy; here I wish to add to these studies a slightly different view, investigating the function of such music-making in Muscovite society as a whole. In chapter 4, I continue the themes introduced in the opening chapter by examining the varied roles musical instruments played within a society that in general had highly negative associations concerning these instruments. Where were such instruments heard, and who might have heard them? What kinds of sources might bind together this complex web of performance traditions, both condemned and cultivated?

Chapters 5 and 6 focus on specific works and events from the 1670s and early 1680s. In chapter 5, I turn to an individual musician, Nikolai Diletskii, and consider how the language and subject matter of his influential music theory treatise might reflect intellectual contexts and concepts about the roles of music and the liberal arts circulating in Muscovy, Ukraine, Belarus, and the West. Diletskii's work is a key document in tracing the ever-shifting context for music-making in late seventeenth-century Muscovy. It is also something of a landmark for Western music theory, for it transmits the first written circle of fifths to appear in any theoretical work, East or West, antedating by decades the well-studied presentations by Western theorists. This chapter considers how Diletskii's work might have been read in multiple ways by its Muscovite audience and how one might establish a wider intellectual frame for this important treatise.

My final chapter surveys the many factors that came together in the creation of the Muscovite court theater, which began its performances for an audience of one—Tsar Aleksei Mikhailovich—in the fall of 1672 and which ran until the tsar's sudden death in January 1676. An examination of the origins and the brief flourishing of the court theater brings together many of the book's central concerns as they were manifested in a single, heady period of creativity that also allows, crucially, for a consideration of gender and its possible role in Muscovite thinking about music and performance. The theater, like Diletskii's theoretical work, has a context in both Muscovy and the West—these final chapters thus also serve to broaden our view to encompass Muscovy's many ways of approaching, appropriating, or rejecting elements of Western culture that were to play such an overwhelming role in the music of Imperial Russia, beginning with Tsar Aleksei's last-born son and eventual heir, Peter the Great. By examining how the court in particular employed and enjoyed music for spiritual enlightenment as well as for entertainment, I hope to emphasize music's varied roles in Muscovite society, to paint a picture of music's "dazzling splendor" in what to many Western readers remains a vast Churchillian enigma.

This study naturally has its own place in the continuum of views of Muscovite music assembled by both Russian and Western scholars, and I gratefully acknowledge my indebtedness to works by historians who have attempted finely tuned specialized studies as well as broader overviews of this period. Indeed, with the renewed interest in Russian church music that has been developing in the post-Soviet period, this is a particularly encouraging time at which to attempt such a synthesis. Works by contemporary Russian scholars, including Nikolai Parfent'ev, S. G. Zvereva, and many others, have revealed the intricacies of the lives of the professional singers as well as the musical concerns of both public and private sponsors, and they have demonstrated formidable archival skills during what must have amounted to extended encampments among dusty payment records and court documents. Their work is built upon the fundamental studies of early Russian music theory by Maksim Brazhnikov and on the multifaceted studies by Vladimir Protopopov, Iurii Keldysh, Nina Herasymova-Persyds'ka, Tat'iana Vladyshevskaia, and their many colleagues, all of whom labored to reveal the depth and quantity of seventeenth-century Muscovy's musical repertoire. Works by these scholars, cited many times throughout this volume, have been punctuated by particularly important large-scale summaries, bracketed by Nikolai Findeizen's monumental efforts in the 1920s and by the multi-volume *Istoriia russkoi muzyki* (History of Russian Music) series begun in the 1980s—both represent an amalgam of contemporary research and thinking, and both have a great deal to offer the historian today. My own writing is meant to add a different perspective to these works, particularly by using a variety of primary sources—travel and diplomatic accounts, newspaper digests, glossaries, play texts—which, although certainly not unknown to previous scholars, have not been fully exploited as music-historical documents.

My work is also part of a similar and much shorter continuum of Western interest in the subject of early Russian music, and my thinking is surely influenced by these works as well. Miloš Velimirović's contributions to the comprehensive surveys in the *New Grove Dictionary* (beginning with the 1980 edition), in addition to his fundamental studies, particularly of liturgical drama in Russia, opened this period to a wide audience in the West. Vladimir Morosan has contributed comprehensive histories and anthologies of Russian music and musical thought in the seventeenth century, and his ongoing translation of Ivan (Johann) von Gardner's important study of Russian church music represents a major contribution to English-speaking readers. Olga Dolskaya has devoted herself to an exploration of the genre of *kant* (spiritual song) in this period, publishing valuable source materials, in particular the full text of a complete *kant* manuscript from the late seventeenth century. Her work, in combination with the textual studies by Hans Rothe, have made it possible for Westerners to comprehend this crucial genre, a genre with important implications for the development of Russian musical thinking in the eighteenth (and even the nineteenth) century as well. Work by these and other scholars is gradually seeping into the mainstream of Western musicology, for example in the expanded coverage of early Russian music in the most recent version of *New Grove* (issued in print in 2001, with important contributions again by Velimirović) and in general surveys of the music of the seventeenth century, especially those by George Buelow and Joel Lester, both of whom have included considerations of Muscovite music in their authoritative surveys of Western music and theory in the seventeenth and early eighteenth centuries.[18] Western scholars have also produced sophisticated studies of Russian culture and its ceremonial, and my dependence on works by specialists such as Daniel Waugh, Michael Flier, Nancy Kollmann, Valerie Kivelson, Robert Crummey, and many more, in addition to related approaches by their Russian colleagues, is evident throughout this work.

A paragraph on transliteration would seem an unlikely place for introspection and meditation, but in the context of the intersecting Muscovite, Ukrainian, Belarusian, and Polish musical cultures of the seventeenth century, it turns out to be an excellent point at which to ponder important issues and influences. When writing about the composer Nikolai Diletskii, does one transliterate his name from Russian (Diletskii) or Ukrainian (Dylets'kyi)? Such choices go beyond the normal difficulties routinely encountered in transliteration, and the resolution of this dilemma says a great deal about how one views this musical world. Soviet-era writings, for example, often focus on general unity (usually expressed through Russian spellings), as did church historians at an earlier time. Many writers today, facing the same thorny issues of transliteration, often use spelling to emphasize the distinctness of Ukrainian-Belarusian-Ruthenian cultures.[19] Here I use the Russian spelling for Diletskii, as his works were apparently compiled or re-compiled in Muscovite territory—Smolensk and Moscow—and circulated in copies intended for a Muscovite audience. Did Diletskii study in Vilnius or Wilno? Did Arsenios work in L'viv (Ukrainian), L'vov (Russian), or Lwów (Polish)? I generally follow current spelling of geographical locations, thus Vilnius and L'viv, although I also use anglicized forms for some familiar cities: Moscow, St. Petersburg, Kiev. I use the spellings Belarus and Belarusian in place of the earlier Belorussia, Belorussian. I have applied the Library of Congress transliteration system strictly throughout, with, naturally, a few exceptions for names and terms frequently encountered in histories of Muscovy: Peter the Great and Simeon Polotskii, for example, and the more familiar anglicized "boyar" rather than the strict rendering as "boiar" ("boiarin"). Dates are generally given in either Russian fashion (which ran ten days behind the Western calendar) or in combination (e.g. the False Dmitrii was killed on 17/27 May 1606). Dates on some of the primary source material used here are written using the Byzantine calendar, which reckoned time from the creation of the world, with the New Year beginning on 1 September. The Russians adopted this system with the acceptance of Christianity, and it was in use until the time of Peter the Great. A convenient reference point is the year A.D. 1492, which corresponds to the year 7000 from the creation of the world in the Byzantine/Russian system.

All references are given in the notes using a short form of the title; full references are found in the bibliography. For some multi-part articles, I have included full references in the notes in order to specify the volume or section clearly.

1

The True False Dmitrii and the Death of Music in Moscow

We all think we know what happened to the False Dmitrii, the imposter of Modest Musorgskii's opera *Boris Godunov*, who schemed with the calculating Jesuits and power-hungry Poles who supported his claim to be the miraculously living son of Ivan the Terrible. If we know the first version of Musorgskii's opera, we lose track of Dmitrii (called Grigorii at that point) early on, during the Inn Scene when, as Richard Taruskin says, the character jumps "out of the window—and out of the opera!"[1] If we are more familiar with the second version of Musorgskii's work, we know that Dmitrii returns on a white steed to a blast of heralding trumpets at the end of the opera, in the Kromy Forest scene of revolution and brigandry. Musorgskii, as Taruskin has shown, was meticulous in his use of source material, and in *Boris* he went to considerable effort to examine historical surveys and primary sources. In the case of the Kromy Forest scene, however, Musorgskii's accuracy may have been even greater than he realized, for Dmitrii— the true False Dmitrii—was indeed heralded by trumpets and more as he made his way through Russian territory in late 1604 and 1605, on his way to Moscow.

The tale of the Pretender is not just an account of a specific period of political and social upheaval in Russia in the early seventeenth century. It is also a tale of the clash of cultures on a massive scale, a clash not simply magnified by the musical accoutrements of Dmitrii's Polish entourage but rather, in a very real sense, a conflict that was crystallized by that music. Contemporaries perceived this as events unfolded. The Muscovite populace not only killed Dmitrii himself in a frenzy of violence that stunned foreign observers in the capital but they targeted music specifically, in the form of the visiting foreign musicians who had taken part in Dmitrii's wedding to Marina Mniszech (of Fountain Scene fame in Musorgskii's opera). Dozens of Polish musicians—one source claims up to one hundred—were killed, representatives of the despised and decadent culture they were seen to have embodied. As a final blow, Dmitrii's corpse, bloodied and mutilated, was decorated with musical instruments, a mask, and money, the tools and wages of a sinful musician.

Why was music such a powerful image in this Time of Troubles, and how might we disentangle the various strains of music as they are represented in Russian and foreign accounts? Music historians have long acknowledged the uneasy role of instrumental music in Orthodox Muscovite society, pointing to its dual nature as bawdy secular entertainment and as proper court embellishment, and we see this dichotomy at several points in the Dmitrii tale.[2] Indeed, a focus on music as it functioned during the reign of the False Dmitrii reveals a series of unique and defining events inside the Kremlin itself, in which ancient, secular, even evil associations with certain types of music and musical instruments played themselves out in the public theater of Muscovite political life at the highest levels and for an extended period. Yet the story takes us even further. With the penetration of such flagrantly secular music and musical instruments into the holy and public ceremonies of royal marriage and coronation, music encapsulated the threat not just to the throne but to the very culture of Holy Russia itself. In one form or another, this confrontation was to play itself out many times over the course of the seventeenth century.

Dmitrii's rise and fall were both spectacular and short, and scholars are as divided about Dmitrii's true identity today as contemporary witnesses and participants were in the first years of the seventeenth century.[3] In general, however, Musorgskii's operatic treatment gives a basic idea of what happened. After securing military and financial aid from Polish political and ecclesiastical authorities, Dmitrii began his march to Moscow in the fall of 1604, when he crossed into Russian territory. The Pretender made his way north and east to Moscow through a combination of military maneuvers and personal charisma; many towns simply opened their gates to him with offers of bread and salt, the traditional Muscovite greeting of hospitality. When Tsar Boris died suddenly in April 1605, the road was clear, and what had been a military march became largely a hero's welcome. Dmitrii made his grand entrance into Moscow on 20 June 1605 and he was crowned a month later, on 21 July.

Dmitrii immediately set about getting his intended Polish bride and tsaritsa, Marina Mniszech, from Poland to Moscow, and he dispatched envoy Afanasii Ivanovich Vlas'ev to Cracow to make the arrangements. A proxy marriage, with Vlas'ev standing for Tsar Dmitrii, took place in November 1605, and Marina set out for Muscovy the following spring. It was a long and difficult journey lasting almost two months, in a procession made up of what one participant calculated as almost two thousand people.[4] Marina finally made her own triumphal entry into Moscow on 2 May 1606 and was promptly shuttled to her future mother-in-law's residence, at the Convent of the Ascension so that, as one source says, she could learn Russian customs.[5] It was a lesson she failed, or, perhaps more accurately, one she had no intention of learning. Marina hated the food and requested Polish chefs, and to help alleviate her fears of the convent, Dmitrii sent some of her attendants to comfort her.[6] The double ceremony of Marina's coronation and wedding took place on Thursday, 8 May, to great fanfare, and the following week was taken up with a series of increasingly elaborate banquets and balls held in Marina's honor and for Marina's Polish suite. Just over a week later, on Saturday, 17 May, the uprising, about which rumors had been swirling for several days, erupted in full force. Dmitrii was killed and Marina and her father were detained and then banished, lucky to escape with their lives.

Music per se was not at issue. The least controversial performances had sounded out at Dmitrii's entrance into Moscow in June 1605, setting the stage for whatever musical harmony might have been possible. The German Conrad Bussow, who worked for the Poles, the Swedes, and eventually for the Russians, wrote a detailed account of the events and gives us an eyewitness account of Dmitrii's entrance into the city:

> The tsar was preceded by many Polish horsemen in full armour, twenty men with shawms and kettledrums in each group. Behind the tsar and boyars [high-ranking Muscovite nobles] rode as many squadrons of Polish horsemen, in the same marching order and with the same joyful music as those who went before. All day, as long as the entry continued, all the bells in the Kremlin pealed, and everything went so magnificently that nothing of the kind could be better.[7]

Another source, the *Tragoedia Moscovitica* (Cologne, 1608), which is related to a cluster of early accounts, reinforces this description, noting that there were both Polish and Muscovite military musicians playing in separate groups but with the same kinds of instruments.[8] This shared military-processional music was appropriate and expected, and it afforded one of the only possibilities for common musical ground. This was the kind of music that accompanied Marina as she made her own entrance into the city, although, as Tsar Dmitrii himself had made the arrangements, her music was somewhat more elaborate than that of his own, earlier parade. Both Bussow and another foreign eyewitness, the Dutch merchant Isaac Massa, describe the festivities, which included a special platform for the musicians. Massa writes that when Marina, "coming through the third city wall, reached the great square before the Kremlin, musicians posted on platforms built for this purpose and on the city gates made the air ring with the sound of their shawms, trumpets, and many kettledrums."[9]

Bussow provides a few more details, underscoring the separate-but-equal status accorded military musicians, and he specifies that the musicians at the gates were Muscovite:

> Ahead of her on foot went three hundred haiduks [musketeers] whom she had brought with her from Poland, with their own shawms and drums. Behind them followed, in full armour, Dmitrii's veteran Polish cavalry, which had served him in his campaigns, ten men in each rank, accompanied by their own drums and kettledrums . . . [Then, following the noble Muscovites and the Polish aristocrats who had come with Marina] came the cavalry which had arrived from Poland, in full armour, with trumpets, kettledrums, and shawms, followed by the Russian cavalry with drums of greater diameter than any other drums or kettledrums . . . At the outer, middle, and inner city gates stood Muscovite musicians, who produced a clamorous noise with their trumpets and drums.[10]

The festivities were bombastic but essentially benign, and they raised no objections among the Russians, who indeed participated equally and enthusiastically.

The Poles did not attempt to take part in the second type of music that functioned throughout these events—liturgical and religious music—although they were present (wearing objectionable clothing and carrying weapons into the church) at the service for Marina's coronation-wedding at the Cathedral of the Dormition in the Kremlin.[11] The liturgical ceremony was described by the Greek prelate Arsenios of Elasson, whose informed account mentions the many processions of various church hierarchs, liturgical singing and prayers, the ceremony of the vestment of the new tsaritsa (which was also accompanied by singing), and so forth.[12] In contrast, one of the Polish observers, Stanisław Niemojewski, was baffled by the proceedings and described the scene dismissively and incuriously: "[A] few clerics sang something from books, but it was impossible to understand anything except 'Gospodi pomilui' [Lord, have mercy], because they repeated that more than a hundred times."[13]

But the seeds of conflict over religious music had already been sown, almost as soon as Marina had set foot on Russian soil and weeks before she arrived in the capital. On 12 April 1606, four days after she crossed the border near Smolensk, an account written by an anonymous member of Marina's party describes the Russians' amazement at hearing the music at a mass celebrated by the Polish entourage (whose number included priests, monks, and numerous additional assistants): "The music during the mass really surprised the Russian folks and, crowding around, they even broke down the barrier."[14]

Although the account of Marina's Polish mass does not give specifics, it seems reasonable to suggest that the services that so amazed the Russian listeners might have included not only polyphonic singing, which would certainly have been familiar in the context of an Orthodox liturgical service at this date, especially in a border town such as Smolensk, but instruments as well. As we shall see below, we do know that the Polish party included a large choral ensemble and instrumentalists who played at banquets and for dancing. In addition, Marina herself had at least one singer associated with her retinue, and there was a Polish organist, Gabriel, who came with his own assistants.[15] Certainly some Russians knew that instrumental music was used in other religious traditions. Just a few years before Marina made her trek to Moscow, for example, Tsar Boris's envoy to London, Grigorii Ivanovich Mikulin, had attended church services with Queen Elizabeth in January 1601 and reported back about the music he had heard. The context was unfamiliar and Mikulin apparently asked his hosts for clarification about the proceedings, but his report described the service without comment, although emphasizing that the performance did indeed actually take place in the church itself: "And when the queen entered the church, at that time they began to play organs and horns and on many other instruments in the church, and to sing, and the officers said that they were singing the psalms of David."[16]

If someone like Mikulin was aware of such musical practices, why should there have been such astonishment among the Russians, to the point that they even "broke down the barrier" at hearing the music of Marina's party, whatever it may have been? One might suggest that diplomatic reports such as Mikulin's, which had only limited circulation within the Kremlin itself, were a far cry from bringing this

Western-style music, with or without instruments, right into Russia itself and performing non-Orthodox religious services there in public, barriers or no barriers.[17] The impact would only have been heightened by the realization that this music was being performed for the woman who was to be the new tsaritsa, a woman whose Orthodoxy was, and would continue to be, seriously and legitimately questioned.[18] As an indication of the depth of feeling religious music engendered among Orthodox Russians, one only needs to recall the anguished *cri de cœur* sounded a few years later by Patriarch Germogen, in the context of the next phase of the Troubles, when the Poles were occupying the capital: "The Latin singing in Moscow," the Patriarch declared, "I can bear to hear no longer."[19]

So although no one objected to the use of military and fanfare instruments in specific contexts and the Poles had no intention or interest in taking part in Orthodox religious music, the boundaries between religious music and instruments were nevertheless dangerously vulnerable to misunderstanding. Ultimately it was in the third musical arena, encompassing instrumental music for entertainment purposes, that all of the Poles, to their great peril, displayed their ignorance of Muscovite traditions. One of Orthodox Russia's weightiest associations with instrumental music came into play after the Polish party settled into the capital: an association with Russia's pagan past, a past virulently derided by an ever-vigilant clergy but evidently a living tradition in many aspects of Russian life. This was music associated with the ancient, usually itinerant bands of *skomorokhi*, who had been dispersed as their base around the city of Novgorod was enveloped into the Muscovite fold but who nevertheless survived and even flourished well into the seventeenth century.[20] *Skomorokh* musical entertainment involved singing (generally songs of highly questionable taste) and a mixed ensemble including the *gusli* (a plucked multi-stringed instrument of ancient Slavic origins, similar to the psaltery), the *domra* and the *gudok* (plucked and bowed stringed instruments, respectively), various flutes or reed pipes (*svireli, dudki, surny,* and others), and certain types of percussion.[21] These instruments accompanied the entertainments typically proffered by the *skomorokhi*, including dancing, costuming, and masking, all of which the Poles unwittingly duplicated in their own musical performances while they were in Moscow.

Although we do not know exactly what kind of music was played for Marina's party at that mass just across the border, we do know that a few weeks later, when the long Polish train approached Moscow, Marina's brother, Stanisław Mniszech, went on ahead. On 6 May Stanisław entered Moscow and headed for Dmitrii's quarters in the Kremlin, where forty of his musicians played for the tsar and a Muscovite audience. "The Russians," reports the anonymous Polish author, "were highly astonished at the orchestra's performance. . . . [Tsar Dmitrii] enjoyed the music, which lasted almost the whole night." If this figure of forty musicians is even approximately accurate, it would represent an exceptionally large ensemble even by Western standards at this date. In Russia this would have been the largest gathering of instrumentalists until the eighteenth century, for even the Muscovite court theater of the 1670s apparently used an instrumental ensemble less than half that size.[22]

Instrumental music as entertainment rather than as military fanfare was acceptable within the Kremlin walls, but only in certain contexts and using certain instruments (as we shall discuss further in chapter 4). The English diplomat Jerome Horsey, for example, describing his preparations in London for a return trip to Russia in 1586, emphasized that he had assembled various keyboard instruments at the court's request: I "had made my provicion of . . . organes, virgenalls, musicions . . . and of other costly things of great value," Horsey wrote in his later account, "according to my commissions" from the Russian court.[23] Yet there were limitations to such entertainments, and the Russian court seems to have stressed the qualities of privacy and scale. The subsequent court performances by Horsey's musicians, which would appear to contradict the horror of association with degenerate, instrument-laden *skomorokhi,* were essentially private and employed only small numbers of players. Horsey's statement confirms this in a somewhat roundabout fashion. He describes how his musicians were invited to play for the royal family but paints their roles there as invisible: nameless but necessary servants. Horsey himself was often not allowed to join his musicians, for as a foreigner and particularly as a spectator, his presence might have suggested the public music-making associated with the professional secular entertainers. The musical ensemble he goes on to describe also seems to have been a small one, and the "thousands of people" he mentions (a number that certainly requires verification) appear to be those admitted into the presence of the tsaritsa herself or at least into the Kremlin residences, thus confirming the notion of a select, if large, audience. Horsey writes:

> [T]he Emporis [Irina, Boris Godunov's sister] . . . admired especially at the organes and vergenalls, all gilt and enambled, never seinge nor heeringe the like before, woundered and delighted at the lowd and musicall sound therof. Thousands of people resorted and steyed aboutt the pallace to heer the same. My men that plaied upon them [were] much made of and admitted into such presence often wher myself could not com.[24]

The royal family, then, did not shy away from instrumental entertainment entirely but enjoyed it in a properly private and limited scope, and in an unquestionably Orthodox context. All these requirements were entirely lacking in the performances of the large mixed instrumental ensemble—with dancing!—provided by Marina's brother for a mixed Polish (that is, Roman Catholic) and Russian audience. Even without the other offenses so abundantly supplied by the oblivious Polish party, this sort of unrestricted, large-scale musical performance was guaranteed to raise Russian suspicion and ire.

Furthermore, the entertainment provided by Marina's brother, at the tsar's invitation and within the Kremlin walls, echoes in many ways the numerous warnings against the emphatically non-Orthodox, publicly performing *skomorokhi* issued over many years by exasperated Russian clergy. The Stoglav Council of 1551, for example, had dealt with the question of music repeatedly. One of its resolutions concerned weddings, a longtime *skomorokh* stronghold which particularly distressed Orthodox hierarchs and which makes the connection to the Polish merrymaking in the Kremlin quite clear:

> **Question:** At secular weddings, trouble-makers, *organniki,* merry-makers, and *gusli* players play and they sing devilish songs. And when people go to get married in the church and the clergyman goes with the cross, before him with all such devilish games they roam, and the priests cannot prohibit them . . .

> **Answer:** At a marriage the *skomorokhi* and trouble-makers are not to go to the holy church before the wedding, and the priest must prohibit this very firmly . . .[25]

Another complaint, from 1636—thirty years after Dmitrii's time and more than seventy-five years after the directives issued by the Stoglav Council—details the kinds of secular celebrations that accompanied the Feast of the Ascension, which involved instruments, dancing, and masks; the petitioner tells Patriarch Iosaf that the celebrations included the following:

> bear-men with bears and dancing dogs, jesters and players [*skomorosi i igretsy*] with masks and shameful instruments of debauchery, with drums and [double-reed] pipes (*surny*) and all sorts of satanic attractions to debauchery and, lord, creating evil devilish attractions, getting drunk, dancing and beating drums, sounding the pipes and going in masks and carrying shameful things in their hands and doing other improper things such as Satan taught them to oppose to the Festival of Christ's Ascension.[26]

The references to dancing, the mixed instrumental ensemble, merrymaking, and even masking sound ominously in two reports about music associated with Dmitrii's wedding. The first is Massa's account of the wedding ceremony, which was followed by a banquet: "A richly ornamented stage had been set up, where an orchestra of musicians played all manner of instruments. These musicians had been brought from Poland by the palatine of Sandomierz [Marina's father]. They were Polish, Italian, German, and Brabançon. Their sweet harmonies added joy to the feast."[27] Bussow's report is similar: "The days of the wedding festivities were celebrated splendidly and joyfully with food, drink, singing, and acrobatics. There were not only all imaginable kinds of musical instruments playing but also an excellent choir with thirty-two voices, as fine as any potentate might desire, which Dmitrii had summoned from Poland."[28]

It was not necessarily the presence of a large choral ensemble but rather the content of the ensemble's performance that would have raised concern. Muscovites, certainly those in the capital city itself, would have been familiar with the singing of the sovereign and patriarchal choirs, which were of comparable size at this time; indeed, the liturgical singers had just taken part in the wedding ceremony, as the Greek cleric Arsenios tells us.[29] But such singing did not belong with a mixed instrumental ensemble and acrobats, and these imported singers were certainly not performing Orthodox religious music.[30]

An enumeration of the events of that fateful week in May 1606, from wedding to massacre, reads like a Greek tragedy: the Poles, oblivious, doing everything possible to ensure their own destruction; and the Russians, with their nuanced and completely foreign context for understanding instrumental music—a context the Poles had no wish to understand—perceiving these wedding festivities as nothing less than an attack on Holy Russia itself.

After the ceremony, the new royal couple returned to their apartments for the wedding banquet to the sound of trumpets and percussion; everyone agreed that the sound was deafening and no one objected, at least in terms of cultural practice, to the incessant fanfares, which were part of the traditional Muscovite wedding ceremony.[31] Then, in a perfect musical juxtaposition, the couple presided over the celebration where, as Massa describes, the foreign orchestra played "all manner of instruments." Dmitrii and Marina thus left the Russian marriage ceremony only to attend a Polish wedding banquet. The festivities continued throughout most of the following week, with many days devoted to receiving gifts and guests. Again there were two distinct types of musical celebrations, fanfares alternating with Western-style *Tafel-* and *Tanzmusik*. Many observers kept careful track of the clothing worn by the royal couple, and Arsenios describes with concern that on Sunday, 11 May, when the patriarch and many high-ranking clergy brought gifts to the newlyweds, Marina was wearing Polish dress. This was apparently Dmitrii's gesture of thanks rewarding Marina's highly reluctant agreement to dress herself *à la russe* for the wedding ceremony itself. The anonymous Polish account notes that at a gathering apparently held later that day, both Marina and Dmitrii wore Polish clothing.[32] Even worse, some of this merrymaking took place on the Feast of St. Nicholas (9 May), a very important and holy day in Muscovy, and the blasphemy was clear to all who cared to note it. Massa, for example, observed the Russians' anger that Dmitrii would "profane this solemn day."[33]

On Monday, 12 May, the Polish writer in Marina's suite noted that the meals were prepared and served by Polish cooks and waiters, the parties continued, and they "danced until dawn."[34] The anonymous Polish writer gives a fairly detailed picture of the dancing that took place on the following day, Tuesday, 13 May. Although the hierarchy of the elaborate partnering involved in this dancing, with its emphasis on rank and precedence, would have been familiar to Muscovites involved in court ceremonial, the dancing itself, no matter how decorous and processional in nature, would certainly have been disturbingly foreign, particularly as it involved men and women dancing together in public.

> After dinner, the Polish gentlemen retainers [*pany priblizhennye*] danced. The tsar changed into Hussar's clothing and danced first with the tsaritsa and then with Pan Voevoda [Marina's father]. The following ceremonies took place at the dance: all the Polish gentlemen who wished to attend [or escort] in the dances in the tsaritsa's presence first kissed the tsar's hand, then went in their proper order, their hats removed, with Pan Voevoda and the ambassador [Vlas'ev] positioned at the very end, and passed in front of the tsar. When only the gentlemen danced, they all removed their hats, all except the ambassador, who removed his only when he passed before the tsar. When Pan Voevoda danced with his daughter, he attended her on the left. The tsar danced with Pan Voevoda and the tsaritsa and [the Polish] Princess Koshirska attended them. A great deal of all kinds of drink was consumed. No Russians were there on that day except Afanasii and Mosal'skii. They broke up at sunset.[35]

This description is quite similar to Niemojewski's detailed account of the dancing and other festivities held a few days later, on Thursday, 15 May. Niemojewski, who attended the celebration, paints a vivid picture of what almost seems to have been a multi-act performance: a banquet accompanied by music, at which only three top-ranking Muscovites were present; elaborate toasts; dancing; a change of costume for the tsar, who disappeared and then reappeared in a splendid hussar's outfit, as above; and more dancing, sometimes with female members of Marina's retinue. The first dance segment featured the same kinds of elaborate pairing and leading as described above:

> After the meal, the Grand Prince [Dmitrii] went to dance with the Sovereign [Marina]; the Voevoda of Sandomierz, the Castellan of Małogość, and several pair of these Lords' friends attended him. Then the Voevoda danced with the Grand Princess [his daughter, Marina], and she led; then came Pan Małagoski, but in this case, he led her.[36]

Rumors of a plot against Dmitrii flew throughout the week, and the anonymous Polish writer says that the tsar was warned but did not listen. The *Reporte* observes ominously that on Wednesday, 14 May, a fast day, the city was "all verie silent"; the linked accounts by Stadnicki and the anonymous Polish writer in Marina's suite both note that Marina invited the Muscovite aristocracy to her quarters that night and that crowds were gathering in the street.[37] Several reports comment on the activities at the end of that week, describing what might have been the last straw. The *Reporte* describes plans for a "mummerie," and Massa tells us that "[t]he same night [Friday, 16 May], joy reigned in the chambers of the tsar. The Polish lords were busy dancing with great ladies. The tsarina [Marina], with her maids of honour, was preparing disguises for a masquerade that she was planning to offer the tsar as an entertainment on the Sunday following."[38] Stadnicki's account describes what sounds like an all-night bacchanal on Friday that ended, abruptly and dramatically, with the sounding of the bells signaling the attack on Dmitrii and his court.

> The tsar's chambers ring with all kinds of music. The Muscovite Hymen dances with the Polish Venus, who is assisted by Bacchus. Filled goblets pass from hand to hand among the Polish gentlemen . . . Everyone got drunk, some from *Falernskoe* [Italian] wine, some from love . . . All are visited by Hymen—no one thinks about Mars. All of a sudden, they struck not the drums, but all the bells. Countless armed men flow from every direction.[39]

The ferocity of the attack, when it came on Saturday, was stunning. As Bussow said, "[t]his day, 17 May, will be remembered as long as the world endures."[40] Dmitrii himself was naturally the primary target; obviously the opposition, headed by Vasilii Shuiskii, needed to remove him in order to claim the throne. The accounts are in overall agreement as to the course of events on that day. Dmitrii did indeed jump out of a window, not in an inn on the Lithuanian frontier, as Musorgskii would have it, but out of a Kremlin window after a pitched battle. He was injured by the fall and unable to escape, and he died at the hands of his former subjects.

Bussow's account of Dmitrii's death includes a detail that ties many of the disparate musical threads together. After the injured Dmitrii was hauled back to his apartments, he was surrounded by a group of angry Russians:

[A] fourth [Russian] struck him on the face, saying: "you, son of a whore, say who are you? Who is your father? Where is your home?" He answered: "All of you know that I am your crowned tsar and the son of Ivan Vasilievich [Ivan IV]. Ask my mother in the convent, or bring me to the platform on the Red Square and permit me to speak." Then a merchant named Miulnik sprang forward with his musket, and said: "It is not permitted for a heretic to justify himself; thus shall I bless this Polish piper!" With these words he shot him through.[41]

Bussow's "Polish piper" is telling. He reemphasizes this crucial association a few lines later, when he describes how the Russians moved into the Kremlin. Bussow, using the Russian term, reports that someone then asks, "What news of the Polish *scammaroth*?"[42] The *skomorokh* image is apt, for how else could the Muscovites interpret the dancing, the costumes, the instrumental music, and the masking? These are all ancient attributes of *skomorokh* life, and Dmitrii and the Poles could not have played their minstrels' roles more faithfully if they had tried.

The associations did not end there, however, for the gruesome tales of Dmitrii's postmortem fate reveal the full implications of the Poles' unwittingly faithful emulation of *skomorokh* traditions. The anonymous *Tragoedia Moscovitica* describes how the Russians put a mask, which they had found in the women's quarters apparently as a remnant of Marina's planned masquerade, on Dmitrii's corpse, stuck a flute (*fistula*) into his mouth, and scattered money about, as wages for singing. The related *Reporte* tells the same story:

There went every day thither great numbers of men and women, to see this hideous sight [of Dmitrii's mutilated corpse], and they put an ugly vilard [mask] upon the Emperours belly, which they had found amongst the Empresses spoyls, and in his mouth the flute, with a kind of little bagpipe, under the arme with a peece of money of the valew of halfe a Pater, giving to understand by this, that for the peece of money hee gave them a hunts up, or fit of an old song.[43]

This deliberate mockery carried echoes of recent Russian history, for Ivan IV himself, not exactly restrained in his love of earthy *skomorokh* entertainments, had also invoked this potent imagery in his humiliation of the archbishop of Novgorod, who was tied onto his horse and paraded around with typical *skomorokh* instruments hung about his neck.[44]

The scholars Boris Uspenskii and Maureen Perrie, in their studies of the phenomenon of pretenders throughout Russian history, show that these references go beyond the actual *skomorokhi* themselves to encompass the traditions of sorcery and black magic with which these entertainers were associated. As Uspenskii says, dressing up or masquerading, including the very act of royal imposture itself, was regarded as a kind of anti-behavior, characterized by the unruly, even blasphemous, activities so abundantly demonstrated by Dmitrii and his followers.[45] The masks, particularly their placement not on Dmitrii's face but on his stomach or groin, were manifestations of a topsy-turvey Uspenskii calls "the inverted world of the sorcerer," in which masks, not icons, were venerated and the holy icons were placed on the floor.[46] The power of this imagery was not simply humiliation—tsar as *skomorokh*—but an overturning of all that was right and ordained—tsar (and *skomorokh*) as worshipper and cohort of the devil. In the short reign and early death of the true False Dmitrii, there was a peculiarly fatal confluence of events as the Poles' ribald, *skomorokh*-like music and behavior, which was bad enough, unwittingly unearthed deep and disturbing associations with sorcery and blasphemy.

Dmitrii's death did not end the matter, and the rumors that immediately sprang up underscore the theme of the *skomorokhi* and their associations with unclean and even satanic behavior.[47] The foreign accounts tell us that Dmitrii, when visiting his bride-to-be in the convent before the wedding, had made music, partied, and performed (and forced the nuns to perform) "filthie songs." Although Marina was the focus of his amorous attentions (and only for a week!), dozens of nuns were subsequently discovered to be pregnant. As the *Reporte* slyly noted, although Marina was at the convent in order to learn about the Orthodox faith, "I rather suppose, seeing Demetrius frequented thither so daylie, and was there so privately, that he taught her an other Catechisme."[48] Russian accounts describe the strange happenings that occurred after Dmitrii's death, invoking familiar musical associations: "many people in the middle of the night, even until cockcrow, heard much dancing and playing of drums [or tambourines] and pipes [*bubny i svireli*], and other devilish games being enacted over his accursed body; for Satan himself was rejoicing at his coming."[49]

Several related accounts trace the musical motif in Dmitrii's life to the early and murky period before he emerged in Poland as the resurrected tsarevich, offering a kind of pre-history of the Pretender. These accounts portray Dmitrii, in an extension of the masquerade theme, as a musical mole who had burrowed his way into the elite professional singing ensemble associated with the Russian patriarch. As the *Reporte* says, Dmitrii had "sometimes serued in the Patriarkes Court, for a Singing man and a Musitian, euer carefully obseruing whatsoeuer might further his intentions."[50] By this account, then, music not only contributed to Dmitrii's downfall but also figured in his rise.

The visiting Polish musicians fell victim to the same rage that was directed against Dmitrii; indeed, their deaths were probably inevitable, given their visible participation in the external trappings of *skomorokh*-like musical entertainment and their consequent association with the deeper meanings such activities evoked. The foreign musicians were apparently known to the Russians not only through hearsay (for, with the exception of the first large-scale musical performance by the retinue assembled by Marina's brother, only a few, select Russians witnessed the music and the dancing, at least as invited guests), but also because they had been lodged in quarters scattered throughout the city.[51] Massa reports that "nearly all the musicians were killed," and the *Reporte* says that although five or six of the musicians escaped, the rest, about twenty, were all killed.[52] Bussow's numbers are much larger: "All the musicians, singers, and instrumentalists—boys, youths, and grown men—who had been lodged in the monastic houses within the Kremlin were killed immediately after the tsar and [his Russian supporter] Basmanov, a hundred innocent, skilled, and honourable people."[53]

Niemojewski's account, part of his harrowing description of the day's events, agrees with the number in the *Reporte*. Niemojewski himself was apparently not an eyewitness to the musicians' fate, yet the fact that he seems to have believed their pleas for mercy to be true (or at least a worthy artistic embellishment) indicates the cultural chasm between the two groups. He writes:

> There were a few dozen various musicians, which they call entertainers [*po-cieszniki*]. They had their quarters in the Kremlin, near the church, into which [churches], at the beginning of the attack, the attackers ran after them. Several of them were killed right then, and others, barricading themselves, yelled out to them: "Is this how you treat the entertainers, and who is going to entertain you after this?" [The attackers] broke in and got them all, with the exception of a few young singers, wounded and stripped naked, who were left for dead. A few others escaped to a neighboring church, but they got at them via the roof and continued to kill them, unarmed and stripped naked.[54]

In his listing of those killed in the uprising, Niemojewski included twenty musicians and two servants working for an organist. The Polish diplomats Oleśnicki and Gosiewski listed thirteen people associated with the organist Gabriel and seventeen of the "tsaritsa's musicians" as killed, plus another eight wounded.[55]

Whatever the exact body count, the prompt and deliberate murders show that the musicians were a viable, indeed a logical, target, and that the Muscovites wasted no time in seeking them out. Later that day, the Russians captured Marina and her father in his Kremlin quarters, and several accounts include a series of charges the captive Poles addressed to the Russians, reproaching them for their behavior. After all, said the Polish prisoners, it was the Russians themselves who had accepted Dmitrii as the living son of the true tsar, it was they who had abandoned Tsar Boris and welcomed Dmitrii into their cities. The Poles also brought up the matter of the musicians. In Bussow's account, Marina's father asks: "How will you answer before eternity for such evil deeds and fearful slaughter? Even if my late son-in-law was not the legitimate sovereign and heir to the throne—and we can prove the opposite from your letters and documents—wherein lies the guilt of the hundred inno-cent musicians?"[56] The deaths were regrettable, the Russians replied, but the deed was done.

No one would argue that Dmitrii died simply and solely because of the music he played at his wedding. Music, however, was a potent shorthand for both foreign culture and *skomorokh* decadence, both literal and symbolic. As Vladimir Moro-san has demonstrated, even the word "music," *musikiia,* could in sixteenth- and seventeenth-century Russian usage carry a special and specific meaning: singing (*penie*) was what one heard in church but *musikiia* implied instrumental (and therefore secular) entertainment, of the sort Dmitrii enjoyed for his wedding celebrations.[57] Music historian Nikolai Findeizen assembled a series of definitions of *musikiia* from sixteenth- and seventeenth-century Muscovite glossaries, all of which refer to instruments or to playing, and sometimes in a very negative man-ner.[58] A Russian account of Dmitrii's wedding festivities uses the term in the same way. After describing the ceremony, with some references to the sung portions of the liturgy, the chronicler noted that "there was no music on the first day, but there was [music later] at the Faceted Palace at the great feast."[59]

Defining proper roles for *penie* and *musikiia* was a difficult and complex question in which context was paramount, and it was an issue that was to be at the heart of Muscovite musical practice throughout the seventeenth century, until the sweeping changes initiated by Peter the Great mooted much of this delicate cul-tural balancing act. This set of negotiations with respect to music and music-making forms the central focus of this study: Who were the music-makers of Muscovy, who were their audiences, and under what circumstances might they have performed? As we trace the roles of music and performance through the seventeenth century, we shall also consider how such issues were addressed dif-ferently as the century progressed, and how these changes mirror larger influences on Muscovite culture in this pivotal century.

2

"Wondrous singers and exceptional voices"

Singers and Singing in Muscovy

The story of the False Dmitrii includes both liturgical singing by Russian performers, at the coronation-wedding ceremony, and secular singing by foreigners during the week of celebrations following. In spite of the dramatic and hostile Russian reaction to the foreign musicians, each of these singing traditions— liturgical and secular—formed an important element of Muscovite music-making, particularly at court and in the capital city, throughout the seventeenth century. This chapter begins a consideration of music's presence in Muscovy, starting with the professional singing ensembles. These groups formed an indispensable part of court and religious ceremonial and because of this, they were a visible musical presence to a wide spectrum of the populace in the capital (and even, to a lesser extent, in other cities as well). The ensembles, largely engaged in liturgical singing, helped define the external, public space carved out by church and state through formalized ritual and display, and they also provide a rare window into the interior, private occupations of the royal family inside the Kremlin. The path we trace here explores the possibilities for sanctioned extra-liturgical or non-liturgical singing in Muscovy. We start by surveying the makeup and activities of the liturgical ensembles, and then track the singers' activities as they move outside the cathedral to participate in religious processions, liturgical dramas, and dramatic readings. In chapter 3 we will consider the non-liturgical singers at the Muscovite court, examining the distribution and transmission of the song-like *kant* repertoire as evidence for domestic religious music-making.

Liturgical Singers and the Continuum of Sacred Singing

Richard James, an Oxford-educated cleric, was interested in anything and everything he saw during his trip to the Russian Far North from 1618 to 1620. James knew several languages (some of them displayed in the record of his Russian journey), and on his return to England he published or compiled a variety of sermons and historical works. "A very good Grecian," said his contemporaries, "[a] poet, an excellent critic, antiquary, divine, and admirably well skilled in the Saxon and Gothic languages," or, less flatteringly, "an atheistical, profane scholar, but otherwise witty and moderately learned."[1]

James's Russian trip was probably confined to the northern port city of Arkhangel'sk, on the White Sea at the mouth of the Northern Dvina River, and to the town of Kholmogory, about ninety miles upriver. These were familiar places to foreign traders, especially the English merchants of the Muscovy (or Russia) Company, and the mission in which James took part was one of the last in the fifty-odd years during which England had enjoyed a powerful trading monopoly in Russia.[2] James attacked his assignment with the gusto one might expect from a "profane and witty scholar," producing a Russian-English glossary in which he recorded over two thousand words and short phrases reflecting his experiences. He names fish and plants, numbers and weather patterns in an indiscriminate enthusiasm that also embraced music, musical instruments, and musical ceremony. He also includes useful phrases for the traveler ("nos osenobil, your nose is frozen").[3] James must have heard enough liturgical singing during his stay to become curious about the proper terminology, and he included the term "diaca" (*d'iak*) in his glossary, defining it, in a brief cluster of ecclesiastical words all explained in Latin, as "homines qui canunt et cantus instruunt."[4] Both of the elements he singles out, singing and teaching, were important components of the liturgical singers' daily routine and duties.

The ultimate origins of the Russian singing ensembles are in the Byzantine traditions imported to Kiev at the end of the tenth century, but their proximate origins, as highly organized professional ensembles attached to important ecclesiastical figures and to the tsar himself, date from the early sixteenth century, with scattered references stretching back into the previous century.[5] By 1573, toward the end of Ivan IV's reign, a substantial choir of twenty-seven members was attached to the court, organized in a clear and hierarchical fashion that was to be maintained throughout the following century, even as its membership expanded. The singers were called the *gosudarevy pevchie d'iaki* (the sovereign's singing clerics or deacons), and they were arranged in a series of groups or ranks called *stanitsy,* each with about five singers. In general, singers moved up from the lowest *stanitsy,* the fourth or fifth rank, to the top, with salaries increasing as they progressed. Over the course of the seventeenth century the number of *stanitsy* increased; ultimately there were around seventy singers associated with the court, although they were attached to various members of the royal family or to different Kremlin churches and apparently did not all sing together.[6]

There was a parallel organization, the *patriarshie pevchie d'iaki,* associated with the patriarch. The sovereign's singers and patriarchal singers frequently performed together on important occasions, with the sovereign's singers taking precedence, standing to the right. The singers stood at the *kliros,* which refers to raised platform areas on either side of the altar but can also refer to the ensembles of singers who were positioned on these platforms. The duties and repertoire of the two ensembles certainly overlapped, but there is also evidence that some pieces were known in a distinct patriarchal variant.[7] There were similar ensembles, arranged in the same hierarchical fashion although generally smaller in size, attached to other church hierarchs and in monasteries.

The group was fully involved in the day-to-day business of the court.[8] The singers received board, clothing, and housing allowances, along with numerous bonus payments for performances and special gifts to individual singers. Their primary tasks were, of course, musical, singing at the liturgical services attended by the tsar or the patriarch, although on occasion they performed privately for a member of the royal family.[9] When these services were celebrated out of town, a frequent occurrence given the many pilgrimages that both leaders undertook on a regular basis, the singers went along. They also ran errands, transporting books, documents, and religious objects from one location to another, and they sometimes worked as scribes, copying mostly musical manuscripts but also some nonmusical documents as necessary.[10] There was a separate group of music scribes who were centered at the "little house by the river" along with the bookbinders and who received regular salaries and supplies for their work.[11]

If the sovereign's singers and patriarchal singers represented the public expression of the liturgical music of Muscovy's state and church, another group reflected the private, domestic side of such singing. The *krestovye d'iaki* (deacons or clerics of the cross), who were also divided into sovereign and patriarchal groups, were responsible for private services for the royal family and the patriarch.[12] They were not primarily singers, although singing represented an increasingly important part of their duties as the seventeenth century progressed. Rather, they were responsible generally for the preparations and celebrations of the royal family's private devotions, including both reading and singing the sacred texts, as well as for accompanying the royal family on pilgrimages and for the same kinds of miscellaneous errands carried out by the more numerous sovereign's singers. The *krestovye d'iaki* also sometimes participated, along with the sovereign's singers, when the tsar celebrated a public liturgy, and they were involved in the events marking the royal family's domestic realm: christenings, funerals, memorial services, and the like. The sovereign's *krestovye d'iaki* increased greatly in number throughout the second half of the seventeenth century, as the demands on domestic services increased with the growing royal family. They were attached to the tsaritsa and the royal children, as well as to the other female establishments at court—the royal aunts, the widowed wives of the royal sons, and so forth—and provide a glimpse of the trained and organized music taking place within the *terem*, the private, secluded arena in which upper-class Russian women spent their lives.

Another distinct group of singers was made up of performers from Ukraine and Belarus. Their names begin to appear in Muscovite documents in large numbers in the 1650s, during Patriarch Nikon's tenure, and especially after the 1654 Union linked Kiev, as well as a host of southwestern towns formerly in the Polish orbit, with Muscovy. Many of the earliest groups of these singers came to the capital at the request of the court or the patriarch; others came to Muscovy with visiting clerics.[13] The new singers, particularly at first, were distinguished by title in the Muscovite documents, where they are called not *pevchie,* but rather *vspevaki* (both translated as "singers"). Both groups performed liturgical music for the tsar, although a 1657 document indicates that at least on this early occasion, they performed in separate groups, the *vspevaki* for the All-Night Vigil and the *gosudarevy pevchie d'iaki* for the Divine Liturgy. Later on, they appear to have been integrated into the rolls of the sovereign singers and the other ensembles, generally without distinguishing labels.[14]

Muscovy also hosted singers associated with visiting foreign clerics, as we saw in descriptions of the 1589 ceremonies marking the establishment of the Russian patriarchate. Similar musical exchanges continued in the seventeenth century. The best-known representative was Meletios, a Greek cleric who by 1657 was established in Moscow as a teacher of "Greek singing." He remained in Russia (with trips to the

Orthodox East) until his death about three decades later, and among his many duties during this period, he was active as a singer and teacher, compiling musical manuscripts and composing liturgical works. He and another Greek singer, Dionysios, sang many times during the 1666–67 church councils, as did other visiting clerics attending the meetings.[15] Private families also supported singers and singing. The Stroganov family, who had a large estate in the Urals, maintained a long-standing interest in liturgical music in the sixteenth and seventeenth centuries. Several important singers were associated with the family and many notated sources attest to their active efforts at compiling a comprehensive musical collection. Their singers also kept up with the latest musical styles. One of the surviving copies of Nikolai Diletskii's music-theoretical work, which was concerned with teaching the new Western-style part singing and which circulated widely in Muscovy, was dedicated to Grigorii Dmitrievich Stroganov. Singers associated with the family were not only known to the court but were requested for their expertise in the new styles.[16]

One of the most valuable witnesses to Russian singing practices in mid-century is Paul of Aleppo, a cleric who accompanied his father, Patriarch Makarios of Antioch, on two trips to Muscovy (once in the mid-1650s and again for the councils in the mid-1660s). He is one of the few foreigners who not only observed Russian church ceremony and celebrations but also understood the liturgical context for the singing he heard there.[17] Paul's account enlarges the scope of what we know about liturgical singing in Muscovy through his many references to trained female singers. Although there were no women among the various assemblies of *d'iaki*, Paul's descriptions of a visit to the large and wealthy Novodevichii (New Maiden) Convent just outside Moscow indicates that the nuns in effect undertook the roles of the *pevchie d'iaki*. His reference to two separate singing groups in the passage below suggests an antiphonal performance by trained, specialist singers:

> On our arrival at the convent, they [the nuns] all came out to meet us; and then walked before us, chaunting with a melody that charmed the heart . . . Whilst we paid our devotions to the images, they sang the *'Axión estin*; and delightful was the harmony and sweetness of their tones and voices, which they continued to modulate, till the Patriarch had given to all of them his benediction, one by one . . . They chaunted also the responses of the Mass, in two choirs . . .[18]

Other sources suggest a familiar organization of singers at the convent. Early in the seventeenth century, payment records refer to groups of "bol'shie kryloshanki" and "men'shie kryloshanki" (greater and lesser female singers at the *kliros*), which suggests a division of duties or experience reflected in the different pay scales.[19]

Although the male ensembles also performed at convents, a later document shows us that the nuns were fully capable of singing liturgical music on their own.[20] This reference again comes from Novodevichii Convent, to which Sofiia Alekseevna, daughter of Tsar Aleksei and half-sister of Peter the Great, was banished in 1689. About a decade later, in 1698, when Peter received information indicating that Sofiia was involved in an uprising by the musketeers, security around her was tightened, and she was finally forced to take her vows as a nun. Peter was concerned with isolating her entirely, and his efforts included the male singers who performed in liturgical services there. To this end, he directed in October 1698 that "no choristers [*pevchie*] should be admitted to the monastery. The nuns sing well enough . . ."[21] The nuns also functioned as music scribes. An Irmologii (a collection of hymns sung at Matins) written in staff notation by nuns at the convent is dated 1660, and the extant collection from the convent includes other notated manuscripts.[22]

The busy and constant preoccupation of the *pevchie d'iaki* with the tools of their musical trade suggests how deeply the value of liturgical singing was embedded in the culture of the royal family and of Muscovy itself. Tsar Aleksei, for example, tried his hand at composition, and one scholar even suggests that Aleksei composed a four-part chant setting written not in neumes but in staff notation. This points to another of the singers' duties, that of instructing the royal children in liturgical singing.[23] Tsar Aleksei learned his lessons well, as indeed did many of Russia's other rulers. Ivan IV wrote either text or music for liturgical hymns; Aleksei's successor, Fedor, wrote church music; and Peter the Great enjoyed performing with the liturgical singers during services.[24]

Tsar Aleksei seems to have been particularly keen in his knowledge of singing practices, as shown in one unnerving incident recounted by Paul of Aleppo. At a Vespers service conducted at the St. Savva Monastery outside Moscow, Aleksei sharply criticized the reader for committing serious errors (the unfortunate cleric did not use the terminology proper when reading in the presence of a patriarch), calling him a "stupid fellow" and providing him with the proper text. The tsar then turned his attention to the singers:

> From the commencement of the service, to the end, he [Aleksei] had been busy teaching them the order of the Ritual; saying to them, as he went round, "Chaunt so": repeating such a Canon . . . or such a Troparion, in such a tune. If they went wrong, he scolded them, and made them go back; being particularly desirous, as I suppose, that they should not do amiss in the presence of our Patriarch [Makarios]. In a word, he was as it were the *Tipokhari*, that is, master of the *Tipikhon*, going round to them and teaching them.[25]

Music manuscripts preserved from the seventeenth century reveal the rich array of liturgical singing styles that constituted the repertoire of these various ensembles. The singers and scribes had to know a variety of monophonic and polyphonic chant styles as well as the new chant dialects that flowered during the late sixteenth and seventeenth centuries (outlined briefly in the introduction). There was also a major linguistic reform in the seventeenth century, in which the sung liturgical texts were revised so that they reflected the pronunciation of texts as they were spoken or read. This entailed important adjustments in the neumes to which these texts were set, and there came to be specialist masters of *narechnoe penie,* that is, song as it sounded in speech.[26] The singers were also engaged in efforts to reconcile the many regional and individual variants that had cropped up in liturgical singing, and in the early years of the century, they had undertaken a thorough attempt at evaluating different variants for individual chants. The Novgorodian tradition remained strong well into the seventeenth century, and other regional traditions and individual ensembles suggest, at times, considerable expertise. Each of the singers in the choir of Archbishop Simeon of Vologda and Belozersk in the mid-1660s, for example, knew multiple parts in polyphonic settings of an extensive liturgical repertoire.[27]

By the seventeenth century, polyphonic settings were well established in Russian liturgical practice.[28] Three-part settings, in which the cantus firmus (called the *put',* or path, way) was placed in the middle voice, were the most common, as in musical example 2.1, a setting of the Cherubic Hymn. The added voices follow the contours of the chant, both melodically and rhythmically, with the upper voices tending to move in parallel motion and the lowest voice moving sometimes in contrary motion, sometimes in parallel. The movement (both melodic and rhythmic) overall is smooth, the vocal ranges close together. It is this style of three-part (*troestrochnoe*) singing that one of the sovereign's singers, Samoilo Eftifeev (or Evtikhiev), taught when he was sent to Tobol'sk, in Siberia, on a multi-year mission in the early 1620s to instruct two *stanitsy* of the archbishop's singers there.[29]

Polyphonic writing of all types was facilitated by the important notational changes that took place over the course of the seventeenth century as the traditional *znamennyi* neumed notation was reworked to indicate specific pitches rather than designating movement through intervallic space. The origins of this process are generally associated with the Novgorodian singer Ivan Shaidur around 1600, and over the course of the century several different types of specialized signs were developed. These notational changes were eventually codified by the Second Commission on church practice (1669–70), but as we shall see, events had already overtaken these efforts. By this time, after the large influx of Ukrainian singers who

EXAMPLE 2.1. Three-part (*troestrochnoe*) setting of the Cherubic Hymn
(from Morosan, *One Thousand Years of Russian Church Music,* pp. 91–92,
used by permission)

brought the Western five-line staff with them, the new staff notation was widely used in Muscovy, where it was known as Kievan notation.[30]

This notation brought a different kind of polyphonic repertoire and singers of different training and expertise into Muscovite practice in mid-century. This initially occurred largely at the behest of Patriarch Nikon, who was a strong promoter of Ukrainian and Belarusian singers. It is from this period that *partesnoe penie* (part singing) begins to circulate in earnest in Muscovy—its very name, from the Latin *partes,* proclaims its origins in Western-style polyphonic writing. Nikon's interest dates from his time as metropolitan of Novgorod, when he began the practice of including Greek and Kievan (polyphonic) singing; according to his contemporary biographer, he "assembled *klirosy* of wondrous singers and exceptional voices [who produced] animate singing far better than an inanimate organ; and no one else had such singing as Metropolitan Nikon." In addition to employing individual *vspevaki,* as did other important Muscovites, when he became patriarch, Nikon sponsored the new styles at the Voskresenskii Novoierusalimskii (Resurrection-New Jerusalem) Monastery, which he founded outside Moscow.[31] The patriarch's musical concerns are also linked with another of the institutions he founded, the Iverskii Monastery near Novgorod. In ordering preparations for a visit he and the tsar were to make to this monastery in 1657, Nikon requested that the hierarchs select from the brethren the best singers for performing the new part-singing style ("po portesu"); a few years later, Nikon ordered the archimandrite there to send polyphonic musical sources to the New Jerusalem Monastery.[32] At the end of the century, Johan Sparwenfeld, a member of a Swedish delegation to Muscovy, visited the Iverskii Monastery and reported on the pleasing polyphonic singing he heard there, describing harmony in five or six parts and the singing of "harmonious hymns."[33]

The new vocal *partesnoe penie,* particularly the large-scale settings known as *kontserty,* introduced stylistic features to listeners and ensembles already familiar with the challenges of polyphonic singing. Instead of the smooth and consistent homophony of the familiar three-part chant settings, however, the *kontserty* featured alternations and contrasts of all sorts, all of which were knitted together with some care, at least by the most successful composers. The liturgical texts they employed (frequently settings of the Divine Liturgy) formed a bedrock of continuity that was varied by alternations in texture and dynamics, often shifting between a smaller three-part ensemble and a larger group, and by the profusion of musical ideas, word painting, and changes in meter and tempo. Musical example 2.2 is the "Kyrie eleison" section from a late seventeenth-century anonymous setting of the Divine Liturgy. Such five-part settings are very common in the

EXAMPLE 2.2. Five-part Kyrie from a setting of the Divine Liturgy
(from Morosan, *One Thousand Years of Russian Church Music*,
pp. 155–57, used by permission)

EXAMPLE 2.3. Vasilii Titov, *kontsert* "Beznevestnaia Devo" (O Virgin unwedded) (from Morosan, *One Thousand Years of Russian Church Music,* pp. 206–207, used by permission)

kontsert repertoire, and here the composer frequently alternates between various combinations of three voices and the full ensemble, with deliberate and careful consideration of color and timbre.

Composers sometimes created clear large-scale formal structures in their *kontserty,* and often they wrote for larger ensembles, generally eight voices, but sometimes for larger multiples of the basic four-part ensemble. Musical example 2.3 is by Vasilii Titov, a member of the sovereign's singing ensemble and one of the best and most sensitive of the composers in this style. In this example he uses repetitions of the words "Beznevestnaia Devo" (O Virgin unwedded) not only as a means of emphasizing the plea of the supplicant, but in order to articulate the work's musical structure as well. The phrase is consistently set for three voices (tenors 1 and 2 and bass 1), acting as a foil for the full eight-voice setting, which is itself divided into a constellation of timbres and colors.[34]

It is this kind of large-scale polyphonic singing that was the focus of Nikolai Diletskii's important theoretical treatise, surviving in several extant versions dating from between 1677 and 1681 (discussed below in chapter 5). The style by this time was well known in Muscovy. The composer Pavel Chernitsyn wrote a five-part *kontsert* for the wedding of Tsar Fedor Alekseevich in 1682, for example, and this is the type of music that was the subject of an exchange about the liturgical singing practiced in Smolensk. Church authorities were sent to this western border city in 1685 to investigate what were considered to be inappropriately sumptuous liturgical performances, including elaborate polyphonic choral music, cultivated there by Metropolitan Simeon, who justified his musical practices by saying that his parishioners were used to such music and without it, they would be bored.[35]

Flames and Angels: Sacred Singing and Performance in Muscovy

The established, regulated, and ever-growing professional choirs interacted readily, producing a perfect setting for the widespread transmission of musical styles and works. The singers in the capital city's choirs lived together in clusters of housing, mostly in the vicinity of the Kremlin.[36] They came from a variety of cities and towns throughout Muscovy, and not only did singers move from one choir to another but they also interacted with the many regional choirs that frequently visited the capital.[37] The effect of these massed choirs must, on occasion, have been particularly impressive, even by the Russian Orthodox Church's high standards of magnificence, as a look at a series of especially solemn ceremonies in the spring of 1669 shows. These events honored the memory of Tsar Aleksei's wife, Mariia Il'inichna, who had died in March of that year.[38] For reading psalms at the funeral, thirty *pevchie* and *krestovye d'iaki* were given a total of 336 rubles, and for the funeral itself, forty-three *d'iaki* were given a total of 133 rubles and change. In the payment record, each of the singers is named, placed in order within the *stanitsa*, and each paid according to his rank. Apart from the spiritual solace afforded by the ceremony, there may also have been an element of personal comfort for the tsar. There were familiar faces at the funeral services, for some of the participating singers had been in the sovereign's employ for more than a decade.[39]

Payment records also preserve the same hierarchical ordering even when the singers were participating in non-liturgical traditions. For example, in 1673 a large group of ecclesiastical singers was assembled at court to sing Christmas music. The carolers (*slavel'shchiki*) were associated with an impressive array of metropolitans and archbishops, all of whom were represented by at least two ranks of *d'iaki* and in some cases, by additional sub-clerics (*pod'iaki*) as well.[40] Surviving payment records for this event do not list individual singers in each category, so it is not possible to determine exactly how many singers entertained the tsar on this occasion, and it is not clear from the record if polyphonic music was performed. The metropolitan of Krutitsa brought a *putnik*, Grigorii, and the *nizhnik* Fedor, but these labels may indicate the singers' customary titles rather than the lines they actually performed on this particular occasion (*put*, path, indicates the vocal line carrying the cantus firmus, and *nizhnik,* the singer of the lowest line). But what is certainly clear is that the walls of the Kremlin residence were ringing with choral music that night in a five-hour performance by a series of large, trained choirs from all over the tsar's realm—a fitting Christmas gift to bestow upon the ruler. Seasonal, non-liturgical caroling, particularly at Christmastime, produced a wealth of music and was an ancient part of Russian life; the documents cited here show that the most highly trained singers of the state took part, perhaps even singing the newest styles (the polyphony that may be suggested by the terms *nizhnik* and *putnik*), lending the performance an unexpected aura of professionalism and official sanction.[41]

But Yuletide caroling was only one of the non-liturgical duties of the professional choirs; indeed, Paul of Aleppo seems to have encountered the singers almost as often outside the church as inside. In such performances—liturgical and non-liturgical alike—the choirs functioned as official and public representatives of high church and court culture, introducing liturgical singing styles to foreign diplomats and visitors as well as presenting polished and professional singing to the Muscovite public at large. Their music was thus a shared experience for many people, a rich and dynamic component of Muscovy's political and cultural discourse.[42]

Banquets were frequently ornamented with readings from the Gospels and singing, as we saw in Arsenios's account of the installation of the first Russian patriarch and as Paul recounts enthusiastically about a banquet for Patriarch Nikon in the mid-1650s: "How wonderful are these things which we witnessed . . . You had a reader to read from the Fathers, and chaunters, hour after hour, to sing before you!"[43] This was a long-standing duty for the singers, and not only in the context of religious celebrations but also for political displays. An English party that had visited the Russian court in the sixteenth century described the same sort of entertainment when, at a state dinner, Tsar Ivan IV entertained his guests with singing. "In the dinner time," writes the English chronicler, "there came in six singers which stood in the midst of the chamber, and their faces towards the Emperor, who sang there before dinner was ended three severall times."[44]

The singers also participated in outdoor processions of all kinds, both religious and secular. Most important and most elaborate were the great church holidays marked by stylized and symbolic movements around the city of Moscow (and duplicated elsewhere in other urban settings), for example the celebration of the Blessing of the Waters on Epiphany (6 January). Richard James witnessed such a procession in Kholmogory in 1619, briefly describing the singing that accompanied the physical actions in the ceremony:

> [U]ppon Twelve day, they digge a greate square on the ice, and in that a little hole, which after manie praiers and singinge, with other ceremonies of candles and images, the priest breaks up, and the water suddenly rises in which they at Colmogrod dipt at least 20 yonge children over head and years [ears] thrice, and every one tooke a little cup of the water which they keep etc. [T]his place they call Yordan in imitation of X. baptisme.[45]

James was one of many travelers to describe this ceremony, one of the most important and impressive in the Russian church calendar and which seems to have been especially fascinating to visitors, most of whom were unaccustomed to the spectacle of frozen rivers and cutting through ice. Indeed, Paul of Aleppo, who participated in the procession held in the capital city about twenty-five years later, had little to say that was not weather-related (a running theme of his account). Although Paul managed to make it through the day, "though our hands and feet and noses were nearly bitten off by the frost," he pays little attention to the ceremony itself. He is more informative about the Lesser Blessing of the Waters, a smaller ceremony held on the more congenial date of 1 August, and his description is quite similar to James's for the more imposing Epiphany Day ceremony:

> When we arrived near the bank of the [Moscow] river, we ascended upon a large scaffold of boards, which had been raised by the janissaries, on the

preceding day, over the river . . . As the choristers chaunted, the Patriarch went down to incense the water, the pictures [icons] around, and the attendants . . . Then he took the cross, and advanced near to the water; and having formed over it the sign of the Cross, he dipped the Cross in the water . . . chaunting all the time, "Save, O God, thy people!" and adding the name of the Emperor. The choristers still answered him with the same chaunt, whilst he washed the cross in a vessel of silver.[46]

Music formed part of the deeply layered symbolism of the elaborate Muscovite Palm Sunday procession, which Michael Flier has described as a "dynamic manifestation of the Palm Sunday icon," a "living tableau" in which the participants become "tangible representations of the intangible."[47] The singers in this context function not only as transmitters of the sacred texts but as performers or actors in a theatricalized rendition of the ritual. Paul describes the setting for the boy singers in the ceremony:

In front of all [in the procession] was a large tree, formed of those branches we mentioned [pussy willows, substituting for palm fronds], which they had been preparing from the dawn of day till now . . . They had then placed it in two sledges, fastened together, and formed around in benches of boards, on which they placed six little Anagnostae in their surplices, chaunting the Hymn of St. Lazarus with a very loud voice; the whole drawn by two horses, at a quick pace.[48]

The singers also performed in outdoor processions unconnected to a specific church holiday or liturgical action. Paul describes the splendid procession assembled to meet Tsar Aleksei, who was returning to the capital from his military expedition to Smolensk. The road was lined with fabric, the clergy were carrying banners and jeweled icons, and the two patriarchs took part in the procession. They walked for an hour, says Paul, although the tsar was concerned that the distance and the cold weather might be placing too great a strain on Patriarch Makarios:

Every moment there came, on the part of the Emperor, an archon to the Patriarch, to beseech him to stop where he was, for fear he should be fatigued with walking along the road. But he would not; and we moved on at a quick pace, the choristers chaunting all the while, with the intent to meet the Emperor at the earthen wall.[49]

The most elaborate and the most overtly theatrical of the singers' performances was in the annual production of a liturgical drama based on the Old Testament story of the three boys in the fiery furnace (Daniel 3). This was performed every year, generally on the Sunday of the Forefathers but with adjustments depending on the day on which Christmas fell. The tradition stretched back to the first half of the sixteenth century at least, with some references indicating a much earlier familiarity with the rite.[50] The Muscovite version, as it emerges from sixteenth- and seventeenth-century sources, represents a combination of Byzantine and Western elements, the former supplying the basic liturgical setting as a drama, and the latter some scenic effects. The Muscovite production was staged during Matins, after several days of preparation inside the cathedral and several weeks of costume and prop repair and instruction for the boy singers.[51] The central action involves the three children who are threatened by the Chaldeans (who do not appear in the Byzantine rendition) with death in the fiery furnace if they do not renounce their belief in God. The children refuse and are led to the furnace, where alarming quantities of real fire were produced by means of powdered stag-horn moss, carefully distributed but not always without incident, by experienced players.[52] A loud noise accompanies the descent of the angel from the ceiling, the Chaldeans fall to their knees, and the children emerge unscathed; appropriate liturgical verses are sung throughout by the boys, the deacon, and the choir. The play was enacted widely throughout Muscovy, with performances recorded in many different cities, as emphasized in one of the early descriptions by Giles Fletcher, the English emissary who was in Moscow in 1588–89:

> Another pageant they haue [in addition to the Palm Sunday procession] . . . the weeke before the natiuitie of Christ; when euery Bishop in his Cathedral Church, setteth forth a shew of the three children in the Ouen. Where the Angell is made to come flying from the roofe of the Church, with great admiration of the lookers on and many terrible flashes of fire, are made with rosen, and gun-powder by the Chaldeans (as they call them) that run about the towne all the twelue dayes, disguised in their plaiers coats, and make much good sport for the honour of the Bishops pageant. At the Mosko, the Emperour himselfe, and the Empresse neuer faile to be at it, though it be but the same matter plaied euery yeere, without any new inuention at all.[53]

The presentation was cultivated intensively from 1613 (when Mikhail Romanov took the throne) through the early 1630s. The Play (or action, *deistvo*) of the Furnace seems to have afforded the possibility for interaction between liturgical personnel and secular players. It appears that non-liturgical actors took the roles of the evil (non-singing) Chaldeans. Records from the Moscow performances in this period show a series of payments to men (or boys?) taking the roles of the Chaldeans, who were often performed by the same players year after year, suggesting at least a stable pool of actors who were able to show up every December. It has been suggested that the Chaldeans were in fact played by *skomorokhi*, who might have been considered appropriate for taking on such evil roles (although, as the traveler Olearius noted, the Chaldeans were required to cleanse themselves in the river on Epiphany, after the revelries were concluded).[54] Existing payment records, however, do not specify that these roles were taken by *skomorokhi* or *veselye liudi* (merry folk), terms which do appear in other official records. Given the varied and numerous personnel at the disposal of the patriarch and the court, one might suggest that the Chaldeans were drawn from a different pool, neither professional singer nor *skomorokh*. Indeed, one of the stalwarts in the role of a Chaldean jailer, Sava Vasil'ev, who performed from 1613 to 1633, is identified in one source as a treasury employee (*kazennyi storozh*). Others with this job title were also intensely involved in the productions at this time (although not as actors).[55]

Whatever their day jobs might have been, however, the behavior of the Chaldeans certainly does recall that of the *skomorokhi,* for example as recounted by Olearius, based on his experiences in Muscovy in the 1630s (and echoing Fletcher's earlier account). Olearius describes only their antics outside the church and does not discuss their context in the drama itself, which he appears not to have witnessed. The Chaldeans, he says,

> often burned the beards of passersby, especially the peasants. While we were there, they burned up a peasant's load of hay, and when he began to resist them, they burned his beard and the hair on his head. Whoever wanted to be spared had to pay a kopek. They were dressed as carnival revelers [*Fassnachts-Brüder*], wearing on their heads painted wooden hats, and their beards were smeared with honey to prevent their being burned by the fire they were casting about . . .
>
> During their escapades the Chaldeans were considered pagans, and impure. It was even thought that if they should die during these days they would be damned. Therefore, on the Day of the Three Saintly Kings [Epiphany] . . . they were all baptized anew.[56]

The Play of the Furnace seems to have died out around the late 1640s. Olearius was in Russia several times in the mid-1630s, with his final trip in 1643, and he specifies that he viewed the wild behavior "while we were there." In the first edition of his book, from 1647, he simply describes the mayhem, but in the expanded edition from 1656 he adds that because of the danger of such escapades, "the Patriarch has entirely abolished their ridiculous games and masked running about."[57] Paul of Aleppo does not describe the play in the voluminous record of his trip from the mid-1650s, and Jacob Reutenfels, who was in Russia in the 1670s, describes the Chaldeans and their connections to the performance as something that belonged to the past.[58] There is, however, a late description in the account of the Moscow embassy headed by Charles Howard, the first Earl of Carlisle, in 1663–

64, when the party witnessed the play and the accompanying revels in Vologda, where they were detained over the winter on their way to the capital. Perhaps this was an isolated remnant of the once-thriving tradition, or perhaps it indicates that the production survived into the second half of the century in outlying areas; at any rate, the English party's observations, which appear to be first-hand accounts, coincide closely with Olearius's earlier description:

> In the 18. of December we saw that strange representation, that is annually made by the Moscovites of the fiery furnace in which Shadrech, Mesec, and Abednego were cast by the King of Babilon. The Persons that act in it are disguised, their beards rubbed over with honey, their hats of wood with which they run up and down the streets, and with wild fire in their hand burn the hair or beard of any body they meet, with great insolence.[59]

It is not clear why the performances ceased. The 1640s was the period of Tsar Aleksei's most austere frame of mind, in which he even forbade the traditional instrumental fanfares at weddings, to be replaced by solemn singing by the *pevchie d'iaki* (see chapter 4); this was also the beginning of a fairly severe crackdown on the *skomorokhi* by the central government, with orders flying to all corners of the country ordering an Epiphany-like cleansing of their influence. Whether actual *skomorokhi* participated or whether the actions of the players were only uncomfortably close to such behavior we do not know—at any rate, the productions apparently did not continue in significant numbers into the second half of the century, nor were they revived when Aleksei began to express an interest in secular theatrical productions (although there was a play on the same Biblical story, written with flamboyant staging by the poet Simeon Polotskii).

Another, later kind of performance in which the singers were engaged takes us one step further away from liturgical conventions and one step closer to the performance ideas embodied in the court theater of the 1670s. Both the genre and the performance traditions are mixed; if this chapter traces a larger continuum of situations in which the *pevchie d'iaki* might have participated, ranging from liturgical services to outdoor processions to liturgical dramas, so the declamations, orations, and dialogues popular at court from the 1660s on display a similar variety of performances, some closely connected with liturgical rites (name-day celebrations, for example) and some far removed from such services (greetings, pastoral dialogues, and so forth). As literary historian Aleksandr Panchenko emphasizes, not only is there a continuum of appropriate venues linking such performances (in church, at banquets, in the royal living quarters), there is also a similar concept of performance style joining these pieces: a performed reading that links liturgical readings of the sort Paul of Aleppo describes to readings of the rhymed, syllabic poetry of the declamations, structurally different but thematically related.[60]

The best known of these stylized performed readings are the declamations (*deklamatsii*), which were introduced in polished fashion into Russian practice in 1656, when Simeon Polotskii, a monk at the Bogoiavlenskii (Epiphany) Monastery in Polotsk, greeted Tsar Aleksei, who had accompanied his troops to the city, with a declamation performed by twelve children. The young performers (*otroki, otrosi*) were students at the monastic school, and they were demonstrating a performance based on their training in the academic curriculum common in non-Muscovite Orthodox schools, that is, a series of courses based on Western classical models; the declamations were part of the curriculum covering rhetoric and poetics.[61] Simeon brought some of his students with him when he went to Moscow for a visit in 1660, and they performed a series of twelve-part declamations during the few months they spent in the capital city. The students performed first for the tsar himself; then for the birth of Tsarevna Mariia; for Tsarevich Aleksei Alekseevich in honor of his patron saint; for the tsar again on his own name-day; and on a few other occasions.[62] These performances were unstaged, without the special costumes, props, and role playing that had been associated with liturgical drama.

Although Polotskii's declamations seem to be the first of their kind in Muscovy, other greeting ceremonies, readings at banquets, and so forth were common in Muscovite practice, as we have seen, for example, from Paul of Aleppo's account. The new, formal *deklamatsiia* style seems to have influenced Patriarch Nikon, who in 1657, shortly after the performance in Polotsk, ordered a similar twelve-part greeting ceremony to take place at the Iverskii Monastery for a visit by Tsar Aleksei and himself:

> You should select some twelve brothers from the Iverskii Monastery who will deliver an oration [*oratsiia*] in front of the tsar and me, it should be short, religious, and laudatory; also select twelve youngsters or more, as many as you can find, and teach them an oration for the arrival of the tsar and myself, short, religious, and laudatory; also prepare an oration to be delivered at the time of the tsar's and my departure from the Iverskii Monastery.[63]

Nikon's references to groups of twelve presenters, as well as his use of the Latin term *oratsiia,* suggests that he was influenced by Simeon Polotskii's performances. Apparently he wished for a greeting at his own Iverskii Monastery that would be as impressive as the recent ceremony in Polotsk.

There were other such declamations and orations in Moscow, written by

Polotskii and others, and some of these works suggest that the *otroki* who performed the verses may have been young singers. This would make sense, not only because such boys would have been literate and trainable, accustomed as they were to memorizing and performing, but also because they were available as a group. Some of the recitations, for example, were closely connected with liturgical texts, that is, texts (and music) with which boy singers would already have been familiar. An example is Polotskii's "Stikhi kraesoglasnyia na Rozhdestvo Khristovo, glagolemyi v tserkvi vo slavu Khrista Boga" (Rhyming verses on the Nativity of Christ, pronounced in church in praise of Christ the Lord), which is written for eight pairs of boys. Each declaimed verse is paired with a text that in liturgical practice would have been sung (an *irmos,* a model stanza in a hymn text). The pairs of texts are closely linked by means of repeated words and phrases and, as befitting a performance "pronounced in church," it certainly seems possible that the *irmos* texts would have been sung.[64] Indeed one source, from the 1690s, even includes some staff notation, apparently indicating the incipits of several declamations.[65]

Another work, by Simeon's student Sil'vestr Medvedev, further supports the notion that young singers were involved and also indicates a different, more private performance venue. A note following Medvedev's "Skazanie o strastekh Khrista" (The story of the Passion of Christ), which dates from the early 1680s, reads: "These verses were sent to the Great Lord in the evening with Lavrin, on the 7th day of April, and were divided out among twelve people, and by this singer they were written in a booklet on sheets of paper." Panchenko has identified Lavrin as Lavrii (Lavrentii) Kuz'min Burmistrov, a sovereign singer whose career can be traced throughout the decade of the 1680s and who was indeed associated with Medvedev. In the 1680s and 1690s, singers were involved in the orations written for the court by the poet and teacher Karion Istomin.[66]

We also know of a young singer associated with both Polotskii and Medvedev, and although there is no evidence that he performed in any of the various recitations, spoken or sung, his biography indicates that both of these writers not only had a general acquaintance with singers while in Moscow but had specific knowledge of specific performers. Vasilii Repskii was a "foreigner from Lithuania" who was sent to Kiev as a fourteen-year-old *dyshkant* in the retinue of Bishop Mefodii. When Mefodii went to Moscow in 1665, Vasilii accompanied him and came to the attention of the authorities there. On his way back to Kiev Repskii was recalled to Moscow, against the wishes of his parents. He ended up as a singer in the royal living quarters, where he remained for four years, a duty unaffiliated with the sovereign's or patriarchal *pevchie d'iaki* and just the sort of supplementary position in which other *vspevaki* were typically engaged at that time. Although the chronology is somewhat confused, it appears that at about this same time both Repskii and

Medvedev studied Latin with Simeon Polotskii. A later court petition outlines Repskii's travails after becoming involved with Artemon Matveev, the architect of Tsar Aleksei's court theater in the 1670s; we shall return to Repskii in chapter 6.[67]

The declamations and other performed readings are thus linked to liturgical traditions and texts and, at the same time, take us further in the direction of secular (or at least, non-liturgical) performance and away from church ritual. Through their ties to the *pevchie d'iaki,* they indicate that the singers, too, played a variety of roles as performers of liturgy and performers of secular poetry, as readers of psalms for the faithful and as readers of verses for what may have been the very same group, now an assembled audience waiting to be entertained.

Avvakum's Distress: Music in Muscovy's Mid-Century Cultural Conflicts

Tsar Aleksei is often depicted as curious and open, especially at the end of his reign, and this curiosity seems to have been activated with respect to the new singing styles so heavily promoted by Nikon in mid-century. What these invited, non-Muscovite singers offered, and what seemed to have fascinated both tsar and patriarch, was not simply a new set of arrangements of the familiar sung texts but rather a new musical sound, a different approach to performance. Paul of Aleppo expresses this clearly and shows that this is not solely a matter of repertoire or the use of polyphony, but rather encompasses performance practice as a whole, both reading and singing. For example, on that same trip to the St. Savva Monastery, when Aleksei so sternly corrected the singers, the tsar discovered that Paul had been studying Russian and asked him to do the readings on the following day:

> I read the Prone in Russian [reports Paul], but in such a manner as to astonish them; for the manner of reading of the Muscovites is heavy and harsh; whereas I read in the light Grecian tone, so that the Emperor was both amazed and delighted. It is usual for the singers at every verse to chaunt *Kirie eleison;* but he would not suffer them to raise their voices, that he might hear distinctly what I said; and every now and then he nodded his head with delight, as I was afterwards told by the persons present.[68]

It is such lightness over heaviness that Paul emphasizes time and again. Paul is certainly aware of his own tastes and prejudices; he states them frankly and indeed frequently, yet passages like the following serve also to point out the difference in singing practice he observed on this trip:

> [T]he chaunting of the Cossacks [in Ukrainian churches] dilates the breast and clears the heart of care. With a vehement love for psalmody, and a strict

attention to the rules of music, they give forth, in a sweet high tone, from their very souls as it were, and from one mouth, the most delightful sounds; whereas the chaunt of the Muscovites is without science, just as it happens: it is all one to them; they find no fault; and the finest in their estimation is the low, rough, broad voice, which it is far from being pleasant to hear. As with us these gross tones are found fault with, so by them our high intonation is deemed vicious; and they laugh at the Cossacks, and reproach them for their music, telling them that theirs is the music of the Franks and Poles.[69]

Although elsewhere Paul does have more positive comments to make about the Russian singers, he points to this basic contrast in performance several times, for example in his description of singing at a banquet in the presence of the tsar and Russian patriarch, both of whom appear to have been fascinated by what they heard:

> For a little while, the singers came and chaunted: but, for the most part, the patriarch and the Emperor delighted only in the chaunting of the Cossack children; many of whom the Emperor brought with him from Poland, and gave them to the Patriarch . . . They always took the lead in singing; and their music was greatly preferred to the harsh and gross intonation of the Muscovites.[70]

Paul's preferences also account for his approval of the nuns, which reaches a fever pitch in his description of nuns singing Divine Liturgy at the Convent of the Divine Ascension in Ukraine; many of the nuns, apparently, were from Polish families. "[T]hey commenced singing and chaunting," he writes, "with a sweet voice and tune which affected the heart and drew tears from the eyes: it was a soothing searching melody, greatly to be admired above the chaunting of men."[71]

Paul's descriptions also help us to understand how other foreigners might have perceived the singing they heard in Muscovy. In some cases the musical differences they point to seem to reflect context more than execution. The mid-sixteenth-century English visitors noted above remarked that the Russian singing they heard at a banquet "delighted our eares little or nothing." This certainly may have been true, but not necessarily because of the quality of the singing itself. Westerners might have expected banquet music to be light-hearted entertainment, *Tafelmusik* of the sort played at Dmitrii's and Marina's wedding, whereas Muscovites saw it as an opportunity for solemn and uplifting, rather than "delightful," liturgical-style singing.[72] Other references to Muscovite singing by foreigners, largely negative, seem to reinforce the visitors' difficulties in approaching a completely foreign liturgy and its accompanying singing styles. Most foreigners, when they are able to observe anything of Russian religious practice, thus seize on the lack of musical instruments in the services.[73]

But some observers emphasize the same vocal qualities Paul had fixed upon. For example, in a frequently cited account from the early eighteenth century, Friedrich Wilhelm von Bergholz describes the seasonal caroling at Christmas and points to the powerful bass voices, with the familiar observation that the singing style was not particularly to his liking:

> On the first day of Christmas, the Russian court singers have a custom of going around to the upper classes with vocal music and best wishes for the season. They thus appeared at our residence right after dinner with about forty people. Among them were wonderful voices, especially the splendid basses, which in Russia are better and more powerful than anywhere else, although their manner of singing might not be the best. The voices of some of the bass singers are as clear and deep as an organ, and in Italy they would make a lot of money.[74]

Even a witness as reliably and provocatively negative as the Englishman Samuel Collins, who was in Russia between 1660 and 1669 as physician to the tsar, can, in light of Paul's more informed observations, tell us something. He too gives a grudging acknowledgment of the power of Russian voices, in a description of Russian mendicant singers: the "strenuous voice [in which they sing] looseth nothing by its harsh notes." Collins describes a four-part singing style and unmeasured performances ("[s]ometimes they will run hard upon a scent, as though they meant to imitate the Italian Recitative Musick"). He also notes the presence of music schools, and he includes several liturgical texts that he "had prick't down by one of the Patriarchs Choristers," implying some sort of exchange between the irascible foreign physician and the professional singers.[75]

Most important, however, is the glimpse Paul's descriptions provide into the variety of singing styles acceptable to those most concerned, Aleksei and Nikon. By appreciating their responses (at least insofar as we can assume that Paul's prejudices did not lead him too far astray), we have another way to provide some context for the enormous changes occurring in Muscovite liturgical singing throughout the century. The series of changes and official reforms in notation, texts, and in the liturgy as a whole are certainly crucial. But the long experience in Muscovy of exposure to a wide variety of (Orthodox) singing, by many different kinds of singers, seems to have been equally influential.

Mid-seventeenth-century Muscovy was concerned with the establishment of an authoritative body of laws and procedures in many arenas. Law codes were compiled and revised, and even the tsar's favorite sport of falconry was regulated and recorded to the smallest detail. Liturgical music did not escape this impulse, but in Nikon's reforms of the 1650s and in the councils of 1666 and 1667 that followed (upholding the reforms but marking Nikon's final removal from the patriarchal throne), only certain types of liturgical singing practices were considered. Thus the cacophony of the simultaneous singing of multiple texts (called *mnogoglasie*, many-voicedness) was denounced, and there had been ongoing efforts at notational (and textual) reform, beginning with the special commission that met in the early 1650s.[76] The councils also addressed the issue of singing at domestic worship services, noting that the singing there should be regulated as in a church, and that in either venue, if no priest or celebrant were present, no singing should occur. Problems created by ill-trained or vain and oblivious singers were, of course, perennial and their discussion not limited to special commissions or assemblies of patriarchs.[77]

Oddly enough, though, what would seem to be one of the most important musical issues—the introduction, on a very large scale and through the special efforts of the patriarch himself, of the Kievan, Western-based *partesnoe* styles—was ignored both by the councils and, largely, by the singers themselves.[78] This does not mean that there was no opposition to *partesnoe penie*, but it does suggest that the professional singers were not leading the charge in questioning the style's authority and validity. Perhaps they considered this music unremarkably similar to the chant-based polyphony familiar from over a century of use, or perhaps they were thoroughly accustomed to hearing *partesnoe* "translations" (*perevody*) themselves by this time, either in their own performances or through the renditions offered by the imported *vspevaki*. From the singers' point of view, then, such musical diversity might have seemed natural, even traditional, and in this light it is perhaps less surprising that a challenging or verification of the Western-based *partesnoe penie* (or its specialist practitioners, the *vspevaki*) did not emerge from professional singers' circles.

Non-musicians, however, were anxious to establish, one way or another, the appropriateness of such music and of other innovative practices they observed in liturgical services, and in 1668 a group of parishioners from the Church of St. John the Apostle in Moscow addressed their concerns to a natural authority, the visiting patriarchs who had been in the capital for more than a year presiding over the councils at which they had ruled upon just such issues. The parishioners inquired about several new practices they had observed, including the use of "Greek and Kievan singing" in services. The patriarchs responded to their queries (in a slightly indirect fashion), saying that "the singing called *partesnoe*," although not of the practice of the Eastern Church, "is used here [in Muscovy] and its use is not frowned upon by anyone." They thus expressed no objection to Western-style polyphonic music playing a role in Orthodox liturgical services.[79] The patriarchs' sweeping answer, a kind of coda to the formal councils, is something of a puzzle: how did the Eastern patriarchs have the temerity to pronounce upon such matters, particularly when they were not familiar with this type of music from their own traditions? Their response, though, seems to have emerged not only from strictly musical considerations but also from the different approaches to reform and from the different kinds of authority with which each of the parties was engaged.

From their first grand entrance into Moscow in late 1666, the visiting patriarchs Makarios of Antioch and Paisios of Alexandria had been heavily involved in the usual liturgical ceremonies and processions, in addition to their work on the commissions. The celebrations welcoming their arrival to the capital included singing by the sovereign's and patriarchal singers plus a host of singers associated with regional hierarchs, and throughout their stay the patriarchs heard singers performing in processions, at banquets, and of course in the context of the liturgy. On several occasions the Russian patriarchal ensemble was specifically detailed to attend the foreign hierarchs on excursions to outlying monasteries. Indeed, when one looks at records of the visitors' stay, it is difficult to find a page on which liturgical singing by the specialist ensembles is *not* listed. At this mid-seventeenth-century convocation, as at the gatherings of foreign hierarchs in Moscow in previous years, there was singing in both Greek and Slavonic by the Russian patriarchal and sovereign's ensembles, as well as performances in Greek both by foreign specialists (especially by the singers Meletios and Dionysios) and by the foreign clergy as a whole.[80] There were also many different styles of singing displayed over the course of the commission's tenure, including a performance of *troestrochnoe penie* (three-part chant-based singing) in the presence of the visiting patriarchs.[81] Such wide and constant exposure does not establish the visitors as experts in Muscovite musical practice but it does show that they had some familiarity with its diversity, especially Patriarch Makarios, who was on his second extended Muscovite sojourn.

The patriarchs' response to the parishioners' queries was, in many ways, just what one might have expected. They had heard a variety of singing styles performed by the tsar's, the patriarch's, and the regional hierarchs' *pevchie d'iaki* throughout their stay and had evidently concluded that such varied practices constituted normal religious singing for their hosts. Their response therefore pointedly notes the acceptance of such practice in local tradition, even though this was a style they did not employ in their own churches. In this emphasis on acceptance of the local norm, the visiting patriarchs were following a process that had been explicitly and recently set out for the Russian church by Paisios, Patriarch of

Constantinople (1652–53 and 1654–55). In a letter of 1655, Paisios responded to a lengthy series of questions Nikon had raised about a range of liturgical practices. Paisios prefaced his answers with a careful explanation of the long-standing acceptance of divergences within the larger church. Thus Patriarch Paisios, in an apparent attempt to rein Nikon in somewhat, emphasized that "if it happens that a certain church differs from another in certain practices which are not important and essential to faith, or which have nothing to do with the chief articles of faith, but only in insignificant practices . . . then this should not cause any division, as long as one and the same faith is preserved." Thus, he told Nikon, "we must not think even now that our Orthodox faith is spoiled if someone has liturgical practices which differ somewhat from another in non-essentials . . ."[82]

This is the spirit—a fairly open concept of local tradition within a larger essential unity—in which the visiting patriarchs seem to have made their decision about Muscovite musical practice after the council concluded its official work, an approach perhaps in keeping with the less formal nature of the inquiry itself. Their response was not necessarily delivered in a fit of musically ignorant high-handedness (although, to be sure, the patriarchs had not hesitated in making sweeping pronouncements in their decisions for the council), but rather reflects an established context of allowing local practices their due if they did not interfere with the fundamental tenets of the faith. As far as the visiting patriarchs could tell, *partesnoe penie* fit this bill.

The official answer, however measured and predictable, did not really resolve anything, for this exchange proved to be only the beginning of a series of debates about musical style, debates that were waged using much the same terminology, and by the same foot soldiers, as were the larger debates about the purity of Muscovite Orthodox traditions (or in other words, the validity of Nikon's reforms) as a whole during these tumultuous decades. Excesses and abuses of liturgical music, whatever their sources, had long been a subject of dispute, and in addressing the issue of *mnogoglasie* the council had taken up a serious and widely acknowledged problem. In the succeeding decades, after the council's ruling on Nikon's reforms gave a hard edge to the boundaries between the official church and the traditionalist views of the Old Believers (or Old Ritualists, who rejected the Nikonian reforms), the musical debates began to take on a somewhat different focus. The participants did not represent simple oppositions: pro- or anti-Western or pro- or anti-reform. Everyone was in favor of respectful and well-regulated singing in church. But what constituted respectful performance, and whose rules were to regulate it? Like the False Dmitrii and his Polish cohorts blundering their way through Muscovite tradition, or the visiting patriarchs and their unfamiliar notions of local usage as opposed to the absolute authority the Russian parishioners were seeking, the Muscovite debaters were themselves often at cross purposes in their assumptions and in the language and images by which they expressed them.

The debates, of which music forms only one strand, were complex and subtle.[83] One can get a sense of the multi-layered tensions by exploring a single image—the organ—as it appears in writings representing different points of view. Archpriest Avvakum and others linked to the hardening split within the church consistently pointed disdainfully to the organ-like sound of the new liturgical singing styles they heard around them, often coupling this with a reference to the offensive physical movements that accompanied such performances. Avvakum's view has been widely and routinely quoted: "In many churches in Moscow they sing songs (*pesni*) instead of divine singing (*bozhestvennoe penie*), in Latin; [they] wave their arms and nod their heads and stamp their feet, as is usual with the Latins' [singing] with the organ."[84] Avvakum's is the best-known complaint, but he was not alone. The whole panoply of associations appears in a consciously apocalyptic passage written in an Old Believer account of liturgical musical practices observed in Tobol'sk in the mid-1660s: singing with organ-like sounds; comparisons to the dance-inducing organ tones of the Roman church; even references to *skomorokh*-style instruments.[85]

The elements Avvakum and others single out are apt targets, for they point to an unacceptable source of influence on Muscovite singing: the musical practices of the non-Orthodox West. But why the organ? Had these critics ever actually heard an organ in Muscovite liturgical practice (or, for that matter, in foreign religious worship in Moscow)? Although in later chapters we examine the organ's role in some Uniate services and even in Muscovite music theory, there is nothing to suggest that the instrument ever sounded in the liturgy as celebrated in Muscovite churches. There were many organs and other keyboard instruments at court and in the private homes of the elite, so it may be that Avvakum had some familiarity with such instruments, at least tangentially. In any case, as Max Okenfuss notes, there were a few Ukrainians among the Old Believers who may have had some first-hand knowledge of such traditions. Avvakum, however, seems not to be reacting to actual Russian liturgical practice; rather he is criticizing the sources of the new musical styles by invoking an instrument associated with Western religious practice and, in a more general fashion, with the vexing antics of the *skomorokhi*, long associated with instrumental performances of all types. Other writings and other people may have reinforced these associations, even (or perhaps especially) if those other writers were referring to the organ in matter-of-fact, non-metaphorical fashion. The learned Ukrainian/Belarusian cleric Epifanii Slavinetskii had come to

Muscovy to translate liturgical books and, after over twenty-five years in Moscow, his oeuvre encompassed a huge number of topics. In one of his works, he not only approves of organ playing but recommends it as appropriate for youths; still worse, this appears in a manual for the proper education of children, *Grazhdanstvo obychaev detskikh,* which was a translation of Erasmus of Rotterdam's *De civilitate morum puerilium.* No wonder Avvakum and his cohorts felt themselves under siege.[86]

Avvakum levels the same sort of criticism, using the same allusions to Western practice, in his equally familiar denunciation of new influences in Muscovite icon painting:

> Icon painters of an unfitting kind have multiplied in our Russian land . . . they paint the image of the Savior Emmanuel with a pudgy face, red lips, curly hair, fat fingers, and legs, with fat hips, in all, completely like a German, only the sword is lacking at his hip . . . Rus', why do you desire the customs and habits of the Germans . . . ? Do not bow down . . . to unsuitable images painted in the German tradition.[87]

The same hyperbolic language appears in an extraordinary Old Believer report sent, apparently, to Avvakum in exile in Pustozersk and written shortly after Tsar Aleksei's death in early 1676. It concerns another manifestation of the increasing Westernization evident at Aleksei's court, the elaborate theatrical productions that had appeared between 1672 and 1676, when performances were shut down in mid-rehearsal at the tsar's sudden death. In this anonymous account, Aleksei's death is linked explicitly to the "utterly shocking" entertainment in which the court indulged, so shocking that even hardened non-Orthodox disapproved:

> This is what was performed in these plays—the crucifixion of Christ, his burial, his descent into Hades and his ascension into Heaven. And even the non-Orthodox were surprised by these plays and said, "There are in our countries such plays, called comedies, but not among very many of the confessions." How strange and frightening it is to hear that a simple peasant in Christ's image is nailed to a cross, a crown of thorns is put on his head, and a bladder with blood is hidden under his armpit so that he bleeds between the ribs when stabbed. Moreover, instead of the image of the Virgin, a foreign damsel [a Polish peasant-girl, *pan'ia-zhenka*] with loose hair weeps; and instead of John the Theologian being summoned, the body of Christ is handed over to a young beardless man.[88]

Did the horrified author really observe or hear about such things actually taking place at court in the tsar's presence? None of the plays Tsar Aleksei did indeed enjoy in the last years of his reign are on themes of the Passion of Christ, although the plays did recreate some biblical stories, largely from the Old Testament and the Apocrypha. None of the productions, however, employed female actors, although foreign boys did take part, performing both male and female roles. The declamations presented to the court during Aleksei's lifetime were unstaged and performed only by boys; some of these were on the events of Christ's life but with no hint of the gory realism detailed in the account above. The language in this anonymous Old Believer account, as in the case of descriptions of music and icon painting, is deliberately and consciously hyperbolic and provocative, as befits the nature of the threat to the very fabric of Orthodoxy the author describes. This author, who was apparently fairly well informed about events at court during Aleksei's last years, seems to be recounting performances he had heard about, not witnessed directly, and possibly conflating Aleksei's well-known penchant for theatrical entertainment at his court with the plays depicting the Passion of Christ performed as part of the curricula of Jesuit-influenced school dramas in Ukraine and Belarus or even in the West.[89]

Those defending musical and artistic innovations in Muscovy sometimes took their opponents head on, in the case of music, for example, referring specifically to the organ in their replies ("if we were to do away with singing that is similar to the sound of the organ, we would be obliged to do away with all singing"). Perhaps this is why Patriarch Nikon's biographer specifically mentions that as metropolitan of Novgorod, Nikon supported improvements resulting in singing that was "better than an inanimate organ."[90] The supporters of the new musical styles also take a different route, by some measures a more traditional defense, pointing to the well-known levels of confusion and ignorance in some musical circles and placing their own efforts as a way to combat this. This approach was also adopted by Aleksandr Mezenets and the other members of the commission assembled to standardize neumatic notation. They were certainly no fans of Ukrainian/Belarusian musical styles and their notation, but they did share the goals of formulating clarified and uniform notational and singing practices.

Other music theorists, especially Nikolai Diletskii and Ioannikii Korenev, also embraced these overall goals of rationality and professionalism but sought very different models for achieving them, looking for solutions in the organizational frameworks familiar to them: classical educational models, rhetoric and its categories, and analogies to language and other liberal arts. Diletskii, as we shall see in chapter 5, posits a series of rules open to every student and applicable to all music—a sharp contrast to the intricate and transformational "mysteries" of music described in chant and notation treatises.[91] Korenev also invokes mastery and training, the "science" of music, saying that it is not surprising "that someone praises the old and the customary while downgrading the newly-corrected, because of his ignorance, for he has not mastered musical and literary science."[92] In a passage guaranteed to inflame the fires even further, Korenev makes the point that disorder cannot produce any kind of musical harmony, an unexceptionable statement, except that he illustrates this point by means of the *gusli,* which, with its harmonious construction, produces harmonious music.[93] Iosif Vladimirov, a mid-century icon painter and theorist who advocated a Western-style naturalistic approach to art, echoes Korenev in his own treatise: "Simpletons and ignorant people do not understand correctly . . . what has happened in icon painting; whatever has grown old, that they adhere to. And if something long ago grew dark or decrepit, this they especially take as a reason to praise its age and dinginess."[94]

Even the title of Diletskii's music-theoretical treatise, *Grammatika musikii-skago peniia* (A Grammar of Musical Singing), has a context in these debates. As a science and a means of classification, grammar, like rhetoric and philosophy, marks the differences between those who supported the Nikonian reforms, with their extensive changes in the very words themselves of the liturgy and scripture, and those who resisted such changes. As the scholar Boris Uspenskii has written, the resistance to alterations in liturgical texts was not simply obscurantism but rather reflects awareness of a new and disturbing attitude toward language itself: grammar "sets out the rules for the composition of a text—of any text in a given language, irrespective of its content. The rules allow for the manipulation of meaning—and, thereby, for the modelling of the world."[95] In some ways, Diletskii approaches his musical grammar in similar fashion: as a means of manipulating sound "irrespective of its content," that is, outside the context of the liturgy. Along these same lines, just as Korenev and Diletskii rely upon traditional Western music-theoretical constructs and linguistic models in order to ensure proper mastery of regulated "musical science," so Vladimirov and, even more strikingly, Simon Ushakov and Simeon Polotskii set out a means of artistic organization and evaluation drawn from Western classical sources.[96]

As we shall see throughout this volume, the debate over sources of influence and inspiration, and the desire to regulate, either through reliance on Orthodox tradition (as in the very different activities of the visiting Eastern patriarchs, Avvakum, and Mezenets) or through concepts drawn from what was to some of the players an equally familiar classical tradition within Orthodoxy (this is especially true for Polotskii and Diletskii), shaped the cultural climate of late Muscovy in many ways. In this, the professional liturgical singers were something of a bellwether, reflecting as they did the deep and abiding importance of liturgical singing, in its multiplicity of forms, styles, and influences, within Muscovite culture as a whole and within the court culture specifically. But they were not the only singers at court, nor was theirs the only singing.

3

~❧~

"Sweet and harmonious singing"

Domestic Singers and Domestic Singing

𝒲ho were the other singers at court, apart from the professional ranks of the sovereign and patriarchal singers and the *krestovye d'iaki*? Court documents refer to a group of domestic singers (or perhaps more accurately, domestic spiritual helpmates who also sang) whose repertoire was sacred but not liturgical, suggesting a less regulated, more intimate and informal setting for making music. This type of singing was especially popular at court during the first part of Tsar Aleksei Mikhailovich's reign, when his ascetical tendencies were in ascendance and he favored spiritual singing over the traditions of storytelling and other entertainments, including music, long established at court. The singers Aleksei promoted were called the *bogomol'tsy* or *vyshie* (or *verknye*) *bogomol'tsy;* that is, the official, court religious seekers or pilgrims. They were highly valued at court, where the expanding domestic establishments, which increased throughout the late seventeenth century as the royal family itself grew, were each provided with a complement of *bogomol'tsy,* just as they were supplied with the appropriate *krestovye d'iaki* to celebrate liturgical services.[1]

The *nishchie* (poor folk) and *bogomol'tsy* had long been associated with the tradition of mendicant alms collecting and were well known for their singing. Samuel Collins noted this link in his 1671 account, in which he included comments made in Holland by a visiting Russian ambassador. Collins did not, unfortunately, describe the music itself:

> The Hollanders willing to gratifie his [the Russian ambassador's] ears with the best Musick in all Holland, both Vocal and Instrumental, asked him how he liked it, to which he replied; very well, for the Beggars use to beg in such Tunes in Russia. What tunes they were I know not. But all the Beggars here [in Russia] beg singing, as well Prisoners as Cripples.[2]

Tsarevna Kseniia Borisovna, the long-suffering daughter of Tsar Boris Godunov, was also said to have favored this type of private religious, non-liturgical singing. In a contemporary account extolling her beauty, her wisdom (as literate and well-spoken), and her humility (the shedding of tears only made her more pleasing), Kseniia was also described as enjoying singing and listening to spiritual verses.[3] This kind of singing would have been entirely appropriate for the "monastic" lives of the royal women, as portrayed by Grigorii Karpovich Kotoshikhin in his mid-century account of the Russian state. The royal women spent their time in prayer, in fasting, and in tears or weeping, says Kotoshikhin; all of these highly valued spiritual qualities echo the description of Kseniia and provide a context for the spiritual singing of the *bogomol'tsy.*[4]

The *bogomol'tsy* were also exposed to the singing of the professional ensembles. In May 1665, the court paid several different groups in connection with the funeral of the *bogomolets* David, including Fedor Koverin (a leader of the *krestovye d'iaki*), the first and second ranks of the sovereign singers, and apparently two other members of the *d'iaki,* who appeared but did not sing at the funeral. The professional singers thus sang for the tsar's pious, in-house pilgrims.[5]

But what, exactly, did they sing? Although there is a rich record of the texts, and a few melodies, associated with the mendicant singers from a later period, it is difficult to reconstruct the repertoire of the *bogomol'tsy* inside the Kremlin in the seventeenth century. There seem to be no records of music copied for them, unlike the many references to manuscripts copied by and for the *pevchie d'iaki* or by the squadrons of specialist music scribes who provided them with written music. Nevertheless, a literate paraliturgical genre, although strongly associated with monastic use, may also reveal links to a more popular tradition, one that may be associated with the mendicant singers who came in from the cold and took up residence in Kremlin. The *pokaiannye stikhi* (penitential verses) are paraliturgical pieces expressing themes of supplication or lament, although their texts cover a variety of subjects, some quite intimate and lyrical. The penitential verses were conceived with music and are preserved in monophonic neumed manuscripts, sometimes in liturgical books and sometimes in separate collections, and they were written and organized with specific reference to the eight-mode structure of liturgical singing. One of the best-known of these verses is also one of the earliest, the beautiful "Plach Adama" (Adam's Lament), which originated in the fifteenth century. The genre as a whole developed fully only in the following century, with codification into an organized cycle towards the middle of the sixteenth and the beginning of the seventeenth centuries. The verses were originally, and naturally, associated with Lent and with the monastic tradition related to the familiar practice of music performed at mealtime.[6]

There are several reasons to associate *pokaiannye stikhi* with the popular mendicant traditions of singing, in spite of the fact that the *stikhi* were conceived in terms of literacy, both musical and textual, a tradition that does not otherwise seem to belong to mendicant singing practices. The wide dissemination of *stikhi* texts indicates their popularity; the texts reflect contemporary moods and, apparently in a few cases, actual events. It may be that their popularity was boosted by the turmoil of Ivan IV's reign and the following Time of Troubles, several decades during which a genre such as the repentance verse would have been able to claim a nearly universal audience in Russia.[7] Some texts were particularly long-lived, surviving in a variety of musical genres and in many different contexts. Adam's Lament, for example, is preserved in neumed liturgical sources and in separate manuscript collections ranging from the end of the fifteenth to the end of the seventeenth centuries; it is mentioned as a well-known example in Nikolai Diletskii's theoretical treatise from the late 1670s; the text is set as a Western-style polyphonic *kontsert* in the early eighteenth century; it is recorded in Pavel Bezsonov's collection of mendicants' texts from the nineteenth century; and it appears in Aleksei Markov's collection of texts from the White Sea area, as provided to him in a songbook by a "literate girl" in the early years of the twentieth century.[8] This particular text seems to have been extraordinarily popular, but there may also be echoes of *stikhi* texts in other musical settings as well.[9]

Another reason to associate penitential verses with a broadly popular tradition relates to their circulation in manuscript sources. The *stikhi* were copied widely, not only in monastic and liturgical sources, but also in a series of remarkably encyclopedic musical manuscripts associated with the Stroganov family and dating from the late sixteenth century. These sources include a range of pieces, including many penitential verses, which seem to have been carefully selected, often listing several variants of the same piece, and many unique settings as well. The *stikhi* themselves thus seem to have been of particular importance, and the collection as a whole indicates the high level of music-making—and apparently also the importance of such non-liturgical, possibly domestic styles—connected with the Stroganov family.[10]

Finally, an extraordinary document from the 1660s provides an additional reason to link penitential verses to mendicant singing practices, and this source further muddies the waters in our thinking about traditions that appear to be fairly clearly divided between literate and oral. The figure of the *iurodivyi*, the holy fool or fool-in-Christ, is another facet of the mendicant tradition, one that was particularly honored throughout Muscovite Orthodox society, including at court.[11] In a remarkable piece of high-tech scholarly deduction, Natal'ia Ponyrko has shown that the *iurodivyi* Stefan, who traveled in the 1660s, was a trained church musician in his previous life in the world, as an *ustavshchik,* or choir leader. After he took up his life as a fool-in-Christ, he continued to write—and notate—religious music, including three *pokaiannye stikhi.* The texts he chose to set, as Ponyrko demonstrates, are windows into Stefan's conception of the wandering, stateless being of the *iurodivyi.* Because of this aspect of personal expression, and because we know that Stefan was the author, it seems reasonable to conclude that he would have performed such pieces in his travels.[12] Stefan's unique source thus supports the manuscript and thematic evidence indicating that penitential verses were widespread and popular, and that they may indeed have formed at least part of the repertoire of the court *bogomol'tsy* or *iurodivye* as well.

Kanty: *Singing "with sweet voices"*

There is another type of non-liturgical religious music that was very popular in Muscovy in the last third or so of the seventeenth century, and which is tied, through surviving manuscript sources, to the court itself. These manuscripts contain works later called *kanty,* their origins revealed in their Western name (*cantus*). Indeed, the earliest of these sources to circulate in Muscovy, from the mid-1670s on, include many pieces written in transliterated Polish or in Slavic with Ukrainian or Belarusian inflections. The *kant* texts are religious and spiritual in nature but with no liturgical connections (unlike the *pokaiannye stikhi,* which were sometimes used in the context of the liturgy and which sometimes circulated in liturgical sources). The *kanty* are homophonic strophic songs, written in score for three voices using five-line staff notation. Their music is accessible and fairly simple, with the top two voices frequently moving in parallel thirds. Most of the *kanty* are

EXAMPLE 3.1. *Kant* "Kako vozmozhem dostoino khvaliti" (How may we worthily praise Thee), attributed to Epifanii Slavinetskii (from Morosan, *One Thousand Years of Russian Church Music*, pp. 110–11, used by permission)

short enough to be written across one opening of a manuscript source, with the text appearing as a block below the three staves. The first half of the strophe is repeated to a new line of text, producing a three-part, A A B form. In some *kanty*, the lowest voice proceeds in a flurry of rhythmic activity, a compositional technique called *ektsellentovyi bass*, described in Diletskii's theoretical treatise and used in other polyphonic compositions in this period. Musical example 3.1 presents the opening of a *kant* attributed to Epifanii Slavinetskii.

A survey of surviving *kant* manuscripts reveals an extensively cultivated, literate, non-liturgical musical culture widely shared throughout Muscovite society. In the neat quarter-century period between the first known Russian *kant* source, manuscript RGB, f. 178, No. 10944, dated 8 September 1675, to the turn of the century, there are about two dozen sources transmitting hundreds of texts and musical settings in multiple variants for a total figure running into the thousands. The manuscripts show a mixture of languages, generally with the Polish linguistic inflections heaviest in the earlier sources and less prevalent in the large group of sources from the first half of the eighteenth century, although certain Polish texts, in "russified" form, were popular for many decades and certain individual sources show heavy Polish influence. The textual sources for the *kanty* include psalms, passages from the Song of Songs, penitential or prayer-like texts (although generally not employing the "canonical" *pokaiannye stikhi* texts, at least not in available listings of textual incipits), some historical songs, carols, and so forth. The musical influences are similarly varied, with evidence of melodic turns from Muscovite chant and Ukrainian songs, Polish dance rhythms, and other sources. The overwhelming impression produced by both texts and music is of popularity, abundance, and variety, within the limits of the uniformly accessible singing style and straightforward strophic form. Some songs seem to have been immediately popular and are preserved in many sources from the very beginnings of the surviving manuscript tradition; a few of the songs were popular into the nineteenth century.[13]

Manuscript 10944 is the earliest Muscovite source known, although it is somewhat anomalous not only because it transmits just fifteen texts (most of the sources contain *kanty* numbering in the hundreds) but because it contains no musical settings. Nevertheless, this source does lay out some of the basic characteristics of the *kant* repertoire at our earliest knowledge of this tradition in Muscovy, for it presents a firmly non-liturgical, even secular, setting for the *kanty* and makes the early links to Polish traditions obvious. The manuscript is titled (in Cyrillic): "Psalmy pol'skie sirech' stikhi krasnye pevaemi po raznym golosam" (Polish psalm settings; that is, pleasing verses sung by various voices), and the texts themselves are also written in Cyrillic. The compiler inscribed his name on the last page, in Latin letters: "Pisal syi psalmy Petr Matyaczew syn Skrzolotowicz" (Petr Matyaczew Skrzolotowicz wrote these psalms [i.e., songs]). Skrzolotowicz added another comment, also in Polish, that points to the strong Polish influence on the earliest group of Muscovite *kanty*: "Tak pisano grubo dlia tego coby rosumiel każdy ruski czlowiek" (Written roughly in this manner so that any Russian might understand).[14]

This inscription is more than just the idle boast of a bored Pole in far-off Muscovy, for it helps to explain a remark made in the account of the Dutch ambassador in Moscow at that very time. Koenraad van Klenk noted that there were many music-lovers among upper-class Russians and that they often kept Polish musicians, both instrumentalists and singers, in their houses to entertain them.[15] We do not know if Skrzolotowicz was a musician (one might think not, otherwise he would have scribbled down some tunes, too), nor do we have any reason to think that he was employed in a private Muscovite home. However, his clear intent to make these songs available to a Russian-speaking audience shows the same kind of direct musical exchange that van Klenk's remark indicates. Whatever the specifics, the general milieu was one of free and rapid exchange among literate singers.

The inscription in manuscript 10944 also helps us to understand another, far more important document of Muscovite-Polish literary interchange: Simeon Polotskii's versified translation of the Psalter, published in Moscow in 1680, in which he also made reference to the popularity in Russia of singing Polish psalm texts. In the second, prose foreword to his translation, Polotskii noted that many people in all the Russian lands and in Moscow itself, "having become fond of the sweet and harmonious [*soglasnoe*] singing of the Polish Psalter, set in verse, became accustomed to singing these psalms, knowing the language little or not at all, obtaining only sweet spiritual entertainment." This kind of singing was certainly not possible in a liturgical context but was obviously popular among the Muscovite faithful in a less formal, domestic role, as Polotskii notes in his third foreword, in verse: "I have endeavored to set [the psalms] in verse / not only to be read in church, / But to be read frequently in homes / or sung with sweet voices."[16] Polotskii himself was an accomplished poet in the Polish language, and his Slavic translation of the Psalter was modeled after the popular Polish version by Jan Kochanowski, the *Psałterz Dawidów* (1579).[17]

In the mid-1680s, just a few years after Polotskii's verse treatment of the Psalter was published, the entire cycle was set to music by Vasilii Titov, a member of the sovereign's singers and one of Muscovy's most skilled composers.[18] Titov set Polotskii's texts as a collection of three-part *kanty,* a natural stylistic choice for works intended, as Polotskii indicated, to be widely accessible. The dedications of two presentation copies of the joint Polotskii-Titov Psalter reflect the familiarity of the *kant* style at the court itself, where both authors had long served. The earlier of these sources mentions the original publication of Polotskii's Psalter translation and includes Titov's dedication to the young co-tsars Ivan and Peter, implying a date no earlier than 1682, when they jointly came to the throne. The second source is an elaborate presentation copy for Sofiia Alekseevna, sister and regent to the two young tsars, dated 1687.[19] Polotskii, who lived in Moscow from 1663–64 to his death in 1680, was not only court poet to the tsars but tutor to the royal children as well, including Sofiia and Fedor (who succeeded Tsar Aleksei), so the royal family would naturally have been interested in the musical setting of his monumental work. The manuscript gifts might also reflect Titov's aspirations as well, and indeed he became something of a semi-official court composer in later decades, writing polyphonic *kontserty* to celebrate Peter's military victories.[20] These two presentation copies also suggest that the *kant* style was considered appropriate for and appreciated at court; perhaps there was even a singer—Titov himself, one hopes—who might have performed these pieces for the royal dedicatees. It does not seem beyond the realm of possibility, given what we know about the rigors of the royal children's musical training, that someone in the royal household itself may have been able to sing along.

The Polotskii-Titov Psalter also reveals important monastic connections for the *kant* style. A few of the surviving sources, in addition to the royal presentation copies, are linked to monasteries or to individual clergy, and another copy belonged to one of the sovereign's singers.[21] Other early *kant* sources share similar patterns of ownership. The important source GIM, Muz. sobr., No. 1743, discussed below, is associated with Damaskin, a deacon (*ierodiakon*) at the Chudov (Miracles) Monastery in Moscow and previously at Nikon's New Jerusalem Monastery. Manuscript GIM, sobr. Khludova, No. 126d, a *kant* source from the late 1680s to early 1690s, apparently belonged to archdeacon Iona Grigorov of the Uspenskii Cathedral.[22]

A consideration of the authorship of *kant* texts underscores the genre's monastic and clerical connections. Although most *kant* settings are anonymous, some texts are attributed to a handful of clerical poets. The most important are the several texts by German (pronounced with a hard *g*), who by the time of his death in 1681 (that is, just at the time the earliest surviving *kant* manuscripts begin to appear) was the archimandrite of the New Jerusalem Monastery. This was a natural place for the cultivation of *kanty*, reflecting the enthusiasm of its founder, Nikon, for the new *vspevaki* and their Western-influenced singing styles. Other surviving *kant* texts attributed (sometimes tentatively) to Polotskii, Slavinetskii, and others strengthen this clerical association.[23] Musical example 3.2 is a *kant* setting by German, "Khristos razhdaetsia" (Christ is born), and shows a somewhat more complex musical style, with some imitative writing, and an acrostic revealed by the first letters of the text.

This monastic link, like the textual, musical, and notational influences from Ukraine, Belarus, and points west, was present at the beginning of the genre's circulation in Muscovy. The earliest preserved source, Skrzolotowicz's little booklet (manuscript 10944), represents an interesting mix. Six of its fifteen texts are unique to this source, but all the remaining texts are concordant with texts appearing in later seventeenth-century *kant* manuscripts. Some of the pieces in this early source proved to be extremely popular. Three of the songs he included—"Ditiatko sia

EXAMPLE 3.2. German, *kant* "Khristos razhdaetsia" (Christ is born; final two lines of first strophe) (from Morosan, *One Thousand Years of Russian Church Music*, pp. 134–35, used by permission)

narodilo" (A Child is born), "Ezu Khriste pane milyi" (Dear Lord Jesus Christ), and "Mesiash prished" (The Messiah came)—each have seven or more concordances in later *kant* manuscripts, and two of these songs are mentioned in Diletskii's theoretical treatise. The popularity of the *kant* style, and even of certain individual pieces, was thus well-established by the mid-1670s, when manuscript 10944 was compiled.[24] In other words, even a visiting foreigner like Skrzolotowicz knew, at least in part, what was popular and made an effort to write it down.

Sheer numbers reinforce the notion of the wide popularity of *kanty* in Muscovy. The figures in Hans Rothe's index of textual concordances reach to nearly 900 entries, although he does include texts for which no music exists, or texts which may not have been set as *kanty*. Reducing these numbers somewhat seems therefore to be in order, and brings us closer to the figure of around 400 song texts, preserved in nearly 2,000 (textual) variants, suggested by Russian specialist Aleksandr Pozdneev.[25] With the exception of the contents of one source, very few of these texts survive as unica; that is, as songs unique to a single source. The exception is the collection RNB, sobr. Pogodina, No. 1974, from the early 1680s. This source includes a high proportion of transliterated Polish pieces—130 of its total of 150—and 60 of these Polish texts are unique to this source, suggesting the same kinds of Polish-Muscovite interchange illustrated by Skrzolotowicz's little music book and by Polotskii's translation of the Psalter. Other Polish texts in manuscript 1974 have concordances in other sources, as do its non-Polish texts.[26]

This source, however, represents something of an anomaly in the face of the overwhelming evidence of a large, shared corpus of *kanty* which appear time and again in sources from before about 1700. The surviving manuscripts begin to appear in bulk around 1680, which is also the time of Simeon Polotskii's Psalter translation. Many of the factors stimulating the emergence of the *kant* as a popular genre in Muscovy were already in place by that time: the regular presence of foreigners in Moscow as well as the influx of the *vspevaki* and, equally important, their integration into the ranks of the *pevchie d'iaki;* the multi-national composition of Nikon's New Jerusalem Monastery; and the presence there of the prolific poet German. The period around 1680, however, seems to represent not the beginning of the Muscovite *kant* tradition but the tipping point, the time at which it became a widespread part of Muscovite culture.[27] It was at this point that scribes could compile sources containing hundreds of overlapping *kanty,* and it was at this point that Simeon Polotskii realized that as long as people were singing these songs, even in Polish, it would be useful to have some of them available in Russian. It was also around this time that Skrzolotowicz did exactly the same thing on a somewhat more down-to-earth scale, jotting down some of these popular texts in a way in which Russian readers could recognize them.

Another measure of the genre's popularity is its inclusion, at this same early period around 1680, in non-*kant* sources, specifically in Nikolai Diletskii's important theoretical treatise. We know that Diletskii was in Muscovy after around 1675, so either he chose song texts and tunes based on his familiarity with the style outside Muscovy (certainly a possibility, given his ties to Kiev and Vilnius), or he heard the tunes after he came to Muscovy and used them as a means of connecting with his audience. The truth probably includes elements of both suppositions. No matter how he learned of the songs, Diletskii apparently took care to choose popular examples, for several of his selections appear in nine or more early Muscovite *kant* sources (see appendix). The texts of two of the pieces he used are by Simeon Polotskii (whose work in Moscow overlapped briefly with Diletskii's time there), and one text has been attributed to Dimitrii Rostovskii; Diletskii does not refer to any of German's works.[28] Diletskii's choices also reflect the linguistic influences in other *kant* sources, such as the Polish texts (in Latin script) included in an early eighteenth-century source with Ukrainian linguistic elements that transmits his work. The *kanty* in Diletskii's treatise are thus a kind of microcosm of the genre's early circulation patterns, outlining the broader influences we have begun to examine here in connection with singing practices.

We can trace the same trends by taking a closer look at a single *kant* source, GIM, Muz. sobr., No. 1938, an early Muscovite manuscript from the beginning of the 1680s. The source in its present state contains 167 *kanty* (plus a few additional texts); a later numbering of the surviving songs indicates that pieces are missing from the beginning and the end of the manuscript. The texts, according to editor Olga Dolskaya, fall into three groups: songs 39–49 (following the numbering in the source) are generally set to Slavic texts; songs 51–100 use transliterated Polish texts and include several settings by the Polish poet Jan Kochanowski; and the largest section, songs 101–201, presents a mixture of Slavic and Polish texts along with texts showing strong Ukrainian influences, with the songs arranged in alphabetical order. No Kochanowski texts appear in this last section, which includes texts by German, Polotskii, and others. No attributions, however, appear in the source itself.[29]

Although manuscript 1938 is one of the earliest surviving Muscovite *kant* sources, it nevertheless has concordances with almost all of the other extant seventeenth-century *kant* manuscripts. Indeed, there are no unica in manuscript 1938—every song appears in at least one of the other surviving sources from this period. The overlap in the repertoire is immense. About two-thirds of the pieces in manuscript 1938 appear in six or more Muscovite *kant* sources and about a quarter of its songs appear in eight or more sources; to put these figures in a slightly different way, there are seventy-five or more concordances with each of seven contemporary *kant* manuscripts.[30] These statistics suggest a readily accessible network of popular pieces. Furthermore, the partial alphabetical ordering in 1938 implies that these songs (or at least their titles) were chosen in advance. The same selective process must have been at work for GIM, sobr. Khludova, No. 126d, which is also arranged alphabetically (and which has more than seventy-five concordant pieces with manuscript 1938) and for GIM, Muz. sobr., No. 1743, which has twice that number of concordances.[31] A scribe would need a stock of songs at hand in order to carry out an alphabetical plan, and although one is tempted to make analogies to the circulation patterns observed for some Renaissance songs in the West, such evidence is thus far lacking for the Russian *kanty*.[32] We know at least that German owned some musical manuscripts, which were left to fellow monks at his death.[33]

Although manuscript 1938 shares concordances with nearly the entire corpus of early Muscovite *kant* manuscripts, it has a particularly close relationship to one of these sources, GIM 1743, with which it shares more than 165 songs (*kanty* frequently appear multiple times in 1743, which accounts for what would seem to be an inordinately high number of concordances between these two sources). The concordances with 1743 cut through all linguistic categories in manuscript 1938, suggesting that there may be a particular association between these sources. Although we know nothing about the origins of manuscript 1938, we do know much more about 1743. It was compiled by Damaskin, a monk at the New Jerusalem Monastery in the 1670s who, by about 1700, had moved to the Chudov Monastery. Damaskin was an author himself, one of several people to whom German left his varied collection of books and music at his death in 1681. It can certainly be no coincidence, then, that manuscript 1743 contains so many of German's pieces.[34] Given the extremely close relationship between the two manuscripts, it may be that 1938 came from this same milieu as well. This would also account for its emphasis on German's works and for the wide variety of songs in both sources—this is the sort of repertoire entirely apt for the international collection of monks at New Jerusalem, who seem to have been instrumental, so to speak, in establishing (or at least writing down) the new style in Muscovy. Thus although direct Polish models, for example via Polotskii's translation, the presence of transliterated Polish texts (including some by Kochanowski), or a collection such as Skrzolotowicz's, were important sources of influence, there were other paths by means of which the *kant* style permeated Muscovite musical consciousness.[35] The New Jerusalem Monastery specifically, and monastic settings in general, seem to have been quite important.

This manuscript tradition can tell us something of the intended singers. Although simple strophic songs may certainly have formed part of the repertoire of popular and mendicant singing, the surviving *kant* sources themselves point to a literate tradition for both texts and staff-notated music. If one looks for literate singers who might have performed these songs from these sources, one comes up with some familiar faces: the various professional ensembles and especially the *vspevaki*, as well as monastic singers, all of whom were engaged in both liturgical and non-liturgical performances. What about the *bogomol'tsy* at court and in the countryside? Although the existence of the *iurodivyi* Stefan does show us that

mendicant performers might indeed have been literate and had musical training, one must also take into account that we have no evidence that the court
bogomol'tsy ever required notated sources of any kind. They may have played a role
in disseminating and popularizing the *kanty*, for the songs are certainly simple
enough to have been learned and performed without notation. In the genre's
earliest documented Muscovite phase, however, literate musical traditions, specifically the use of the five-line staff and the appearance of voluminous sources, seem
to have played a dominant role. This does not rule out significant influence from
popular spiritual singing traditions (caroling, for example), but literacy, and particularly musical literacy, was a scarce commodity in Muscovy and must figure in
any assessment of the genre's development.

If we take our cue instead from the singers we know were involved in the
production and transmission of *kanty*, we find generally that the people who
appreciated Polotskii's psalm translations came from the same ranks as those who
were interested in compiling these documents of an intimate, devotional, non-
liturgical singing, often based on these very same psalm translations. These are the
people who wrote such pieces, for example German at the New Jerusalem Monastery, these are the people who compiled or owned such manuscripts, and these are
the people to whom such manuscripts were dedicated. *Kanty* long remained in
Orthodox Russia's cultural consciousness, circulating into the nineteenth century
and retaining their lively roles in the religious culture of this later period.[36] The
extensive seventeenth-century manuscript tradition emphasizes, apparently from
its very beginnings in Muscovy, a musical genre and notation involving a substantial and literate ensemble of musicians and poets.

One of the early scholars focusing on *kanty*, the distinguished literary historian Vladimir Peretts, considered what appears to have been a fundamental turning point, when, as Simeon Polotskii said in his Psalter, people liked the new *kanty*
so much that they sang them even when they did not understand the words. Why,
in other words, was the style so popular in Muscovy, particularly when the same
group of professional and monastic singers had long cultivated another non-
liturgical (or paraliturgical) genre in the *pokaiannye stikhi*? Why did such penitential verses no longer suffice on their own?[37] Part of the answer may be that the *kanty*
did not necessarily replace the penitential verses, which circulated throughout the
seventeenth century and beyond. It may be that with the importation of so many
Ukrainian and Belarusian singers (and clerics and poets) concentrated at court, in
the capital, and in certain monasteries, the *kant* brought some of its audience

ready-made, at least in its initial stages in Muscovy. The accessible musical style and the wide range of *kant* texts, which enhanced and broadened the themes of the *stikhi* texts but generally did not re-set them, invited wide participation among the Muscovite "early adoptors," the singers and clerics who had the training to perform and transmit them and who were at the same time familiarizing themselves with Western-style singing in other types of *partesnoe penie*, which also used a five-line staff. In this context, the *kanty* may be seen as another representative of the eclecticism Max Okenfuss points to as one of the hallmarks of late Muscovite culture, emanating from the same Polish and non-Russian Orthodox sources that created the same mix in Muscovite book culture and education at this time.[38] The places that apparently nurtured such composition—the New Jerusalem Monastery and other monastic centers, Simeon Polotskii's circle, and the court itself—are the places in which one sees Polish and Ukrainian/Belarusian influences expressed strongly in other areas of Muscovite culture. But such singing would not have become so popular if it had not answered a need in Muscovite society, one identified clearly by Simeon Polotskii—adept at cultural translations of all kinds—in his setting of the Psalter. Just as the declamation was translated for Tsar Aleksei and his court, and just as Nikolai Diletskii translated compositional rules for his Muscovite students, so the *kanty* inspired new kinds of composition from German and others. Were there other Russian singing traditions from which German and the many anonymous *kant* composers might have drawn? One point of departure lies in a tiny, humorous detail in one of German's texts.

Historical Texts and Singing of History

One aspect of the *kanty* links them to traditions associated with both public, secular, and high-ranking state occasions as well as with a humbler, more popular tradition of singing: the presence of texts depicting or commemorating actual historical events, a phenomenon they share with the *pokaiannye stikhi*. There are a few historical texts among the *kant* sources, although they are not the most characteristic topics for the genre, particularly in the seventeenth century. Texts reflecting the 1654 Union between Muscovy and part of Ukraine appear in some seventeenth-century *kant* sources, and a few of German's texts refer to events connected with the New Jerusalem Monastery.[39] But in one of German's acrostics he reveals personal, even humble, details of his life, reporting that he was sick in May.[40] This is *Augenmusik* of the most intimate sort, for who else, other than the brethren at the New Jerusalem Monastery, would have been concerned with the state of German's health? And because the message was coded in an acrostic clearly meant to be seen and not heard, who else, besides his literate fellows, could German have intended as reader-performers of this music?

The historical texts appearing in the *kanty* point in two directions. The most direct line points to the future, for the *kant* style became a staple of the music used to celebrate Peter the Great's military victories, beginning in the late 1690s and continuing throughout his reign and beyond. Such *kanty* thus become documents commemorating specific historical events.[41] These celebratory works were often meant to be performed in the large outdoor processions so beloved in Peter's reign. As Vladimir Protopopov has observed, these large collections of triumphal *kanty* (and associated *vivaty,* fanfare-like works featuring the Latin word "vivat") were musical suites, each meant to contribute to the overall effect of the spectacular, ambulatory whole. Some were written and performed by the *pevchie d'iaki*—Vasilii Titov's *kontsert* in honor of the Poltava victory, for example—and we also know that students at the Greek-Latin-Slavonic Academy sang at these celebrations; for neither group was this a new role. The *d'iaki,* as we have seen, traditionally participated in the private and public events of the court, and declamations had consistently been associated either with students or with the young (apparently unaffiliated) performers listed in the sources.[42] The music for Peter's many celebrations, both public and private, thus illustrates how new musical styles combined with older types and traditions of singing and singers, an adaptability familiar from many musical practices throughout the seventeenth century.

The same commemorative approach can also be traced back to the long-established acclamation or toast (*chasha,* or literally, cup), a practice which in Russia appeared widely at court and in monasteries; as we saw in the celebrations marking the installation of the new Muscovite patriarchate, toasts were offered to religious figures, church hierarchs, and the ruling family. Like many other aspects of Muscovite religious life, toasting was increasingly regimented as the seventeenth century progressed, settling what was originally extra- or paraliturgical singing into ever more specific and elaborate liturgical contexts.[43] It was also performed in ornate musical settings, using both the elaborated *demestvennyi* chant style as well as being set polyphonically (or both).[44] Although these pieces (both text and music) have other liturgical positionings, the texts in the rite were selected in order to present a unified idea focused on saving, greeting, and acclamation, and incorporating the tsar's actual title, thus imparting the historical element to the genre.[45] The traditions of toasting proved naturally adaptable. Liturgical sources from the second half of the seventeenth century include acclamations to be used for secular figures, and Tsar Fedor's musical library included "voinskie stikhi" (military or war verses), which may refer to religious pieces performed in the context of greeting, dispatching, or memorializing soldiers, as in a ceremony in Paul of Aleppo's account, where he describes the public reading of names of fallen soldiers in the context of a memorial service.[46]

There is another side to the historicism hinted at in the *kant* texts, and one that while not transmitted in notated sources may also have important ties to the kinds of singing we have been considering. Again, the Englishman Richard James provides us with fascinating source material, for during his stay in Russia between 1618 and 1620, he had six song texts written out for him by a Russian informant.[47] These texts belong to the category of "historical song," although the label is something of a misnomer, for the events they describe were, for the most part, vividly experienced contemporary subjects at the time they were recorded for James: the death in 1610 of the popular military leader M. V. Skopin-Shuiskii, who rallied the Russians against the Polish troops during the Time of Troubles; a song about the Crimean raid on Moscow in the late sixteenth century; and a soldiers' song about spring military service (difficult but, as the song says, not as difficult as winter service). The Time of Troubles provided rich fodder for song texts in general, and some of the topics covered in the James collection are represented in other, later songs as well. Skopin-Shuiskii was a particularly popular subject.[48]

The remaining texts in the James collection are also concerned with vital contemporary events: two lovely laments in the voice of Tsar Boris's daughter, Kseniia Godunova, in which she mourns the state of Muscovy after the takeover of the imposter, Grisha Otrep'ev, and mourns equally her own fate; and the return from Polish captivity of Filaret, father of Tsar Mikhail Romanov, in 1619. Filaret's return took place while James was in Russia, and Kseniia Godunova was still alive at the time these poignant lament texts were recorded. She died only in 1622.

The first of Kseniia's laments in James's collection begins as follows:

There weepeth a little bird,
a little white quail:
   "Alas, that I so young must grieve!
   They wish to burn the green oak,
   to destroy my little nest . . ."

The text then turns to Kseniia herself:

In Moscow the Princess weepeth:
   "Alas that I so young must grieve!
   for there comes to Moscow the impostor

> Grishka Otrepiev, the defrocked monk,
> who wants to take me captive,
> and having captured make me a nun . . ."

Finally, Kseniia turns to the fate of her country:

> And in Moscow the Princess weepeth,
> the daughter of Boris Godunov:
> "O God, our merciful Savior!
> wherefore is our Tsardom perished—
> is it for father's sinning,
> or for mother's not praying?
> And you beloved palace halls!
> who will rule in you . . ."[49]

Kseniia's two lament texts bring with them a host of associations. We already know, from contemporary sources, that Tsar Boris's daughter enjoyed singing and listening to music, so the attribution of such songs to her as a singer (and while she still lived) may be something more than reflex artistic embellishment. The texts are full of wedding imagery—indeed, the genre of the lament itself is associated with brides in traditional Russian wedding ceremonies, during which the bride laments her change in status and her move to her husband's family.[50] Kseniia's texts extend the imagery, depicting the events of her own sad fate as it is intertwined with that of her father and of Muscovy itself. Although the imagery is different, the themes coincide with those of the penitential verses, which were also quite popular during the catastrophic events of the Troubles. The two laments in the James collection, with their lyrical and evocative language, thus straddle the traditions of penitential verse and folk recounting, and, as we shall see, laments uttered in female voices appear in the Muscovite theater of the 1670s.[51]

Another cluster of secular texts from the end of the century brings forth some of the same associations between domesticity and music-making, leading also to a consideration of the links between the culture of the court and its service person-nel and the worlds of folk poetry and songs. A series of lyrical texts, perhaps meant to be sung and at least some of them clearly related to folk songs and folk poetry, are preserved in the papers of Petr Andreevich Kvashnin-Samarin (1671–1740s). The texts merge the author's own poetic ideas with what appear to be reworkings, jogged by memory, of folk tunes the author encountered in Ukraine during his military tour in Azov in the mid-1690s. The poems are drafted on the backs of family documents and so even in their transmission preserve a kind of domesticity and intimacy. In addition to their possible connections to Kvashnin-Samarin's own marriage in the late 1690s, one wonders if the texts might preserve something of the author's service at court, where in the late 1680s and early 1690s he served as a *stol'nik* (a job held by youths and roughly equivalent to a page) for Tsaritsa Praskov'ia Fedorovna, wife of Tsar Ivan Alekseevich. As in the case of the *kanty*, particularly the Polotskii-Titov Psalter setting presented to Tsarevna Sofiia Alekseevna, one must use a light touch to tease out the relevant influences from behind the closed terem doors, but the Kvashnin-Samarin texts offer another hint of the intimate styles—music included—that may have emerged from the court and its ranks.[52] At least one *kant* source comes from this same milieu: the collection of songs in RNB, sobr. Pogodina, No. 1974, which has so many Polish texts and unica, was associated with the household of Princess Avdot'ia Ivanovna Cherkasskaia, widow of boyar Grigorii Cherkasskii.[53]

These various song texts span the seventeenth century, ranging from those associated with James and Kseniia Godunova to the folkish settings by Kvashnin-Samarin. What can they tell us about singers and performance? Unlike the *kanty*, this group of texts does not seem to be associated with notated polyphonic musical settings, and therefore they would appear to belong to a somewhat different tradition and perhaps a correspondingly different performing ensemble. Olearius seems to have heard one of these contemporary "historical" songs in 1634 in Ladoga, as he was traveling to Moscow; the subject of the song was the current ruler, Tsar Mikhail:

> At midday of the 23rd [of July], while we were at table, two Russians with a lute and a fiddle ["mit einer Lauten und Geigen"] came to entertain the ambassadors. They played and sang about the Great Lord and Tsar, Mikhail Feodorovich. Observing that we liked their performance, they added some amusing dances and demonstrated various styles of dancing practiced by both women and men.[54]

This kind of entertainment was the provenance of the storytellers and other musicians both at court and in the countryside, not the *pevchie d'iaki* or Diletskii's intended music theory pupils nor, one presumes, the main focus of monastic singing. The presence of the instruments in Olearius's tale suggests a wide gulf between the singing we have been considering—by monks and literate Muscovites, by poets and professional singers—and the world of storytellers and dancers. But a closer look might help us bridge this gap, suggesting not only a broader investigation into the use of instruments at court but whispering, however tenuously, of a possible link between the *kanty* and instrumental music. In his will, German of the New Jerusalem Monastery not only left books and music to his friends but also a *liutnia*, possibly a lute or at least some sort of plucked stringed instrument.[55] We know that German wrote the texts and, presumably, the music to a dozen or so *kanty,* and we know that several early *kant* manuscripts are strongly linked to monasteries. Could German's *liutnia* imply not only a means of working out the composition of the three-part *kanty* but also indicate that they might have been performed with instrumental accompaniment? (At the very least, German's bequest seems to indicate that it was possible to own such an instrument openly and pass it on to another monk.) If so, the New Jerusalem Monastery, with its focus on Western-style music-making and with its varied population, would seem to be a natural place for such activity.

Other scattered accounts suggest that musical instruments were not unheard of in Muscovite monasteries. Archpriest Avvakum himself supplies one such reference. In describing his incarceration at the Pafnut'ev (St. Paphnutius) Monastery, not far from Moscow, Avvakum mentions with great distaste the presence of musical instruments there; his reference seems to be a simple statement of observed fact, as opposed to his symbolic (and hyperbolic) references to organs and other instruments we considered earlier:

> There [at the monastery] the cellarer Nikodemus was good to me at first, but he, poor fellow, smoked of tobacco of which more than sixty *puds* they seized when they searched the house of the [Greek-born Paisios] Metropolitan of Gaza, and they seized a *domra* [a plucked stringed instrument] too and other hidden things of the monastery on the which [sic] they played and made merry withal. It is a sin to speak of it, forgive me; it was not my business, let him look to it, to his own Lord he must stand or fall.[56]

Indirect evidence supporting Avvakum's observation comes from an account written more than a century earlier by Sigismund von Herberstein, who visited Muscovy as a member of diplomatic missions from the Holy Roman Empire in 1517 and 1526. Herberstein heard various types of music and singing during his stay, including performances by the singers associated with the court at this early period, and he also attempted to describe the unfamiliar rites of the church to his Western readers. In his discussion of Orthodox monasteries, Herberstein noted that their rules were quite strict, implying also that these rules were not always followed: "They dare not indulge in any sort of amusement. If any one is found to have a harp or any musical instrument, he is most severely punished." Herberstein's observations are echoed much later, in an eighteenth-century collection of

Old Believer writings that refers to punishments to monks for music-making (including playing the *gusli*) and dancing.[57]

If we began with the paradox of the False Dmitrii's musicians, surveying many avenues for the expression of sanctioned but non-liturgical or extra-liturgical singing in Muscovy, we finish with a similar paradox concerning musical instruments: if the instrumental music at Dmitrii's court engendered such overwhelmingly negative associations and such a deadly end for its performers, how is it that we find hints of a similar musical tradition—discouraged but extant, even if only faintly—in Muscovite monastic life? And if instrumental music existed in monasteries, how much more lively was the tradition at the tsars' courts?

4

Tavern and Wedding

The Instrumental Traditions
at the Muscovite Court

*O*n January 1648, the third year of his reign, the young Tsar Aleksei Mikhailovich celebrated his wedding to Mariia Il'inichna Miloslavskaia. Aleksei was well known for his piety, which was reflected in the somewhat unusual musical arrangements made for the ceremony. The festivities included all the traditional elements of the lengthy Russian wedding: the assigned roles for the bride's and the groom's family representatives as well as for matchmakers, candle-bearers, torch-bearers, and the like; the distribution of traditional wedding foods, and so forth. At the church service (which comprised only a small portion of the multi-day ceremony), the sovereign's singers performed several times, including singing an elaborate *mnogoletie*, described as "demestvo bol'shoe" (great or elaborate chant in the *demestvennyi* style), for the tsar and his new wife.[1] The musical novelty came later, when the new couple went to the bedchamber, where they were together "for a time," after which the tsar departed to the bath. The consummation of the marriage was traditionally marked by an instrumental fanfare, as had been the case at Tsar Mikhail's weddings in 1624 and 1626. At Mikhail's first wedding, sources note that the trumpets, drums, and *surny* (shawm-like military instruments)—more than a hundred of them—sounded out at this point in the ceremony, and at his second wedding the fanfare lasted all day long.[2] But Tsar Aleksei had different ideas, their novelty clearly spelled out in the documents:

> It is true that at previous royal weddings there would occur at this time, when the Lord goes to the bath, all day from morning to night at court they would play *surny,* and trumpets, and beat the drums; but the present Great Lord, the Tsar and Grand Prince of all Russia Aleksei Mikhailovich, on his royal wedding, did not permit the playing of drums and trumpets. And, instead of trumpets and *organy* and all the wedding entertainment, the Lord ordered at his royal banquets his sovereign singers to sing in alternation *strochnye* and *demestvennye bol'shie* verses, from the Prazdniki and from the Triod', with quietude, joy, and greatest decorum.[3]

The singers performed the same kind of music on the second day, and on the third day they sang before the tsar throughout the meal.[4]

There are several new elements in this account, beginning with what appears to have been the tsar's own decision to forgo the traditional instrumental fanfare in favor of well-ordered singing by *d'iaki.* The instrumental fanfare was a long-standing tradition, which is why the documents seem to need to explain rather carefully the tsar's decision to leave it out. The mid-sixteenth-century household guide, the *Domostroi,* describes this fanfare, which always sounded at the same point in the proceedings, as the groom goes to the bathhouse after the couple's first night together. The visiting Polish contingent at Dmitrii's wedding complained about the tumultuous fanfares following the ceremony, and both Kotoshikhin and Olearius noted the same kind of instrumental music at the same point in the celebrations in their own discussions of Muscovite wedding practices.[5]

Aleksei's musical prohibitions also appear to include not just the fanfare but also the "trumpets and *organy* and all the wedding entertainment" that traditionally formed part of the festivities, a decision the writer praises for its quietude and decorum. The *organy* here might indeed refer to actual organs, for as we shall see below, organs formed part of the court's entertainment at this time, including appearances at weddings. The word might also have a more general meaning, indicating an assembly of instruments. There is a wedding context for such a general interpretation as well, for Tsar Mikhail's wedding was celebrated not just by the traditional fanfare, but with other performances on various musical instruments, including *organy.* The music that Tsar Aleksei did permit at his wedding, however, was certainly not austere. The singers performed polyphonic music (the *strochnye* pieces) as well as pieces in the *demestvennyi* chant style, which could have been polyphonic or monophonic. These were the most elaborate and up-to-date singing styles in Muscovy, performed by the best singers the court had to offer and drawn from a wide range of liturgical pieces.

The real surprise, however, is that musical instruments had an important role in a Russian royal wedding in the first place, and the meticulous lengths the documents take in this instance to explain their absence, implying that such instruments had a customary and accepted place at court. Such appearances (or carefully explained non-appearances) of musical instruments at the Muscovite court, particularly in connection with a royal wedding, fly in the face of the terrible fate of the Polish musicians in Dmitrii's entourage, and also contradict the relentless anti-instrument (and more importantly, anti-*skomorokh*) campaign in which the church was engaged throughout the seventeenth century. The church's consistently scorched-earth policy with regard to instruments is illustrated in one of the best-known stories (indeed, one of the *only* known stories) about Muscovite music to have percolated into general consciousness: Olearius's tale of the burning of five wagonloads of musical instruments, at the behest of the patriarch:

> [T]he present Patriarch considered that music was being misused in taverns and pothouses, as well as in the streets, for all kinds of debauchery and obscene songs. Accordingly, two years ago he ordered the destruction of any tavern musicians' instruments seen in the streets. Then he banned instrumental music altogether and ordered the seizure of musical instruments in the houses; once five wagonloads were sent across the Moscow River and burned there.[6]

Olearius's story would seem to bring to a logical conclusion the moral of the Dmitrii tale: instruments are associated with the *skomorokhi*, and the church would rigorously and tirelessly rid the country of this blight. And indeed Olearius's account, written around mid-century, does mark the end game in the state's relentless persecution of the *skomorokhi*. A series of edicts culminated at about this time, and, although the *skomorokh* tradition persisted into the eighteenth century, their presence appears to have been drastically reduced and references to their music are scarce.[7] However, in spite of the church's campaign, throughout this same period the Muscovite court rang with the sounds of instruments—sometimes the very instruments the church was simultaneously denouncing or destroying when found in the hands of a *skomorokh*. Even in Muscovite religious services, where there was never a question of allowing instruments, there was an important instrumental presence, most obviously expressed in the Psalms, with their wealth of references to all kinds of instruments (and supplemented by an equally broad range of visual images related to these sacred texts).[8] As in the realm of singing, then, so for musical instruments there was a flexibility in Muscovite culture that runs through the practices of the seventeenth century. Not all instrumental music was *skomorokh* music, and not all the instruments the *skomorokhi* played automatically carried blasphemous associations. How and under what circumstances such distinctions may have been made is the subject of this chapter.

"A confusion of glory": Fanfares and Processionals

The account of the short reign and early death of the False Dmitrii introduced distinct instrumental components: processional music to accompany, for example, the grand entrance of Dmitrii's bride Marina into the city, employing the percussion, trumpets, and *surny* associated also with military practice; and music for indoor entertainment, featuring a mixed instrumental ensemble. There was also a third category, hinted at by the presence of the Polish organist and his assistants, who also died during the uprising. It is not clear how the Poles employed their organist, although apart from church services, it seems reasonable to assume that he would have taken part in the various indoor entertainments and ceremonies. All these traditions were known in Muscovy as well. A series of glossaries compiled by foreigners immediately before and after the Time of Troubles indicates not only how widespread Muscovite instrumental traditions were, but how distinctly these traditions were categorized in the minds of the Russian informants.

Richard James proves himself again to be an excellent guide, and his glossary offers a revealing glimpse into the thoughts and associations of his hosts. Many of the words in James's glossary appear in clusters: days of the week, names of fish, labels for people. This is also the case, in several instances, for his musical terminology. The word *skomorokh*, defined in musical terms, apparently brought to mind a spate of equally dubious characters, all presented together in a single grouping:[9]

> skomoroke [*skomorokh*], a fidler
> rosboinic [*rozboinik*], a robber
> tat [*tat'*], a pilferer
> shish [*shish*], a rouge of the woods
> spoine, a jestinge rouge[10]

James also lists a variety of *skomorokh*-type instruments. Two different stringed instruments, *gusli* ("a kinde of Russe harpe") and *domra* ("a kinde of R[usse] lute"), are paired, as is *lyra* or hurdy-gurdy ("a kinde of instrument which goes with a wheele, in sounde much like our Bagpipes") with another kind of entertainment, *kukli*, "the poppet thinges." One of Olearius's illustrations reinforces these connections, pairing a *skomorokh* puppet show with a *gusli* player and with someone playing the *gudok*, a bowed stringed instrument (see figure 4.1, below).[11]

There are other instrumental associations in James's glossary. The phrase "peasna [*pesn'*], a songe," for example, is followed by "rogha, a horne" and "pastuke, a heardsman," and James also includes, in separate listings, "trubense, a trumpetter," "nabat, a drumme," "strone, a stringe of an instrument," and "duda, a pipe."[12] Other percussion instruments are included together in a separate, brief listing of military terminology:[13]

> snamena [*znamena*], the colours of an armie
> litavera [*litavra*], a kettle drumme
> tolumbaz [*tulumbas*, also a kind of drum; James provides no separate
>   definition]
> copia [*kop'e*], a launce

Other contemporary sources retain the same rough categories, separating military instruments from other types. A vocabulary written in a slightly different format was compiled by the French trader Jean Sauvage during his short stay in Kholmogory in 1586. Sauvage's work is a phrase book, with words and sentences covering various topics clustered together. He includes a separate section on music, in which he names many of the same instruments that James listed, with the addition of a reference to a keyboard player; he does not include the term *skomorokh*:[14]

> Ung Musicien, Piesselnicq [*pesel'nik*]
> Ung Joueur de luth, Doumernicq [*domernik, domershchik*]
> Ung Joueur d'espinette, Samballenicq [*tsymbal'nik*]
> Ung Joueur de violon, Semousenicq [*smychnik, smytsnik*]
> Ung cornet a bouquin, Doudenicq [*dudnik*]
> Ung joueur de hault boys, Sounachay [*surnachei*]
> Ung joueur de musette, Doudenicq [*duda* can also indicate a bagpipe][15]

Sauvage also compiles a separate military section, including the instruments "Le tambour, Nabamchicq" [*nabatchik*] and "Une trompette, Troubenicq."[16] The Trondheim vocabulary, a thematic Slavic-German glossary from the mid-seventeenth century, includes a section listing musical instruments and other vocabulary related to entertainment, and a separate, military section, which includes various percussion and trumpets.[17]

The Englishman Mark Ridley, who served as physician to the tsar in the 1590s, compiled an extensive glossary that lists many of the same musical terms appearing in the other contemporary foreign sources, especially James's: *skomorokh"*, *domora* [*domra*], *gusli*, *rog"*, *dudka*, *skrip"* (*skripka*, fiddle), and so forth. His inclusion of both *tsimbaldi* ("virginals") and *organi* ("organs") may reflect his experiences at court, where such instruments were popular.[18] Ridley's stay in Russia began just after Jerome Horsey had brought his "organes and virgenalls" from London, so we know at least that such instruments were at court when Ridley was there. He mentions only some of the terminology associated with military instruments: *tulombas"* [*tulumbas*] and *truba,* but not *baraban* or *litavra,* for example.[19] Taken as a whole, these vocabularies reveal a rich, varied, and accessible repertoire of instruments that reflect common Russian practice both in the Far North, where James and Sauvage stayed, as well as in the capital, where Ridley worked.[20]

The instruments included in the military category were widely known for their roles in the elaborate processions staged for ushering visiting ambassadors into Moscow. Dmitrii's own careful preparations for Marina's entrance into the capital, which required a wait of several days outside the city, were repeated throughout the century. The ceremonies for the 1663–64 mission headed by the Earl of Carlisle, for example, used the same kinds of instruments Dmitrii had had at his disposal, with trumpets, percussion, and "howboys" corresponding to the "Drometen, Heerpaucken und Schallmeyen" of Bussow's earlier account. Guy Miege's record of the Carlisle embassy is both admiring and critical of the Russian musicians. When they finally entered the city, the English party found that

> there were so many Trumpets, Kettle-drums, Howboys, and other such instruments of war, which they had disperst in parties thorow all their Troops, that for two miles we were in no want of Musique. But they having battered our ears with one continued aire above two hours together all the way as we marcht, the noise of those Instruments which at first had delighted us with their melody, became now obstreperous and troublesome.

The party finally reached the city gates, where, just as in Dmitrii's spectacle, a special musical interlude had been planned:

> And here the Moscovian Trumpets all stopt, to sound at the time as the Ambassador past the Gate, and was entred into the Town, which was exactly performed: but with so confused a noise, it might very well be compared to that which the Geese made in the Capitol, whilst the Gauls were climbing over the Walls.[21]

Many other visiting parties received the same treatment. The Klenk mission from Holland, for example, noted the presence of Russian trumpets and drums, in groups of six, eight, ten, or more, scattered throughout the various military units. They also heard pipers or flautists, drummers, and *surny* ("pijpers, trommels, schalmeyen") in the procession, with a special flourish of percussion and trumpets at the gates.[22]

Both the Carlisle and the Klenk missions brought along their own, similar instruments. Miege notes that the English party included two trumpeters along with six musicians and a "Musique master." The English trumpeters sounded out as the party approached a town of any size on their way to Moscow. On one occasion, they remained silent as a means of rebuking the Russians for what the English considered to be their poor preparations. They also participated in the English party's entrance into the capital, along with the Russian musicians, and similarly at the ambassador's procession to his audience with the tsar.[23] The Dutch party also included a drummer and three trumpeters, whom they arranged carefully for the entry procession, positioning their first trumpeter, "ein Moor," immediately following the ambassador, with the drummer and the two other trumpeters behind.[24]

Similar fanfare music was used to accompany the tsar. When Aleksei returned to Moscow from his military campaigns in 1655, the entry procession included trumpets, percussion, and *surny* as well as a contingent of clergy, including boys in white clothing who sang from papers they held in their hands.[25] Adolf Lyseck, documenting the Imperial embassy to Moscow in 1675, described the tsar's departure to the Trinity-St. Sergius Monastery as accompanied by trumpets and drums.[26] Peter the Great was to build upon such festive traditions in his elaborate victory celebrations, which included instrumental music and military fanfares along with specially written vocal pieces.

All of the Muscovite fanfare music sounded out of doors. None of the many diplomatic reports by seventeenth-century visitors mentions any music indoors during their audiences with the tsar. The Russian account documenting the Carlisle mission, for example, notes that the English party was accompanied by (Russian) drums and banners, along with the English trumpeters, inside the Kremlin walls from the Cathedral of the Annunciation as they were going to their audience with the tsar. There was no reported music, however, as they or any of the other visiting parties entered the tsar's receiving chambers, where other aspects of ceremony took precedence over fanfare. Perhaps mere music would have been superfluous. Miege describes passing through numerous ranks of the tsar's soldiers, mounted and on foot, and through various courtyards and halls, until the English party finally entered the reception hall itself. "And here," he writes, "it was we were like those who coming suddainly out of the dark are dazled with the brightnes of the Sun: the splendor of their jewels seeming to contend for priority with that of the day; so that we were lost as it were in this confusion of glory."[27]

High-ranking Muscovites imitated the tsar's ceremonial accoutrements. Olearius describes how boyar Boris Ivanovich Morozov's musicians serenaded his party as they were beginning a journey from Moscow to Persia: "and his [Morozov's] trumpeters came up, bringing all sorts of costly drinks . . . Then he rode alongside us in a special little boat for quite some time, having his trumpets play gaily, and ours answered them." Tsar Aleksei requested that his cousin, Nikita Ivanovich Romanov, lend him a trumpeter and some of his singers, and boyar I. D. Miloslavskii left "14 German trumpets" after his death in 1668. The inventory of the Golitsyn princes Vasilii and his son Aleksei includes extensive military or fanfare instruments, with *truby* and paired sets of *litavry* in various sizes, along with banners or hangings as decorations for the instruments, as well as *nakry* and *surny*.[28]

The Muscovite government actively and consistently recruited skilled musicians to perform in such processional and military ceremonies, drawing both from the pool of visiting foreigners as well as directly from abroad. One of the trumpeters in Olearius's party eventually went into service in Moscow, and two German musicians (*muzykanty*) attached to an Imperial mission remained in Moscow after their embassy departed and eventually performed in the tsar's theater.[29] John Hebdon, while in England in 1660, was commissioned by the Russian court to look for "royal horns and percussion," and Paul Menzies, the tsar's envoy to Rome in 1672, was instructed to hire qualified trumpeters while he was abroad.[30] Muscovite payment records in the 1660s and 1670s include many foreign trumpeters on the payrolls in connection with the military, which also included a considerable number of percussionists. These players are always referred to in the records as *barabanshchiki* (in contrast to the different percussionists listed at court), and apparently many were children, probably related to the soldiers themselves.[31]

Just as foreign embassies brought a few trumpeters and percussionists along with their diplomatic suites, so Muscovite ambassadors took their own musicians with them when they traveled abroad. An English account, "The Arrival of Peter John Potemkin, from the Czars of Muscovy," describes the disembarkation of the Russian suite in London in November 1681, an event that included Russian musicians: "The Czars Trumpetts & Kettle Drums having one of them [a small boat] to themselves, with the Tilt [canopy or cover] taken off, that they might sound, as the Amb[assador] desired, in their coming up."[32] Later that month, as Potemkin prepared to attend the London theater, he entertained the English guests in his lodgings with his own musicians: "He [Potemkin] sate till it was almost time to go to the Play; and then he Entertained us with his Kettle Drums and Trumpetts, while he changed his Cloaths."[33] An ensemble performing similar processional music was even sent to Siberia for the signing of the 1689 Sino-Russian Treaty of Nerchinsk. Thomas Pereira, a Portuguese Jesuit who took part in the proceedings, described the Muscovite contingent, which was "preceded by some bands of well-harmonized *charamellas* [shawms] and four *trombetas* [trumpets] which from time to time united their tunes with those of *charamellas* with much applause. They were followed by some drums mounted on horses." Later, "the Moscovites played trumpets and *charamellas*, which to the angels of peace seemed like heavenly melody."[34]

These descriptions are consistent in their repertoire of fanfare instruments: percussion of some sort, trumpets, and usually also the *surna*, which corresponds to the *Schalmei* mentioned in many of the foreign sources. These are, for the most part, the same sorts of instruments used in the same sorts of situations that Muscovite officials would have read about in the *kuranty* or *vesti-kuranty*, summaries of Western European newspapers drawn up by the Diplomatic Chancellery for use by the court. (They are named after Dutch newspapers, which were important early sources, with the word *Courante* in their title; the Russian *vesti* means "news.") The *kuranty* were compiled throughout the seventeenth century and were intended for use by upper-level government officials—just the sort of people who were responsible for arranging the ceremonies for diplomats visiting Russia. These summaries are full of references to music, generally that of military trumpets and drums, as it sounded in Western parades, processions, and gatherings of all sorts. A dispatch from 1643, for example, lists the suite of the Danish King Waldemar, which included a percussionist, twelve trumpeters, and two groups of "musicians."[35] Although the primary function of such reports was to keep Muscovite policymakers and diplomats up-to-date on European politics, their frequent references to details of ceremony and celebration must also have functioned as a kind of inventory of appropriate and customary behavior among Western courts. As we shall see later, on rare occasions the *kuranty* reports may also have introduced new kinds of musical entertainment to Muscovy's foreign specialists.

The Private Music of the Court

The Russian tsars who followed Dmitrii were entertained, as Dmitrii himself had been, by a contingent of instrumentalists who performed regularly at court. The instruments they played, particularly the *gusli,* the *domra,* and fiddles (*skripki, skrypki*), were not only quite distinct from the music used in outdoor processions and military and wedding fanfares, but formed part of the instrumental toolkit consistently associated with *skomorokh* musicians in the sixteenth and seventeenth centuries. These instruments are listed frequently and consistently in Muscovite directives, generally in the context of enumerating the undesirable activities they accompanied when played by *skomorokhi.* Although we have seen that the *skomorokhi* carried disturbing connections with blasphemy and the devil, they also had much simpler associations with drunken rowdiness, as Olearius makes clear in his statement on the burning of the wagonloads of instruments, quoted above. A 1653 directive similarly emphasizes the connection between tavern and *skomorokh,* with reference to the additional dangerous connections with games, animals, and masks:

> At the pot-house jesters [*skomorokhi*] with *bubny* [little drums or tambour-ines] and *surny,* with bears and with little dogs should not come, and no devilish games at all should be played by any means . . . if any jesters are discovered . . . and are brought in a second time, I order those jesters to be beaten with the knout, and I order a fine of five rubles a man to be exacted from them; and I order the *bubny, surny, domry,* and *gudki* to be smashed to pieces; and I order the masks to be burnt . . .[36]

The same behaviors, with the same kinds of musical instruments, were ex-hibited on important feast days, for example in the 1636 complaint, quoted in chapter 1, issued by a group of priests in Nizhnii Novgorod. The complaint details the abuses typical at the Feast of the Ascension, listing *skomorosi* and players (*igretsy*) with their *bubny* and *surny* and their accompanying blasphemous be-havior (masks, dancing, bears, drinking, and "other improper things").[37] A similar listing of forbidden *skomorokh* musical instruments comes in a series of edicts from just after mid-century, including one from 1657, issued by the metropolitan of Rostov, stating that "there shall no longer be *skomorokhi* or bear leaders allowed, that they shall no longer play on *gusli, domry, surny,* and bagpipes, or play devilish games and sing satanic songs, and no longer entice lay people."[38] These are the instruments shown in Olearius's famous illustrations of *skomorokhi* (figure 4.1), and these are the instruments enumerated, at least partially, by James and other writers around 1600. Such comparisons do not necessarily show that James and the other foreigners who listed these instruments heard actual *skomorokhi* play, al-though the tradition was strong in the Russian North, but rather that these were the familiar instruments of everyday life, which they themselves heard or which

FIGURE 4.1. Olearius, *Vermehrte Newe Beschreibung* (1656), *skomorokhi* playing the *gusli* and the bowed *gudok* and giving a puppet show (from Findeizen, *History,* 1:121, used by permission)

their informants described, readily accessible under many circumstances. In some cases, their observations come from their own experiences, for example Olearius's description of the music he heard in the town of Ladoga, when the two Russians with what he described as a lute (probably a *domra*) and a fiddle sang a song about Tsar Mikhail and then danced for the foreign party.[39]

The same kinds of instruments were associated with weddings. As the writers of the Stoglav Council confirm in their listing of the "trouble-makers, *organ-niki,* merry-makers, and *gusli* players" who disrupt weddings, such *skomorokh* connections were strongly associated with the large portion of the Russian wedding ceremony unconnected to the church. This complaint does not concern the groom's instrumental fanfare but rather the instrumental celebration that accompanied the wedding, which included instruments also consistently associated with *skomorokh* practice. These associations continue even into the Kremlin, where the same sorts of instruments (in addition to the groom's fanfare) sounded out at royal weddings. The description of Tsar Mikhail's second wedding, in 1626, forms a stark contrast to Aleksei's musical austerity (and shows why the sources were at such pains to describe Aleksei's break with tradition). Court records not only include payments to performers on keyboard instruments (*tsynbaly* and *vargany*) but also list payments to the following *veselye* (merry-makers, merry folk, a term used in connection with *skomorokhi*) who entertained the tsar at his wedding:

> the *veselye:* Paramonka Fedorov, the *gusli* players Uezda and Bogdashka Vlas'ev, the *domra* players Ondriushka Fedorov and Vaska Stepanov, and the fiddlers [*skrypotchiki*] Bogdashka Okat'ev, Ivashka Ivanov, and Onashka, and to the foreigner, the newly christened Armanka.[40]

The records specify that the entertainment took place "v Verkhu," that is, upstairs in the private family quarters.

Given the violent Russian reaction to the Polish musicians at Dmitrii's court, such entertainment would seem to constitute surprising—and dangerous—territory. The difference appears to lie in context: in certain situations, even instruments linked to *skomorokh* practice had other, approved uses. In spite of some outward similarities in their approaches to music and musical entertainment, the seventeenth-century Russian tsars thus navigated these treacherous waters very differently from Dmitrii and his Polish entourage, in ways sometimes difficult to appreciate. For example, although the *skomorokh* imagery relating to Dmitrii's court and his death was clearly and consistently articulated by both Russian and foreign observers alike, there is no indication that Dmitrii invited actual *skomorokhi* to perform. They would have been superfluous, whatever his Polish audience might have thought of their antics, for Marina's brother had brought his own *skomorokh*-like entertainment along with him. The account of the Polish merchant Niemojewski mentions Antonio Riati, an Italian jester who formed part of the Polish party and who figured prominently in the wedding entertainments.[41] The *skomorokh* imagery surrounding the events of Dmitrii's wedding was just that, imagery naturally and inevitably called forth to Muscovite and even to foreign observers by the mixed instrumental ensemble (although not necessarily by the specific instruments being played) and by the accompanying dancing, costumes, masks, and general revelry.

Mikhail and other Russian tsars, on the other hand, were able to enjoy the same instruments, but within the bounds of privacy, propriety, and scale. The instrumental music played in connection with Mikhail's wedding presupposes a stationary, accessible group of musicians who performed in the tsar's private quarters; as we shall see, some of them were regular court employees. Although the instruments they played were part of a long-standing *skomorokh* tradition, can we assume that the performers were themselves considered to be *skomorokhi*?

Scholars have noted that census and taxation records change their vocabulary in the late sixteenth and especially the seventeenth century, referring less and less frequently to *skomorokhi* and more often to specialists: *domra* players, *gusli* players, instrument makers with stalls in the markets, and so forth, as we shall see in the 1638 Moscow census records below. Some *skomorokhi* (or at least those with skills traditionally associated with *skomorokhi*) thus seem to have become defined by musical specialties and were often concentrated in towns and cities. It may have been from such settled and urbanized musical traditions that some of the instrumentalists for the court wedding were drawn. The musical entertainment at Tsar Mikhail's wedding was thus no less secular than Dmitrii's had been, but it was comprehensible and contained within established court and wedding traditions.[42]

Musical and other kinds of entertainments also formed part of the activities within the royal family's living quarters, a venue that further underscores the importance of privacy. The antics of various storytellers, jesters, dwarves, Moors, and Kalmyks were favorite pastimes for the royal family, as described by the Englishman Giles Fletcher, who was in Russia in 1588–89. After evening worship, he notes, "for the most parte [Tsar Fedor] recreateth himself with the Empresse till supper time, with iesters, and dwarfes, men and women, that tumble before him, and sing many songs after the Russe manner. This is his common recreation betwixt meales, that hee most delightes in."[43] Such private entertainment also included musical instruments. Some of the performers, such as the string players mentioned above in the context of Mikhail's wedding, may have been temporary (or at least do not appear in available court payroll listings). In contrast, at least some of the *domra* players (one of whom doubled as a storyteller) maintained a constant presence at court from the outset of Mikhail's reign; performers on *gusli* and *domra* are also listed by occupation in the 1638 census (indicating housing outside the court).[44] The court also maintained a large group of blind *domra* players, some of whom were paid from the coffers of the tsaritsa's treasury in the late 1620s, suggesting intimate, female-centered, and thus by definition private, entertainment. Ivan Zabelin suggests that the performers' close association with the intimate atmosphere of the terem might have been facilitated by their blindness—further insurance of privacy, perhaps (although not a prerequisite, for not all of the entertainers who performed in the terem were blind).[45]

Musical amusements for the royal children also fit into the category of the mixed suite of instruments. The young Tsarevich Peter Alekseevich (the future Peter the Great) was famous for his ranks of soldiers, including drummers and wind players, first as the result of boyish enthusiasm and then organized into real military regiments, but he was certainly not the only Russian tsarevich to play such musico-military games.[46] Peter's father, Tsar Aleksei, had also been supplied with organized squads of percussionists during his childhood. These *nakra* players (*nakry* were small military-type drums) were part of a miniature mirror court set up to duplicate the real court of his father, Tsar Mikhail. (Young Aleksei's court also included liturgical singers.) Tsarevich Aleksei had other types of military toys, both weapons and various kinds of percussion instruments, as did his own sons, Aleksei Alekseevich (1654–70) and his eventual successor, Fedor Alekseevich (1661–82).[47] The royal children also had their own collections of musical instruments, again duplicating their parents' collections and familiar from the listings in the glossaries by James, Sauvage, and others. In addition to various toys, birds, books, and games, Tsarevich Aleksei Mikhailovich was supplied with two *domry* and a *rylia* (or *lira;* hurdy-gurdy) purchased from Domra row (Domernyi riad) at the Moscow market, and he had a *gudok,* also purchased at the market. The royal daughters had some of the same toys, although with a greater emphasis on puppets or dolls and, with at least one exception, without the military playthings. The exception refers to Tsarevna Irina Mikhailovna who, as a five-month-old in 1627, was entertained by "girls beating the drums" ("devki po litavram b'iut")—an entertainment which, in truth, is difficult to appreciate at this distance. Irina and other seventeenth-century tsarevny also had *domry,* small tambourines or drums (*bubenchiki*), and little bells to play with.[48]

The court's keyboard players formed another important component of royal musical pastimes.[49] These musicians performed on organs (*organy;* the term is used in the plural), which were generally small portative models, although there were some larger, but still portative, instruments at court as well. Although the Poles had brought a single, ill-fated organist with them to Moscow, Tsar Mikhail institutionalized the presence of organs at court by hiring a series of invited foreign masters (including Poles) whose positions at court, in various and overlapping configurations, were maintained throughout the seventeenth century.[50] The foreign masters were required to teach Russian students in their craft, and a great deal of effort was devoted to the repair and upkeep of the court's instruments.

The other important keyboard instrument at court was the *tsynbaly.* Leonid Roizman has parsed the difficult, sometimes overlapping terminology used to indicate keyboard instruments in this period, determining that *tsynbaly* were harpsichord-like instruments; the term *klevikorty* (or *okhtavy* for a small instrument) referred to a clavichord-type keyboard instrument.[51] There were many *tsynbaly* players—called *tsynbal'niki*—at the Russian court beginning in 1613 and continuing throughout the century. Some of them also played the organ. The earliest group of *tsynbal'niki* seems to have been Russian: Tomila Besov, Meletii [or Melentii] Stepanov, and Andrei Andreev, whose tenure at the Poteshnaia palata (Entertainment Hall) spans the period from 1613 into the early 1630s. In the late 1620s and 1630s, the Polish organist Iurii Proskurovskii worked in Moscow and was listed as "Iurii tsynbal'nik" in the 1638 Moscow census.[52]

The best-known organists of the period were two Dutch brothers, Johann and Melchior (or Melchert) Luhn and their two foreign assistants, whose employment in the 1630s overlapped with that of some of the Russian keyboardists. The Luhn brothers brought an instrument with them, which they worked on while in Moscow. The organs and keyboard instruments were elaborately carved and ornamented, and the Luhn brothers' model was purchased by the court for the fantastic sum of 2,676 rubles. The tsar heard and saw the instrument twice, after which he bestowed additional gifts upon the two brothers. The Luhns remained at court for most of the decade. Johann died in Moscow in 1637 and Melchior received permission to return home in 1638, leaving behind his Russian student, Iakushka Timofeev (who is mentioned generically as a *poteshnik* [entertainer] in the census records of that year). In that same year, the Pole Fedor Zaval'skii was hired as an organist, presumably as a replacement.[53]

In spite of Tsar Aleksei's lack of interest in musical instruments around the time of his first marriage, Roizman notes that in the 1640s and early 1650s the instruments remained at court nevertheless, citing a fascinating, if difficult, passage in support. Two Muscovite envoys had been dispatched to the Persian Shah Abbas II in 1653. Before their return to Moscow, the diplomats relaxed in the warm southern gardens, sipping a grape beverage called *chikhir,* admiring the flowers, and listening to the shah's musicians playing *domry, gusli,* and fiddles (*skripki*). The shah asked whether or not Tsar Aleksei enjoyed such music, and the envoys replied: "Our Great Lord has many such instruments and people who know how to play them. However His Highness does not amuse himself with such playing, but rather with spiritual entertainments. *Organy* sing before him, praising God with many-voiced singing . . ." Roizman suggests that the term *organy* here refers not to an instrument, but rather to voices (and it is paired with the verb *pet',* to sing, which is not used in connection with instruments); nevertheless, this passage appears to confirm the presence at Aleksei's court of various types of musical instruments, even if they were not particularly favored at that time.[54]

The instruments themselves, and presumably the associated performing traditions, were revived soon afterwards, when the Polish organist Simeon Gutovskii came to Moscow from Smolensk, just after the city changed to Russian hands in 1654. Gutovskii was a highly skilled craftsman, a wood and metal worker and a musician, who created and performed on the instruments at court. He built a large organ to be given as a gift to Shah Abbas II in the early 1660s—confirming the shah's taste in music—and he accompanied the precious gift to Isfahan, where he assembled and, one presumes, performed on it. Gutovskii was also charged with repairing the various keyboard instruments (*tsynbali, klevikorty,* and *argany* [*organy*]) belonging to the royal children. The children also had *stramenty,* which were apparently mechanical instruments with a turning handle and metal strings.[55] Gutovskii was also involved with the instrumental ensemble assembled for the court theater. He was a dominant musical presence at court for some thirty years and, following his marriage to a Russian woman, he was succeeded in his duties by his sons after his death in 1685.[56]

Muscovy's elite families also owned these same kinds of keyboard instruments. Prince V. V. Golitsyn and his son Aleksei had several expensive organs, valued at between 120 and 200 rubles, with a smaller or less elaborate model worth the still-considerable sum of 30 rubles. They also owned much less expensive *klevikorty* and *tsynbaly;* Prince Aleksei had an organ and *klevikorty* in his bedroom, and the two other costly organs were in the princes' dining chambers. These keyboard instruments were generally inventoried with other mechanical or artistic objects, particularly clocks. The Golitsyn inventory also included a large *domra* and two "German flutes."[57] An organ and *tsynbaly* from the estate of the tsar's uncle, N. I. Romanov, were given to I. A. Vorotynskii in 1657; Vorotynskii, in turn, gave the tsar *tsynbaly* in 1671.[58] As we shall see in our discussion of the court theater, A. S. Matveev, the theater's prime organizer and the head of the Diplomatic Chancellery, also had access to musical instruments, including an organ.

Fletcher's comments above about the male and female "iesters and dwarfes" who so entertained Tsar Fedor and Tsaritsa Irina in the late sixteenth century, as well as the reference to the *litavra*-playing girls who soothed Mikhail's young daughter, raise the possibility of female instrumentalists at court. Just as the court enjoyed female dwarves, Moors, *bogomolitsy,* and *nishchie,* so one wonders if there were female instrumentalists as well.[59] The available records do not refer to any female instrumentalists at court—the names seem to be uniformly male for this category of entertainer (and the girl drummers, however amusing to the infant tsarevna, probably do not belong to the class of professional instrumentalists). Yet there is some evidence that whispers of the presence of female court musicians, although from a significantly later period. For example, in 1725, Peter the Great, his wife, and other members of the court attended the wedding of his female *gudok* player (*gudoshnitsa*), Nastas'ia, to another court employee; all the other court *gudok* players attended. (This was at a time, of course, when female entertainers, both native and foreign, had begun to appear in Russia.)[60] Even as early as the 1670s, the court's theatrical planners tried fairly seriously to hire Anna Paulsen, the director of a troupe employed in Denmark, to bring her actors to Moscow. The group did not go to Russia, and one can only speculate as to whether or not Paulsen herself would have performed on a Muscovite stage; the actors ultimately chosen (young people from Moscow's Foreign Quarter) were all male, as were the musicians.

One of the most powerful sources attesting to the familiar, even casual, acceptance of a mixed instrumental ensemble at the Russian court comes from a primer written by Karion Istomin for the young Tsarevich Aleksei, published in 1694.[61] Istomin's *Bukvar'* (Alphabet) depicts ordinary objects through pictures and verses laid out in alphabetical order, with creatively contorted human figures forming each letter. For the letter *O* Istomin includes a picture of a small portative organ, or *organy* (figure 4.2) The instrument is encased in a squarish, decorated box, with a keyboard and twenty-four pipes visible, and seems to be just the sort of small, compact instrument indicated in other descriptions; the value of the instruments seems to have been a matter of external ornamentation as much as size. Istomin also corroborates the court's familiarity with other sorts of instruments, for he includes a large *gusli* as well as drums (*barabany,* in a vivid battle scene under the letter *B*) and various horns and trumpets. One of his most famous illustrations is under the letter *Ps,* for "psalter," "psalms" (illustrated by an open book showing musical notation using a five-line staff), and the related concept "Musika. Penie sladkoe" (Music. Sweet singing), which is meant to accompany the Psalms and Psalter (and which only confirms the popularity of the various *kant*-style settings of psalms, including Vasilii Titov's; see figure 4.3). The illustration combines the lively instrumental presence at court with the Ukrainian and Belarusian influences we considered in chapters 2 and 3, for it depicts not only the staff notation typical of such settings, but an ensemble of four (male) instrumentalists playing a large violin or *skripka,* a *gusli* (also illustrated under the letter *G*), a wind instrument held vertically, possibly with some kind of reed, and a *bandura,* a large plucked instrument with a bowl- or lute-shaped body associated closely with Polish and Ukrainian practice. As Nikolai Findeizen points out, the *gusli* player in Istomin's *Alphabet* is positioned in the same way, holding the same style of instrument and seated on the same throne-like chair, as in many Russian depictions of King David. One cannot help but recall the *liutnia* left behind at the death of poet-musician German of the New Jerusalem Monastery.[62]

In spite of the obvious *skomorokh* connections—real ones, not just analogies— associated with at least some of the tsars' musical entertainments, this kind of music-making with mixed instruments may have been regarded in some instances

FIGURE 4.2. Istomin, *Bukvar'* (1694), illustration of organ under the letter *O* (from Findeizen, *History*, 1:157, used by permission)

not only as appropriate, but even perhaps as Orthodox, and not just because of the unquestionably Orthodox milieu of the royal family itself, a quality conspicuously lacking for the False Dmitrii, his bride Marina, and their guests at the beginning of the century. The reference above to the fiddlers at Tsar Mikhail's wedding includes the names of three Russians plus a foreigner, the "newly christened Armanka."[63] Armanka may have been foreign born, but unlike the imported foreign musicians who played for Dmitrii and Marina, he was described as a properly baptized Orthodox subject of the tsar. This was not uniformly the case. Although the Polish organist Fedor Zaval'skii was required to swear on the cross that he would perpetrate no "sly tricks" upon the sovereign's *argany,* there is no evidence that he or any of the other foreign keyboardists were required to convert (although Gutovskii must have been Orthodox if he married a Russian woman). Similarly, the fact that Melchior Luhn was given permission to leave Russia permanently indicates that he had not converted to Orthodoxy, for an Orthodox subject of the tsar would not have been allowed to emigrate.[64] The other performers in Mikhail's ensemble, however, seem to have been Russian, and perhaps this is why Armanka is specified as "newly christened."[65]

FIGURE 4.3. Istomin, *Bukvar'* (1694), illustration of *Psaltir'—musika, psalmy,* and *penie sladkoe* (from Findeizen, *History,* 1:156, used by permission)

Furthermore, not only was this musical entertainment apparently on a fairly small scale (no forty-member orchestra for Tsar Mikhail, as there had been for Dmitrii), but the available sources describing the events of Mikhail's weddings include no references to dancing, particularly dancing in mixed company, or to masks, costumes, or "mummerie," all of which played such a conspicuous part in Dmitrii's and Marina's celebrations. Mikhail's wedding music thus seems to have represented an appropriate extension of earlier, private court music, along the lines of Horsey's "organes and vergenalls" or Fletcher's "iesters and dwarfes" for an earlier Russian royal family. Indeed, the question of dancing seems to have been an extremely important one, and one that differentiates Dmitrii's entertainments from those of the following Russian tsars at least as much as their choice of music. Grigorii Kotoshikhin flatly denies that there was any dancing at the Russian court, and we should probably take his statement at face value, for although there are a few accounts of dancing, particularly in connection with weddings, such references do not encompass the royal family.[66] An account by the Pole Samuel Maskiewicz underscores this. Maskiewicz, after observing the non-church festivities at a Russian wedding in 1611, noted that the Muscovites considered dancing to be inappropriate and undignified for a high-ranking person. He describes dancing performed by *szuty* (jesters or fools; he does not use the term *skomorokhi*), who also sang unseemly songs and played the *lira* (hurdy-gurdy, which he describes

carefully) at the wedding.[67] Dancing may have been considered especially dangerous because of its associated behaviors: masking, costumes, and the accompanying
lascivious movements. Such a strong prohibition against public dancing may account for the reticence with which the Russian upper classes (women especially)
initially joined in Peter the Great's new assemblies of the early eighteenth century,
which enforced social mingling between the sexes, including dancing.[68]

The supreme importance of context in understanding the roles of music at the
Muscovite court is underscored by the conclusion of Olearius's remarks on the
banning and burning of musical instruments. When, at the height of the church's
campaign against the *skomorokhi* and their music in mid-century, the patriarch
was forced to acknowledge concessions to the total ban on instruments, his allowances were not to the *skomorokhi* themselves, but to the styles and contexts that
were acceptable and familiar in court circles. As Olearius says: "The Germans,
however, are permitted to have music in their homes, as is the great magnate Nikita
[Romanov], the friend of the Germans ["dem Deutschen Freund"], who has a
positiv and many other instruments in his palace. There is little the Patriarch can
say to him."[69] Olearius's comment suggests that foreign instruments, musicians,
or both played some role in influencing Muscovite musical practices in styles
not limited to the military fanfares or keyboard instruments, but in the arena of
mixed instrumental ensembles for private entertainment. Did they in fact do so,
and if so, how?

Music from the Outside

One of the points Leonid Roizman makes in the most forceful manner in his
important book on organs in Russia is that in the seventeenth century, Russian
organ practice was not tied to churches in Moscow's Foreign Quarter. In the first
half of the century, the Foreign Quarter did not exist as a specific, distinct locale,
and in the second half of the century, when it did, the small churches there did not
contain any organs. Furthermore, as we have seen, the Russian court enjoyed
performances on organs and other keyboard instruments from at least the late
sixteenth century, if not earlier. Roizman's related statement, that the foreigners
themselves did not own organs and therefore, again, Russian organ performance
was a native rather than an imported practice, is somewhat more problematic.[70]

It is certainly true, as Roizman points out, that there are reports of Muscovite
musicians playing for foreigners, suggesting that the visitors were dipping into the
pool of Russian musical talent rather than vice versa. Employees of the Vorotynskii and Dolgorukii families, for example, were loaned out on request to resi-

dents of the Foreign Quarter, where they played "*organy* and *tsimbali* and violins [*skripki*]."[71] However, the fact that Horsey brought keyboard instruments and performers to Russia in the late sixteenth century, that the Luhn brothers also brought an important instrument in the 1630s, along with their own assistants, and that there was a series of Polish organists throughout the century does point to a certain level of foreign influence on Muscovite organ and keyboard practice (although, as Roizman says, centered at court rather than among the city's foreign population). A slightly different example of such musical interchanges might be drawn from the court's efforts to procure an organ for their theatrical productions in the early 1670s. In this case, no suitable instrument was to be found at court, so a large instrument, valued at 1,200 rubles (bettered only by the value of the Luhn brothers' organ), was purchased from a "foreign trader," Timofei Gazenkrukh (Hasenkruch; see chapter 6).

These observations are not meant to dispute Roizman's main point, which was intended to underscore the important role of musical instruments, especially keyboards, at the Muscovite court throughout the seventeenth century, a development that was primarily, if not solely, homegrown, with timely infusions of talent and material from invited foreign masters. However, the evidence from foreign accounts suggests at the very least some degree of interchange or exposure to Western musical practices on the Russian side. Furthermore, this exposure tends to be among the small circle of high-ranking members of Russian society and top government officials that was responsible for engaging in and monitoring the activities of the visiting foreign parties. Members of the Klenk mission, for example, remembered seeing Polish musicians employed by upper-class Muscovites, and Skrzolotowicz wrote his little song booklet in Cyrillic with the specific intent of making it accessible to Russians. To paraphrase Olearius's statement on the musical independence of Nikita Romanov, there was little the patriarch could do to control such exposure.

Several foreigners mention their own music-making in an unexceptionable context: private religious devotions. Such activities, certainly not an influence on Muscovite practice, nonetheless indicate that the visiting foreigners came equipped to make music. Andrei Rode, who wrote the account of the Danish embassy in Russia in 1659, remarks, for example, that they celebrated their own Easter services quietly and simply, singing psalms, reading the Gospels, and praying. Olearius, in Moscow awaiting an opportunity for an audience with the tsar, notes that the party "gave thanks to God for our safe arrival, with prayers, a sermon, and music."[72] But the foreign religious celebrations were not always so discreet; one recalls the religious services held by Marina's party, which so startled the Russians that they "broke down the barrier." Even later, foreign services were not necessarily either quiet or private. Like many outsiders, Bernard Tanner, a member of the Polish embassy of 1678, was fascinated by Russian Easter celebrations, and he mentions the Russian customs of men and women exchanging kisses, giving one another dyed Easter eggs, and exclaiming "Christ is risen!" He goes on to compare Russian practices to those of his party—unfavorably, of course—when they celebrated their own Easter festivities on their way to Moscow, and where the Russian audience made an automatic connection between instrumental music and dancing:

> We celebrated Easter in our own fashion, solemnly with trumpets and drums. Our agreeable music and our singing to [notated] music, which so caressed the ear, was extremely unusual to our uneducated listeners. They all stood, mouths agape, in amazement that we could pray to God to the accompaniment of such agreeable singing and playing of instruments; it seemed to them that this rather inclined one's soul to dancing.[73]

A more typical context for such invigorating foreign instrumental music was in the non-religious activities of a visiting ambassadorial party. The Carlisle embassy spent the winter months of 1663–64 in Vologda, on their way to Moscow, and their account describes how the English visitors sought to alleviate their boredom with music and dancing. As in the case of Tanner's description, an interested Russian audience was present for music-making:

> Our Musique was most commonly at Dinner, at which time there was nothing to be heard but Trumpets and Viols, whose delightful and agreeable Harmony, did sometimes so charm the Russes, that it drew great Company of them to hear it. And indeed the Musique was very good, being managed by one of the best experienced Musicians of England, who from time to time composed new airs.[74]

The Klenk embassy had a similar musical exchange. In January 1676, after a session in conference between the ambassador and the tsar's advisors, the visiting Dutch party sent a page to entertain the Russian court: "In the evening, a young page was again sent to the tsar, in order to play there on the drums and also on the violin and the organ. He was sent home in the same sledge, after they gave him jam and sweet wine. This occurred again on several occasions."[75]

Another route by which information about organs in particular might have made its way to Moscow is through Uniate and Uniate-influenced religious practice in the areas south and west of Muscovy. (The Uniates, or Eastern Rite Catholics, acknowledged the Western Catholic pope as head of the church but retained the Orthodox liturgy.) When Paul of Aleppo traveled through Ukraine on his way to Moscow, he encountered organs performing in services in several churches. He described how the organ accompanied the singers in the town of Uman' (about 120 miles south of Kiev): "In this church are lofty pillars; with galleries looking over the choir, in which the musicians stand, and sing from their musical books to the organ, making with it a noise that emulates thunder." Later in that same town, Paul notes that "after reciting the Gospel, they chaunt with the organ the words "Doksa soi, Kirie, doksa soi" [Glory to Thee, O Lord, glory to Thee]."[76] Paul gives a similar description of the music he heard at another church, in the town of Sakoka: "Above the Great *Narthiks* are galleries; with balustrades, looking over the choir, in which the singers stand and chaunt to the organ."[77]

Paul also observed that, at least on occasion, Ukrainians recycled churches that had been built by the Poles for Catholic services. Such buildings would have been constructed with organ participation in mind, and the Ukrainians might even have taken over an instrument. Although he does not mention this specifically, Paul does say that at the Church of St. Nicholas in Sakoka, "the choristers are continued the same as in the time of the Poles."[78]

Paul's observations are supported by a mid-seventeenth-century musical source linked to Uniate practice. Manuscript 10002 from the Jagellonian Library in Cracow (BJ 10002) contains primarily secular music, with over sixty Polish songs and dance melodies. It also includes several Cyrillic liturgical texts set to both Kievan square notation and standard Western (oval) notation, along with a selection of "Amin'," "Aleliuia," and "Kirie" settings, also in Cyrillic. These Cyrillic texts are set to figured bass notation, which Jerzy Gołos, who discovered and edited the manuscript, believes is consistent with Uniate musical practices; this would also support Paul's reports on organ music in some Ukrainian churches.[79] Diletskii, too, mentions figured bass notation in his music-theoretical work, as noted below in chapter 5.

The various and fluid combinations of texts and notational systems in this source highlight the larger issue of musical innovations emanating from the Uniate Church and their impact on Muscovite practice. We have already observed the important influence of Polish and Belarusian/Ukrainian song styles on the Muscovite *kant*, and although manuscript BJ 10002 is largely secular, it contains two songs of special interest to Russian singing traditions. The text "Jesu Christe, Panie mily," which appears as a two-part song in BJ 10002, was transmitted widely in the *kant* sources discussed in chapter 3, including the earliest *kant* manuscript (texts only), which was written by a Pole in Moscow in 1675, as well as two settings in another early source (GIM, Muz. sobr., No. 1938). Another song in BJ 10002,

"Dayci Boze dobranoc," appears in Polish in a source displaying Ukrainian linguistic influences that transmits Nikolai Diletskii's *Grammatika*, a source including several other Polish song texts.[80]

Manuscript BJ 10002 also supports the broader picture of the influences from Belarus and Ukraine on Muscovite music. For example, we have seen how Simeon Polotskii brought the performed recitation (*deklamatsiia*) from the Orthodox Epiphany Monastery in the city of Polotsk to Aleksei's court in Moscow. Gołos makes a strong case for placing BJ 10002 in Polotsk as well. The manuscript was discovered as part of the binding material for a Uniate missal from that city, which was also an important Jesuit center. There is evidence that the Uniate archbishop of Polotsk, Cyprian Żochowski (d. 1693), sponsored what Gołos terms "interfaith" religious celebrations with the Jesuits there. He points out that there are some Polish instructions noted next to the Cyrillic liturgical texts, for example, the remark "A Po tych te Kirieleson" (After those [melodies] this Kyrie eleison) or, at the bottom of the page, the note "wprod Te grac" (first play these). The situation was not unique to Polotsk, for the fraternal organizations associated with Catholic, Orthodox, and Uniate churches throughout Belarus participated in some celebrations together; for example, when Orthodox singers took part in a Catholic procession of Corpus Christi in the town of Mohilev in 1695.[81]

The Blagoveshchenskii (Annunciation) Monastery at Supraśl, near Białystok, also seems to have played an important role in incorporating aspects of Western music into its ritual, and it too had musical ties to Muscovy. The monastery was founded in the late fifteenth century by Orthodox monks from the Kievo-Pecherskii (Kievan Caves) Monastery, and it adopted the Union in 1614. From this monastery came the earliest known translation of traditional *znamennyi* melodies to the five-line staff (the Irmologii of 1598–1601; that is, before it adopted the Union), the earliest examples of liturgical polyphony in the *partesnoe* style (several four-part settings in the Irmologii of 1638–39), and one of the earliest extant examples of printed music (a *tropar'* from 1697).[82] The monastery apparently enjoyed good relations with Muscovy, for a 1645–54 inventory lists copies of the Irmologii, including three staff-notated versions (plus another two in a 1668 inventory) and many books written in the *partesnoe* style; it also includes seven Muscovite copies ("Irmoloev sem', moskovskikh") and notes that seven unidentified books from Supraśl had been sent off to Moscow. The exchange recalls a similar dispatch of books, including musical sources, from the Orthodox Iverskii Monastery to the New Jerusalem Monastery.[83]

By the middle of the seventeenth century, the Supraśl monastery owned a substantial collection of Latin and Polish books, including Jan Kochanowski's verse setting of the Psalter. Kochanowski's settings not only appeared (transliterated into Cyrillic) in some of the early *kant* sources we examined in chapter 3, including Skrzolotowicz's, but they prompted Simeon Polotskii's versified psalm translations into Slavic, which were later set to music by Vasilii Titov. Even taking into account the heavy losses of manuscript material throughout the entire area (and the heavy losses sustained by the monastery itself in 1944), the Supraśl establishment seems to have been an important musical center. One can only hope that the discovery and publication of other sources from these important meeting points, where Catholic, Orthodox, and Uniate musical practice existed side by side, will allow scholars to expand upon this dynamic interchange.[84]

All of these various influences, styles, practices, and traditions come together at Tsar Aleksei Mikhailovich's court in the early 1670s, particularly in the two important cultural milestones of this time: his second marriage, in 1671, and the formation of the court theater shortly thereafter. The musical entertainments at Aleksei's second wedding are generally invoked as a contrast to the liturgical singing at his first wedding, serving as an illustration of the increasingly Western cultural orientation at the Muscovite court in the intervening years.[85] Muscovite records describe the tsar's 1671 wedding as including a mixed instrumental ensemble, with an organ played by a foreigner, as well as traditional Russian instruments, which may hint at the customary wedding fanfare:

> [A]fter the banquet, the Tsar ordered entertainments, and the Great Lord was entertained by organs, and a foreigner [*nemchin*] played the organ, and they played on *surny* and blew on the trumpets, and played *surenki* [small *surny*], and they beat on the *nakry* and *litavry* throughout.[86]

Each of these elements—the presence of an instrumental ensemble, the choice of instruments, the inclusion of an organ, and the performance by both Russians and a foreigner—also reflect long-standing musical traditions at the Muscovite court, deliberately cultivated. Aleksei's tastes may have changed over the course of a quarter-century, but the court's music, in its essentials, did not. The real aberration was not the foreign organist and the instrumental entertainments at Aleksei's second wedding but their absence at his first.

Yet there were still lingering, and telling, fears of the infectious power of the dangerous *skomorokh*-like behavior associated with musical entertainment. The theorist Ioannikii Korenev, writing in the 1670s, emphasized that it was the bawdy songs, particularly at weddings, that created the greatest offense, and he was even prepared to permit quiet, private instrumental performance in order to stave off such music: "[I]t would be better for you to permit lay people to praise God . . . in their home even on inanimate instruments, rather than sing prodigal and indecent songs during weddings . . ."[87] Such fears were, at the very same time, expressed immediately following Aleksei's own wedding, as the court prepared for a new and highly Westernized entertainment: the first court theater in Russia. In trying to convince the tsar of the necessity of music and dancing for the theater, the organizers, led by Artemon Matveev (the head of the Diplomatic Chancellery and guardian of the tsar's new wife), ran into opposition that was both natural and ancient. As one of the foreign participants wrote:

> At first, it is true, the tsar did not want to allow music [in the theatrical productions] as being new and in some ways pagan, but when they pleaded with him that without music it was impossible to put together a chorus, just as it is impossible for dancers to dance without legs, then he, a little unwillingly, left everything to the discretion of the actors themselves.[88]

Why should Aleksei hesitate, given the musical entertainment he had just enjoyed at his wedding? The tsar could be entertained at his wedding and on other occasions by musical instruments, as his father had been before him, but the associations connected to the theater were of a different nature. The theater involved not only music, but dancing and costumes as well, perhaps a bit too close to the masking of the *skomorokhi* (or the masquerades planned for Dmitrii's oblivious Polish guests). These were the musical associations the tsar justifiably feared in the context of the new theater, and Aleksei's hesitation echoes age-old negotiations and navigations between pagan licentiousness and proper entertainment, between public and private, and between foreign and Orthodox.

The strength of such traditional Muscovite prohibitions is emphasized in an even later document, from the final years of the seventeenth century and the beginning of the eighteenth, during the early part of Peter the Great's reign. Peter had sent a number of aristocrats abroad in a campaign to advance Russian military knowledge, including Prince Petr Alekseevich Golitsyn (1660–1722), who was sent to Venice to study naval technology. Golitsyn traveled throughout Italy and while in Florence he also sought out singers, for Tsar Peter "ardently wanted musicians at his court." (This was not the mission's sole musical engagement, for Golitsyn's group included three other Russians who learned to play the theorbo, two of them rather successfully.) Thus when Golitsyn returned to Moscow in late 1698, he brought with him a young castrato, Filippo Balatri, who lived with the family for two years (with a short stint at court) and who then returned with them to Vienna, where Golitsyn served as Russia's first permanent ambassador to the Holy Roman

Empire from 1701 to 1703.[89] Balatri, although only fourteen when he moved east with Prince Golitsyn, was already a trained musician who had studied in Florence and had frequently sung for Cosimo III, and his nine-volume account of his stay with the family reveals him to be curious and clever (he quickly learned Russian), and a natural and ever-willing performer. The Golitsyns, on their part, treated him as a beloved favorite, defending him against accusations of heresy (he adhered strictly to the Catholic faith) and even providing him with transportation to the Foreign Quarter to attend mass every Sunday. Balatri's ambiguous sexual status, which may not have been understood in Muscovy, and perhaps also his youth gave him free access to the closed quarters of the terem—he even learned to embroider in order to sit with the ladies of the house there, telling stories, singing songs, and generally entertaining everyone in his orbit. "I think," he declared early in his account, "I could be called the 'Orpheus of Moscow.'"[90]

Balatri also performed at Peter's court, where he lived for a short time (he was given the status of *spal'nik,* a page or attendant, but he preferred to return after a short time to the more congenial situation at the Golitsyn home). He also accompanied Tsar Peter on various trips, during which he provided musical entertainment, and he even traveled with a Russian embassy to the Kalmyk Khan Aiuk, where, of course, he sang for the hosts and even, at one point, feared for his future, for the khan so enjoyed his performances that he requested to purchase the singer.[91] "Filippushka" also sang for other foreigners in Moscow's Foreign Quarter, where he spent a great deal of time with Anna Mons, Peter's *inamorata,* eventually being assigned as her music teacher. Tsar Peter arranged to have a keyboard instrument brought to Anna's home so Balatri could accompany himself, and Peter also played the instrument "fairly passably." Balatri says that he sang "Muscovite arias in the Italian manner," and he recorded the Russian text of one of his showpieces, a song that was preserved in many variants throughout the eighteenth century.[92] He even, in a refreshing change of pace for a foreigner in Russia, praised the Russian language, regarding it as superior for singing to English, German, and French (not to Italian, though).

Balatri's diary is an intimate portrait of a traditional Muscovite household, and his singing there, although unusual in that a foreigner had such unrestricted access to the private world of Russian women, shows the kinds of musical entertainments one might readily expect: domestic singing that included women and girls; public singing at court and on the embassy; and the mixed entertainments at the Foreign Quarter, a harbinger of the changes Peter was in the process of instituting.[93] But the diary also emphasizes the strength of Muscovite traditions regarding music and theater. Princess Dar'ia Golitsyna's stay in Vienna with her husband was very difficult for her, requiring public appearances, Western dress, and other such unfamiliar indignities, which she seems to have handled with gracious aplomb. While in Vienna, she took the opportunity to explore the city's various theatrical venues. This was unusual for a woman of her rank, for as Balatri recorded, based on his many conversations with her, Muscovite ladies did not go to "impertinent comedies or to masquerades (those damnable occasions)." Princess Golitsyna found some of the Viennese comedies to be "immodest and indecent for so noble an audience," but others, including a Harlequin comedy, she approved.[94] While in Vienna, it was appropriate to enjoy some Viennese theater, but there was a limit and that limit touched on long-standing traditions and prohibitions of Orthodoxy.

Defining a proper role for non-liturgical music, particularly instrumental music, was thus a continuing theme in Muscovite cultural history, a set of negotiations that both encompassed and transcended the stark and specific events of Dmitrii's brief reign and that help us understand the musical impulses of his Romanov successors. With the ever-increasing contacts with Western governments during the seventeenth century, the role of *musikiia* had particular resonance in Muscovy as a marker of grandeur as well as a continuation and extension of traditional entertainments, with all their attendant associations. Yet at each step of the way, there were specific considerations to keep in mind and a tenuous balancing act to maintain. As they did with the varieties of vocal music pouring into Muscovy in the seventeenth century, so the Russian cultural elite made their decisions about musical instruments in a spirit of both tradition and curiosity, the greatest example of which was their exhilarating experience with theater, which we shall examine in chapter 6.

5

Nikolai Diletskii

Language and Imagery in
Muscovite Music Theory

The musical changes we have traced—the introduction and popularity in Muscovy of *kanty, kontserty,* and the notational practices they brought with them, the increasing numbers of Ukrainian and Belarusian singers and singing styles, and the lively range of instrumental entertainment—are mirrored by equally great changes in the language and methodology by which music was taught. The enormous, even confusing shifts over the course of the century engendered many writings on music, heated attacks on or defenses of various singing styles and practices. Our focus here is on the works devoted to the language and techniques of music-making, and there are two especially important and serious theoretical efforts in this category, by Aleksandr Mezenets and Nikolai Diletskii. The two theorists and their works are very different. Mezenets had been engaged since before the middle of the century in a series of notational reforms that would clearly prescribe pitch in the context of neumed notation. These efforts were to be joined in the service of textual reforms to create accurate, reliable musical sources for liturgical singing. Mezenets's collaborative work represented a tremendous and serious effort made by expert church singers and at the highest levels over a period of several years. It was an effort very much in the descriptive mold of traditional Russian chant theory; that is, concerned heavily with notation, following the pattern of the older *azbuki* (listings of neumes). Although it would be an overstatement to call this effort stillborn, the work was not in tune with the Western-style polyphonic music that was becoming so popular in Muscovy at that very time, and the tools of that new style—its theoretical language, Western-based precepts, and use of staff notation—were soon applied to chant itself, especially via the *dvoznamenniki,* sources that presented the traditional chant melodies by means of two (or more) notations, usually neumes and staff notation. Thus, although inconceivable only a few years earlier, the other landmark theoretical work, by Nikolai Diletskii, was not concerned with traditional church singing per se but rather with the new *partesnoe penie* repertoire. Diletskii was careful to note, however, that his rules were universal and so could be applied to liturgical singing. Diletskii's theoretical language clearly reflects the sources of this newly popular music—even his biography, with a career spanning (at least) the centers of Kiev, Vilnius, Smolensk, and Moscow, mirrors these musical influences. This Western-oriented approach is evident in other theoretical works from later in the century, some clearly modeled on Diletskii's treatise and some blending traditional approaches to chant with this new vocabulary.[1] We thus begin here with a survey of Diletskii's life and his treatise, which, judging from its widespread manuscript transmission, its longevity, and its influence on other theorists, was an enormously successful work. We then consider in more detail how Diletskii's work followed other cultural trends in Muscovy, and how other theorists developed his (or similar) precepts in their own writings.

Nikolai Diletskii and His Grammatika: *Mapping Musical Culture*

Although the broad outlines of Diletskii's biography are fairly firmly established, the details remain elusive.[2] A comment in a musical treatise by another theorist, Ioannikii Korenev, is the only preserved reference to Diletskii's association with Kiev. Korenev describes Diletskii as a "resident of the city of Kiev" who translated his own theoretical work from Polish into Slavic ("slovenskii"). Although this remark does not necessarily establish Diletskii's ultimate origins, it does at least provide a foothold on his career path.[3] Korenev's information should be reliable, for the two musicians apparently knew one another. As we shall see below, the version of the *Grammatika* written in Moscow in variants from 1679 and 1681 was often joined with Korenev's treatise in manuscript sources, and one source indicates that Diletskii prepared this translation while in Korenev's home.[4]

The major source of information about Diletskii's life is the *Grammatika* itself, in its three preserved versions: from Smolensk 1677; from Moscow 1679; and from Moscow in variants dated 1679 and 1681. We do not know when the author was born or when he died, but because there seems to have been no further work on the *Grammatika* after 1681, it may be that Diletskii died shortly after this date. Scholars have suggested a birth date in the 1630s simply by projecting back from this hypothesized date of death. Diletskii's apparently short career in Muscovy, documented only from the late 1670s to 1681, might thus account for the archival silence on the theorist.

Some have challenged this rough outline, based on their interpretation of one of the *Grammatika* sources, a manuscript with some Ukrainian linguistic elements written in St. Petersburg in 1723. They suggest that this source is actually an autograph: it shows evidence of Ukrainian—suggestive, given Diletskii's ties to Kiev—and several passages seem to indicate that Diletskii was alive at the time it was produced, suggesting a correspondingly later birth date. The signature in this source is followed by a mark which might be deciphered as МП (in Cyrillic; *manu propria*).[5] This interpretation was quickly challenged. Some pointed to errors in the musical examples in this manuscript, somewhat disconcerting if one believes Diletskii wrote them out himself. The passages that seem to indicate that Diletskii was alive at the time the manuscript was produced turn up in other, later copies of the treatise and thus would not necessarily carry special biographical significance for this source. Finally, the *manu propria* sign might also be deciphered as a cursive letter T, indicating simply *tvorets* (author). Although the jury is still out regarding the question of exactly who wrote this manuscript, St. Petersburg in the early years of the eighteenth century would have been a comfortable milieu for a musician with Diletskii's skills and training (and for his treatise as well).[6]

The first and only reference to Diletskii in a source independent of his treatise and musical compositions concerns his stay in the Polish-Lithuanian city of Vilnius. Diletskii wrote a pamphlet there entitled *Toga złota* (The Golden Toga), which was published in 1675. The work is lost, preserved only through the citation of its title page in a nineteenth-century bibliography: "The Golden Toga in the new metamorphosis of the world, dedicated to the noble Vilnius magistrate (council) on the new year, written by Mikołaj Dilecki, a Vilnius academic, printed in Vilnius. The Franciscan Press, 1675. In quarto, 7 unnumbered leaves. [In the] Krasiński [Library]."[7] Most scholars agree that the seven leaves specified for *Toga złota* could scarcely have represented even a preliminary version of the very long *Grammatika*. It may instead have been a panegyric, a genre popular in Vilnius and one that often employed unusual or fanciful titles. Such works were published there in great numbers in the sixteenth and seventeenth centuries, usually in Polish or in Latin, and were often read at public ceremonies or processions that typically would also include music. Diletskii's possible contribution to the genre might thus speak to his familiarity and facility with these traditions.[8]

In spite of the thin documentation for this period in Diletskii's life, it is worth pausing to speculate about the author's time in Vilnius, especially because he mentions his studies there in his *Grammatika*. What did Diletskii mean by calling himself an "akademik Wileński" in the title page of *Toga złota*? There was a Jesuit College in Vilnius, the largest and most important school in the city and one of the largest in Eastern Europe. Was Diletskii a student or a teacher there? The jury, again, is out. On the one hand, *akademik*, which carried strong associations with the Platonic school, seems to have indicated either a student or a teacher in seventeenth-century Poland. Diletskii's "akademik Wileński" might thus be interpreted simply as "Vilnius academic," without necessarily implying a specific position or level of instruction.[9]

On the other hand, a musician—either a teacher or a student—would have been exposed to a great deal of music at the College, which followed the pattern of the classical grammar school established at other Jesuit institutions, beginning with the basics of grammar, poetics, and rhetoric, and advancing to the upper levels, where students attended the advanced courses in philosophy and theology. As part of this curriculum, the Jesuit colleges (and the Orthodox schools modeled after them) maintained active schedules of dramatic productions (school dramas) as well as public readings and performances, most of which employed some sort of vocal or instrumental music.[10] The Vilnius College supported an extensive musical establishment, including many instruments in addition to the organ, as well as providing instruction in liturgical singing. The published works by Sigismund Lauxmin, a student, teacher, and eventually pro-rector at the College, encapsulate the institution's broad, classical approach. In 1667 Lauxmin published three practical chant treatises: *Ars et praxis musica in usum studiosae iuventutis in Collegiis Societatis Jesu; Graduale pro exercitatione studentium;* and *Antiphonale ad psalmos.* He also published textbooks on rhetoric and Greek.[11]

Diletskii may have had other connections in Vilnius as well, for *Toga złota* was published not at the Jesuit College but rather at the city's Franciscan press. The list of titles from the Franciscans' Vilnius post is sketchy, possibly because their output was overshadowed by the larger printing concern at the Jesuit College, but it operated from 1670 to at least 1711, offering a small list of titles primarily devotional in character. Without the text of Diletskii's work, it is difficult to determine how *Toga złota* might have fit into their publications. It appears that the College's courses in philosophy and theology were attended by members of other orders, including the Franciscans, so publication of Diletskii's pamphlet at the Franciscan press does not rule out study at the Jesuit College.[12]

No matter where Diletskii studied in Vilnius or with whom, the most important fact of his stay there was the composition of his music theory treatise. Korenev said that Diletskii originally wrote his work in Polish, and although this Polish version is now lost, Diletskii referred to it frequently in his three subsequent translations. He did not repeat the phrase "akademik Wileński" in his later translations, but in the dedication of one version he mentioned that he had studied the liberal arts (*svobodnye nauki*) in Vilnius, extolling his familiarity with both Orthodox and Latin sources: "Now I begin to write [my music treatise], having written it earlier in Vilnius, where I studied the liberal arts, and using as a basis for it the works of many skillful masters, creators of singing for the Orthodox Church as well as the Roman [Church], and many Latin books on music."[13] Given Diletskii's previous contacts, this was no idle boast. A musician in Vilnius (or indeed, in Kiev or Smolensk) might easily have learned from "many Latin books on music" and participated in the city's frequent "interfaith" processions, learning the song of both the Orthodox and Roman churches.

We are on somewhat firmer ground when we turn to the three chronologically distinct versions of Diletskii's musical treatise.[14] Diletskii's first Muscovite home was Smolensk, a western border city that had been under dispute with Poland for most of the century, and definitively brought under Muscovite control in 1654. The author arrived there within two years of his stay in Vilnius, for copies of the translation of his musical treatise are dated 1677. The Smolensk version of his treatise is titled *Grammatika musikiiskago peniia* (A Grammar of Musical Singing), and Diletskii also composed an eight-voice "Smolenskaia sluzhba" (Smolensk Service), which was excerpted in the 1677 redaction and presented more fully in later versions of the *Grammatika* written in Moscow. This setting reflects what we know of the prominence of polyphonic singing in Smolensk, where Metropolitan Simeon's elaborate musical performances, mentioned above in chapter 2, drew unwelcome attention from the Moscow hierarchy only a few years after Diletskii's stay there.

Because we know so little of this period in Diletskii's career, Vladimir Protopopov's proposed identification of the dedicatee of one of the Smolensk *Grammatika* sources is significant. The name and patronymic of the dedicatee, Timofei Dementianovich, were preserved in published fragments from a *Grammatika* source now lost. Protopopov suggests that this is Timofei Dementianovich Litvinov, a clerk (*d'iak*) employed in various government departments in Moscow during the second half of the seventeenth century. Protopopov makes this identification through letters written by Sil'vestr Medvedev (a poet and student of Simeon Polotskii), in which Medvedev mentions two Polish translations of Aristotle that Litvinov had borrowed, as well as books that Medvedev had apparently borrowed from Litvinov.[15] There is no evidence that Diletskii was involved in this book exchange but if Protopopov's identification is correct, at least we know that Diletskii was aiming high, trying to link himself to some of Muscovy's leading writers and thinkers. It also demonstrates the types of reading favored by educated, Western-oriented intellectuals in Muscovy, a milieu congenial to Diletskii as well.[16]

Diletskii had arrived in Moscow by 1678 or 1679 (7187 in the Muscovite reckoning).[17] This is the date on the next version of his treatise, *Idea grammatikii musikiiskoi* (An Idea of Musical Grammar; the word "idea" here suggests a conception or formulation), which was dedicated to the wealthy and influential Grigorii Dmitrievich Stroganov. A line in Diletskii's dedication indicates that he was commissioned to write this version: "And thus you directed me, your humble servant, by your Lord's wishes [to write] this grammar, which is on music—useful to you to teach others . . ." This last phrase might refer to other musicians in Stroganov's employ (and we know there were many), but Diletskii's own position within the family's vast establishment (if indeed he did have a formal job with them) is unknown.[18] The family had a long-standing interest in liturgical music and singing, as we have seen in previous chapters, with many comprehensive chant manuscripts in their possession and singers who knew the latest polyphonic styles in their employ. The *Grammatika's* practical and didactic tone would have meshed readily with the requirements of such an ensemble, and Diletskii himself alludes to some sort of teaching or conducting experience of his own: "I, in many years of singing and directing [*masterstvuiushche*], rarely saw this [musical procedure done] or wrote it myself."[19]

The other Moscow version of his treatise, associated with Ioannikii Korenev, is preserved in variants from 1679 and 1681 and is titled *Grammatika peniia musikiiskago* (A Grammar of Musical Singing). One source includes an inscription noting that the author wrote the work in May 1681.[20] Diletskii was thus apparently alive and well at this time but after this date we have no further information about him, apart from the disputed attribution of the 1723 source, which would appear after a silence of over forty years. The author may have died, retired, or left for another city—as is so often the case, we can only speculate.

The *Grammatika*, in all its various incarnations, is less important as a biographical marker (ambiguous as it is in this capacity) than as a musical treatise.

What does it say, how does it teach, and to whom is it addressed? Why was it so popular and what specific needs did it fill in Muscovy? As Diletskii says in his dedication to Stroganov, he had a comprehensive purpose in writing his treatise: "not only [for the purpose of] singing, but also to compose song."[21] Diletskii taught a compositional style he knew well and one that was currently of great interest to many Muscovite musicians: the *kontsert*. In the *Grammatika*, Diletskii outlines the elements of the *kontsert* style—word painting, imitation and repetition or sequence, bass patterns, and so forth—and then parses them systematically, building up a repertoire of musical devices, a language with which the most up-to-date composers were producing popular pieces. In order to write fluently in this language, the student needed to know the fundamental parts of musical speech, the irreducible elements of music. These Diletskii lays out in his opening chapters.[22]

In presenting the rudiments of music and the advanced topic of composition, Diletskii frequently relies on terminology borrowed from a variety of disciplines. He often relates musical problems to more common situations with which his readers might be familiar. In his explanation of how to take musical dictation, for example, Diletskii observes that the composition must not be sung quickly; after all, he says, one cannot write down someone's words if they are spoken quickly. He also advises composers to study pieces by other musicians. Just as rhetoricians study books and icon painters and other artists have models for their works, he explains, so a composer should write down and study musical works in order to understand how they are constructed.[23]

The musical examples sprinkled generously throughout the work are generally short in the first section: brief melodic figures designed to illustrate a specific theoretical point and presumably devised by the author himself. Many of the examples in the section on composition appear to be drawn from larger works, mostly anonymous, but a few of which Diletskii identifies as his own. He also mentions compositions by Kalenda, Ziuska, and Zamarevich, and by two well-known Polish composers, Marcin Mielczewski and Jacek Różycki. When written explanation and musical example seem insufficient, for instance in a technical issue such as enharmonic equivalence, Diletskii advises the reader to consult an experienced organist. There were organists working in varying capacities in all the locations with which Diletskii was associated; nevertheless, the assumption that music students in Moscow or musicians associated with the Stroganovs would have had ready access to the instrument suggests an unexpected role for the organ as a kind of Muscovite monochord.[24]

Diletskii opens his *Grammatika* with a traditional and fundamental question harkening back to Boethius: What is music ("Chto est' musikiia")? Any collegium-

EXAMPLE 5.1. Diletskii, *Grammatika,* illustration of happy music (RGB 107, p. 16)

EXAMPLE 5.2. Diletskii, *Grammatika,* illustration of sad music (RGB 107, p. 16)

educated musician would have been familiar with Boethius, who is mentioned by name later in the *Grammatika* and also in Korenev's treatise. The question-answer, catechism-like format of Diletskii's work would also have been familiar from many other models, particularly grammars and rhetoric treatises. One might pause over Diletskii's choice of the word *musikiia* here, a term familiar from just about any Western treatise one might care to name, from any century. As we have seen, in the Muscovite context of the late seventeenth century, *musikiia,* as distinct from *penie* (liturgical singing), referred to precisely the kind of mixed singing and instrumental styles Diletskii presents throughout his work. The author juxtaposes both terms, and both sets of associations, in his title (A Grammar of Musical Singing).

Diletskii provides two answers to his opening question. The first is a subjective definition stating that music is that which moves one's heart to happiness or to sadness by means of singing or playing. He follows this with a somewhat more objective definition of music as the movement of voices up and down.[25] Diletskii does not offer precise definitions of the music that evokes these two emotional states, relying instead on the brief examples meant to illustrate the two types. These musical examples do emphasize melodies using either major or minor thirds or triads, and his category of a mixed emotional state (both happy and sad) includes both. Thus, in example 5.1, which illustrates music that creates happy feelings, Diletskii obviously emphasizes the major triads on the pitches C–E–G and G–B–D; in example 5.2, he stresses the minor third D–F; and in example 5.3, illustrating mixed emotions, he juxtaposes the major triad C–E–G with the minor triad A–C–E. Nevertheless, in his prose descriptions, Diletskii does not isolate the qualities of the thirds or triads, nor does he say explicitly that they alone determine happy or sad feelings. Indeed, in the Moscow 1681 version of the treatise, the example of

EXAMPLE 5.3. Diletskii, *Grammatika,* juxtaposing major and minor triads
(RGB 107, p. 16)

EXAMPLE 5.4. Diletskii, *Grammatika,* fanfare figure in the Moscow 1681
version (RGB 146, p. 60, from OLDP Izdaniia 128, from the collection of
the University of Washington)

music creating happy emotions does not contain any thirds at all, presenting a
bouncy, fanfare-like procession of fifths, as shown in example 5.4.

Diletskii then divides music into two categories, according to its meaning or
sense (*smysl*) and according to its key (*kliuch*). Music's meaning is three-fold:
happy music, sad music, and a mixture of the two. The Smolensk versions of the
Grammatika, which do not include notated examples in their opening definitions
of music, explain the three subdivisions of *smysl* in familiar, non-technical language that refers to secular song. Diletskii's listing of various musical venues in this
passage recalls similar lists in rhetoric treatises specifying appropriate situations
for different kinds of speeches: funerals, greeting a church hierarch, and so forth.

> Happy [music] is when one's ears and heart are moved to happiness and to this
> type belongs all church, joyful, and popular [*mirskoe*] singing. Sad music is
> when one's heart is moved to sadness and sorrow as in weeping, sobbing, and
> funereal singing and others. Mixed [music] is when one's ears are first moved
> to happiness and then to sadness, as in some sad popular singing.[26]

At this point in his presentation, Diletskii remarks that *ut–mi–sol* indicates
happy music and *re–fa–la* indicates sad music. Immediately following this observation, the author lists, for the first time and without comment, the six musical
notes (or signs or voices) *ut* through *la,* and repeats the division into happy and sad
music: "The six musical signs are these: *ut, re, mi, fa, sol, la,* and they are divided
into two: *ut–mi–sol* is happy singing, and *re–fa–la* is sad."[27] Diletskii refers here to
a long-standing and very well-developed method used in Western theory to specify
not just single pitches but the constellation of surrounding pitches and their
interrelationships. The system uses a set of six solmization syllables, *ut, re, mi, fa,*

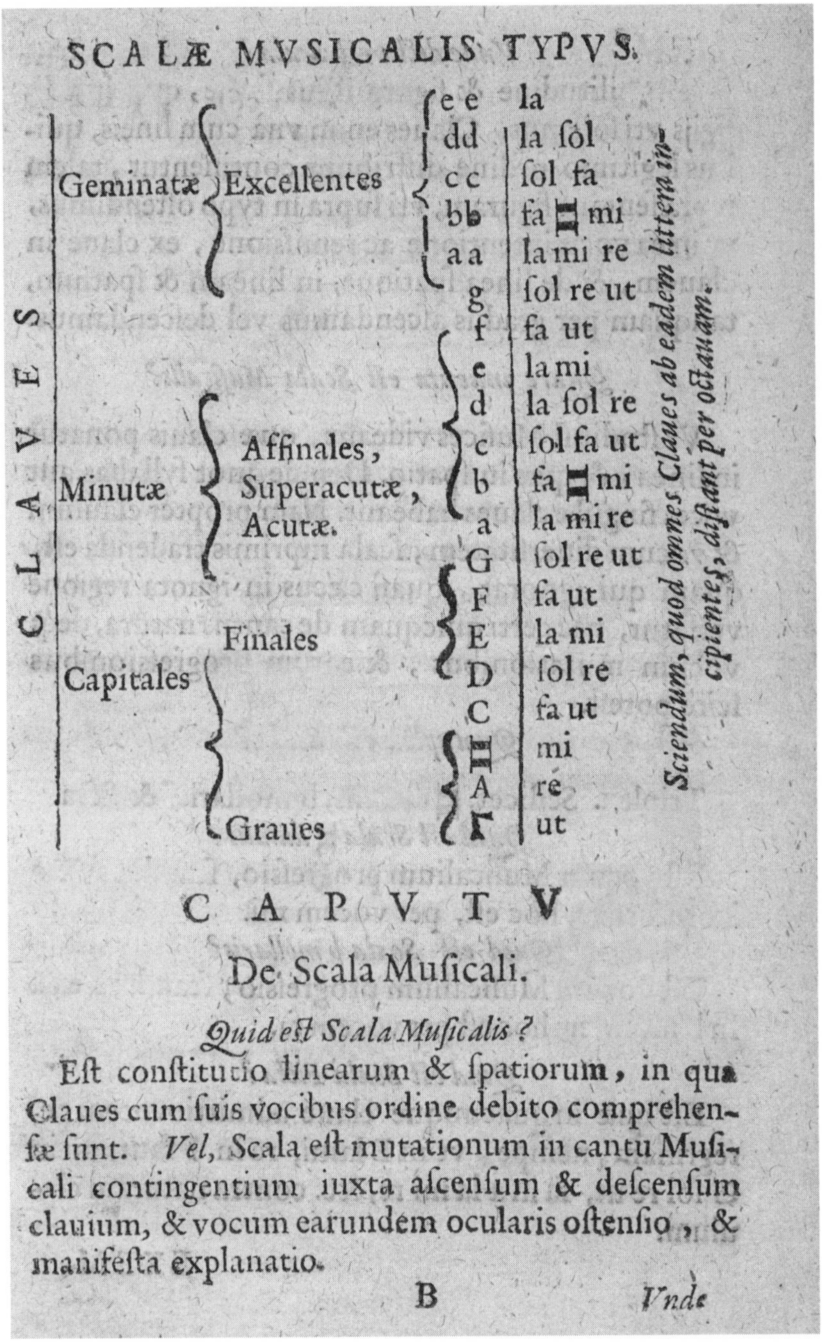

SCALÆ MVSICALIS TYPVS.

		e e	la
		dd	la ſol
Geminatæ	Excellentes	cc	ſol fa
		bb	fa ♮ mi
		a a	la mi re
		g	ſol re ut
		f	fa ut
		e	la mi
		d	la ſol re
	Affinales,	c	ſol fa ut
Minutæ	Superacutæ,	b	fa ♮ mi
	Acutæ.	a	la mi re
		G	ſol re ut
		F	fa ut
	Finales	E	la mi
Capitales		D	ſol re
		C	fa ut
		♮	mi
		A	re
	Graues	Γ	ut

C L A V E S

Sciendum, quod omnes Claues ab eadem littera in-cipientes, diſtant per octauam.

C A P V T V

De Scala Muſicali.

Quid eſt Scala Muſicalis ?

Eſt conſtitutio linearum & ſpatiorum, in quâ
Claues cum ſuis vocibus ordine debito comprehen-
ſæ ſunt. *Vel,* Scala eſt mutationum in cantu Muſi-
cali contingentium iuxta aſcenſum & deſcenſum
clauium, & vocum earundem ocularis oſtenſio, &
manifeſta explanatio.

B   *Vnde*

FIGURE 5.1. Starowolski, *Musices practicae erotemata* (1650), layout of the overlapping
sets of hexachords (Brussels, Royal Library of Belgium, used by permission)

EXAMPLE 5.5. Diletskii, *Grammatika,* flat sign signals immediate change to *bemmoliarnyi* key (RGB 107, p. 19)

sol, and *la,* which comprises the basic unit: the hexachord. These six syllables were combined with pitch-letter names (A through G) to carve out musical space, defining the position of whole and half steps and setting out the parameters by which a singer might move through this space. The diagram in figure 5.1, taken from a mid-seventeenth-century publication by the Polish writer Szymon Staro-wolski (*Musices practicae erotemata,* Cracow, 1650), is a typical presentation of this material. It shows three overlapping sequences of pitch letters and solmization syllables. In each case, there is a half step between the syllables *mi* and *fa;* the various combinations of syllables attached to each pitch letter show both the immediate context for the pitch as well as the ways in which each pitch might be reinterpreted. Thus, the label C *fa ut* indicates that the pitch C functions as *fa* in the first hexachord outlined and as *ut* in the next hexachord.[28] Diletskii refers readily and frequently to the six solmization syllables throughout his treatise, but he does not explain—even here, when these terms are introduced for the first time—how these syllables indicate a specific set of intervallic relationships.

Diletskii then introduces a second category of music, *kliuch* (or *kliavish,* key), which refers to the presence or absence of sharps or flats in a composition. He lists four types of music, labeled with terminology derived from Western practice: *duralnaia musikiia,* with no flats or sharps, from the Latin term *dur* (referring to the hard, or square, pitch letter B, indicating B-natural, as in figure 5.1); *bemmoliar-naia,* which uses flats (referring to the rounded B, or B *moll,* that is, B-flat); *diezisovaia,* which uses sharps (the Latin *diesis* indicated a sharp); and *smeshennaia* (mixed), which begins, for example, with no flats or sharps and then adds one or the other during the course of the piece.[29] He employs these four categories throughout his treatise and presents them consistently as descriptive rather than as hierarchical: the categories simply indicate the presence, absence, or introduction of sharps or flats but do not propose any of the categories as primary or norma-tive.[30] As Diletskii says: "When you see the ♭ go immediately to the *bemmoliarnyi* [*bemmuliarnyi*] key and the same is true for *diezisovaia* music," as shown in musical example 5.5.[31]

The categories of *kliuchi* or *kliavishi* appear to be independent of Diletskii's classification of music according to its meaning as happy, sad, or mixed. Happy music, for example, might be in any of the four keys; conversely, knowing that a piece is in the *duralnyi* key does not help to ascertain the underlying quality of happiness or sadness. In a passage in the Moscow 1679–81 version, for example, Diletskii lays out the steps necessary in order to take musical dictation. He separates out his various classification systems, explaining that one must first determine whether the composition is happy or sad, and only then turn to its rhythmic characteristics and its key:

> If you want to write down some fantasy [*fantaziia*] that you have heard, whether played or sung, then you have to determine which fantasy the music is in, either happy or sad. Then, having figured this out, you have to determine if there is triple time in this fantasy or not, or whole notes, half notes, quarter notes, eighth notes, and so forth. Then you may write it down easily . . . The fantasy will be of the *duralnyi* or the *diezisovyi* or the *bemmoliarnyi* key.[32]

The second chapter of the *Grammatika* introduces the fundamental pitch letters A through G.[33] Diletskii assembles a long series of illustrations showing how to combine the letters and hexachordal syllables in the various keys [*kliuchi;* also *penie*]. In *duralnyi*, for example, the combinations begin with A *la re,* Be *mi,* C *fa ut,* and so forth. He offers a brief bit of information: "The first notes go below, the last [notes go] above, for example A *la re. La* is below, *re* above."[34] Here the author has in mind again the overlapping sets of hexachordal syllables as they are appended to pitch letters. For the pitch A, the syllable *la* indicates its context in a hexachord beginning on C, and *re,* its context in a hexachord beginning on G (see figure 5.1). This is Diletskii's only prose explanation of the relationships among the interlocking hexachordal sets. Although his lengthy presentation demonstrates his own ease in manipulating the hexachordal combinations and shows that he considers this a necessary skill for his students, he nevertheless makes no other explicit integration of the letters and syllables.

After listing his *kliuchi,* which include *bemmoliarnyi* and *diezisovyi,* and after musical examples that contain flats and sharps, Diletskii finally defines these two signs: "*Diezis* in Greek, in Latin *semitonium,* half steps [*polnoty*] above and ♭—half steps below."[35] In the context of the *Grammatika* this statement is quite abstract, for he has not defined *polnoty* nor indeed has he introduced formally the concepts of whole and half steps, although such concepts are obviously implicit in his reliance on hexachordal constructs. He therefore adds a bit of practical advice: "and you will understand this more clearly from performance on the organ or below from my work." At such an apparent impasse, one is only left to imagine that some classroom explanation would have rounded out the presentation (which again points to the importance of the organ as a teaching tool).

In his discussion of sharps, Diletskii emphasizes matters of convenience for singers. There are four sharps—on G, C, D, and F—and sometimes a fifth, on A. (Diletskii's terminology again refers to the hexachords: he labels the sharps *gis mi, cis mi,* etc., in which the designation *mi* locates the placement of the half step.) On the organ, he adds, A-sharp is the same as B-flat. He adds another practical comment about the sharp sign when encountered as an accidental: "sing it thus in the following manner in mixed music: hold *mi* in your head, on your tongue and [in your] voice [sing] *fa.*"[36] This rule is intended to simplify things for the singer. A sharp used as an accidental (especially involving adjacent pitches) would create a new half step, which would therefore require a change of hexachord, but Diletskii says that the singer can ignore this. The performer needs to acknowledge that there is a half step, which would be signaled by the syllable *mi* ("hold *mi* in your head"), but for the sake of simplicity, the singer does not need to change hexachords and can situate the raised note in the hexachord as if it were not altered (thus, "on your tongue and in your voice sing *fa*"). Such hexachordal license for the sake of convenience was familiar in the same context in Western theory books into the seventeenth century.[37]

The rest of the chapter continues the emphasis on practical aids for performers. Diletskii presents an elaborate array of clefs (also called *kliuchi* or *kliavishi*) derived from the pitch letters C, G, and F and labeled according to the vocal ranges discant, alto, tenor, and bass.[38] Next he presents a system of transposition designed to help the performer avoid key signatures. He shows that one might reduce or eliminate flats or sharps in the signature by moving a piece from one hexachordal positioning to another by means of changing the clef. For example, the author says that in order to avoid the *bemmoliarnyi* key with two flats, one might keep the position of the notes on the staff the same but change the clef from alto to tenor (thus transposing the melody down by a third, as shown in musical example 5.6) and sing the tune with no flats. The hexachordal relationships spelled out by the syllables above the tune remain the same, although the pitch level is altered. A student would rarely have needed this handy system to work through the *Grammatika,* for most of the musical examples in the treatise have no more than one flat in their signatures. Late seventeenth-century *kontserty* likewise do not often exceed a notated signature of one flat.

Diletskii retains his primary divisions of music into *kliuch* and *smysl* in the second half of the *Grammatika,* which focuses on techniques of composition, and he offers an additional concept in order to show how these categories are

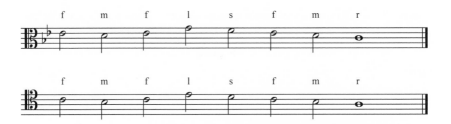

EXAMPLE 5.6. Diletskii, *Grammatika,* transposition to avoid key signature (RGB 146, p. 71, from OLDP Izdaniia 128, from the collection of the University of Washington)

fundamental to the structure of a musical work. The important distinction be-tween happy and sad music is encompassed by the word *ton* (tone); as the author explains, "Tone is differentiated [*raznstvennyi*], that is, happy or sad."[39] *Ton* exists independently of any particular composition and is fundamental to all music; it is expressed by means of the voices (or instruments) in a composition but these voices themselves do not establish the *ton:*

> You ask me, my student, how *ton* is different from *musikiia*. I answer you in this way: *ton* precedes the sounding of the voices in singing, that is *ut mi sol* or *re fa la,* and so forth; music, that is, singing, comes forth at the sounding of the voices and by means of its singing or playing expresses to people's ears the composer's idea in the *kontsert.* When you give the tone *ut mi sol* or *re fa la* one does not hear the singing [*penie*] until you sing the music, which is the singing itself.[40]

Ton applies even to the music of the Irmologii. Diletskii explains that he brings up the Irmologii, even though it is not the subject of the *Grammatika,* to show that the qualities of happiness and sadness belong to all music: "The church Irmologii tones as I said above are not our subject except happy, sad, and mixed; these make up the Irmologii and all singing." *Ton* thus transcends the type of music being performed, and Diletskii maintains throughout his treatise that a single set of theoretical rules applies to all kinds of music: "for both secular and spiritual, church singing have *ut, re, mi, fa, sol,* and *la* in their voice and singing."[41]

In the second part of the treatise, Diletskii outlines a series of rules for compos-ing *kontserty.* He begins by laying out his rules of ascent and descent, each of which is defined by a musical pattern that can be used as the building block for a composi-tion. Each pattern is made up of rising or falling intervals progressing diatonically from a whole step through a fifth. Brief musical examples after each rule show how

EXAMPLE 5.7. Diletskii, *Grammatika,* illustration of the interval of an ascending second, by Marcin Mielczewski (RGB 146, p. 98, from OLDP Izdaniia 128, from the collection of the University of Washington)

the melodic cell might be used to construct a composition, and here, as in other similar passages, Diletskii introduces several works by other composers; he labels musical example 5.7, illustrating the pattern of ascending seconds, as a work by Marcin Mielczewski. Musical example 5.8 shows the interval of an ascending fourth, which Diletskii calls the most beautiful of all (*spetsialissima*). Each example is prefaced by an illustration of the basic melodic pattern.

Other rules follow, covering different aspects of composition and generally illustrated with at least one musical example. Diletskii's mixed rule (*pravilo smeshennoe* or *miksta*) combines patterns of rising and falling intervals. The *khoralnoe* rule describes imitation, which is especially effective when presented using alternating blocks of voices, and the natural rule (*pravilo estestvennoe* or *naturalnoe*) describes word painting. The *dudalnoe* rule discusses pedal notes in the bass, and is followed by the rule of cadences.[42] The fundamental (*fundamentalnoe* or *osnovatelnoe*) rule describes a style in which the bass moves by fourths, fifths, and octaves, while the upper voices feature imitative patterns. A sad song may be turned into a happy song by means of the opposite or contrary (*protivnoe*) rule, and the series ends with the untexted rule (*pravilo bezrechnoe* or *atekstalis*). According to this rule, a composer may write a piece of music to which he fits a text only later. The section concludes with a demonstration of how to vary a given melody, illustrated by a sample tune with ten different embellishments.

Diletskii devotes an entire chapter to *kontrapunkt* or, in a literal translation, *protivotochie,* which he defines as an imitative style using primarily dotted

EXAMPLE 5.8. Diletskii, *Grammatika,* illustration of the interval of an ascending fourth, the most beautiful of all (RGB 146, p. 99, from OLDP Izdaniia 128, from the collection of the University of Washington)

rhythms.[43] He demonstrates this procedure with a series of musical phrases ascending or descending in intervals ranging diatonically from a whole step through a fifth. This is followed by another chapter with a similar emphasis on methods of constructing a composition, showing how to build a piece around rising or falling leaps, again ranging diatonically from a whole step through an octave.[44]

The final large section in the *Grammatika* is aptly entitled "On things I forgot to write about earlier."[45] Here Diletskii clarifies or adds to topics he had covered previously, beginning with the placement of accidentals and their appearance in cadences, and including intervals and text setting. He follows this with observations on procedures that are contrary to musical grammar (parallel fifths, for example) and gives additional information on notation and rhythm. The *Grammatika*'s final section also includes advice to composers on how to begin a piece ("O inventsii"), on laying out a musical work ("O dispozitsii" or "O razlozhenii"), and on varying the opening phrase of a piece ("O eksordii"). The section headed "On amplification" ("O amplifikatsii") explains how to expand a piece and includes the circle of fifths as one way to do so; we discuss this diagram separately below. In some versions of the treatise, this final section includes a method for teaching children, an updated Guidonian hand in which the five fingers serve as a model for the staff (also discussed below).

In spite of the rather miscellaneous character of his last large section, Diletskii's overall intent is clear. In the first part of the treatise, he provides the reader with a theoretical system based on the contrast between happy and sad music and on a series of *kliuchi* defined by the presence or absence of flats and sharps. In the second part, he breaks the process of composition into a series of rules and steps, presumably guided by his own experiences as a composer. Both sections are practical, using short musical phrases as examples or models and referring to an organ or an organist as a handy source for musical consultation in case of any particular technical difficulties. The same basic concepts are preserved in each of the three versions (although not necessarily in the same order or with precisely the same terminology), which suggests that this was the fundamental information and approach the author considered most beneficial for his Muscovite audience. It is not difficult to put his presentation, particularly in the opening chapters, under a scholarly microscope and criticize its ordering, vocabulary, and even some aspects of its basic clarity, but one must also keep in mind that these important criticisms may have been mitigated by the book's apparent function within a classroom setting, as two different accompanying illustrations suggest.[46] What we read in the existing sources therefore may not have constituted, nor been intended to constitute, the whole of Diletskii's presentation. It is far more important to try to understand how and why Diletskii's language and systems proved so useful in Muscovy, what students might have learned from the *Grammatika*, and how its precepts served the existing repertoire.

"The inexhaustible waters of the sea": Rhetoric and the Liberal Arts in the Grammatika

Diletskii, like many of his contemporaries in the West, perceived and emphasized a unity between the linguistic and the musical arts, and he drew repeated analogies in the service of his primary goal: to present a practical, comprehensive guide to composing the popular polyphonic styles he heard in Kiev, Vilnius, and Muscovy. Given Diletskii's origins and education, it is not surprising that his intellectual assumptions—what Lawrence Gushee has called "intellectual style"—should rest upon the foundations of grammar and rhetoric, the fundamentals of the Latin grammar school and widely taught in Diletskii's part of the world, both in Ukraine and in Vilnius.[47] In order to understand how and why he transported these approaches wholesale to Muscovy, we examine some of the terminology he uses in his treatise, speculating at the same time about the Muscovite intellectual style he was attempting to blend with his own.

Diletskii seems to have regarded his treatise as an advanced and well-rounded collection of information necessary to the modern musician, emphasizing its comprehensive character in the dedication to Stroganov and also at the beginning of the section teaching composition. He returns to this theme in his final section, where he compares his work to grammars that teach language. His own treatise, he says, is as different from an elementary work on music as the linguistic grammar is from the simple alphabet sheet:

> There are many textbooks of musical grammar which teach singing imperfectly and which are incorrect, because [musical] alphabets do not lay out everything, just A *la re* and A *la mi re;* these are neither for advanced studies of music nor for elementary studies and they are not grammars but alphabets, which [present to] children for study A, B, C, and other letters. Linguistic grammars are those that teach the eight parts of speech; just as this is a real grammar and not an alphabet because it teaches about the parts of music, not only how to sing well, but [how] to create songs, with counterpoint, with *kontserty,* with rules of ascent and descent . . .[48]

Ioannikii Korenev lays out a similar analogy in his own treatise. "Music," Korenev writes, "is the second philosophy and grammar, measuring the voices by intervals, just as literary philosophy and grammar consists of the proper usage of words and their properties, syllables, phrases and reasoning, the knowledge and nomenclature of the elements, all of their properties and strengths."[49]

The *grammatika* of Diletskii's title thus reflects the comprehensive character of the treatise and its equal standing relative to linguistic grammars. The comparison would have made sense to his readers, for grammars and simple alphabet sheets had been issued in manuscript and in print in Muscovy and Ukraine throughout the seventeenth century, with some, for example the grammar by Meletii Smotritskii, published in several editions in both places. The stability of the work's title is thus quite meaningful, for although each of the three separate versions transmits a slightly different title, the word—and the concept— *grammatika* is common to all of them.[50]

In the section headed "On amplification" Diletskii offers detailed examples drawn from linguistic practice in order to illustrate a specific musical point: how to prolong or stretch out a composition. He compares a musician who is unsure of the rules of composition to a student of rhetoric or poetics in similar ignorance of the rules of his discipline. Although they may have some talent, such untrained artists will be incapable of evaluating their works and they will not know how to proceed with their writing once they have begun.[51] Along these same lines, Diletskii compares a musician who plays the organ well but does not know the rules of music to a scribe who skillfully copies out various documents but cannot compose them on his own (again assuming that organists were available and familiar to Muscovite students).[52] He also maintains that it is useful for a composer, like a rhetorician or an icon painter, to take other musical works as models for his own. The advice seems aimed at students, who would have studied a whole series of such model speeches in their rhetoric course.

> Just as a rhetorician who does not read books will not be a real composer of speeches and, in addition, will not write a great deal, so a rhetorician who reads [books] writes for himself various informative pieces, well-formed speeches, parables, etc., and he applies them when he is creating speeches or lessons. And note also the icon painters and other artists who make for themselves models of icon painting or other [artistic] work. Thus you, the creator of song, when you hear somewhere the song of a skillful master, put it down on your tablet, where you can see what rules of construction or laying out the song [follows] . . .[53]

Contemporary Muscovite art theory also took this same practical approach. One of Diletskii's contemporaries, the icon painter Simon Ushakov, did indeed make large-scale studies of Byzantine and old Russian icons, as Diletskii prescribes. Ushakov also turned to a different type of model-making, one similar to Diletskii's approach to composition in which he breaks a musical work into its constituent parts. In his art theory treatise, Ushakov proposed to compile a series of model figures that artists could use for reference or for study; he called it an alphabet for art ("alfavit khudozhestva"). The project, unfortunately, was not realized.[54]

Diletskii's deliberate analogies between language and music indicate that he viewed his subject within the broader intellectual tradition of the seven liberal arts (see also above, chapter 2). He mentions his study in Vilnius of "svobodnye nauki" (literally, free sciences) in his dedication to Stroganov, a section which is itself a dense display of erudition, packed with classical references, derivations of words in Greek, Latin, and Slavic, references to Orthodox church music, and heartfelt good wishes for Stroganov's health and long life—in other words, a perfect example of the author's self-professed course of study. It is in this portion of the treatise that Diletskii says he consulted "many Latin books on music" in compiling his treatise. He also drops references to mythology, listing Jupiter, Pallas Athena, Amphion, Orpheus, and the Vale of the Tempe.[55] Wherever he was educated—Vilnius, Ukraine, or somewhere else—Diletskii clearly wanted to make sure that Stroganov was made aware of the extent of his training, and he obviously assumed that his dedicatee would be properly impressed by this intellectual resume.

The dedication also provided one of the best opportunities for Diletskii to showcase his own rhetorical skills. (The lost *Toga złota* would presumably have offered another chance to scrutinize Diletskii's literary prowess.) The author took full advantage of the opportunity, listing his literary talents by the convenient means of disclaimer:

> There are a great number of rhetoricians who begin their works with a lesson, and many place in their oration introductory speeches [*arkhi*] which are derived from the topic itself. Thus the great poet Maro [Publius Vergilius Maro] begins his historical book [the *Aeneid*] this way: "I write of heroic war and of brave men." There is, I repeat, much artistry [in their] lessons: when they set out the beginning either working from analogy, for example "in his wisdom he resembles Solomon"; or [working] from a place: The Vale of the Tempe; or from a person: "a person more beautiful than all of mankind's sons"; or from epigram, for example Dimitrii-*mitra* [mitre], Grigorii-*gory* [mountains], *gory zhe vysoki* [high mountains], Mariia-*more* [sea], Simeon-*sion* [Zion]; . . . or from *iroglifik* [symbol, figure] and etymology: Vasilii-*vasis* [which means] foundation, Ioann-*blagodat'* [paradise, grace], Feodor-*dar bozhii* [gift of God]; . . . But I [begin] from the very thing itself . . .[56]

Diletskii's dedication in the Smolensk version of the treatise includes many of the same concepts, suggesting that the author had definite ideas about what such a passage should properly include. This dedication opens with an invocation to God, to whose honor and in whose praise the work was composed. It is from God, says Diletskii, that all wisdom and learning comes, including rhetoric, philosophy, and theology, all subjects part of the familiar curriculum. He also uses other terminology familiar from classical and rhetorical studies in this dedication, for example, *epilog* and *apostrofiia*.[57] Elsewhere in his treatise, Diletskii acknowledges the connection between the different branches of learning and the importance of learning itself. In one of the most felicitous and enthusiastic passages in his treatise, he describes for his students the vast sea of knowledge: "You know that the waters of the sea are inexhaustible. [If you used] not only barrels but also tubs as large as 1,000,000,000,000 fathoms in their height and breadth, you could draw [the water] out, but you could never exhaust it. Thus also is learning."[58] Diletskii's enthusiasm is echoed slightly later in another groundbreaking Russian treatise with similar roots in Western humanistic practice, the *Arifmetika* by Leontii Magnitskii (1703). "Numbers are without end," writes Magnitskii at the opening of his book. "Our minds cannot grasp them. / No one knows their end / Except God the Creator of all."[59]

In his dedications Diletskii shows his readers that he is well versed in recognized literary practice. Contemporary Kievan treatises, for example, discuss the popular device of deriving names from various words, a trick appearing also in poetic works, for example those by Simeon Polotskii.[60] Similarly, Diletskii's references to classical literature and places mark his familiarity with the kinds of works studied at the Vilnius College and at other institutions run or inspired by the Jesuits. The dedication was thus a natural place for Diletskii to mention his stay in the city and his studies of the liberal arts there. However, these topics—the core curriculum at the Vilnius Jesuit College—would also have been taught at the Kievan College or, for that matter, at almost any of the Orthodox schools in Ukraine or Belarus, which essentially duplicated the coursework of the Jesuit schools, right down to the choice of the basic Latin grammar text.[61] The *Aeneid*, which Diletskii quotes for Stroganov, was part of the curriculum at Latin schools as well as Orthodox.[62] Diletskii's references would also have been in good company in Moscow, for the classical names he invokes appear abundantly in the works of Simeon Polotskii, who for example in his *Orel rossiiskii* (The Russian Eagle, 1667, written for the elevation of Tsarevich Aleksei as designated heir to the throne) mentions many of the figures Diletskii lists in his dedication to Stroganov: Orpheus, Amphion, Athena, even Aeneas.[63]

Diletskii's numerous and creative analogies would also have been readily comprehensible to his students through the large and accessible body of Muscovite writings that placed music among other scholarly and creative disciplines, particularly in the context of the seven liberal arts. The Ukrainian and Belarusian clerics who were coming to Moscow in important numbers in the second half of the century took this framework for granted from long familiarity through their collegium educations. Simeon Polotskii, for example, in his early, Polish-language works, wrote a poem extolling the seven liberal arts that also displays a ready command of classical references, and the last decades of the century produced a flurry of texts on rhetoric and poetics from the ever-productive faculty of the Kievan College.[64] The Muscovite monastic centers that cultivated *kanty* and *partesnoe* singing also appear to have embraced some of the same kinds of humanistic educational approaches. The *kant*-composing monk German at the New Jerusalem Monastery, for example, owned a copy of Alvarez's Latin grammar (listed as "Alvar latinskii"), and he also owned other books in Polish, Latin, and Greek.[65]

Similar writings emanated from the Muscovite court. In 1671 the Moldovan scholar Nikolai Spafarii Milescu (1636–1708) came to Moscow, where he worked as a translator at the Diplomatic Chancellery. In the early years of that decade, Spafarii wrote or translated many treatises, including the *Kniga izbranaia vkrattse o deviatikh musakh i o sedmikh svobodnykh khudozhestvakh* (A Brief Book on the Nine Muses and on the Seven Liberal Arts, 1672). This is one of four books apparently comprising a didactic cycle, possibly written in connection with private tutorials; a presentation copy was prepared for Tsar Aleksei Mikhailovich.[66]

This book, like many of Spafarii's writings, was based on earlier works from the West as well as from Muscovy itself. As Ol'ga Belobrova has demonstrated, the illustrations of the seven arts in Spafarii's book were based on engravings by Western artists, and the text is related to a widely circulating anonymous tract entitled *Skazanie o sedmi svobodnykh mudrostekh* (A History of the Seven Liberal Arts).[67] In Spafarii's work, each of the seven arts begins with an introductory section that defines the subject and lists reasons to study it. This opening passage concludes in each case with a line similar to that for music: "And music speaks in person thus."[68] At this point, each chapter switches from third to first person, and each of the arts defines itself, explains its origins, and so forth. In each of the seven chapters, Spafarii's work coincides with the anonymous *Skazanie* at the very point at which the subject begins to speak for itself, suggesting that Spafarii's contribution was confined to the introductory passages for each of the seven arts.

Spafarii's original material, brief though it may be, adds other humanistic traditions to the subject of music in Muscovite writings. He explains in his preface that music is made up of *obraz* (form or manner) and *dvizhenie* (movement or motion), which he defines as the voice or instrument that performs the music. *Obraz* he defines as *glas* (literally voice, but used here in the sense of mode), and with no further ado, Spafarii gives examples of various *glasy*: "1, which is called Dorian; 2, which is called Lydian; 3, which is called Phrygian, and so forth."[69] This appears to be the first—and, for seventeenth-century Muscovy, the last—mention of the traditional Greek names of the modes. Spafarii also includes the story of Pythagoras and his discovery of musical proportions. (Korenev, too, mentions Pythagoras, but only in a listing of famous ancients associated with music.)[70]

The origins of the anonymous *Skazanie*, in its turn, are somewhat clouded, but for our purposes it is the work's wide circulation in Muscovy from the first half of the seventeenth century that is important.[71] The ordering of music within the seven arts is not the same in the anonymous *Skazanie*, where it is listed in fourth position, as it is in Spafarii's treatment, where it is listed fifth. This distinction is useful in situating other independently circulating texts, such as *Mudrost' chetvertaia Musi-*

kia (The Fourth Art: Music), as belonging to the *Skazanie* tradition. Korenev, too, listed music as the fourth of the seven liberal arts: "in Polish, liberal arts [*nauka vyzvolona*], of which there are seven; among these, the fourth is music."[72]

The complex of manuscripts transmitting the *Skazanie* and the Spafarii texts leads us to another large group of sources that are related in theme and in overall outlook. The bulk of a rhetoric treatise attributed to Makarii, Metropolitan of Novgorod (d. 1626) was translated from a Latin original; some versions include additional material taken from the *Skazanie*. The work circulated in Muscovy in more than thirty sources ranging in date from the early seventeenth century to the time of Peter the Great. Although its ultimate origins in Russia are somewhat in question (did the translation itself originate in Muscovy, or was it an import?), the fact that it circulated in Muscovy in such impressive numbers throughout the century shows that the liberal arts in general, and rhetoric in particular, would have been familiar to at least some Muscovite readers.[73]

Kievan treatises also provide a useful model for the production of textbooks. The *Grammatika* is certainly didactic in character, and the depiction of classroom scenes in two of the sources appear to advertise its suitability for schoolroom use. Some of the Kievan rhetoric treatises, too, are textbooks, representing specific courses given at individual institutions. Other texts were actually lecture notes; theological works from Vilnius, for example, made their way south as notes compiled by Kievan students who went to the Vilnius College to take the course in theology, which was not offered in Kiev until late in the seventeenth century.[74] It is possible that the *Grammatika* had similar beginnings as student notes, from Vilnius or Ukraine, subsequently expanded and formalized.

There is a particularly close relationship between Diletskii's *Grammatika* and the subject of rhetoric. These parallels are evident at every level, from the largest sectional headings to the use of individual words and phrases. At the smallest level, for example, one notes Diletskii's use of the word *iroglifik* in his dedication to Stroganov. This term is routinely used in Kievan rhetoric treatises in describing ways to ornament a speech.[75]

But rhetorical terminology guides Diletskii's approach in a more fundamental way. Two of Diletskii's titles match the Slavic terms used to outline the major divisions of rhetoric. The section entitled "On disposition" ("O dispozitsii" or "O razdelenii," "O raspolozhenii") appears in the first part of the *Grammatika* and describes how to lay out a text that is to be set to music. This rule instructs the composer to decide on the musical treatment for each phrase of the text. In rhetoric treatises, *raspolozhenie* is the second division of the subject and, as in the *Grammatika,* it refers to the way in which a work is laid out or presented: "*Raspolozhenie,* according to Cicero and other rhetoricians, is the orderly distribution of the topics that have been invented."[76] Rhetoric treatises discuss various procedures for setting out long or short speeches. In the *Grammatika,* Diletskii shows how to lay out a text in preparation for its musical setting. Using a text from the Divine Liturgy, "Edinorodnyi syn" (Only-begotten Son), he outlines how one might alternate textures:

> "Only-begotten Son" will be a *kontsert;* "deign [for our salvation]"—all [voices] together; "incarnate"—*kontsert;* "and Ever-Virgin Mary"—all [voices]; "crucified"—*kontsert;* "[trampling down] Death by death"—all; "One of [the Holy Trinity]"—*kontsert;* "glorified together with the Father"—all, one after another or all together, as you choose.[77]

Diletskii follows this explanation with a setting of the concluding section, "sproslavliaemyi ottsu" (glorified together with the Father), drawn from one of his own works. Evidently he intended this passage simply as an illustration of how a text might be laid out, for his other settings are treated in different ways.[78]

A second Latin title heads the section teaching composition. Diletskii's "O inventsii" or "O izobretenii" explains that the musical rules provide the information necessary in order to begin or invent a song. In rhetoric treatises, "Ob izobretenii" is generally the first major division of the subject. A definition from a Kievan work from the late seventeenth century also highlights the importance of rules or structure, defining this term as "the invention of means which support the topic."[79]

Diletskii's heading "O eksordii" or "O nachale" (On the beginning) suggests a parallel to the divisions of a speech or prose composition into beginning, middle, and final sections. The *Grammatika* does not define this term in quite the same manner, focusing instead on a methodical series of ways by which a composer might vary rhythmically the opening of a composition. A composer might also begin a piece by means of *kontrapunkt,* close imitation between voices using dotted rhythms.[80] Diletskii does note the importance of the beginning, middle, and ending sections of a composition elsewhere in the treatise: "On the beginning—briefly, on how to begin a *kontsert* with three voices or four or five or many, see numerous works of musical composers and in my *kontserty* . . . On the end and middle of these *kontserty,* give some study to how to end, for the end crowns the work."[81] There is a small chart near the end of the Moscow 1679–81 version of the *Grammatika* summarizing the important elements of poetics, rhetoric, and philosophy, all of which Diletskii discusses over the course of his work.[82]

Diletskii's *pravilo naturalnoe* (natural rule) addresses a concern common to many seventeenth-century composition treatises from the West, advising the composer how to depict in music the meaning of specific words or phrases: "The natural rule, in Latin *naturalnoe,* is when the composer writes according to the strength [effect, meaning] of the words or the substance of the song." He gives two examples, one describing descent to earth ("Snide na zemliu"), which is set to descending lines, and the other describing ascent to heaven ("Vozshedyi na nebesa"), set to ascending music. Diletskii follows this rule faithfully in his own compositions. In his eight-part setting of the Easter *kanon,* for example, he writes an extended imitative passage on a descending melodic line at the word "snide" (descending) and at the word "skakashe" (leaping), he places another rhythmically active imitative passage beginning in the bass.[83]

Diletskii also believes that performers should strive to portray a work's meaning through expressive vocal inflections. In rhetoric treatises, the proper expression of a text comes under the general heading *vyrazhenie* (expression), especially the under subsection *iziashchestvo* (elegance, grace), which emphasizes a refined manner of speaking appropriate to the words. Diletskii refers here only to his own natural rule; he does not introduce analogies to texts nor does he use the term *vyrazhenie:*

> When you are singing, you should consider how and where you display your voice, not exceeding the limits of your voice or singing beyond your strength. And you should know how to sing a sad song and how to sing a happy song; a sad song requires your voice to sing tenderly, for example in the verse "Svete tikhii" (Gladsome light)—here you must sing in the softest voice. Sing in a strong voice, expressing the nature of the verse as in "Veleglasno zovushche" (In full-voiced proclamation)—here you must sing in the most elevated and biggest voice.[84]

Korenev, too, stresses the importance of the artist's inflections in performing a sacred work: "Let them through singing better understand the divine words, sung in hymns emotionally, quietly, and clearly . . . The *prichasten* (Communion Hymn) must be sung with fear and trembling, so that all would hear wisdom and not the voice."[85] Late seventeenth- and early eighteenth-century Muscovite sources do use dynamic markings on occasion. For example, in one of Vasilii Titov's eight-part settings of the Divine Liturgy, the opening measures are performed by three voices (tenors and bass) and are marked "tikho" (softly), and when the rest of the ensemble joins in the parts are marked "golosno" (full voiced). These markings alternate, somewhat redundantly, throughout the piece, "tikho" appearing in the sections for reduced forces and "golosno" when all voices sing together.[86]

Even Diletskii's general observations of the emotional power of music show some parallels to descriptions in rhetoric treatises about the ways in which language can evoke emotions in listeners. Diletskii's catalogue of the qualities of happy and sad music at the beginning of the *Grammatika* are similar to a listing in a late seventeenth-century rhetoric treatise describing how, through speech, one's heart might be moved "to anger or hatred, or to sorrow and tender emotion, or to fear and apprehension, or to joy and love."[87]

Diletskii maintains that the composer is responsible for transmitting texts accurately. He does not approve of repeating incomplete words in a composition, and in warning against this practice, he emphasizes the relationship between the musical rules and the rules of language: "[The composer] Kolenda's writing 'raduem, raduem, raduemsia' [rejoi-, rejoi-, rejoice] is not only contrary to the musical grammar but also contrary to the linguistic grammar."[88] In spite of his concern for the setting and expression of the text, however, Diletskii does include the untexted rule, which allows the composer to write music without a text and then add appropriate words later. Although he insists that the added text must fit the music, his examples show texts that are suitable or unsuitable by virtue of their syllable count rather than by any specific expressive elements (which would in any case have been transmitted responsibly by the wise performer). At the end of this passage, Diletskii notes that the untexted rule "is especially useful for harps, the *lira, gusli,* organs, and also for singing."[89] This list of musical instruments is familiar from the assortment used at court and among high-ranking aristocrats for entertainment; presumably Diletskii's intended readers would also have had knowledge of such instruments as well.

Diletskii's intellectual style is thus very broad, encompassing different types and functions of vocal and instrumental music and using literary and rhetorical concepts as basic points of departure. Given Diletskii's own background, this approach is not at all surprising; what is more revealing is that the author seemed confident that his Muscovite audience would consider such analogies and examples as valid and comprehensible organizing principles for a music-theoretical work. The *Grammatika* was successful because it reflected, at least to some degree, his audience's intellectual style, their own exposure to a wide range of musical genres and contexts.

Musical Circles: Music Theory in Words and Images

If Diletskii's writing has a comprehensive and specific position in the complex culture of late seventeenth-century Muscovy, how then might it fit into contemporary musical debates among Western theorists? Specifically, are Diletskii's conception and presentation of the hexachordal syllables and the qualities of happy and sad to be equated with modern concepts of two modes, major and minor? After all, the author says: "I teach you in this [work] a two-fold [system of] musical voices or tones—*ut* and *re*—and a two-fold [system of] music: happy, which is *ut,* and sad, which is *re.*"[90] Furthermore, Diletskii observes many times that a composition might begin on any pitch letter. Generally he simply lists the letters A–G, sometimes with the syllables *ut–la* appended to each, without specifying whether it is possible to begin on a letter such as B-flat or G-sharp.[91] Other passages suggest that the author might include the full chromatic range: "On every letter (remember this always) may be *ut, re, mi, fa, sol,* and *la.* On every key of the organ you see that you distinguish between happy song, which is *ut,* and sad song, which is *re.*"[92] The L'viv source has a more explicit statement: "In my grammar I said that on an instrument one may work from any letter, on *ut, re, mi, fa, sol, la* . . . Similarly [one may work] with any sharp on the *positiv,* not only with the letters A, B, C, D, E, F, and G, but one may have *ut* and *re* on G-sharp and on the other sharps."[93]

A listing at the end of the two early Moscow 1679–81 sources suggests that Diletskii did indeed recognize *ut* on every letter, with or without chromatic alteration. This statement is preceded by a listing of letter-syllable combinations, with musical examples, showing the four kinds of *kliuchi;* the presentation is similar to that in his second chapter:

> By means of these alphabetical listings true mixed music [is produced] on every letter:

A	*ut re mi fa sol la*
b dur	*ut re mi fa sol la*
b mo[l]	*ut re mi fa sol la*
c	*ut re mi fa sol la*
cis [c-sharp]	*ut re mi fa sol la*
d	*ut re mi fa sol la*
dis [d-sharp]	*ut re mi fa sol la*
e	*ut re mi fa sol la*
e ♭	*ut re mi fa sol la*
f	*ut re mi fa sol la*
fis [f-sharp]	*ut re mi fa sol la*
g	*ut re mi fa sol la*
gis [g-sharp]	*ut re mi fa sol la*[94]

Diletskii does therefore include many of the components that would constitute a two-mode, major-minor system. One nevertheless hesitates to ascribe modern tonal thinking to his work. For example, the listing above emerges directly from the long summary series of examples of *kliuchi* in *duralnyi*, *bemmoliarnyi*, and so forth, for each of which the pitch letter–solmization syllable combinations are listed along with a short musical example. The *duralnyi kliuch* lists A *la re*; *bemmoliarnyi* with one flat lists A *la mi*; *bemmoliarnyi* with two flats lists A *mi fa*, and so forth, resulting ultimately in a series of examples in which each solmization syllable is indeed appended, in one context or another, to each pitch letter. Thus, "by means of these alphabetical listings, true mixed music [is produced] on each letter."

There are other ways in which Diletskii's approach does not fit with modern concepts of major-minor thinking. For example, he does not isolate explicitly the quality of the third in his definition of happy and sad music, and his differentiation between the two types does not necessarily carry with it the particular set of interrelationships that would define a theoretical system based on major and minor triads and generating a full range of twenty-four keys. In his third chapter, Diletskii lists concordant notes, building successive triads on the pitch letters A–G. The hexachordal syllables he appends to each note distinguish between *ut* and *re*; that is, in the major triad C–E–G, he labels the letter C with the syllable *ut*, and in the minor triad A–C–E, he labels A with the syllable *re*. But he does not describe these concordances with his terms happy and sad, nor does he distinguish between major and minor in his definition of the term *tertsiia*, which he defines simply as the third note.[95] The section "O notakh" (On notes) similarly presents the third without describing it as representing *ut* or *re*, happy or sad, or major or minor. In this section, Diletskii simply lists his concordant intervals as *obyknovennyi* (usual, including thirds and fifths) and *neobyknovennyi* (unusual, including sixths, fourths, sevenths, and seconds).[96]

A more important example of Diletskii's approach appears in his discussion of the contrary rule (*pravilo protivnoe*), which shows how to change music from happy, for example, to sad. Diletskii discusses the contrary rule from two angles. In one context he considers this rule as a means of lengthening a composition by changing a melody from one type of music to another and then repeating it. He refers to this approach twice but in neither case does he give technical advice on how to make such a change, saying simply: "I said that one may expand singing in a *kontsert* especially by means of the contrary rule, that is, when first the singing was happy and then in expanded form [it is] sad or the other way around, happy [singing] following sad" (as illustrated in musical example 5.9).[97]

He also speaks more specifically about the contrary rule in several passages. The change from happy music to sad or vice versa would require a full range of

EXAMPLE 5.9. Diletskii, *Grammatika,* the *pravilo protivnoe* as a means of lengthening a composition (RGB 107, p. 151)

EXAMPLE 5.10. Diletskii, *Grammatika,* a melody presented in happy music (RGB 107, p. 138)

EXAMPLE 5.11. Diletskii, *Grammatika,* the same melody, now changed into sad music (RGB 107, p. 139)

accidentals, and the author's enumeration of the flats and sharps, listed above, indicates that he recognized just such a wide range of chromatic alterations. But there are difficulties in integrating his presentation of the contrary rule with an interpretation of the *Grammatika* as expressing a modern conception of a two-mode system generating twenty-four keys differentiated by major or minor thirds. First, in his examples of moving from happy to sad, Diletskii never repeats the melody at the same pitch level, changing simply the quality of the third. In each example he moves the melody to a different position on the staff, where the major or minor third occurs without the use of accidentals. An example is his rendition of the Cherubic Hymn first in happy music (example 5.10) and then in sad (example 5.11).

Second, Diletskii says that sometimes it is impossible to change a piece note-for-note ("nota na notu"); when moving from one type of music to another, one must sometimes bend the shape of the melody:

> I already spoke of the contrary rule when one changes happy singing to sad and sad to happy, not only when the change is note-for-note, but when it is not possible to make such a change, then place [the notes] such that in the change they follow the first melody [musical example 5.12]. However you see in this song that it is impossible to change note-for-note, [thus] I change it as follows [musical example 5.13].[98]

EXAMPLE 5.12. Diletskii, *Grammatika,* presentation of a melody to illustrate the *pravilo protivnoe* (RGB 107, p. 115)

EXAMPLE 5.13. Diletskii, *Grammatika,* the same melody, impossible to change note-for-note (RGB 107, p. 115)

Perhaps here the problem of changing (in this passage Diletskii consistently uses the verb *prevrashchat'* [to change, convert, transform] and derivatives) note-for-note arose because the original melody outlined both the minor third and the major third, with the pitches C and C-sharp in the opening measures. Diletskii had used this same melody earlier, in his initial presentation of the contrary rule.[99] In this first presentation, his change from happy to sad also involved more than simply altering the quality of the third, requiring some recomposition and repositioning as shown in musical examples 5.14 and 5.15. In a two-fold system in which the types are defined and differentiated solely by the quality of the third, it would never be impossible to change a given melody note-for-note from happy music to sad. Furthermore, such a change would require only an alteration in the third itself, not a move from one location to another.

Diletskii's discussion of cadences is equally difficult to fit into a modern conception of tonality. The Moscow 1679–81 *Grammatika* defines cadences in chapter 3, at a point earlier in the treatise than in the other versions. Here, the author defines an *obyknovennyi* cadence (usual, normal; corresponding to the term *sovershennyi,* which has the sense of complete or full, used later in other redactions). An *obyknovennyi* cadence is one that ends on the same note with which the piece began; a *neobyknovennyi* (unusual) cadence does not end on the

EXAMPLE 5.14. Diletskii, *Grammatika,* the same melody, in happy music
(RGB 107, p. 76)

EXAMPLE 5.15. Diletskii, *Grammatika,* the same melody, changed to sad music
(RGB 107, p. 76)

same note with which the work began.[100] Diletskii repeats his definition in all three
versions of the treatise in the section entitled "On cadences." Here he emphasizes
the movement of the bass line as the determining factor in labeling the cadence,
explaining that an *obyknovennyi* (or *sovershennyi*) cadence occurs when the bass
falls a fifth or rises a fourth. Conversely, a *neobyknovennyi* (or *nesovershennyi*)
cadence requires a falling fourth or a rising fifth in the bass: "*Obyknovennye*
cadences are when the bass falls from an upper fifth to a fifth or [moves up] from a
fourth, that is, making the cadence by means of the lower fourth note . . . *Neobyk-
novennye* cadences are when the bass makes the cadence down by a fourth or up by
a fifth."[101] These melodic considerations cause Diletskii to classify the passage in
musical example 5.16 as a *neobyknovennyi* cadence, even though the bass begins
and ends on the same note.

His later discussions of cadences also emphasize melodic rather than vertical
classifications. In a passage at the opening of the final chapter, Diletskii gives the
reader additional information on the use of sharps in cadences. He says, for
example, that "one places G-sharp [*gis mi*] when the bass moves frequently up
from the letter A to E."[102] Diletskii's example (musical example 5.17) shows what
would be described in modern tonal terms as the use of the leading tone in a
cadential progression from tonic to dominant to tonic. But Diletskii keeps to his
earlier criteria in this and in all the examples in this passage, focusing on the

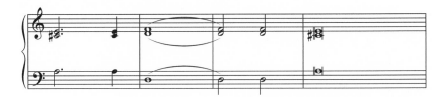

EXAMPLE 5.16. Diletskii, *Grammatika,* a *neobyknovennyi* cadence beginning and ending on the same pitch (RGB 107, p. 220)

EXAMPLE 5.17. Diletskii, *Grammatika,* the melodic movement of the bass in a cadence (RGB 107, p. 100)

melodic movement of the bass. His discussion relates to the appearance, rather than to the function, of the sharp. Because the sharp appears in the example when the bass moves from A to E, that is the movement Diletskii isolates. This definition recalls his four-fold division of music according to *kliuch,* in which the system is determined by the appearance of a flat or sharp rather than the function of a particular key signature or accidental in a particular musical context.

Diletskii's discussions of happy and sad music, the contrary rule, and cadences all point to a system based on hexachords and the descriptive categories of *smysl* and *kliuch.* Yet one important construct in the *Grammatika* seems to fly in the face of all this: the diagram of the circle of fifths. Taken alone, Diletskii's musical circles do appear to violate the unity of the author's hexachord-based approach to music, for they present in vivid, literal form the full range of twenty-four major and minor keys, none described as transposed, transformed, or specially derived—the very definition of a modern two-mode system. But in the context of the *Gram-matika,* the circles encapsulate all the elements of Diletskii's methodology: his vocabulary describing *kliuch;* his reliance upon literary and rhetorical models; and his practical and didactic approach, including many references to the organ as a teaching device. An appreciation of the *Grammatika's* intellectual style, then, again provides a sound starting point for a consideration of the most spectacular element of Diletskii's theory.

Diletskii's two musical circles are part of a section entitled "On amplification" ("O amplifikatsii" or "O razmnozhenii").[103] This section appears in the final chapter of the treatise, and it explores various ways of spinning out a musical idea. Diletskii begins by explaining that one might expand a piece by using the methods discussed in the previous section, "On the beginning" ("O eksordii" or "O nachale"), which considered ways to begin a composition. A composer might lengthen a work by repeating the text, contrasting happy and sad music, varying the meter, or employing the numerous compositional rules outlining melodic patterns to be used throughout a piece. Diletskii gives examples to illustrate his advice. His first example is meant to show expansion through text repetition, although only two of the available sources actually include a text. Other sources, however, show melodic repetitions presumably intended to reflect those that would appear if the text were repeated.[104] His next example shows expansion through changing the music from sad to happy; this is amplification by means of the contrary rule, as shown above in musical example 5.9.

Diletskii then shows how to expand a musical idea by means of similar letters ("cherez litery sebe podobashe"), by which he means letters with similar hexachordal positionings. If a melody in the tenor begins on D *sol*, for example, one might shift it to G *sol* and place it in the alto, as in musical examples 5.18 and 5.19.[105] This strategy might also be combined with a change in meter. Another way to expand a piece is by exchanging melodic fragments among the voices.

This section also includes a passage on organ or keyboard writing ("O organakh"), in which Diletskii gives advice on how to interpret figured bass notation. He says that it is an error to add a sharp to a note that does not require one. This occurs, he says, in changing Latin *kontserty* to Russian ("prevrashchaiushche latinskie na rosskiia kontserty"). The sharp is placed in the score for the sake of the organist: in musical example 5.20, which accompanies this passage, the sharp in the bass is placed not in order to produce A-sharp in the lowest voice, but rather to produce C-sharp in the upper voice.

The author strays from his main point in his next few examples, where he mentions word painting and varying the texture of opening phrases. He returns, in the Moscow 1679 and L'viv sources, to the idea of musical expansion by introducing a literary analogy. He says that just as in a sermon, in which one might reverse the order of the words to make the presentation last longer, so in a musical work a composer might reverse the order of the notes for the same reason. He gives short

EXAMPLE 5.18. Diletskii, *Grammatika,* expansion by means of similar letters, beginning on D (RGB 146, p. 157, from OLDP Izdaniia 128, from the collection of the University of Washington)

EXAMPLE 5.19. Diletskii, *Grammatika,* expansion by means of similar letters, shifted to G (RGB 146, p. 157, from OLDP Izdaniia 128, from the collection of the University of Washington)

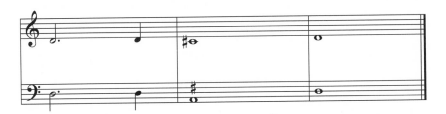

EXAMPLE 5.20. Diletskii, *Grammatika,* explanation of figured bass notation in translating Latin *kontserty* to Russian (RGB 146, p. 155, from OLDP Izdaniia 128, from the collection of the University of Washington)

examples of this procedure as it occurs in texts, for example "gospodi pomilui"/ "pomilui gospodi" (Lord, have mercy). The L'viv manuscript presents a slightly different and more accurate analogy. Here the palindrome (*polindromon*) appears as the literary model, illustrated by means of the phrases "sygna te signa temere me tangys et angys" and "Ronia [*sic*] tyby sybyto motybus ibyt amar."[106] In the Moscow 1679 sources, the textual examples are followed by a melody which is presented forward and then backward.[107]

The musical circle finally makes its appearance as yet another way one might expand a composition. Diletskii explains that a melody might pass through all the letters in the circle and end up back at the beginning, an effective if somewhat long-winded way of spinning out a musical idea. Each of the three versions refers to the organ or to an organist for verification or further clarification of the musical circle.[108]

The two musical circles are diagrams drawn in the form of circular staves, with additional staves filling in the interior. Each circle resembles the face of a slightly skewed clock, with numbers beginning at the top with one and moving around to twelve. These numbers mark the progress of a short musical phrase as it passes through each of the twelve happy or sad keys.[109] In some sources, hexachordal syllables are entered at the first appearance of the melody, showing that in happy music, the tune begins on *sol* and moves to *ut*, which in turn becomes *sol* as it passes to the next iteration.

In each of the sources, the melody moves first through *bemmoliarnaia* music and then switches to *diezisovaia,* as shown in figure 5.2 (transcribed in musical example 5.21). The first circle contains additional theoretical material inside the ring. A box outlined by four staves illustrates and labels each of the four kinds of *kliuchi: duralnaia, bemmoliarnaia, diezisovaia,* and *smeshennaia.* Angled inside this square is another, which again illustrates the different kinds of music as defined by *kliuch: duralnaia, bemmoliarnaia, bemmoliarnaia* with four flats, and *diezisovaia* (in some sources combined with *smeshennaia*). The diagram of sad music includes only the circular staff, with a melody beginning on *la* and passing to *re* in each of the twelve keys. Diletskii again moves through *bemmoliarnaia* music first and then changes to *diezisovaia* music, as shown in musical example 5.22.

Diletskii describes the circles using the theoretical vocabulary he has employed throughout the treatise, as in his explanation of the happy circle:

> Note the following circle and by what means a fantasy may move through all the letters (see this from the organ, or if you do not know how to play it, then ask knowledgeable organists) and return to the first voice [*glas*] and to its first key [*kliuch*] and letter, from which you began.[110]

He gives a slightly more technical explanation of the second circle. In the Moscow 1679 sources, Diletskii writes: "and thus see that in any letter you may construct *ut, re, mi, fa, sol,* and *la.*" This explanation is expanded in other versions:

> Understand that in any letter you may depict all voices and notes [*glasy, noty*], that is, in any letter you may find and create *ut, re, mi, fa, sol,* and *la,* which you see on the organ . . . You may change any desired fantasy through all the keys [*kliuchi*] in the alphabet—*bemmoliarnyia* and *diezisovyia*—twelve times and then return around, going to the first letter from which you began . . . This is most easily grasped on the organ.[111]

The musical circles are thus wholly consistent with Diletskii's overall approach. They conform to the author's literary analogies in general and to his rhetorical analogies specifically, for the term *amplifikatsiia* is also used in Kievan rhetoric treatises in the context of expanding or lengthening a speech.[112] The circles also reflect Diletskii's reliance upon the organ as an all-purpose reference for students, particularly in such tricky matters as enharmonic equivalence or the use of multiple

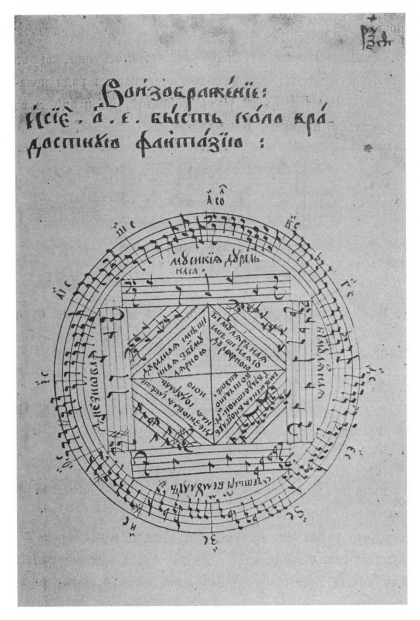

FIGURE 5.2. Diletskii, *Grammatika,* the musical circle (RGB 146, p. 160, from OLDP
Izdaniia 128, from the collection of the University of Washington)

EXAMPLE 5.21. Diletskii, *Grammatika,* the musical circle (transcription of figure 5.2, from RGB 146, p. 160, from OLDP Izdaniia 128, from the collection of the University of Washington)

flats and sharps. They are also consistent with Diletskii's frequent use of pictures and diagrams as supplements to written rules. All these elements derive from the author's practical approach to the process of composition and all are invoked frequently throughout the treatise. Diletskii reinforces this context in his explanations of the circles, which rely completely on his system of four *kliuchi* and the solmization syllables.

Diletskii seems to have worked on the *Grammatika* for the half-decade between the mid-1670s in Vilnius and 1681, the date of the final Moscow version. Western European theoretical treatises of this period have no diagrams comparable to Diletskii's. The first simple listing of all twenty-four major and minor

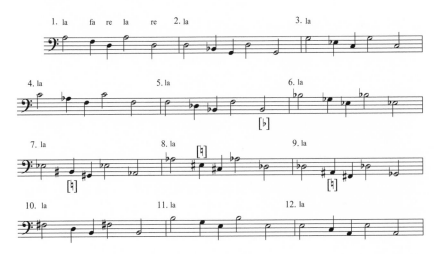

EXAMPLE 5.22. Diletskii, *Grammatika*, the musical circle (RGB 107, p. 134, barlines added)

keys—a listing that does not recognize them as equal in derivation—follows by a decade the final version of the *Grammatika*, appearing in 1691 in Jacques Ozanam's *Dictionnaire mathématique*. Ozanam lists the keys by letter, dividing them into three groups, including a category labeled "Les Modes Transposez."[113] The twenty-four keys were first presented as equal in derivation in Thomas Janowka's little-circulated *Clavis ad thesaurum magnae artis musicae* (Prague, 1701). In his definition of "tonus," Janowka lists the major-minor pairs of scales on every note, beginning with A and proceeding chromatically.[114] A few years earlier, Andreas Werckmeister had included a non-circular listing of a series of triads passing through the circle of fifths or fourths in his general bass treatise, *Die nothwendigsten Anmerckungen und Regeln, wie der Bassus Continuus oder General-Bass wol könne tractiret werden* (Aschersleben, 1698). He repeated the diagram later in his *Musicalische Paradoxal-Discourse* (Quedlinburg, 1707). Johann Heinichen made the first pictorial representation of the "musicalischer Circul" in chapter 4 of his *Neu erfundene und gründliche Anweisung . . . des General-Basses* (Hamburg, 1711).[115]

Diletskii's circles appeared more than thirty years before Heinichen's. Could there be any relationship between the two diagrams? We must turn again to a broad consideration of context in order to understand both Diletskii's circles as well as the early Western formulations. Of course Diletskii was influenced by Western theoretical concepts and language—one only needs to read a page or two of his treatise, with its solmization syllables and *duralnaia* music, to be convinced of this. Indeed, all the preceding chapters in this study have been devoted to an exploration of how Muscovite music and musicians interacted with, responded to, and might have comprehended the Western music they encountered with increasing frequency as the century progressed. Nevertheless, Diletskii did not necessarily derive his own musical circles from the same theoretical base from which Werckmeister or Heinichen developed theirs. The vociferous exchanges in the West about modes, psalm tones, keys, tunings, and the like—to which Ozanam, Werckmeister, and Heinichen were responding—would not have affected Diletskii or, even less so, his intended Muscovite audience in the same manner or to the same degree.[116]

Diletskii's language starkly illustrates such differences. He presents his circles solely as practical devices in the context of amplifying a composition, and describes them only in terms of their melodic content, saying that they are "without beginning and without end." Nowhere does he use labels such as "Circul der quinten oder quarten," as Werckmeister does, or "Quartenzirkel," as a later reader of the L'viv manuscript inscribed helpfully in bold pink ink.[117] Nor does Diletskii label each key area as it appears. In this his diagrams differ from Heinichen's, which include no music but are simply listings by letter of the major and minor keys together, arranged in the form of a circle. Although a number of issues hotly debated in the West are implicit to Diletskii's circles—equal temperament, recognition of a two-mode major-minor system, and the equal derivation of all the keys— Diletskii introduces the diagram in his *Grammatika* simply to show a student how to expand a piece of music. The circles do not appear in order to illustrate or make tangible a point of theory but rather as vivid, literal examples of the repetitions "without beginning and without end" with which the student composer might beef up a too-short piece.

Such a rigidly utilitarian description, paradoxically, also helps us situate Diletskii's circles within the larger context of European music theory. Two characteristics of the early Western references to circles of fifths suggest a manner of thinking similar to Diletskii's. First, and not surprisingly, the two earliest Western sources indicate that the idea of constructing circles of fifths originated well before an example was actually written out in a theory treatise. Although Diletskii's diagrams precede written examples in Western theory books, the idea of a lengthy progression by fifths or fourths was certainly in general circulation among performing musicians by the 1670s. (Indeed, Diletskii has such a passage in his own setting of the Easter *kanon*.)[118] Second, these early Western sources mention the circle in connection with a keyboard instrument.

In his *Hypomnemata musica* (1697), Andreas Werckmeister mentions the "Circul der quinten oder quarten" as a musical device that had been used three decades earlier by Froberger in a keyboard piece. Werckmeister says that Froberger transposed a theme "through the entire keyboard on all twelve keys . . . through the circle of fifths or fourths."[119] Similarly, as Joel Lester emphasizes, Heinichen himself does not take credit for the "musicalischer Circul" that appeared in his *Neu erfundene und gründliche Anweisung*. Instead, in a later treatise, Heinichen explains that his own teacher, Johann Kuhnau, had told him about a circle constructed by another theorist, Athanasius Kircher. Heinichen writes: "[M]y teacher told me something of the above-mentioned circle of [Athanasius] Kircher [1601–80], but this gave me no satisfaction if I set out to go from a major key to a distantly related minor key and vice versa."[120] Heinichen says only that Kircher's method, although widely acknowledged, was awkward and that he improved on it: "The well-known method of Kircher, to circulate through all the keys by fourths and fifths, is one of the most imperfect. For if one begins, e.g., from a major key, and continues by fourths or fifths until he returns to the first key, all twelve minor keys are left out."[121]

According to Lester, Kuhnau's sole extant treatise, the *Fundamenta compositionis* of 1703, contains only a traditional presentation of the modes, and Kircher's explanation, in the first volume of the *Musurgia universalis* (Rome, 1650), is likewise traditional. Kircher's harmonic circle, writes Lester, appears "only as an abstract concept in the discussion of various types of keyboards."[122]

Lester's evaluation of Heinichen's musical circle brings out two elements that characterize both the early Western examples as well as the diagrams in the *Grammatika*. Lester concludes that Heinichen's musical circle was "presented not as a revolutionary method of establishing a new tonal system, but as a practical convenience to aid in modulation from one key to another."[123] Ozanam, a well-known mathematician, also took an intensely practical, synthetic approach throughout his own work, which was aimed not at professional musicians but at an educated audience interested in the unity of all the mathematical disciplines, including music.[124] The early and widespread existence of the circles as a practical tool used by keyboard players, rather than as a pathbreaking theoretical construct, suggests a context for Diletskii's circles as well. Diletskii's own pragmatic approach to theory and his emphasis on the organ (along with the presence in Ukraine and Belarus as well as in Muscovy of organists, some foreign and some native and performing in a variety of situations) form a reasonable link to this practical, almost informal notion of the musical circle.

There is an equally practical Muscovite context for Diletskii's illustrations. The musical circles are among many diagrams in the *Grammatika,* and some versions of the treatise even include more than one set of circles. An additional circular diagram appears in the Moscow 1679–81 redactions, toward the end of the section on teaching the rudiments of music. It is drawn as a circular staff and is meant to show how the letters repeat as they ascend and descend. The letter names A–G are entered on the lines and spaces, spiraling around the circle up and down again, over a span of about one and one-half octaves.[125] Diletskii also includes charts explaining the various placement of sharps in cadences. The *Grammatika* even opens with a drawing, a cross made of intersecting staves, which in some sources transmit a melody.[126]

Other seventeenth-century Muscovite theoretical works share this pictorial approach. Although the content of Diletskii's treatise and the musical style he teaches are far removed from traditional Russian chant treatises, one wonders if some of his approaches might not have been derived from or echoed, in very general terms, the diagrams and visual aids so commonly used in these sources (see also below). Diletskii's demonstrations of each of his ascending and descending rules (see musical examples 5.7 and 5.8 for illustrations of the ascending rule) recall the earlier practice of listing neumes according to the ascending and descending melodic patterns they represent.

Diletskii may also have been influenced by the visual aspects of contemporary Muscovite and Ukrainian or Belarusian poetry and other literary works. Simeon Polotskii, for example, wrote poems arranged in various shapes suggested by their subjects (a kind of visual word painting), and many of his works were devised in complex labyrinths and cryptograms. The hidden acrostics in German's *kanty* show a similar delight in visual puzzles, and the poets at the Kievan collegium were also noted for elaborate visual constructions in their works.[127] Rhetoric treatises produced in Muscovy, familiar sources for other aspects of Diletskii's thinking, are also full of diagrams and drawings. Andrei Belobotskii included circular diagrams, with texts and letters added in segments, like the face of a clock, in his rhetoric treatise. One might even cite the increasingly pictorial and visual emphasis in children's primers (*bukvari*), a genre with some parallels to the *Grammatika*, as representative of similar trends.[128]

In light of Diletskii's limited and specific purpose for his musical circles, a link to the West is thus only one of many possible sources of influence. Although it is possible that Diletskii became acquainted with the general notion of a circle of fifths or fourths through exposure to Western theoretical writings or from imported performers or compositions, the idea of translating it literally onto a circular staff is not necessarily connected solely to European music theory. In other words, although Diletskii's acquaintance with Western compositions and musical vocabulary is obvious enough, one need not postulate for the author elaborate (and so far undocumented) European trips or academic degrees in order to account for a diagram which, at first glance, appears to represent an astonishing theoretical leap.

The Grammatika *and the Language and Legacies of* Muscovite Music Theory

The concepts and language Diletskii presents in his treatise also appear in the musical compositions—*kanty* and especially *kontserty*—his intended audience was being trained to write and perform. In some cases, the language Diletskii uses for specific concepts or procedures becomes diffused, appearing in non-theoretical sources as descriptive titles. The inventory of the extensive musical holdings of the L'viv Orthodox confraternity provides a good example. The inventory was written in 1697, listing over 350 pieces, most for twelve or fewer voices, but at least one for eighteen vocal parts, a clear indication of the high level of musical activity and training at the confraternity. The listing includes five of Diletskii's compositions: three settings of the Divine Liturgy (labeled as *sluzhby,* or services) for eight voices; an eight-part *kanon;* and another liturgy for an unspecified number of voices. Many other composers are represented in the inventory as well, although most of the works are anonymous. One of the anonymous compositions is described as a "Bemuliarna sluzhba" for eight voices. An independently circulating composition by Diletskii is called "Sluzhba bozhiia preportsialnaia," in accordance with the layout of the piece in triple time, and settings by Vasilii Titov are also labeled "Sluzhba bemuliarna" and "preportsialnaia."[129]

Other terms familiar from Diletskii's theoretical writings percolate into song texts. One song seems to have been written by Diletskii himself, almost as an advertisement of his theoretical wares. This four-part song includes the couplet, in the bass: "These voices were composed by the sinful man / Nikolai Dyletskii, the foreigner and *pan.*" (The Polish honorific *pan* means mister or sir.)[130] The text of each of the four voices in the song announces its range (discant, alto, tenor, and bass) and includes other information on polyphonic singing. The opening of the discant, for example, proclaims:

> My name is discant, above all so high
> By an octave over the tenor I fly
> Pray to God and sing *ut, re, mi, fa, sol, la.*[131]

Although Diletskii passes up the chance to illustrate the solmization syllables in the melody of the song, he does take advantage of the opportunity to criticize the excesses of chant performance (the term *kulizma* below refers to a neume used in chant notation):

> My name is the tenor, I carry the *cantus firmus,*
> When you sing me you will be on *terra firma.*
> Sing with a sweet and beautiful voice ringing,
> Don't contort yourself with *kulizma* singing.[132]

Because of their wide popularity, song texts would seem to be a logical place in which to inject didactic content, and indeed there are other such examples. The "numbers songs," for instance, were a popular category in *kant* manuscripts; they taught the numbers through a listing of important spiritual landmarks (one Son of Mary, two tablets of Moses, and so forth).[133] Diletskii, too, engages the student with the familiar language of the *kant* in his treatise, citing several *kant* texts and their tunes (as single-line melodies), as summarized in the appendix.

But which came first, Diletskii or the terminology? Were other composers or copyists picking up on language used in the *Grammatika,* or was Diletskii himself reflecting the vocabulary and concepts he heard around him in Muscovy, often the same concepts he would have encountered earlier in Vilnius and elsewhere? Indeed, perhaps a widespread knowledge of these fundamental music-theoretical approaches in Muscovy is what prompted Diletskii to relocate and rewrite his Polish-language treatise for Muscovy in the first place. He must have had some sense that his approach and ideas would be valuable in Muscovy: why would he have gone to Smolensk and Moscow at all if he had not anticipated a decent reception? In such a scenario, Diletskii would be cast into the role of (a more organized and intentional) Pan Skrzolotowicz, the Polish visitor in Moscow who certainly did not invent the genre of *kant* nor bring it first and single-handedly to Muscovy in his little manuscript collection, but who picked up on the music he heard around him and reproduced it in his own fashion.

If indeed these were Diletskii's assumptions, then he had judged well. His theoretical views and concepts obviously found a ready audience in Muscovy, and there are two groupings of sources that show how the ground might have been prepared. The first set of sources relates to the innovations in chant theory that emerged throughout the seventeenth century. Many scholars have observed the link between the *soglasie* system, which emerged during this period, and the hexachords of Western practice. The *soglasiia* (plural; accords, concordances, agreements) divided the entire scale used to sing the liturgical repertoire into four consecutive trichords. Each pitch was then labeled according to its position in one of these trichords. The system has obvious parallels to the Western hexachordal layout, and Maksim Brazhnikov and others believe that Muscovite theorists recognized and even deliberately exploited the similarities between the two systems.[134]

The two approaches were linked and blended in many ways, as two brief examples indicate. Many of the instructive, practical chant treatises of the seventeenth century include a triangular diagram called the *gorovoskhodnyi kholm* (ascending knoll), which is meant to show the singer the basic patterns of ascent and descent, marked out by the proper neumed notation. In the second half of the seventeenth century, these diagrams sometimes also included the (Cyrillic) letters used to indicate the *soglasiia;* in some cases, the diagrams also incorporated Western solmization syllables. One source, from the last quarter of the century, gives a simple and obvious listing of the correspondences. Under the heading "The beginning (or foundation) of sacred singing—the two-fold agreement (*soglasie*) of the ascending and descending voice," the author simply lists the concordances: 1. *ut,* entered above the sign indicating the first pitch in lowest trichord in the *soglasie* system; 2. *re,* entered above the sign for the next pitch in the lowest trichord; 3. *mi,* entered over the sign for the third pitch in the lowest trichord, and so forth, throughout the entire range of the *soglasiia.*[135]

If some music-theoretical works recognized the common ground between the two systems, other Muscovite notation treatises brought them together directly. The introductory *azbuki* (listings of neumes) were often associated with collections called *dvoznamenniki,* comparative notated compilations generally focusing on two types of notation, usually neumes and staff notation. The *dvoznamenniki* (from "two signs") did not necessarily give strictly parallel layouts of the different systems. One source, for example, has neumatic notation on one side of an opening and staff notation on the other. In another source, each neume is accompanied by one of the Western hexachordal syllables; there is no other notation.[136] Brazhnikov emphasizes that the *dvoznamenniki* were not written to explain the five-line staff to beginners, but rather that they were intended for people who probably already sang from the new notation. These singers needed the traditional neumatic notation as a guide to the stylistic elements of liturgical chant, which the Western staff did not convey.[137]

Such concordances in theoretical thinking also seem to be reflected in Diletskii's work.[138] For example, the subjects covered in contemporary chant treatises might explain some of the lacunae in the *Grammatika.* As noted above, Diletskii (along with Korenev and others) did not discuss or even define the intervallic relationships (whole and half steps) implied by the hexachordal syllables. Perhaps he was able to assume that because of the widespread use of solmization syllables in elementary chant treatises and *dvoznamenniki,* this concept would already have been quite familiar to his students. Along these same lines, perhaps this is why Diletskii and others writing in Muscovy did not formally introduce the rudiments of staff notation, again assuming that its widespread use in the *dvoznamenniki* (and in manuscripts transmitting all kinds of *partesnoe penie*–style pieces) provided sufficient explanation. And perhaps the content of the *dvoznamenniki* also dictated the relatively lengthy presentation of rhythm and meter in the *Grammatika* and in the theoretical section of Korenev's treatise. The *dvoznamenniki* do not use rests and generally rely on fairly straightforward rhythmic patterns. Readers with some experience singing liturgical chant might thus be assumed to understand staff notation but not complex rhythmic signs.[139]

In other passages, however, Diletskii's relationship to contemporary chant theorists is more difficult to determine. In his dedication to Stroganov, Diletskii says that he consulted works by other Orthodox writers in compiling his *Grammatika,* and elsewhere in his text he mentions a theorist, Tikhon, by name. Is this Tikhon Makar'evskii, whose *dvoznamennik* circulated widely in the late seventeenth century and into the eighteenth? Tikhon Makar'evskii was archimandrite of the Makar'ev-Zheltovodskii (St. Macarius Yellow Lake) Monastery near Nizhnii Novgorod in the mid-1670s, and by the end of the decade was associated with the St. Savva Monastery in Zvenigorod, just outside Moscow; he was later called to the Patriarchal Treasury in the capital. His music-theoretical work, *Kliuch razumeniia* (Key to Understanding), circulates in nearly two dozen sources from the last quarter of the seventeenth century and into the eighteenth. The actual date of composition is unknown, although scholars generally propose a date in the mid-1670s.[140] This work represents, in effect, the end game of the transition from neumes to staff notation in the context of liturgical singing, following the earlier (and not necessarily identical) efforts of Aleksandr Mezenets in his own work.

If indeed Diletskii's reference is to Tikhon Makar'evskii, then it raises more problems than it solves. There are some points of contact between the two treatises. Tikhon, for example, does refer to solmization syllables in the opening illustration of his treatise, which shows a key with three teeth, upon which the syllables *ut, re,* and *mi* are written. He explains that these three syllables constitute all sacred singing, thus touching on both chant as well as hexachords.[141] However, the name Tikhon appears in Diletskii's discussion of the term *ton,* which he uses to mark the basic distinction between happy and sad music. Tikhon Makar'evskii does not employ Diletskii's concepts of happy and sad or his other, related terminology. Even apart from this the reference is curious, for Diletskii, who explicitly declares that the *Grammatika* does not discuss Irmologii singing, would not seem to have much in common with the kind of music Tikhon presents. Furthermore, Diletskii's remark is in the first person, past tense ("as I said in Tikhon's music"), which suggests a variety of possibilities, all fascinating yet wholly speculative.[142]

There is, however, far more direct evidence of specific and even somewhat detailed knowledge of Western theoretical (especially hexachordal) concepts in Muscovy before Diletskii wrote his treatise, and it is in the work of a person with whom we know Diletskii to have been associated: Ioannikii Korenev. Korenev's main objective, both in the hefty polemical section that constitutes the bulk of his original treatise and in his music-theoretical presentations, is a plea for the universality of the rules of music. The two writers share an impatience with the chaotic singing practices they hear around them and a knowledge of historical precedent to support their endeavors; both invoke literary models and terminology in their efforts to create coherent musical rules; and both strive for an expressive music, or as Korenev describes it, a union of word and sound.[143]

Korenev's *O penii bozhestvennom* (On Sacred Singing) was written in 1671, and it circulated anonymously in several manuscript sources with this title and date. A later redaction of the treatise, with Korenev's name attached, is associated with the Moscow 1679–81 *Grammatika;* one early source includes an annotation indicating that Korenev himself wrote out the manuscript.[144] In both versions of his work Korenev presents brief technical discussions of music-theoretical concepts. However, it is in the first (1671) version that we get the clearest sense of his reliance on traditional hexachordal models.[145] It is possible that Korenev drew some of this material from the widespread contemporary references to such models in Muscovite chant books. His presentation, however, has a specificity not seen in such Russian treatises but which rather is quite close to listings standard in Western theoretical works. He says that there are twenty keys or rules (*kliavishi, pravila*) of music and then proceeds to name and categorize them, as summarized in figure 5.3 (Korenev's presentation is in prose listings, not in a diagram).[146]

Not only in its scope but in its divisions into primary, middle, and high groupings (*glavnyi, srednii, vysokii*) and the sub-categories of beginning or primary and ending (*nachinaiushchii* or *glavnyi, konchashchii*), Korenev's listing recalls similar layouts in Western treatises. One particularly close example appears in both prose and tabular form in Szymon Starowolski's *Musices practicae erotemata* (Cracow, 1650), shown in figure 5.1 above. There are other similarities between the two works. Under the rubric "A quo inuenta est Musica?" Starowolski offers a listing including the biblical Tubal, son of Lamech and, among the Greeks,

20. E-e lia mi

19. De-de lia sol' re

    high
    [*vysokie*]
18. Tse-tse sol' fa ut   *kliavishi*

17. Be-be fa ga mi [*sic*]

16. A-a lia mi re

15. E-sol re ut [*sic*]

14. Ef-fa ut

    concluding
13. E-lia mi   [*konchashchii*]

    middle
12. De-lia sol re   [*srednie*]
    kliavishi

11. Tse-sol' fa ut   [primary [*glavnii*]

10. Be-fa ga mi [*sic*]

9. A-la mi re

8. E-sol' re ut [*sic*]

7. Ef-fa ut   concluding
    [*konchaschchii*]

6. E-lia mi

5. De-sol re   primary
    or lowest
4. Tse-fa ut   [*glavnye, nizovye*]
    kliavishi

3. Ga-mi [*sic*]

    beginning or primary
2. A-re   [*nachinaiushchii, glavnyi*]

1. Ga-mi ut

FIGURE 5.3. Korenev, *O penii bozhestvennom,* layout of the *kliavishi*

Pythagoras, Mercurius, Zetus, Amphion, Orpheus, and Linus—all of these names appear in Korenev's own listing of musicians, and in the same order.[147] Thus, although we cannot say with any certainty that Korenev saw Starowolski's (or any other specific) treatise, we can at least suggest that he saw something Western, something with an approach similar to that in Starowolski and others. (Indeed, Starowolski's own sources, in particular the treatises by Johann Spangenberg and Andreas Ornithoparchus, present strikingly similar listings of musical ancients.)[148] Korenev worked for a time at the Sretenskii (Presentation) Cathedral in the Kremlin, so he would have been in the right place and at the right time (Moscow in the late 1660s–ca. 1670) to have come into contact with the kinds of people there who were familiar with such Western writings and approaches.[149]

In the second version of his treatise, Korenev substitutes his fairly detailed listing and classification of hexachordal syllables with another theoretical discussion, a short passage clearly (and deliberately) linked to Diletskii's presentation, which follows in several of the manuscript sources. Korenev begins with a brief recapitulation of an earlier question—"What is music?"—and a quick listing of the three clefs (*kliavishi*). He then inserts what appears to be a disclaimer, which serves to revise his previous, and quite traditional, presentation of the network of hexachords and to link this revised material explicitly to Diletskii's *Grammatika:*

> And in earlier [works] about music it was written that there are twenty rules which are called *gamma ut,* etc., which are called *kliavishi,* and that there are two *abetsadla* [alphabets], seven *duliarnyi* and seven *bemuliarnyi,* which are also called *kliavishi,* first twenty and then fourteen, but these are not *kliavishi* [in the sense of clefs, which he has just discussed]. See the *abetsadla* or *bukvari* [alphabets] ahead in this book, which Nikolai Diletskii, a resident of the city of Kiev, translated from Polish to Slavic in [7]187 [1678/1679].[150]

In the 1671 treatise Korenev had indeed listed twenty *kliavishi* (or *pravila*): *Ga-mi ut, A-re,* and so forth, as presented in figure 5.3. Now he appears to be reconciling his terminology with Diletskii's and referring to the *Grammatika,* which follows directly.[151] Korenev immediately reiterates that the *kliavishi* are the three clefs; the alphabets are written as follows: *gamma ut,* A *la re,* and so forth. He then lists the six solmization syllables *ut–la* in ascent and descent.[152] Korenev devotes considerable attention to rhythmic notation, employing the same terminology Diletskii uses, in two well-organized passages. He defines *takt* (whole note) as the basic unit of measure, relating it to the movement of the hand up and down. Diletskii, too, writes that "*takt* is counting by beats ["udarenie chislitelnoe"] in singing, or in singing or musical conducting [*rukovozhdenie*]." This definition also recalls rare pictorial evidence of conductors in some seventeenth-century choirs.[153]

The vocabulary and approaches we have seen in Diletskii and in other treatises appear in much-distilled form in simpler, less comprehensive theoretical writings from the late seventeenth and the eighteenth centuries. Some suggest the same kinds of cross-pollination we saw in the Korenev-Diletskii complex. One such work is the *Nauka vseia musikii* (The Complete Science [or Study] of Music). The *Nauka* is an introductory treatise, full of examples and tables aimed at the beginning student and clearly requiring the mediation of a more experienced practitioner. Its content is familiar, with discussions of rhythmic values (using both Kievan and Western oval notations); clefs (*kliavishi*), which are positioned on the staff and labeled with hexachordal syllables and pitch letters; rests; meter; and sharp and flat signs. There are four-part musical examples illustrating concords and cadences, tables showing the solmization syllables in *duliarnyi* and *bemmoliarnyi*, and excerpts apparently drawn from individual parts of existing *kontserty*.[154] The language of the *Nauka* thus comes from the same general circles as the language used by Diletskii and Korenev. Indeed the strongest ties may be between the *Nauka* and Korenev, in several ways. The *Nauka* not only uses the term *kliavish* in the sense that Korenev did in his first, 1671, version—that is, as indicating the layout of the hexachordal syllable–pitch letter gamut—but one specific passage in the *Nauka*, covering the "six-fold signs" and the beating of time with the hand (*takt*), is essentially identical in the two treatises (in this case, Korenev's revised music-theoretical presentation in the second version of his treatise).[155]

This blend of elements is reflected in the later circulation of these (and other) treatises, which seem in many cases to have been regarded as a flexible didactic unit, with pieces combined or eliminated as necessary. Diletskii's and Korenev's treatises tend to circulate as a pair; although Korenev's initial effort, *O penii bozhestvennom*, does circulate independently, the second version of Korenev's work rarely circulates without the *Grammatika*, suggesting that Korenev's own link to Diletskii's treatise prompted this pairing in the sources. Tikhon's treatise, as Brazhnikov notes, circulates frequently in mixed collections, in one case with excerpts from Korenev, and in several others, with the *Nauka*. Other treatises combine a reliance upon elements from the "big three" of late Muscovite theorists—Diletskii, Korenev, and Tikhon—with other sources of information, creating still broader rings of influence in later Russian music theory.[156]

One such mixed work, and one that allows us to trace Diletskii's influence quite clearly on later theoretical writing, is the *Kratkosobrannaia mussikiia* (A Brief Resume of Music), preserved in a mid-eighteenth-century manuscript source.[157] The treatise is aimed at beginning singers and provides exactly the sorts of information most useful to such a group: names of the six *noty, ut–la,* which are attached to the seven Latin letters; information on clefs; a relatively detailed discussion of rhythmic notation (especially rests); and a presentation of meter. The anonymous author uses terminology and concepts familiar from Diletskii's presentation: *kliavis* or *kliuch, takty, chvertki, polchvertki,* and so forth. The solmization syllables are joined to the seven letters in *duralnoe* or *prostoe penie* (without sharps or flats), and the author refers by name to the musical styles and genres with which Diletskii was occupied: *partesnoe penie* and *kontserty.* The work touches briefly on some topics relating to composition but it is primarily intended for beginners.[158]

Although the *Kratkosobrannaia mussikiia* invokes familiar theoretical language, the ways in which these concepts are presented indicate a real difference between the anonymous author's understanding of the underlying theoretical constructs and Diletskii's usage. This is most obvious in the ways in which the *Kratkosobrannaia mussikiia* employs the combinations of hexachordal syllables and pitch letter names. The author presents a series of octave scales beginning on G and running through successive pitches to the G an octave above, each illustrating the letter-syllable combination for each pitch in the scale. Unlike Diletskii's presentation, with its meticulously notated accidentals, the *Kratkosobrannaia mussikiia* includes no flats or sharps in this series of examples. For the anonymous author, the entire procedure was apparently mechanical, having lost any real connection to the interlocking sets of hexachordal syllables and their significance in determining the positioning of whole and half steps.[159]

The author does, however, acknowledge his indebtedness to the older writer, for he mentions Diletskii by name in a concluding note on the origin of the solmization syllables, invoking a still more ancient figure of authority (one to whom Diletskii himself also turned):

> At the end of Diletskii's *Music* it is written that the poet Boethius represented the six beginning musical notes by means of the following verse [in Cyrillic]:
>   *Liabiis ratus solve poliutis famuli puorum mia sanktorum retsitare ut kveant.*[160]

The author then provides "Diletskii's translation" of this text. As Protopopov points out, the *Kratkosobrannaia mussikiia* does indeed quote from Diletskii's presentation of the famous "Ut queant laxis" hymn, but presents it backwards. The author's source for the text seems to be the Moscow 1679 *Grammatika*. Although Diletskii presents the text in its proper order, this version of the *Grammatika* does include the same errors in transliterating the Latin text into Cyrillic and offers the same translation.[161] The author must have had available a copy of the Moscow 1679 *Grammatika* (in its entirety or in part) while compiling his own work; even in this mid-eighteenth-century source, Diletskii's name and work survive as acknowledged authorities.

But the author of the *Kratkosobrannaia mussikiia* had other sources at hand, as indicated by his reference to Guido of Arezzo ("Gvido Aretin monakh"). If one wonders why musicians use Latin letters for the names of the notes, he says, and not Hebrew or Greek or Russian letters, this is because they were invented by the monk Guido of Arezzo, who worked in Rome, he says, under Pope Benedict in 1202; this, he adds, is according to Baroni. Protopopov has identified this author as Cesare Baronius (1538–1617), whose *Annales ecclesiastici a Christo nato ad annum 1198* (issued in single volumes as they were finished by the author, beginning in Rome, 1588) has a long and rich tradition in the Muscovite context, with manuscript circulation extending from the early seventeenth century into the nineteenth century and a printed (abridged) edition from 1719. Baronius does mention Guido, under the (proper) date 1022, during the papacy of Benedict VIII, although he includes no specific theoretical information. By the mid-eighteenth century, Diletskii had thus taken his place, along with Guido and Boethius, as one of the standard musical authorities.[162]

Musical Hands and Musical Grammars

One of Diletskii's diagrams, the musical hand, provides an especially direct way to trace his influence throughout the eighteenth century and even into the early years of the nineteenth. In the *Grammatika,* the drawing of the musical hand is in the section headed "On a manner of teaching children," which appears in widely separated positions in the different versions of the treatise and is aimed at different audiences. The basic form of the diagram, however, is consistent in each of the three versions, where it is presented as a model for a five-line staff: "For the hand has five fingers, just as music [*musikiia*] has five lines or strings."[163] The accompanying drawing shows a left hand, tipped on its side, with a clef and letters entered on and between the fingers to illustrate how the notes fall on the lines and spaces of the staff (figure 5.4).

One mid-eighteenth-century copy of the *Grammatika* shows a special fascination with the musical hand, prefacing the text of the Smolensk 1677 *Grammatika*

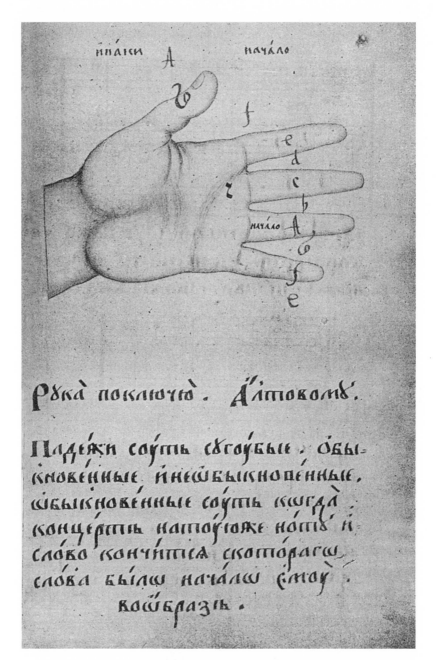

FIGURE 5.4. Diletskii, *Grammatika*, musical hand (RGB 146, p. 83, from OLDP Izdaniia 128, from the collection of the University of Washington)

with a series of more than forty hands meant to illustrate how to combine letters and solmization syllables in the four different systems (*kliuchi*) and in different clefs. These diagrams thus represent not only an expansion in sheer numbers over Diletskii's presentation but also contain more information than in their presentation in the *Grammatika*.[164] Another source from the early eighteenth century transmits a similarly comprehensive series of hands, in this case linking them to concepts and vocabulary drawn from chant theory. This source includes a somewhat more modest collection of twenty-three hands labeled according to vocal range, with letters and syllables written on and between the fingers. Melodic patterns entered on staves drawn in the palms of each hand also include solmization syllables. This manuscript continues with a section entitled "The birth of the Russian *soglasiia*," equating the hexachordal syllables to the Cyrillic letters of the *soglasie* system. It concludes with a *dvoznamennik*.[165]

Diletskii's musical hand naturally recalls the traditional Guidonian hand, which although devised to illustrate a different, equally practical musical task, might easily have served as a visual model for Diletskii or one of his contemporaries, searching for a way to explain the new staff notation to their students. There are also other, more direct possible models. One such possibility is a diagram of a hand used, like Diletskii's, as a model for the staff, in a Polish-language music treatise by Jan Aleksander Gorczyn (ca. 1618–after 1694). Gorczyn was a Cracow printer and publisher who wrote the *Tabulatura muzyki* (1647), an elementary music treatise and the first to be written by a Pole in the vernacular.[166]

The first two chapters of Gorczyn's treatise are devoted to definitions and classifications of music (divided, traditionally, into *muzyka choralna* and *figuralna*), clefs, solmization syllables, *ton* (the vocal ranges discant, alto, tenor, bass), and a thorough discussion of the staff and the effects of flats and sharps. The hand appears in the third chapter, headed "How to remember the scales of these voices on the fingers." The diagram is labeled "The *partes* on the discant hand" and shows a right hand tipped on its side, with the four fingers representing the lines and spaces of the staff. The lowest finger is marked with a C-clef and the pitch letters C–B are entered on the resulting lines and spaces. Gorczyn gives a thorough explanation of the position of the pitches on and between the fingers, starting at the bottom and moving up (figure 5.5).[167]

Diletskii says that he consulted many theoretical works, including Latin treatises and works associated with the Catholic church, in writing the *Grammatika*. His *Toga złota* shows that he was involved (or wished to be involved) with Polish-speaking circles in Vilnius, and his references to works by Mielczewski and Różycki, as well as some of the vocabulary he employs, indicates that he was

FIGURE 5.5. Gorczyn, *Tabulatura muzyki* (1647), musical hand (Polskie Wydawnictwo Muzyczne S. A., Cracow, used by permission)

familiar with the Polish-speaking musical world.[168] If Diletskii did seek out Western sources, he might have been drawn to a work such as Gorczyn's, written in an accessible language and compatible in its musical aims.

Muscovite sources, too, might have inspired Diletskii's musical hand (or at least reflect the same desire for immediately comprehensible analogies), along with the strong pictorial bent in Muscovite chant theory as a whole. The hand, for example, serves as a unifying theme for a rhetoric treatise written by one of the best-known teachers at the Kievan College. Stefan Iavorskii's *Ritoricheskaia ruka* (The Rhetorical Hand) was originally written in Latin and was translated into Slavic by Fedor Polikarpov in the early eighteenth century. Iavorskii's work appears to have been written during the author's tenure as professor of rhetoric at the College in 1690–91 and so would not have been a direct influence on Diletskii. The texts produced for such courses, however, frequently evolved from material the teachers themselves had covered as students, so the hand used as a teaching device in a rhetoric course might well have originated earlier. The title of Iavorskii's work derives from a picture of a hand, tipped on its side, on which each finger is labeled with one of the five fundamental elements of rhetoric. Each chapter in Iavorskii's treatise is labeled according to its subject finger; chapter two, for example, is called "The Second finger of the rhetorical hand: laying out a subject."[169] Diletskii uses the same term, *raspolozhenie,* to describe the laying out of a musical subject.

Diletskii's musical hand may represent the author's longest-lasting contribution to Russian music theory, for the diagram appears in several smaller-scale treatises, both published and in manuscript, from the second half of the eighteenth century (and, of course, the *Grammatika* itself was also copied throughout this time). Most of these later works refer also to Diletskii's primary organizing principle—the analogies between music and language as signaled by the *grammatika* of the title—suggesting a perhaps unexpectedly long-term humanistic context for music theory in Russia.

Diletskii's language, his emphasis on music and grammar, and his diagram of the hand appear in two works preserved in RGADA, f. 381, Nos. 1195 and 1474, from the second half of the eighteenth century. The longer of the two treatises (entered at the beginning of manuscript 1195) is an untitled anonymous work offering a brief summation of some fundamental rules of music. Although the author defines the work as a *grammatika,* emphasizing composition as the true center of music, he acknowledges that his rules are only an introductory guide to a deeper understanding of the subject. This short treatise lays out a system combining letters and hexachordal syllables grouped into three types of alphabets (*bukvari*), labeled according to the presence or absence of sharps and flats. This layout is familiar from the *Grammatika,* and the anonymous treatise also borrows Diletskii's concepts of happy and sad music. The work also includes a drawing of a hand, explaining that students might more easily comprehend the various hexachordal syllable–pitch letter combinations through analogy to the hand, which has five fingers and four spaces in between, just like the lines and spaces on a staff. The drawing shows a hand on which the pitches, reading from the bottom, are F *fa,* G

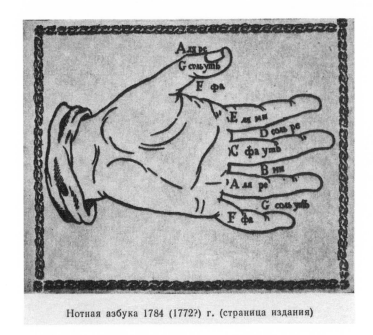

Нотная азбука 1784 (1772?) г. (страница издания)

FIGURE 5.6. *Azbuka* (issued by Synodal Press, 1784), musical hand (from Vol'man, *Russkie pechatnye noty XVIII veka,* following p. 32, from the collection of the University of Washington)

sol ut, A *la re,* and so forth, corresponding to the *duralnyi* alphabet that has just been presented. The author's setup for the hand, as a model for the lines and spaces of the staff, is thus like Diletskii's, but as in the other eighteenth-century examples it includes additional theoretical information.[170] This terminology is very similar to the language used in the second work in manuscript 1195, entitled *Azbuka nachalnago ucheniia* (An Elementary Alphabet); this treatise also appears twice in manuscript 1474.[171] The *Azbuka* does not include a drawing of a musical hand but a small engraved hand, with F *fa* on the lowest finger, is bound into manuscript 1474.

Both works reflect the singing practices of the Synodal choir. The *Azbuka* in both manuscript sources is inscribed by three people, the cleric Ivan Nikitin and singers Andrei Popov and Ivan Timofeev, who "verified these alphabets with the originals."[172] It is fairly easy to suggest a candidate for this original, for a booklet bearing the same title was published by the Synodal Press and is extant in a second edition from 1784. It is a small work, only four folios long, presenting familiar rhythmic terminology and the solmization syllables in a series of ascending and descending scalar patterns. The manuscript *Azbuki* correspond almost completely to the printed version.[173] The printed *Azbuka* also has a musical hand (figure 5.6),

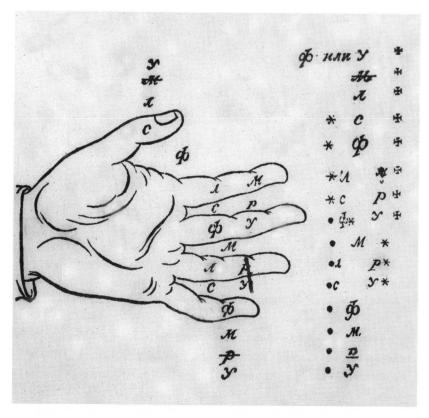

FIGURE 5.7. *Opyt irmoloinago peniia* (1798), musical hand (from the microfilmed series accompanying *Svodnyi katalog russkoi knigi grazhdanskoi pechati XVIII veka,* from the collection of the University of Washington)

which apart from its decorative border is the same as the engraved hand bound into manuscript 1474. The names in the inscriptions in the RGADA sources reveal a further link to the Synodal Press edition, for Nikitin and the two singers were among those primarily responsible for the Synod's ambitious publication of the liturgical service books in 1772.[174] The watermarks in the manuscript sources point to a date in the 1760s or 1770s, a time frame consistent with Vol'man's hypothesis that the first edition of the *Azbuka* dates from 1772, when the Synod published the complete set of service books. The work seems to have been popular and useful—there is a manuscript version of the treatise from the nineteenth century.[175]

The Synod's final music-theoretical publication of the century confirms both the continuity of some of Diletskii's basic terminology as well as the continuing appeal of the musical hand itself. The *Opyt irmoloinago peniia* (A Method of Irmologii Singing) was issued in 1798 and reprinted in 1801 as a practical guide for students. Although the work does not use Diletskii's system of *kliuchi,* it does employ familiar terminology in describing rhythm and it introduces the syllables *ut–la* to explain the three octaves (the middle octave, called the octave of the Irmologii, is the most commonly used; it overlaps with the upper and lower octaves). The musical hand illustrates the three overlapping octaves, which are labeled with pitch names on the fingers and with sets of hexachordal syllables to the side. The actual drawing of the hand in the *Opyt* resembles the other printed hands very closely, down to the details of the lines inscribed in the palm, although it encompasses a wider pitch range, with ledger lines entered above and below the fingers/lines (figure 5.7).[176]

Diletskii's treatise, like the inexhaustible waters of the sea of knowledge he so rapturously cites, is thus a document of broad resonance. It is not Muscovy's only music-theoretical treatise, but it represents an especially rich summary of the many trends and ideas of late seventeenth-century Russian music and culture, helping us to make sense not only of the many contexts for Muscovite music but of important currents in Western thinking as well. It is a work that was written to be used, to be wrestled with in the trenches of hands-on teaching and learning, and its usefulness is documented through the many copies that were produced for more than a century. The *Grammatika* was a product of a culture in transition, and its openness, its breadth of subject matter, and its willingness to borrow from many sources and disciplines is mirrored in another series of events taking place in Muscovy at very nearly the same time and which also involved a large musical component: the court theater of the early 1670s, the subject of our final chapter.

6

The Muscovite Court Theater

The evening of 17 October 1672 was an event to remember. This was the opening night of Moscow's first-ever court theater, and the production was a resounding success. The tsar watched from a seat placed in front-row center, his wife, Tsaritsa Natal'ia, observed from behind a screen, and the rest of the audience—high-ranking figures all—ranged themselves in unobtrusive positions behind the primary spectator; some of them may even have observed the proceedings from the stage itself. One of the people involved in the production was Laurent Rinhuber, who had come to Moscow several years earlier as an assistant to the tsar's Saxon physician. He described how Tsar Aleksei sat entranced throughout the ten-hour (!) performance, and added that it was this marvelous first impression that cemented the theater's success at the outset.[1] The theater continued, with new productions and encore performances of the older plays, until Aleksei's sudden death in January 1676. After this, the theater was disbanded and the equipment dispersed on the order of his son and successor, Fedor Alekseevich, who had no interest in continuing the productions. It was only in the reign of Peter the Great, several decades later, that the first public theater opened in Russia.

The Muscovite court theater of 1672–76 is the highlight of what has been called the renaissance of Tsar Aleksei Mikhailovich's last years. The plays, elaborate and increasingly secular, were the result of detailed and expensive planning and rehearsals, and they demonstrate the close ties between two familiar and inter-related circles in Moscow: Artemon Matveev's Diplomatic Chancellery, with its affiliated, often non-Muscovite staff, and the community of the capital's Foreign Quarter, the *Nemetskaia sloboda*. But the tsar's theatrical architects were also draw-ing upon long Muscovite traditions of theatrically presented liturgical dramas, declaimed poetry, and panegyrics. The court plays themselves, widely and pen-etratingly studied, begin with a series of biblical stories: Esther (in the play *Artak-serksovo deistvo* [The Play of Artaxerxes]), Judith, the Prodigal Son, the Fiery Furnace, and others; the plays also branch out into secular territory, with treat-ments of Bacchus and Venus and a setting of the historical story of Tamerlane.[2]

All the plays are full of musical references, and here too, the Muscovite plan-ners had broad experiences from which they must certainly have drawn, ranging from the musical tradition of genres such as Adam's Lament and other *stikhi* to the instrumental fanfares staged for visiting diplomats. No written music survives from the Muscovite theater, and perhaps none was ever written down, for there are no preserved references concerning copying or preparing music. Surviving rec-ords, however, do indicate the care Matveev and his subordinates took in attempt-ing to locate and hire the proper musicians for their theater and in acquiring appropriate instruments. Their assumptions and expectations concerning theatri-cal music and its realization thus fit readily into the continuum of Muscovite musical experiences.

Fish, Clouds, and Flying Horses: Antecedents to the Muscovite Court Theater

The scope of these experiences is suggested in a book by Jacob Reutenfels, who was a participant in some of the activities leading to the establishment of the theater and who recorded the events of his stay in Moscow in his *De rebus Moschoviticis* (Padua, 1680). Reutenfels's account of the Moscow premiere is the most extended preserved statement on the theatrical productions by a foreign observer, and his remarks give us a clue as to where to begin our examination of the Russian court theater:

> A few years ago he [Aleksei Mikhailovich] ordered the foreigners who lived in
> Moscow to put on a theatrical performance, comprised of dances and the story

of Ahasuerus [Artaxerxes] and Esther, presented comically. The fact is that hearing from many ambassadors that theatrical presentations were often given for European monarchs, with choruses and other amusements, in order to pass the time and disperse boredom, he, somewhat unexpectedly, ordered the presentation of a similar small production for himself, in the form of some sort of French dance ("specimen eius rei in tripudio aliquo Gallico"). For that reason, in view of the shortage of time, in one week with all possible haste everything necessary for the chorus was prepared. In any other place but Moscow, the performance would not have been able to be seen without anticipated apologies but to the Russians it appeared so unusual and artistic that everything—the new costumes, never seen before, the unfamiliar sight of the stage, even, finally, the word "foreign" and the graceful strains of the music—easily created a sense of wonder. At first, it is true, the tsar did not want to allow music as being new and in some ways pagan, but when they told him that without music it was impossible to put together a chorus, just as it is impossible for dancers to dance without legs, then he, a little unwillingly, left everything to the discretion of the actors themselves. With respect to the entire farce, the tsar sat before the stage proudly on his throne, the tsaritsa's and the royal children's place was through a lattice, or rather through a special slit marked out by boards, and the aristocracy (for no one else was admitted) stood on the stage itself. The celebratory verses, declaimed by Orpheus, before he began to dance between two moving pyramids, I find necessary to put down here, out of respect to the most honored Aleksei, although they were, actually, neither sonorous nor complex.[3] On that same day, Saturday in *maslenitsa* [Shrovetide], the tsar also organized a hunt on the Moscow River, which was frozen over, in which large dogs from England and other countries fought with Samoyed white bears. The spectacle was very entertaining because time and again they could not remain on their feet on the slippery ice. In the evening, the tsar went there to see fireworks.[4]

Reutenfels's description, although it may not be entirely accurate (it was written several years after the event), nevertheless reflects with some precision the conflicting impulses of Aleksei's character, the combination of curiosity and hesitation that indeed characterizes much of late Muscovite culture as a whole. A single word in Reutenfels's description, the reference to "pagan" instrumental music, brings a host of associations stretching, in the seventeenth century at least, back to the dramatic—one might even say theatrical—events associated with the False Dmitrii and the deaths of his musicians. We take our point of departure from Reutenfels's reference to those "many ambassadors" and begin by examining some of the proximate sources influencing Muscovite theatrical thinking. These various sources are not stepping stones we can use to trace a clear path to that grand opening night at Tsar Aleksei's court, but rather stages in a converging constellation of events, joined together by the common elements of curiosity about and exposure to Western practice, combined with strong existing traditions of public readings and staged pageantry. These theatrical pathways reflect the varied musical influences we have already seen, bringing them together in a package that itself represents a multitude of traditions.

Aleksei had shown some interest in plays and theatrical presentations in the decades preceding the establishment of the regular court theater. One path by means of which the court might have learned about such theatrical pastimes and about their suitability for royal entertainment was through the *kuranty,* the digest compilations of Western newspapers prepared by the Diplomatic Chancellery for the tsar and his advisors. The *kuranty,* as we have seen, are full of references to public music-making in parades, ceremonies, and processions. In several instances, however, they also transmit to their Russian court audience the language of Western theater. The *kuranty* report on a comedy (*komediia*) performed in Innsbruck in 1646 in honor of a royal wedding, and another account, from Nuremberg in May 1650, describes a comedy staged for royalty and diplomats to which fireworks and other amusements were added. A 1649 report from Denmark carefully describes a ballet performed for the rulers: "[T]he ambassador was at an entertainment called a ballet and the king himself and the queen were at this ballet and the ballet ran until six the next morning."[5]

Reports like this must have served only to reinforce what Muscovite diplomats themselves had long reported upon returning home from their assignments abroad. The Russian envoy to Elizabeth I, Grigorii Mikulin, had been royally entertained during his stay in London. At a state dinner he saw what appear to have been elaborate musical performances by the Children of the Chapel, whose "many players performed many pieces"; at that same dinner, apparently, the children also performed a traditional Twelfth Day carol. During the course of his visit, from May 1600 to July 1601, Mikulin also heard what another visitor, Virginio Orsino, Duke of Bracciano, described as "wondrous music" at the Queen's Chapel, which included organs and other instruments as well as singing.[6]

The Muscovite emissaries who went to Poland in 1635 for the signing of the eternal peace between the two countries also attended a dazzling church service, where music resounded from the four corners of the building. They then went to the king's banquet, similarly adorned with musical performances. The musical *pièce de résistance* came on the following day (April 24/May 4), when the Poles put on a theatrical entertainment for their guests, which included singing by an Italian castrato. The Russians identified this as a play on the story of Judith, which they called in their report an entertainment (*potekha*); a description by one of the

Polish attendees labels it an Italian comedy called a *recitativa*.[7] When two Russian emissaries went to Warsaw to bring gifts to the newly married Polish king a few years later, they attended a performance of an Italian opera on the subject of Daphne. The librettist was Virgilio Puccitelli, who worked for the court through the 1630s and 1640s. The composer is unknown, but was probably one of the several composers at the court during this period (Marco Scacchi, Kaspar Förster, Marcin Mielczewski, and Bartłomiej Pękiel).[8]

One of the most important Russian diplomatic accounts documents the extensive theatrical performances witnessed by Vasilii Likhachev, the tsar's emissary to Florence. Likhachev and a party of nearly thirty arrived in Italy in early January 1660 and, after making their way to Florence in the middle of the month, remained there for about four weeks. Their Florentine hosts arranged for a variety of diversions, ushering their guests through their many palaces, showing off their magnificent art collections, and taking them for carriage rides around the city (although the Russian party avoided visiting Catholic churches, with the exception of the chapel of San Lorenzo, which was not yet consecrated). They spent days engaged in such pleasures, including strolls through the Boboli gardens, where the Russians described in some detail the fragrant cedar and cypress trees, the fruit trees, the exotic fish, and, most astonishing, the complete lack of snow (in January!). They also heard music in the gardens: "[T]here were many performances [or playing; *igr*"], *organy, kimvaly,* and music. And other people played the organs but no one set them in motion. And it is hard to describe this differently, because no one who did not see this can understand it." At a lavish banquet held on 20 January, which featured huge confectionary double-headed eagles studded with gems, the Muscovites were also treated to performances of instrumental music. Following a series of toasts to the members of the Russian royal family, "at that time they played [instrumental] music ('po muzyke') and *kimvaly* and *organy,* and [there were] two trumpets and eight instrumentalists [*vosem' gudtsov*]."[9]

The best was yet to come, for the Florentines, who seemed to take great delight in displaying their treasures and arranging excursions for their wide-eyed guests, also showed them a grand theatrical entertainment. Likhachev was astonished at the scenic spectacle he witnessed—flying horses, oceans, battles!—and described it carefully in his report. The production seems to have been marvelous and overwhelming; one senses the author struggling to find language with which to express the events he witnessed. For example, the official account uses the word *palaty* (chambers or rooms) to describe theatrical sets or stages, which must indeed have appeared to the visitors as a series of small, ever-changing rooms. The spectacle was lavish, employing the traditional and considerable staging effects of seventeenth-century Italian theater. Likhachev notes that it cost 8,000 *efimki* (silver thalers) and that a similar comedy had been given as a present to the Spanish king, in honor of the birth of a son—in other words, the Muscovites were honored by an appropriate, and appropriately costly, production:

> The prince ordered the entertainment to start and chambers appeared and [first] there was one chamber, which then sank out of sight, and in this manner there were six changes [of scenery]; and in those chambers the ocean appeared, disturbed by waves, and there were fish in the sea and people rode on the fish, and at the top of the chamber was the sky and people sat on the clouds. And the clouds with the people on them sank down, and they grabbed a man on the earth under his arms, and they went back up again. And the people sitting on the fish also rose up to the sky after them. And then a man sitting in a carriage was lowered from the sky, and across from him in another carriage there was a beautiful maiden, and the valuable horses beneath the carriages moved their legs as if they were alive. And the prince said that one represented the sun and the other, the moon.
>
> And in a different scene ("v inoi peremene"), in the chamber there appeared a field full of human bones, and blackbirds flew in and started pecking at the bones. And then the sea appeared in the chamber and on the sea were small ships and people inside were sailing [them].
>
> And in a different scene, there appeared fifty men in armor; they started fighting with sabers and swords and they shot from firearms and it was as if three men were shot. And young men and girls came out from behind the golden curtain and danced and did many marvelous things.[10]

The Italian summary of these events is far more laconic, listing a "comedie" along with "i calci divisi" (apparently some sort of gymnastic routines, which might explain the "many marvelous things" enacted by the young men and women at the end of the show). According to the Italian account, the performance took place in the Pitti Palace, which the ambassadorial party also visited on their departure from the city.[11]

Who could resist such an event and such a description? Likhachev and his party arrived back in Moscow in early June 1660.[12] Later that month, the court sent agent John Hebdon (Ivan Gebdon) to the Netherlands and London with commissions to purchase important supplies for the Muscovite military and to hire all kinds of craftsmen and specialists: glazers, builders, translators, clockmakers, and many others. Among these necessary personnel was an unsurprising musical category, for the tsar instructed Hebdon to scout out "royal trumpeters and percussionists" ("trub i litavr korolevskikh"). Another category of skilled craftsmen on the tsar's list, however, is far more interesting. Hebdon's assignment also included, in a notation believed to be in Aleksei's own hand, a request to find "masters to stage a comedy" ("*masterov komediiu delat*'"). (The tsar's hand also appears in another annotation, requesting other "people who play the trumpet" in addition to the royal fanfare musicians listed above.) The tsar's explicit interest in comedies, coming as it does hard on the heels of Likhachev's return, strongly suggests that this desire to witness theatrical productions was influenced by Likhachev's fantastic experiences in Florence. Interest in court theater appears to have come from the very top.[13]

The curiosity at the highest levels seems to have been infectious, and perhaps led to a certain spirit of freedom and exploration on the part of the tsar's ambassadors. Another Muscovite emissary, Petr Potemkin, also took the opportunity to see Western theatrical spectacle at first hand. Potemkin, who enjoyed a long and important diplomatic career, was sent to Spain and France in 1667–68 as part of the tsar's effort to create an alliance against the Ottoman Turks and to inform Western leaders about the 1667 peace treaty between Poland and Muscovy, resolving, finally, a conflict that had spanned the century. This was the first official embassy from the tsar to the Spanish court, and the Muscovite party traveled widely through Spain during the first half of 1668. They toured palace buildings and gardens in Seville, Madrid, and other major cities, and Potemkin's official report makes several brief references to various entertainments (*potekhi*) they witnessed, including visits to the theatrical halls at the Palacio Real during an audience with the young king, Charles II. Their trip, however, fell within the nearly five-year ban on theatrical performances following the death of Philip IV in 1665, and it appears that they saw no large-scale play or theatrical production during their stay.[14]

The Muscovite visitors were luckier in their next destination: Paris. During their stay in the French capital, Potemkin's party attended, with great fanfare, a production of *Les Coups d'amour et de fortune* at the Théâtre du Marais, and they saw the Molière company perform *Amphitryon*. The Sieur de Catheux, who was responsible for overseeing the Muscovite mission in Paris, described the elaborate proceedings in his own account, beginning on 6/16 September 1668:

> On the sixteenth the Ambassador, his son, the Chancellor, and all their entourage attended the performance of the comedy *Les Coups de la fortune*, performed by the Marais troupe with set-changes and ballet entrées, which they greatly enjoyed. They requested some wine, which was brought to them. On the eighteenth the troupe of Sieur de Molière performed *Amphitryon* with machines and ballet entrées, which greatly pleased the Ambassador and his son.[15]

Other French sources corroborate Catheux's description and provide additional details showing that the Russian visitors witnessed the full panoply of French theatrical entertainment. The gazetteer Charles Robinet, for example, says that in addition to their visit to Molière's theater, the Russians saw Fiorilli's *commedia dell'arte* company perform (they shared the Théâtre du Palais-Royal with Molière's actors) and that the Troupe du Roi performed *Amphitryon* with "ample collation, pas de ballet, & symphonie."[16]

Potemkin's spirit of freedom, however, apparently had its limits, for he passed over this and several other sightseeing tours of the city in his own official report, and his theatrical excursions are known only through Catheux's journal entries. In spite of this reticence, however, it is difficult to believe that the ambassador's sampling of the delights of Parisian theater remained entirely unknown to his interested superiors back home, and his experiences certainly reinforce Likhachev's account of his own wondrous visions in Florence.[17] As Reutenfels said, Tsar Aleksei would indeed have had plenty of opportunity to learn of Western theatrical practice from his ambassadors.

Foreign ambassadors visiting Muscovy would also have contributed to this knowledge. Many European embassies brought their own musicians with them to Moscow, as we saw in chapter 4, primarily trumpeters to sound out during the elaborate ceremonies accompanying their entrance into the capital, and Russian embassies abroad did the same. The 1663–64 mission headed by Charles Howard, first Earl of Carlisle, however, went beyond traditional pomp and fanfare. The English mission included a music master, six musicians, and two trumpeters in their party, and Guy Miege's account describes how some of these musicians might have helped to entertain their fellow travelers. After arriving in Moscow, members of the Carlisle embassy found their activities and their access to important court figures severely restricted, and they turned to other means to pass the time until summoned for official business. Hunting, which had been a favorite pastime as the party whiled away the winter in the town of Vologda, was not possible in the capital, but at their residence in Moscow the Englishmen "fell immediately to making of Horse-matches" and got up a twelve-member team "to play at Football." They also turned to theatrical entertainment. "Our Musique-master," reports Miege, "composed a handsome Comedie in Prose, which was acted in our House."[18] Miege does not say that any Muscovite officials were present, although one might assume, given the English party's complaints about their heavy restrictions and supervision, that their actions were not unknown to their Russian hosts. Indeed, Miege specifies that earlier, in Vologda, their dinner music by trumpets and viols, "being managed by one of the best experienced Musicians of England," drew crowds of Russian spectators. "Our dancing also [in Vologda], which the Ambassador used sometimes upon occasion of this Musique, was no less admired by them, who in their Dances knew nothing but brutish and uncomely Postures."[19] Perhaps such casual mixing was possible only in the looser atmosphere outside the capital. At any rate, the specifics of the private "handsome Comedie" probably had little or no impact on the later Muscovite court theater, but its existence and its suitability as high-level entertainment most likely did. Carlisle's wife accompanied him to Moscow and would surely have enjoyed the performance along with the rest of the party, perhaps also signaling that such amusements were appropriate for genteel women as well as men.[20]

The tsar himself is said to have attended private theatrical performances held in the home of Artemon Matveev, head of the Diplomatic Chancellery, and these performances have been cited as the direct inspiration for the formation of the court theater.[21] We know little about such performances. Matveev was linked to "comedies"—or perhaps more accurately, had evidence of such reprehensible activities flung in his face—by Archpriest Avvakum in the mid-1660s. The two men had met in a fruitless attempt by the government to persuade the unpersuadable priest to tone down his rhetoric and cease his criticism of the official church. One of the issues Avvakum raised with Matveev was the fact that new and additional supporters of Latin (that is, Western, non-Russian, non-Orthodox) ways were increasing in Moscow, and that they were promoting the performance of comedies. It is not clear what kinds of performances Avvakum had in mind. There is no evidence of plays being performed at court in the 1660s, and Matveev himself, although a close and long-standing friend of the tsar and the royal family, was not at that time the dominant political and cultural figure he would become after Aleksei's second marriage in 1671. One wonders if Avvakum might have been thinking of the series of declamations presented at court by Polotskii and his students, which were popular with the tsar during these years; indeed, Polotskii accompanied Matveev on his visit to Avvakum.[22] Perhaps Avvakum raised the issue at this meeting because he knew of Matveev's interest in things foreign and, as it would turn out, his particular interest in Western-style theatrical works. Later references to Matveev's private performances, whatever they may have been, seem to center on the figure of Vasilii Repskii, a singer and instrumentalist whose story, even incompletely understood, links music and theater even more closely to the circles of the Diplomatic Chancellery and to Matveev himself.[23]

Vasilii Repskii, mentioned earlier as one of the many Ukrainian *vspevaki* brought to Moscow, began his service as a singer but moved to other kinds of activities, in particular studying Latin with Simeon Polotskii along with several other students.[24] In late 1668, Repskii and his fellow students accompanied the Muscovite diplomatic mission to the Baltic Duchy of Courland headed by Afanasii Lavrent'evich Ordin-Nashchokin, Matveev's powerful predecessor at the Diplomatic Chancellery. Although the mission failed in its diplomatic purpose (neither Poland nor Sweden, the two invited parties, showed up), one assumes that Repskii and the others would have been exposed to at least some degree to the ceremonial culture of the ducal court, including its music, an important consideration as Courland provided Muscovy with theatrical musicians a few years later. Ordin-Nashchokin remained in Courland until being recalled in early 1669; it is not known for how long Repskii stayed.[25]

After his return to Moscow, Repskii went to Izmailovo to study painting ("v zhivopistsekh") and *perspektivy* with a foreigner, Peter Engels, who also worked on the court theater's productions later. The term *perspektivy* was used to indicate theatrical decorations, and Repskii himself makes this connection, testifying that he did *perspektivy* and other tasks relating to theatrical productions for three years, which would coincide with the first year or two of the tsar's theater.[26] It was this artistic work that drew Matveev's attention.

Repskii's fate then takes a dramatic turn, for while in Matveev's employ, he signed (willingly or not) papers redefining his status as a legal bondsman, an onerous duty that included performances on musical instruments in connection with some sort of theatrical performances. Repskii describes it as follows in his 1676 petition, addressed to Tsar Fedor Alekseevich:

> And seeing, Lord, my knowledge and study, boyar Artemon Sergeevich Matveev took me unwillingly by force to court and held me, Your servant, confined to the Diplomatic Chancellery in chains ("skovana . . . v zhelezakh") for a long time and starved me nearly to death. And, Lord, when I was with him, at his command I played the organ and violin many times against my will at comedies ("na komediiakh na arganakh i na skrypkakh igral nevoleiu").[27]

The instruments Repskii lists are exactly the sorts assembled for the court productions, and we know that Repskii had musical training, so this particular use (or misuse) of his talents seems beyond question. His forced performances were not at Matveev's home, however, but at the Diplomatic Chancellery, one of two venues used for teaching and rehearsing the plays.[28] Although Repskii's sad tale dramatically illustrates Matveev's vigilance in acquiring trained personnel for theatrical entertainments, it is difficult to read this particular petition as providing irrefutable proof of private performances in Matveev's own home. Nevertheless,

Repskii's career demonstrates that Matveev and the other planners had plenty of resources at their disposal when embarking on their new enterprise. In addition to his experiences with Repskii, we know that Matveev had access to other musicians at this time (possibly his own, possibly those at court), and he knew about and was able to commandeer the large organ belonging to the foreigner Hasenkruch, who was also involved in the court productions.[29]

Orpheus in Muscovy

All of these various influences come together in what appears to be the most direct and immediate spur to Aleksei's theater: a Moscow entertainment involving the character Orpheus. Reutenfels hints at the existence of such a performance, casually mentioning the character Orpheus in his passage, quoted above at greater length, on the court theater: "The celebratory verses, declaimed by Orpheus, before he began to dance between two moving pyramids, I find necessary to put down here, out of respect to the most honored Aleksei, although they were, actually, neither sonorous nor complex." Reutenfels continues by saying that "[o]n that same day, Saturday in *maslenitsa*, the tsar also organized a hunt on the Moscow River."

This frustratingly laconic reference has become enshrined in histories of Russian music. Nikolai Findeizen's account is both typical and influential: "[A]t Aleksei Mikhailovich's court, a complete work by a foreign master was performed, namely, the ballet *Orpheus and Euridice,* staged in Moscow at the end of Carnival week in 1673." Findeizen goes on to identify the piece as being composed by Heinrich Schütz, with text by the Wittenberg professor August Buchner, performed in Dresden in 1638.[30] What, then, was Orpheus doing in Muscovy, when was this work performed, and is it possible that this was really a production of the nearly fifty-year-old Schütz ballet (now lost)?

Using Reutenfels's account, scholars have proposed a variety of dates for the Orpheus performance, ranging generally between 1673 and 1675, that is, in the mid-to-late period of the theater's brief existence. If these dates are correct, Orpheus would be simply one more among the increasingly varied productions at Tsar Aleksei's theater.[31] Apart from Reutenfels's rather confusing passages on dancing and Orpheus, other references to ballets or to dancing appear in Russian theatrical documents between January 1673 and January 1676. Supplies for "four *balety*" are included in a long accounting of items purchased for the theatrical performances in January 1673. On 9/19 December 1674, Hermann Dietrich Hesse, who had remained behind in Moscow in order to learn Russian after his embassy returned to Prussia, mentioned a ballet and two comedies, one on the story of Judith (by Polish youngsters) and one about Esther (by German youngsters) performed for the tsar over the past three weeks. In January 1676 there are more detailed references to dancing, costumes, and dance instruction.[32]

Sources from Scandinavian archives, however, suggest that Orpheus actually *preceded* the formation of the court theater and may in fact have been the final catalyst for its formation.[33] These sources, in their turn, present difficulties in dating but taken as a whole, and in connection with Reutenfels's account, they suggest a new and formative role for Orpheus in Muscovy.

We begin with two securely dated sources preserving identical texts. These are enclosures in larger packets sent by the Swedish agent in Moscow, Simon Grundel Helmfelt. One is from Helmfelt to King Charles XI, in which the enclosure is dated Moscow, 13 February, inside a larger packet dated 29 February 1672; the other is to the Swedish official Bengt Horn, in which the enclosure is also dated Moscow, 13 February, sent inside a larger packet dated Narva, 1 March 1672.[34] Both sources refer to "Butterwoche" and continue on, describing an unnamed ballet being organized by Matveev with foreign residents; they also describe other festivities associated with *maslenitsa,* including fireworks, bears, and additional entertainments. *Maslenichnaia subbota* (the Saturday of *maslenitsa,* before the beginning of Lent) was on 17 February in 1672, and because of the long tradition of celebration, including masking and role-playing, associated with this period, a theatrical performance would make a great deal of sense for this time of year. Helmfelt's descriptions should certainly be taken at face value.[35]

The other Scandinavian source, far richer in its information on the Orpheus production, is also from Helmfelt. It too is an enclosure in a larger packet, this one dated Narva, 29 December 1671. The enclosure is labeled "Extract schreiben von Moscow" and carries a notation in a different hand explaining that it is an addition (*bilag*) to the December report; it has no internal date of its own.[36] This "Extract" includes a long description of a "ballet" entertainment that includes Orpheus among its cast of characters, the whole enterprise supervised by Matveev and performed by foreigners.

There are several key points one might glean from Helmfelt's "Extract" and these, in turn, help us to clarify some of the puzzles of the Reutenfels account. It appears likely that the undated "Extract" has been misfiled and belongs instead to the February 1672 time frame, along with the two short, dated enclosures described above.[37] In the "Extract," for example, Helmfelt identifies the general time period as "in dieser Fastenzeit," with a date of the twenty-sixth of an unnamed month.

There is no particular reason he should be reporting on pre-Lenten activities in December (and this date falls outside the Nativity fasting period), but every reason to suggest that his description, which matches so closely the references to "Butter-woche" in the two dated enclosures, relates to the same pre-Lenten celebrations of February 1672. Helmfelt's dated enclosures from 13 February are brief, suggesting a quick mention of events which are to take place in the near future. The "Extract" appears to complete this process, describing in some detail a performance that had just occurred; again, a proposed date in February 1672 makes far more sense than the December 1671 date of the handwritten notation. Finally, a quick sentence in the midst of his description of the performance settles the matter. Here, in a casual aside, Helmfelt notes that on the next day ("Dass andern morgens") the patriarch died. Patriarch Iosif died on 17/27 February 1672, which would correspond to Helmfelt's "next day," that is, the day after the performance on the twenty-sixth. It therefore seems reasonable to conclude that all three accounts describe the same event, which took place in connection with *maslenitsa* in February 1672.

This interpretation allows us to make some sense of Reutenfels's account, presented in full at the beginning of this chapter. Reutenfels clearly begins by describing the Esther play, but he then mentions the mystifying presence of the character Orpheus dancing between moving pyramids and declaiming a poetic text. Orpheus obviously has no business appearing in the biblical story of Esther, with or without pyramids; indeed, only the first line of Reutenfels's description seems to apply to the Esther play, with the rest describing the groundwork for the separate Orpheus production.[38] Reutenfels was in Moscow at the time of this proposed dating of the Orpheus performance, in February 1672, but he left before the premiere of *The Play of Artaxerxes,* which took place in the fall of that year. After leaving Russia, he went first to Rome and then to Florence, where he wrote his book-length description of the Russian state for Cosimo III, which was completed before 1680 (the book was published in that year, after the manuscript was discovered in Cosimo's library by a visitor). Although Reutenfels had not seen the Esther play, he might have found a reliable source of information about the event in the figure of Laurent Rinhuber, who had also been in Moscow at the time of the Orpheus production and who had been heavily involved in the much more complex preparations for the full-length play. Rinhuber had left Moscow with the Menzies mission immediately after the Esther premiere and, after two intervening trips back to Russia, he too eventually found his way to Florence, arriving there probably by late 1678 and apparently staying for some time—both men, therefore, were in Tuscany at the end of the 1670s.[39]

In Reutenfels's famous description of the Muscovite theatrical pastimes, then, there seem to be references to two different productions using two kinds of information: Reutenfels's own first-hand account of the Orpheus performance, and what appears to be a second-hand description (possibly via Rinhuber) of the Esther play. Both productions were under Matveev's direction, at least one of the performers appeared in both presentations, and both included music in a richly decorated setting attended by the highest ranks at court. It is easy to see why Reutenfels, several years after the event, might have generalized.

Reutenfels mentions *maslenitsa* (*bacchanalia*) immediately following his reference to Orpheus and the poetic declamations, describing the bear fights on the frozen Moscow River later in the day and the fireworks that evening. Helmfelt's "Extract" also mentions fireworks and bears.[40] Even Reutenfels's description of the special enclosed viewing area for the tsaritsa and the royal children matches the description in Helmfelt's "Extract." This construction may indeed have been used in the court theater's productions, but Helmfelt describes a similar setup in connection with Orpheus. Finally, placing the Orpheus production in February might also explain Reutenfels's insistence on the hasty preparations for the spectacle, which, he says, took only one week. The preparations for the court theater itself were detailed, expensive, and time-consuming, involving several months of well-documented work. The arrangements for the foreigners' production in February would certainly not have been nearly as extensive, even if they did take longer than the single week Reutenfels stipulates.

Helmfelt's "Extract" describes a lavish affair produced at the Miloslavskii residence (the home of the late tsaritsa's family; her father had died in 1668 and Helmfelt refers to the tsar's mother-in-law's home).[41] He calls it a ballet, and says it was attended by the tsar, his wife, and their children, along with a group of retainers, including women, who watched by peering through openings in some sort of partitions. Helmfelt himself attended with a group of visitors. The tsar, Helmfelt emphasizes, was in a jolly mood ("lustige humeur"), and the royal audience sat for more than three hours "with the greatest enjoyment." The decorations were lavish: green hangings decorated with gold leather, tapestries, a large mirror, elaborate costumes, and other costly ornaments. The evening's entertainment was performed by a group of foreigners, all of whom served the tsar in varying capacities, including Dr. Rosenberg and his two sons; Trautenberg and his students; a Herr Leutinant and his students; C. Rodan; Kantenberg; and Hasenkruch. The last-named is especially important, for he was also involved in the later court theater, as was one of Dr. Rosenberg's sons. Hasenkruch's role as "ein artiger Pikelherung" (Pickleherring) refers to a stock comic character popular from the

German stage (although ultimately originating with the traveling English acting companies that toured the continent in the early seventeenth century). Pickleherring was traditionally associated with music, and we know from later documents that Hasenkruch had some musical connections, so this may have been a good role for him. Both the character and the choice of player thus derive naturally from the experiences and abilities of the German cast.[42] Pickleherring was the hit of the evening, and the tsar "laughed a great deal" over his antics; indeed, Helmfelt says that the audience "shook noticeably with laughter" at the performance.

Helmfelt also names some of the other characters in the evening's entertainment: Mercury, who was costumed with wings at his head and feet; Orpheus; "ein Moohr"; "ein Jäger"; and others. He does not mention pyramids of any sort, although he does refer to Mercury standing in front of a realistic green mountain, which stood in front of a two-headed red painted eagle; the whole was illuminated effectively and, as Helmfelt says, "it was truly amusing and all was done with great success." Reutenfels's pyramids thus unfortunately remain a mystery.

The ballet also featured music. Heinrich Munter sang a newly composed song, accompanied by viola da gamba, which Helmfelt praises as being quite beautiful, and the production also had music by two viols and flutes (including transverse flutes). There was also some sort of silhouette presentation ("Schattenwerk"), which Helmfelt says was very amusing. The tsar would happily have seen more, Helmfelt reports, but there was "no more to present." "Thank God," he concludes, "that his Majesty and the others were so pleased." After the tsar departed, the audience was thanked by Artemon Sergowitz (Matveev), who was already busy trying to arrange a second performance.[43]

The music, the comic antics of Pickleherring, and the elaborate sets and stage decorations obviously needed no translation in order to appeal to the royal Russian audience, but how might they have understood the role of Orpheus? To the foreign performers, the Orpheus theme would have seemed natural in the context of an evening of musical entertainment, and there are many ways in which the Muscovite audience, too, might have made such a connection. A few years before the Orpheus of Helmfelt's account, for example, Simeon Polotskii invoked the figure in his *Orel rossiiskii* (1667). In this work, as we saw in chapter 5, Polotskii listed a constellation of figures from Greek mythology and history, among them not only the musician (*igrets*) Orpheus, but also Ovid, who tells the tale in his *Metamorphoses*. Polotskii would certainly have learned Greek history and mythology in his studies in Kiev; if the details of the story were hazy, he might have checked the copy of Ovid's work in his personal library collection.[44]

Other sources also carried the legend to Muscovy. Orpheus was known generally as a foreign musician in the many *azbukovniki,* the dictionaries that circulated in Muscovy throughout the seventeenth century. In two such sources he was identified specifically as a Thracian *gusli* player.[45] The Orpheus legend was also known in court circles close to the time of the foreign production. Nikolai Spafarii mentions Orpheus as a musician in his book on the seven liberal arts (1672), a copy of which was produced for Tsar Aleksei's collection. There is no evidence that Spafarii was active in the production of the Muscovite Orpheus or in the court theater, but Spafarii and Polotskii knew each other (indeed, Spafarii seems to have come to the attention of the court after an impromptu debate with several learned figures, including Polotskii).[46] Ioannikii Korenev's *O penii bozhestvennom* also dates from this time (1671), and he too includes a passing reference to Orpheus as an example of a Greek musician. He also includes Amphion as another musical figure from the ancient world, and as we have seen, both names appear in Nikolai Diletskii's 1679 *Grammatika.*[47]

Although none of these references offers any details about the Orpheus legend, taken as a whole they indicate that the court audience would probably have recognized the character on stage. Indeed, this may have been the *only* Muscovite audience for which this production would have made any sense at all. As Max Okenfuss observes, this is precisely the milieu in which knowledge of characters such as Orpheus and writers such as Ovid circulated in Muscovy: among non-Russian Orthodox (figures such as Polotskii, Repskii, and Spafarii), and among the Diplomatic Chancellery circles centering around Matveev.[48] These, of course, are the very groups responsible for the formation of the court theater only a few months later.

If Orpheus has at least a tentative toehold in Muscovite court culture through these literary and theatrical productions, there remains a final element that would link this performance directly to the larger circles of Western theatrical traditions. Does Helmfelt's "Extract" describe a Moscow production of the lost Schütz ballet?

Schütz's work was written for the wedding of the Saxon Electoral Prince Johann Georg II to Princess Magdalene Sibylle of Brandenburg, which took place on 14 November 1638, and the ballet was one of several presented a few days later. August Buchner was the librettist and his text is the only surviving remnant of the production.[49] On the surface, it would seem highly unlikely that this ballet was somehow transported, in toto, to Moscow and performed by amateur foreign actors for the Russian court, and there is simply not enough evidence, either from the German or the Muscovite side, to suggest that this did indeed happen. Helmfelt's description paints a picture rather of a succession of performances or skits involving different combinations of characters and talents. (The two productions do have at least two characters in common, Orpheus and Mercury, but one assumes that these two characters might easily appear in unrelated stagings based in some fashion on the Orpheus legend.)

There are, nevertheless, interesting links between the productions. Even if the Moscow Orpheus is not a reproduction of Schütz's ballet, it certainly has a context beyond the confines of the tsar's court. Both were intended for special festivities and it may be that apart from its comfortable place in the context of traditional *maslenitsa* entertainment, the Moscow Orpheus was staged in honor of the first anniversary of Tsar Aleksei's second marriage, to Natal'ia Naryshkina (they had been married on 22 January 1671). As the *kuranty* show, the Russian court was certainly aware of the Western custom of celebrating weddings with elaborate theatrical presentations.

The poetry preserved from the Dresden and Moscow productions shows Orpheus's links to both Muscovite and Western practice. Reutenfels includes the German text of Orpheus's verses, which were uttered before the pyramid dance (both the tsar and the pyramids are mentioned in the text), although it is not clear exactly where in the production these verses would have appeared. It is difficult to find anything comparable in Buchner's surviving libretto, although there is a final chorus, sung by a choir of shepherds and nymphs, wishing long and successful rule to the newlyweds, who are mentioned by name in the text. Such a vague topical similarity seems unremarkable; both poems were appropriately designed to celebrate and honor their royal viewers. Verses of this type would have been familiar to Matveev and the rest of the court from their long acquaintance with Polotskii's orations and other readings—although the poem in Rinhuber would have been remarkable for its apparent performance in German—yet such verses would have been equally familiar to the German cast through their similar experiences with the same sorts of celebratory poems and performances at home. There are also Saxon connections (and lots of them) to the tsar's theater. Pastor Johann Gregorii, for example, who wrote the earliest plays for the Russian court, was in Dresden in 1661–62 and again in 1667, and other Saxons involved in the court theater or in the Orpheus show include Rinhuber, the family of the court physician Dr. Blumentrost, and others.[50] While it seems very unlikely that the Moscow Orpheus represented a wholesale (or even partial) reproduction of the Schütz ballet, musical score and all, on Russian soil, one might easily appreciate that the foreign cast brought their understanding and experiences of German theatrical and performance traditions to the tsar and his court (as in the case of the Pickleherring character, for example). The blend was obviously successful, for preparations for the permanent, if ultimately brief, court theater began just after the curtain fell on Orpheus's Moscow debut.

The Moscow Orpheus, then, represents a crucial step among the many that came together to form Aleksei Mikhailovich's court theater of 1672–76. The production was a logical extension of the Muscovite government's continuing interest in the entertainments of their royal brethren in the West and their decade-long efforts to hire musicians, producers, and actors from abroad. Work on the production gave Matveev a chance to become acquainted more closely with the resident foreigners in the capital, and, judging from Helmfelt's account, Matveev was already working the crowd immediately following the hugely successful evening of entertainment. He certainly realized a good thing when he saw it, and the royal family shaking with laughter and clamoring for more was definitely a good thing. This collaboration with the foreign residents of Moscow jumped into high gear several months later with preparations for *The Play of Artaxerxes.*

The Impresario: Artemon Matveev and the Musical Preparations for the Theater

For the second phase of the Muscovite theater, the productions staged for the court between October 1672 and January 1676, we are fortunate to possess extensive documentation describing the preparations for the performances, in addition to the accounts by Rinhuber and Reutenfels. These records, published as a group by Sergei Bogoiavlenskii, provide many clues about the theater's vocal and instrumental music. Indeed, in the absence of any notated musical sources from the theater, these documents, along with the play texts themselves, must serve as our primary guide to the kinds of music the tsar and his court might have heard.[51]

Matveev was the court theater's impresario, issuing orders and keeping tabs on every aspect of the effort, both at home and abroad. He had dispatched Col. Nicholas von Staden to Western Europe on a mission to recruit theatrical specialists and other skilled workers, and Staden sent back frequent reports detailing his progress (or lack thereof). Matveev's deep involvement may have derived from his earlier success with the Orpheus evening; at any rate, outsiders remarked on his dual role as the chief political as well as the chief artistic advisor to the court. Mons Giøe, a Danish diplomat in Moscow in the early 1670s, mentioned in a report from November 1672 (a few weeks after the theater's premiere performance) that Matveev was responsible for maintaining order among the young actors: "Since they have recovered from the fear the Turks inspired in them, the most important occupation of this first minister is to produce comedies, even appearing in the theater himself, in order to maintain discipline among the children who are performing."[52]

The published theatrical documents begin in May 1672. The earliest, from 10 May, concerns provisions to be sent to the projected theater site and, as Bogoiavlenskii observes, suggests that the preparations actually had begun a bit earlier.[53] The next document, from 15 May, orders Staden to go abroad to find various specialists willing to work in Muscovy: those knowledgeable about ores and mining; two excellent and learned horn players; and two people who "know how to put on all kinds of comedies."[54] This first list is much the same as those given earlier to John Hebdon, with requests for assorted specialists, including horn players, who are not linked explicitly to the theater. Staden was ordered to begin his search in Courland and, if he could find no suitable candidates there, to go on to Sweden and Prussia. At about the same time, the tsar's agents were working in Moscow to find someone who would be able to produce a play. Pastor Gregorii's contract, to write a play on the Esther story, is dated 4 June.[55] Apparently Staden's specialists were not considered indispensable and, as it turned out, the musicians Staden did eventually hire arrived in Moscow only after the first performances had taken place.

On 18 July 1672 Staden wrote to Matveev from Riga, saying that he had not found any trumpeters, although he had offered a great deal of money, but that he had found two musicians who had only recently learned their instruments but could play various songs and might also teach others, whereas real, full-fledged trumpeters did not teach at all. Staden's reference to full-fledged or complete trumpeters ("polnye trubachi") may be to the strictly ordered music guilds set up in Riga in the seventeenth century. Staden would thus have been unable to find a guild member to come to Muscovy, but he did succeed in finding musicians not associated with the guild.[56] Staden continues his report to Matveev, saying that the two musicians, in addition to their salary of six rubles per month, were also to have permission to play wherever else in Moscow they wished (implying that there were indeed other venues in Moscow that the musicians considered, or at least hoped to be, lucrative). This guarantee was given to other musicians Staden hired later, and it confirms the suggestion that Moscow's Foreign Quarter was not a primary source of instrumental talent for the theater.[57] Finally, Staden explicitly links the musicians to the theater in this report, saying that the two trumpeters were well-suited as actors ("a k komediantom one gorazdo godny"). Staden also noted his success in hiring (non-trumpet-playing) actors. In later reports, the number of actors fluctuates; ultimately he failed to bring back any actors at all (in any case, as Bogoiavlenskii observes, Staden exceeded his original mission, which was to hire directors or producers for the theater). The two trumpeters were mentioned again in a report from the tsar to officials in Pskov, ordering them to give the musicians passage to Moscow.[58]

On 10 October, just a week before the premiere, Staden reported again from Riga, saying he had just returned from Stockholm, where he had hired a trumpet player and three young musicians who played on all kinds of (unspecified) instruments "not ever heard in Moscow."[59] According to a message from the confused agents in Pskov, however, Staden showed up with a trumpeter and four other musicians. This tally corresponds to a summary compiled in Moscow on 3 December 1672 and to the actual contracts signed by the foreigners. (The contracts were preserved in later documents, entered as proof that the Muscovites were remiss in fulfilling their financial obligations.)[60] These contracts tell us where the musicians were hired, in some cases where they had worked previously, what instruments they played, and what their duties in Moscow were to be.

Staden hired four musicians (*muzykanty*) in Courland; the contract was signed on 25 August 1672 in Mitau (Jeglava), Latvia. All four, although of different origins, had previously been in the employ of Duke James of Courland and were hired together as a group. In the Muscovite documents they are always called the *muzykanty* and their contract was a single one, signed by all four. In the contract the four musicians—Friederich Platenschleger of Prussia, Iacob Philips from Courland, Gottfried Berge of Danzig, and the Saxon Christophor Achermann—listed the instruments they knew: "Orgeln, Trompeten, Trompeten-Marinen, Cinchen, Dulcian und Posaunen, Violen and Viol de Gambe, auch die vocalische Music dabey, und noch andere Instrumente mehr verstehen."[61] Trumpeter Johann Waldonn was always listed separately and rated a higher salary than the *muzykanty,* eight rubles per month instead of only six. Waldonn signed his contract with Staden in Stockholm on 10 September 1672.[62] There is no information in this document about his previous employment and apparently he was not expected to play other instruments.

Taken together, the five musicians formed a varied ensemble: organ, brass (trumpet, trombone, and cornet ["Cinchen," probably "Zincken"], in addition to the trumpet specialist), winds (the "Dulcian" or "Dulzian" is an early bassoon), and strings (including the tromba marina, definitely an instrument "not ever heard in Moscow"). Staden himself apparently approved the ensemble, and again he greatly exceeded his original commission to hire two trumpet players. But the arrangements evoked no comment from Moscow (only from officials in Pskov, who were scrambling to arrange proper passage relying on second-hand information relayed from the capital).

In addition to hiring the instrumentalists from Sweden and Courland, Staden made another attempt to acquire musicians and performers from abroad after the theater opened. He had previously made contact with a Danish acting troupe headed by Anna Elisabeth Paulsen. She wrote to him from Copenhagen in April 1673, saying that she did indeed wish to come to Moscow and confirming that in accordance with Staden's earlier wishes, she was trying to supplement her group with a good singer and a lutenist. She also added that they would just have to do the best they could regarding the transport of their stage machinery.[63] Ultimately, Paulsen's troupe did not go to Moscow, but the requested lutenist would have added to the musical ensemble already assembled and the singer would have joined the vocal talents claimed by the group of *muzykanty.*

Although the Courland musicians included the organ among their many musical skills, there would have been no need to transport an instrument to Moscow, and the surviving documents are silent on the issue.[64] The Muscovite court, as we have seen, had long employed organists and organ builders, some Russian and some foreign, so there would have been no need to transport a bulky instrument from abroad for the theater. Matveev commandeered the large (or at least costly) organ for the Muscovite theatrical performances from Timotheus Hasenkruch (Gazenkrukh in the Russian records), the foreign trader who had recently triumphed as Pickleherring in the Orpheus entertainment and who was to play an active role in the formation of the court theater. We know something of Hasenkruch's organ from a petition he later wrote to Tsar Fedor after the theater was closed down. Although the transaction worked out badly for Hasenkruch, his sad tale illustrates the resources Matveev and the other planners were able to employ in arranging the music for the theatrical performances. It also demonstrates how the Muscovite planners made strategic use of a valuable resource—the foreign residents in the capital—in order to create their theater.

In July 1676, about six months after Tsar Aleksei's death, Hasenkruch petitioned Tsar Fedor for payment for his organ, describing how Matveev had discovered the instrument at his home (an interesting point in itself) and had promised him a large sum of money in payment:

> In the previous year 1672, in the month of October . . . Boyar Artemon Sergeevich Matveev saw the organ at his, Timofei's, residence and he [Matveev] bought the organ from him, from Timofei, for the theater for 1,200 rubles. And the clerk Afonasei Dmitriev got the organ from Timofei and took it to the Vladimir Office and transported it to Preobrazhenskoe and placed it in the theater and he [Timofei] was never given the money for the organ.

Hasenkruch continues, saying that

> if they had not taken his organ for the theater, he [Hasenkruch] would have sold it to the Persians, and they would have given him 1,200 rubles for it at that time. But now the organ has been ruined by the moves, as it was moved from Preobrazhenskoe to Moscow many times, and from Moscow to Preobrazhenskoe in winter and spring.[65]

Hasenkruch's organ was apparently larger or more elaborate than the instruments at court or those belonging to the aristocracy, none of which was valued at more than about 200 rubles and many at significantly lower amounts.[66] These smaller or plainer instruments must not have been considered appropriate for the theater or its royal audience—this is why they needed Hasenkruch's organ in the first place. His troubles in collecting payment are unfortunately typical. All the musicians Staden hired engaged in similar struggles to collect their wages, and all left Moscow before the theater closed, either legally (Johann Waldonn) or otherwise (the *muzykanty*).[67]

The last information in Hasenkruch's petition, that the instrument was ruined, apparently speaks ill of those in charge. It was the job of the tsar's Smolensk-born Polish organist, Simeon Gutovskii, to transport the organ to the different theatrical sites, a job that may have been doomed to failure by the weather and the state of transportation. Gutovskii certainly had the knowledge and experience to be placed in charge of the theater's organ, given his earlier work on the instrument built for the Persian shah and his work in 1668 on an even larger instrument intended for the same court (a long-term hotbed of organ enthusiasts, a fact Hasenkruch was evidently well aware of). The fate of this second instrument is not known, but it must have been unavailable at the time of the court theatricals, making Hasenkruch's organ a desirable and necessary commodity.[68] It is not clear from the documents if Gutovskii played the organ for the court theater; the records speak only of his role in caring for the instrument. Hasenkruch, on the other hand, was listed among the theater's players (*igretsy*), a position consistent with his part in the Orpheus event and separate from the musicians and from "Simeon arganist."[69]

Staden and Matveev thus gathered a small but varied ensemble of instrumentalists for the court theater. These musicians may have been intended to form the ensemble in its entirety or they may have been hired to supplement musicians already assembled in Moscow. The documents do not clarify this point and, at least initially, it did not signify, for none of the foreign musicians Staden hired was in Muscovy at the time of the premiere, in October 1672. Given Staden's unhurried pace and the plans going on simultaneously in Moscow, perhaps there was no expectation that these musicians were necessary for the theater to go on. If music was required for the first performances, Matveev would have to improvise from sources within his reach.

As we have seen from the documents concerning the Repskii affair, Matveev was well able to lay his hands on instrumentalists. A series of Muscovite documents describing events in the fall of 1674 illustrates the ways in which Aleksei's theater represented both the new and the old, a new interpretation of long-held Muscovite instrumental practices. Documents from October describe events associated with the royal family and show the continuity of instrumental performances at court. Like the court organists and heralding trumpets, the instrumentalists were an accepted if not everyday part of court ceremony. The first document, from 1 October 1674, records the tsar's private entertainment: "[T]he tsar ordered boyar and *oruzhnichii* [armorer] Bogdan Matveevich Khitrovo to arrange for his Lord's entertainment with trumpets and *nakra* and *surna* players and *litavra* and *nabatchik* players at the place where the old Monastery Prikaz was."[70] The same kinds of instruments, with the addition of an organ, were named a few weeks later at a banquet: "And after the meal the tsar permitted entertainment by all kinds of playing ("vsiakimi igry"). And they entertained the tsar and played the organ, and a foreigner [*Nemchin*] played the organ, and they blew on the *surna* and on the *truby,* and played the *surenki* and beat on the *nakry* and the *litavry* throughout."[71]

In documents from December of that year, describing theatrical performances that had taken place in the previous month, the new musical element lies not so much in the use of instruments for court entertainment but in the choice of instruments and the choice of entertainment (which included dancing as well as music). These documents, combined with the contracts for Staden's musicians, give us an idea of the kind of ensemble chosen to accompany the tsar's plays:

> And foreigners [*Nemtsy*] and boyar Artemon Sergeevich Matveev's people entertained the tsar [with the play] "How Artaxerxes ordered Aman to be hanged, according to the petition of the tsaritsa and Mordecai's wise advice," and they played the organ and *fioly* and *stramenty* and danced . . .

A very similar description follows, listing the same kinds of instruments and entertainment, including dancing, and although this following passage does not specify that a play was performed, it seems reasonable to link this description (with its "various other entertainments") to the descriptions immediately preceding, which mention performances of the Judith and the Esther plays:

> And in that same year [1674] in the same village of Preobrazhenskoe, the tsar had an entertainment before the fast ["na zagoven'e"], and foreigners, Germans ["inozemtsy Nemtsy"], and boyar Artemon Sergeevich Matveev's people entertained His Highness on organs and *fioly* and *stramenty* and danced and [there were] various other entertainments.[72]

There was thus a fairly specific set of instruments accompanying the tsar's various entertainments, including the royal theatrical evenings. Matveev, Staden, and the other planners, perhaps taking their cue from the musicians of the Orpheus event, went to some effort to assemble a European-style ensemble with strings and winds, in addition to the horns, organs, and percussion already available and commonly used for the court's pleasure. This sort of ensemble stands in contrast to the squadrons of *domra* and *gusli* players and the military-style horns and percussion also associated with the royal family's entertainments. Staden searched abroad for a mixed ensemble—defined by the contracts with the Courland musicians he eventually hired—and Matveev found additional musicians in Moscow, commandeering Hasenkruch's organ and enlisting musicians with appropriate training on appropriate instruments (possibly Repskii himself, probably others as well).

Drawing such distinctions among various instrumental ensembles helps to decipher a series of otherwise puzzling requests made at the time of the theater's premiere. In October 1672 Paul Menzies, a Scottish military officer in the employ of Tsar Aleksei, was sent to Rome as part of a widespread diplomatic initiative aimed at assembling a unified front against the Turks, who had just crossed the Danube with a large army. In addition to his diplomatic mission, Menzies was also assigned the familiar task of hiring specialists to work in Muscovy, including not only gold and silver workers, but also two trumpeters who "can play dances on the high trumpet." Menzies's instructions are repeated in several different documents, all from precisely the time of the theater's premiere. The first such order appears to date from 11 October, and the order is repeated on 17 October, the day of the first performance, and again on the following day. The instruments would be appropriate for just the sort of dancing mentioned in the theatrical documents cited above; indeed, given the customs of the Muscovite royal family, there can scarcely be any other context. Menzies's party, which departed on 20 October, was certainly familiar with the music and dancing of the court theater, for accompanying Menzies as a private secretary was the very Laurent Rinhuber who had been so deeply involved in training the young performers for the premiere performance.[73]

Opening Night in Muscovy: Music's Indispensable Role in the Tsar's Court Theater

Rinhuber's account of the premiere, written several months after the event, emphasizes the many months of preparation (under his own unerring guidance) that occurred after the tsar had heard about theatrical presentations. He also notes the participation of the foreign playwright and the foreign youngsters and especially, the resounding success of this ambitious enterprise:

The great tsar of Muscovy, hearing of dramatic works, avidly desired to see a play. The question was whether there was anybody who could take charge of the matter. Nobody daring it, Master M. Gregorii the Pastor was secretly recommended. It was reported that he was able to write a play. He [Gregorii], willingly or unwillingly, was required to engage in this effort and wrote, with my help, the tragi-comedy of Ahasuerus [Artaxerxes] and Esther. Over the course of three months, I prepared youngsters for participation in this performance in German and in Slavic. The performance itself took place on 17 October 1672. The tsar was so entranced by the performance that he watched it for ten hours straight, without moving from his place. This no doubt was the source of later successes.[74]

Russian scholars have skillfully situated the tsar's new theater within the larger context of the highly theatricalized life of the Muscovite court: the production was truly a play within a play, the world of the court mirrored in the world created on the stage. The subject of the first play, the story of Esther, had obvious resonance. The play, in which a wise ruler chooses a second wife, who brings a trusted counselor to the king's side, was performed before a real-life wise tsar, recently remarried, whose new wife also brought a trusted and powerful counselor to the court. The tsar for whom the play was produced sat enthroned, surrounded by his own advisors, just as the king onstage was surrounded by his own wise counselors. The actors addressed one another using the titles and symbols of their audience, and the concepts they discussed on the stage court concerning order, obedience, and humility—even images of the scepter of authority and the bright eyes of the king—were concepts fundamental to the larger theater of the Muscovite court itself. In a very real and deep sense, this new theatrical entertainment brought to life not just the familiar biblical stories and characters but the lives of its audience as well.[75]

Our exploration of this first Russian theatrical experience focuses on a single element. All the planning, dispatching, hiring, and rehearsing recounted above illustrate one central and crucial fact about the productions: they were conceived from the outset as being realized through musical performances, both vocal and instrumental, as well as through spoken dialogue. Music was as necessary as the actors, the costumes, and the sets, all of which received detailed attention from the planners. As Reutenfels said, "[W]ithout music it was impossible to put together a chorus, just as it is impossible for dancers to dance without legs." Every scrap of information the Muscovite government had received about theatrical entertainments produced abroad had included references to music, and the Muscovites' own liturgical dramas, even if not a particularly vital part of their experience at this date, had been similarly supplied. Closer to home, the Orpheus evening had featured instrumental music and singing prominently and successfully. How did this necessary element function within this first play, and how did this newest court endeavor reflect the musical tastes and traditions of the Muscovite court as well as those of the Westerners who brought it to life?[76]

Music articulates the structure of Pastor Gregorii's *Play of Artaxerxes* at several levels. The play is preserved in both a Slavic version (in a manuscript from Vologda) and in a bilingual German-Slavic version (primarily in a source from Lyon, with missing segments preserved in a fragment from Weimar).[77] On the largest scale, the play is divided into four segments laid out in the form of a palindrome, with the shorter outer segments framing two larger inner groupings, as follows:

Prologue
Act 1, scenes 1–4
Interscenium 1

Act 2, scenes 1–6
Act 3, scenes 1–6
Interscenium 2

Act 4, scenes 1–6
Act 5, scenes 1–6
Interscenium 3

Act 6, scenes 1–3
Act 7, scenes 1–3
Interscenium 4
Epilogue [lost][78]

The opening prologue is addressed to Tsar Aleksei and it invites the royal audience into the world of Artaxerxes while at the same time, by drawing parallels between the court of the Persian king and the still greater court of the Muscovite tsar, it also calls deliberate attention to the essential artifice of the performance to follow. The prologue was performed by Laurentius Blumentrost, son of the court physician, who gives Aleksei credit for the creation of the theater: "[Y]our royal command brings him [Artaxerxes] on stage, alive in the shape of a young man who is eager to tell you" his story through this "childlike comedy." He concludes by proclaiming that if, "God willing, our feeble efforts, oh tsar, can well please your highness, then do not shed the radiance of your grace on Persia but let the people of Artaxerxes be none other than these Germans."[79] Act 1 is fairly short (four scenes instead of the usual six in most of the other acts). It opens with a flourish at a royal banquet and then traces the story told in the first book of Esther: King Artaxerxes calls his queen, Astin' (the biblical Vashti) to him; she refuses to appear and is banished. This segment ends with the performance of the first *interscenium,* as it is called in a contemporary annotation.[80]

The second large section of the play is made up of acts 2, 3, and the second *interscenium.* Acts 2 and 3 each comprise six scenes, continuing the biblical story laid out in Esther 2 and 3. Act 2 is devoted to the selection of Esther as the new queen, in spite of the worries of Mordecai, her beloved uncle and guardian, and act 3 develops the plot to kill Artaxerxes and its subsequent unraveling, due to Mordecai's timely information, and follows the elevation at court of the malevolent Haman. These two acts are then followed by the second *interscenium.*

In the third large section, acts 4 and 5 are also made up of six scenes each. Act 4 is devoted to Haman's orders to destroy the Jews, laments by Mordecai and by Esther herself (Esther 4:3–4), and Esther's invitations to her banquets as part of her plan to save her people. Act 5 focuses on Haman at the height of his power and the sharp reversal of his fate, as the king orders him to elevate the despised Mordecai to the highest honor of the court. "Oh shame, oh disgrace, oh vile rebuke and humiliation!" wails Haman. "I thought that the tsar was going to exalt me; instead I am obliged to raise my enemy."[81] These two acts are followed by the third *interscenium.* The proportions of the play's last large segment mirror those of the first. Acts 6 and 7 are short, only three scenes each, and conclude the story with the hanging of Haman and the rejoicing of the populace. A final *interscenium* wraps up the action, and there was apparently a concluding epilogue (now lost), also read by Blumentrost.

The four *interscenia* apparently trace the main themes of the play, reduced, so it seems, to formulaic comedic form. The texts are lost, but the listing of the characters includes the lovers (or married couple) Elena (also called Gelenka) and Mops (the word refers to a pug dog). Two additional characters, both played by the boy Snikkert (who also took the role of Hatach in the play), appear in the *interscenia:* Thraso, the boasting soldier and a stock comic figure, and Muischelow (another canine reference; the name indicates a mouse-hunting dog). An anonymous soldier rounds out the small cast of characters appearing in the *interscenia.* One of the surviving play texts includes a summary listing of the plot, which suggests that the *interscenia* lay out, in John Stone's succinct formulation, "a romantic triangle involving violence."[82] The first *interscenium* is summarized as

"Mops et Elena amorosi" (Mops and Elena are lovers). In the Vologda source, they are described as a married couple, which would correspond to the relationships between the king and Astin' and later, the king and his new queen. The two inner scenarios seem to revolve around normal *commedia*-like roughhousing: the second *interscenia* is reduced to "Sibi imminent" (they threaten each other) in the short-hand annotation, and the third as "Semet percutiunt" (they hit each other). The final *interscenium* is labeled "Mops strangulat Muischelowum" (Mops strangles Muischelow), an act that would parallel the main action of the play, particularly as the character Mops has, in act 6, stepped out of the world of the *interscenia* to appear in the play itself as Haman's hangman.

Music articulates the play's structure at each step of the way on both the large and the small scale. The opening banquet scene is described in the shorthand summary as beginning with horns or a fanfare ("epulum Artax. incip. cum tubis"), a musical marker calling the audience to attention, perhaps, and setting the proper festive and brilliant mood. The notation, with its call for horns, may suggest why the Muscovite planners collected such a variety of brass instruments: not only would they have been able to function in extra-theatrical fanfares and greeting ceremonies, but they could lend a touch of realism to the similar situations de-picted on the new stage. The structural role of music is most clearly evident at the end of act 1, which carries the annotation: "Sequitur musicam mutatio Theatri et Interscenium primum" (Music and the first interlude precedes the changing of scene).[83] In this case, then, music and the *interscenium* are linked, and deliberately so, forming a transitional element signaled by music. The same sort of linkage seems to appear later. Act 2 ends with the injunction to rejoice at the king's wedding feast, which might cue in some musical fanfare. This act leads without an intervening *interscenium* to act 3, which represents a large plot shift (act 3 revolves around the machinations kill the king). The final scene of act 4 does not include a musical cue, but act 5 opens at a banquet (which we know from act 1 to require some sort of music) and includes references to singing in praise of Esther, so music might indeed be seen as a marker separating these two segments. (There are other passages in this act that hint at some sort of musical element, particularly the "Triumphus Mardochei," in which Haman is forced to lead his enemy, who is seated in glory on a horse.) Acts 6 and 7, the final large segment, are short, and act 7 is filled with musical cues in its three brief scenes (and even the hangman who appears at the end of act 6 is accompanied by soldiers and a drummer).

The hangman's drummer and the banqueting cues for music and singing are important (and realistic) touches, but far more important are the large-scale musi-

cal interludes carefully placed throughout the play. They too are rendered natu-
ralistically, arising readily from the plot and in forms generally familiar to the
Muscovite audience. There are several pieces labeled "lament" (*plach*) or "song"
(*pesn'*) or "aria" in the polyglot sources. The first such opportunity is seized by
Queen Astin' as she laments her futile stubbornness in having refused to appear
before her king (act 1, scene 4). This passage is labeled "Plach' otverzhennoi As-
tiny" (The weeping or lament of the rejected Astin') and is described in shorthand
form as "Vasthi perturbatio et lamentatio" in the summary listing of the play. The
scene opens as she receives from the king's messengers the news about her banish-
ment. The stage then empties for a soliloquy by the unhappy queen, who laments
her pride and her bitter fate.[84] The disposition of the queen's text strongly suggests
a musical performance. Astin' laments in three large rhymed sections, each divided
into three smaller segments: 1) an opening quatrain in which she states her grief
and pain; 2) a quatrain beginning in each case with "O" ("O ponos [ponoshenie], o
sramota," "O ponoshenie," and "O gorkaia lest'" [Oh mockery and shame; Oh
mockery; Oh bitter flattery]);[85] and 3) a series of direct appeals to the king, each of
which begins "O Artakserks" followed by a rhyming couplet. The passages are
structured in the same way in both the Slavic and the German versions, and they
rhyme in both languages. Music sounded at least at the end of this soliloquy, for
this is where the notation "Sequitur musicam mutatio Theatri et Interscenium
primum" appears. It is difficult to believe that the lament itself was not either sung
or punctuated by some sort of instrumental interlude (or both).

An "aria" appears in the act 2–act 3 unit; indeed, the last scenes of act 2 include
several places naturally suggesting some sort of musical accompaniment or fanfare
(and provide a sharp contrast to the serious nature of the plot—regicide—worked
out in act 3). Act 2, scene 4 is described in the preliminary summary as including:
"Aria. Ermuntre den[n] nun." The word "aria" (in Cyrillic) appears in the text of
the Weimar fragment (where this act is preserved) at the beginning of a series of
seven sets of praises uttered by Esther's female attendants. Each is declaimed in
turn by a different servant—Naomi, Dina, Judith, and so forth—and all are six-line
recitations ending (except for the final strophe) with some variation of the phrase
"iako esi ventsa dostoina" (worthy of the crown), an attribute Esther modestly
denies. The first strophe, by Naomi, begins "Vospriani zhe nyne" (Rejoice then),
which would correspond to the German-language cue in the summary: "Aria.
Ermuntre den[n] nun." There is little doubt that these passages were, indeed,
conceived of as a series of sung praises.[86]

Both scenes 5 and 6 in act 2 begin with statements of rejoicing, the former by
Mordecai and his friends, and the latter, more promisingly in terms of music, by

the king at his court in honor of his newly chosen queen. At the end of scene 6, which concludes act 2, each of the male courtiers in turn praises Esther in joyous, formulaic one-line exclamations, concluding with the king's final command: "Come, counselors, follow me to the royal hall. Be joyous at my wedding feast."[87] It is difficult to believe that the laboriously assembled instrumental ensemble was silent at such a command, particularly as act 3 provides little scope for music (and the change of scene would presumably require something to occupy the royal audience, for whom a wedding feast—with musical entertainment—was a recent and joyous event).

It is during act 4 that the musical elements of the play reach their height. This is (surely not coincidentally) the structural mid-point of the work, preceded and followed by the symmetrical distribution of acts, *interscenia*, and the prologue and (now-missing) epilogue. The first scene of act 4 opens with a formulaic lament utterance by Zadok, Mordecai's friend ("Alas, alas, alas"), followed by a brief recapitulation of the events that have transpired, including Haman's order to destroy all the Jews. The scene shifts abruptly to the court, juxtaposing Mordecai's mournful musings to the triumphant revenge expressed by Haman: "Land of my ancient ancestors, rejoice and consider your good fortune!"[88] The third scene takes us back to Mordecai and his friends; it is labeled "Lamentationes Judaeorum" and "Plach' Mardokheina s zhidami" (The Lament of Mordecai and the Jews). The lament sequence is carefully structured, using psalm texts written out in transliterated Hebrew and then summarized in Slavic translation by one of the characters immediately following. (The transliterated Hebrew also appears in the German text, which is not complete.) These psalm recitations alternate with sections of dialogue in which the characters discuss Haman's devastating edict and express their hope that Esther will somehow save them. There are four such large psalm segments (some with multiple citations) layered into this scene.

The presentation of the psalm texts, in which the verse is intoned in Hebrew and then summarized in translation, is clearly articulated in the second utterance of the first large psalm segment of the scene:

> **Mordecai** *[reciting a psalm text in Hebrew, written in Cyrillic]:*
> *Elogim, zanakh falanezakh*
> *ieskhan, appekha bezon maritekha?*
> *zekhor adafkha kanitfa kedem*
> *gaalikha skhefatf makhalafekha*
> *khar' zion zef, skhaanfa bo!*

[*Partially transliterated in the German text:*
Elohim Zanach Ihalanezah
Jeschan appecha bezon maritecha
zechor adathcha kanitha kedem.]

[*Psalm 74:1–2, King James translation:*
O God, why hast thou cast us off for ever?
why doth thine anger smoke against the sheep of thy pasture?
Remember thy congregation, which thou hast purchased of old;
the rod of thine inheritance, which thou hast redeemed;
this mount Zion, wherein thou hast dwelt.]

Azaria [*summarizing the text, in Slavic*]: Oh God! Why have You forsaken us and why are you scorning Your people?

Zadok [*continues the summary*]: Why are You wrathful with Your chosen? Remember Your pasturing sheep!

Mordecai [*continues the summary*]: Oh, remember Your heirs! You are dwelling in us, yet You let us be annihilated.[89]

What might the distinguished Muscovite audience have made of these psalm recitations? The fact that Gregorii added the translations immediately after the Hebrew passages for almost every utterance suggests that he intended his audience to understand what was being pronounced on stage. It also suggests that Grigorii feared his audience might not have understood the texts (or perhaps—initially at least—even recognized the language) had they not immediately been provided with such a translation. The first psalm reference in the scene may have been confusing (and one should note that although this first reference is quite short, just a few exclaimed lines, it is not fully translated, either), and one senses that Gregorii was stepping fairly gingerly at this point, acclimating his audience by means of an initial series of quick, one-line interjections.[90]

Although there is no evidence that the royal audience had any familiarity with Hebrew, Gregorii seems to have been correct in assuming that the court would readily have made the basic link between Hebrew and the psalm texts. Simeon Polotskii, for example, in his verse translation of the Psalter (which he worked on in 1678 and which was published in 1680), included several fairly casual references to the Hebrew psalm texts in his introductions (although, to be sure, he does not actually offer any examples in Hebrew and his translations were based on Polish verse renditions).[91] The audience knew that Mordecai and his friends were Jews and that they were lamenting; if they then heard familiar psalm verses in Slavic as the scene unfolded, it would not have been an unreasonably large step for them to conclude that they had also just heard these same verses in Hebrew.

How were these psalm verses performed? There are no annotations indicating any sort of performance directions at this point in the play, apart from the designation at the head of the scene labeling it as a series of *lamentationes* and a *plach*. It would, however, seem safe to suggest that these verses were intended to be delivered in a manner that differentiated them from the less heightened exchanges that follow. Perhaps the simple fact of reciting the lines in Hebrew would have been enough, but everyone in the audience knew through long experience at church and through countless images of King David composing the Psalter surrounded by singers and instrumentalists that psalms were commonly intoned or sung. The sung *plach*, too, was a long-familiar musical outpouring. It does not seem too risky to propose that these texts were performed in some musical fashion.[92]

There is no doubt about the presence of singing in the next scene, about which the brief summary in the Lyon manuscript says: "Ariae binae. 1. Gott der du Einig all. 2. O Unschuld flieh'!" The two arias specified here are preceded by a brief introduction that ties this scene to the previous one. Esther, at court in scene 4, continues the lamentations of her kinsmen in the previous scene, even taking up their psalm-flecked laments in her own, which is also written in transliterated Hebrew:

> **Esther:** *Mi iitten mizzio ieshiuatkh Israil'!*
> *Beshkhuv iovakh s'shkhefutkh ammo,*
> *Iagal iaakov, iizmakh israel'.*

> *[Partially transliterated in the German text:*
> *Mi jitten mizzyon jeschuath Israel]*

> *[Psalm 14:7, King James translation:*
> *Oh that the salvation of Israel were come out of Zion! when the Lord bringeth back the captivity of his people, Jacob shall rejoice, and Israel shall be glad.]*

Esther then immediately addresses her maidens, giving a sense of the Hebrew text, as in the previous scene, but not actually summarizing it fully:

> **Esther:** *Children, children, let us now pray. In such peril, let us all call to the God of our fathers, to the God of Abraham, Isaac, and Jacob!*

*Cry out together with me, and let rivers of tears flow. Let us then start
sobbing and cry out together how our heart is grief-stricken.*

She then proclaims a series of seven numbered, rhyming, six-line strophes, to each
of which the group of maidens replies in unison with some variant of the phrase
"Priidi, priidi i nas izbavi!" (Come, come and free us!). The first of her statements
begins with the textual incipit cued in as the first of the "ariae binae," namely,
"Gott, der du einig all-regier'st" (Bozhe, vsemi narody obladaia; Oh God, Lord of
all peoples). After this "aria," Esther then explicitly bids her attendants to sing
a song:

> **Esther:** *And you, my maidens of beautiful countenance, all that are here,
> praise God so that He will appear, and reveal Himself in a divine
> miracle; and add a song besides, for I am cast down in sorrow and
> grieve in great distress, so that I cannot utter a song.*[93]

Following the direction "Liki dev poiut pesn'" (The chorus of maidens sings a
song), the text lays out a series of ten numbered, four-line verses, beginning with
the second textual incipit listed above: "O Unschuld, flieh' zum Throne" (O nevin-
nost', bezhi k prestolu; Oh innocence run to the throne). This is, indeed, exactly
what Esther (innocence) does, in the pivotal action of the drama. Just as the
maidens finish their exhortatory song, Hatakh, one of Esther's male servants,
enters and tells her that the king is alone. Esther resolves to go to him unbidden (an
act punishable by death) to plead for her people, and she orders Hatakh to inform
Mordecai of her action. The maidens' song, then, has given her the courage to act
as she knows she must; the "choro virginum" has functioned as a conscience,
telling her in song what she must risk.

The three scenes of the final act are given over almost entirely to music. Act 7,
scene 1 is labeled "Aria Judaeorum. Israil da radu[etsia]!" (Israel, be happy!) in the
summary (combining Latin and Cyrillic), and "pesn'" (song) in the Lyon text of
the play. It is called forth by Mordecai, who urges his companions to "pray to the
almighty God and bow down with thanks for His grace which defeated the pride of
the enemy!" and concludes with a prayer to "hear this humble song." The song falls
into twelve numbered strophes of (mostly) rhyming text, the first and the last
almost exact duplicates and thus forming a rounded textual structure. In the
dialogue immediately following, several characters refer to the song or to singing.[94]

The second scene of act 7, at court, offers a resolution: although the king's
order to kill the Jews cannot be rescinded, it can be mitigated by publicly announc-
ing that the Jews have the right to defend themselves. The final lines spoken by the

king on stage invite the royal audience seated before them to participate in the rejoicing: "Now trumpets and timbrels proclaim that the proud perish in their chains, that meekness is crowned, faithfulness rewarded, the crowns are saved, and innocence is free. Sing and dance joyously all day. Be full of joy!" To which everyone on stage replies: "Yes, yes, yes, yes! Great Moscow, join us in our celebration." This is immediately followed, in the play's final scene, by the performance of another "pesn'," this one with a military edge: "So! Blankke Waffen" (Se svetloe oruzh'e; Thou shining weapon), performed by the ensemble.[95] The last *interscenium* provides a final wrap-up of the main action. Mops, just seen on stage as Haman's hangman, strangles Muischelow.

The music of *The Play of Artaxerxes*, excluding the *interscenia*, thus falls into two clearly demarcated categories. The instrumentalists, either "Matveev's people," who supplied the music for the premiere, and/or the hired performers who came shortly thereafter, were apparently kept busy with a variety of incidental music: for staged banquets, fanfares, processions, hangings, and the like. Such music is often cued by the play's text, and would have been readily supplied by the mixed instrumental ensemble assembled for the event. Wherever they came from—Muscovite court circles or from abroad—the instrumentalists would have been familiar with music's role in such circumstances. The fanfares and military flourishes were familiar musical touches in Muscovy, and even the instrumental music of the play's staged banquets, which in the Muscovite context tended to use a somewhat different set of instruments (and would apparently, as in the documents quoted above, have been performed after a banquet, not during the meal), was doubly familiar from reports by Russian diplomats who had witnessed such music on their tours. One assumes that this music was fairly simple, worked out during the long period of rehearsal and preparation. At any rate, the ensemble would not have needed extensive written scores, and the simple and commonplace effects might account for the lack of written music from the theater.

The other important musical style is quite different: the large, formal, and highly structured vocal numbers. These are labeled *pesn', plach, lamentatio,* or *aria* in the texts, and all are strophic: the lament of Astin' (act 1, scene 4); the "aria" performed in sequential strophes by Esther's maidens (act 2, scene 4); and the "ariae binae" of act 4, scene 4, in which Esther sings a strophic song punctuated by one-line responses from her attendants, who then sing their own strophic song. What appear to be large, triumphant choral numbers in act 7, scenes 1 and 3 are also strophic: the "aria Judaeorum" and the concluding military song. These strophic songs might also have employed instrumental accompaniment, although this is not specified in the meager stage directions. Presumably, in the case of the laments, there would have been less emphasis on the trumpeting brass and more from the organ and the strings. At any rate, one would again presume fairly simple accompaniment, consistent with the lack of notated music (at least so far discovered) associated with the theatrical productions.

Why the emphasis on strophic singing? The form is simple and direct, important considerations both for the young actors as well as for the equally inexperienced audience. Strophic texts would have been readily understood (and memorized), and strophic musical settings would have been relatively easy to compose or compile, again fitting comfortably with the lack of references to specialist composers or singers for the theater. Apart from its simplicity, however, the form itself would have resonated with both performers and audience. Strophic singing was certainly part of the repertoire of the young Protestant actors, who would have grown up with hymn singing even in the remote environs of Moscow's Foreign Quarter. (In the fall of 1674, for example, Rinhuber signed for the transport of fifteen "Gesangbücher" to the Lutheran church in Moscow.)[96] For the same reason, strophic singing would have been a natural musical reflex for the German pastor-playwright.

The form would have been equally comfortable, in a somewhat different context, for the Muscovite audience, familiar with the *kanty,* the strophic, non-liturgical religious songs which at just this time were becoming so popular in Muscovy. The earliest preserved collection of such texts in Muscovy dates from 1675; Polotskii's verse translation of the Psalter a few years later pointedly observes the popularity in Muscovy of singing such texts in Polish; and Vasilii Titov's musical settings of Polotskii's texts in the *kant* style—a setting by a court singer of the court poet's translations—comes from less than a decade after the abrupt closing of the theater. In the case of strophic texts, then, one size does indeed fit all. The songs may have been performed in unison or in simple harmonizations. If the theater's planners were able to teach their foreign-born youngsters such a lengthy and complex drama and expect that they could perform it for the high-stakes production at court, one must believe that they would also have been able to teach simple and familiar hymn-like homophony.

In addition to the similarities in form, the featured dramatic solo singing in *The Play of Artaxerxes* was of a specific type: the lament. The genre would have been familiar from many biblical examples or references, and to Pastor Gregorii and the other Westerners involved, whatever their specific experience in theater and performance, laments would have been standard fare. However, these important musical moments have another element in common, for all solo singing in the play is performed by female characters (played of course by the young male actors). Male characters engage in the hearty choral finales of act 7 but the central dramatic laments were given solely to female characters. This distribution of the vocal numbers may result in part from the cues in the biblical story, where for example, Esther laments in a general way (although with no specific written text). In the Western theatrical traditions from which the performers would have drawn, however, sung laments had a specific connotation, one that was developed and cultivated with some deliberation: laments were female affairs, signaling a loss of emotional (and often musical) control. The musical vocabulary of laments was fairly rigorously formulated, and applying such vocabulary to a male character instantly feminized him, in ways complex and subtle.[97] Does such an association function here, in the Moscow play?

Yes and no. Laments had a long pedigree in the Muscovite context, where they were a familiar part of both liturgical and extra-liturgical worship and devotions through the penitential verses. The dramatic and popular Adam's Lament—itself a stylized, even theatrical work—might even have prepared the Muscovite audience for the transfer of such emotions to the new stage. Adam's Lament, as we have seen, circulated widely in musical settings and in visual images; Diletskii, for example, in his *Grammatika,* which was written within a few years of the court's theatrical experiences, emphasized its character as an outpouring of weeping and sobbing.

There is also a secular precedent for laments in Muscovy, a tradition that might also have made the transition from private to public performance, highlighted by the laments of Kseniia, Boris Godunov's forsaken daughter, as recorded in the texts written down for Richard James at the beginning of the century. Secular laments also appear in other popular tales throughout the seventeenth century, for example in the narrative poem recounting the tale of Misery-Luckless-Plight (which begins with the story of Adam and Eve, or, as Diletskii calls Adam, "the first singer of sad music").[98] The specific context for the genre within a staged play was new to Muscovy, but the general concept of a formal lament (sacred or secular, spoken or sung, and by men or women) was not. Gregorii's approach, then, would have been acceptable from either the Western or the Muscovite side of the equation. The author's ability to ferret out the familiar within the novel event he was preparing ensured that this play and his others were easy for the royal audience to grasp. No wonder they were so popular.

On the other hand, the male lamentation in *The Play of Artaxerxes,* by Mordecai and his friends, is handled quite differently than the other laments. For this scene Gregorii abandons the strophic form he uses in connection with all the other laments in favor of the series of psalm readings or intonations in Hebrew. There are many reasons Gregorii might have chosen this type of setting. This scene is natural and even powerful dramatically; structurally, however, a strophic lament at this point would only undercut the two such settings that appear in the following scene. Did Gregorii's choice of form also take into consideration that this lamentation was assigned to a male character, with the support of a male chorus? Nothing similar to these psalm segments appears in the later Muscovite repertoire. Perhaps this was due to the complexity of the scenic construction rather than to its genre and the gender of the characters assigned to sing it. Perhaps, more simply, the Hebrew texts in this scene were confusing enough, without adding other formal elements on top of them. At any rate, neither Gregorii nor any of the later playwrights tried anything like this again.

No matter what musical styles and forms Pastor Gregorii used, the surviving texts of this first play make clear the care the author took in building and linking scenes, and confirm his intention from the outset to incorporate some sort of music within the drama. The musical portions of the play were not solely decorative, although they do have that function as well, but serve to delineate and even motivate the actions of the players on stage. The theater, we know, was successful almost from the instant the curtain was raised. *The Play of Artaxerxes* was performed multiple times over the next few months, until Gregorii was able to get a new play, on the story of Judith, ready for performance in February 1673. Even after that date, *The Play of Artaxerxes* was repeated in the growing repertoire of the theater up to the end of its existence. After *Iudif'* (Judith) opened, the next work, also apparently by Gregorii, appeared in the fall of 1673 (a retelling of another story from the Old Testament Apocrypha, Tobit, a text which is now lost). We see another cluster of works in February of the following year, 1674; a series of works produced in the following February and November; and a final set of new works in preparation in January 1676. Altogether we know of eleven titles, which apparently rotated in revolving performances.[99]

Music remained a key element in each of these later works but there were subtle shifts (insofar as we can track them in light of the several lost or only partially preserved texts). Never again did Gregorii or any of the other playwrights attempt the structural complexity, linkage, and symmetry achieved in the Esther story. Gregorii's Judith play is shorter and its mood somewhat different, with more emphasis on comic elements (performed in quick exchanges by groups of characters, mostly soldiers), which are juxtaposed with lengthy and serious speeches delivered by the biblical figures. Perhaps the shorter length and ponderous exchanges by the major characters, as opposed to the (relatively) more fluid dramatic exposition in *The Play of Artaxerxes,* reflect the fact that Gregorii and the other theatrical workers had less time to polish this production.

The music of *Judith* reflects, in part, the same two types we have already observed: instrumental music (often cued by the text) and strophic ensemble singing. Where are the laments or, more generally, solo singing? The character Judith has a moment of prayer and reflection (act 5, scene 5), which might have been set, as in the Esther drama, as a lament-style solo song, but here Gregorii chooses not to employ this approach. Perhaps this was a result of haste and distraction, but in light of the ways in which music functioned in all the later plays, one begins to wonder if this shift might not reflect something of the court's level of comfort with its theatrical presentations. Judith is the only important female character in this play (her maid, full of snappy one-liners, is a comic character); indeed, after Esther and Judith (and Eve, in the play about Adam and Eve), there are no featured female characters in the Muscovite plays, at least judging from the surviving sources (after all, in the lost Bacchus and Venus there must have been at least one fairly prominent woman!).[100] After Esther and Astin', there are no more (preserved) solo lament texts in the main action of the plays. Is there a link between gender and genre? The plays as a whole also tend to become shorter, with Simeon Polotskii's two contributions—retellings of the stories of the Prodigal Son and of King Nebuchadnezzar and the fiery furnace—so short as to make one wonder if they were produced as a double bill. Perhaps there was simply no time or dramatic space for such leisurely musical moments.

Indeed, the lament tradition survived after a fashion in one later play, the setting of the story of Adam and Eve (*Zhalobnaia komediia ob Adame i Eve*; The Mournful Comedy of Adam and Eve), but there are instructive, perhaps telling, changes in approach. This is a shortish work, preserved only incompletely, whose authorship is somewhat cloudy. It is generally attributed to Gregorii, who died in February 1675; the play was produced in November of that year, so other writers may have contributed as well.[101] The singing is structured, at least in part, in a fashion reminiscent of Gregorii's other works, that is, as a means of concluding a scene and marking the change to the next. In this play, the first two of the surviving acts end with music performed by an ensemble of angels (the play breaks off in act 5). Act 1 ends with a series of brief musical events: the three angels sing a short praise of God together; the first two angels each sing a line of praise in sequence; and they conclude with a final series of exclamations performed by all three together. The stage directions are carefully noted in the text for each element.

The sung finale to act 2 is a brilliant, if modest, tribute to Gregorii and his German and/or Russian collaborators, touching on deeply ingrained traditions of both groups yet immediately and meaningfully accessible to all. Act 2 is a monologue for Adam, who kneels in prayer after he and Eve have tasted the forbidden fruit. Following his lengthy prayer, the stage directions state: "Here they sing a song" ("Zde poiut' pesn'"). The text that follows is thus not a solo lament but rather performed by an ensemble, presumably by the three angels who had concluded act 1 (and who open act 3, scene 1, which follows immediately). They sing the following text:

> Chrez adamovo padenie vsi
> Vsi rody pogubleny,
> Zane tot iad na nas priide,
> I uzhe ne mozhem zhiti bez
> Bozhiei ruki silnei.
> Iazhe nas vyruchila:
> Egda Zmiia Evvu zvela,
> Kazn' na nas vsekh navela.

This is a translation of the first strophe of the very well-known Lutheran hymn "Durch Adams Fall," which would certainly have been part of Gregorii's (and his student performers') repertoire.[102] It is difficult to imagine any of the Germans involved in the production as conceiving this song without the traditional melody; the text reads as follows:

> Durch Adams Fall ist ganz verderbt
> Menschlich Natur und Wesen.
> Dasselbe Gift ist auf uns geerbt,
> Daß wir nicht konnten genesen
> Ohn Gottes Trost, der uns erlöst
> Hat von dem großen Schaden,
> Darein die Schlang' Evam bezwang,
> Gotts Zorn auf sich zu laden.

The English translation of the hymn text serves both the German and the Russian versions:

> Through Adam's fall human nature
> and character is completely corrupted,
> the same poison has been inherited by us,
> so that we would not be able to recover health
> without comfort from God, who has redeemed us

from the great harm

that was done when the serpent overcame Eve

and led her to bring God's wrath upon herself.[103]

Yet to the Russian audience, although this specific text would have been new, the theme was equally familiar from the long-popular Adam's Lament.[104] The doubly familiar text, then, is a testament to the kinds of collaboration engendered by the Muscovite court theater and the ways in which the planners were able to draw upon multiple traditions, a monument to the felicity of collaboration. This musical moment, however, is performed not as a solo lament by the character Adam but by an ensemble, the plural "they" who are directed to sing the song. Adam's long solo scene of prayer and grief—a spoken lament—is thus followed by a kind of Greek chorus (or Lutheran congregation) commenting on the emotions he expressed. The reconfiguration of the solo laments of *Artaxerxes* in this play— divided and redistributed as spoken monologue and vocal ensemble—seems to reflect the evolving context of Muscovite theatrical preference.

Most of the music, both instrumental and vocal, of the later plays is of the banqueting-and-rejoicing, trumpets-and-timbrels type heard throughout *The Play of Artaxerxes*. The setting of the Tamerlane story, which premiered in February 1675, for example, was an obvious place for military music. *Temir-Aksakovo deistvo* (The Play of Tamerlane) was the first of the Muscovite plays to be based on a historical, rather than a biblical, story, one with very real connections to political events of the time. The prologue carefully spells out for the audience the work's historical and didactic character, but the real mood is set in act 1, scene 1 with a spectacular and noisy (and unique) appearance by the character Mars, who calls for the trumpets to sound the alarm, followed by the stage direction: "Trivoga [trevoga]. Trivoga bolshaia" (A military alarm. A great alarm). In this pervasively martial atmosphere, there is no room for formal laments (and no real place for prominent female characters), although there is a strophic drinking song in one of the comedic scenes.

Decorative music of this type sounds throughout Simeon Polotskii's two short plays. A copy of his setting of the story of Nebuchadnezzar (*O Navkhodonosore tsare, o tele zlate i o triekh otrotsekh, v peshchi ne sozhzhennykh*; King Nebuchadnezzar, the Golden Idol, and the Three Boys Who Were Not Burned in the Furnace) was bound in February 1674, so the work was, at the latest, written by that date. Polotskii's other play, *Komidiia pritchi o bludnem syne* (The Parable of the Prodigal Son), appears to date from about the same time.[105] Both plays, but particularly the Nebuchadnezzar setting, suggest elaborated treatments of Polotskii's rhymed, spoken declamations, the works that brought him to the attention of the Muscovite court in the first place. With these plays Polotskii had, after a fashion, come full circle in his career at court.[106] The plays are written in rhyming couplets throughout and were presented by the same kind of performer Polotskii had introduced to the Muscovite court, that is, a trained ensemble of youths such as the group he had brought to recite for the tsar almost a decade earlier. The scripts have fairly detailed information on staging, especially on music, of the sort one can only dream of for the more dramatically complex Esther play.

Throughout both works, the musical elements generally occur fairly naturally, for example in part 2 of *The Prodigal Son* a drinking scene, which includes music within the scene as well as at the end; toasts; a *mnogoletie* (offered by increasingly inebriated characters); and a final request for some "merry playing," which is concluded by the direction "the singers sing and there is an Intermedium" ("Pevtsy poiut, i budet Intermedium"). In part 3, the Prodigal Son wakes up with a hangover ("My head hurts!" he whines), whereupon the servants take up drinking again, with more singing, playing, and toasting.

The Nebuchadnezzar play is not divided up into acts or scenes but it is punctuated by musical segments called forth by the drama and which are used, especially in the first section, in a brilliant, festive manner, complementing the dramatic and specific stage directions.[107] For example, the play's first major segment is the discussion of the idol, and it concludes with the king ordering a musical celebration. The stage direction notes that "the musicians enter" and then, following a brief couplet pronounced by the king, another note specifies "then there is dancing" ("Priidut musikii" and "zde budut likovstvovaniia"). The idol is then revealed with dramatic flourish from behind a curtain or screen, and the dialogue, in which the characters marvel at the object's beauty, includes the lines: "Before the idol bow to the ground / and let trumpets, organ, and pipes resound!" ("Pochtiti obraz; a veli igrati / v truby, organy i svirelstvovati"). A character called A Player (Gudets) calls for more music, and the stage directions specify horns and pipes, the common musical currency of the Muscovite theatrical ensemble.[108] The next main section of the drama, in which the three boys do not bow to the idol and are thrown into the furnace, focuses on singing. Polotskii cues in dialogue from the biblical text (Daniel 3), and the three boys first say and then sing, "Blagosloven esi, gospodi" (Blessed art Thou, O Lord), one of the texts spoken and sung in the old liturgical drama's rendition of the story.[109] After the second, sung statement of the text, one of the witnesses refers to the boys' sweet singing. The action wraps up quickly, with a final epilogue, following which Polotskii directs a *mnogoletie* to be performed, and then a final *igranie* (literally, a playing; that is, for instruments). In this play, then, music helps to articulate the gulf between the unbelievers and the faithful, between Nebuchadnezzar's court and the true church.

We know very little about individual *interscenia* or *intermedia* in the Muscovite repertoire but it appears that as a whole, these interludes trace the same sorts of changes over the years of the theater's existence as do the plays themselves; that is, an overall streamlining, yet retaining a strong musical component. There might easily have been some sort of music associated with the *interscenia* listed in *The Play of Artaxerxes* summary: light-hearted, one presumes, and comic, in keeping with the very little we know of the characters who appear in these scenes. The storyline in these *interscenia* is more Western than Muscovite: the character Thraso, for example, as well as Mops and Muischelow.

After *The Play of Artaxerxes,* some of the *intermedia* characters and situations were integrated into the plays themselves. Perhaps the cycle of two separate but related actions was too complex, or perhaps such elaborate material simply made the evening's entertainment too long. At any rate, in later plays, the comic scenes and their comic music tend to become part of the main play and are not performed as separate cycles. In *Judith,* for example, there are several scenes devoted to comic action (mostly involving drinking and soldiers), sometimes with strophic singing (the drinking song in act 5, scene 2, for example). There is also a concluding strophic song in which the rejoicing performers sing a text based very closely on the song of praise in Judith 16. Each of the five strophes in Gregorii's version ends with an invocation to rejoice, and the first strophe calls upon instruments to praise God.[110]

Judith includes only one segment labeled "Mezhdosenie" (*interscenium*). It is not comic, however, but has an important dramatic and musical component. The *mezhdosenie* is clearly related to the action of the play, with one of the characters appearing in both and with references in its dialogue to the main events of the play. The primary action of the *mezhdosenie* is the spoken laments of the four kings taken captive by the Assyrians. It concludes with a song (*pesn'*) which, according to the preserved stage directions, each of four kings sings sorrowfully or mournfully (*zhalobno*) one after another. The text is written as a series of six-line strophes. It is, then, a strophic lament sung in sequence by male characters.[111] Although the kings themselves do not appear outside this scene, the dramatic situation of the *mezhdosenie* clearly serves to highlight the events and mood of the play. Yet this segment is at the same time set apart, not only by its label and by the four unique characters, but through their sung lament as well. Thus in *Judith*, one section of the play, with dramatic acting and a sung strophic lament, is called a *mezhdosenie*, but another section, with comic action and also with strophic singing, is simply part of the play's main action. Were the two segments performed in different theatrical spaces? Was the *mezhdosenie* considered separate precisely because of its "mournful" song? The net result is that in *Judith*, although the *interscenia* are reduced in number relative to *The Play of Artaxerxes*, the comic action as a whole is more evident and is tied closely to the main storyline.

This appears to be the case for other Muscovite court plays, some of which, as in the earlier Orpheus entertainment and in the Esther play, refer to Western comic characters. In the Tamerlane play, for example, there are no specific segments labeled as *intermedia* or *interscenia*. There are, however, several comic scenes, generally involving soldiers and drinking, in one of which the characters end up singing a song that concludes in inebriated nonsense syllables (act 2, scene 2). Act 1, scene 5 looks very much like a Western-style *intermedio*. It is composed primarily of comic clowning, yet is related to the events of the main text, and it concludes the first act of the play. The four characters who appear in this scene are Pickleherring (Pikel'gering), who, true to form, steals, drinks, and generally creates havoc; two soldiers with the obviously foreign names Leonardo and Valerio (spelled variously); and another fellow called simply *muzhik*, a courier whom the others waylay. These characters, although they refer in their conversations to the primary action of the play, do not appear elsewhere. Although no music is specified for Pickleherring and friends, and the scene in which they appear has no special label in the text, this would seem to be a typical *intermedio*-type interlude, reintroducing the character to the Muscovite court after his highly successful debut in the pre-Lenten Orpheus entertainment. Similar antics also take place in *Judith*, where the character Susakim pursues a single-minded obsession with sausages and has his head temporarily cut off with a fox tail in the last scene of act 6, prefiguring the action to befall, with permanent consequences, to Holofernes in the next act. (In the traditions of the Western European stage, the fox tail is an attribute of the Pickleherring character.)[112]

Simeon Polotskii was especially fond of *intermedia*, which are meticulously specified at the end of each of the six sections of *The Prodigal Son* with some variant of the direction: "The singers sing, and there is an Intermedium" (the final word written in Latin script at each appearance). Polotskii's intentions for these *intermedia* are difficult to fathom with any certainty. The author came from the rich tradition of Jesuit-influenced school dramas in Belarus and Ukraine, which would have relied upon stock comic situations and figures similar to those appearing in the Moscow Orpheus and the *interscenia* in *The Play of Artaxerxes;* at the same time, such elements are amply demonstrated in the other Muscovite plays as well.[113] Polotskii does not specify any characters, texts, or songs to be performed in his *intermedia,* which suggests that they did not belong to the elaborate, play-within-a-play approach of the Esther drama. The playwright's silence on the specifics of his *intermedia* also indicate they were not necessarily related to the main action of the play (otherwise, the author would have needed to specify particular characters and song incipits at the least). This contrasts to his approach in his play texts where, for example in Nebuchadnezzar, he noted specific biblical passages to be inserted into the action. Polotskii's *intermedia* may have provided some comic diversion, which was generally integrated into the other play texts (especially in *Judith*) but not especially featured in Polotskii's works (apart from the drunken singing in *The Prodigal Son*). The *intermedia* may also have given a bit more substance to the otherwise quite short texts.[114]

Another dramatic work with a possible connection to the court's productions combines a variety of approaches, although still in the general direction of an overall streamlining in terms of length and complexity of scenic construction. The story of *Aleksei chelovek bozhii* (Aleksei, Man of God) was popular in Muscovy, with obvious resonance during Tsar Aleksei's reign. For a planned (but ultimately unrealized) royal visit to Kiev, the tsar's recently appointed governor there, Iu. P. Trubetskoi, planned a theatrical version of the story at the Kievan collegium, and the work survives in a printed playbill (dated 1674) and in the manuscript copy of the play's text.[115] The production called for two sections labeled "Intermedium, ili smekh" (Intermedium, or comedy [literally, laughter]), placed in the middle of act 1 and again in the middle of act 2 in the two-act production. The first *intermedium* is a comic drinking scene set at a wedding and is derived from the action of the main drama. It includes stage directions calling for *tsymbali* and *skrypki* to play and for dancing.[116]

The second *intermedium* relies instead on a bit of local color—Cossack life—for entertainment. The brief reference in the surviving playbill reads: "An Italian comes to the Zaporozhian Cossacks and they dress him up as a Cossack." This sort of down-home, vernacular humor is typical of the Polish-Belarusian-Ukrainian tradition of school drama with which Trubetskoi himself was familiar.[117] In the complete text of the play, this second *intermedium* is also called an "igralishche" (a "playing" of instrumental music), although no stage action or text is preserved.[118] (One wonders if this is also what Polotskii had in mind for his own *igranie* at the conclusion of the Nebuchadnezzar play.) There are also references to singing throughout the play's text, including sections in which Aleksei's parents and bride lament his death; in one case, there may be a hint of strophic structure but there are no other indications that these passages were set to music.[119]

The setting of *Aleksei, Man of God* is relevant because Trubetskoi may have had personal experience with the tsar's theater in Moscow. He was in the capital at the time of the 1672 premiere and as a boyar, may have attended the performance of *The Play of Artaxerxes;* he left for Kiev in February 1673, so he would only have seen that first production.[120] Trubetskoi would thus have been well aware of the tsar's enthusiasm for theatrical performances, which is probably why he went to such lengths to prepare one for Aleksei's intended trip to Kiev, and also accounts for the many references to the current political situation with the Turks that are embedded in the play's text. The same approach was taken later in the Muscovite rendition of the Tamerlane story. So although some of Trubetskoi's production decisions may reflect the resources at the Kievan collegium and the somewhat different traditions of school drama there, he would also have been aware of the value of theatrical productions to Aleksei. The Kievan production of *Aleksei, Man of God* thus seems to represent an initial reaction, by a sensitive politician, to the court theater's first presentation (and indeed, even if Trubetskoi did not actually attend the premiere, he, like all top-ranking government figures, would certainly have known about it).

A final, late reference to the Muscovite passion for entertainment illustrates the popularity and importance of the sort of knock-about comic routines that appear to have been regular features of the court productions. A description by Adolf Lyseck in 1675 ties together many of the elements featured in the various *interscenia,* overlaid with a deep and familiar wariness on the part of the Muscovites when confronted with magical—devilish—stage tricks. Although Lyseck's account may refer to one of Aleksei's theatrical evenings (he describes events of November 1675, which does coincide with known theatrical performances), his tale also reminds us how important the Orpheus-like variety entertainment was to the court, and the lengths to which they were prepared to go in order to supply it:

> A few days after our departure [from Moscow on 7 November 1675] German players were going to present a comedy [*comoedia*] which, as they said, would be highly pleasing to the tsar if only one of our servants would take part. This servant was a tightrope-walker, whose amusing and graceful tricks aroused widespread astonishment, especially among the Russians, all of whom declared that he was a sorcerer who deceived worthy people with devilish powers. At any rate, one really had to puzzle over his tricks. . . . The Germans and a few Russians asked the Ambassador [Battoni] to let him stay in Moscow so he could

show his talents to the tsar and tsaritsa. Their wishes, however, were not fulfilled. Word of our departure got back to the tsar, and he immediately dispatched General Menzies, a former envoy to Vienna and Rome, after us, along with a translator, in order to return our servant-magician to Moscow. They caught up to us on the third day in postal sleds. After explaining the tsar's wishes, they asked the servant to return and assured him that the tsar would reward him handsomely and would immediately send him back. The messengers let him decide on his own. The servant returned to Moscow and performed his tricks there at the royal palaces twice, amazing the tsar and the tsaritsa.[121]

Lyseck concludes his tale by noting that the servant rejoined the party as they were still on the road, having squandered everything the tsar had given him.

The series of Muscovite plays points generally in the direction of a paring down of Gregorii's original and complex work, moving from the full-out laments and elaborately layered *interscenia* of *The Play of Artaxerxes* to the rapid-fire comic exchanges in *Judith* and the quick-moving storytelling of *The Prodigal Son*. Gregorii's audience enjoyed their theatrical entertainment mightily but seemed to want to retain the spectacle in simpler form and presented in more forthright fashion. All the plays emphasize music in some of the ways Gregorii had used it initially, as a structural element defining the large divisions of a given work and as a natural and decorative expression of the dramatic events, through fanfares, banquet music, and the like. Strophic singing by an ensemble also seems to fit into this celebratory and decorative category. Each of these elements was familiar: the plays themselves from the old liturgical dramas and from diplomatic reports; instruments from long use at court; and even strophic non-liturgical singing in the form of the new *kant* styles.

It is the solo sung laments that seem to have been the least comfortable in the Muscovite context and which were prominently featured only in the first play. Did the laments (and the characters who performed them) seem the most "foreign" in this process? In Polotskii's setting of Adam and Eve, the lament is not by Adam himself but rather about Adam, in which his—and our—sad fate is pondered, quite appropriately, by the three angels. The Hebrew psalms, another sort of lament, also appear to have been an uncomfortable fit, for nothing similar follows in the extant texts, even when, as in *Judith,* such an approach would seem appropriate. Perhaps the performance concept interfered with the dramatic flow of the evening, or perhaps the available singers simply could not carry it off. At any rate, the surviving play texts trace a streamlining in terms of both dramatic construction and music in which, although music is used more simply (by eliminating the laments, for example), musical expression in general might feature more prominently. The short *Prodigal Son,* with its many *intermedia,* would have presented a more concentrated impression of music than the much longer *Play of Artaxerxes,* which also had a great deal of music but spread out over a longer and more complex dramatic narrative. Ironically, for the music of the Muscovite theater, less was clearly more.

In his famous account of the Muscovite court theatrical productions, Jacob Reutenfels gives a sense of both hesitation and achievement, of tradition and of possibilities transcending those traditions. The Russians' obvious willingness to explore (or, as Reutenfels said, to leave "everything to the discretion of the actors themselves") was still tempered by the powerful customs of society long after Aleksei's theater closed its doors. Both approaches were in full operation some twenty-five years later, when the Golitsyn family lived in Vienna with their beloved companion, the young castrato singer Filippo Balatri. The intrepid Princess Golitsyna had found a few appropriate theatrical performances in Vienna—and still others of which she did not approve—and on one occasion, she and Balatri conspired together to persuade the Orthodox priest in her household there to accompany them to one of the approved venues. As Balatri recounts, they were able to persuade the priest "to attend a drama of Judith and Holofernes by telling him it was an edifying biblical story *with no masks*" (emphasis added), commenting that even cloistered nuns might attend such a drama. Balatri explained in his diary that the princess held such an opinion because the Orthodox Church forbade the use of masks. The princess's characterization of the production elicited the same kind of automatic horror that had greeted Marina Mniszek's fatal masquerade nearly a century earlier—and this after the exhilarating experience of the court theater—and shows just how powerful the customs and traditions of Russian life really were and, at the same time, how flexible and curious the Russian audience was.[122] Something of the same special Muscovite reaction to masks finds its way into an account written by another Russian exploring Western European culture at just this time: the travel journal written by Petr Tolstoi, a fifty-year-old official sent by Peter the Great to study maritime skills in Venice in 1697–99. Although Tolstoi's description reflects the attractive licentiousness made possible—even encouraged —by such masquerade, his account simultaneously conveys the special reserve carried from long Muscovite custom:

> [A]ll through the carnival all the men and women and girls walk in masks, and
> they stroll about freely, wherever they please, and no one knows anybody. And
> this is how they always make merry in Venice, and they never want to be

without amusement, and in this gayety they sin much and, when they come together on the square at San Marco, many girls in masquerade hold hands with visiting foreigners, and stroll with them and amuse themselves without shame.[123]

Aleksei's theatrical enterprise did not survive him. Court poet Simeon Polotskii praised the young successor, Fedor Alekseevich, in his *Gusl' dobroglasnaia* (The Sweet-Sounding Psaltery), a poetic work composed on Fedor's ascent to the throne, by comparing him to the "great tsar Artakserks," a figure of some consequence in the reign of Fedor's father. In the more conservative atmosphere of the new court, however, this image and the wealth of allusions it engendered—the Westernized aesthetics, the foreign planners and players, even, perhaps, down to the lowly musicians—no longer had the same appeal. As Andrei Robinson says, it was far easier for Tsar Fedor to close the theater than to support its continuation.[124] As early as February 1676, only a few weeks after Aleksei's death, the Danish diplomat Giøe was reporting that "it is said that the state will be conducted according to ancient custom, that is to say, that the comedies and ballets will cease for ever ... it is the old boyars who press the abolition of all these things."[125] By 1684 the Saxon visitor Georg Adam Schleussing, whom we encountered earlier urging foreigners to sneak into Russian churches in mufti, was proclaiming that although previously the court had employed German musicians and actors, this was no longer the case: the patriarch "believes that Russia will perish if any kind of novelty is introduced." Although Schleussing is not necessarily the best informed of witnesses (he prefaces his remark on the foreign musicians, for example, by stating that Russians do not like music), on this particular subject he may have had some inside knowledge. Schleussing attended the same diplomatic reception in Moscow in 1684 as did fellow Saxon Laurent Rinhuber, who was certainly quite familiar with the hiring of foreign specialists for Aleksei's theater.[126] Rumors of vast theatrical enterprises carried out by Tsarevna Sofiia Alekseevna (regent to the young co-tsars Ivan and Peter after the death of her brother, Tsar Fedor, in 1682) are not substantiated, although one might note that Sofiia's powerful and influential advisor, Vasilii Vasil'evich Golitsyn, owned, along with the musical instruments inventoried in chapter 4, four manuscript books labeled "On the production of Comedy."[127]

Private royal theater did, after a break of several decades, re-emerge, and in interesting quarters, suggesting the many changes that had swept through Russian society in the intervening years. Two of Peter's relations, his sister-in-law, Praskov'ia Fedorovna (Tsar Ivan's widow), and particularly his sister, Natal'ia Alekseevna, both continued and cultivated theatrical performances in the first decade and a half of the eighteenth century, at a time when the first Russian public theater made its brief appearance in Moscow. Natal'ia's theater, established first in the familiar residence of Preobrazhenskoe and then in St. Petersburg, shows important links to her father's productions, including the recycling of some of the texts and equipment. Her theater and the new public establishment on Red Square in Moscow represent a new chapter in the history of Russian theater—but that is a history that belongs to a different chapter in a different book.[128]

Epilogue

Reversing Our Gaze: A Case Study

If there is a single, overarching theme of this study it is surely this simple idea: an appreciation of the multiplicity in the worlds of Muscovite music-making and in the sources that can tell us about these activities. This book has focused on music and musical practices associated with a very small segment of the Muscovite population of the seventeenth century—that of the literate, generally non-clerical establishment—and even a very small segment within this group; that is, the upper echelons of the ruling class, confined largely to the capital city and especially to the inner sancta of the Kremlin. Yet even within this small group, the choices and use of music were profuse, a true "inexhaustible sea," to quote Diletskii again. Within this diversity of singing styles, approaches to entertainments and instruments, and musical vocabulary, there were some common touchstones that regulated one's basic views, prohibiting or restraining the all-too-easy licentiousness music could so easily stimulate. These rough parameters, then—which I summarized earlier as privacy, propriety, and scale—provided the guideposts for the myriad ways in which those at the top of Muscovite society navigated their choices in music.

In its emphasis on richness and variety in Muscovite musical life, this study fits comfortably with many other recent investigations that stress multiplicity and avoid rigid characterizations of this society. The editors of a recent collection focusing on religious practices, for example, make the same point (oddly echoing the pleas of Paisios, Patriarch of Constantinople, to Nikon cited in chapter 2), when they conclude that "Orthodoxy was an enterprise capacious enough to accommodate a community of conversation, with room for disagreement, negotiation, and even contradiction."[1] The musical cultures we have considered throughout this volume share in this capacious and generous abundance. Olearius's tale of the burning of instruments can no longer suffice as a shorthand for musical Muscovy.

What was the legacy of the many kinds of singing, playing, and music-making we have considered in previous chapters, or did this complex and vibrant approach to musical culture simply wither away in defeat when the first Western opera singers made their entrances onto the stages of Imperial Russia? The Russian musical world changed profoundly in the eighteenth century, with the wholesale importation of European performers, composers, and impresarios beginning in earnest with Peter the Great's successors in the 1730s. Yet the musical legacy of seventeenth-century Muscovy, which had itself incorporated borrowed musical styles, composers, and theoretical language, was still strong. This is seen readily enough in some relatively straightforward instances. The long-standing institution of the *pevchie d'iaki* remained, for example, although as a result of the extensive institutional and administrative reorganizations that occurred throughout Peter's reign, the singers' titles and assignments came in for some revision. Nevertheless, they were still the professional singing ensembles of state and church (or Synod), and they still had important roles in processions and ceremonies both sacred and secular—these are the singers that Friedrich von Bergholz praised for their sonorous bass voices, ringing out like organ pipes.[2] Peter himself sang with the *d'iaki*, and reports of his traditional royal musical training circulated throughout the realm. Visiting clerics from the far-away provincial city of Viatka (Kirov), for example, described Peter's singing at celebrations on New Year's Day in 1705, noting also that the service was followed by public dining accompanied by violins, organ, and trumpets, familiar accoutrements of earlier court entertainment although displayed in a more public venue.[3]

Outdoor music was cultivated enthusiastically under Peter and at the ceremonies marking the victory at Poltava over Sweden (1709), for example, developed into elaborate, multi-sectional concerts-in-progress. Outdoor musical suites of this type, although on a more modest scale, had long been part of Muscovite practice to mark sacred and secular occasions. The *kant*, which was developed so intensively in the late seventeenth century, continued to circulate in even greater numbers in the following century and was the crucial ingredient in the formation of the emerging Russian solo song.[4] The Petrine-era assemblies, so striking for their exceedingly non-Muscovite mixed socializing, especially dancing, also included entertainment by musical instruments that would not have been entirely out of place (in simpler and reduced form) at the Muscovite court.[5] Even the spectacular public concert life that grew so rapidly in Imperial Russia, which certainly had no direct precedents in the Muscovite past, might have been prefigured in part by the performances at Tsar Aleksei's wondrous theater. After all, the earliest productions of Western opera in Imperial Russia were, like Tsar Aleksei's theater, created largely for an audience of one—Empress Anna—and confined initially to annual performances to commemorate Anna's birthday. No matter how tempting it is to make the seventeenth century into a brief prelude to the exciting world of divas and drama that we see in Imperial Russia, as so often happens in surveys of Russian music, this study shows how thoroughly much of eighteenth-century Russian music and musical thinking was grounded in earlier practices and approaches. This again supports recent scholarship in Russian culture, for example in the history of theater. Scholars such as Liudmila Starikova have been revealing the wealth of influences and experimentation in the theatrical practices at the courts of Peter's immediate successors, a process only too familiar from similar experimentation in Aleksei Mikhailovich's reign.

The treatment of music theory provides yet another example of continuity. As we saw in chapter 5, Nikolai Diletskii's *Grammatika* circulated throughout the eighteenth century, and the author himself served as a quotable authority on theory for much of that time. Some of his teaching tools outlasted the *Grammatika*, and other Muscovite-era theory treatises survived into the eighteenth century along with his. At least in certain circles, seventeenth-century Muscovite music theory lived on in Imperial Russia, even as the new secular presses issued musical works by well-known Western writers. Such works, by Georg Simon Löhlein, David Kellner, and others, may indeed have been new but the concept of comprehensive, didactic theoretical treatises with a strong infusion of Western musical constructs and vocabulary was certainly a familiar one.[6]

The foundations of eighteenth-century Russian musical life are thus deeply rooted in seventeenth-century practice and experience, and we conclude this study by considering a final illustration of this legacy as it was reinterpreted in the eighteenth century, not in Russia but in the West. Such an approach, in lieu of a more traditional concluding chapter, not only affords us a chance to broaden our appreciation of the strengths of Muscovite culture but it brings us back to our opening chapter, for we end where we began, with the Time of Troubles and its aftermath. This time, however, we see its lingering and powerful influence on Western thinking about Russia and in artistic works expressing that influence. By reversing our perspective, we can appreciate that even in the eighteenth century Westerners often saw Russia through the lens of the previous century.

The False Dmitrii and Les faux Moscovites *on European Stages*

This concluding study revolves around two different constructions of "Russianness" on Western stages, one a quick satire based on a real-life encounter with a representative of the tsar's realm in Paris in 1668, and the other a more elaborate invocation of Russian history based on long-familiar imagery. Westerners had been writing about Russia for well over a century by the time these two theatrical works appeared. Some accounts written by travelers to Muscovy were especially well known and influential in the West: Herberstein's *Rerum Moscoviticarum commentarii* (Vienna, 1549) was one such authoritative source, issued in almost twenty-five editions, in a variety of languages, before 1600.[7] Giles Fletcher's *Of the Russe Commonwealth,* although suppressed after its initial publication in 1591, was an influential source for English audiences through the seventeenth century, with a readership including Raleigh, Jonson, Beaumont, the playwright John Fletcher, Milton, and possibly also Bacon, Spenser, Shakespeare, and others.[8] In the seventeenth century, Adam Olearius's account circulated widely, with editions in the original German and in French, Dutch, English, and Italian issued into the early decades of the eighteenth century.[9] Many of the images of Russia in these accounts sounded the same themes: tyranny and unfettered power wielded by the tsar (especially Ivan IV) over the long-suffering populace—the "slave-born Muscovite" of Sir Philip Sidney's poem—along with hardships and casual cruelty meted out, especially to women.[10] Even geography was a special theme: the northern locale and the extreme cold were topics that transcended the meteorological, touching on resonant images in mythology and biblical writings of the evil associated with the earth's far northern regions. Frightening images of the power of ice thrilled Europeans in more temperate landscapes through the widely published experiences of Dutch explorer William Barents, who wrote vividly of his party's miraculous survival on the ice floes in the Russian Far North.[11]

The splendor of the tsars' court and the mysterious animals and native peoples the travelers found in Muscovy were also fascinating subjects, and descriptions of such alien beings complemented the notions of exoticism developed early on in the West. The masquerade Henry VIII held on Shrove Sunday in 1510 was an early and influential example of such a view. It featured elaborately costumed courtiers attired "after the fashion of Russia or Ruslande, with furred hattes of greye on their hedes," accompanied by torchbearers "appareyled in Crymosyn satyne and grene, lyke Moreskotes, their faces blacke." The long description of Henry's revelries appeared in Edward Hall's *Chronicle,* published in 1548 and 1550 and reissued in 1587, at a time when English interest in Russia ran high due to important commercial ties. The "Masque of the Muscovites" in *Love's Labour's Lost* presents a similar parade.[12]

Travel accounts included Russian music in a similar fashion, that is, emphasizing what was different and strange to the Western reader, as we have seen throughout this volume. Curiosity about Russian music continued in the West throughout the eighteenth century in writings with a somewhat more knowledgeable evaluation of at least some of Russia's musical styles.[13] The earliest substantive treatment, coming from a time when the Russian court was hiring Western academics and artists at a frenzied pace, was by Jacob von Stählin, who lived in Russia from 1735 until his death fifty years later. Stählin wrote a series of observations of Russian musical life, which he published in a German-language periodical in St. Petersburg and which were then collected and issued in 1769–70 as "Nachrichten von der Musik in Russland."[14] At around the same time, the *Essai sur la littérature russe* (Livorno, 1774) offered its own readers an "Histoire abregée de la musique en Russie" that included a discussion of contemporary musical life, religious music, and folk practice. This history was taken from Stählin's publication, including the "Melodie pour le chant du peuple en Russie" that concludes the French work.[15] English readers in this period were (relatively) well informed about Russian songs through publications of individual compositions in popular journals, and particularly through the work of Dr. Matthew Guthrie, a physician who lived in Russia from 1770 until his death in 1807. Guthrie devoted himself to studies of Russian history and folklore, and his *Noctes Rossicae, or Russian Evening Recreations,* although unpublished in its full form, was issued in a partial French translation in St. Petersburg as *Dissertations sur les antiquités de Russie* (1795); the work was for sale in London, where it received a substantial notice in the *Monthly Review.* Guthrie's musical examples were taken from the recent large-scale publication of Russian folk songs collected by Jan Prach (St. Petersburg, 1790).[16]

For ordinary Westerners, however, there were far more tangible elements influencing their views of Russians: the visiting ambassadorial parties—real Russians in the real Europe—who appeared in increasing numbers throughout the seventeenth century. Just as Western affairs and ceremonies were summarized in the *kuranty* for the tsar's court, so visits by these colorful guests were reported extensively in European newspapers and in other writings. Although Western images of Russia and Russians in the late sixteenth and seventeenth centuries were formed by many experiences, an important part of this formulation came from the highly staged, almost theatrical appearances of these alien visitors. The guests' striking costumes and manners are consistently singled out in contemporary accounts, recalling the description in Hall's *Chronicle* of the previous century. Samuel Pepys, for example, observed the huge crowd that assembled to witness the procession of the Muscovite embassy to London in 1662, describing the Russians "in their habits and fur caps very handsome, comely men, and most of them with hawkes upon their fists to present to the King," and noting that the ambassador's son wore "the richest suit for pearl and tissue, that ever I did see, or shall, I believe."[17] The portrait of Ambassador Potemkin painted during his 1681–82 trip to Europe only reinforces the impressive and quite foreign appearance of the Muscovite visitors, "star'd at . . . by a number of Gawdy spectators": floor-length, heavy robes dripping with furs and jewels; conical hats adorned with still more fur; luxuriant beards; and no wigs. Combined with the diplomats' stately and ponderous choreography, the grave insistence on protocol to the tiniest detail, and the exotic gifts—heaps of furs, hawks, and the like—such figures were a magnificent and entertaining curiosity to Western eyes.[18]

These external features and impressions were transferred to Western stages. Ambassador Mikulin's highly visible time in London in 1600–1601 may have prompted the incidental but realistic appearance of a Muscovite ambassador in Thomas Heywood's *If You Know Not Me, You Know No Bodie* (published 1605), set in the time of Queen Elizabeth. Two years later, the exploits of the Sherley brothers in their ongoing and dangerous series of diplomatic adventures were depicted on stage in *The Travels of the Three English Brothers*, which features a dumb-show depiction of their entertainment in Moscow.[19] Generic stage Russians appear in the "Troisième Entrée" of the *Ballet Royal de l'Impatience* (1661), where the dancing masters in the ballet "grow impatient while teaching the courante to some Muscovites." Although both Schleussing and Miege made unflattering comments about Russian dancing, the masters' impatience in this instance may refer as much to the general inability of *any* foreigner to perform to exacting French standards as it does to any specifically Russian choreographic blunders—although the frequently invoked association with lumbering bears might have made the Muscovites a particularly inviting target to depict foreign clumsiness.[20]

The most vivid and direct appearance of Russians in a seventeenth-century Western theater came from Paris in the second half of the century, during a period of regular and large-scale diplomatic exchange between Muscovy and Western Europe. This is a portrayal "from life," based on Ambassador Petr Potemkin's visit—or, more accurately, non-visit—to a Parisian theater, which prompted the production of a farce that emerged directly from contemporary Franco-Russian interactions (and from a showman's quick ability to profit from adversity). Like the scenario it resembles, the Turkish act in Molière's *Le bourgeois gentilhomme* (1670), this Parisian work has a broader context in terms of Western notions of the exotic. But both scenes also emerged from real-life contact and diplomacy.

Ambassador Potemkin witnessed two spectacular performances during his 1668 trip: *Les Coups de la fortune* by the Marais troupe and the Molière company's performance of *Amphitryon* "with machines and ballet entrées." However, the ambassador's third planned visit, to the Hôtel de Bourgogne, failed to materialize, for the very good reason that the diplomats were having an audience with the king on that day. Charles Robinet, in the *Gazette rimée* of 29 September 1668, composed a verse account of the events:

> [T]he comedians of the Hôtel [de Bourgogne], / not with mediocre pomp, / but beautifully . . . / have been three times awaiting / the Muscovite Excellencies, / with magnificent dances, / with lovely plays, with concerts, / and even with sweet treats: / but having this time other business . . . / they could not show up.[21]

The envoys themselves were apparently quite a draw for the theater, and the company was naturally upset that the showy, revenue-producing visit was cancelled. In revenge, actor Raymond Poisson wrote a wicked one-act farce called *Les faux Moscovites* in order to remedy the deficiency (or, as he explained, "not being able to have the real Muscovites, [I was obliged] to cook up some fake ones").[22]

The play is a veritable catalogue of European stereotypes about Russians, based on the less-than-stellar behavior of some earlier Muscovite missions. In Poisson's play, the innkeeper Gorgibus is awaiting the arrival of a Muscovite nobleman, and in the meantime, he has been catering to two supposed interpreters, who have been living in luxury at the innkeeper's expense. In reality, these two have actually been sent by a local gentleman to carry off Gorgibus's daughter. They engage another conspirator to impersonate the much-awaited Muscovite, who finally appears in magnificent style, babbling in "Russian" all the while and consuming the feast Gorgibus has prepared. Eventually all are revealed and Gorgibus's daughter is properly married, with the other sundry characters dispatched appropriately.[23]

The Russian impostors behave as the French audiences apparently expected: they drink heavily, toast constantly, eat heroically, and perform violent physical activities (a drunken chase after one of the female characters is described as a simple post-prandial siege, normal exercise for the guests). Although the French did take note of hearty eating by Potemkin and his party, the caricature does not really fit his behavior. The 1654 Russian embassy to France, however, had not been so well behaved. Observers reported that the head of this earlier party "passed every afternoon getting intoxicated with his secretary and another attaché; and that the three of them consumed eight pints of hard liquor each day, and that, in their drunkenness, they quarreled and even fought like lackeys."[24] Poisson and his troupe also take aim at all Russian emissaries' preoccupation with finances, which were of constant concern to the visiting party (and Potemkin was no exception). As Sir Charles Cottrell, Master of Ceremonies at the English court, observed after receiving disappointing parting gifts from a Russian delegation in 1673: "[I]t is their Custome, to think, whatsoever they get, too little, and whatever they give, too much."[25]

Some of the most elaborate satire is directed at language, which again is not necessarily specifically related to Russian habits (although the Russian diplomats were notorious sticklers for absolute fidelity in titles and address, to the point of having multiple documents recopied multiple times). The pretend Muscovite, the character Lubin, is directed to give "a long speech in pidgin Russian while cutting the meats and presenting them to the others" at a banquet for their gullible French host. The other pretenders, Jolicœur and La Montagne, respond in turn:[26]

> **Jolicœur:** *Cracq.*
> **La Montagne:** *Cricq.*
> **Lubin,** *while swallowing he jabbers nonsense: Crocq.*
> **Jolicœur:** *The pig, he says, is admirable.*
> **Lubin** *jabbers at length with glass in hand.*
> **La Montagne,** *to the ladies: He drinks to your health.*
> **Mme Aminthe:** *How idiotic this language is!*
>   *What! to talk on and on in order to say but one word!*

As John Powell has pointed out, the situation recalls French amusement with another foreign tongue spoken by other imposters on the Parisian stage. In Molière's *Le bourgeois gentilhomme* (act 4, scene 4), the Mufti says simply: "Bel-men." The interpreter launches into a lengthy translation, at which one of the characters asks, disbelievingly: "So many things in just two words?" Yes, is the reply, the Turkish language is like that. The association probably went beyond equally incomprehensible languages: the bearded Russians, enveloped in their long caftans and protocol-obsessed, must, like the Turks, have seemed to the French the epitome of the foreign.[27]

Potemkin did not include his theatrical experiences in his own report but they surely made an impression, for when the ambassador returned to the West in 1681–82, he again enjoyed several nights at the theater, arranged at his own request. In an entry dated 12 January 1682, the Calendar of State Papers noted that in London, "By the ambassador's particular command a play called the Tempest was played yesterday, at which he [Potemkin] was present. On Friday the second part of the Siege of Jerusalem is acted by his particular command and on Monday he goes home." (The performances were Thomas Shadwell's adaptation of Shakespeare's *The Tempest* and part 2 of John Crowne's *The Destruction of Jerusalem* by Titus Vespasian.) True to form, as the Master of Ceremonies reports after a performance on 10 January:

> [Upon] the invitation of Mr Killegrew, Master of the Revells and of the Kings Play House, to the Amb: to see a Play, he went this day; was placed in the Kings Box; he was entertained with very fine Daunces between the Acts; and at the end of the first with a great Basket of Fruit; and as I think, he gave not one farthing either for that or the Play.[28]

In Paris on the same trip, Louis XIV regaled the ambassador with a banquet, a comedy, and some ballet *entrées*.[29]

Poisson's revenge was certainly sweet and apparently quite entertaining. But more complex views of Russia also found a place on European stages along with Poisson's broad satire. This deeper and more serious vein brings us back to the era of the False Dmitrii and its many players.

The great German theorist Johann Mattheson spent part of the year 1710 working on an opera, *Boris Goudenow*. (The work was completed in a kind of rough draft form, but it was not performed.)[30] The story of Boris's elevation to the throne—the familiar prologue to the horrific events of the Time of Troubles—was old news, and would seem to be a curious choice for an operatic subject in early eighteenth-century Hamburg. Mattheson's work was certainly not a direct artistic response to the specific events of the century-old story.

The most obvious immediate context for Mattheson's *Boris Goudenow* is the aftermath of Peter the Great's stunning victory over Sweden at Poltava in 1709, an event of the greatest import to the European powers. Things Russian suddenly became intensely and vitally interesting, a view that was only enhanced by Peter's earlier ill-disguised incognito visit to Holland and England in 1697–98.[31] This context in contemporary politics may also have been heightened by Mattheson's own contacts with the diplomatic world. Mattheson worked from 1704 as tutor to Cyrill Wich, the son of England's resident in Hamburg; he later served as secretary to Ambassador John Wich and was well acquainted with the events of the Great Northern War. Young Cyrill himself was eventually appointed English ambassador to Hamburg, and in 1741 he was sent as English ambassador to the court of St. Petersburg. Mattheson met both Charles XII of Sweden and Peter the Great (whom he entertained in Hamburg in May 1716). In the year of Peter's victory at Poltava, a Russian ambassador was sent to Hamburg; as Stephen Stubbs, one of the editors of Mattheson's opera, asks, "Can it be coincidental that Mattheson chose this moment [1710] to write an opera on a Russian theme?"[32]

The answer must be both yes and no. The general interest in Russia is well established for Mattheson's time and place, but one must still ask why this particular story from this particular time in Russian history? Mattheson fashioned his libretto from published accounts of Russian events, particularly the well-known book by Peter Petreius, a Swedish diplomat who had been in Russia during the Troubles and whose work appeared in Swedish in 1615, with a German translation issued in Leipzig in 1620.[33] Some of the incidents dramatized in the opera appear in Petreius's work, for example a deathbed scene in which Tsar Fedor Ivanovich offers the scepter to each of four Romanov brothers, all of whom decline it. This dramatic incident also appears in one of Petreius's own sources, the account written by Conrad Bussow; indeed Petreius, although he had witnessed many of the events of the Troubles at first hand, took much of his material from Bussow's work, a "shameless plagiarism" that stole some of Bussow's thunder as he attempted to publish his own account. Bussow also includes the story of the passing of the scepter among the Romanovs, and his work may be the ultimate source for this and other incidents in Mattheson's libretto.[34]

The deeper context for Mattheson's work is the West's continuing fascination with Russian affairs both specific and general, an interest that shifted from the pamphleteers' presses to the stages and entertainment halls of Europe. Such images were concentrated in realizations of the story of the False Dmitrii and in broader treatments of the era of Ivan, Boris, and the Time of Troubles—the very essence of the violence, tyranny, and ruthlessness European audiences had come to expect. Like the extensive pamphlet literature cited in chapter 1, which supplied a deliciously horrified Western readership with the gory details of the chaos in Russia, this period also provided fuel for Western stages. As historian Matthew Anderson observed, the Troubles "made it possible to think of the country, more even than in the age of Ivan the Terrible, in terms of cruelty, violence, blood, and suffering."[35]

These images are quite different from the satire of *Les faux Moscovites*. Indeed, one might argue that although there had been a visible Muscovite diplomatic and ecclesiastical presence in Europe since at least the Council of Florence in the fifteenth century, and Muscovy had been an important trading partner, especially for the English and increasingly the Dutch since the sixteenth century, it was the shocking and spectacular events of the life and death of Boris Godunov, the young tsarevich Dmitrii, and Dmitrii the Pretender that lodged Muscovite affairs firmly in Europe's cultural consciousness—this was, in short, a great story, ready-made for the stage.[36]

Western observers couched their commentary on the Time of Troubles in specifically theatrical terms. In a 1605 pamphlet describing Thomas Smith's trip to Russia for the Muscovy Company, the anonymous author characterized the events in Russia as "the Poeticall Furie in a Stage-action, compleat yet with horrid and wofull Tragedies: a first, but no second to any Hamlet." Another English observer uses the same imagery, describing in "this vnhappie countrey" a "woefull Sceane and publicke stage whereon so many bloudy parts haue bene acted on all hands."[37] Only a few years after Dmitrii's dramatic career, his life and the horrific surrounding events moved to the real "publicke stage" in Western dramatic works. The Spanish playwright Lope de Vega produced his influential *El Gran Duque de Moscovia y emperador perseguido* only a few years later (the play was published in 1617 but had apparently been produced somewhat earlier).[38] Several later plays were in turn based on Lope's influential drama; as Anderson notes, of all the events in Russian history known to Western writers and audiences in the seventeenth century, it was only the Time of Troubles that was dramatized on European stages.[39]

In England, where interest in Russian affairs was intense due to the Crown's trade monopoly, Russian images had long held special associations and had often appeared in writings and theatrical works, most importantly Shakespeare's.[40] John Fletcher's *The Loyal Subject* (1618) appears to have some resonance with the specific events of Dmitrii's time, although the work's meaning has and continues to be debated. At any rate, John Fletcher was the nephew of the diplomat Giles Fletcher, who had served as Elizabeth's ambassador to Russia, and John seems to have used his uncle's important *Of the Russe Commonwealth* as a source while working on his play.[41] Another English dramatist, Mary Pix, took up the subject at the end of the century in her play *The Tsar of Muscovy* (1701), and dramatic presentations of the tale cropped up in Italy as well, with Giuseppi Theodoli's *Il Demetrio Moscovita* (1652).[42]

Interest in current Russian events continued in the Western press, for example, with brief spurts of reporting after Stenka Razin's rebellion and execution in

1671 and the *strel'tsy* (musketeers) revolt in 1682.[43] But the Dmitrii affair retained its prominence—its preeminence for the West as *the* representative Russian event—both in historical works and in more fanciful renditions. Sometimes both approaches were combined, as in Sir Roger Manley's *The Russian Impostor: or, the History of Muskovy, under the Usurpation of Boris and the Imposture of Demetrius, Late Emperours of Muskovy* (1674 and 1677). Manley, like Mattheson, relied on previous accounts in his retelling of history, including Petreius's work, and his account is meant to be an impartial and scholarly study, told in lively and entertaining fashion.[44] In his second edition, however, Manley adds a purely imagined history of Dmitrii's days in Poland, courting the beautiful Marina and dueling with a rival, in an appendix titled *The Amours of Demetrius and Dorenski, Rivals in the Affections of Marina*. In a single volume, the Dmitrii tale thus passes from scholarly history to bodice-ripping fiction.

So no matter what Mattheson relied upon for his immediate sources and inspiration in setting his own *Boris Goudenow*, there was a century's worth of Western European history, fiction, and stage work from which he might have learned of the tale and formed his own views of its dramatic capabilities. Indeed, the story had such a tenacious hold on the Western imagination precisely because it vindicated the stereotypes already in hammered into place, pamphlet by pamphlet, book by book, over nearly two centuries' worth of observations by Western writers. In this light, it would almost have been more surprising if Mattheson had chosen a different scenario for his foray into Russian history. Although *Boris Goudenow* is based largely on a superficial knowledge of long-past events, it nevertheless reflects vividly held images of Russia in the contemporary Western imagination and in contemporary Western theatrical culture.[45]

The long, muddy roads that stretched between Moscow and Paris, Florence, Vienna, and all the other great Western European cities were indeed two-way streets, opened long before Peter the Great's energetic push to the West. Names, characters, and even playwrights reappear on both ends of the road: Molière's *Amphitryon*, which Ambassador Potemkin had glimpsed in Paris in 1668, was part of the repertoire of the early eighteenth-century Russian public theater as *Poroda Gerkulesova, v nei zhe pervaia persona Iupiter* (The Origin of Hercules, wherein the Principal Person is Jupiter), and Molière was represented by two additional plays in this period, with his *Komediia o doktore bitom* (The Comedy of the Doctor Drubbed, or *Le médecin malgré lui*) and *Dragyia smeianyia* (Dear Ones Laughed At, in Simon Karlinsky's heroic translation of the Russian rendition of *Les précieuses ridicules*).[46] This next generation of Russian audiences was entertained by Pickleherring, the clown who had caused Tsar Aleksei Mikhailovich to "shake with laughter" at the Orpheus production, in the play *Prints Pikel'-Giaring, ili Zhodelet, samyi svoi tiur'movyi zakliuchnik* (Prince Pickleherring, or Jodelet, Himself His Own Prisoner; ultimately based on Calderon, via Corneille).[47] These were not necessarily direct borrowings from the experiences of wide-eyed Muscovite ambassadors in Paris or Florence in the 1660s any more than the appearance of the Judith play at the Muscovite court can be said to have been an import from the 1635 performance that entertained the Russian delegates in Poland. Yet each contributed to the whole and each brought its own luster to, in Guy Miege's felicitous phrase, that "dazzling splendor" that traces the history of music and theater in seventeenth-century Muscovy and beyond.

Appendix

Kanty in Nikolai Diletskii's *Grammatika*

This appendix represents a preliminary attempt to illustrate the range of concordances among various *kant* manuscripts, focusing on the examples appearing in Diletskii's work. In some cases, *kanty* circulated into the late eighteenth century; see, for example, the listings in Titov, *Rukopisi slavianskie i russkie,* 2:374, from a late eighteenth-century source that includes the popular text "Messiia priide vo mir," a work that also appears in the earliest preserved Muscovite source, RGB 10944, from 1675. Most of the concordances listed below are based on Rothe, *Verse und Lieder bei den Ostslaven,* and thus refer only to textual concordances unless musical concordances are listed in addition. Full listings of the manuscript sources are in the bibliography.

"Bozhe laskavyi"

Diletskii: as both à 1 and à 2 in the following available sources: RGB 107, p. 123; GIM 168, fol. 65v; GIM 777, fols. 99v–100; Tver' 651a, pp. 176–77; RGB 146, p. 145; GIM 1340, fol. 131; RGADA 541, fols. 58v–59; Tver' 553, fol. 62v; and L'viv, p. LI (title only).

Literature and published examples: Rothe, *Verse und Lieder bei den Ostslaven,* No. 64; Dolskaya-Ackerly, "The Early Kant," 106; Dolskaya, *Spiritual Songs in*

Seventeenth-Century Russia [GIM 1938], Nos. 54 and 116; Pozdneev, *Rukopisnye pesenniki*, 112–13.

Concordances: GIM 1743; GIM 1938 (appears twice); GIM Shchuk. 61; GIM Sin. 927; RNB Pog. 426; RNB Pog. 1974; RNB Q.XIV.25; RNB Tit. 4172; RNB Q.XIV.141 (from Peretts, *Iz istorii russkoi pesni*, 183).

"Dieciątko sie narodziło"

Diletskii: L'viv (in Latin letters, p. XXVI), as a title; the à 1 melody (untexted) is presented following the title and repeated with the text "Alliluiia."

Literature and published examples: Rothe, *Verse und Lieder bei den Ostslaven*, No. 204; Dolskaya, *Spiritual Songs in Seventeenth-Century Russia* [GIM 1938], No. 137; *IRM* 1:231 and example 56 (from GIM 1743). The readings in GIM 1743 and GIM 1938 are extremely close; the reading in L'viv is transposed and has significant melodic and rhythmic variants. *IRM* 1:316, example 57, is a Polish version of the piece printed in Nowak-Dłużewski, *Kolędy polskie*, 2:313 and 317–19, a setting of "Puer natus" followed by several settings of the Polish translation, "Dieciątko się narodziło." The pieces are from four songbooks, extant in sources from 1586, ca. 1600, and 1637. Pozdneev, "Svetskie pol'skie pesni," esp. 58–60, includes an important discussion of the influence of published Western sources on some Russian *kant* manuscripts.

Concordances: GIM 1743 (appears twice); RGB 10944 (text only); RGB 9498; GIM 1938; GIM Khlud. 126d; GIM Shchuk. 61; RNB Pog. 426; RNB Pog. 1974; RNB Q.XIV.25; RNB Tit. 4172.

"Est' prelest v svete" (Simeon Polotskii, *Rifmologion*)

Diletskii: as à 1 in Tver' 553, fol. 60; L'viv, p. XLIX; title as "Est' zdrada v svietsie" in RGADA 541, fol. 56; RGB 146, p. 142; GIM 1340, fol. 128.

Literature and published examples: Rothe, *Verse und Lieder bei den Ostslaven*, p. 310; Dolskaya, *Spiritual Songs in Seventeenth-Century Russia* [GIM 1938], No. 140. On Simeon Polotskii's version in the *Rifmologion*, see Eremin, "Poeticheskii stil' Simeona Polotskogo," 142; Dolskaya-Ackerly, "The Early Kant," 124 and 266; Aravin, "U istokov," 111–12; Peretts, *Iz istorii russkoi pesni*, 129–50; Pozdneev, *Rukopisnye pesenniki*, 51. Published as example 67 in *IRM* 1:319 (based on GIM Shchuk. 61).

Concordances: GIM Shchuk. 61; GIM 1938; GIM Khlud. 126d; RGB 9498; RNB Q.XIV.25.

"Messia priide vo mir"

Diletskii: as à 1 (corresponding to lowest line in GIM 1938) and as à 4 in RGB 107, pp. 123–24; GIM 168, fol. 66; GIM 777, fols. 100–100v; and Tver' 651a, pp. 177–

78; RGADA 541, fol. 59; L'viv, p. LI, and Tver' 553, fol. 63; RGB 146, pp. 145–46; and GIM Barsova 1340, fols. 131–131v.

Literature and published examples: Rothe, *Verse und Lieder bei den Ostslaven*, Nos. 388–89; Dolskaya, *Spiritual Songs in Seventeenth-Century Russia* [GIM 1938], No. 156; Aravin, "U istokov," 113; and Pozdneev, *Rukopisnye pesenniki*, 95–96.

Concordances: RGB 10944 (text only); GIM 1743; RGB 9498 (twice); GIM 1938; GIM 2469; GIM Khlud. 126d; GIM Shchuk. 61; GIM Sin. 927; RNB Pog. 426; RNB Q.XIV.25; RNB Tit. 4172; RNB Q.XIV.141 (cited in Peretts, *Iz istorii russkoi pesni*, 183).

"Nakłon o Ewropo"
Diletskii: in L'viv (in Latin letters), p. LXXVI; the melodic outlines are similar to the example in GIM 1938, No. 73, but the two versions have different rhythmic settings, although both are in duple time.

Literature and published examples: Rothe, *Verse und Lieder bei den Ostslaven*, No. 423; Dolskaya, *Spiritual Songs in Seventeenth-Century Russia* [GIM 1938], No. 73; Pozdneev, *Rukopisnye pesenniki*, 111.

Concordances: GIM 1743; GIM 1938; GIM Shchuk. 61; RNB Pog. 426; RNB Pog. 1974; RNB Q.XIV.25; RNB Tit. 4172.

"Nekh monarhove"
Diletskii: as title in L'viv, p. LIV preceding an untexted example, à 2, which also appears in RGB 107, p. 129; GIM 168, fols. 68–68v; GIM 777, fol. 101v; and Tver' 651a, p. 180. The tune does not match that in GIM 1938, No. 162.

Literature and published examples: Rothe, *Verse und Lieder bei den Ostslaven*, No. 453; Dolskaya, *Spiritual Songs in Seventeenth-Century Russia* [GIM 1938], No. 162.

Concordances: GIM 1743; GIM 1938; GIM Shchuk. 61; GIM Sin. 927; RNB Pog. 1974; RNB Q.XIV.25; RNB Q.XIV.141 (cited in Peretts, *Iz istorii russkoi pesni*, 183–84).

"Pokhvalu prinesu"
Diletskii: à 3 setting in RGB 107, p. 154; GIM 168, fol. 88v; GIM 777, fols. 132–132v; Tver' 651a, pp. 242–43; RNB Q.XII.4, fol. 82.

Literature and published examples: Rothe, *Verse und Lieder bei den Ostslaven*, p. 311; Dolskaya, *Spiritual Songs in Seventeenth-Century Russia* [GIM 1938], No. 179 (attributed to Rostovskii, p. 328); attribution to Dimitrii Rostovskii also in Aravin, "U istokov," 114; and in Pozdneev, *Rukopisnye pesenniki*, 47; see also Dolskaya-Ackerly, "The Early Kant," 111–12 and 256.

Concordances: GIM 1938; GIM Khlud. 126d.

"Raduisia radost' tvoiu vospevaiu"

Diletskii: as à 1 in RGB 146, p. 108; GIM 1340, fol. 97v; and GIM 184, fol. 26, where the tune is presented twice, first set to this text and then to the liturgical text "Slava ottsu." This version corresponds to the top line of the setting in GIM 1938, No. 182. Tver' 553, fol. 31v, transmits no text for the two settings. In a later passage, L'viv lists "Raduisia radost'" as a title but has no musical example (p. XXVIII).

Literature and published examples: Rothe, *Verse und Lieder bei den Ostslaven,* No. 646; Dolskaya, *Spiritual Songs in Seventeenth-Century Russia* [GIM 1938], No. 182 (attributed to Slavinetskii on p. 328); see also Livanova, *Russkaia muzykal'naia kul'tura,* 1:499.

Concordances: GIM 1743 (appears three times); RGB 9498; GIM 1938; GIM Khlud. 126d; GIM Shchuk. 61; RNB Pog. 426; RNB Q.XIV.25; RNB Tit. 4172.

Notes

Introduction

1. Arsenios had been sent to Moscow as a patriarchal exarch in 1585–86; after this he remained in L'viv, where he taught at the Orthodox confraternity school at the Church of the Dormition. In May 1588, still in L'viv, he received a letter from Patriarch Hieremias, who requested his former pupil to accompany him on a trip to Moscow. The primary sources on Arsenios are Demetrakopoulos, *Arsénios Elassónos,* and Dmitrievskii, *Arkhiepiskop elassonskii Arsenii,* a parallel Greek-Russian edition of Arsenios's memoirs, which are otherwise lost; the Russian translation is reprinted as Arsenii Elassonskii, *Memuary iz russkoi istorii,* 163–210. Brief surveys are in Demetrakopoulos [Demetracopoulos], "On Arsenios, Archbishop of Elasson," and *SKK XVII v.,* pt. 1:108–10, and *SKK XVII v.,* pt. 4:671–72. Arsenios also wrote a poem describing the 1589 ceremonies; there is a prose Russian translation in Pitirim, "Arsenii, Arkhiepiskop elassonskii." See further Papadopoulos and Jensen, " 'A Confusion of Glory.' " Many thanks to George-Julius Papadopoulos for his translation of the Greek materials used here.

2. See Nikolaevskii, "Uchrezhdenie patriarshestva v Rossii," and *RIB* 2: No. 103: cols. 314–27 (where the document is incomplete, beginning only with the banquet following the installation ceremony). Nikolaevskii uses a series of quotations from several contemporary sources; he does not include details about Iov's attendants, including singers, at this point in the proceedings. Many thanks to Gregory Myers and to the late Miloš Velimirović for advice on terminology in the following discussion. On the complex proceedings leading to the establishment of the Russian patriarchate, see for example Makarii, *Istoriia russkoi tserkvi,* 10:3–34 and ff.; additional bibliography is in Papadopoulos and Jensen, " 'A Confusion of Glory,' " and Gudziak, *Crisis and Reform.*

3. Pitirim, "Arsenii, Arkhiepiskop elassonskii," 263; the Greek text is published in Sathas, *Biographikón Schedíasma perí toû Patriárchou Hieremíou B',* 50, vv. 512–13. In both Greek and Russian usage, *domestikos (domestichos)* or *domestik* is a lower ecclesiastical official, typically a cantor; the sources in question here refer to a skilled singer, specifically the leader of a choir; see Papadopoulos and Jensen, " 'A Confusion of Glory,' "

9, n. 15, and Morosan, *Choral Performance in Pre-Revolutionary Russia,* 10. The singer Paschales is mentioned by name in the Russian documents in Buganov and Lukichev, *Posol'skaia kniga po sviaziam Rossii s Gretsiei,* 49, and an unnamed "pevchii diiachok" (or "diiak") is listed among the members of Patriarch Hieremias's suite on pp. 13 and 41.

4. The Monday banquet is described in *RIB* 2: cols. 322–23: "i potom posovetovali patriarkhi promezh soboiu da veleli peti d'iakom pevchim Eremeevym patriarkhovym Dmitreiu s tovaryshchi, po grecheski."

5. The Russian sources describing the installation ceremonies tend to distinguish between performance of an "Ispolaeti despota" (usually for the Greek hierarchs or by the Greek singers) and a *mnogoletie* (generally by the Russian singers for a Russian hierarch), suggesting that the pieces may have been performed in different languages; see for example *RIB* 2: cols. 323 (a *mnogoletie*) and 319 (singers in Iov's second rank performing the "Ispolaiti" for Patriarch Hieremias).

6. Russian documents on the Greek party's trip to the monastery are in Buganov and Lukichev, *Posol'skaia kniga po sviaziam Rossii s Gretsiei,* 40–41.

7. On the liturgical singers in the sixteenth century, see Zvereva, "O khore gosudarevykh pevchikh d'iakov," and on the Novgorodian singers, see Parfent'ev, *Drevnerusskoe pevcheskoe iskusstvo,* chap. 1. English-language surveys are in Morosan, *Choral Performance in Pre-Revolutionary Russia,* chap. 1, and Gardner, *Russian Church Singing* 2:193–205 and 261–74.

8. A survey of the *demestvennyi* repertoire and its origins is in *IRM* 1:147–51, and see Parfent'ev, *Drevnerusskoe pevcheskoe iskusstvo,* 80–91, on the changing repertoire of the singers. In English, see Gardner, *Russian Church Singing,* 1:108–10, 2:232–34 and 292–305; *NG2* ("Russian and Slavonic Church Music," by Miloš Velimirović); and the updated bibliography in Findeizen, *History,* 1:333–34.

9. Quoted in Morosan, *"Penie* and *Musikiia,"* 166.

10. The unfamiliar liturgical practices are described in Leonid, "Svedenie o slavianskikh pergamennykh rukopisiakh," 165–67; see also Kapterev, "Snosheniia ierusalimskikh patriarkhov s russkim pravitel'stvom," 31ff. On Arsenios and his role as liaison, see Fonkich, *Grechesko-russkie kul'turnye sviazi,* 58, and Demetrakopoulos, *Arsénios Elassónos,* esp. 91–116. A later account, describing Theophanes's return trip through Kiev, does mention one of Patriarch Theophanes's singers, the monk Gavriel, who would also have been in the patriarchal party in Moscow and would have taken part in Filaret's installation; see Yurchyshyn-Smith, "The Antimension," 98 (citing Papadopoulos, *Hoi patriárchai Hierosolýmōn,* 60), and Makarii, *Istoriia russkoi tserkvi,* 11:249–50.

11. On Filaret, see Kazanskii, "Ispravlenie tserkovno-bogosluzhebnykh knig"; Makarii, *Istoriia russkoi tserkvi,* 11:1–75 passim; and briefly, Yurchyshyn-Smith, "The Antimension," 95. There is a survey of Filaret's tenure in Keep, "The Régime of Filaret." A recent survey of the voluminous literature on Patriarch Nikon is in *SKK XVII v.,* pt. 2:400–404 and pt. 4:757–61, and see Meyendorff, *Russia, Ritual, and Reform.*

12. Both English accounts are discussed further below. Fletcher's remarks are in his *Of the Russe Commonwealth* (1591); see Berry, *The English Works of Giles Fletcher,* 297, and Berry and Crummey, *Rude and Barbarous Kingdom,* 238, where Horsey's comments appear on pp. 321 and 325. On Horsey, see also Bond, "Russia at the Close of the sixteenth century, Comprising the Treatise 'Of the Russe Common Wealth,' by Dr. Giles Fletcher; and the Travels of Sir Jerome Horsey, Knt," 217 and 222 (henceforth "The Travels of Sir Jerome Horsey").

13. Quoted in Findeizen, *History,* 1:195; see also Fennell, *The Correspondence,* 242–

43. (The correspondence between Ivan and Kurbskii, from the latter's self-exile in Lithuania, is controversial; Keenan, *The Kurbskii-Groznyi Apocrypha*, considers it to be a later forgery.) Additional bibliography on *skomorokhi* appears below.

14. Koshelev, "'V tserkvi—obraza, a v kel'e—gudochnik'" and the same author's "Ispol'zovanie Pistsovykh knig v istoricheskikh issledovaniiakh" emphasize the economic consequences of interactions with *skomorokhi.*

15. "The voyage, wherein Osep Napea the Moscovite Ambassadour returned home into his countrey," 1:435.

16. Theophanes's edict was issued in Kiev in 1620–21. Makarii, *Istoriia russkoi tserkvi,* 11:264, and Yurchyshyn-Smith, "The Antimension," 98, citing *Arkhiv iugozapadnoi Rossii* 5, part 1: No. 1 (p. 8). Makarii paraphrases the gravesite practice as taking place "s muzykoiu," implying instrumental music rather than liturgical singing (*penie*); Papadopoulos, *Hoi patriárchai Hierosolýmōn,* 65 (probably using Makarii as his source) refers unambiguously to "mousikà órgana." Makarii, *Istoriia russkoi tserkvi,* 11:264, n. 208, notes that the document is dated 1620 but includes the names of the hierarchs Theophanes consecrated in January 1621. Theophanes also commented on wedding practice, saying that he had observed that some sort of drink was served at the singing of the *kanonik* [*koinonik*] ("Receive the body of Christ" ["telo Khristovo priimite"]). Adam Olearius, who accompanied the Duke of Holstein to Muscovy in the 1630s and early 1640s, also described how the bride and groom drank three draughts of wine and sang a psalm at the wedding ceremony (Olearius, *The Travels of Olearius,* 167). Earlier, Patriarch Hieremias had noted food-related transgressions in Ruthenian practice; see Gudziak, *Crisis and Reform,* 204. The implications of the term *musikiia* are discussed in Morosan, "*Penie* and *Musikiia.*"

17. [Miege], *A Relation of Three Embassies,* 147.

18. George Buelow has been particularly vigorous in his efforts to include East Slavic practice in his general surveys of seventeenth-century music, for example in his *History of Baroque Music* and in the contribution by Velimirović, "Warsaw, Moscow and St. Petersburg," in *The Late Baroque Era.* Joel Lester, for example in *Between Modes and Keys,* has also noted developments in Eastern European and Russian practice; see further chapter 5 below.

19. Gudziak, "The Sixteenth-Century Muscovite Church," esp. 201–207, gives a brief historiography focusing on just such issues; see also Okenfuss, *The Rise and Fall of Latin Humanism.*

1. The True False Dmitrii and the Death of Music in Moscow

1. Taruskin, "Musorgsky versus Musorgsky," 237. Some of the main themes of this chapter were presented at the annual meeting of the American Musicological Society, Seattle 2004.

2. Findeizen, *History,* 1: chap. 8, discusses this point carefully in the context of the Time of Troubles, clearly delineating the different roles and interpretations of music in this series of events. See also the discussions of instruments by Keldysh in *IRM* 1, esp. pp. 66–79, and Roizman, *Organ,* and the extensive bibliography cited in these sources. In English, see Velimirović, "Warsaw, Moscow and St. Petersburg." Uspenskii [Uspenskij], "Tsar and Pretender," discusses elements of musical symbolism in Ivan IV's earlier reign, and see below for Uspenskii's interpretation of events in Dmitrii's story.

3. There is a great deal of literature on this period. English-language sources

include two studies of Dmitrii himself, by Perrie, *Pretenders and Popular Monarchism*, and by Barbour, *Dimitry Called the Pretender*. Platonov, *The Time of Troubles*, is a translation of a classic study of the period, and see also Dunning, *Russia's First Civil War*, and the concise summary by Orchard, "Time of Troubles," in *MERSH* 39:49–57. Investigations at the time of his death determined that the child Dmitrii had died in 1591 in an accident incurred during an epileptic seizure. Ivan had killed his eldest son himself in a fit of rage, immortalized by the painter Il'ia Repin; he was succeeded by his second son, the physically and mentally weak Fedor, who died without issue in 1598. Fedor, in turn, was succeeded by Boris Godunov, his brother-in-law, who had served as Fedor's regent throughout his reign.

4. *Dnevnik Mariny Mnishek*, 36. In spite of the title traditionally applied to this work as Marina's diary, it was not actually written by the tsaritsa but was rather the record of an unidentified member of her suite; see the discussion of authorship, esp. pp. 13–19. A. I. Vlas'ev is first mentioned, as a diplomat, in 1595, and his life is documented through 1610; see the brief biography by Orchard in *MERSH* 42:186–88.

5. *The Reporte of a Bloudie and Terrible Massacre in the Citty of Moscow* (London, 1607; henceforth *Reporte*), published in Howe, *The False Dmitri*, 36. See below on the relationships among the various foreign accounts.

6. *Dnevnik Mariny Mnishek*, 52.

7. Bussow, *The Disturbed State of the Russian Realm*, 50 (although the phrase "20 Mann mit Schollmeyen und Kesselpauken" has been rendered here as "shawms and kettledrums," replacing the translation as "trumpets and kettledrums"). The German text is published in [Bussow], *Moskovskaia khronika [Die Moskauer Chronik]*, 235 (henceforth *Die Moskauer Chronik*). Bussow worked in Russia under Tsars Boris and Dmitrii and remained there until 1611; his treatise was written in several recensions between 1612 and 1617. On the complex issue of versions and collaborations, see Orchard's introduction to *The Disturbed State*, esp. pp. xxxi–xxxvii.

8. The *Tragoedia Moscovitica* was published in a dual Latin-Russian edition as *Moskovskaia tragediia*; Dmitrii's entrance is on p. 34. This is one of a cluster of early, interrelated works on Dmitrii that appeared in Western Europe between 1606 and 1608. Three are available in modern reprints or editions: *La Légende de la vie et de la mort de Demétrius* (Amsterdam, 1606, listed as "Traduicte nouvellement l'an 1606"), published in van der Linde, *Histoire des guerres de la Moscovie*, 1:287–310 (there are several separate items in van der Linde's edition, and this short treatise is henceforth referred to as *La Légende*); *Reporte* (London, 1607, written by an anonymous Dutch merchant and translated by William Russell; see above); and *Tragoedia Moscovitica* (1608). These three published sources are close (in places extremely close) but not identical. In his edition of the slightly later treatise by Massa, *A Short History*, xxi–xxiv, Orchard suggests that the common source for all three is *Warachtige ende eygentlijcke Beschryvinghe vande wonderbare ende seer gedenckweerdighe geschiednissen die in Moscovia zyn voorgevallen*, which appeared in 1606 (and has not been republished; Orchard, however, provides many references to this source in his edition of Massa). According to Orchard, the crucial sections relating to the death of Dmitrii in Massa's important account are close to the presentation in *Warachtige ende eygentlijcke Beschryvinghe*. Although Massa's work relies primarily on the notes he took during his long residence in Moscow between 1600 and 1609, Orchard suggests that he incorporated information from or perhaps knew the author of *Warachtige ende eygentlijcke Beschryvinghe*, and included this information in his own, later account (which covers the period to 1610); there is thus some overlap between all four of these sources.

9. Massa, *A Short History*, 129. Van der Linde, *Histoire des guerres de la Moscovie*, 1:1–219, reproduces Massa's text in the original as *Een cort verhael van begin en oorspronck deser tegenwoordighe oorloogen en troeblen in Moscouia totten jare 1610* (henceforth *Een cort verhael*); on p. 153 the instruments are listed as: "veele scalmeijen en trompetten gespeelt ende ooc op veele keteltrommen geslagen." (Orchard's translation has been changed here to read "shawms" instead of "flutes.") *Dnevnik Mariny Mnishek*, 46, notes that the musicians were placed in a specially built "theatrum" (the author uses the Latin term) at the Kremlin walls beyond the third gate into the city. *La Légende*, 293–94; *Reporte*, 35; and *Tragoedia Moscovitica*, 45–46, all mention the platform or scaffolding. A similar fanfare had sounded out earlier as Marina's party passed through Smolensk. This is described in the narrative poem (1606) by the Greek hieromonk Matthaios Koletzides, who was in the city at the time of her arrival. He describes cavalry and infantry, drums and horns, all assembled in profusion: "The queen arrived in great magnificence / she passed right through the ranks of the foot soldiers; / the horns began to sound and the drums began to beat." The poem is published in Knös, "Une version grecque," where these lines appear on p. 244; translation by George-Julius Papadopoulos. Koletzides' poem is discussed further in Papadopoulos and Jensen, " 'A Confusion of Glory,' " 13–14.

10. Bussow, *The Disturbed State of the Russian Realm*, 58, with transliteration modified to conform to the system used here. In the passage describing the Polish cavalry in full armor, "mit ihren Drometen, Heerpaucken und Schallmeyen," Orchard's translation has been changed from "drums, kettledrums, and shawms" to "trumpets, kettledrums, and shawms"; see the German text in [Bussow], *Die Moskauer Chronik*, 241–42.

11. Massa, *A Short History*, 132, clearly saw the implications for trouble: "Oh, how vexed the Muscovites were when they saw the Poles enter the church with plumes on their heads and weapons in their hands! Had anyone stirred them up, they would have thrown themselves upon these miscreants and killed every one of them, for they regard their churches as profaned by the presence of pagans."

12. Dmitrievskii, *Arkhiepiskop elassonskii Arsenii*, 108–12, and Arsenii Elassonskii, *Memuary iz russkoi istorii*, 181–82.

13. Stanisław Niemojewski (ca. 1560–1620) was a merchant in Marina's retinue; some of his writings are published in Russian translation in an appendix to *Dnevnik Mariny Mnishek* (where he describes the wedding ceremony on p. 185). His account is published in Niemojewski, *Pamiętnik Stanisława Niemojewskiego*, where his comment on the Russian liturgical singing is on p. 49, and in Russian translation in [Niemojewski], "Zapiski Stanislava Nemoevskogo," 59.

14. "Muzyke vo vremia messy 'Moskva' ochen' udivlialas' i dazhe, tolpias', lomala ograzhdenie" (*Dnevnik Mariny Mnishek*, 37). It is not clear what kind of barrier or railing the author had in mind; in the very closely related account by Martyn Stadnicki, who was related to the Mniszech family and headed Marina's court, the Russians are reported to have broken the benches ("lomali dazhe skam'i"; in [Stadnicki], "Istoriia Dimitriia Tsaria moskovskogo," 146). This account does not mention the celebration of a mass but it is clearly labeled as taking place on a Sunday. Both sources were available in Russian translation only. Niemojewski mentions the celebration of a mass on this date, but does not refer to the musical incident (Niemojewski, *Pamiętnik Stanisława Niemojewskiego*, 8, and "Zapiski Stanislava Nemoevskogo," 24–25). The religious figures in the Polish party are listed in *Dnevnik Mariny Mnishek*, 35–36.

15. Marina's singer and Gabriel and his crew were among those killed in the 1606 uprising; see below.

16. Mikulin's report is published in Bestuzhev-Riumin, *Pamiatniki diplomatiche-*

skikh snoshenii moskovskogo gosudarstva s Angliei, 335 ("v vargany i v truby, i v-ynye vomnogie igry, i peti"), reprinted in Likhachev, *Puteshestviia russkikh poslov,* 176. Additional biographical information is in *SKK XVII v.,* pt. 2:350–51 and pt. 4:748–49, and in Mikulin, "Kommentarii k naznacheniiu rossiiskogo poslannika v Angliiu." The organ and its use in Uniate practice in mid-century Ukraine is discussed in chapter 4 below.

17. Mikulin did, however, apparently describe his trip to some people back home. The Englishman Richard Barne wrote from Arkhangel'sk that "[t]here come many to him [Mikulin] to whom he imparteth at large every particular of his entertainment: in which discourse he intermingleth commendations of our country and people." Quoted in Evans, "The Meeting of the Russian and Scottish Ambassadors," 528.

18. For a discussion of the deliberately double interpretation of this double ceremony of wedding and coronation, see Uspenskii, "Svad'ba Lzhedmitriia"; Barbour, *Dimitry Called the Pretender,* 255–56, also calls brief attention to the deliberate duality of the ceremony. In the *Relazione della segnalata, e come miracolosa conquista del Paterno Imperio, conseguita dal Serenissimo Giovine Demetrio Gran Duca di Moscovia* (Venice, 1605, with additional editions and translations between 1606 and 1609), which is written from a Jesuit point of view and ends with Dmitrii's wedding plans, Marina is portrayed as a good Catholic girl and the wedding as a triumph for the Catholic church; a Russian translation is in Obolenskii, *Inostrannye sochineniia i akty,* 1–17, and see Poe, *Foreign Descriptions,* 141.

19. Quoted in Gardner, *Bogosluzhebnoe penie,* 1:551, and also (in a slightly different English translation) in Gardner, *Russian Church Singing,* 2:340, and in Morosan, "*Penie and Musikiia,*" 159. (There is a somewhat different reading of this passage in the chronicle source in *Kniga nazyvaemaia Novyi letopisets,* 354.) Germogen (Hermogen), the Metropolitan of Kazan', was appointed patriarch by Vasilii Shuiskii in 1606, replacing the patriarch Dmitrii had installed the previous year. He subsequently served as a unifying figure in the last years of the Troubles (Platonov, *The Time of Troubles,* esp. 143ff., and *MERSH* 14:11–13).

20. General surveys of *skomorokhi* and their musical roles are in Findeizen, *History,* 1: chap. 5; Koshelev, "Skomorokhi novgorodskoi zemli," reevaluates some of Findeizen's source material, concluding that *skomorokhi* may have been more numerous than he thought. Other surveys include *IRM* 1:60–61 and 123–24; Belkin, *Russkie skomorokhi;* Koshelev, *Skomorokhi: Problemy i perspektivy izucheniia,* and the same author's *Skomorokhi: Annotirovannyi bibliograficheskii ukazatel'.* Some English-language discussions are in Zguta, *Russian Minstrels,* and Smith and Christian, *Bread and Salt;* additional bibliography is in chapter 4 below.

21. On these instruments, see the sources listed in n. 2 above and in Aumayr, *Historische Untersuchungen an Bezeichnungen von Musikinstrumenten,* and Keldysh, *Muzykal'nyi entsiklopedicheskii slovar'.*

22. *Dnevnik Mariny Mnishek,* 42. Stadnicki's account also mentions the forty musicians ("Istoriia Dimitriia," 152). These two accounts are extremely close throughout these initial sections (at least as far as the death of Tsar Dmitrii), with *Dnevnik Mariny Mnishek* slightly more detailed in general and more accurate in listing specific dates. In this passage, however, there is significant added material in Stadnicki's account (pp. 151–52), which begins under the date 6 May, with no specific indication for 7 May, when the forty-member orchestra apparently performed. The later Muscovite theater orchestra is discussed in chapter 6 below.

23. "The Travels of Sir Jerome Horsey," in Bond, "Russia at the Close," 217; and

Berry and Crummey, *Rude and Barbarous Kingdom,* 321 (the editors also include an overview of Horsey's mission). The nature of Horsey's commissions is somewhat unclear and judging from the reaction to the musical instruments, at least, it appears that he was asked to bring back a variety of interesting and amusing objects but not specifically to bring a collection of keyboard instruments. This general commission is evident from the full listing of items Horsey was packing for his return trip, which involved a "provicion of lyons, bulls, doggs, guilt halberds, pistolls, peces, armor, wynes, store of druges of all sorts, organes, virgenalls, musicions, scarletts, perrell chaines, plate of curious makinge and of other costly things of great value, according to my commissions."

24. Bond, "The Travels of Sir Jerome Horsey," 222, and Berry and Crummey, *Rude and Barbarous Kingdom,* 325.

25. Emchenko, *Stoglav,* 309–10. A slightly different version of this passage is quoted and translated into modern Russian in Rogov, *Muzykal'naia estetika Rossii,* 53–54.

26. Smith and Christian, *Bread and Salt,* 138–39 (material in square brackets added to their translation), quoting Rozhdestvenskii, "K istorii bor'by s tserkovnymi bezporiadkami," 26–27.

27. Massa, *A Short History,* 133, and *Een cort verhael,* 158. Arsenii, *Memuary,* 182, indicates that the patriarch and the high-ranking Muscovite clergy left after the services and did not attend the banquet along with the other Russian and Polish guests (see below). On the other hand, Jacques Margeret (d. after 1619), who served in both Tsar Boris's and Dmitrii's armies, reported that only Russians attended the banquet held immediately after the wedding; see Margeret, *The Russian Empire and Grand Duchy of Muscovy,* 72. In the account of the two rather prickly representatives from the Polish king, Mikołaj Oleśnicki and Alexander Gosiewski, the envoys say that Dmitrii told them that everyone was tired from the long coronation-wedding ceremonies and that there was to be no feast until the following day. Their account is in Ustrialov, *Dnevnik Mariny Mnishek i poslov pol'skikh,* 150 (henceforth *Dnevnik poslov pol'skikh*). Due to disagreements over various issues of protocol, the envoys did not attend any of the banquets or functions until Sunday.

28. Bussow, *The Disturbed State of the Russian Realm,* 61 (transliteration modified), and *Die Moskauer Chronik,* 244.

29. Arsenii, *Memuary,* 181–82, notes the singers at the wedding (he does not specify to which of the ensembles they belonged), and see also the references to liturgical singing in the Russian account included as an appendix to *Dnevnik Mariny Mnishek,* 179–83. Zvereva, "Muzykal'nye chernoviki," 105, speculates on the role of the singer Fedor, possibly the important singer Fedor Khrest'ianin, at Dmitrii's wedding.

30. This part of the celebration was similar to the festivities following the proxy wedding in Cracow, which was held according to the Roman rite and which concluded with dancing (the Muscovite ambassador declined, saying he was not worthy of dancing with the new tsaritsa). Although no specific dances are listed, the dancing appears to be of the same type that the Polish party brought to Moscow, with several named attendants escorting the people of rank who were dancing. The Polish king and Marina, for example, danced while being attended by four others. A dispatch describing the proxy wedding is cited in an appendix to *Dnevnik Mariny Mnishek,* 175 (this is a Polish source from 1605, printed in Polish and in Russian translation in *RIB* 1, where the dancing is in cols. 64–66).

31. The fanfare is reported in Massa, *A Short History,* 133; *Tragoedia Moscovitica,* 47; *Reporte,* 37; [Stadnicki], "Istoriia Dimitriia," 159–60; and [Niemojewski], "Zapiski Stanislava Nemoevskogo," 60, 66, and 71. In his entry for 9 May (p. 60), Niemojewski estimated

that there were fifty drums and thirty trumpeters. The fanfares lasted for most of the week, and some of the informants found them increasingly irritating (for example, Niemojewski's entry on p. 71; in *Pamiętnik Stanisława Niemojewskiego* these references are on pp. 51, 58, and 64). See also chapter 4 below.

32. Arsenii, *Memuary*, 182–83, describes the patriarch's visit, at which he himself was present, adding that this sort of breach of etiquette and tradition contributed to the subsequent deaths and riots in Moscow. The festivities apparently held later that day are described in *Dnevnik Mariny Mnishek*, 54, and in [Stadnicki], "Istoriia Dimitriia," 160; both sources note that on the previous day, Saturday, 10/20 May, there were "no elaborate dishes, no ceremony, and no music" but various Polish military figures were invited to the meal, for which Marina wore Polish dress and Dmitrii appeared in Muscovite clothing. On the music that Sunday, see also Ustrialov, *Dnevnik poslov pol'skikh*, 162; the two ambassadors had been absent from the earlier festivities due to diplomatic disagreements.

33. Massa, *A Short History*, 133. Bussow, *The Disturbed State of the Russian Realm*, 61, notes that Dmitrii "no longer went to church as diligently as before, he lived by adhering in all things to foreign ceremonies and customs, ate unclean food [veal], went to church without cleansing himself [and] did not revere the icon of St. Nicholas." Most of these transgressions are linked to the celebrations noted above, and they were recapitulated in the list of charges laid against Dmitrii after his death.

34. *Dnevnik Mariny Mnishek*, 54.

35. *Dnevnik Mariny Mnishek*, 54–55. The Russian Prince Vasilii Mikhailovich Mosal'skii was close to Dmitrii; the party had met up with him earlier in their journey (see *Dnevnik Mariny Mnishek*, 36 and n. 88, where he is identified and his career reviewed briefly). The Afanasii mentioned in this passage is ambassador Afanasii Vlas'ev. The identity of the Princess Koshirska noted here is unknown, but the same person is also mentioned in [Stadnicki], "Istoriia Dimitriia," 160, where the account is extremely close to that of *Dnevnik Mariny Mnishek* but the specific date is lacking; she also appears on several occasions in Ustrialov, *Dnevnik poslov pol'skikh*, which notes that on Tuesday, 13 May, "everyone made merry and danced to the sounds of the tsaritsa's musical ensemble" (p. 163). On dancing in connection with a Muscovite boyar's wedding, see below.

36. Niemojewski, *Pamiętnik Stanisława Niemojewskiego*, 66 (which uses different titles for Dmitrii and Marina: "Po obiedzie szedł Wielki Kniaż w taniec z Hospodarynią"), and "Zapiski Stanislava Nemoevskogo," 73. The Castellan of Małogość was the Polish envoy Mikołaj Oleśnicki (*Dnevnik Mariny Mnishek*, 145, n. 117, and Barbour, *Dimitry*, 181). There is some discrepancy between Niemojewski's account and that of the anonymous author of *Dnevnik Mariny Mnishek* (p. 55), who speaks of no entertainments on this date, and indeed says that things were a bit quieter although, unbeknownst to the Poles, the Russians were planning various accusations and plots against them. Niemojewski's account clearly indicates that he was present and participating in these activities, so perhaps one of these accounts is misdated, or perhaps the author of *Dnevnik Mariny Mnishek* did not attend or was not aware of this particular gathering. Ustrialov, *Dnevnik poslov pol'skikh*, 170, also mentions dancing on this day but does not note the presence of either Dmitrii or Marina. Many thanks to Michael Biggins for his advice on these translations from Polish.

37. *Reporte*, 41; *Dnevnik Mariny Mnishek*, 55; and [Stadnicki], "Istoriia Dimitriia," 160. [Niemojewski], "Zapiski Stanislava Nemoevskogo," 72, attributes the silence to a general need for rest after all the celebrating but he does note the rumors the day before

the massacre (p. 74). Bussow, *The Disturbed State of the Russian Realm,* 60 and 62, also mentions warnings that Dmitrii brushed aside.

38. Massa, *A Short History,* 136, and *Een cort verhael,* 162. The "mummerie" is described in *Reporte,* 42, and *Tragoedia Moscovitica,* 50. Niemojewski does not mention these preparations, but he had a private audience with Dmitrii that evening to display the jewels he had brought to sell. As in Massa's description, the accounts in *Reporte* and *Tragoedia Moscovitica* do not mention Dmitrii in connection with the masks, describing only Marina's activities and the general dancing at court. On Niemojewski's business transactions, see his *Pamiętnik Stanisława Niemojewskiego,* 69, and "Zapiski Stanislava Nemoevskogo," 75–76; and Barbour, *Dimitry,* 275.

39. [Stadnicki], "Istoriia Dimitriia," 162, entered under 17/27 May, the Saturday of the attack. The switch to present tense in this passage is abrupt, suggesting that Stadnicki might have turned to a different source or informant at this point. This passage does not appear in *Dnevnik Mariny Mnishek.* Stadnicki's account may represent an expanded depiction of the general celebrating described above in *Reporte* and *Tragoedia Moscovitica.* Although both Stadnicki and Massa note that the activities took place in the tsar's chambers, neither source places Dmitrii himself there, so these sources do not appear to conflict with Niemojewski's account, in n. 38 above. According to Ustrialov, *Dnevnik poslov pol'skikh,* 173, "They say that Dmitrii did not sleep the night of 17/27 May and everyone made merry." Other accounts, for example Massa, *A Short History,* 136, and Bussow, *The Disturbed State of the Russian Realm,* 62, also put the time of the attack in the morning; Bussow even says that it occured "after the tsar and the Polish lords had gone to bed and were sleeping off their revelries."

40. Bussow, *The Disturbed State of the Russian Realm,* 69, and *Die Moskauer Chronik,* 251.

41. Bussow, *The Disturbed State of the Russian Realm,* 66, and *Die Moskauer Chronik,* 249. Orchard's translation of the phrase "ich will diesem polnischen Pfeiffer einen Plaslabith geben" has been changed here from "this Polish minstrel" to "this Polish piper."

42. Bussow, *The Disturbed State of the Russian Realm,* 66 and 208, n. 55, and *Die Moskauer Chronik,* 249: "Was doch der polnische Scammaroth gutes gesaget." Although Bussow was not an eyewitness to Dmitrii's death, his choice of this particular word is nevertheless revealing, indicating that either he or his informant clearly understood the implications of the term; as both editions state, there is a marginal note in the manuscript: "Scammaroth ein Spielmann."

43. *Reporte,* 47; *Tragoedia Moscovitica,* 53–54; and *La Légende,* 301 (where the phrase "ugly vilard" is rendered as "masque hideuse"). Bussow, *The Disturbed State of the Russian Realm,* 77, tells the same story: "A boyar came out of the Kremlin with a mask and a bagpipe, and laid the mask on the tsar's stomach next to his privy parts, but placed the pipe in his mouth, and laid the sack of the bagpipe on his chest. Then he said: 'You son of a whore and betrayer of the land, you forced us for so long to pipe for you, now you can give us a tune' " (see also *Die Moskauer Chronik,* 257). Massa, *A Short History,* 138, focuses on the masks: "Some conspirators went behind and ahead of this sorry procession [escorting Dmitrii's corpse], carrying masks, and calling to the people: 'Here are the gods whom he adored!' Now these masks had been taken from the apartments of the tsarina, where they had been prepared for the masquerade that was to have been held for the tsar's entertainment. Not knowing what these objects were, the Muscovites believed, and still

believe today, that these masks were really Dmitrii's gods" (transliteration modified). Ustrialov, *Dnevnik poslov pol'skikh*, 175–76, also reports on the mask, which Dmitrii was accused of having used as an icon, but added: "and why they gave [Dmitrii's body] a *dudka*, I do not know."

44. This story was recounted in Olearius, *The Travels of Olearius*, 91–92; see also Findeizen, *History*, 1:195, and Uspenskii [Uspenskij], "Tsar and Pretender," 282, n. 59.

45. Uspenskii [Uspenskij], "Tsar and Pretender," esp. 272–73.

46. Ibid., "Tsar and Pretender," 276 (and see also p. 287, n. 84), and Perrie, *Pretenders and Popular Monarchism*, esp. 98–104. Both authors also include insightful discussions of these themes as they appear in seventeenth-century song texts. Niemojewski said that the masks belonged to a Pole named Marsylio; Marina borrowed his masks and took them to the tsar's chamber. When the Muscovites found them later under the tsar's bed, they concluded that these were Dmitrii's idols, which he wanted to force the Muscovites to worship (*Pamiętnik Stanisława Niemojewskiego*, 95–96, and "Zapiski Stanislava Nemoevskogo," 98).

47. See for example the discussion in Findeizen, *History*, 1:202–203. Dunning, *Russia's First Civil War*, 236–37, also refers to the *skomorokh* imagery applied, postmortem, to Dmitrii, and see below for Perrie's and Uspenskii's discussions. Shuiskii naturally reinforced the doubts about Dmitrii's faith when he took power; thus his proclamations detailing Dmitrii's transgressions, his intent to convert all of Russia to Catholicism, and so forth. See, among others, the listings in Massa, *A Short History*, 146–49, and Shuiskii's statements in *RIB* 13: cols. 66ff.

48. *Reporte*, 36; the "filthie songs" and Dmitrii's violation of the nuns is on p. 58, and see also *La Légende*, 307–308, and Massa, *A Short History*, 143.

49. *RIB* 13: col. 831; translation from Uspenskii [Uspenskij], "Tsar and Pretender," 276 (where the term *bubny* is translated as bells); see also *RIB* 13: col. 59, quoted in Findeizen, *History*, 1:202. Uspenskii continues (pp. 275–76), noting that Dmitrii's body was eventually buried, but as the Muscovite accounts said, "the earth itself did abhor" the body, so the corpse was exhumed and burned. Perrie, *Pretenders and Popular Monarchism*, 100–101, also recounts the travails of Dmitrii's corpse.

50. *Reporte*, 54, and see *Tragoedia Moscovitica*, 58, and *La Légende*, 305. Massa, *A Short History*, 146–47, which is related at this point to these three treatises, says only that Dmitrii, as Grigorii Otrep'ev, had been in a monastery but does not mention the musical angle.

51. "Several Moscow merchants," reported Massa, "were obliged to give up the best apartments of their own dwellings for a time to accommodate the Poles invited to the wedding" (Massa, *A Short History*, 125). Dunning, *Russia's First Civil War*, 227–28, points to the dispersal of the guests throughout the city as an important error on Dmitrii's part, particularly when coupled with the guests' riotous behavior.

52. Massa, *A Short History*, 140, and *Reporte*, 47.

53. Bussow, *The Disturbed State of the Russian Realm*, 67; on p. 54, Bussow notes that earlier, Dmitrii had displaced some clergy near the Kremlin so his foreign guard could be quartered near him. See also Bussow, *Die Moskauer Chronik*, 239.

54. Niemojewski, *Pamiętnik Stanisława Niemojewskiego*, 91, and "Zapiski Stanislava Nemoevskogo," 94–95. Both editions contain two versions of Niemojewski's account: the L'viv text, the primary text used in the edition, which includes annotations by Niemojewski himself and apparently belonged to the Mniszech family; and the Vilnius account, preserved in an eighteenth-century manuscript ("Zapiski Stanislava Nemoevskogo," 13).

In the Vilnius version, Niemojewski identifies the Polish musicians specifically as the tsar's musicians, brought by Marina's brother (*Pamiętnik Stanisława Niemojewskiego,* 87–88, and "Zapiski Stanislava Nemoevskogo," 91). Otherwise the story contains the same elements, with the exception of the somewhat theatrical pleas for mercy ("who is going to entertain you after this?").

55. Niemojewski, *Pamiętnik Stanisława Niemojewskiego,* 93–94, and "Zapiski Stanislava Nemoevskogo," 96–97. Oleśnicki's and Gosiewski's listing of the dead musicians is in Ustrialov, *Dnevnik poslov pol'skikh,* 191; on p. 189 they also list as dead one Talashko, a musician/cook, and Nitovskii [Nitowski], Marina's singer (p. 191). They do not give a specific account of the deaths of the musicians in their description of the events of 17 May, which includes both eyewitness and reported material.

56. Bussow, *The Disturbed State of the Russian Realm,* 73; the Russian reply is on p. 74. See also Bussow, *Die Moskauer Chronik,* 254–55.

57. Morosan, "*Penie* and *Musikiia,*" esp. 152.

58. Findeizen, *History,* 1:148–49, and see also the definitions from earlier periods in Sreznevskii, *Materialy dlia slovaria drevnerusskogo iazyka,* 2: col. 196.

59. "A musike na pervyi den' ne byt', a byt' v Granovitoi polate za bolshim stolom," in *Dnevnik Mariny Mnishek,* 183 (citing *SGGD* 2:293). If the writer were a member of the clergy, he would not have known about the celebrations immediately following the ceremony, for Arsenios reports: "After the wedding they went to the court, according to rank . . . When they entered the court—the tsar, the tsaritsa, all the Russian and Polish boyars and their wives and all the clergy—there was great joy and everything that follows a wedding. Whereas the patriarch and the hierarchs went home after Divine Liturgy" (according to the Greek version of the text in Dmitrievskii, *Arkhiepiskop elassonskii Arsenii,* 112; cf. Arsenii, *Memuary,* 182; thanks to George-Julius Papadopoulos for advice on this translation). The term *musika,* in this context, also apparently did not refer to fanfare music.

2. *"Wondrous singers and exceptional voices"*

1. These views of James (1592–1638) are quoted in *DNB,* s.v. "James, Richard," which is the major source of biographical information used here; see also *SKK XVII v.,* pt. 1:255–56. James was chaplain for the unsuccessful English mission headed by Dudley Digges, described in Phipps, "Britons in Seventeenth-Century Russia," 113–15.

2. According to Larin, *Tri inostrannykh istochnika,* 196, James and the rest of the English party were in Kholmogory from late July 1618 to the spring of 1619; some of the Englishmen went to Moscow in the summer of 1619, returning to Kholmogory in August, where they remained for nearly a year. They left for England in August 1620. It is not known if James went to Moscow or remained in the north, but it appears that most of James's work was compiled in Arkhangel'sk or Kholmogory. Extensive bibliography is in Anderson, "English Views of Russia in the 17th Century"; Phipps, "The Russian Embassy to London of 1645–46"; Jansson and Rogozhin, *England and the North;* and *MERSH* 32:27–33.

3. Larin, *Tri inostrannykh istochnika,* 177–508, is an edition of James's glossary; this phrase is on pp. 219/410 (transcription/facsimile). James's Russian terms are written in transliteration, generally with English translations following.

4. Ibid., 257 (as "nomines")/435.

5. On the origins of the ensembles, see Zvereva, "O khore gosudarevykh pevchikh

d'iakov," and Parfent'ev, *Professional'nye muzykanty*, 7–8. The same authors have produced other excellent surveys; see Zvereva, "Gosudarevy pevchie d'iaki posle 'Smuty,'" and Parfent'ev, *Drevnerusskoe pevcheskoe iskusstvo*, esp. chap. 2. Earlier surveys include Razumovskii, *Patriarshie pevchie diaki i poddiaki* and his "Gosudarevy pevchie d'iaki XVII veka."

6. Zvereva, "Gosudarevy pevchie d'iaki posle 'Smuty,'" examines the *stanitsa* structure in the first third of the seventeenth century, noting that each *stanitsa* was regarded as a unit, made up of specialist singers who could sing (and copy) specific lines of two-, three-, and four-part polyphonic settings.

7. Parfent'ev, *Professional'nye muzykanty*, 84–85 and 98–99, and his *Drevnerusskoe pevcheskoe iskusstvo*, 87–89, discusses the patriarchal singers and the patriarchal variant noted in some musical sources. English-language discussions of the *kliros* and its several meanings are in Gardner, *Russian Church Singing*, 2:24, 204, and 273–74, and in Morosan, *Choral Performance*, 9–10.

8. This brief description is based on the impressive archival survey by Parfent'ev, *Professional'nye muzykanty*, part 1.

9. For example, Parfent'ev, *Professional'nye muzykanty*, notes that sovereign's singer Rodion Grigor'ev sang "O divnoe chiudo" for the tsar in 1675 (p. 183), and patriarchal singer Ivan Lebedkin sang a *partesnoe* (Western-style polyphonic) piece for the patriarch in 1684 (p. 270).

10. Patriarchal singer Osip Novgorodtsev, for example, was paid throughout the 1680s and 1690s for copying numerous *perevody*, translations from neumes into staff notation, and in the early years of the eighteenth century he copied a long series of Christmas pieces for boyar I. A. Musin-Pushkin (Parfent'ev, *Professional'nye muzykanty*, 309–10). At his death in 1672, sovereign's singer Nikita Kazanets left a variety of chant manuscripts, including some polyphonic ones (Parfent'ev, 236). Music manuscripts copied by patriarchal singer Fedor Konstantinov, whose long and distinguished career is documented from 1620 to 1675, are recorded in a listing of sources in the tsar's collection (Parfent'ev, 250).

11. Many of the music scribes enjoyed long and steady careers. Potap Maksimov, for example, worked for more than twenty-five years as a music copyist; see *RIB* 23, kn. 3:477 (April 1664, with later references throughout the 1660s and 1670s), and Protopopov, "Notnaia biblioteka," 121, where he is listed as a music scribe in 1687. Apparently there were other ways to learn musical notation, as revealed in the accounts of a nasty dispute in 1688 between Timofei Stepanov and his pupil, Kuz'ma. Timofei, who is identified only as a scribe (*pisets*) and is not otherwise linked to the *pevchie d'iaki* or to the official music scribes, taught from printed and manuscript chant sources and also taught the most up-to-date polyphonic *partesnoe penie* and *kontsert* styles (described below). See Kotkov, Oreshnikov, and Filippova, *Moskovskaia delovaia i bytovaia pis'mennost' XVII veka*, 287–90; a brief reference to this dispute is in Petrovskaia, "Ob izuchenii russkoi muzykal'noi kul'tury," 235.

12. Information here from Parfent'ev, *Professional'nye muzykanty*, esp. 9–11, 54–58, and 100; as he notes (pp. 57–58), the roles of the patriarchal *krestovye d'iaki* are difficult to assess but they seem to have encompassed the same kinds of domestic services and preparations with which the sovereign's *krestovye d'iaki* were charged. See also Parfent'ev, *Drevnerusskoe pevcheskoe iskusstvo*, 77–79. Zabelin, *Domashnii byt russkikh tsarei*, pt. 1:384ff., discusses the roles of the *krestovye d'iaki* in the tsar's daily routine, and see also Fletcher's description in Berry and Crummey, *Rude and Barbarous Kingdom*, 236–37. The

krestovye d'iaki in the sixteenth century are covered in Zvereva, "O khore gosudarevykh pevchikh d'iakov," esp. 127–28.

13. Lists of singers from this early period are in Kharlampovich, *Malorossiiskoe vliianie,* 72–74 and 317–22. These singers often went to the Andreevskii Monastery near Moscow, which had been specially built to accomodate the activities of the learned Ukrainian monk and teacher Epifanii Slavinetskii; see *SKK XVII v.,* pt. 1:309–13. Okenfuss, "Education in Russia," 120ff., makes the point that the Andreevskii Monastery did not constitute a formal school. Even so, there is some evidence of regular instruction there, at least for a time; see Rumiantseva, "Andreevskii uchilishchnyi monastyr'," esp. 298–99.

14. The 1657 performance is in Zabelin, *Opyty izucheniia russkikh drevnostei i istorii,* 1:289. None of the singers from the 1650s listed in Kharlampovich, *Malorossiiskoe vliianie,* 72–74 and 317–22, appears in Parfent'ev, *Professional'nye muzykanty,* which lists singers in the established choirs in Moscow. Later singers (from the 1680s and 1690s) identified as Ukrainian in Kharlampovich, 324–29, do appear in Parfent'ev's listings; occasionally a singer is also labeled as a *vspevak.*

15. Meletios's biography is reviewed in Fonkich, "Meletii Grek," and see also *SKK XVII v.,* pt. 4:494–96. On his work as a singing teacher, see Protopopov, "Notnaia biblioteka," 123–24, where he notes that the references to teaching "Greek singing" confuse the issue of the so-called "Greek chant" in Muscovite practice (references to which first seem to appear, not surprisingly, at the New Jerusalem Monastery in the 1650s; see *IRM* 1:218 and n. 31 below). The origins of "Greek chant" are surveyed in Igoshev, "Proiskhozhdenie grecheskogo rospeva," and Papadopoulos and Jensen, "'A Confusion of Glory,'" esp. 22–23. Meletios worked closely with his countryman Paisios Ligarides to remove Nikon from the patriarchal throne. References to Meletios's and Dionysios's singing at the 1667 council are in *DAI* 5:105–106, 116, and 132; there are many references to singing in Greek during the proceedings.

16. The Stroganov establishment is surveyed in Parfent'ev and Parfent'eva, *Usol'skaia (Stroganovskaia) shkola,* and in Parfent'ev, "Usol'skaia shkola v drevnerusskom pevcheskom iskusstve"; his "Prikaznye dokumenty" focuses on the singers in the late seventeenth century. Musical sources associated with the Stroganov family are surveyed in Seregina, "Pevcheskie rukopisi iz knigopisnoi masterskoi Stroganovykh," where the author notes, on pp. 205–206, the presence of a musical "primer," supporting the notion that there was a singing school or at least, structured training associated with the Stroganov establishment.

17. Paul of Aleppo's important account is available in three translations from Arabic: by F. C. Belfour in *The Travels of Macarius* (the version printed in Palmer, *The Patriarch and the Tsar,* vol. 2, is taken from the Belfour translation, with some corrections); by G. A. Murkos in "Puteshestvie antiokhiiskogo patriarkha Makariia v Rossiiu" (Murkos refers to, and corrects, the Belfour translation and employs some additional sources); and by Basile Radu in "Voyage du Patriarche Macaire d'Antioche" (with continuous pagination noted in square brackets; Radu's translation covers only part of Paul's trip, through Ukraine). These editions are henceforth referred to by translator and volume: page number. On Paul of Aleppo, see two studies by Charles J. Halperin, both with extensive bibliography: "In the Eye of the Beholder" and "Friend and Foe."

18. Paul of Aleppo, Belfour 2:272 (during Lent 1656) and Murkos 4 (1898): 152 (where Belfour's phrase "in two choirs" is translated as "na oboikh klirosakh"). Paul says that the nuns are not Muscovite but Belarusian or Ukrainian (see the note in Murkos).

Nuns of the Convent of St. Savva also sang to accompany the procession of the patriarchal party; see Belfour 2:168 and Murkos 4 (1898): 51 (these were also apparently non-Muscovite nuns).

19. Shvedova identifies the nuns as singers in "Tsaritsy-inokini Novodevich'ego monastyria," 78, citing a document dated 1603–1604. The term *kryloshanka* is discussed in Senyk, *Women's Monasteries*, 172 (see also 182).

20. Paul observed male singers at a funeral at Novodevichii (Belfour 2:82–83 and Murkos 3 [1898]: 166–67), and he also apparently refers to male singers at the Feast of the Translation of the Image of Our Lady of Smolensk at the convent (Belfour 2:165–66 and Murkos 4 [1898]: 49). Senyk, *Women's Monasteries*, 173, notes an instance in which a convent hired seven male singers.

21. Quoted and translated in Hughes, *Sophia Regent of Russia*, 255, citing *Pis'ma i bumagi Imperatora Petra Velikogo*, 1:268 (document No. 254). Two decades later, the Spiritual Regulation refers to nuns singing in the choir of convent churches (Muller, *The Spiritual Regulation of Peter the Great*, 79–80).

22. The 1660 source is GIM NDM 122, with the inscription (fol. 3) reading (in part): "[copied] by means of the diligence and labor of nuns from this same [Novo-devichii] convent" ("Tshchaniem i trudom togo zhe monastyria inokin'"), in Chistia-kova, *Monakhini "s Beloi Rosi" v Novodevich'em monastyre*, 151–52. A color facsimile of another staff-notated Irmologii (1667) from the collection is in Trutneva and Shvedova, *Novodevichii monastyr'*, 96 (No. 56, identified on p. 111 as NDM 123/457, from the convent's "[m]anuscript workshop"). Other notated books are mentioned in Shvedova, "Tsaritsy-inokini Novodevich'ego monastyria," 83 (which also notes Paul of Aleppo's comments), and see Senyk, *Women's Monasteries*, 182–83. Findeizen, *History*, 1:265, states that Tsarevna Sofiia, as the nun Susanna, copied a notated Oktoechos (citing Kazanskii, *Selo Novospaskoe*, 57; an Oktoechos is another notated collection of liturgical hymns). This document is not mentioned in Hughes, *Sophia*.

23. Works ascribed to Tsar Aleksei are in the inventory of his successor, Tsar Fedor Alekseevich; see Protopopov, "Notnaia biblioteka." Tsar Aleksei's compositional activities are surveyed in Bylinin and Pososhenko, "Tsar' Aleksei Mikhailovich kak master raspeva," and in Protopopov, "Chetyrekhgolosnaia khorovaia kompozitsiia tsaria Alek-seia Mikhailovicha." Parfent'ev, *Professional'nye muzykanty*, 45, outlines the roles of the singers in teaching the royal children, and see also Zabelin, *Domashnii byt russkikh tsarei*, pt. 2:107 and 165–66, and the payment records cited in the accompanying *Materialy*, pt. 2:612.

24. An exploration of the contentious issue of Ivan IV as composer is in Ramaza-nova, *Moskovskoe tsarstvo v tserkovno-pevcheskom iskusstve*, 151–67. On Peter the Great's singing abilities, see Findeizen, *History*, 1:267, and the epilogue to the present volume.

25. Paul of Aleppo, in Belfour 2:246 and Murkos 4 (1898): 126. Paul discusses the proceedings carefully, transcribing and translating the tsar's Russian comments at some length.

26. These linguistic shifts are discussed in English in Gardner, *Russian Church Singing*, 2:275–81. Patriarchal singer Fedor Konstantinov, mentioned above, worked with five others at the Printing Office on the corrections; see Parfent'ev, *Professional'nye muzykanty*, 249.

27. Findeizen, *History*, 1:100–101 and 105, quotes extensively from Novgorod's St. Sophia *chinovnik*, which was published in Golubtsov, "Chinovnik Novgorodskogo Sofiiskogo sobora." (A *chinovnik*, or Ordinal, includes instructions for various services in

accordance with local custom.) On the evaluation of regional variants, see Zvereva, "Muzykal'nye chernoviki." The repertoire of the Vologda singers is in Belonenko, "Pokazaniia arkhiereiskikh pevchikh XVII veka."

28. The origins of polyphony in Russian liturgical music are somewhat cloudy and beyond the bounds of the present, limited discussion of liturgical singing, but the practice was certainly known in the sixteenth century; English-language discussions are in Gardner, *Russian Church Singing*, 2: chap. 4, and Velimirović, s.v. "Russian and Slavonic Church Music" in *NG2*.

29. Zabelin, "Dopolneniia k Dvortsovym razriadam," *ChOIDR* 3 (1882), pt. 1: cols. 505–506; see also Parfent'ev, *Professional'nye muzykanty*, 203.

30. English-language summaries of the wide literature on these seventeenth-century notational developments are in Velimirović, "Russian Musical *Azbuki*," and his "Russian and Slavonic Church Music" in *NG2*. On a revised dating proposed for some of these changes, see Parfent'ev, "Avtografy vydaiushchegosia russkogo muzykal'nogo teoretika." Parfent'ev has done important work on the re-dating of the two commissions, summarized in his article "Aleksandr Mezenets" in *SKK XVII v.*, pt. 1:63–68 and pt. 4:664, which includes additional bibliography; an English-language summary by Velimirović is in Findeizen, *History*, 1:374–75. Mezenets's treatise, *Azbuka znamennogo peniia*, was first published by Smolenskii and there is a new edition by Guseinova and Parfent'ev; see [Mezenets], *Aleksandr Mezenets i prochie*.

31. Nikon's biography was written in the 1680s by I. K. Shusherin, published as *Izvestie o rozhdenii i vospitanii i o zhitii sviateishego Nikona;* see p. 42 on the many foreigners at the monastery and p. 13 (and note) on his music as metropolitan. Translation from Morosan, *Choral Performance*, 42. Nikon's interest in Greek singing ("grecheskoe penie") and polyphonic singing in the new, imported style "by means of Kievan concordances" ("soglasiem kievskim") are in Shusherin, 43 and 54 (and quoted in Leonid, "Istoricheskoe opisanie stavropigial'nogo Voskresenskogo Novyi Ierusalim imenuemogo monastyria," *ChOIDR* 3 (1874), pt. 1:19–20). Individual singers associated with Nikon included five "Polish-born *vspevaki*" (including a "Pole who sings in Latin") and twenty-eight "litovskie" (Lithuanian) singers (whose identity is unclear); on these and other non-Muscovite singers in Muscovy, see Kharlampovich, *Malorossiiskoe vliianie*, 318ff.

32. A survey of musical references relating to the Iverskii Monastery is in *IRM* 1:171–72, and see the general context laid out in Sazonova, *Literaturnaia kul'tura Rossii*, esp. 462–66. The monastery held a copy of an icon from the Iviron Monastery on Mount Athos, thus its name; a brief overview of this monastery and its place in Nikon's earliest years as patriarch is in Bushkovitch, *Religion and Society in Russia*, 124. Nikon's request to send musical manuscripts to New Jerusalem refers to pieces in the new style. He includes a request to send the "Minevskii Mass" as well as three-part *kontserty* ("tregolosnye kontserta") and other polyphonic pieces; the reference to Minevskii has sometimes, and erroneously, been assumed to refer to the Polish composer Mielczewski (*IRM* 1:171, n. 7). These sources are also summarized in Kharlampovich, *Malorossiiskoe vliianie*, 318.

33. [Sparwenfeld], *J. G. Sparwenfeld's Diary*, 1:102 and 105 (the harmony in five or six parts), and 104 and 105–106 (the harmonious hymns).

34. On the various polyphonic vocal styles discussed here, see for example several works by Herasymova-Persyds'ka (in Russian publications as Gerasimova-Persidskaia): *Ukrains'ki partesni motety; Khorovyi kontsert na Ukraini;* and *Partesnyi kontsert v istorii muzykal'noi kul'tury*. In English, see Morosan, *One Thousand Years of Russian Church Music* and the stylistic discussion in Dolskaya-Ackerly, "Vasilii Titov and the 'Moscow'

Baroque"; all of these works include important additional bibliography. See also below, chapter 5.

35. The Smolensk practices are reported in Popov, "1685 g. O poezdke v Smolensk k mitrop. Simeonu," 42; the elaborate music is described on p. 39. On pp. 42–43, the envoys accuse Simeon of using part singing in the Western polyphonic style ("poiut u tebe s partes, a ne ruskim soglasiem"), to which Simeon again answers that his people like this kind of singing ("a to de penie v zdeshnei strane prilichno, i liudem liubezno"). The *kontsert* for Tsar Fedor is in Sazonova, *Literaturnaia kul'tura Rossii,* 332.

36. Parfent'ev, *Professional'nye muzykanty,* 111ff.

37. Visiting clerics also attended the tsar's private services, providing another opportunity for exchange; see Zabelin, *Domashnii byt russkikh tsarei,* pt. 1:385.

38. Longworth, *Alexis, Tsar of All the Russias,* 197–98, describes the funeral, and see Zabelin, *Domashnii byt russkikh tsarits,* 332–37, on the series of services following Mariia's death. The visiting patriarchs were still in Moscow following the adjournment of the councils over which they had presided, and they too participated in some of these ceremonies; see *DAI* 5:139ff.

39. *RIB* 23: cols. 998–99 (25 March 1669; totals taken from the summary on col. 999). Each of the singers is listed in Parfent'ev, *Professional'nye muzykanty,* but this published payment record brings them together conveniently. Of the singers listed in *RIB,* F. Koverin, E. Gavrilov, I. Gavrilov, E. Evstrat'ev (or Evstratov) (Kostromitin), P. Pokrovets, N. Nesterov, Stepan Aleksandrov, Savva Arkhipov, and Kuz'ma Rodionov (Karpov) had all been in service since or before 1659.

40. *RIB* 23: cols. 197–99. Parfent'ev, *Professional'nye muzykanty,* 41, and his *Drevnerusskoe pevcheskoe iskusstvo,* 70, also discusses this tradition, and there are many examples in the records in Zabelin, "Dopolneniia k Dvortsovym razriadam." Zabelin, *Domashnii byt russkikh tsarei,* pt. 1:407–10, describes a regular tradition of *slavlenie* (praising, honoring) at court for both tsar and tsaritsa in which many singers participated and for which they received special payment; he also discusses the special Christmas practice. On p. 410 he notes an occasion in 1659 at which Tsarevich Aleksei Alekseevich was "praised" by two of his dwarves.

41. Such singing may also represent an important link between folk traditions and the church; see for example, Vladyshevskaia, "K voprosu o sviazi narodnogo i professional'nogo drevnerusskogo pevcheskogo iskusstva," 334. Paul of Aleppo also heard caroling at Christmas; see Paul of Aleppo, in Belfour 2:232–33 and Murkos 4 (1898): 112, for the year 1655, and for the previous year, Belfour 1:351 and Murkos 4 (1897): 191. He also mentions house-to-house processions at Easter (Belfour 2:284–85 and Murkos 4 [1898]: 164). The patriarchs presiding over the church council in 1667 were also included in the caroling (*DAI* 5:119 and 138). Examples of this tradition from the early eighteenth century are in Voznesenskii, "Khorovoe iskusstvo petrovskoi epokhi," 148–49.

42. See Kollmann, "Pilgrimage, Procession and Symbolic Space," esp. 179–81.

43. Paul of Aleppo, in Belfour 1:391; see also 1:417, where Paul says that at a banquet, the visitors were called upon to sing in Greek and in Arabic (Murkos 3 [1898]: 25 and 53–54); in Ukraine, Paul read in Arabic and Greek (Belfour 1:219; Radu 26 [1949]: 703, and Murkos 4 [1897]: 62). There are numerous references to the *pevchie d'iaki* singing at banquets during the ceremonies surrounding the 1667 council; see *DAI* 5: 113, 123–24, and passim.

44. "The voyage, wherein Osep Napea the Moscovite Ambassadour returned home into his countrey," 421 (see also below, where the author notes that they did not particu-

larly enjoy the singing). The reference to singing "three severall times" may suggest a toast (see below). Zguta, *Russian Minstrels,* 55, believes that these singers were *skomorokhi,* but the strong tradition of *pevchie d'iaki* performing at banquets supports the idea that this was religious singing.

45. Larin, *Tri inostrannykh istochnika,* 279–80/451.

46. Paul of Aleppo, in Belfour 2:170 and Murkos 4 (1898): 53; the passage describing the Epiphany ceremony, quoted above, is in Belfour 1:354 and Murkos 4 (1897): 195. Singing had been an integral part of the Russian Epiphany ceremony from its beginnings, in the first quarter of the sixteenth century. Dmitrii Gerasimov, an emissary from Grand Prince Vasilii III to Pope Clement VII in 1525–26, described the Russian practices with which he was familiar. His descriptions were repeated in an account by Paolo Giovio, who says that the Russians "sing hymns in a large chorus" at the riverbank, where they had set up a structure. See Bushkovitch, "The Epiphany Ceremony of the Russian Court," 10 and n. 14. Poe, *"A People Born to Slavery,"* 24ff., discusses Giovio's meetings with Gerasimov and the circulation of his treatise. Russian descriptions of the ceremony appear, for example, in *DAI* 5:119 (January 1668) and 133 (August 1668; for both of these dates the patriarchal parties in Moscow for the church councils participated and there was singing in Russian and in Greek), and there is a brief reference to the ceremony in January 1669 on p. 138.

47. Flier, "Breaking the Code," 232, and see also his "The Iconology of Royal Ritual," 66.

48. Paul of Aleppo, in Belfour 2:90 and Murkos 3 (1898): 175–76. Flier, "Breaking the Code," 218–19, explains that the Lazarus hymn, one of the musical and theatrical high points of the ceremony, serves to link Palm Sunday simultaneously with the preceding Palm Week, celebrating Lazarus's resurrection, and with Passion Week, beginning with Christ's entry into Jerusalem and culminating with the Resurrection on Easter Sunday. Flier, "Court Ceremony in an Age of Reform," esp. 85–89, emphasizes the theatrical element in Nikon's reformed version of the Palm Sunday procession as a whole (which dates from 1656).

49. Paul of Aleppo, in Belfour 2:215 and Murkos 4 (1898): 95–96, describing events in 1655; Paul concludes, as he so often does, by recounting the effects of the weather: "[We] returned to our convent [monastic quarters], an hour after nightfall, almost perished and dead, with the fatigue of walking, the excessive cold, and extreme hunger" (Belfour 2:217).

50. Miloš Velimirović's fundamental article "Liturgical Drama in Byzantium and Russia" discusses the liturgical calculations for the time of performance on pp. 355 and 370; the actual dates might range from 16 to 22 December. A reference by Ignatius of Smolensk in 1389 to a Byzantine production of the play suggests that the drama may have been familiar in Russia quite early; see Velimirović, 363 and 365, and the survey in Spitsyn, "Peshchnoe deistvo i khaldeiskaia peshch'" (some of the payment records are translated in Velimirović). A recent survey is in Swoboda, *"The Furnace Play."*

51. See Velimirović, "Liturgical Drama," esp. 362–63, 365, and 374–75, on the mixed origins of the play, with special reference to the presence of Zoe (Sofiia) Paleologue, niece to the last Byzantine emperor, who was raised in Italy and married the Russian Grand Prince Ivan III in 1478. This was soon after Russian delegates had attended the Council of Florence, where they witnessed theatrical presentations; see Velimirović, 374. (Russian accounts of the council are reprinted in *Biblioteka literatury drevnei Rusi* 6:464–87, and *DRV* 17:178–85.) Zabelin, *Materialy dlia istorii, arkheologii i*

statistiki goroda Moskvy, 1:59, notes payments for teaching the children, and see also Velimirović's "Liturgical Drama," appendix II for a summary of these documents, outlining the preparations for the plays. Other payments for instructing the boy singers are in Zabelin, "Dopolneniia k Dvortsovym razriadam," *ChOIDR* 1 (1882), pt. 2: cols. 12–13 (1613); col. 124 (payment in February 1618 for the previous year); 285–86 (payment in February 1622 for the previous year); and *ChOIDR* 3 (1882), pt. 1: col. 550 (1628). See also Parfent'ev, *Professional'nye muzykanty,* 45, and listings for individual singers, for example on p. 213 (singer B. I. Zlatoustovskii).

52. Velimirović, "Liturgical Drama," 371–72.

53. Fletcher, *Of the Russe Commonwealth,* quoted from Berry, *The English Works of Giles Fletcher,* 293; see also Berry and Crummey, *Rude and Barbarous Kingdom,* 234.

54. On the possible participation of the *skomorokhi,* see for example, Velimirović, "Liturgical Drama," 373; Swoboda, *"The Furnace Play,"* 229–30, appears to equate the Chaldeans with *skomorokhi.* Some reservations are expressed in *IRM* 1:154, n. 3, citing Moleva, "Kaftany dlia khaldeev"; Moleva (writing in a popular style in a non-academic context) believes that the *d'iaki* took the roles of the Chaldeans; their names do not appear in the listings in Parfent'ev, *Professional'nye muzykanty,* however. The payment records in Spitsyn, "Peshchnoe deistvo i khaldeiskaia peshch'," 115–31, and those listed in n. 55 below do not employ the term *skomorokh.* Likhachev, Panchenko, and Ponyrko, *Smekh v drevnei Rusi,* 156–75, discuss the symbolism of the Chaldeans' actions and their context in other forms of Yuletide entertainment.

55. Payments to Sava (or Savka) Vasil'ev for his role as a Chaldean are in Zabelin, "Dopolneniia k Dvortsovym razriadam," *ChOIDR* 1 (1882), pt. 2: cols. 12–13 (1613); cols. 76–77 (1616); col. 283 (1621); *ChOIDR* 3 (1882), pt. 1: col. 360 (1623); col. 550 (1628); and *ChOIDR* 2 (1883), pt. 1: col. 652 (1630); and also Zabelin, *Materialy dlia istorii, arkheologii i statistiki goroda Moskvy,* 1:55–58 (1626–1630, 1633). Sava is paired with Kharka Ontsyforov in 1627, 1628, and 1630. Spitsyn, "Peshchnoe deistvo i khaldeiskaia peshch'," 96, singles out his continuing presence, but in his lengthy series of excerpts (pp. 122–30) from the payment records published in Zabelin, *Materialy dlia istorii, arkheologii i statistiki goroda Moskvy,* Spitsyn does not include the 26 Nov. 7136/1627 payment listing Sava as a *kazennyi storozh* (Zabelin, 1:56). The other *kazennyi storozh* frequently involved in the productions at this time was Vas'ka Shakhov.

56. Quoted in Olearius, *The Travels of Olearius,* 241–42; the reference to "Fassnachts-Brüder" is from Olearius, *Vermehrte Newe Beschreibung,* 284, and is noted in Velimirović, "Liturgical Drama," 373, n. 62. Likhachev, Panchenko, and Ponyrko, *Smekh v drevnei Rusi,* 158, also refer to Olearius's description. Apparently the Chaldeans were not the only mischief makers at this time of year. An edict was issued by Patriarch Filaret in December 1627 warning against such wild and inappropriate behavior (including music) but without reference to Chaldeans, *skomorokhi,* or to the play, although this was during the drama's most heavily-documented period (*Akty istoricheskie* 3:96 [document 92, part 10], cited in Peretts, *Iz istorii russkoi pesni,* 195).

57. Olearius, *The Travels of Olearius,* 242; on p. 12, editor Samuel Baron notes that Olearius had been at the Russian court in 1634, 1636, 1639, and 1643. Olearius's remark that the patriarch abolished the wild behavior appears in the 1656 edition (*Vermehrte Newe Beschreibung,* 284). In the 1647 edition, *Offt begehrte Beschreibung der Newen Orientalischen Reyse,* 183–84, the description is very similar but omits the last sentence, on the banning of the Chaldeans' wild antics.

58. Paul does, however, mention the Chaldeans, somewhat confusingly, in connec-

tion with the consecration of a bishop, describing how following the ceremony, the Chaldeans accompany the new bishop for three days; he adds that "we did not succeed in learning the reason and design of this" (Paul of Aleppo, in Belfour 2:130 and Murkos 4 [1898]: 18, where Murkos adds in n. 2 that the Chaldeans were figures in the Play of the Furnace, which was abolished by Patriarch Nikon—he has no other explanation for their appearance at this point in Paul's narrative). Likhachev, Panchenko, and Ponyrko, *Smekh v drevnei Rusi,* 161, n. 26, also call attention to this passage. Reutenfels's account is in Reutenfels, *De rebus Moschoviticis,* 216 (Russian translation as Reitenfel's, *Skazaniia,* 367 (and see chapter 6 below on this important account).

59. [Miege], *A Relation of Three Embassies,* 104–105. Spitsyn, "Peshchnoe deistvo i khaldeiskaia peshch,'" 114, also discusses the gradual demise of the play, noting a late performance in Vologda in 1643 (with payment records on pp. 116–18)—perhaps, then, the performances did survive later in outlying areas, as Miege's account suggests.

60. Panchenko, "Deklamatsiia Sil'vestra Medvedeva na temu strastei Khristovykh," esp. 116–21.

61. On the context of these works in the Jesuit curriculum adopted in non-Muscovite Orthodox schools, see Okenfuss, "Education in Russia" and his *The Rise and Fall of Latin Humanism,* chap. 1 (both with extensive bibliographies). On Simeon Polotskii's roles, see the excellent English-language survey by Hippisley, *The Poetic Style of Simeon Polotsky,* esp. chap. 1, and the survey in *SKK XVII v.,* pt. 3:362–79 and pt. 4:790–93.

62. These early declamations are discussed in Hippisley, *The Poetic Style of Simeon Polotsky,* chap. 1 (p. 24 lists the names of the pupils who went on the trip to Moscow); see also Eremin, "'Deklamatsiia' Simeona Polotskogo," and Prashkovich, "Iz rannikh deklamatsii Simeona Polotskogo."

63. Translation from Findeizen, *History,* 1:214 (citing *Akty istoricheskie* 4, No. 110:251). See Sazonova, *Literaturnaia kul'tura Rossii,* 462–82, for context and analysis of the texts; she also suggests a connection to the earlier performances in Polotsk.

64. Shcheglova, "Deklamatsiia Simeona Polotskogo," and Panchenko, "Deklamatsiia Sil'vestra Medvedeva na temu strastei Khristovykh," 118–19.

65. Sazonova, *Literaturnaia kul'tura Rossii,* 333, citing Vienna, Österreichische Nationalbibliothek, Cod. slav. 174.

66. Lavrin is identified in Panchenko, "Pridvornye virshi 80-kh godov XVII stoletiia," 68, where he notes that the singer fled from Moscow along with Medvedev and that both were exiled to Siberia; Medvedev was executed in 1691. See also Panchenko, "Deklamatsiia Sil'vestra Medvedeva na temu strastei Khristovykh," 117 and 119. Burmistrov's career is outlined in Parfent'ev, *Professional'nye muzykanty,* 151–52, which traces him to September 1689; the orations are mentioned on p. 106. There are other such associations: the son of patriarchal singer Afanasii Kurdiumov, for example, performed several such recitations, one of them for the patriarch, in the late 1670s through the mid-1680s (Parfent'ev, 260). Vsevolodskii-Gerngross, *Istoriia russkogo dramaticheskogo teatra,* 1:56–57, suggests that the declamations were on occasion performed in private homes. Istomin and his context in court culture is surveyed in Sazonova, *Literaturnaia kul'tura Rossii,* 73–84.

67. Repskii's biography is reconstructed primarily from a later petition to the court in which the singer recounted his abuse at the hands of Matveev, published in Starikova, "K istorii domashnikh krepostnykh teatrov," 56–60; see also Kharlampovich, *Malorossiiskoe vliianie,* 320–22, and Eingorn, "O snosheniiakh malorossiiskogo dukhovenstva," 368–69, n. 483. Repskii and his parents were originally from Poznań, and his

brother was employed by the Polish king. Repskii's father had sent him to Kiev to study; Polotskii calls him a *cherkass* in his own statement.

68. Paul of Aleppo, in Belfour 2:247 and Murkos 4 (1898): 127–28 (where the choir repeats the phrase "Gospodi pomilyi").

69. Ibid., in Belfour 1:324 and Murkos 4 (1897): 165–66. As Halperin, "In the Eye of the Beholder," 412, explains, Paul edited his notes after the completion of his first trip, thus his comparisons of the various singing styles from different points in his voyage. Johannes Herbinius, a clergyman who spent time at the Kievan Caves Monastery, also admired the choral part singing he heard in Ukraine. His work is reprinted in Lewin, *Seventeenth-Century Writings on the Kievan Caves Monastery;* a Russian translation is in Razumovskii, *Tserkovnoe penie v Rossii,* vyp. 2:208–209 (reprinted in Gardner, *Bogosluzhebnoe penie,* 2:60; on p. 61 Gardner reproduces the sample of staff-notated music appearing in Herbinius). Vladyshevskaia, "Stanovlenie stilia barokko i istoriia mnogogolos'ia Rossii," 27, also cites this passage from Paul as demonstrating that Muscovite and Ukrainian styles were still quite different at this point.

70. Paul of Aleppo, in Belfour 2:231 and Murkos 4 (1898): 111. More positive comments are in, for example, Belfour 2:48 (where he describes the reading and singing at a Lenten service, "chaunting with a voice concentrated and softened. Such is their practice; and excellent it is"; the translation in Murkos 3 [1898]: 135, appears to refer only to the readings in this passage). He also notes favorably the singing he heard on a trip to Novgorod, mentioning "delightfully sweet chants" (Belfour 2:181 and Murkos 4 [1898]: 63).

71. Ibid., in Belfour 1:216; Radu 26 (1949): 698 [462]; and Murkos 4 (1897): 58.

72. "The voyage, wherein Osep Napea the Moscovite Ambassadour returned home into his countrey," 421.

73. A disappointing lack of instruments in services is noted, for example, in Meierberg, *Puteshestvie v Moskoviiu,* 106, and in [Lyseck], *Relatio,* 43 (a Russian translation is in [Lyseck], "Posol'stvo Battoni," *Otechestvennye zapiski* 33 [Jan. 1828]: 310). Another important stumbling block was that non-Orthodox foreigners were not allowed to attend Orthodox services. The Saxon Adam Schleussing (or Schleussinger), who was in Russia in 1684, suggested that foreigners might circumvent this difficulty by visiting the private chapel of some wealthy Muscovite or simply by disguising oneself in Russian clothing and walking into a church. He presumably speaks from experience but nevertheless has nothing to say about church singing; see Lapteva, "Rasskaz ochevidtsa o zhizni Moskovii," 117. Sparwenfeld's favorable account of the hymn-like singing he heard at the Iverskii Monastery came from observations made from the doorway.

74. Bergholz, *Dnevnik,* 177 (Christmas 1723). Bergholz was part of a diplomatic mission to Russia in the 1720s, and his diary, written in Moscow and St. Petersburg, covers the first part of that decade; see Sander, *Social Dancing.* Other foreigners' observations on music in Peter's reign are summarized in Voznesenskii, "Khorovoe iskusstvo petrovskoi epokhi."

75. Collins, *The Present State of Russia,* 32 (where he concludes: "Finally, when they have brought up these children to a perfection, what with Bases, Tenors, Contratenors, and Trebles, you shall hear as good a Consort, as ever was sung at a Cats Vespers"), and 34. On Collins, see also Loewenson, "The Works of Robert Boyle"; Anderson, "English Views of Russia in the 17th Century"; and *DNB* 12:731–32.

76. The 1666 and 1667 pronouncements on music are published in *Deianiia moskovskikh soborov,* fol. 38 (first council) and fol. 5v (second council, separately foliated in the published edition); these passages are quoted in Metallov, *Ocherk istorii pravoslavnogo*

tserkovnogo peniia, 83, n. 1, and general context is set out in Meyendorff, *Russia, Ritual, and Reform.* The issue of *mnogoglasie* was an important one and had been the subject of much discussion at the series of councils in mid-century (and much earlier, for example, at the Stoglav Council of 1551); see Belokurov, "Deianie moskovskogo tserkovnogo sobora 1649 goda." The problem persisted; Collins, *The Present State of Russia,* 4, mentions multiple simultaneous readings in church services, and it was noted as a "bad and harmful custom" in the Spiritual Regulation, which Peter the Great signed in 1720 (Muller, *The Spiritual Regulation of Peter the Great,* 15). Uspenskii [Uspensky], "Schism and Cultural Conflict," 124–26, rightly situates the issue of *mnogoglasie* into the larger cultural contexts for the Nikonian reforms; the problem, however, was not limited to the mid-seventeenth century, as the previous and continuing efforts noted above indicate. The work of the commissions for notational reform has been reexamined recently, as noted in n. 30 above. The first commission worked from 1652 to 1654; there was ongoing work in the mid-1660s; and the second commission assembled in 1669 and 1670. Thus, although the notational efforts were not specifically linked to the 1666–67 councils, the commissions were part of the larger efforts begun by Nikon and continuing after his departure and final removal from the patriarchal throne.

77. The inappropriate vocal gymnastics of the singer Login in the early seventeenth century are reported in Morosan, *"Penie* and *Musikiia,"* 164–65 (quoting Rogov, *Muzykal'naia estetika,* 66–69). The council's decrees on domestic services ("a bez sviashchennika v domekh i tserkvakh peniia ne peti i ne nachinati") are in *Deianiia moskovskikh soborov,* fol. 46 (first council), and in Rogov, 86. One might read this statement, in part, as a confirmation of the professionalism of the *pevchie d'iaki.*

78. The report of the final commission on notation did state pointedly that staff notation, which was used in the *partesnoe penie* styles and by the imported singers, was unnecessary for those who understood the neumes; see Morosan, *"Penie* and *Musikiia,"* 171–72.

79. "[I] peniia imenuemogo partesnoe, ashche i ne ou ot seia tserkve vostochnyia priiatoe, ibo i stranam priemshym e vo upotreblenie nikimzhe okhuzhdaemi." The document is published in Preobrazhenskii, "Iz pervykh let partesnogo peniia v Moskve," 38–39, and in Gardner, *Bogosluzhebnoe penie,* 2:65–66. The petition also includes inquiries about other church practices; there is a brief reference in Gardner, *Bogosluzhebnoe penie,* 2:65.

80. In his highly opinionated history of the council, Paisios Ligarides, Metropolitan of Gaza, mentions singing on several occasions during the time of the patriarchs' stay, noting that when the visitors and their choirs came to sing a *mnogoletie* for Tsar Aleksei at Christmas 1666, the right *kliros* sang in Slavonic and the left, in Greek—something new in Muscovy and meant to show, as he says, "the unity of the Church, divided only by a difference of language" (Palmer, *The Patriarch and the Tsar,* 3:200). Although the alternation of languages by the right and left choirs in a single piece may have been new, Russians had long been accustomed to hearing singing in both languages at services and holidays (as we saw, for example, in the singing celebrating the creation of the new Muscovite patriarchate). Paisios also mentions a more relaxed style of singing by the Greek visitors at one of the banquets celebrating the election of the new patriarch: "And, as the banquet went on, and the mutual good-fellowship grew, we Easterns made a singing like that of the sirens" (Palmer, 3:283). All references to singing and singers are from *DAI* 5:98–144 (covering the arrival of the visiting patriarchs in November 1666 to the departure of Patriarch Paisios in July 1669).

81. Metallov, *Ocherk istorii pravoslavnogo tserkovnogo peniia,* 83, singles out this

performance of polyphonic music in the presence of the visiting patriarchs and notes the possible connection to their later decision approving the use of polyphonic *partesnoe* singing; he refers to Razumovskii, *Patriarshie pevchie diaki i poddiaki*, 22 (from *DAI* 5:122). There are also references to *strochnoe* singing and to singing with *stroki* (*DAI* 5:136 and 144), but these took place after Patriarch Makarios had departed. One is probably safe in assuming that some of the references to other styles and types of singing performed for the visitors also included polyphony, although it is not explicitly described as such.

82. Meyendorff, *Russia, Ritual, and Reform*, 56; see also Scheliha, "The Orthodox Universal Church," 273. Paisios's letter is published in "Gramota konstantinopol'skogo patriarkha Paisiia I," where this passage appears in *Khristianskoe chtenie* no. 3–4: 316–17. The date of Paisios's letter is discussed on pp. 304–307.

83. Good discussions of the ramifications of these debates are in Baranova, "Muzykal'naia estetika," and Zabolotnaia, "Barochnye formy."

84. Morosan, "*Penie* and *Musikiia*," 173; all bracketed material is Morosan's. Later Old Believer sources continued to link Nikon unfavorably to Kievan *partesnoe penie*; see for example Peretts, *Iz istorii russkoi pesni*, 199, citing an eighteenth-century Old Believer collection (Viazemskii manuscript O.V, described in Sheremetev, *Opisanie rukopisei kniazia Pavla Petrovicha Viazemskogo*, 485–90). Gardner, *Bogosluzhebnoe penie*, 2:63–64, notes the emphasis on physical gestures, which did not conform to the regulated and calm appearance the singers were meant to display.

85. This passage is discussed (in a slightly different context) in Baranova, "Muzykal'naia estetika," 362–63, quoting Rogov, *Muzykal'naia estetika*, 162–63; other such complaints are in Rogov, 161–66.

86. Okenfuss, *The Rise and Fall of Latin Humanism*, 42. Kononovich, "Epifanii Slavinetskii," identifies Slavinetskii's work as a translation from Erasmus (1526) that is based on a later, abridged version by Reinhard Hadamarius, *Civilitas morum Erasmi, in succinctas* (Nuremberg, 1555; there are also several earlier editions of the abridged text). A recent overview of Slavinetskii's career is in *SKK XVII v.*, pt. 1:309–13, with substantial bibliography in *SKK XVII v.*, pt. 4:700–702.

87. Quoted and translated in Murphy, "Cicero and the Icon Painters," 151.

88. This account is discussed in Bubnov and Demkova, "Vnov' naidennoe poslanie iz Moskvy v Pustozersk," where the passage quoted is on p. 143. The translation is from Uspenskii [Uspensky], "Schism and Cultural Conflict," 127.

89. Uspenskii [Uspensky], "Schism and Cultural Conflict," 127, notes that the Western mystery play "was accepted at the Mohyla Academy in Kiev and from there found its way to Moscow"; surviving Muscovite texts, however, are from a later period. Bubnov and Demkova, "Vnov' naidennoe poslanie iz Moskvy v Pustozersk," 139, observe that the performance by the loose-haired "pan'ia-zhenka" reported in this account would represent something entirely new to Muscovite theatrical history. Although the full implications of this document would take us rather far afield, I would tentatively argue for a less literal interpretation of this passage, acknowledging, however, that there were declamations on the Passion of Christ later at the Muscovite court under Tsar Fedor, by Polotskii's pupil and follower Sil'vestr Medvedev. In addition, to muddy the waters still further, Uspenskii, 126, points out that Avvakum, in his *Kniga tolkovanii i nravouchenii*, refers to a theatrical production when he mentions a peasant who was "costumed as the Archangel Michael" and who "found himself in a palace" (quoting from *RIB* 39: col. 466). Avvakum's work was written in the last years of Tsar Aleksei's life, and at about that same

time the Archangel Michael does indeed appear as a character in a play produced at court, *Zhalobnaia komediia ob Adame i Eve* (The Mournful Comedy of Adam and Eve); see chapter 6 below.

90. Nikon's music in Novgorod is in Shusherin, *Izvestie o rozhdenii i vospitanii i o zhitii sviateishego Nikona,* 13 (and note). The comparison of singing to the organ is translated in Morosan, "*Penie* and *Musikiia,*" 173 (citing Preobrazhenskii, *Kul'tovaia muzyka v Rossii,* 47–48). It is worth citing in full:

> Why cannot we today favor the sweet singing of our brethren? We know your answer: because it has the sound of an organ. But understand, you schismatics, does not our ancient singing have the sound of an organ as well? Yes, it has. For if we were to do away with singing that is similar to the sound of the organ, we would be obliged to do away with all singing. For all singing bears similarity to the sound of an organ, just as the organ can play all tones and singing.

91. See Baranova, "Muzykal'naia estetika," esp. 363–65.

92. Morosan, "*Penie* and *Musikiia,*" 174, citing the translation into modern Russian in Rogov, *Muzykal'naia estetika,* 124. The original is excerpted in Rogov, 105, from Ioannikii Korenev's theoretical work (p. 7 in the published version of RGB, f. 205, No. 146 discussed in chapter 5, n. 3, below). Zhivov, "Religious Reform and the Emergence of the Individual," 194, even views rhetoric and rhetoric manuals as wide-ranging cultural guides in seventeenth-century Muscovy. A larger and somewhat different context for the meaning of grammar itself is laid out in Uspenskii [Uspensky], "The Attitude to Grammar and Rhetoric," and see also chapter 5 below.

93. This passage is highlighted in Baranova, "Muzykal'naia estetika," 367, quoting Rogov, *Muzykal'naia estetika,* 121 and 137 (RGB, f. 205, No. 146, p. 48).

94. Quoted in Murphy, "Cicero and the Icon Painters," 153. The discussion in *IRM* 1:173ff., also places Korenev and Vladimirov within the circle of artistic debates in the last third of the century, and see also *SKK XVII v.,* pt. 2:110–11 and pt. 4:727–28.

95. Uspenskii [Uspensky], "The Attitude to Grammar and Rhetoric," 494; see also Zhivov, "Religious Reform and the Emergence of the Individual," esp. 193ff., and Okenfuss, *The Rise and Fall of Latin Humanism,* 41–44 (with many references by Old Believers to the disciplines of rhetoric, grammar, and philosophy).

96. Murphy, "Cicero and the Icon Painters," links Polotskii and Ushakov together as joint composers of an art treatise, "Slovo k liubotshchatel'nomu ikonnago pisaniia" (A Discourse to a Lover of Icon Painting). Several recent writers have reevaluated Ushakov's works, seeking to balance an earlier view of the artist as a representative of Western trends with a recognition of the equally important traditionalist elements in his work; see, for example, Smirnova, "Simon Ushakov—'Historicism' and 'Byzantinism,'" and for a more general appraisal, Hughes, "Secularization and Westernization Revisited." Murphy's discussion of the clear use of Western classical source material in this treatise gives Ushakov another interesting twist, placing him squarely on both sides of the debate.

3. "Sweet and harmonious singing"

1. General information on the establishment of the *bogomol'tsy* at court is in Zabelin, *Domashnii byt russkikh tsarei,* pt. 1:82–83 and 391–92, and pt. 2:296–301.

2. Collins, *The Present State of Russia,* 31–32. The Spiritual Regulation is less charitable: "those indolent rogues [alms collectors or beggars] compose certain insane and

spiritually harmful songs, and sing them before the people with sham groaning. Then, accepting remuneration for it, they madden yet more the simple oafs" (Muller, *The Spiritual Regulation of Peter the Great*, 54–55).

3. This description of Kseniia is in "Povest' knigi seia ot prezhnikh let," transcribed and translated into modern Russian in *PLDR konets XVI–nachalo XVII vekov*, 424–25 ("i pesni dukhovnyia liubezne slysheti zhelashe"). Sources are surveyed in *SKK XVII v.*, pt. 3:55–59. There is an English translation in Zenkovsky, *Medieval Russia's Epics, Chronicles, and Tales*, 390 (where the phrase "pesni dukhovnyia" is translated simply as "church music"), and the passage is discussed in Maiasova, "Literaturnyi obraz Ksenii Godunovoi," 294.

4. Thyrêt, *Between God and Tsar*, 136, points out that Kotoshikhin's description, which has generally been interpreted negatively, in fact demonstrates the importance of the royal women in the spiritual life of Muscovy. The passage from Kotoshikhin is in his *O Rossii v tsarstvovanie Alekseia Mikhailovicha*, 22.

5. The funeral payments are cited in Zabelin, *Domashnii byt russkikh tsarei*, pt. 2:299. On Koverin's career, see Parfent'ev, *Professional'nye muzykanty*, 244–45.

6. There is a large literature on Adam's Lament, and a comprehensive bibliography in Petrova and Seregina, *Ranniaia russkaia lirika*, 155–58. Two works by Savel'eva give a good overview: "Strukturnye osobennosti kratkoi i prostrannoi redaktsii 'Placha Adama'" and "'Plach Adama.' Krug istochnikov i literaturnaia sem'ia pamiatnika." Sergeev, "Dukhovnyi stikh 'Plach Adama' na ikone," focuses on the work's liturgical context, with references to the discussion in Findeizen (see below). The survey article "Stikhi pokaiannye" by Panchenko, in *SKK XIV–XVI v.*, 2: pt. 2:421–23, emphasizes the monastic context; see also the historical survey in Petrova and Seregina, *Ranniaia russkaia lirika*, and in individual sources listed below. Some texts are published and discussed in *PLDR vtoraia polovina XVI veka*, 550–63 and 635–40, and in Panchenko, *Russkaia stikhotvornaia kul'tura*, 19ff. There is a brief English-language description in Gardner, *Russian Church Singing*, 2:328, and in Findeizen, *History*, 1:205–11.

7. On historical themes in the *stikhi*, see the surveys in *SKK*; Peretts, "K istorii drevne-russkoi liriki"; Malyshev, "Stikhotvornaia parallel'" and "Stikh 'pokaianny' o 'liute' vremeni i 'poganykh' nashestvii"; and Petrova and Seregina, *Ranniaia russkaia lirika*, which emphasizes the everyday, down-to-earth quality of the texts. Korableva, "Pokaiannye stikhi kak zhanr drevnerusskogo pevcheskogo iskusstva," 9, emphasizes the connections between Ivan IV's time and the flowering of the *stikhi*.

8. The settings of Adam's Lament as neumed *stikhi* are listed in Petrova and Seregina, *Ranniaia russkaia lirika*, 155; on Diletskii's reference, see chapter 6 below; polyphonic settings in the Western-influenced *partesnoe penie* style are discussed in Gerasimova-Persidskaia, "Srednevekovye stikhi v partesnoi interpretatsii," and *Partesnyi kontsert v istorii muzykal'noi kul'tury*, 163–65; an example is published in Herasymova-Persyds'ka, *Khorovyi kontsert na Ukraini v XVII–XVIII st.*, 94–96. Later examples are in Bezsonov, *Kaleki perekhozhie* (cited in Petrova and Seregina, 155), and Markov, *Belomorskie stariny i dukhovnye stikhi*, 761 (text No. 328, "Stikh o Adame"), 768, and 755, where there is data on the informant, from the White Sea village of Pertozero. The texts were taken from a verse book (*stikhovnik*) containing several religious *stikhi*. The editors note that formerly there had been an Old Believer community there; *pokaiannye stikhi* circulated quite late among Old Believers. Markov recorded this text in 1909. Gerasimova-Persidskaia, "Partesnoe mnogogolosie i formirovanie stilevykh napravlenii," esp. 130, also ponders the relationships between *stikhi* and *kontserty*.

9. See the brief discussion in Dolskaya, *Spiritual Songs in Seventeenth-Century Russia*, xxii–xxiv, for example.

10. Markelov and Frolov, "Stroganovskie rukopisi v Pushkinskom dome," and Seregina, "Pevcheskie rukopisi iz knigopisnoi masterskoi Stroganovykh."

11. On *iurodstvo*, see Likhachev, Panchenko, and Ponyrko, *Smekh v drevnei Rusi*, 72–153, and in English, the review essay of the first edition of their book in Pope, "Fools and Folly in Old Russia," and Fedotov, *The Russian Religious Mind*, 2: chap. 12. Zabelin briefly mentions the presence of *iurodivye* at court as part of the *bogomol'tsy* in *Domashnii byt russkikh tsarei*, pt. 1:391–92, and in the *Materialy*, 713 (accompanying vol. 2, *Domashnii byt russkikh tsarits*), he lists payments to *iurodivye* and *bogomol'tsy*.

12. See the fascinating articles by Ponyrko, "Avtor stikhov pokaiannykh i raspevshchik iurodivyi Stefan," and "Stikhi pokaiannye galitskogo iurodivogo XVII v. Stefana" (where the author notes the influence of the language of existing *stikhi* on Stefan's farewell letter to his family). Some of the texts were published originally in Likhachev, Panchenko, and Ponyrko, *Smekh v drevnei Rusi*, 205–13.

13. English-language studies of the seventeenth-century *kant* are by Dolskaya-Ackerly, "The Early Kant," and her edition of an entire *kant* manuscript, GIM, Muz. sobr., No. 1938, in Dolskaya, *Spiritual Songs in Seventeenth-Century Russia*. This is the only seventeenth-century *kant* source published in its entirety (apart from the Polotskii-Titov Psalter; see below). Concordances among the early anonymous *kant* texts are in Rothe, *Verse und Lieder bei den Ostslaven*. The brief survey by Barbara Krader, in Brown and Mazo, *A Collection of Russian Folk Songs by Nikolai Lvov and Ivan Prach*, xiii and 10–13, takes the genre through the eighteenth century and demonstrates its lasting influence on Russian musical thinking. Russian-language surveys include *IRM* 1:226–49, and the article "Kant," by Vasil'eva and Lapin, in *MP* 1: pt. 2:20–37. There are many important works (cited below) by A. V. Pozdneev, the most extended of which is his *Rukopisnye pesenniki* (a posthumous publication of his dissertation, with the addition of a large and important introductory chapter), portions of which are summarized in his "Rukopisnye pesenniki XVII–XVIII vekov"; an overview of Pozdneev's contribution to the field is in Smith, "A. V. Pozdneev and the Russian 'Literary Song.'" See also Livanova, *Russkaia muzykal'naia kul'tura XVIII v.*, 1:453–525 (an overall survey focusing on the eighteenth century), with a separately published book of transcriptions and facsimiles from GIM, Otd. ruk., No. 2473, issued as *Sbornik kantov XVIII veka*; Findeizen, *History*, 2: esp. chap. 18; and the monograph by Kostiukovets, *Kantovaia kul'tura v Belorussii*. Additional works by Iu. V. Keldysh are cited below. Pozdneev, *Rukopisnye pesenniki*, 96ff., discusses *pokaiannye* texts, referring to the subject matter and emotional content of these works, not to the set of *pokaiannye stikhi*.

14. My deepest thanks go to Hans Rothe, who generously supplied a copy of this important source. The inscriptions appear on fols. 1 and 24v–25, and they are transcribed in *IRM* 1:229 and n. 8 (and thanks to Katarzyna Dziwirek for advice on the translation). On the somewhat fuzzy term "psal'm" in early usage (apparently antedating the term *kant*), see *MP* 1: pt. 2:482–97.

15. Klenk, *Posol'stvo Kunraada fan-Klenka*, 235 (Dutch) and 540 (Russian translation).

16. Polotskii's forewords are in Polotskii, *Izbrannye sochineniia*, 213 (the prose text) and 215. The first foreword (p. 211) also makes reference to singing and music. The title page of the Versified Psalter (by Simon Ushakov, engraved by A. Trukhmenskii) depicts King David with a small, Western-style harp and is reproduced in Derzhavina, "Simeon

Polotskii v rabote nad 'Psaltyr'iu rifmotvornoi,' " 121. Serman, " 'Psaltyr' rifmotvornaia' Simeona Polotskogo," 220–21, also calls attention to Polotskii's emphasis on singing, noting that the poet's advice to sing the psalms in lieu of secular songs may fit into the context of the struggles to ban the *skomorokhi;* see also Pozdneev, *Rukopisnye pesenniki,* 20–21 and 86, on Polotskii's observations and on the popularity of Jan Kochanowski, Polotskii's poetic model, in Muscovy. Sazonova, *Literaturnaia kul'tura Rossii,* 333–34, suggests that Polotskii had musical settings in mind, noting particularly the multiplicity of strophic forms in his settings. A listing of holdings in the icon workshop (Obraznaia palata) includes, among a substantial collection of books, a manuscript volume "on domestic singing" ("o domashnem penii"); it is not clear what its contents might be, although the book collection as a whole is of course religious. The listing is in Viktorov, *Opisanie zapisnykh knig i bumag,* 1:209.

17. Lewin, "Jan Kochanowski: The Model Poet," 433, notes that even though Polotskii did not mention Kochanowski by name in his own translation, others made the link. Patriarch Ioakim and a monk from the Chudov (Miracles) Monastery said that Polotskii's Psalter "was not that one which had come to us from the Holy Spirit by David's good offices. It was collected by him from Polish books or even taken ready from a certain Jan Kochanowski, a true Latin." (Lewin quotes from Serman, " 'Psaltyr' rifmotvornaia' Simeona Polotskogo," 216; see also Sazonova, *Literaturnaia kul'tura Rossii,* 55–56).

18. On Titov, see Dolskaya-Ackerly, "Vasilii Titov and the 'Moscow' Baroque," and her edition of some of his choral works in Titov, *Vasilii Titov i russkoe barokko.* See also Protopopov, "Tvoreniia Vasiliia Titova," his *Muzyka na Poltavskuiu pobedu,* 228ff., and the survey in *IRM* 1:243–49 and 287–93.

19. The first of the presentation copies is RNB, Q.XIV.41. The later presentation copy to Sofiia is BAN, sobr. Petra I A 66 (16.15.11) (see Bobrova, *Biblioteka Petra I,* No. 182, and the facsimiles and discussion in Findeizen, *History,* 1:236–40).

20. Protopopov, *Muzyka na Poltavskuiu pobedu,* 230, suggests that Titov's success in setting the psalms may have contributed to his rise through the ranks of the *stanitsy* as a singer. On Polotskii as tutor, see *SKK XVII v.,* pt. 3:367, and Hughes, *Sophia,* 33.

21. *IRM* 1:249 and n. 40, notes that RNB, Sol. sobr., No. 800/692 belonged to the Solovetskii Monastery and RGB, f. 310, No. 899, which contains some of the Polotskii-Titov settings, was associated with Ioakim, a deacon (*ierod'iakon*) who may have been at the Voznesenskii (Ascension) Convent in Moscow. According to Leonid, *Sistematicheskoe opisanie slaviano-rossiiskikh rukopisei,* 520, manuscript GIM, sobr. Uvarova, No. 760, from the late seventeenth or early eighteenth century, includes an inscription on fol. 122 linking it to "diiakon Kiril Beznikovets." Manuscript BAN, sobr. Petra I B 117 (16.15.9), another Polotskii-Titov source, belonged to Andrei Nizhegorodets, a singer in Peter's choir in the 1690s whose career lasted into the 1720s (see Parfent'ev, *Professional'nye muzykanty,* 296, and Bobrova, *Biblioteka Petra I,* No. 183).

22. There is a brief biography of Damaskin in *SKK XVII v.,* pt. 1:246–47, and the inscriptions in GIM 1743 are discussed in Pozdneev, "Knizhnye pesni XVII veka," 227 and n. 6, and in his "Nikonovskaia shkola pesennoi poezii," 423–24. The inscriptions in GIM, sobr. Khludova, No. 126d are also discussed in "Nikonovskaia shkola," 426, and "Knizhnye pesni XVII veka," 227. The manuscript RGIA, f. 834, op. 3, ed. khr. 3764, of mixed contents but which includes a *kant* on the birth of Tsarevich Aleksei Petrovich in 1690, was associated with the Pafnut'ev (St. Paphnutius) Monastery, according to Protopopov, "Panegiricheskii kant 1690 g.," 241. Livanova, *Russkaia muzykal'naia kul'tura,* 1:467ff., examines the contents of the *kant* manuscript GIM, Otd. ruk., No. 2473 from

ca. 1739–48 (substantial excerpts published separately as *Sbornik kantov XVIII veka*), which contains some of Polotskii's psalm translations and a few of Titov's musical settings, which tended to fare worse than the texts; some of Polotskii's psalm texts in this source are set to new music. *MP* 1, pt. 2:27, also discusses the circulation of the Polotskii-Titov settings in the eighteenth century, and see also Pozdneev, *Rukopisnye pesenniki*, 51–54, 85–88, and 181n, and Peretts, *Iz istorii russkoi pesni*, 202–204.

23. Pozdneev, *Rukopisnye pesenniki*, 23–55, discusses German and the Nikon school centered at the New Jerusalem Monastery; on German, see also *SKK XVII v.*, pt. 1:198–200 and pt. 4:681; Pozdneev, "Pesni-akrostikhi Germana," and "Poet XVII veka German"; Tschiževskij, "Akrostikhi Germana i starorusskie akrostikhi"; Dolskaya-Ackerly, "German Voskresenskij: A Seventeenth-Century Poet-Musician"; and Vasil'eva, "Tri Voskresnykh gimna arkhimandrita Germana."

24. According to the listings in Rothe, *Verse und Lieder bei den Ostslaven*, the following texts in manuscript 10944 have concordant versions in later sources: "Angel pastyrem movil" (No. 15 in Rothe's listing, four concordant versions, and see also the discussion in Peretts, *Iz istorii russkoi pesni*, 169–75); "Dai nam Khriste vspomozhene" (No. 196, three concordances); "Ditiatko sia narodilo" (No. 204, nine concordances, and the text appears in Diletskii's *Grammatika* with the Polish text "Dzieciątko sie narodziło"; see appendix); "Mesiash prished" (No. 388, listed as unique in Rothe, but No. 389, "Mesiia pride vo mir istinnyi" has ten concordances and appears in Diletskii's *Grammatika*); "Khristos z mertvykh vstal est' " (No. 776, four concordances); and "Ezu Khriste pane milyi" (No. 831, seven concordances). The text "Nasventsha panno i matko bozha" (No. 426) is also listed as unique to manuscript 10944, but the text "Nasventsha panno slichna Mariia" (No. 427) appears in one other source. Rothe does not list individual textual variants, so the spellings listed here may not correspond precisely to those of manuscript 10944.

25. See the statistics in Pozdneev, *Rukopisnye pesenniki*, 15–16, and in his "Pol'skii element v russkikh rukopisnykh pesennikakh," 335. Neither Rothe nor Pozdneev considers musical variants specifically, and no list of musical incipits is available (the most extensive examples are in Dolskaya-Ackerly, "The Early Kant," 226–36); some variant musical readings are evident from comparing isolated published examples (see appendix).

26. Pozdneev, "Svetskie pol'skie pesni," focuses on the Polish content of manuscript 1974. Some of Pozdneev's figures vary slightly in his different articles, apparently because some Polish texts appear more than once in this source.

27. Pozdneev, *Rukopisnye pesenniki*, esp. 15–20, makes this point clearly.

28. Ibid., 47ff., discusses Dimitrii Rostovskii.

29. The texts are categorized in Dolskaya, *Spiritual Songs in Seventeenth-Century Russia*, x (and see also p. 335, an editorial note by Hans Rothe). The non-*kant* texts (described on pp. 241 and 279) include sketches for the Cherubic Hymn text; some folios are ruled but have no music entered and some song numbers are lacking. Texts attributed to Epifanii Slavinetskii are discussed on pp. xxxvii–xxxviii; in Pozdneev, *Rukopisnye pesenniki*, 55–79, and his "Die geistlichen Lieder des Epifanij Slavineckij."

30. The seven sources with which manuscript 1938 shares seventy-five or more works are: GIM 1743; RGB 9498; GIM Shchuk. 61; RNB Pog. 426; RNB Q.XIV.25; RNB Tit. 4172; and GIM Khlud. 126d (full citations are listed in the bibliography under Manuscripts Cited). These statistics are based on the listings in Rothe, *Verse und Lieder bei den Ostslaven*, which include only anonymous pieces (and only textual incipits), so they are not accurate for the pieces in manuscript 1938 which are attributed to a known

author; this set of concordances has been drawn from various sources and is certainly not complete.

31. Dolskaya-Ackerly, "The Early Kant," 96, notes the alphabetical ordering of GIM, Khlud. 126d; and on the ordering of GIM 1743, see the important study by Keldysh, "Rannii russkii kant," 69 and n. 3, where he also notes the significance of such ordering.

32. It is difficult to reconstruct pairs or consistent small groupings of *kanty* from the listings in Rothe, *Verse und Lieder bei den Ostslaven*, although these listings do include folio numbers. However, songs frequently appear several times in a single source (especially GIM 1743) and the manuscripts are quite long; one can only hope for the publication of additional individual sources.

33. Pozdneev, "Poet XVII veka German," 155, describes German's book collection as including both chant and *partesnoe* musical sources; in the more extended description in *Rukopisnye pesenniki*, 32, he describes German's books as including "knigi kievskogo prostogo peniia" (books of Kievan simple [monophonic] singing).

34. All but two of the fourteen works attributed to German listed in Pozdneev, "Pesni-akrostikhi Germana," appear in GIM 1743.

35. Pozdneev, "Svetskie pol'skie pesni," 58–59, focuses on another critical and little-explored aspect of transmission: via printed Western sources. He notes that the *kant* source RNB 1974 includes several annotations pointing to songs that are found in such published sources ("est' v kantychkakh").

36. There is a broad survey of the *kant* in eighteenth- and nineteenth-century practice in Dolskaya-Ackerly, "The Early Kant," 175ff. and chap. 7.

37. Peretts, "K istorii drevne-russkoi liriki," 479.

38. Okenfuss, *The Rise and Fall of Latin Humanism*, esp. p. 63, but see chap. 1, passim. Parfent'ev, *Drevnerusskoe pevcheskoe iskusstvo*, 163ff., characterizes some of the singing ensembles associated with private families as early adoptors of the *partesnoe* style.

39. Pozdneev, *Rukopisnye pesenniki*, 111–16, discusses texts associated with historical events, and see also his "Knizhnye pesni XVII veka." Senyk, *Women's Monasteries in Ukraine and Belorussia*, 171, points to another historical (and of course religious) context for *kanty*: an association with pilgrimages to specific sites. On historical elements in chant and chant sources, see the interesting discussion in Ramazanova, *Moskovskoe tsarstvo v tserkovno-pevcheskom iskusstve*, especially 151ff., on the works attributed to Ivan IV; another consideration of liturgical sources as historical documents is in Seregina, "Muzykal'naia letopis' Rossii," and in Parfent'ev, *Drevnerusskoe pevcheskoe iskusstvo*, esp. 165, where he characterizes the Stroganov collection. A brief English-language study of one such verse is in Velimirović, "An Unusual Russian 'Spiritual Verse.'"

40. The acrostic reads "maiia mesiatsa boleznen" and it is one of two acrostics in the text of "Pamiat' predlozhiti smerti," as quoted in Pozdneev, "Poet XVII veka German," 153 (and see also *SKK XVII v.*, pt. 1:199). Some of German's acrostics are quite intricate, both in terms of their structure and in their interplay with the themes presented in the main text; see Vasil'eva, "Tri Voskresnykh gimna."

41. An early example of a commemorative *kant* is the work written for the birth of Peter's son, Tsarevich Aleksei Petrovich, described in Protopopov, "Panegiricheskii kant 1690 g."; another early example commemorated the Russian victory at Azov (1696), for which a *kant* extolling General-Admiral Lefort (named in the text) was composed; see Protopopov, *Muzyka na Poltavskuiu pobedu*, 202; Pozdneev, *Rukopisnye pesenniki*, 109–16 and 124–29 and passim; and Findeizen, "Petrovskie kanty." Keldysh's discussion of Pe-

trine public music in *IRM* 2:37ff., also notes the relationship between the new *pane-giricheskie kanty* and the older traditions of acclamation and *mnogoletie*. Parfent'ev, *Drevnerusskoe pevcheskoe iskusstvo*, 81–82, uses the term "panegyrical music" in a discussion of some of the extra-liturgical singing in which the *d'iaki* engaged.

42. Protopopov, *Muzyka na Poltavskuiu pobedu*, 206ff., describes these *kanty* as suites, and he ponders the question of the composers and performers of these various works throughout his study. See also the works by Keldysh, Findeizen, and Pozdneev listed above, n. 13.

43. Burilina, "Chin 'za prilivok o zdravii gosudaria,'" lays out the developing liturgical settings for toasts; Findeizen, *History*, 1: chap. 9, surveys the practice, based primarily on Orlov, "Chashi gosudarevy"; and see *SKK vtoraia polovina XIV–XVI v.*, 2: pt. 2:508–11. Many visitors describe the toasts they observed at banquets in the capital. See Paul of Aleppo, in Belfour 2:232 and Murkos 4 (1898): 112; Herberstein, *Notes Upon Russia*, 2:132 (private toasts offered in the ambassador's quarters); and Olearius, *The Travels of Olearius*, 65 and 98 (toasts in the context of ambassadorial exchanges and receptions). Richard James provides two different definitions for the word "chasha" (cup). The first, as "chash," appears in a series of terms describing various types of wooden cups; following this definition, he adds the phrase "chasha sudariva," defining it, somewhat confusingly, as "the Emperors health of others they say" (Larin, *Tri inostrannykh istochnika*, 243/424, and as a toast on 297/466).

44. Burilina, "Chin 'za prilivok o zdravii gosudaria,'" 212–13. Burilina uses the term *deistvie* (action) in her study, echoing other such "actions" which enjoyed their greatest development during the same period in the late sixteenth and seventeenth centuries: the Palm Sunday procession; the Play of the Furnace; and even, to a certain degree, the later plays performed at the new court theater in the 1670s—all of these are actions of a sort, developed and systematized with the organizational and theatrical flair typical of this period.

45. Ibid., 210–11.

46. The rite of acclamation for secular figures is in ibid., 213, n. 54. The "voinskie stikhi" are in Protopopov, "Notnaia biblioteka," 125; the document is transcribed on p. 132. Paul of Aleppo describes the recital of the names of Russian soldiers who fell "in defence of their religion," a procedure he clocked at over three hours in the bitter cold, in Belfour 2:273 and Murkos 4 (1898): 153.

47. These songs are preserved in Oxford, Bodleian Library, ms James 43. The manuscript sources were published in facsimile and in transcription in Simoni, *Velikorusskie pesni*, and the texts are readily available, for example in *PLDR konets XVI–nachala XVII v.*, 536–40. Translations of some of the texts are in Zenkovsky, *Medieval Russia's Epics, Chronicles, and Tales*, 501–505 (the song about the Crimean Tatars, the return of Filaret, and Kseniia's first lament), and in Brown, *A History of Seventeenth-Century Russian Literature*, 82–84 (portions of the song of the Crimean Tatars, the song on the death of Skopin-Shuiskii, and the same lament by Kseniia Godunova).

48. There is a brief survey of the topics addressed in the James songs in *SKK XVII v.*, pt. 1:255–56. The subject of the song about the Crimean raid is disputed; see Danilov, "Sborniki pesen XVII stoletiia," and Sheptaev, "Zametki o pesniakh, zapisannykh dlia Richarda Dzhemsa." The collection in Alekseevna, *Istoricheskie pesni XVII veka*, lists a series of songs on Skopin-Shuiskii on pp. 47–89, and another (later) song on Filaret on pp. 99–100; there are dozens of songs about the events of the Time of Troubles.

49. Translation from Zenkovsky, *Medieval Russia's Epics, Chronicles, and Tales*, 503–504.

50. Sheptaev, "Zametki o pesniakh, zapisannykh dlia Richarda Dzhemsa," 306–308, discusses the wedding imagery in these laments, and see also below, chapter 4.

51. On the lament and its appearance in written documents preserving folk traditions in this period, see the discussion in Malyshev, "Stikhotvornaia parallel' k 'Povesti o Gore i Zlochastii'"; the tale, as "Misery-Luckless-Plight," is translated in Zenkovsky, *Medieval Russia's Epics, Chronicles, and Tales,* 489–501.

52. The Kvashnin-Samarin texts are discussed in many works, including *IRM* 1:188–89, where their links to folk song are emphasized. A good summary of the literature is in Teletova, "Pervyi russkii liricheskii poet P. A. Kvashnin-Samarin," and in *SKK XVII v.,* pt. 2:154–56. A selection of texts is published in *PLDR XVII vek, kniga pervaia,* 595–602 and 703–704; English translations of some texts are in Zenkovsky, *Medieval Russia's Epics, Chronicles, and Tales,* 515–17, and Brown, *A History of Seventeenth-Century Russian Literature,* 84–86. The position of *stol'nik* was usually held by youths from around age ten to sixteen from important (although not the highest-ranking) families; see Zabelin, *Domashnii byt russkikh tsarits,* 403–405, where he also quotes from Kotoshikhin's account. Another set of similar, lyrical texts is preserved from the 1680s, written by Semen Ivanovich Pazukhin (d. 1709). The texts come from the same service milieu and seem to reflect the same influences from folk songs and texts; see Kudriavtsev, "Dve liricheskie pesni, zapisannye v XVII veke."

53. Pozdneev, "Svetskie pol'skie pesni," 57.

54. Olearius, *The Travels of Olearius,* 48, and *Vermehrte Newe Beschreibung,* 19. Findeizen, *History,* 2:235, notes it is possible that secular songs were notated by means of neumes; he cites an admittedly flawed paper by Odoevskii, "Mirskaia pesnia."

55. Pozdneev, *Rukopisnye pesenniki,* 32, and "Poet XVII veka German," 155–56. The term *liutnia* does not appear in the seventeenth-century glossaries excerpted in Findeizen, *History,* 1:148, although two sources define *arfaliutnia* as a *gusli,* that is, a plucked stringed instrument (1:144–45, where one of these sources also defines it as a violin). Johan Sparwenfeld includes *liutnia* in his *Lexicon Slavonicum,* which, although compiled somewhat later, was based on his years in Moscow studying Russian in the mid-1680s; see [Sparwenfeld], *Lexicon Slavonicum,* 1: no. 3932 (listed with a series of stringed instruments, mostly plucked: *gusli, skrypitsa, garfa,* and others).

56. Translation (slightly modified) of Avvakum's *vita* from Zenkovsky, *Medieval Russia's Epics, Chronicles, and Tales,* 437–38 (where *domra* is translated as "lute"), and see *PLDR XVII v., kniga vtoraia,* 381.

57. Herberstein, *Notes Upon Russia,* 1:58. His *Rerum Moscoviticarum commentarii* originally appeared in Vienna in 1549 and was reprinted; this translation is based on the 1556 Basle edition. On Herberstein, see *Notes Upon Russia,* 1:lxxxvi–cxlvii; *MERSH* 14:6–10; and Poe, "*A People Born to Slavery,*" esp. chap. 4. The eighteenth-century Old Believer source is cited in Peretts, *Iz istorii russkoi pesni,* 200 (referring to a manuscript in the Viazemskii collection, O.VI, described in Sheremetev, *Opisanie rukopisei kniazia Pavla Petrovicha Viazemskogo,* 490–92).

4. Tavern and Wedding

1. *DRV* 13:205. The *mnogoletie* is also described as being performed "demesvom bolshoe" in records of Tsar Mikhail's 1626 wedding, in *DR* 1: cols. 779–80; see also Parfent'ev, *Professional'nye muzykanty,* 33, 333, and 358.

2. See the general survey in Martin, "Archival Sleuths and Documentary Trans-

positions" and his "Choreographing the 'Tsar's Happy Occasion,'" where he refers to 101 musicians playing the fanfare at the 1624 ceremony on p. 806 (and, in a personal communication, details the several important families who contributed their own musicians for this fanfare). The description of the all-day fanfare for the 1626 wedding is in *DR* 1: col. 785.

3. *DRV* 13:214. The Prazdnik mentioned in the passage quoted is a book that contains Proper hymns for the great feasts; the Lenten Triod' contains Propers for Lent; and the Festal Triod' contains Propers for Easter through Pentecost. Aleksei's wedding is described in much the same way (although in less detail) in the *vita* of Ioann Neronov; an English translation is in Zhivov, "Religious Reform and the Emergence of the Individual," 192, citing Subbotin, *Materialy dlia istorii raskola*, 1:272; and see also Longworth, *Alexis, Tsar of All the Russias*, 35. The term *radost'* (literally, "joy," "happiness"; translated here as "marriage") in the context of Russian weddings is discussed in Samodelova, "Opisaniia drevnerusskoi svad'by," 805–807. Thanks to Russell Martin for his advice on this text.

4. On the second day, they performed "strochnye i demestvennye stikhi izo Vladychnykh prazdnikov, i iz triodei," and on the third, the ranks are described as singing throughout ("vo ves' stol peli"); *DRV* 13:221–22 (and many thanks to Russell Martin, who provided the text for this passage from RGADA, fond 135, sec. IV, rub. II, no. 24, fols. 46–46v).

5. Some versions of the *Domostroi* include an extensive discussion of traditional wedding procedures; see Kolesov and Rozhdestvenskaia, *Domostroi*, 73–87, and the English translation by Pouncy, *The Domostroi*, 204–39 (with the fanfare on p. 226). Olearius's remarks are in *The Travels of Olearius*, 168, and see chapter 1 on the fanfares for Dmitrii's wedding. Kotoshikhin, *O Rossii v tsarstvovanie Alekseia Mikhailovicha*, 21 and 132, notes that the fanfare is the only music ("muzyka") allowed at weddings. Foreign accounts describing Russian weddings are summarized in Samodelova, "Opisaniia drevnerusskoi svad'by." English-language discussions of early Russian weddings, in addition to Russell Martin's works listed in n. 2 above, include Kaiser, "Symbol and Ritual in the Marriages of Ivan IV," and Rabinovich, "The Wedding in the Sixteenth-Century Russian City."

6. Olearius, *The Travels of Olearius*, 262–63 (this is the 1656 edition of his work). The translator of this edition, Samuel Baron, cites an order of 16 August 1653 in the context of this passage, so the "present patriarch" would refer to Nikon (see *AAE* 4: no. 63 [pp. 95–97], which was issued in the name of the tsar). Olearius was not in Russia after 1643 and this passage does not appear in the first edition of his work, from 1647; this information may thus have come from his meeting with a Muscovite embassy in Holstein in 1653 (according to Baron, p. 15, Olearius met "daily" with this embassy). The story is repeated in Klenk, *Posol'stvo Kunraada fan-Klenka*, 235 (Dutch) and 540 (Russian); the Klenk embassy arrived in January 1676, just before Aleksei died. It also appears regularly (although not necessarily attributed to Olearius) in English-language surveys of Russian music, for example Leonard, *A History of Russian Music*, 24, and Seaman, *History of Russian Music*, 41, and in popular accounts of Russian history, for example Massie, *Land of the Firebird*, 80.

7. Zguta, *Russian Minstrels*, chap. 3, passim (especially notes 87 and 89), discusses the decline of the *skomorokhi* in the seventeenth century and their fate in the eighteenth century. Belkin, *Russkie skomorokhi*, 73ff., reviews the government documents of the seventeenth century (as does Findeizen, *History*, chap. 5). As both Zguta and Belkin note, there has been a great deal of discussion about the eighteenth-century collection of folk

texts assembled by Kirsha Danilov, which some believe are attributable to a *skomorokh;* see for example Gorelov, "Kem byl avtor sbornika 'Drevnie rossiiskie stikhotvoreniia.'" The collection is published in Evgen'eva and Putilov, *Drevnie rossiiskie stikhotvoreniia.* The word *skomorokh* does appear in Sparwenfeld's late seventeenth-century lexicon, associated with *medvednik* (bear leader); see [Sparwenfeld], *Lexicon Slavonicum,* 2: No. 2547. A similar pairing appears in the *vita* of Ioann Neronov, written in the 1670s but describing events from the first half of the century (Subbotin, *Materialy dlia istorii raskola,* 1:260–61).

8. There is a difficult passage in Reitenfel's, *Skazaniia,* 289, that seems to hint at the use of organs in Orthodox churches in Moscow. In his description of Aleksei's piety, the author notes that the tsar was always accompanied by his confessor; it was under his influence, along with Tsaritsa Mariia's, that Aleksei decided to remove the elaborately decorated organ that was located in the main church of the Kremlin. This would be a highly unlikely place for an organ in Muscovy. Roizman, *Organ,* 47, although not addressing the issue of the instrument's location, suggests that Reutenfels refers to the Luhn brothers' organ (see below), which was located not in a Kremlin church but at court in the late 1630s, before Aleksei took the throne (and of course, well before Reutenfels was in Russia).

9. Larin, *Tri inostrannykh istochnika,* 219/410 (transcription/facsimile).

10. James's *spoine* (Larin, *Tri inostrannykh istochnika,* 219, suggests *s"pyn'*) is something of a puzzle; James Augerot suggests that it may come from the verb *pet'/spet'* (to sing). Thanks also to John Hall for his advice on this term.

11. *Gusli* and *domra* are paired in Larin, *Tri inostrannykh istochnika,* 243/424; *lyra* and *kukli* are nearby on 243/425.

12. Ibid., as follows: "peasna," "rogha," and "pastuke" on 235/419; "trubense" (220/411); "nabat" (237/420); "strone" (293/462); and "duda" (299/467).

13. Ibid., 234/418.

14. Captain Jean Sauvage spent about a month in 1586 in Kholmogory, where the glossary was compiled. It was reworked to some degree by André Thevet in Paris in that year; see Larin, *Tri inostrannykh istochnika,* 24–27, and for the listing of musical terms, 102.

15. On the term *duda,* see Protopopov, PRMI 7:620, n. 40 (see chapter 5 below on this source), and Aumayr, *Historische Untersuchungen an Bezeichnungen von Musikinstrumenten,* 29–32.

16. Larin, *Tri inostrannykh istochnika,* 138.

17. Lunden, *The Trondheim Russian-German MS Vocabulary,* lists the instruments in chap. 56 ("O penii i o vsiakikh igrakh / Von singen undt aller spielen," fols. 90v–91 in the facsimile): "*svirel*—eine Pfeiffe"; "*surenka*—ein Schallmey"; "*truba*—ein Trmpet" [*sic*]; "*organy*—ein Orgel"; "*organshik*—ein Organist"; "*rygaly*—ein Real"; "*tsymbaly*—ein Rausimbel"; "*volynka*—ein Sakspfeiffe"; and "*gudok*—ein Geige." The military section is on fols. 82v–83v. There is a discussion of appropriate military music in the *Politika* by the Croatian cleric and scholar Juraj Križanić (Iurii Krizhanich), who was in Russia, under varying circumstances, from 1659 to 1677; his listing is not a record of Muscovite military practice *per se,* however, but a set of recommendations based on a variety of sources, including classical studies and contemporary musical treatises and encyclopedias. See Letiche and Dmytryshyn, *Russian Statecraft,* 65–66, and Vidaković, *Yury Krizanitch's "Asserta Musicalia,"* 52–53.

18. Stone, *A Dictionarie of the Vulgar Russe Tongue,* is an alphabetical listing of the

terms in Bodleian Library, Laud misc. 47a (the word lists, which focus on the vernacular, spoken language as opposed to Church Slavonic, plus a series of specialist lists including birds, plants, and diseases) and Laud misc. 47b (a largely overlapping listing), which date from the end of the sixteenth century. The musical terms appear on the pages of the edition as follows: *skomorokh*" ("a minstrell," p. 373); *domora* ("lute," p. 130); *gusel'* ("an harpe") and *guselnik* ("an harper"; p. 117); *rog*" ("an horne," p. 343); *dudka* ("a pipe," p. 134); *skrip*" ("a fidle," p. 374); *tsimbaldi* ("virginals," p. 437); and *organi* ("organs," p. 264). On p. 117, Ridley defines *gusli* (as opposed to *gusel'*) as "a timbrell." The association is unclear; a timbrel is generally a small, tambourine-like drum.

19. Stone, *A Dictionarie of the Vulgar Russe Tongue,* where *tulombas*" is defined as "a taber for the saddle" on p. 416 and *truba* ("a trumpett") and *trubnik* ("a trumpiter") on p. 415.

20. On northern linguistic influences in Ridley, though, see Stone, *A Dictionarie of the Vulgar Russe Tongue,* 29ff., where the editor suggests that he may have gathered such words en route to Moscow from the north.

21. [Miege], *A Relation of Three Embassies,* 129–30 and 134. Konovalov, "England and Russia: Three Embassies," 71–72, discusses the entry (it was not without its difficulties, which was the case for the entire trip). An earlier English account, by the traveler Peter Mundy, offers the same mixed evaluation of the instrumental music he heard in the Russian north in 1641: "Musick they use like thatt in Turky. Noe greatt art in thatt, Nor painting, allthough the one Make a pretty shew and the other yeild No unpleasantt sounde" ([Mundy], *The Travels of Peter Mundy in Europe and Asia,* 4:151). Križanić recommended setting up a music school in Moscow for military musicians and suggested not only that the Muscovite government recruit such players from abroad (which they were doing), but that they might form an orchestra and give regular public concerts, for "[n]othing would add more to the splendor of the tsar's court than good music played on wind instruments." He also recommended that musicians should learn to play nonmilitary instruments for weddings and at other events; see Letiche and Dmytryshyn, *Russian Statecraft,* 66.

22. This series of references is in Klenk, *Posol'stvo Kunraada fan-Klenka,* 101–104 (Dutch) and 389–91 (Russian). Other travel accounts refer to trumpets and percussion on their entry into Moscow, for example Meierberg, *Puteshestvie v Moskoviiu barona Avgustina Meierberga,* 81, and for the embassy sent by Emperor Leopold in 1675, in [Lyseck], "Posol'stvo Battoni," *Otechestvennye zapiski* 33 (Jan. 1828): 298, and *Relatio,* 35. Later in the century, Sparwenfeld describes their party's entrance into Novgorod as being heralded by a contingent of twenty-four shawm players who "sounded like small geese." He also describes their own trumpeters and drummers as well as the Russian musicians who played for the entrance of the Imperial embassy into Moscow; see [Sparwenfeld], *J. G. Sparwenfeld's Diary,* 82–83, 135–37, and 159–65.

23. [Miege], *A Relation of Three Embassies,* mentions the trumpeters, the six musicians, and the music master on pp. 4 and 142; on the trumpet fanfares or deliberate silences, pp. 111–12 and 116; and pp. 145–48 on the procession for their audience with the tsar.

24. Klenk, *Posol'stvo Kunraada fan-Klenka,* 100 (Dutch) and 387 (Russian).

25. *SGGD* 3:539–40; the same procession is described in the diary written by a member of the Swedish delegation to the tsar in 1655, published in Semenov, "K istorii snoshenii so Shvetsiei," 19; and see also Paul of Aleppo's account in Belfour 2:214–17 and Murkos 4 (1898): 95. On an earlier occasion, however, Paul observed a royal entrance into

the city, mentioning only percussion instruments playing with the military contingent, and specifying that the tsar himself was accompanied by no musical instruments, but "only [by] the chaunters singing hymns" (Paul of Aleppo, in Belfour 1:367–68 and Murkos 3 [1898]: 5).

26. [Lyseck], "Posol'stvo Battoni," *Otechestvennye zapiski* 35 (Sept. 1828): 316, and *Relatio*, 68.

27. The Russian account of the Carlisle mission's procession is in *DR* 3: col. 558, and the "confusion of glory" is in [Miege], *A Relation of Three Embassies*, 147–48. Bernard Tanner, who wrote the account of the Polish mission to Tsar Fedor Alekseevich in 1678, also described the splendor at their reception by the young tsar; their party included three trumpeters and drummers (not listed separately but apparently part of the mission's military contingent). His account of the party's entry into the city and their procession to meet the tsar is similar to Miege's; see Tanner, *Legatio Polono-Lithuanica in Moscoviam,* 17 (the three trumpeters), 44 (their entrance into Moscow), and 52–55 (the procession to the first meeting with the tsar), and "Opisanie puteshestviia pol'skogo posol'stva," 19, 43, and 50–54.

28. Olearius, *The Travels of Olearius,* 287. Findeizen, *History,* 1:393–94, n. 381, refers to Nikita Ivanovich Romanov's musicians, citing *Sobranie pisem tsaria Alekseia Mikhailovicha,* 45; he also mentions the inventory of I. D. Miloslavskii's possessions, which also included organs, citing Viktorov, *Opisanie zapisnykh knig i bumag,* 2:394 and 1:207. Olearius mentions Romanov's love of foreign music in *The Travels of Olearius,* 130 and 263. The references to military instruments in the Golitsyn inventory are in *Rozysknye dela o Fedore Shaklovitom,* 4: cols. 133–38, 167–68, and 316. They also employed at least one trumpeter; see col. 605, where the *trubach'* Ian Stanislavov was given money to replace a lost mouthpiece. The Golitsyn inventory is analyzed in Hellie, *The Economy and Material Culture of Russia,* chap. 24, where he also surveys the 1608 inventory of Mikhail Tatishchev, who owned *tsymbaly* (p. 617; not cymbals but a keyboard instrument) and a large military drum (*tulumbas*).

29. Olearius, *The Travels of Olearius,* 54, and Bogoiavlenskii, "Moskovskii teatr," 62, from 2 November 1675, where two foreign musicians, probably the same pair, are mentioned in a document from 8 November 1675. This document is also published in Findeizen, *History,* 1:395, n. 384.

30. The Menzies mission is described in Charykov, *Posol'stvo v Rim,* 28, and see also chapter 6 below. On Hebdon, see Gurliand, *Ivan Gebdon,* 48.

31. On trumpets, see Protopopov, "Neizvestnoe posobie po teorii muzyki," 294, citing *Perepisnye knigi goroda Moskvy 1665–76 gg.,* col. 174, from April 1671; see also cols. 175–83 and col. 173, where *surna* and *nakra* players are mentioned. The *barabanshchiki* appear, for example, in *RIB* 21:1118 (October 1665), which also refers to widows whose children are among the *barabanshchiki;* cols. 1434–35 (November 1668) describes them as children of soldiers. Records of such instrumentalists date to the early years of Mikhail's reign; see Zabelin, "Dopolneniia k Dvortsovym razriadam," *ChOIDR* 1 (1882): pt. 2:45, 270–71; *ChOIDR* 3 (1882): pt. 1:625; and *ChOIDR* 2 (1883): pt. 1:697, payment records spanning the years 1615 through 1631 and which include both Russian and German players.

32. Vinogradoff, "Russian Missions to London," 55. The Russian musicians appeared again in the ambassador's quarters, although apparently only to eat, not necessarily to perform: "He [Potemkin] desired there might be a little Table placed at the lower end of the Room for the Czars Trumpets, which he said he did use to have eat in the same

Room with him: but that they should have a Dish or two off from his Table" (Vinogradoff, "Russian Missions to London," 56).

33. Ibid., 62.

34. In Sebes, *The Jesuits and the Sino-Russian Treaty of Nerchinsk,* 230–31 and 286–87, where *charamella* is translated variously as flute or fife; it seems, however, to correspond to the *Schalmei/chalemelle/cialamella,* which, in turn, corresponds to the Russian *surna;* see *NG2,* s.v. "Shawm" and "Escobar, André," who is listed as a shawm-player or *charameleiro.* See also Petrovskaia, "Ob izuchenii russkoi muzykal'noi kul'tury," 233–34. Pereira's opinions are valuable because he himself was a skilled musician (Sebes, 135–36).

35. *V-K 1642–1644 gg.,* 35.198–200, and see also P[rilozhenie] 10.219–22. References here are to the document number and page numbers within each document, following the editions. On the *kuranty,* see Waugh, "The Publication of Muscovite *Kuranty*"; Maier, "Newspaper Translations in Seventeenth-Century Muscovy"; and Maier and Pilger, "Second-hand Translation." All three articles include extensive bibliography. Other examples of fanfares and processions are in *V-K 1642–1644 gg.,* 6.65ff.; *V-K 1645–1646, 1648 gg.,* 61.148 and 62.134; *V-K 1648–1650 gg.,* 3.207–209, 4.191–92, 5.9, 27.47, and many others.

36. Translation from Smith and Christian, *Bread and Salt,* 156–58, with the original names of the instruments replacing the suggested translations; the original document is in *AAE* 4, No. 63 (p. 97), also referred to above, n. 6. The revelry included singing, of course; Smith and Christian, 140–41, cite a source from the town of Sol' Vychegodsk, where there was a cathedral church with cellars used to store the alcohol from the two taverns next door. "If anyone buys spirits under the church . . ." states a directive, "they are to drink those spirits on the spot. When they sing matins or vespers in the church, the revellers sing songs and engage in every sort of disrespect." One might note that bearbaiting was extremely popular at the Muscovite court throughout the seventeenth century, especially around the time of *maslenitsa* (Carnival).

37. Smith and Christian, *Bread and Salt,* 138–39, quoting Rozhdestvenskii, "K istorii bor'by s tserkovnymi bezporiadkami," 26–27.

38. Quoted in Findeizen, *History,* 1:124 and 348, n. 213, citing *AAE* 4, No. 98 (col. 138).

39. Olearius, *The Travels of Olearius,* 48, and *Vermehrte Newe Beschreibung,* 19.

40. Zabelin, "Dopolneniia k Dvortsovym razriadam," *ChOIDR* 3 (1882): pt. 1:440, from 10 Feb. 1626, with additional payments to Meletii Tsynbal'nik (col. 443) and to Patrekeik Luk'ianov (cols. 445–46) for playing *tsynbaly* and organ; the document is summarized in Zabelin, *Domashnii byt russkikh tsarei,* pt. 2:283. On the terminology relating to *tsynbaly,* see note 51 below. In the seventeenth century, the term *vargany,* used in the plural, generally referred to an organ; see Roizman, *Organ,* 45, and Aumayr, *Historische Untersuchungen an Bezeichnungen von Musikinstrumenten,* 106–109. In an earlier period, *vargan* indicated a military instrument (Roizman, 39ff.), and Aumayr, 69, and Findeizen, *History,* 1:180, note that the term was also sometimes used to indicate a Jew's-harp.

41. Niemojewski mentions Riati at a large celebration on the day after the wedding and at the elaborate festivities on 15 May; see Niemojewski, *Pamiętnik Stanisława Niemojewskiego,* 56–57 (and note) and 66, and "Zapiski Stanislava Nemoevskogo," 64–65 (and note) and 73. In the listing of those who died in the Moscow uprising, Ustrialov, *Dnevnik poslov pol'skikh,* 189, lists a jester (*shut* in the Russian text), Baltser Zidek.

42. It is a difficult question (and one that takes us far beyond the bounds of this study): were all *domra* players or instrument makers considered to be *skomorokhi,* or did

they use musical skills traditionally associated with *skomorokhi* in order to settle into recognized and profitable occupations in urban areas? Are these two activities necessarily distinct and separate? Petukhov, "Svedeniia o skomorokhakh," 411–12, labels as *skomorokhi* the keyboard players associated with court and listed in the Moscow census of 1638, along with all others associated in any fashion with instrumental practice. See also Zguta, *Russian Minstrels,* esp. 32ff. and throughout chap. 3. In some cases, such musicians are clearly not *skomorokhi,* for example the sovereign's *nakra* players; *nakry* were military drums (see Zguta, 56 and n. 54, and Petukhov, 418, referring to *Perepisnaia kniga goroda Moskvy 1638 goda,* col. 218). Findeizen, *History,* 1:117 and 122–23, mentions domestic *skomorokhi* associated with important landowners in the first half of the seventeenth century; throughout the chapter, he also mentions settled *skomorokhi* from roughly the period 1550–1650 who owned shops and paid taxes or ploughed land and harvested crops. On the changing labels for the *skomorokhi,* see the discussion in Belkin, *Russkie skomorokhi,* esp. 105–108. One might note, however, that in the 1638 census, there is no one called *skomorokh,* as there were in earlier documents cited in Findeizen, although the term *veselyi* (used to describe instrumentalists at Tsar Mikhail's wedding celebrations) does appear (*Perepisnaia kniga goroda Moskvy 1638 goda,* cols. 86 and 131, noted in Koshelev, "V tserkvi—obraza," 89, and in Petukhov, 416–17; there are many lacunae in the published records of the 1638 Moscow census so it is entirely possible that the *skomorokh* label is simply lacking in this source).

43. Berry, *The English Works of Giles Fletcher,* 297. The same sort of entertainment may be hinted at in Jerome Horsey's account of Tsar Fedor's coronation, in 1584. Horsey describes a slow and dignified public ceremony, with many processions accompanied by liturgical singing, but he does mention private entertainment, remarking that the "solemnitie and triumph lasted a whole weeke, wherein many royall pastimes were shewed and used" (Bond, "The Travels of Sir Jerome Horsey," 274).

44. Zabelin, "Dopolneniia k Dvortsovym razriadam," *ChOIDR* 1 (1882): pt. 2:103, lists a *domra* player in April 1617, and see also *Perepisnaia kniga goroda Moskvy 1638 goda,* col. 244 (the *gusel'nik* Liubimka Ivanov) and 78 and 83 (references to *domershchiki*). Liubim Ivanov apparently worked at court, for in July 1629 he was given an entire suit of clothing; see Zabelin, *Domashnii byt russkikh tsarei,* pt. 2:282–83 (where Zabelin wonders whether or not the *gusel'niki* lived at court or only worked there at certain times).

45. Zabelin, *Domashnii byt russkikh tsarei,* pt. 2:281–83, and see the series of payment records in the accompanying *Materialy* to vol. 1, pt. 2:662f. A general discussion of the tradition of the blind musician in the Slavic context is in Kononenko, *Ukrainian Minstrels.*

46. In 1688, for example, Peter requisitioned several groups of drummers and fifers from Gen. Patrick Gordon's regiments; see Gordon, *Passages from the Diary of General Patrick Gordon,* 165. English-language studies of Peter the Great's play regiments include Hughes, *Russia in the Age of Peter the Great,* 16ff., and Massie, *Peter the Great,* 68ff.

47. On the military instruments among the toys of earlier tsarevichi, see Zabelin, *Domashnii byt russkikh tsarei,* pt. 2:90ff., and on Tsarevich Aleksei's *nakra* players and singers, see Zvereva, "Gosudarevy pevchie d'iaki posle 'Smuty,'" 362.

48. Aleksei Mikhailovich's *domry* and *rylia,* purchased in 1634, and his *gudok,* from 1642, are listed in Zabelin, *Domashnii byt russkikh tsarei,* pt. 2:89; a listing of his toys, including the *barabany* and *nakry,* is on pp. 81–82 and 101–108. The listing of the tsarevnas' toys, from which all references above were drawn, is on pp. 121–37, and Zabelin compares the instruments given to the royal children on p. 98. On pp. 77–80, Zabelin notes that in

addition to the toys manufactured by the royal workshops, the tsaritsas often purchased simple toys for the children as they were traveling on a pilgrimage or visit. For example, Mikhail's wife, Tsaritsa Evdokiia, purchased toys, including bells, on a journey in 1632; see Zabelin, "Dopolneniia k Dvortsovym razriadam," *ChOIDR* 2 (1883): pt. 1:725–26.

49. Material in the following paragraphs is taken from Roizman, *Organ,* esp. 45–92, the standard source on keyboard instruments in Muscovite practice; see also Zabelin, *Domashnii byt russkikh tsarei,* pt. 2:283–86, on keyboards in the Poteshnaia palata (Entertainment Hall). An English-language survey of organs and organists in seventeenth-century Russia is in Velimirović, "The First Organ Builder in Russia."

50. Although the present work focuses on organs at the Muscovite court in the seventeenth century, there is evidence that such instruments were used at court considerably earlier. There was an organist in the suite of Ivan III's bride, Sophia Paleologue, the Italian-raised niece of the last Byzantine emperor who married the tsar in 1472; see Roizman, *Organ,* 28–30. Even earlier, there is a depiction of an organ (along with other instrumentalists) in the frescoes at St. Sophia in Kiev, from the mid-eleventh century, which reproduces familiar elements from Byzantine practice; see the updated and corrected discussion and bibliography in Findeizen, *History,* 1:310–11, and also Roizman, 22–23, and the illustration following p. 48. An example of organs in Muscovy early in the seventeenth century comes from the diplomatic account written by Georg Tectander describing his trip, via Muscovy, to the Persian shah Abbas I. The party lingered in Moscow in late 1602 in order to hire an organist who had his own organ (a *Regal*), who was to accompany them on the rest of the trip. Although the organist died, they delivered the instrument because the shah "was inordinately fond of the organ, although he played it very poorly." The account is translated into Russian in [Kakash and Tektander], "Puteshestvie v Persiiu," 17.

51. Roizman, *Organ,* 53–55, focuses on the materials used for the strings and for repair of the instruments. Although *tsynbaly* (sometimes *tsinbaly* or *tsymbali*) could refer to a dulcimer-like instrument, in seventeenth-century court practice it generally indicated a harpsichord-like keyboard instrument, as it does in Sauvage (where "samballenicq" [*tsymbal'nik*] is defined as "Ung Joueur d'espinette" [*épinette*], in Larin, *Tri inostrannykh istochnika,* 102), and in Ridley (where "tsimbaldi" is defined as "virginals," in Stone, *A Dictionarie of the Vulgar Russe Tongue,* 437).

52. *Perepisnaia kniga goroda Moskvy 1638 goda,* col. 14. Tomila Mikhailov (Besov) is listed in Zabelin, "Dopolneniia k Dvortsovym razriadam," *ChOIDR* 1 (1882): pt. 2:8 and 22 (1613 and 1614), and Meletii Tsynbal'nik is listed in connection with Mikhail's wedding in n. 40 above

53. Information on the Luhn brothers, in Roizman, *Organ,* 61–63, is from *RIB* 8: cols. 284–89. Luk'ianka Timofeev is listed as a *poteshnik* in *Perepisnaia kniga goroda Moskvy 1638 goda,* col. 244, and see also Roizman, *Organ,* 63 and note. The organs were at the Granovitaia palata (Faceted Palace) in the Kremlin and remained there throughout the century (Roizman, *Organ,* 58). Moleva, "Muzyka i zrelishcha," 150, includes excerpts from a reference suggesting that at a banquet at the Granovitaia palata, some of the guests were seated "where the organ is" ("gde argany stoiat"); this does not necessarily imply that organs sounded at the banquet, and indeed no other source suggests that this was the case. Moleva's reference is inaccurately identified and undated. See also n. 8 above.

54. Roizman, *Organ,* 67, and on pp. 10–11 he cites examples of the term *organ* used to indicate human voices; see also the definitions in Findeizen, *History,* 1:149 and 154. The diplomatic report is partially summarized, partially quoted in Solov'ev, *Istoriia Rossii s*

drevneishikh vremen, 6: books 11–12:543; on p. 605, the editors identify Solov'ev's source as RGADA, f. 77, Snosheniia Rossii s Persiei, 1653, d. 3–5, which is unpublished. (In Soloviev, *Tsar Alexis*, this embassy is discussed on pp. 75–79.)

55. Roizman, "Iz istorii organnoi kul'tury v Rossii," 596–97, assesses the meaning of the term *stramenty*, which appeared widely among the royal children's toys. He discusses Gutovskii's involvement in the repair of the various keyboard instruments in *Organ*, as noted above, and see also the references in Zabelin, *Domashnii byt russkikh tsarei*, pt. 2:90. On the musical toys belonging to the royal children, see Zabelin, pt. 2:119–21, 126, and 133, and see above, nn. 47 and 48. Roizman, *Organ*, 64–65, also discusses organs at the court in Astrakhan (on the way to Isfahan), citing Olearius.

56. Roizman, *Organ*, 69–79, focuses on Gutovskii, who was also the first to attempt music printing in Russia. See also Roizman, "Iz istorii," 569ff. A contemporary description of Gutovskii's Persian organ, in Roizman, *Organ*, 73–74, is translated in Velimirović, "The First Organ Builder in Russia," 222. Discussion and facsimiles of Gutovskii's printed music are in Vol'man, *Russkie pechatnye noty*, 15–17, and in his "O nachale notopechataniia v Rossii," 79–80.

57. The Golitsyn instruments are inventoried in *Rozysknye dela o Fedore Shaklovitom*, 4: cols. 5, 12, 18 (the two "fleity nemetskiia"), 20, 40, 105–106, and 137 (see also Roizman, *Organ*, 85). There is an annotation in the Golitsyn inventory (see for example *Rozysknye dela*, across cols. 21–22 and 139–40) stating that "Mikita the painter evaluated the organs" ("Mikita Maliar argany tsenili"), suggesting that the instruments' appearance accounted for much of their value. Hellie, *The Economy and Material Culture of Russia*, 616, summarizes the Golitsyn musical instruments (although the *tsynbaly* were not cymbals).

58. The *tsynbal* (here in the singular) and the organ ("argany nemetskie") are listed in Barsov, "Rospis' vsiakim veshcham," pt. 1:60 (repeated on p. 115), with another *tsynbaly* listed on p. 42 (repeated on p. 107); he also owned *surny* (p. 106) and a *tulumbas* (p. 61). See also Roizman, *Organ*, 67–68, where Vorotynskii's later gift to the tsar is mentioned.

59. Zabelin, *Domashnii byt russkikh tsarei*, pt. 2:302–305, lists the names of the male and female dwarves and others associated with the tsar, the tsaritsa, and various other royal women.

60. Findeizen, *History*, 1:356, n. 251 (9 January 1725; see also Hughes, *Russia in the Age of Peter the Great*, 260). Findeizen's reference is also mentioned in Gorelov, "Kem byl avtor sbornika 'Drevnie rossiiskie stikhotvoreniia,'" 306. On female theatrical performers in the early eighteenth century, see for example the documentary evidence in Starikova, "Russkii teatr petrovskogo vremeni." Upper-class Russian women performed on the keyboard at a slightly later time, and a woman, Gertrude Koening, was hired as a court harpsichordist in 1738; see Karpiak, "Culture of the Keyboard." See also the discussion below on the Moscow diaries written around 1700 by the Italian singer Filippo Balatri.

61. Istomin's *Alphabet* is published in facsimile in Istomin, *Bukvar' sostavlen Karionom Istominym*. There is a biographical summary, with substantial bibliography, in *SKK XVII v.*, pt. 2:140–52 and pt. 4:729–31, and Sazonova, *Literaturnaia kul'tura Rossii*, 73ff., emphasizes his ties to court culture; in English, see Okenfuss, *The Discovery of Childhood in Russia*, esp. 22–35.

62. Findeizen, *History*, 1:155–57 and 185, discusses the Istomin illustrations, suggesting that the musicians were Ukrainian, judging not only by the instruments they hold but also by their costumes. Findeizen believes that the wind player is performing on a straight

wooden trumpet; Roizman, *Organ*, 66, note, apparently defines this instrument as some kind of flute or pipe (*tsevnitsa, fleita*).

63. See n. 40 above. Armanka is described as a *nemchin*, which literally means a German but was used more generally to indicate a foreigner.

64. Roizman, *Organ*, 63–64, discusses Zaval'skii and his oath; the document giving M. Luhn permission to leave Russia is in *RIB* 8: cols. 285–86. Polish organist Iushka Proskura (or Proskurovskii) worked at court beginning in September 1625, that is, before the February 1626 wedding. He performed at the wedding and was rewarded for his services (Roizman, 58); there are no published references to his being Orthodox, newly baptized or otherwise. Judging from a description of Iushka's clothing, Zabelin, *Domashnii byt russkikh tsarei*, pt. 2:287, suggests that he might have been one of a number of visiting entertainers whose skills included not only music but acrobatics and other such tricks.

65. This quality of "Russianness" was consciously cultivated by means of musical instruments (and of course by many other means) at court in the late eighteenth century, with the official *bandura* and *gusli* players; see Findeizen, *History*, 2: esp. 241ff., on Vasilii Trutovskii, the last of the court *gusli* players. Trutovskii was also responsible for compiling the first printed collection of Russian folk songs with their tunes; in English, see Brown and Mazo, *A Collection of Russian Folk Songs*, 16–19; Brown, "Native Song and National Consciousness"; and Taruskin, *Defining Russia Musically*, chap. 1.

66. See Kotoshikhin, *O Rossii v tsarstvovanie Alekseia Mikhailovicha*, 21, in the context of a royal wedding. He also says that there is no music (i.e., instrumental music) at such royal wedding festivities, which was true for Aleksei's first marriage. Kotoshikhin wrote his work abroad in the late 1660s, before the celebration, with instruments, of Aleksei's second wedding. Reitenfel's, *Skazaniia o Moskovii*, 343, mentions bagpipes and dancing in the context of a peasant wedding, and Adam Schleussinger notes dancing in another general description of Russian weddings, only to criticize the awkwardness of the Russian style (Lapteva, "Rasskaz ochevidtsa o zhizni Moskovii," 116). Olearius, *The Travels of Olearius*, 168, mentions the wild celebrations at a boyar's wedding, describing how the two days following the church ceremony were "spent in great and extravagant eating, drinking, dancing, and every manner of amusement they can think of. They also have all sorts of music." He includes an illustration of some of the events comprising the church portion of a boyar's wedding, in which he shows several people involved in a round dance, and he notes that at the church, the priest "leads [the couple] around in a circle, while singing the 128th Psalm. They sing the verses after him and dance" (p. 167 and *Vermehrte Newe Beschreibung*, 213). Dancing in the church itself is scarcely possible, and one wonders if Olearius confuses the religious procession with dance movements. There is a reference to dancing in terms of rope dancing or tightrope walking ("po konatam khodit' i tantsovat'") as entertainment at court; see Zabelin, *Domashnii byt russkikh tsarei*, pt. 2:102, 105, and 107, referring to the entertainer (*poteshnik*) Ivan Semenov Lodygin.

67. Sajkowski and Czapliński, *Pamiętniki Samuela i Bogusława Kazimierza Maskiewiczów*, 141–42, translated in Ustrialov, *Zapiski Maskevicha*, 60–62 (in which the translator does employ the term *skomorokh*).

68. Judging from the detailed diary kept by Friedrich von Bergholz in the early 1720s, the Russian aristocracy had by then become accustomed to such dancing, particularly in connection with wedding celebrations. See the specialized study of dancing as

described in Bergholz's work in Sander, *Social Dancing*. It was not an easy road, however, as revealed in the remarks, discussed below, by Princess Dar'ia Golitsyna in the early stages of Peter's social reforms, ca. 1700, showing how reluctant Muscovite women were to conform to the new social requirements.

69. Olearius, *The Travels of Olearius*, 263 (where *positiv* is translated as "harmonium"), and *Vermehrte Newe Beschreibung*, 302.

70. Roizman, *Organ*, 79–82, and in his "Iz istorii," 578–80.

71. Bogoiavlenskii, "Moskovskaia Nemetskaia sloboda," 231 (from 1671); also cited in *IRM* 1:194, and see Roizman, *Organ*, 81.

72. Rode, *Opisanie vtorogo posol'stva v Rossiiu datskogo poslannika Gansa Ol'delanda*, 21; Olearius, *The Travels of Olearius*, 59.

73. Tanner, *Legatio Polono-Lithuanica in Moscoviam*, 32–33, and in "Opisanie puteshestviia pol'skogo posol'stva," 33. Many thanks to Robert Fradkin for his advice on the Latin text.

74. [Miege], *A Relation of Three Embassies*, 99–100; see also Olearius, *The Travels of Olearius*, 51–52.

75. Klenk, *Posol'stvo Kunraada fan-Klenka*, 129–30 (Dutch) and 422 (Russian). The instruments are listed in the Dutch version as "om daar op de staafjes, en ook op de viool en orgel te spelen." The phrase "op de staafjes," in the Russian version translated as "na palochkakh," is somewhat unclear; a document in Zabelin, *Domashnii byt russkikh tsarei*, pt. 2:102, suggests that it indicates drumsticks. Thanks to Robert Fradkin and Goedele Gulikers for their advice on the Dutch text.

76. Paul of Aleppo, in Belfour 1:185–86, Murkos 4 (1897): 22–23, and Radu, 26:637–39. The passage Radu translates as "avec accompagnement d'orgue" reads in the original "bi-l-'urġhun" ("with the organ"). For his advice on the Arabic original of Radu's translation, I am indebted to Robert Fradkin.

77. Ibid., in Belfour 1:191; Murkos 4 (1897): 27; and Radu, 26:646. In Murkos, 24, the town is called Makuka or Man'kovka; this is another southern town, near Uman'.

78. Ibid., Belfour 1:191, Murkos 4 (1897): 27, and Radu, 26:646.

79. BJ 10002 (*olim* 127/56) is published as Gołos and Stęszewski, *Muzyczne Silva Rerum*. Transcriptions of the Cyrillic texts ("Velichit dusha moia gospoda," "Teb[e] bozhe," "[Poi]dete [sic] poklonimsia," and others) and some of the Kievan notation are on pp. 1–3 and 86–89, with facsimiles (following p. xliii) of fols. 1v–2 and 59v–60. There is an English summary of the introductory notes on pp. xxxix–xliii, and see also Gołos, "A New Source of Old-Polish Secular Music," and the same author's brief survey, "Manuscript Sources of Eastern Chant," 76, where he notes the use of instruments in some Uniate practice.

80. "Jesu [Jezu] Christe, Panie mily" is No. 102 in BJ 10002; there are clear melodic similarities, particularly at the opening, with the versions in GIM 1938, published in Dolskaya, *Spiritual Songs in Seventeenth-Century Russia*, nos. 85 and 139; see also the textual concordances listed in Rothe, *Verse und Lieder bei den Ostslaven*, No. 831. "Dayci Boze dobranoc" is No. 47 in BJ 10002, and it appears, with some similarities in melodic outline, as a melody in the *Grammatika* source L'viv, Natsional'nyi muzei, No. 87/510804 (discussed in chapter 5 below, and see also the appendix).

81. Gołos and Stęszewski, *Muzyczne Silva Rerum*, xii–xv (English summary on p. xxxix), discuss the manuscript's probable origins in Polotsk and suggest an explanation for the performance notes in Polish. The performance instructions are transcribed and translated on p. 130 of the edition; the annotations to the pieces are on fol. 60r. On

Orthodox participation in the Catholic Corpus Christi procession, see Kotliarchuk, *Prazdnichnaia kul'tura,* 89–90. Krajcar, "Religious Conditions in Smolensk," also points to a generally fluid exchange among the Catholic, Uniate, and Orthodox communities in that city.

82. The musical sources from the Supraśl monastery are discussed in Konotop, "Suprasl'skii irmologion"; his "Suprasl'skii irmologii 1638–39 gg." (where on p. 239 he dates the four-part *partesnyi* pieces no later than 1644); and his "Struktura Suprasl'skogo irmologiona." See also Pichura, "The Podobny Texts and Chants of the Supraśl Irmologion." On the printed *tropar',* see Labyntsev, "Neizvestnyi pamiatnik notnoi pechati"; this postdates Gutovskii's experimental music printing in Moscow.

83. Konotop, "Suprasl'skii Irmologii 1638–39 gg.," 234–35, discusses the inventories, citing *Arkheograficheskii sbornik dokumentov,* 9:205 (the 1645–54 inventory) and 9:243 (the 1668 inventory). See also Rogov, "Suprasl' kak odin iz tsentrov," 328–29 and 334.

84. In addition to the general studies cited above and in previous chapters, see, for example, Trilupaitene, "Muzykal'nye rukopisi XVI v. vil'niusskogo bernardinskogo monastyria." Gołos, "Manuscript Sources of Eastern Chant," 78–80, includes a preliminary list of sources reflecting Orthodox and/or Uniate practice currently in Polish collections. See also Isaievych, *Voluntary Brotherhood,* passim.

85. See, for example, Findeizen, *History,* 1:248, and Roizman, *Organ,* 76. Keldysh, in *IRM* 1:195, points to the decade of the 1660s as a kind of tipping point, when what he terms the *skomorokh* influences seem to have dissipated and were supplanted at court by other, more Westernized kinds of instrumental music for entertainment. Perhaps this might be characterized as Tsar Aleksei's personal tipping point as well.

86. Quoted in Findeizen, *History,* 1:248 (he gives his source only as *DR;* the passage does not appear in the published description of Aleksei's wedding in *DR* 3:871–79, so Findeizen may have been quoting from an unpublished manuscript collection). Findeizen's reference is quoted elsewhere, for example in Roizman, *Organ,* 76.

87. This passage is singled out and translated in Morosan, "*Penie* and *Musikiia,*" 176, quoting the modern Russian translation in Rogov, *Muzykal'naia estetika Rossii,* 130. The original is excerpted in Rogov, 113, from RGB 146, p. 28 (see chap. 5, n. 3, on this source). Samuel Collins made note of the "prodigal and indecent" drinking songs himself, noting that after the wedding (he is not describing royal weddings), the bride and groom are led home and are seated at the table, at which point "a Quire of Boys and Girls standing aloft, sing Epithalamiums, or nuptial Songs, so bedawb'd with scum of bawdry and obscenity, that it would make Aretines ears glow to hear them" (*The Present State of Russia,* 7); Maskiewicz, too, emphasizes the dirty songs (see n. 67 above). Korenev also referred to the use of organs in Polish churches in Ukraine (see RGB 146, p. 32, and Rogov, 114 and 131), and as we shall see in chapter 5, theorist Nikolai Diletskii frequently relies on the organ as a teaching device in his treatise.

88. Reutenfels, *De rebus Moschoviticis,* 105, and Reitenfel's, *Skazaniia,* 301.

89. Filippo Balatri (d. 1756) wrote three accounts based on his time in Russia. The first was a journal his Florentine employer, Duke Cosimo, had ordered him to keep; it is now lost. The second is the *Vita e Viaggi di F. B., nativo di Pisa,* a prose narrative that survives in nine manuscript volumes, written between 1725–32, in RGB, f. 218, No. 1247. The third is a shorter version reworked in verse in 1735, *Frutti del Mondo,* published in an edition by Karl Vossler in 1924. The present discussion is based on excerpts and information on the *Vita e Viaggi* in Gerasimova, "Vospominaniia Filippo Balatri"; Schlafly,

"Filippo Balatri in Peter the Great's Russia"; the same author's "A Muscovite *Boiarynia*"; and Di Salvo, "Kastrat Petra Velikogo." On the other Russians in Golitsyn's party and Peter's desire for musicians, see Gerasimova, 170 and 174, and Schlafly, "A Muscovite *Boiarynia*," 249 and n. 3. Schlafly, "Filippo Balatri in Peter the Great's Russia," 182, gives a brief biography of the singer (after his stay in Russia, he met Handel in England; met Louis XIV; sang with Faustina Bordoni; and retired as a priest in a Cistercian monastery near Munich).

90. On the Golitsyn family's support of Balatri's religious faith, see Schlafly, "A Muscovite *Boiarynia*," 258–59, and his "Filippo Balatri in Peter the Great's Russia," 185, 192, and passim. The "Orpheus of Moscow" is quoted in Schlafly, "A Muscovite *Boiarynia*," 251. Di Salvo, "Kastrat Petra Velikogo," 437, emphasizes that Muscovites may not have understood his sexual status as a castrato because the tradition was completely foreign to them.

91. The embassy, headed by Golitsyn's brother, is discussed in Gerasimova, "Vospominaniia Filippo Balatri," 184–85, and Schlafly, "Filippo Balatri in Peter the Great's Russia," 184 (on p. 182, Schlafly notes that when Balatri met Louis XIV, the king admired a robe Khan Aiuk had given him on that trip).

92. On music at Anna Mons's house, see Schlafly, "Filippo Balatri in Peter the Great's Russia," 188–89 (where he calls the instrument a harpsichord; no Italian is given for this passage), and Gerasimova, "Vospominaniia Filippo Balatri," 185. Balatri fancied himself in love with Anna and spent a great deal of time with her. The infatuation was not serious, but Princess Golitsyna (and his Catholic confessor) told him that such feelings were immoral (the Catholic Church did not allow castrati to marry); see Schlafly, "A Muscovite *Boiarynia*," esp. 260. Hughes, *Russia in the Age of Peter the Great,* treats the Mons affair briefly on pp. 393–94, and see also Massie, *Peter the Great,* 116–17, 234, 262, and 373. The text to Balatri's song, which he transliterated as "A sarocca, biela bocca" (The white-sided magpie), is in Schlafly, "Filippo Balatri in Peter the Great's Russia," 184, n. 21. Sheptaev, "Russkoe skomoroshestvo v XVII v.," 61–63, traces other variants of this song text ("A soroki-beloboki") in eighteenth-century collections, linking it to the late *skomorokh* tradition.

93. Balatri's memoirs also give a sense of the disruptions Peter's measures caused to traditional women and their families; see Schlafly, "A Muscovite *Boiarynia*," esp. 261–62.

94. Schlafly, "A Muscovite *Boiarynia*," 264–65.

5. Nikolai Diletskii

1. Baranova, "Muzykal'naia estetika," deals elegantly with this transitional period. Many thanks are due to Evgenii Vorob'ev for his generous and careful suggestions throughout this chapter, based on his forthcoming "Gvidova sol'mizatsiia v Moskovskom tsarstve."

2. The most important source on Diletskii's life and works is Protopopov's edition (listed in the bibliography under Diletskii, *Idea grammatiki musikiiskoi*), which includes a facsimile of one of the *Grammatika* sources (RGB, f. 173, No. 107, abbreviated here as RGB 107) and the editor's extensive commentary (referred to here as PRMI 7); see also Protopopov, *Russkaia mysl' o muzyke,* 58–65, and the bibliography in *SKK XVII v.,* pt. 1:257–58 and pt. 4:687–88. The most comprehensive published source for Diletskii's compositions is Dylets'kyi, *Khorovi tvory;* other accessible published examples of Dilets-

kii's works are in Morosan, *One Thousand Years of Russian Church Music*, 191–97, as well as short excerpts in *IRM* 1 (and see also n. 22 below).

3. The language of Diletskii's translations is Early Modern East Slavic, which would have been widely understood in all the Slavic-speaking areas in which Diletskii lived (my thanks to James Augerot and Evgenii Vorob'ev for their advice on the descriptions of Diletskii's translations). Korenev calls Diletskii a "zhitel' grada Kieva" in the source published in OLDP Izdaniia 128, p. 53 (this is Stepan Smolenskii's edition of RGB, f. 205, No. 146, henceforth referred to as RGB 146, with references to the page numbers in Smolenskii's edition). This is the only source to give Diletskii's patronymic as Pavlov (p. 1; facsimile on p. 175). It was in Moscow that Korenev and Diletskii might have met, fairly soon after Diletskii's arrival there sometime after 1677/1678. As Evgenii Vorob'ev points out, this link to Kiev does not necessarily establish Diletskii's origins; Avvakum, for example, in his autobiography said that Simeon Polotskii described himself as being from Kiev, although his origins were in Belarus (*SKK XVII v.*, pt. 3:365). Although this statement may represent Avvakum's desire to link Simeon to the dangerous latinizing heresies of Kiev and Ukraine, it does illustrate the care with which such labels must be approached.

4. "[V] domu diakona Anikiia Trofimova syna Koreneva izhe ispisa siia" ("at the home of *d'iak* Anikii Trofimov Korenev, who wrote this out") in GIM, sobr. Barsova, No. 1340, fol. 59v. Protopopov, PRMI 7:611, n. 1, speculates that Korenev and Diletskii might have collaborated on the production of a cross made of intersecting staves on which music and text are entered and which appears at the beginning of some *Grammatika* sources.

5. The manuscript is L'viv, Natsional'nyi muzei, No. 87/510804 (see chap. 4, n. 80, above), available in Dylets'kyi, *Hramatyka muzykal'na*, a color facsimile and transcription edited by O. S. Tsalai-Iakymenko. This manuscript is henceforth referred to as L'viv, citing the pagination given in the facsimile in roman numerals, which corresponds to the transcription made by the editor; the signature is on p. LXX. The editor's transcription emphasizes (even enhances) the Ukrainian linguistic elements, as J. Dingley's review points out; the language might be characterized as Early Modern East Slavic (like the other sources), but with some Ukrainian traits. On the proposed revisions to Diletskii's biography, see, most recently, Tsalai-Iakymenko, *Kyivs'ka shkola muzyky*, chaps. 12 and 13 (esp. pp. 346–50, a series of facsimiles illustrating the *manu propria* abbreviation in Eastern and Western Europe). These long-standing debates are summarized briefly in one of the few English-language reviews of the edition, by Stephen Reynolds.

6. Kharlampovich, *Malorossiiskoe vliianie*, 1:327–28 and 821ff., discusses Ukrainian singers in the central choirs from the 1690s–1720s. Protopopov, in PRMI 7:476–78, lists errors in the L'viv source; in most cases, the reading given as the correct version agrees with the readings in the Smolensk, 1677 sources RGADA, f. 181, No. 541 and Tver', f. 103, No. 553 (from the mid-eighteenth century). RGADA 541 was copied by Moisei Arsen'ev; according to an inscription entered by his son, Arsen'ev wrote the manuscript while still in school. In a later autobiographical sketch, Arsen'ev noted his studies with the Likhud brothers at their Moscow academy and later privately in the mid-1690s. See Turilova, "Memuary russkogo raznochintsa." Many thanks to Evgenii Vorob'ev for bringing this reference to my attention.

7. "Toga złota w nowey świata metamorphosi, szlachetnemu magistratowi Wileńskiemu na nowy rok przez Mikołaia Dileckiego, akademika Wileńskiego ogłoszona w

Wilnie. Typis Franciscanis anno 1675. w 4ce, kart 7 nlb. Krasińs.," cited in Estreicher, *Bibliografia polska*, 15:207. Estreicher listed the Krasiński Library as the single location for this print. Much of this collection was destroyed during World War II and no other sources have come to light.

8. A general context for panegyrics in Belarusian cities is in Kotliarchuk, *Prazdnichnaia kul'tura*, esp. 66–67. On *Toga złota*, see Goshovskii and Durnev, "K sporu," 144; Protopopov, "Nikolai Diletskii i ego russkie sovremenniki," 84; and his PRMI 7:520. Goshovskii and Durnev also raise the question of the "noble Vilnius magistrate." As David Frick points out, the magistrate was a collective office (he suggests "magistracy" as an appropriate translation), so Diletskii's appeal is not necessarily to a single person. (My thanks for his advice on this terminology; see also the definitions in *Słownik polszczyzny XVI wieku*, and thanks to Evgenii Vorob'ev for raising this issue.) Goshovskii and Durnev note that the city magistrates were generally Catholic or Uniate, and they suggest that Diletskii was close to this circle, perhaps even embracing Catholicism himself. There is ample precedent for temporary conversions, especially to the Uniate Church, by Orthodox scholars working in Catholic territory or at Catholic universities, for example see Shreer-Tkachenko, Maiburovaia, and Bulat, "Za nauchnuiu ob"ektivnost'," 141. Ronald Vroon, *DLB* 150:293, s.v. "Simeon Polotsky," comes to a similar conclusion regarding Simeon's references to himself as a Uniate (Basilian); it is not clear why or how sincerely Simeon converted, says Vroon, but the action does "testify to his profound personal contact with the intellectual and spiritual world of Roman Catholicism," a context one might keep in mind for Diletskii as well.

9. Goshovskii and Durnev, "K sporu," 144–45. *Akademik* is defined as both "student" and "teacher" in, for example, *Słownik polszczyzny XVI wieku*. The Polish terms *baklarz, magister,* and *doktor* designated specific degrees. Isaievych, *Voluntary Brotherhood,* 165, notes that teachers at some eighteenth-century confraternity schools were known as *bakaliary.*

10. See Kotliarchuk, *Prazdnichnaia kul'tura,* esp. chap. 3; Isaievych, *Voluntary Brotherhood,* esp. 180–83; and Petrov, "Kievskaia Akademiia vo vtoroi polovine XVII veka," *TKDA* no. 10 (1895), esp. 232ff.

11. On Lauxmin's career and the musical life at the Vilnius College, see Trilupaitiene, "Zygmunt Lauksmin w życiu muzycznym Akademii Wileńskiej." Lauxmin's theoretical work is published as Lauxmin [Liauksminas], *Ars et praxis musica.* There were three editions, issued in 1667, 1669, and 1693; see Przywecka-Samecka, *Dzieje drukarstwa muzycznego w Polsce,* 299 (citing Estreicher, *Bibliografia polska,* 21:130), and Trilupaitiene, 102. Protopopov, PRMI 7:584, cites only the 1693 edition, as an example of a work postdating the *Grammatika.*

12. Abramowicz, *Cztery wieki drukarstwa w Wilnie,* 79, describes the Franciscan press as being in operation for a century, but Gidžiūnas, in *Encyclopedia Lituanica,* s.v. "Franciscans," states that it operated only until 1711. On the exchange of students, see Rabikauskas, *Encyclopedia Lituanica,* s.v. "Academy of Vilnius," and Kubilius, *A Short History of Vilnius University,* 21.

13. RGB 107, p. 9 (references are to the later pagination visible in the upper right corner on each page in the published facsimile; Protopopov's transcription and his modern Russian translation are keyed to this pagination). The word *iskusnykh* (skillful) was entered later, squeezed in place using small letters. Goshovskii and Durnev, "K sporu," 144, n. 3, suggest that the change from "akademik Wileński" (in *Toga złota*) to "nauk svobodnykh uchashchesia" (in RGB 107) signaled a small biographical drama:

Diletskii, having failed to receive the anticipated support from the dedication of *Toga złota* and unable to find work in Vilnius, moved to Muscovy, where he no longer described himself as an *akademik* but noted merely that he had studied the liberal arts. Protopopov, PRMI 7:547, combines the two phrases to draw conclusions about the chronology of the *Grammatika*. Assuming that Diletskii studied at the Jesuit College, he suggests that the version of the *Grammatika* in which this phrase appears must be based on a source written before 1675, because in that year in *Toga złota* the author referred to himself as an *akademik,* indicating he had already finished the course of study. On a more general use of the term *akademik,* see above. The "interfaith" excursions noted below were not always benign; see, for example, Frick, "The Bells of Vilnius," 36–37.

14. Although none of the scanty evidence of Diletskii's biography places him west of Vilnius, several scholars have suggested that he spent time in Poland. Lehmann, "Nikolai Dilezki und seine 'Musikalische Grammatik,'" esp. 43–50, and in his "Mikołaj Dylecki a muzyka polska," esp. 43–44, postulates a stay in Warsaw, suggesting that this is where Diletskii might have become acquainted with compositions by the Polish composers Jacek Różycki and Marcin Mielczewski, whose works are cited several times in the *Grammatika.* Tsalai-Iakymenko and Zelins'kyi, "'More neprebrannoe,'" 114, disagree, stating that Warsaw was not a cultural center in seventeenth-century Poland and at any rate, such musical activities as existed there were entirely dominated by Italian opera. Goshovskii and Durnev, "K sporu," 142–43, suggest that Diletskii worked, or tried to work, in Cracow, based on their reading of a passage unique to L'viv (pp. LXXX–LXXXI, and see also Iakymenko and Zelins'kyi, "'More neprebrannoe,'" 115). This passage is a bitter complaint about corrupt publishing practices in Cracow, where printers will issue anything in order to realize a profit and a work is credited with great authority simply because it appears in print. The author refers to the (as yet unidentified) Cracow treatise *Isagog do muziki,* which he says is not bad, although it is dogmatic in its rules, yet people think it is good just because it has been published. Goshovskii and Durnev suggest that this small tirade may reflect Diletskii's own, apparently unsuccessful, experiences in that city. However, if L'viv is not an autograph or authorial source, it is not clear what biographical import this passage might have.

15. The dedication in the lost manuscript is quoted in Sakharov, "Issledovaniia," 185. Protopopov's identification is in PRMI 7:540–45, citing Brailovskii, *Pis'ma Sil'vestra Medvedeva,* 9.

16. Protopopov, PRMI 7:542–43, tentatively extends the hypothesized network of relationships one step further to include Medvedev's teacher, Simeon Polotskii, suggesting that such a link might account for the inclusion of an excerpt from Polotskii's *Zhezl pravleniia* (The Scepter of Authority, written in connection with the 1666–67 church councils), which is inserted, in Polish, in L'viv, pp. LXXXV–LXXXVII. If this passage from Polotskii's work indicates an acquaintance between the two authors, then one presumably would regard this source as authorial; after all, if Diletskii himself was not responsible for inserting the *Zhezl* fragment, then the passage says nothing directly about the author's circle of friends. Elsewhere, Protopopov seriously questions the accuracy and authority of the L'viv manuscript. One might also wonder why this particular passage, no matter who inserted it, might have been of interest among St. Petersburg's musicians fifty years after it was written (although one should also note that Polotskii's work was reprinted in 1753). And why in Polish? Polotskii knew Polish and he even made a transliteration of the *Zhezl* into the Latin alphabet using (at least some) characteristically Polish spellings, but there does not seem to have been a Polish translation of the *Zhezl* in

circulation in Muscovy. On Polotskii's transliteration, see Demin, " 'Zhezl pravleniia' i aforistika Simeona Polotskogo," 66 (describing RGB, sobr. Moskovskoi dukhovnoi akademii, No. 68, dated May–July 1666). The Moscow 1753 reprint is published in Polotskii [Polockij], *Zezl pravlenija*, where the passage that appears in L'viv begins on fol. 73v.

17. Perhaps the evidence of Diletskii's collaboration with Korenev might support Protopopov's suggestion (PRMI 7:544) that Diletskii was in Moscow before going to Smolensk.

18. RGB 107, p. 8. A link between the Stroganov family and Diletskii was assumed, for example, in Vvedenskii, "Biblioteka i arkhiv u Stroganovykh," 95–96, and in Gerald Abraham's article on the composer in *New Grove Dictionary*, 1980, s.v. "Diletsky, Nikolay." Authoritative surveys of the Stroganov musical establishment are in Parfent'ev and Parfent'eva, *Usol'skaia (Stroganovskaia) shkola* and in Parfent'ev, "Prikaznye dokumenty o stroganovskikh 'spevakakh.' "

19. RGB 107, p. 141. Diletskii refers here to pitches upon which a composer might properly begin; he had rarely seen a piece begin and end on B in a system (*duralnyi kliuch;* see below) with no flats or sharps.

20. RGB 146, p. 1. Watermark evidence dates the manuscript as contemporary to this timeframe; see Protopopov, PRMI 7:455.

21. "[N]e tokmo peti no i tvoriti peniia" (RGB 107, p. 9).

22. Gerasimova-Persidskaia, *Partesnyi kontsert*, examines the origins of the style and includes a large section on Diletskii's works, and there is also a survey in *IRM* 1:263ff. Butskaia, "Printsipy obrazovaniia mnogogolosiia v partesnykh garmonizatsiiakh," uses Diletskii's treatise as a starting point for an examination of compositional practice in the period.

23. See these passages in, for example, RGB 146, pp. 146 and 116–17.

24. The monochord was a traditional teaching device used in music theory treatises, its single string serving as a ruler upon which to project the various mathematical ratios described by musical intervals. Roizman, *Organ*, 53, note, points out the insufficiently appreciated importance of Diletskii's assumptions regarding organs. There was another, equally unexpected, instrument used for teaching in eighteenth-century Russia: the *gusli*, which in this later period and in a somewhat redeveloped form was often associated with priests (Findeizen, *History*, 1:177–78). The instrument still seemed to provoke undesirable actions. In March 1777, Archbishop Samuil of Rostov wrote from Moscow to hieromonk Illarion, noting that he was displeased with his singers and that the students were not learning new *kontserty* properly. He requested that *diak* Aleksandr be given a *gusli* with which to teach the boys. A week later, Samuil wrote again, saying that it had come to his attention that Aleksandr had taken the *gusli* and gone out wandering to local houses, which was not at all appropriate; his solution was not to abandon the *gusli* as a teaching tool but rather to make Illarion the keeper of the instrument, which would only be used at lesson time. See Videneeva, *Rostovskii arkhiereiskii dom*, 288–89 (thanks to Daniel Waugh for this reference).

25. See the opening definitions in RGADA 541, fol. 1v; RGB 146, p. 60; and RGB 107, p. 15.

26. RGADA 541, fol. 2 (musical example not included here); see also Tver' 553, fol. 15; L'viv, p. III; and the lost manuscript from the Sakharov library, in Sakharov, "Issledovaniia," 181. The readings in the Smolensk sources RGADA, Tver', and the lost Sakharov source are closer to each other than to L'viv for this passage. The presentation of this material in the three versions of the *Grammatika* is somewhat blurred, with Moscow 1679

presenting the happy, sad, and mixed categories at the outset, with no separate category of *smysl*. The concepts and basic divisions are the same, however.

27. RGB 146, p. 61.

28. The hexachordal system and its origins are laid out efficiently in *NG2*, s.v. "Hexachord" and "Solmization."

29. I have generally retained the spellings as in the original sources; thus, for example, *duralnyi*, although in modern Russian the word would be spelled with a soft sign: *dural'nyi*. (In general, the sources tend to be very sparing in their use of the soft sign.) In summarizing elements of Diletskii's theory, I use regularized spellings; when quoting from a specific source, I add the original orthography, if different, in square brackets.

Diletskii never does explain the origins of the terms he uses to define *kliuch*, even in the Moscow 1679–81 and Smolensk versions, where he generally prefers Russian vocabulary. *Bemmoliarnyi, duralnyi,* and *diezisovyi* are simply self-standing russianized versions of Western terminology, although corresponding Russian labels might have been found. *Duralnyi*, for example, might have been translated literally into Russian as *tverdyi* (hard) or, as in Protopopov's translation into modern Russian, as *prostoi* (simple or plain). In one passage, however, Diletskii himself uses the term *prostoi*, as opposed to *duralnyi*, fairly consistently. *Prostoi* seems to mean simply without qualifying flats or sharps, and is applied to letter names rather than to the four *kliuchi* that indicate the presence, absence, or introduction of sharps or flats in an entire line or piece (RGB 146, p. 135; RGADA 541, fol. 49; and L'viv, p. XLIV). Later theoretical works do use the term *prostoi* for *duralnyi*. The second half of GIM, sobr. Zabelina, No. 168 (a source written in the mid-eighteenth century) includes the following phrase (fol. 129v): "v duralnom (to est' v prostom)" (in *duralnyi* [that is, in *prostoi*]). The term *dur* appears in Russian translations of Western theoretical treatises produced in the second half of the eighteenth century.

30. There may, however, be a suggestion of hierarchy in the Smolensk version's definition of *musikiia fikta*. In this redaction, *musikiia fikta* is defined as indicating the presence of flats or sharps in a key, as opposed to *duralnaia* music, which has neither; the word *fikta* is translated into Russian as "invented" (*umyshlenaia*) and *duralnaia* music is opposed to *bemmoliarnaia* and *diezisovaia*: "*Duralnaia* music is when there is neither a flat nor a sharp. It is called *musikia fikta* or invented [music] when there are flats or sharps in the keys" (RGADA 541, fols. 6–6v, and see also Tver' 553, fol. 17v, where *musikiia fikta* is defined as *vymyshlennaia*).

31. RGB 107, p. 19. The category of *bemmoliarnaia* music thus seems to apply to the part of the piece that begins with the flat in this example; the category of *smeshennaia* music overlaps, describing the change from one type of music to another and applying to the entire piece. Diletskii repeats this prescriptive element later, when he explains that a sharp sign, used as a natural to cancel a flat, shows that the music has changed from *bemmoliarnyi* to *duralnyi* (RGB 107, p. 102). A single piece might have one voice in *duralnyi*, for example, and another in *bemmoliarnyi;* the entire piece, however, is apparently regarded as mixed, as in RGB 107, p. 218.

32. RGB 146, p. 146 (also Tver' 553, fol. 63v). In Moscow 1679, this passage is expanded to include the type of song, *znamennoe* or *troestrochnoe* (a monophonic chant or a three-part harmonization). The two systems, meaning and key, are joined under the general heading "music" in this passage, but the categories are nevertheless separate: "When you want to write down any song, whether vocal or instrumental, then you need to determine in what kind of music the song is: either happy, or sad, or mixed, or

duralnaia, or *bemoliarnaia"* (RGB 107, p. 136; see also other Moscow 1679 sources and L'viv, p. LXIII). The passage does not appear in RGADA 541 in this chapter, but in chap. 1, under the heading "O kliavishakh" (On clefs), the Smolensk sources include a passage that outlines steps to be taken in writing down a piece; these sources recommend determining the clef (*kliuch*) first, and then the system (*musikiia,* that is *duralnaia,* etc., in RGADA 541, fol. 6v, and L'viv, p. VII). Diletskii uses the term *fantaziia* several times. Murphy, "Cicero and the Icon Painters," 156–57, traces this word in Polotskii's writing, where it refers to imagination, which is ultimately Diletskii's general sense as well.

33. The fundamental pitch letters (*pisma* or *litery osnovatelnye*) are in RGB 107, p. 19 (the letters appear also in chap. 1 on p. 17); and see the published sources RGB 146, p. 62, and L'viv, p. IV. In *duralnaia* music, the letter B is written with the letter H.

34. RGB 107, p. 20.

35. Ibid., p. 21.

36. RGB 146, p. 68. The passage in RGB 107, p. 22, reads: "hold *mi* in your head and sing *fa* or *ut.*" Diletskii generally presents the sharps in the order listed above, with the sharp on A always listed as the fifth possibility.

37. Protopopov discusses this passage in PRMI 7:614–15, n. 16. See the discussion in *NG2,* by Jehoash Hirshberg, s.v. "Hexachord," which discusses just such a situation, noting that a sharp or a natural sign "could be used without a change of hexachord, as described in a number of sources from the 14th to 16th centuries—a note prefixed by either of these signs was never solmized as *mi,* but may be either *ut, fa* or *sol* temporarily raised by a semitone." Thanks are again due to Evgenii Vorob'ev for many discussions of this passage.

38. Diletskii also classifies them into usual (or normal) and unusual positionings (*obyknovennyi* and *neobyknovennyi*); a usual alto, for example, is C3 (a c-clef on the third line of the staff) and an unusual alto is C2 or G4, both of which he calls high alto (RGB 146, pp. 69–70). The ordering of the clefs in the three versions differs slightly. Diletskii also warns the reader that the flat sign is not meant to function as a clef, repeating his warning against this offense in the section on the Irmologii (for example in RNB, Q.XII.4, fol. 58v; this source is inserted in Protopopov's edition of RGB 107 in order to fill in a missing gathering). The Moscow 1679–81 sources add that a sharp sign does not signify a clef either. Later, Diletskii warns that the sharp sign does not indicate a slur.

39. RGB 107, p. 187.

40. Ibid., p. 198.

41. These two passages are from RGB 107, pp. 187 and 64. Gerasimova-Persidskaia, "Partesnoe mnogogolosie i formirovanie stilevykh napravlenii," discusses the importance of these two broad categories in the *partesnoe* style as a whole.

42. As Protopopov points out (PRMI 7:620–21, n. 40), the *dudalnoe* rule derives its name from the *duda,* a type of bagpipe; the alternate title for the rule, as *liripippialnoe,* also refers to the same kind of instrument. The late sixteenth-century glossary assembled by Jean Sauvage lists a "doudenicq" as "ung joueur de musette" (Larin, *Tri inostrannykh istochnika,* 102). Here again, I have retained the original spellings, many of which would require a soft sign in modern Russian (*khoral'noe, dudal'noe*). In the series of rules that follows below, modern practice would require some modifications (e.g., "Ob amplifikatsii" instead of "O amplifikatsii"); again, I have retained the (fairly consistent) original orthography.

43. RGADA 541, fol. 36.

44. Presentations of "O ustroeniiakh" or "O sposobstvuiushchikh" are in RGB 146, p. 125, and RGB 107, p. 92.

45. RGB 107, p. 99.

46. Illustrations of classrooms are in RGB 146, p. 4 (reproduced in color in Protopopov, PRMI 7, color plate 13), and in BAN, sobr. Pliushkina, No. 263 (reproduced in PRMI 7:489).

47. Gushee, "Questions of Genre in Medieval Treatises on Music," 366.

48. RGB 107, p. 189.

49. Quoted and translated in Morosan, *"Penie* and *Musikiia,"* 174, from Rogov, *Muzykal'naia estetika Rossii,* 124 (the original text is quoted in Rogov, 105, from RGB 146, p. 11). Protopopov, *Russkaia mysl' o muzyke,* 53–54, discusses Korenev's general meaning of the term "filosofiia."

50. There is substantial bibliography on Smotritskii (Smotryts'kiy), surveyed in *SKK XVII v.,* pt. 2:346–50. In the Moscow 1679–81 and Smolensk versions, Diletskii briefly points to arithmetic as another model familiar to his student readers; just as arithmetic has numbers as its basic rules, so music uses the letter names of the notes (RGB 146, p. 98, and RGADA 541, fol. 20v). Gerasimova-Persidskaia, *Russkaia muzyka XVII veka,* esp. 73f., also calls attention to the term *grammatika* in Diletskii's work.

51. RGB 107, p. 114, which includes the phrase "litoriki [sic] ili poetiki." In his translation of this passage, Protopopov reads the word "poetiki" as two words, "po etiki," and he thus refers to rhetoric and ethics (PRMI 7:377). Given the curriculum of the Jesuit schools and those modeled after them, "poetics" seems more likely. There is a short consideration of rhetorical influences in Diletskii's treatise in Zakharova, "Ritoricheskaia traditsiia v russkoi muzyke," and in the same author's *Ritorika i zapadnoevropeiskaia muzyka,* esp. chap. 2; and see also Lehmann, "Dilezki und die grosse Wandlung der russischen Musik," esp. 347–48.

52. RGB 107, p. 175.

53. Ibid., p. 116. RGB 146, p. 117, includes a comparison to a church figure after the opening analogy to a rhetorician, for both need models for their works.

54. Smirnova, "Simon Ushakov—'Historicism' and 'Byzantinism,'" discusses Ushakov's copies of icons. Ushakov's proposal to create model images is in Dmitriev, "Teoriia iskusstva i vzgliady na iskusstvo," 98, and see the brief discussion in Hughes, "The Moscow Armoury," 214. Murphy, "Cicero and the Icon Painters," 156, draws attention to the references to beginners' alphabets in both Vladimirov and Simeon Polotskii. Note 96 in chap. 2, above, discusses Simeon's role in part of Ushakov's treatise. Vladyshevskaia, "Stanovlenie stilia barokko," esp. 20–24, considers a more general link between artistic practice and music, examining the influence of images depicting the Trinity, especially Andrei Rublev's important icon, and the rise of three-part (*troestrochnoe*) singing. Diletskii's approach would also have been familiar in Muscovite liturgical singing practice through the use of model stanzas for hymns.

55. Diletskii's dedication is in RGB 107, pp. 1–14; Protopopov identifies the classical figures in PRMI 7:612, notes 3 and 4.

56. RGB 107, pp. 1–3. Protopopov translates *arkhi* as *iskusnye voskhvaleniia* (skillful praises), but the term seems to indicate introductory speeches or praises specifically, as Diletskii's examples suggest. The seventeenth-century lexicon by Berynda, *Leksykon slovenoros'kyi,* 181, defines *arkhi* as *nachalo* (beginning), which is the meaning it has in Greek. *Iroglifik* is discussed below, n. 75. Diletskii directly addresses Stroganov again at the end of the treatise (RGB 107, pp. 232–33).

57. The dedication is published in Sakharov, "Issledovaniia," 184–85, and excerpts are also in Protopopov, PRMI 7:541. Protopopov notes that the concluding dedication in the L'viv source is quite similar to that in the lost Sakharov manuscript, although the dedicatees are different (and there are some significant additions, for example, references to "sarabandi i balliati i inie sal'ta [other dances]"); see L'viv, pp. LXIX–LXX.

58. RGB 107, p. 169. A Russian rhetoric treatise associated with Mikhail Usachev, related to the Spafarii-Makarii-*Skazanie* complex (see below) but from later in the century, also has a passage expressing the inexhaustible dimensions of the ocean; see Eleonskaia, *Russkaia oratorskaia proza,* 32.

59. Leontii Magnitskii, *Arifmetika* (1703), 3, translated in Okenfuss, *The Rise and Fall of Latin Humanism,* 76 (where the author, on p. 75, characterizes Magnitskii's book as "the culmination of the impact of the foreign on seventeenth-century Muscovy"). Magnitskii's work, like Diletskii's, is an intensely practical technical manual, using a question-answer format, charts and classification schemes, and Western terminology with explanatory Russian vocabulary.

60. On rhetorical treatises and the study of rhetoric at the Kievan collegium, see Petrov, "O slovesnykh naukakh"; his "Kievskaia Akademiia"; Okenfuss, "Education in Russia," esp. chap. 3; and his "The Jesuit Origins." Examples of name derivations in Polotskii's verses are published in Adrianova-Peretts, *Russkaia sillabicheskaia poeziia,* 166–67. The derivation of names in the Kievan rhetorical treatise *Concha* (1698) is cited in Petrov, "O slovesnykh naukakh," *TKDA* no. 3 (1868): 472; the same procedure is outlined in the treatise by Ioannikii Galiatovskii, from 1659 (see Eleonskaia, *Russkaia oratorskaia proza,* 38–39).

61. As Okenfuss, "Education in Russia," 107, says, the Orthodox schools in the Slavic lands west and south of Muscovy "competed with the Jesuits' institutions by using the most obvious, and yet the most effective tool at their disposal: imitation." On the Kievan College and its curriculum, see Petrov, "Kievskaia Akademiia," *TKDA* no. 10 (1895): 221ff.; Okenfuss, "The Jesuit Origins"; and Kharlampovich, *Zapadnorusskie pravoslavnye shkoly,* 23ff. Sydorenko, *The Kievan Academy in the Seventeenth Century,* chap. 2, does not place as much emphasis on the influence of the Jesuit educators on Orthodox schools; see the review by Sysyn, "Peter Mohyla and the Kiev Academy," esp. 155–60. A brief history of Emmanuel Alvarez's Latin grammar, used in both Jesuit and Orthodox schools, is in Farrell, *The Jesuit Code of Liberal Education,* appendix C. As Okenfuss points out in "The Jesuit Origins," 128, the Alvarez grammar was never published in Russia, although it was used well into the eighteenth century. Texts were compiled by teachers based on their own schooling and passed on to their students.

62. On Virgil in the curricula of colleges in the West and in Kiev, see Petrov, "Kievskaia Akademiia," *TKDA* no. 10 (1895): 217ff., and Okenfuss, "Education in Russia," 108. On the holdings at the L'viv confraternity—well stocked with Classical works—see Isaievych, *Voluntary Brotherhood,* 173–75.

63. Hippisley, *The Poetic Style of Simeon Polotsky,* 62–64, discusses the use of classical references in the *Orel rossiiskii;* the work is published in Polotskii, *Orel rossiiskii.* Korenev also refers to Orpheus and Amphion in a passage listing classical authorities (RGB 146, p. 12), and see also below.

64. Polotskii's poem is translated in Okenfuss, *The Rise and Fall of Latin Humanism,* 60, citing Polotskii, *Virshi,* 120–22. Rhetoric treatises from the Kievan College are listed in Stratii, Litvinov, and Andrushko, *Opisanie kursov filosofii i ritoriki.* Meletii Smotritskii

refs to the seven liberal arts in an introduction to the edition of his grammar published in Moscow, 1648 (for example on fol. 43); see also Rumiantseva, "Andreevskii uchilishchnyi monastyr," 293. Protopopov, *Russkaia mysl' o muzyke*, 50, also calls attention to Smotritskii's work. The art treatise by Ushakov and Polotskii, noted above and in chapter 2, also refers to the seven liberal arts; see Murphy, "Cicero and the Icon Painters," 158, and Dmitriev, "Teoriia iskusstva i vzgliady na iskusstvo," 101.

65. Pozdneev, *Rukopisnye pesenniki*, 32–33.

66. Belobrova, *Nikolai Spafarii*, 6–7. Belobrova discusses this work in "K izucheniiu 'Knigi izbranoi vkrattse'" and in "Allegorii nauk v litsevykh spiskakh 'Knigi izbranoi vkrattse.'" The presentation copy for Tsar Aleksei is listed in Waugh, "The Library of Aleksei Mikhailovich," 315. Additional biographical information is in Belobrova, *Nikolai Spafarii*, 3ff., and in her substantial survey in *SKK XVII v.*, pt. 2:392–400 and pt. 4:755–57.

67. Belobrova identifies the Western artistic sources (images by painter Marten de Vos and engraver Jan Sadeler) in "Ob istochnikakh miniatiur." A color facsimile of the illustration "Music" from Spafarii's work is in Protopopov, PRMI 7, color plate 16.

68. "Glagolet ubo i musika ot litsa svoego sitse," in Belobrova, *Nikolai Spafarii*, 39 (based on GIM, Sin. sobr., No. 527; she publishes the *Skazanie* from GIM, Sin. sobr., No. 353).

69. "1—izhe dorie narechesia, 2—izhe lidie narechesia, 3—izhe frigie narechesia i proch," in Belobrova, *Nikolai Spafarii*, 38, where Spafarii also defines *obraz* and *dvizhenie*.

70. Ibid., 39, and Korenev, in RGB 146, p. 12. Juraj Križanić (Iurii Krizhanich; d. 1683), the scholar from Zagreb who studied in Rome and eventually made his way to Russia, wrote several works on music. His earliest, *Asserta musicalia* (Rome, 1656), does include a recounting (and refutation) of the Pythagoras tale: "The tradition that Pythagoras discovered and determined the proportions of sounds from hammer strokes should be considered a fable." See Vidaković, *Yury Krizanitch's "Asserta Musicalia,"* 118–19, and the discussion on 65ff. Križanić arrived in Moscow in 1659 to promote the Union; by 1661 he had been sent into exile to Tobol'sk, apparently because of his ties to the Western church, although the reasons are unclear. He was able to work relatively freely while he remained in exile, which lasted until 1676. His *De musica*, written in Latin in Tobol'sk, mentions Pythagoras (again negatively) in a different musical context; see Gol'dberg and others, "Traktat o muzyke Iuriia Krizhanicha," where the reference to Pythagoras is on pp. 364 and 388, and the summary in Vidaković, 56–61. Križanić's *Politika* (1663–66) includes passages on military music (Letiche and Dmytryshyn, *Russian Statecraft*, 65–67), and see the general survey in Belokurov, "Iurii Krizhanich v Rossii."

71. Scholars disagree on the date of the *Skazanie* (in the sixteenth century, probably as a translation from a Latin original) and its origins (either from Muscovy itself or from Ukraine or Belarus); see *SKK XVII v.*, pt. 3:442–43.

72. The *Mudrost' chetvertaia Musikia* circulated independently in a source published in OLDP Izdaniia 6: fols. 1–11, a manuscript from the Viazemskii collection (RNB, sobr. Viazemskogo, O.57). This source is described in Sheremetev, *Opisanie rukopisei kniazia Pavla Petrovicha Viazemskogo*, 540; cf. the text published in Belobrova, *Nikolai Spafarii*, 145–47. Korenev's listing is in RGB 146, p. 19. Belobrova, "K izucheniiu 'Knigi izbranoi vkrattse,'" 311, compares the listings in the *Skazanie* and in Spafarii.

73. There is a large literature on the *Ritorika* attributed to Makarii, summarized in *SKK XVII v.*, pt. 2:317–21, and in the recent edition by Annushkin, *Pervaia russkaia "Ritorika"*; see esp. 209–11 and 317–47 (a discussion of sources), and 221–25ff. (a discus-

sion of the various redactions, some of which include introductions taken from the *Skazanie*). The Russian translation was apparently based on Philipp Melanchthon's popular *Elementorum rhetorices,* and the edition includes the Latin text of the abridged version published in Frankfurt, 1577.

74. Petrov, "Kievskaia Akademiia," *TKDA* no. 10 (1895): 204ff., discusses the compilation and circulation of textbooks in Kiev; and see the listings in Stratii, Litvinov, and Andrushko, *Opisanie kursov filosofii i ritoriki.*

75. *Iroglifik* appears in enumerations of elements one might use to embellish a speech, particularly in the context of symbol, emblem, and other indirect illustrations. See Stratii, Litvinov, and Andrushko, *Opisanie kursov filosofii i ritoriki,* nos. 10, 13, 29, 50, 57, 74, and 77 (from the late seventeenth century through the first decades of the eighteenth century). In the same context, *iroglifik* appears, paired with *emblimata,* in Iavorskii, *Ritoricheskaia ruka,* 20.

76. On Diletskii's use of the term, see the published sources RGB 107, p. 44; RGB 146, p. 92; and L'viv, p. XV. Latin headings in the *Grammatika* often appear with Slavic translations in the Moscow 1679 redaction and in the L'viv manuscript; the Smolensk and Moscow 1679–81 versions generally prefer Slavic headings only. On *raspolozhenie* in rhetoric treatises, see Petrov, "O slovesnykh naukakh," *TKDA* no. 3 (1868): 475. There is a similar definition of *razmnozhenie* in the Makarii rhetoric, in Annushkin, *Pervaia russkaia "Ritorika,"* 62 and 129 (modern Russian translation).

77. RGB 107, pp. 44–45. Diletskii cites only excerpts from the text. Petrov, "O slovesnykh naukakh," *TKDA* no. 3 (1868): 475ff., discusses how a speech is laid out in rhetoric treatises.

78. Diletskii's "Sluzhba Bozhiia preportsialnaia" is preserved in GIM, Sin. pev. sobr., No. 712 (a set of seven partbooks; the eighth, for discant 1, is missing); the work is published in Dylets'kyi, *Khorovi tvory,* 199–251, and, partially, in Protopopov, PRMI 7:493–504.

79. "O inventsii" or "O izobretenii" is in the published *Grammatika* sources RGB 107, p. 107; RGB 146, p. 139; and L'viv, p. XLVII. The definition in the Kievan rhetoric treatise ("vymyshlenie prichin, podtverzhdaiushchikh predlozhenie") is quoted from *Concha* (1698) in Petrov, "O slovesnykh naukakh," *TKDA* no. 3 (1868): 471. There is a similar definition in Annushkin, *Pervaia russkaia "Ritorika,"* 23 and 100 (modern Russian translation).

80. "O eksordii" or "O nachale" begins in RNB, Q.XII.4, fol. 60v; RGB 146, p. 155; and L'viv, p. LVIII. Diletskii gives another series of variations of a given melody at the end of the fourth chapter (for example in RGB 107, pp. 78–79).

81. RGB 146, p. 92 (and, in transliterated Latin with a Slavic translation, in L'viv, p. XV). This phrase is repeated near the end of Moscow 1679–81 (RGB 146, p. 167, and see also L'viv, p. LXIX); it appears at a different point in the Moscow 1679 sources (RGB 107, p. 177).

82. RGB 146, p. 172.

83. RGB 146, p. 109. The Moscow 1679–81 and Smolensk versions add information on how this rule obtains in multi-voiced works. Diletskii's composition is in Dylets'kyi, *Khorovi tvory,* 54 and 40ff.

84. RGB 107, pp. 197–98. The terminology used in rhetoric treatises is from Petrov, "O slovesnykh naukakh," *TKDA* no. 3 (1868): 479–80. Thanks to Gregory Myers for his advice on the liturgical texts.

85. Translation from Morosan, "*Penie* and *Musikiia*," 176, quoting Rogov, *Muzykal'naia estetika Rossii,* 134 (Korenev's original passage is in Rogov, 117, and in RGB 146, p. 37).

86. Titov's setting is in GIM, Sin. pev. sobr., No. 712. The dynamic markings are written in red ink and appear in most of the individual partbooks.

87. Eleonskaia, *Russkaia oratorskaia proza,* 32, quoting from the rhetoric treatise associated with Mikhail Usachev.

88. RGB 107, p. 228 (where the composer's name is spelled "Koleda"). See also Protopopov, PRMI 7:625, n. 65.

89. Ibid., p. 77.

90. Ibid., p. 124. Protopopov, PRMI 7:625, n. 72, cites this passage, noting that here, "more clearly than in other places in the *Grammatika,* major and minor are implied (*podrazumevaiutsia*)."

91. For example: "I said earlier that in any letter at times there is *ut, re, mi, fa, sol,* and *la.* For example the letter A: A *ut re mi fa sol la* and A *la sol fa mi re ut.* And the same way for the letter B: B *ut re mi fa sol la* and B *la sol fa mi re ut* [and so forth, through the letters C–G]" (RGB 107, pp. 228–31). Along the same lines, Diletskii says: "In every rule, as you wish, you may lay out a musical song [beginning] from a letter, that is from the letter A and from the letter C, etc., in the happy or in the grieving and weeping *ton*" (RGB 146, p. 101).

92. GIM, Sin. pev. sobr., No. 777, fol. 95v; see also Tver', f. 103, No. 651a, pp. 168–69. The readings in RGB 146, p. 133, and GIM 1340, fol. 119, appear to be garbled. The order of the hexachordal syllables in the latter sources is *ut, re, la, fa, sol, mi.*

93. L'viv, p. LXXI.

94. RGB 146, p. 171. The entire presentation begins in RGB 146, p. 168; see also GIM 1340, fol. 154 (fol. 153 is missing) and L'viv, p. XCII (which omits a listing on B). Pages from these passages in RGB 146 are reproduced (in reversed order) in Lehmann, "Dilezki und die grosse Wandlung der russischen Musik," 360–61. Some eighteenth-century *Grammatika* manuscripts do include long listings of scales built on every pitch.

95. For example, in his discussion of the triad A–C–E, Diletskii writes: "The word A agrees at the third, that is, in the third note, with the word C, and with the word E at the fifth, that is, at the fifth note" (RGB 146, p. 75).

96. RGB 146, p. 81, for instance, where the example illustrates major thirds only.

97. RGB 107, p. 151.

98. Ibid., pp. 114–15.

99. Ibid., p. 76, where there are two sets of examples, both of which involve transposition rather than an alteration of the third.

100. RGB 146, p. 81. Protopopov, PRMI 7:586, offers a different interpretation of Diletskii's treatment of cadences, and in his analysis, this section represents the most important evidence pointing to the *Grammatika's* non-hexachordal, octave-based major and minor system.

101. RGB 107, pp. 71–72.

102. Ibid., p. 100.

103. See the published *Grammatika* sources RNB Q.XII.4, fol. 62; RGB 146, p. 157; and L'viv, p. LIX.

104. For example, RGB 146, p. 157.

105. The text under the first example in RGB 146 reads "Alliluiia."

106. L'viv, p. LXI. The "gospodi pomilui" example is in RGB 107, p. 132.

107. RGB 107, p. 132. In L'viv, p. LXI, the same melody is presented once, without illustrating the retrograde version.

108. The musical circles begin as follows in the published sources: RGB 107, p. 133; RGB 146, p. 159; and L'viv, p. LXI.

109. The circle depicting happy music appears first in all sources, followed by the circle illustrating sad music. GIM 777 and Tver' 651a include a second "happy circle."

110. RGB 146, p. 159.

111. The Moscow 1679 passage is in RGB 107, p. 134; the expanded explanation is from RGB 146, p. 161.

112. See the listings in Stratii, Litvinov, and Andrushko, *Opisanie kursov filosofii i ritoriki*, Nos. 1, 2, 8, and 11.

113. Lester, "Major-Minor Concepts," 234–35, n. 88, and see also his *Between Modes and Keys*, 98–99. Ozanam's listing is in his *Dictionnaire mathématique*, 659–60; the work is discussed in Cohen, "*Musique* in the *Dictionnaire mathématique.*"

114. Lester, *Between Modes and Keys*, 105–106, citing Janowka, *Clavis ad thesaurum magnae artis musicae* (e.g., in the article "Tonus," pp. 287–304, translated in Lester, 167–73). See also Lester, "The Recognition of Major and Minor Keys," 77–78, and the biographical survey by John Clapham and Tomislav Volek in *NG2*, s.v. "Janowka, Tomás Baltazar."

115. Lester, *Between Modes and Keys*, 92 and 108 (where he reproduces Heinichen's diagram), and see Heinichen, *Neu erfundene und gründliche Anweisung*, where the diagram follows p. 260.

116. Lester, "The Recognition of Major and Minor Keys," 77, emphasizes that Janowka's approach was similarly removed from such debates, noting that Janowka "appears to be in total ignorance of the traditional church modes and terms associated with them." Janowka was an organist in Prague (at the Týn Church) for fifty years and his *Clavis ad thesaurum magnae artis musicae*, a dictionary of music, shows him to be well acquainted with contemporary theory and composition (see *NG2*, s.v. "Janowka, Tomás Baltazar"), so he must have had at least some familiarity with traditional modal theory and vocabulary.

117. L'viv, p. LXI. Diletskii's description as "without beginning and without end" ("beznachalnoe, i bezkonechnoe") is in RGB 107, p. 133.

118. Dylets'kyi, *Khorovi tvory*, 23ff.

119. "Es hat der Weltberühmte Froberger schon vor etlichen 30. Jahren eine Canzon gesetzet, da er algemach das thema durch das gantze Clavier in all 12. Claves transponiret . . . und also durch den Circul der quinten oder quarten gebet," in Andreas Werckmeister, *Hypomnemata musica*, chap. 11, p. 37; quotation and translation from Lester, *Between Modes and Keys*, 92, n. 37.

120. "Mein Lehrmeister hatte mir zwar etwas von dem oben gemeldten Circul des Kircheri gesaget, allein dieser gab mir keine Satisfaction, so offt ich mir vorsetzte, aus einen Modo maj. in einen weit abgelegenen modum min. & vice versa zu gehen," in Johann Heinichen, *Der General-Bass in der Composition*, 840–41; quotation and translation from Lester, *Between Modes and Keys*, 109.

121. "Die bekandte Arth des Kircheri, alle Modos per Quartas & Quintas zu circuliren, ist eine der unvollkommensten. Denn wenn man z. E. von einem Modo majori anfänget, und gehet so lange per 4tas oder per 5tas fort, biss man wieder in den ersten Modum gelanget, so sind alle 12 modi minores aussenblieben," in Heinichen, *Der General-*

Bass in der Composition, 837; quotation and translation from Lester, *Between Modes and Keys,* 109. [Trilupaitiené], "Vilnius als Musikzentrum des Grossfürstentums Litauen," 146–47, notes that Kircher was a figure of great authority at the Jesuit College in Vilnius.

122. Lester, "The Recognition of Major and Minor Keys," 81; see also his *Between Modes and Keys,* 108.

123. Lester, "The Recognition of Major and Minor Keys," 79; see also his *Between Modes and Keys,* 110.

124. As Albert Cohen notes, Ozanam's definitions "are a reflection, if not always of the most profound musical ideas of his time, at least of thoughts that were current during the period in which he wrote. They are products of a synthesis that appears to have been made by Ozanam himself in objectively seeking a common understanding for the meanings of the musical terminology of his day" ("*Musique* in the *Dictionnaire mathématique,*" 91).

125. See the facsimile in RGB 146, p. 88 (also in GIM 1340, fol. 82, and GIM, Sin. pev. sobr., No. 184, fol. 14v). The diagram also appears in GIM 777, fol. 43, and Tver' 651a, p. 67 (in these two sources, the circle appears in chap. 3, in the middle of the explanation of concords). This diagram is immediately followed by a pair of grids made up of boxes forming stylized staves. The letters A–G are entered across the top and clefs and key signatures appear on the lines, illustrating triads in *duralnyi* and *bemmoliarnyi* keys; see RGB 146, p. 89, and RGB 107, p. 37.

126. The charts begin as follows in the published sources: RGB 107, p. 117; RGB 146, p. 131; and L'viv, p. XLIII. On the opening diagram of the cross, see n. 4 above.

127. Facsimiles of Polotskii's poems are in Polotskii, *Izbrannye sochineniia,* following p. 160 (heart- and star-shaped poems), and see the discussion in Hippisley, *The Poetic Style of Simeon Polotsky,* esp. chap. 3. Poetic forms used by the Kievan faculty are discussed in Petrov, "O slovesnykh naukakh," *TKDA* no. 1 (1867): 104ff.

128. Ian (Andrei Khristoforovich) Belobotskii was a Pole who worked in Muscovy from about 1680 into the early eighteenth century; his work is a Slavic translation of the Latin treatise by Ramón Lull. See *SKK XVII v.,* pt. 1:128–31 and pt. 4:674–75, and the brief biographical sketch in Lewin, "Polish-Ukrainian-Russian Literary Relations," 260–61. His popular treatise is discussed in Eleonskaia, *Russkaia oratorskaia proza,* 40–47, with facsimiles of the circles on pp. 41 and 48, and in Vomperskii, *Ritoriki v Rossii XVII–XVIII vv.,* 38–53. On the primers, see Okenfuss, *The Discovery of Childhood in Russia.*

129. The L'viv inventory is published in *Arkhiv iugo-zapadnoi Rossii,* 12: pt. 1:62–71, where the "Bemuliarna sluzhba" is on p. 68, and Diletskii's pieces are on pp. 64 and 68. Diletskii's "Sluzhba bozhiia preportsialnaia" is in GIM, Sin. pev. sobr., No. 712 (and see n. 78 above). Protopopov, "Tvoreniia Vasiliia Titova," 858 and 863, refers to the descriptive titles of Titov's works. Overviews of the educational approaches at the L'viv confraternity (and at other such institutions) are in Isaievych, *Voluntary Brotherhood,* and Gudziak, *Crisis and Reform.*

130. "Kamponoval siia glasy chelovek greshnyi / inozemets zhe i pan Nikolai Dyletskii," quoted in Livanova, *Ocherki i materialy,* 211, and see the discussion in Protopopov, PRMI 7:608–10. The song appears in three sources from the late seventeenth or early eighteenth century (GIM, sobr. Shchukina, No. 61 and GIM, Sin. pev. sobr., Nos. 757 and 486), and also in a *Grammatika* manuscript from the mid-eighteenth century in a three-part variant (RGB, f. 218, No. 14).

131. "Imia moe est' dyshkant / bo zovut mia vsi verkhom. / Molisia bogu i poi ut, re, mi, fa, sol', lia . . ." (Livanova, *Ocherki i materialy,* 210).

132. "Imia moe est' tenor, soderzhet v sebe put' / Vypoesh' li mia budet v tebe istinnyi put'. / Vypevai sladkim sim i preblagim glasom / A ne krivisia durno kulez-matskim glasom" (Livanova, *Ocherki i materialy,* 211). The word *put'* means both "cantus firmus" and "path" or "way." Vladyshevskaia, "Stanovlenie stilia barokko," 29–30, notes that this song text also shows the relationship between chant terminology (not only the names of the neumes but also the vocal parts) and the *partesnoe* style.

133. The songs "about numbers" ("o chislakh") are discussed in Dolskaya, *Spiritual Songs,* xxviii and No. 105; the example appears in six other early *kant* sources. See also Pozdneev, "Svetskie pol'skie pesni," 62.

134. Brazhnikov, *Drevnerusskaia teoriia,* 258 and, in general, chaps. 9 and 10; see also Miloš Velimirović in *NG2* (s.v. "Russian and Slavonic Church Music"). Schidlovsky, "Sources of Russian Chant Theory," 93, suggests that even earlier, the introduction of the *pomety* and *priznaki* (other markings used to clarify specific pitch level) during the seventeenth century gave a "new theoretical orientation" to the introductory, notation-based *azbuki* ("alphabets" of chant notation).

135. Shabalin, *Pevcheskie azbuki,* 1:236 (RGB, f. 272, No. 429). In another instance, a treatise presents a listing that not only equates the neumed notation (including *soglasiia*) with the Western solmization syllables but it does so in a manner reminiscent of age-old Western practice. The names of the Western solmization syllables are taken from the first syllables of a hymn, "Ut queant laxis," in which each phrase of the melody begins on the adjacent pitch in an ascending scale: thus, "*Ut* queant laxis" produces the first syllable, *ut;* "*re*sonare fibris" produces the next syllable, *re,* and so forth. In the Muscovite source RNB, Q.XII.1, from the 1680s, the author writes out a musical and textual phrase of chant, picks out specific syllables to produce the equivalent of an ascending scale as defined by the letters used in the *soglasie* system, and then equates the (textual) syllable to one of the Western hexachordal syllables (thus "spa," from the word "spasenie" is equated with *ut;* "io" from "Ionu" is equated with *re,* and so forth). The result is a kind of hybrid *kholm*-solmization chart, listing the syllables in ascending order from *ut* to *la* (or *spa* to *le*); see Shabalin, 1:238.

136. The neume-solmization syllable example is reproduced in Shabalin, *Pevcheskie azbuki,* 1:261–63 (RGB, f. 379, No. 4, from the last quarter of the seventeenth century); the example with notation on opposite sides of an opening is described in Brazhnikov, *Drevnerusskaia teoriia,* 399, citing RGB, f. 379, No. 3, a late seventeenth-century manuscript transmitting Tikhon's *Kliuch* (for a general discussion, see Brazhnikov, chap. 12). The *dvoznamenniki* were not limited to listings of neumes and staff notation. A few manuscripts line up two types of neumed notation (for example, *znamennyi* and *demestvennyi* or *kazanskii* notation). Brazhnikov, 391, mentions a source with three notational types: neumes, Kievan square staff notation, and rounded Western-style staff notation (RNB, Sol. sobr., No. 647/619).

137. Brazhnikov, *Drevnerusskaia teoriia,* 390.

138. See, for example, Brazhnikov, *Drevnerusskaia teoriia,* 412–13. Diletskii even includes a diagram strongly reminiscent (in form if not in function) of a *kholm;* see RGB 107, p. 176. Additional illustrations are in Shabalin, *Pevcheskie azbuki,* 1:239–47 (ranging in date from the seventeenth to the nineteenth centuries); Gardner and Koschmieder, *Ein handschriftliches Lehrbuch der altrussischen Neumenschrift,* Bl. 5b (with hexachordal syllables); and Schidlovsky, "Sources of Russian Chant Theory," 94.

139. Brazhnikov, *Drevnerusskaia teoriia,* 390–91, points out the complete lack of rests in *dvoznamenniki.*

140. Tikhon's biography and works are reviewed in *SKK XVII v.,* pt. 4:31–42, and see also the brief summaries in Protopopov, PRMI 7:565 and 630, n. 101, and his *Russkaia mysl' o muzyke,* 66–67. Many thanks to Evgenii Vorob'ev for sharing his recent research on Tikhon; he emphasizes the work's context in this difficult and delicate transitional period of the last quarter of the seventeenth century, in which there was already a generation of liturgical singers who had grown up with the reality of staff notation.

141. Brazhnikov's discussion of Tikhon's deliberate merging of Western hexachordal syllables and Muscovite *soglasiia* is in *Drevnerusskaia teoriia,* 393 (and see also the general discussion in Velimirović, "Russian and Slavonic Church Music," in *NG2*). A facsimile of Tikhon's key is in Kudriavtsev, *Sobraniia D. V. Razumovskogo i V. F. Odoevskogo,* 11.

142. "[I]akozhe rekokh v tikhonovskoi musikii" (the final two words written in red ink; RGB 107, p. 203); Protopopov discusses this passage in PRMI 7:630, n. 101, and in his *Russkaia mysl' o muzyke,* 67.

143. Protopopov, *Russkaia mysl' o muzyke,* 54–55.

144. On Korenev, see ibid., 44–58; *SKK XVII v.,* pt. 2:181–82 and pt. 4:733; and the excerpts in Rogov, *Muzykal'naia estetika Rossii,* 104–40 (a few extracts are translated in Morosan, "*Penie* and *Musikiia,*" 174–76) and, from *O penii bozhestvennom,* in Shabalin, *Pevcheskie azbuki,* 1:349–54 and 2:391–98 (translation into modern Russian). Korenev was apparently also a composer. A setting of Psalm 60 in GIM, sobr. Khludova, No. 126d (No. 97), a late-seventeenth-century *kant* manuscript, includes an acrostic with the name "diakon Anikii," which some scholars identify with Korenev; see Pozdneev, "Nikonovskaia shkola," 421–22, and Protopopov, PRMI 7:555. The 1671 *O penii bozhestvennom* circulates in the lost Sakharov source (excerpts published in Shabalin, and see Sakharov, "Issledovaniia," 168–71); RNB, Q.I.1101 (third quarter of the seventeenth century; excerpts in Shabalin); RNB, F.I.244; GIM, Muz. sobr., 4072 (Protopopov, PRMI 7:469 suggests a date in the first quarter of the eighteenth century); and NBU, Sof. 127/381 (Protopopov, *Russkaia mysl' o muzyke,* 48, says that this is a seriously flawed text; Tsalai-Iakymenko, *Kyivs'ka shkola muzyky,* 283, n. 182, cites it as a Ukrainian work, assigning it an early date of 1663–65).

Protopopov divides the remaining Korenev sources into two redactions, one from 1679 (with the theoretical section relating to the *Grammatika*) and one from 1681 (which adds verses, a "Note to the reader," and other material). I have not made such a fine distinction in the following discussion, referring simply to a "second version" of Korenev's treatise. This version circulates in its full (or nearly full) form in RGB 146 and GIM 1340 (both very early sources transmitting the Moscow 1679–81 *Grammatika;* it is in GIM 1340 that we find the statement suggesting that Korenev wrote the manuscript); and in RGB, f. 173, No. 116 (Protopopov, PRMI 7:458–59, suggests a date of ca. 1700 and notes that the Korenev text matches that in RGB 146). It circulates in excerpted form (focusing on the theoretical material) in the *Grammatika* sources GIM 777; Tver' 651a; Kostroma, f. 558, op. 2, No. 583; MGK V 68; and BAN, sobr. Pliushkina, No. 263. Excerpts unconnected to Diletskii's work are in Kostroma, f. 670, No. 44.

Oleksandra Tsalai-Iakymenko, most recently in *Kyivs'ka shkola muzyky,* presents a very different interpretation of *O penii bozhestvennom;* her chap. 11, for example, is headed "Traktat 'O pinii Bozhestvennom' (E. Slavynets'koho) [by E. Slavynets'kyi]." Her position has not generally been accepted; the debates are summarized in Protopopov, PRMI 7:558–60, and *Russkaia mysl' o muzyke,* 49 (note).

145. This discussion is necessarily tentative, as Korenev's treatise is in desperate

need of a critical edition comparing the two versions (and in particular, publishing in full one of the 1671 versions). The present discussion is based on the description in Protopopov, *Russkaia mysl' o muzyke*, 44–58, and the same author's "'Musikiia' Ioannikiia Koreneva"; from Protopopov's presentations, it appears that the bulk of the treatise (excluding the music theory section at the end) is basically the same in the two versions. However, no substantial excerpts from the 1671 version (apart from a portion of the theoretical section in Shabalin, *Pevcheskie azbuki*, 1:349–54) have been published. As n. 144 above indicates, the manuscript transmission is complex, with some sources (GIM 777 and Tver' 651a especially) making intelligent excerpts from widely spaced passages from Korenev's work.

146. Figure 5.3 is based on the prose layout in Shabalin, *Pevcheskie azbuki*, 1:353–54.

147. Starowolski, *Musices practicae erotemata*, A5–A5v; Korenev, in the second version, RGB 146, pp. 11–12 ("Eval, Lamekhov syn" and a series of Biblical references, followed by the Greeks "Pifagor, Merkorii, Zetis, Ampfonii, Orfei, Ilinii [*sic*] i Orion," and later in the treatise (p. 52), "Aval, Lamekhov syn" and, several lines later, "Pifagor, Merkurii i prochii."

148. Starowolski's list of names is similar to those in Andreas Ornithoparchus, *Musicae actiue micrologus* (Leipzig, 1517), sig. A5, and Johann Spangenberg, *Quaestiones musicae* (Cologne, 1563), sig. A4; Starowolski's chart laying out the hexachords is closer to the presentation in Spangenberg (sig. A6). A few of the names also appear in the section on music in Spafarii's work on the seven liberal arts (Belobrova, *Nikolai Spafarii*, 38–39), in both Spafarii's introduction and in the section drawn from the *Skazanie*. Protopopov, *Russkaia mysl' o muzyke*, 50, suggests that the introduction to Smotritskii's *Grammatika* (in the Moscow, 1648 edition) and the *Kniga o vere* (Book of Faith; also from Moscow, 1648) provided sources for Korenev's listings of musical authorities. Although the Smotritskii introduction, in particular, does include some discussion of music and of the liberal arts, and both invoke traditional church authorities (as does Korenev), the listings in these two Muscovite publications do not include the same distinctive series of biblical and Greek names. Spangenberg's work was widely printed in Poland; see Przywecka-Samecka, *Dzieje drukarstwa muzycznego w Polsce*, 251 and 261–64 (various Cracow editions), and 294 (editions from Raków).

149. The reference to the Sretenskii Cathedral is in RGB 146, p. 1 (facsimile on p. 175); see also Protopopov, *Russkaia mysl' o muzyke*, 47, on Korenev's possible career in the 1660s. Nikolai Spafarii was in Moscow as of late 1671 (Belobrova, *Nikolai Spafarii*, 4–5).

150. RGB 146, p. 53, with a modern Russian translation in Protopopov, PRMI 7:560, n. 52.

151. Protopopov, PRMI 7:560–62, relates Korenev's passage to one in the Moscow 1679–81 *Grammatika* (RGB 146, pp. 62–63) that refers to old and new practices. Formerly musicians used *gamma ut*, but now they call it *gamma sol ut*, implying an expansion of the scale.

152. Korenev does not divide these six signs, *ut–la*, into happy and sad music, nor does he discuss or classify the different systems (*kliuchi* in Diletskii's terminology). In RGB 146, p. 15 (which precedes the theoretical section), Korenev does refer to various happy and sad emotions. He does not appear to regard these as theoretical categories, however, of the sort we see in the *Grammatika*.

153. Korenev's description is in RGB 146, p. 56; Diletskii's is in RGADA 541, fol. 7.

A detail from a late seventeenth-century Ukrainian icon shows a choirmaster with hand raised, directing an ensemble of twelve singers (including one small boy), all of whom are reading from what appear to be staff-notated sheets. The image is reproduced, for example, in Herasymova-Persyds'ka, *Khorovyi kontsert na Ukraini,* following p. 64, and in Morosan, *Choral Performance,* 52.

154. The *Nauka vseia musikii* has not been published in full, although a fairly substantial excerpt appears in Shabalin, *Pevcheskie azbuki,* 1:364–69; the summary here is also based on Protopopov, *Russkaia mysl' o muzyke,* 71–72; Tsalai-Iakimenko, "Muzykal'no-teoreticheskaia mysl' na Ukraine," 353–59; and Konotop, "K voprosu," 83–85, an important correction to Tsalai-Iakimenko's method of transcription. A later discussion of the treatise in Tsalai-Iakymenko, *Kyivs'ka shkola muzyky,* 305–308, only partially addresses some of the issues brought up by Konotop.

According to Protopopov and Konotop, the *Nauka* appears in RNB, Q.XII.1 (a late-seventeenth-century source that includes other works on music, described in Kalaidovich and Stroev, *Obstoiatel'noe opisanie slaviano-rossiiskikh rukopisei,* otd. 2:285, and the source for Shabalin's excerpt); RGB, Muz. sobr., No. 3893 (late seventeenth century, with Tikhon's treatise); MGK V 68 (1740s, also with Tikhon and Mezenets); and in a lost source from the Sakharov library (Sakharov, "Issledovaniia," 168). The use of the term *nauka* (science or study) in the title recalls presentations of the seven liberal arts.

155. Metallov, "Starinnyi traktat," 1753–54, long ago called attention to this passage (in Korenev in RGB 146, p. 56; Sakharov, "Issledovaniia," 168; and Shabalin, *Pevcheskie azbuki,* 1:364). Metallov was working with GIM 777, which includes excerpts from Korenev's treatise at the opening of the *Grammatika;* he thus compares this text to passages in Diletskii's treatise rather than to Korenev's. See above on Diletskii's references to beating time and conducting. Other passages in the *Nauka* also recall Korenev; the references in the *Nauka* to the notation of the "Romans" and the comparison of Kievan and Western oval notation are illustrated in Shabalin and in Protopopov, "Neizvestnoe posobie po teorii muzyki," 295; see Korenev's discussion in RGB 146, pp. 6–7. The presentation of rhythmic notation in the *Nauka* is also close to that in Korenev. There are also some interesting differences. In the *Nauka,* the sharp sign is used to indicate a slur (Konotop, "K voprosu," 85); Diletskii also mentions this usage but forbids it, saying that only ignorant people do such a thing (RGB 107, p. 122). Protopopov, *Russkaia mysl' o muzyke,* 71, even points to specific Western models, in particular Starowolski, for the *Nauka;* the passages he enumerates are not published and were unavailable for the present study. The close ties between Korenev and the *Nauka,* however, make the idea particularly intriguing.

156. The Korenev-Diletskii pairing is with the Moscow 1679–81 version of the *Grammatika* (including the very early sources GIM 1340 and RGB 146 as well as the later sources GIM 777 and Tver' 651a, which transmit a mixed version of Diletskii's text and excerpts from Korenev's). An exception is the source Kostroma f. 670, No. 44, which includes excerpts from Korenev with Tikhon's *Kliuch.* Brazhnikov, *Drevnerusskaia teoriia,* 392, observes the circulation patterns of Tikhon's work. The late-eighteenth-century source GIM, sobr. Barsova, No. 1382, which includes excerpts from the *Grammatika* along with Tikhon's *Kliuch* and with what are apparently carefully selected examples of *partesnoe*-style works, is surveyed in Aravin, "U istokov russkogo mnogogolosiia." Tsalai-Iakimenko, "Muzykal'no-teoreticheskaia mysl' na Ukraine," 357, n. 11, says that Korenev's *O penii bozhestvennom* circulates with the *Chetvertaia mudrost' Musika* (discussed above under the title *Mudrost' chetvertaia Musikia*) in NBU, Sof. sobr., No. 127/381. The *Nauka*

vseia musikii circulates in collections that also include Tikhon's and Mezenets's works (RGB, Muz. sobr., No. 3893 and MGK V 68; see Protopopov, *Russkaia mysl' o muzyke*, 71–72).

157. This work is discussed in Protopopov, *Russkaia mysl' o muzyke*, 72–74, and in his "Neizvestnoe posobie po teorii muzyki," 295–302.

158. The *Kratkosobrannaia mussikiia* does refer to "many skillful composers" who build a composition beginning with the bass (derived from the Latin word *basis*) because the bass voice is the foundation (*fundament, osnovanie*) upon which the other voices are built; this is, indeed, the advice Diletskii gives in his own treatise. The *Kratkosobrannaia mussikiia* follows up on this advice with some examples of bass motion in a *kontsert*, echoing, although not duplicating, Diletskii's series of compositional rules. Another nod to musical authority lies in the author's deliberate, if not always accurate, use of Latin terminology.

159. The author does present flat and sharp signs at the end of the short treatise but does not refer to *bemmoliarnaia* or *diezisovaia* as specific categories of music; none of the musical examples in the work includes a flat or a sharp. The writer also does not distinguish between B and H, using the letter B throughout. Furthermore, he uses the same solmization syllable-letter names throughout his series of scales, with only two exceptions (F *fa ut* instead of F *fa* in the scale beginning on G, and E *mi* instead of E *la mi* in the scale beginning on A). The author explains, as did Diletskii, that in the letter-syllable pairings, *la* is below, *re* is above (although the example in the *Kratkosobrannaia mussikiia* is slightly different).

160. Protopopov, "Neizvestnoe posobie po teorii muzyki," 301 and n. 12.

161. RGB 107, p. 170. The translation in the *Kratkosobrannaia mussikiia* is almost identical (one word is omitted and several words are reversed in order). The hymn text also appears in L'viv, p. LXXVII, where it is written out in Latin letters (with the same errors in transmission), but with no suggested translation of the text.

162. Protopopov identifies Baronius in *Russkaia mysl' o muzyke*, 73 and note, citing only the 1719 printed edition. This passage appears in a later edition of his work, *Annales Ecclesiastici, auctore Caesare Baronio* (1744), 16:534. On Baronius's long circulation in Muscovy, see Bubnov, "'Deianiia tserkovnye i grazhdanskie' Tsezaria Baroniia." The 1719 publication is described in Bykova and Gurevich, *Opisanie izdanii, napechatannykh kirillitsei*, 208–11 (item No. 122); other copies of the work in Russia are described in Bobrova, *Biblioteka Petra I*, Nos. 893–94, and Pekarskii, *Nauka i literatura v Rossii*, 2:446–47. Baronius's work was well known in Muscovy in the seventeenth century, and Simeon Polotskii had a copy in his library; see Hippisley, "Simeon Polotsky's Library," 53 and 60, and Iusim, "Knigi iz biblioteki Simeona Polotskogo-Sil'vestra Medvedeva." The nineteenth-century manuscript copy is described in Bubnov, *Opisanie Rukopisnogo otdela Biblioteki Akademii nauk SSSR*, vol. 3, vyp. 3:115–16.

163. RGB 146, p. 82. This section is discussed in Jensen, "Nikolai Diletskii's *Grammatika*," 163–72.

164. The source is Tver' 553, where the drawings are headed "A method of teaching young children and anyone who wants to study," followed by a text close to the Moscow 1679–81 version of the "Manner of teaching children." Two hands, one blank and one with the letters A–G, complete this brief introduction. The long series of forty-two musical hands follows (fols. 1v–9). On the date of this source see Jensen, "Nikolai Diletskii's *Grammatika*," 383–84, and Protopopov, PRMI 7:491.

165. Excerpts from this manuscript, RNB, sobr. Viazemskogo, Q.215, are published

in *Znameniia osmoglasnago peniia;* see also Brazhnikov, *Drevnerusskaia teoriia,* 407–408. The ordering of the hands in this source differs from that in Tver' 553. In the Viazemskii manuscript, the hands are listed according to vocal ranges in the different systems. In Tver' 553, the hands are arranged by system (*duralnyi, bemmoliarnyi,* and *diezisovyi*) in the various clefs and vocal ranges.

166. Gorczyn's *Tabulatura muzyki* (1647) was available in photographs generously supplied by the late V. V. Protopopov; it has been reprinted in *Monumenta musicae in Polonia.* Fragments from the treatise are published in Prosnak, "Z dziejów staropolskiego szkolnictwa muzycznego," 14–15, and see also Pamuła, "*Tabulatura muzyki* Jana Aleksandra Gorczyna." Judging from the lists of musical publications in Przywecka-Samecka, *Dzieje drukarstwa muzycznego w Polsce,* few theoretical treatises were published in Poland during the seventeenth century. Gorczyn also wrote another introductory work, *Nowy sposób Arythmetyki* (A New Method of Arithmetic), published in the same year.

167. Chap. 3, "Jako na palcach Scalam tych głosow pamiętać," and the diagram of the hand, "Partes na ręku Diszkantu," in Gorczyn, *Tabulatura muzyki,* sig. C[1]v–C2.

168. Polish theorists were also aware of musical practices to the east. See, for example, the reference to the music of the "Rutheni" in Starowolski, *Musices practicae erotemata,* sig. F6. As noted in chapter 2, another Westerner, Johannes Herbinius, described singing at the Kievan Caves Monastery and provided a notated example.

169. The published translation of Iavorskii's *Ritoricheskaia ruka* is based on a nineteenth-century manuscript from the Viazemskii collection (No. 10, octavo); the chapter heading is on p. 21 and the drawing of the hand on p. 10.

170. RGADA, f. 381, No. 1195, fols. 2–2v. The untitled work in manuscript 1195 is summarized in Jensen, "Nikolai Diletskii's *Grammatika,*" 8–11, with a description of the source (pp. 385–87), which appears on watermark evidence to date from between the 1750s and the 1770s.

171. RGADA, f. 381, No. 1474 is summarized in Jensen, "Nikolai Diletskii's *Grammatika,*" 12–13, with a physical description on pp. 387–89. Again, modern orthography would require a soft sign for the word *nachal'nyi.*

172. "Onye azbuki s podlinnymi svidetelstvoval Ipodiakon Ivan Nikitin," for example, in RGADA 1195, spread across fols. 490ff. (the two sections of the manuscript have separate foliations). "Svidetelstvoval" plus the same three signatures also appear on fols. 485ff., and see also RGADA 1474, fol. 12v.

173. The text of the printed *Azbuka* is published in Shabalin, *Pevcheskie azbuki,* 1:346–48. Facsimiles of two folios are in Vol'man, *Russkie pechatnye noty,* following p. 32, with a brief discussion of the work on pp. 23–24. There is a single line of music in the RGADA sources that does not appear in the printed version in Shabalin.

174. On those involved in the 1772 edition (Irmologii, Oktoikh, Prazdniki, and Obikhod), see Vol'man, *Russkie pechatnye noty,* 20 (citing Razumovskii, *Tserkovnoe penie v Rossii,* 90). Another inscription in the anonymous treatise in RGADA 1195 (beginning on fol. 42) is also tied to the Synod, for it mentions Stepan Beshkovskoi, the head of the Synodal Press.

175. The nineteenth-century manuscript copy is listed in Shabalin, *Pevcheskie azbuki,* 2:634. The engraved hand in RGADA 1474 is blank on its verso, suggesting that it did not belong to the printed edition (which would have had the title on the other side). One wonders if it might represent a separate printing—hands only—recalling the alphabet sheets issued in the seventeenth century.

176. The work's full title emphasizes its practical aims: *Opyt irmoloinago peniia,*

v kratkikh pravilakh v Belogorodskoi dukhovnoi seminarii dlia legchaishago onomu izucheniia napisannyi (A Method of Irmologii Singing, Written in Brief Rules at the Belgorod Theological Seminary for Its Easiest Comprehension) (1798). The diagram of the hand appears on p. 7. The manuscript original of the work is in RGADA, f. 381, No. 1590, with corrections and the approval signature of Bishop Feoktist (Mochul'skii), to whom the work has been attributed; he also wrote other treatises on liturgical singing. Many thanks for this information to Evgenii Vorob'ev, who, in his forthcoming study, calls Feoktist the "last soldier of Guidonian solmization."

6. The Muscovite Court Theater

1. Rinhuber, *Relation du voyage en Russie*, 29: "Quam rem admiratus magnus Czar decem horis imobilis adspexit. Res haec certe melioris fortunae erit initium" (reprinted in Koch, "Die Sachsenkirche in Moskau," 315). Biographical information and a Russian translation of portions of Rinhuber's writings are in Brikner, "Lavrentii Ringuber," where the passage above is translated on p. 401; see also the discussion below. The ten-hour figure is cited ubiquitously and has been justified, for example, on the basis of other lengthy ceremonies favored by the Russian court and church. Judging from the preserved text of the play, however, it is difficult to understand exactly how it might have been extended to such a great length—perhaps with much repetition (and fortitude on the part of all concerned). Kholodov, "K istorii starinnogo russkogo teatra," and his posthumous *Teatr i zriteli*, chaps. 1 and 2, reviews evidence of the tsar's attendance, the positioning of the other spectators, and the date of the first performance.

2. There are excellent studies of these plays, including editions of the surviving texts, in *RRD* 1 and 2, and see below for additional bibliography. An English-language summary of some of this information is in Jensen, "Music for the Tsar." Longworth, *Alexis, Tsar of All the Russias*, chap. 9, for example, refers to Aleksei's last, renaissance, years.

3. Reutenfels, *De rebus Moschoviticis*, 106–107, includes the German-language verses. The poem has been widely reprinted, for example in Koch, "Die Sachsenkirche in Moskau," 306–307; *RRD* 2:311–12; and Proehl, "Eine Beschreibung Moskaus durch den Kurländer Jakob Reutenfels," 470. A Russian translation is in Reitenfel's, *Skazaniia*, 301–302.

4. Reutenfels, *De rebus Moschoviticis*, 104–107 (and Reitenfel's, *Skazaniia*, 301–302). My deepest thanks go to Martha Lahana for providing a copy of this important text, and to Kent Webb for his advice on the translation from Latin.

5. The Innsbruck *komediia* is in *V-K 1645–1646, 1648 gg.*, 45.80; the Nuremburg report is in *V-K 1648–50 gg.*, 51.233–34, where the Danish ballet is reported in 40.112. The *kuranty* are discussed above, in chap. 4.

6. Mikulin's description of the music is in Bestuzhev-Riumin, *Pamiatniki diplomaticheskikh snoshenii moskovskogo gosudarstva s Angliei*, 336 (where he reports that at the banquet "igrali vo mnogie igry mnogie igretsy"). The account is reprinted in Likhachev, *Puteshestviia russkikh poslov*, where the reference to the many players is on p. 177. Orsino's account of the "wondrous music" is in Hotson, *The First Night of "Twelfth Night*," 199, and Hotson cites the payments to the Children of the Chapel on p. 18 (for "a show with music and special songs," although no source is given; the carol is on p. 18, and see n. 1). The passage on the "many players" is in Hotson, p. 194; see also the contemporary references in [Chamberlain], *The Letters of John Chamberlain*, 1:115. Hotson's study is controversial.

After the state dinner (and, unfortunately, after Mikulin and his party left), Orsino describes elaborate musical entertainments, a grand ball, and a comedy (Hotson, 201–202); Hotson believes the play was Shakespeare's *Twelfth Night,* although Orsino does not give the name of the play or its author in his account. There were many other musical preparations made for this state dinner. Mikulin did not mention any additional musical or theatrical events in his account, and such preparations may have been intended to accompany the play that followed the banquet; see the listings in Hotson, esp. 180–81.

     7. The Russian delegation was headed by A. M. L'vov-Iaroslavskii; see *RBS* 10:761–65, and Crummey, *Aristocrats and Servitors,* 183, on his career. Descriptions of the entertainments are in Radziwiłł, *Memoriale rerum gestarum in Polonia,* 2:95–98 (3 and 4 May, 1635, where the description of the theatrical performance reads: "Vesperi comoedia Italica [appellata 'recitativa'] musicis"); a Polish translation is in Radziwiłł, *Pamiętnik o dziejach w Polsce,* 1:449–52. The description in Solov'ev, *Istoriia Rossii s drevneishikh vremen,* 5: books 9–10:173–74, is based partially on Radziwiłł, but Solov'ev seems to have taken the Muscovite account in which the Judith story is identified from unpublished archival sources (apparently from RGADA, f. 79, Snosheniia Rossii s Pol'shei). Solov'ev quotes the Russian description as follows (p. 174): "a potekha byla, kak prikhodil k Ierusalimu assiriiskogo tsaria voevoda Alafern, i kak Iudif' spasla Ierusalim" ("and the entertainment was how the Assyrian tsar Holofernes came to Jerusalem, and how Judith saved Jerusalem," quoted from Soloviev, *The First Romanov,* 240). Robinson, in his introductory essay in *RRD* 1:47, also discusses the mission.

     8. The Russians were invited in mid-1637 to send emissaries to the wedding, which was scheduled for September, but the combination of the tardy invitation and bad roads made this impossible, and they arrived only in April 1638. See Solov'ev, *Istoriia Rossii s drevneishikh vremen,* 5: books 9–10:179–83 (citing unpublished manuscript sources, as above), and cited also in *RRD* 1:58 and 69–70. Solov'ev, 182–83, says that the king invited the Russian envoys to court "to see a comedy, in Russian, an entertainment" ("smotret' komedii, a po-russki—potekha"); the translation in Soloviev, *Michael Romanov, The Last Years,* 8, as inviting the Russian visitors "to attend a comedy and a Russian-style entertainment," is misleading. Berkov, "Iz istorii russkoi teatral'noi terminologii," 281–82, also cites this passage on the use of the terms *potekha* and *komediia.* The performance is identified more precisely in Radziwiłł, *Memoriale rerum gestarum in Polonia,* 2:269 ("Vesperi comoedia cantu musicorum de Daphne recitata"), and in Radziwiłł, *Pamiętnik o dziejach w Polsce,* 2:92 (both editions identify Puccitelli). On Puccitelli's work at the Polish court, see the entry on the librettist in *NG2* by Anna Szweykowska.

     9. Likhachev's report is in *DRV* 4:339–59, where his description of the banquet is on pp. 349–50 (there was dancing afterwards but the Russian party had already departed), and the music in the gardens is on p. 353. Roizman, *Organ,* 68–69, discusses the term *kimvaly* used in Likhachev's report, concluding that it most likely referred to harpsichord-type instruments; he also suggests that in this outdoor garden setting, the people who played the organs were statues. Roizman adds that Likhachev, while impressed by the circumstances of the performance, did not seem to be surprised by the mixed instrumental ensemble, which would have been familiar from Muscovite court practice. The Russians' care to avoid stepping into a Catholic church is recounted in the Italian documents covering this embassy; see Buturlin, *Bumagi florentinskogo tsentral'nogo arkhiva,* 45 (Italian) and 215 (Russian translation), which also lists the other sightseeing tours in the city.

There is another, much less colorful report of the mission, published in *PDS* 10: cols. 309–670, which does not mention the music (nor does it mention the theatrical production discussed below); this description places the banquet on 19 January.

10. Likhachev's description is in *DRV* 4:350–51, where it appears just after the entry for 20 January (although the account at this point may not be strictly chronological, for he follows this description with miscellaneous information about other excursions the party enjoyed). There is a partial English translation of this passage in Longworth, *Alexis, Tsar of All the Russias*, 210. Likhachev mentions no music in connection with this production (although it is hard to believe that it was entirely lacking), suggesting that whatever he saw, it was probably not an opera. Likhachev's amazement at the spectacle must have been obvious, for the prince, as the ambassador himself says, attempted to interpret the events on stage for his guest.

11. The Italian account is in Buturlin, *Bumagi florentinskogo tsentral'nogo arkhiva*, 45 (Italian) and 214–15 (Russian translation). After describing the "marvelous things," Likhachev adds: "and a small man came out and asked to eat and they gave him many [loaves of] unleavened bread and they couldn't fill him up ("i mnogo emu khlebov pshenichnykh opresnochnykh davali, a nakormit' ego ne mogli").

12. A note in the account in *PDS* 10: cols. 669–70, specifies the dates 23 June 1659 to 11 June 1660.

13. Hebdon's list (and the annotations apparently by the tsar himself) is in Gurliand, *Ivan Gebdon*, 46–49; Gurliand discusses the contents of the list and Hebdon's trip on pp. 16ff.; see also the "shopping lists" in Longworth, *Alexis, Tsar of All the Russias*, 120–21 and 133. A follow-up Muscovite mission to Florence in 1662–63, headed by Ivan Zheliabuzhskii, was also entertained with outings around the city. This group did not report any theatrical performances but they did see another staged event: animal baiting, involving lions, leopards, and other wild animals, which the Russian account also describes using the term *potekha* (*PDS* 10: cols. 735–36).

14. The itinerary for the Spanish portion of Potemkin's trip is based on the report published in *DRV* 4:360–457. The party arrived in Cadiz in December 1667 and, after a leisurely trip through Toledo and Seville, made its formal entrance into Madrid on 27 February/8 March 1668. See also Weiner, *Mantillas in Muscovy*, 1. The Muscovite embassy left for France in June. The *potekhi* and the visits to the *poteshnye dvory* (entertainment halls) are in *DRV* 4:428–29 and 439. Potemkin's tour of the Palacio Real is discussed in Weiner, "The Death of Philip IV of Spain," 184 and nn. 25 and 26.

15. Quoted from Jensen and Powell, "'A Mess of Russians,'" 140, n. 17; translation by John Powell from Catheux's journal, published in Galitzin, "Une ambassade russe à la cour de Louis XIV," 22.

16. Jensen and Powell, "'A Mess of Russians,'" 133–34.

17. At least, no such descriptions by Potemkin survive. Likhachev's account of his trip to Florence, after all, survives in versions both with and without a description of the party's theatrical experience, which would have been nearly impossible to reconstruct by relying only on the fairly uninformative Italian references. The differences between Potemkin's report and Catheux's journal are noted in Jensen and Powell, "'A Mess of Russians,'" 133, and see the passages in Catheux's journal in Galitzin, "Une ambassade russe à la cour de Louis XIV," 20–22.

18. The various pastimes are described in [Miege], *A Relation of Three Embassies*, 142. A general description of the restrictions faced by ambassadorial parties in Muscovy is in Poe, "*A People Born to Slavery*," esp. chap. 2.

19. The Vologda entertainments, quoted more fully in chapter 4, are in [Miege], *A Relation of Three Embassies,* 99–100.

20. Countess Anna Carlisle's presence is noted in Konovalov, "England and Russia: Three Embassies," 65. On the flip side of the coin, Ambassador Potemkin, in Paris in 1668, encountered French women in public but declined to make any observations. According to the Sieur de Catheux: "I asked him to tell me what he thought of them [several beautiful women who had been presented to Potemkin], and he responded that he had taken one [for wife] in his country, and that it was no longer permitted him to look upon others at length so as to be able to discuss his feelings" (Jensen and Powell, " 'A Mess of Russians,' " 137). Robinson, *Bor'ba idei,* 129–30, notes the presence of women at the 1637 entertainment the Russian envoys attended in Poland.

21. See for example, Roizman, *Organ,* 82, citing Kliuchevskii, *Kurs russkoi istorii,* 3:293, which, in turn, appears to be based on the sources from *DR* 3 listed below, n. 72. Longworth, *Alexis, Tsar of All the Russias,* 199, mentions the tsar's secret visits to Matveev's home; his sources are not clear.

22. "[N]ovykh . . . [latyn] v Moskve umnozhilosia, nauchili svoemu rukodeliiu kamedieiu igrat'," cited in Malyshev, "Zametka o rukopisnykh spiskakh Zhitiia protopopa Avvakuma," 388 (ellipsis as in Malyshev); he discusses the issue of authenticity on p. 381. Vsevolodskii-Gerngross, *Istoriia russkogo dramaticheskogo teatra,* 1:60, discusses the date of this passage, and Longworth, *Alexis, Tsar of All the Russias,* 185, mentions Matveev's and Polotskii's visit with Avvakum in August 1667, as does Martha Lahana in her un-published "Breaking the Rules in Muscovy: The Example of A. S. Matveev." Chapter 2 above gives another, later instance of Avvakum's concern with theatrical presentations.

23. As noted above in chapter 2, Repskii's varied career is known through a series of petitions he made in 1676; they are published in Starikova, "K istorii domashnikh kre-postnykh teatrov," 56–60, which forms the basis for the present discussion. (There are some inconsistencies in the various testimonies involved in the case; a detailed evaluation goes beyond the bounds of the present, general discussion.) Repskii's petition has been noted in the musical literature, for example in Roizman, *Organ,* 83, and Moleva, "Muzyka i zrelishcha," 152. Lahana, "Breaking the Rules," suggests that Repskii's petition might be read as part of the Miloslavskii family's denunciations of Matveev shortly after Aleksei Mikhailovich's death, and see also Starikova, 55.

24. In his statement, Polotskii lists his other students as including Semen [Sil'vestr] Medvedev and Semen and Vasilii Kazanets. Although Polotskii's influence on Repskii at this time is obvious, one might also consider how Polotskii himself might have responded to being in close contact over the course of several years with a musician of Repskii's training, particularly when considering the roles of music in Polotskii's later plays for the court theater.

25. The Courland meeting and its role in Ordin-Nashchokin's career is discussed in Ellersieck, "Russia under Aleksei Mikhailovich," 188–96. Other sources discuss the prep-aration of the same group of students (with the exception of Repskii) for diplomatic service; see Zabelin, *Opyty izucheniia russkikh drevnostei i istorii,* 1:197.

26. "[I] pisal perspektivy i inye shtuki, kotorye nadlezhit kh komedii; i rabotal tem zhivopisnym pismom velikomu gosudariu goda s tri," in Starikova, "K istorii domashnikh krepostnykh teatrov," 58. The reference to Engels is from Kharlampovich, *Malorossiiskoe vliianie,* 321, n. 4, citing testimony of F. Kazanets. Engels arrived in January 1670; references to his work on the theatrical project are in Bogoiavlenskii, "Moskovskii teatr," for example, on viii, 15, and 32. On Engels and on the term *perspektivy,* see Hughes,

"The Moscow Armoury," 210, and the same author's *Sophia*, 136 and 296, n. 12; *perspektivy* is also used to describe theatrical decorations in [Tolstoi], "Puteshestvie stol'nika P. A. Tolstogo," *Russkii arkhiv* 5 (1888): 36, and in the translation, *The Travel Diary of Peter Tolstoi*, 197, describing monastic theatrical props he saw in Naples in 1698.

27. Starikova, "K istorii domashnikh krepostnykh teatrov," 57; to add insult to injury, Repskii says that Matveev even forced him to marry against his will (p. 58).

28. Bogoiavlenskii, "Moskovskii teatr," xii, where he discusses the two venues for rehearsal, the Posol'skii prikaz and the Meshchanskaia sloboda, and see also the documents he cites on pp. 50–51 and elsewhere. In the description of Matveev's home in [Lyseck], "Posol'stvo Battoni," *Otechestvennye zapiski* 35 (1828), 327–28, there is no mention of musical instruments.

29. Hasenkruch's organ is discussed in Bogoiavlenskii, "Moskovskii teatr," 39 and 75–76, and in Roizman, *Organ*, 84–85; see below on Hasenkruch's role in the Orpheus production. Uspenskii, *Tsarskie ikonopistsy i zhivopistsy XVII v.*, 2:231, refers to Repskii's career as an artist after the 1676 petition.

30. Findeizen, *History*, 1:255. Other excellent studies repeat this information, for example, *SKK XVII v.*, pt. 2:429, and *RRD* 2:311; the association seems to have originated with Koch, "Die Sachsenkirche in Moskau," 306. Keldysh, *IRM* 1:197–98, expresses doubt concerning the Schütz attribution.

31. Kholodov, "K istorii starinnogo russkogo teatra," 155–58, surveys the range of dates assigned to the Orpheus production.

32. Hesse's report is in Hirsch, "Brandenburg und Russland," 292–93 (dispatch from 9/19 December 1674). The Polish children he mentions were probably from Polish or Belarusian merchant or artisan families who had relocated to Moscow (see below, n. 102). The list from 1673 is in Bogoiavlenskii, "Moskovskii teatr," 30, and the references from 1676 are on p. 67. There is also an incomplete reference from November 1675 on p. 57.

33. These sources also indicate that the term *ballet* (*balet*) should not necessarily be taken literally, as it often seems to have been in earlier literature, that is, as a staged, full-length dance, but in a more general meaning as entertainment that included dancing along with music, acting, and comedy. This makes sense, given the strictures about dancing in Muscovite court life. A preliminary study of the Orpheus production is in Jensen, "Orpheus in Muscovy."

34. The two dated enclosures are as follows: Helmfelt to Charles XI, 29 February 1672 (enclosure Moscow, 13 February), Skrivelser från generalguvernörer i Ingermanland (henceforth as Livonica II), vol. 180, Riksarkivet, Stockholm; and Helmfelt to Bengt Horn, Narva, 1 March 1672 (enclosure Moscow, 13 February), Bengt Horns Samlung, vol. 11, Riksarkivet, Stockholm. My deepest thanks to Martha Lahana for generously supplying the texts of these very important documents, and to Daniel Waugh and Ruth Petersky for help in transcribing and translating them.

35. On the dates for *maslenitsa* in 1672, see Kholodov, "K istorii starinnogo russkogo teatra," 156. In general on the traditions of role-playing associated with this season, see Likhachev, Panchenko, and Ponyrko, *Smekh v drevnei Rusi*, 175–202.

36. Simon Grundel Helmfelt to Charles XI, Narva, 29 December 1671, undated enclosure headed "Extract schreiben von Moscow," in Livonica II, vol. 180, Riksarkivet, Stockholm.

37. Ellersieck, "Russia under Aleksei Mikhailovich," 328–29, n. 55, also suggests

that Helmfelt's report is misfiled; see also Martha Lahana's forthcoming monograph on Matveev.

38. Kholodov, "K istorii starinnogo russkogo teatra," 157, also stresses this point; that is, that most of Reutenfels's description appears to apply not to *Artakserksovo deistvo* but to Orpheus.

39. Rinhuber was in Moscow between 1668 and 1672; he left just after the play premiered, in October 1672, to go with Paul Menzies to Vienna and Rome. He returned to Moscow for the first half of 1674, and then again in late 1674 or 1675 to 1678, and again, for a fourth time, briefly in 1684; see Brikner, "Lavrentii Ringuber," 399–417; Rinhuber, *Relation du voyage en Russie*, v–xi, and n. 73 below. Reutenfels's biography is summarized in *MERSH* 31:34–38. Kholodov, "K istorii starinnogo russkogo teatra," 157–58, also makes the link between Rinhuber and Reutenfels in Florence.

40. Other writers described *maslenitsa* using the term *bacchanalia;* see [Korb], "Korbs *Diarium itineris in Moscoviam,*" 1:273–74 (Poe, *Foreign Descriptions of Muscovy,* 189, lists a German-language edition of Korb's work from Leipzig in 1699, and a Latin version from Vienna in 1700 or 1701).

41. As Martha Lahana points out in her forthcoming monograph (citing Bogoiavlenskii, "Moskovskii teatr," 1), Aleksei originally ordered his court theater to be established at the Miloslavskii house, thus providing another connection between Orpheus and the official court theater. Eventually they constructed a new court theater, in Preobrazhenskoe.

42. A general survey of the English players in Europe is in Stříbrný, *Shakespeare and Eastern Europe,* chap. 1. A more detailed study of the Pickleherring character and his association with music is in Schrickx, " 'Pickleherring' and English Actors in Germany." As we shall see below, the character appears (as Pikel'gering) in another of the plays for Aleksei's court, *Temir-Aksakovo deistvo* (The Play of Tamerlane), and he also appears in Russian theatrical productions of the Petrine period (see, for example, Karlinsky, *Russian Drama from Its Beginnings,* 47, and the Tamerlane play text in *RRD* 2:68 and 71). Rosenberg (or Rosenburg) was physician to the tsar and, at the same time, he provided secret information to the Swedish government (Ellersieck, "Russia under Aleksei Mikhailovich," 38–39). One wonders if this might be why Helmfelt, another Swedish employee, was so well informed about the production.

43. One might speculate that in spite of Matveev's obvious desire to repeat the success, the death of the patriarch put an encore performance on hold.

44. Hippisley, "Simeon Polotsky's Library," 61. Greek figures are listed in Polotskii, *Orel rossiiskii,* xiv–xix; the references to Orpheus are on pp. 39 and 71 and to Ovid on p. 38.

45. Findeizen, *History,* 1:149.

46. *SKK XVII v.,* pt. 2:393, and Belobrova, *Nikolai Spafarii,* 4–5.

47. RGB 107, p. 12; Korenev's reference is in RGB 146, p. 12 (and in Rogov, *Muzykal'naia estetika Rossii,* 106 and 125).

48. Okenfuss, *The Rise and Fall of Latin Humanism,* chap. 1.

49. Buchner's text is published in Hoffmann von Fallersleben, "August Buchner," 13–38. General background on Schütz's ballet is in *NG2*.

50. Günther, "Neue deutsche Quellen," 666–67; Koch, "Die Sachsenkirche in Moskau," esp. 276–87; and *SKK XVII v.,* pt. 1:226–30 and pt. 4:684–85. Gregorii would have been a child at the time of the Schütz production, and there is no evidence that he saw it

or even that he was in Dresden at the time. Gregorii's own theatrical experiences remain largely unknown but, as Günther and Koch point out, there were ample sources of influence—school training and productions, Lutheran and Jesuit plays, English comedy, and other public performances—that would have informed Gregorii's general knowledge of public speaking and theater; see also Stone, "The Pastor and the Tzar," esp. 244ff. A discussion of the often strained relationships among the residents of the Foreign Quarter, with emphasis on Gregorii and his circle, is in Lahana, "Novaia Nemetskaia Sloboda," 107ff. and 124ff. The people involved in the theatrical productions were linked in many ways. Gregorii, for example, was Dr. Blumentrost's step-son; many of these figures are discussed in Kovrigina, *Nemetskaia sloboda Moskvy i ee zhiteli*, in addition to the sources cited above. Information on the cast members of *Artakserksovo deistvo*, based on the listing in Mazon and Cocron, *"La Comédie d'Artaxerxès,"* 55, is in Amburger, "Die Mitwirkenden bei der Moskauer Aufführung des 'Artaxerxes.'"

51. Some historians have suggested that there is some music extant from the court theater, based on the short musical pieces published in Shliapkin, *Tsarevna Natal'ia Alekseevna*, v–vi and 82–83, taken from a source dating from the early eighteenth century. However, according to Keldysh in *IRM* 1:199 and *IRM* 2:56 and 280 (musical example 9), the text of the piece Shliapkin assigns to the Esther play matches that of a work written in 1724 for the coronation of Catherine I, and indeed the preserved music looks very much like the top two lines, moving mostly in parallel thirds, of a *kant*. See also Günther, "Neue deutsche Quellen," 672, n. 1. Keldysh describes the song assigned to the character Amarfal (in the Judith play), which appears in Shliapkin's source, as a jumble of later chant motives ("popevki"); this excerpt is discussed below, esp. n. 111. This text does appear in Gregorii's *Judith* as a song (it is the fourth strophe of a song in the *mezhdosenie* between acts 3 and 4; *RRD* 1:399), and the source Shliapkin describes includes excerpts from specific roles from the play. The manuscript was compiled by the court dwarf Georgii Kordovskii (*SKK XVII v.,* pt. 3:280) and it also carries the inscription of the singer Grigorii (Shliapkin, iii). Thus, although there is nothing linking this tune specifically to Pastor Gregorii's earlier productions, one might at least regard it as representing an acceptable musical rendition (as far as one can judge from the published transcription) for Natal'ia's later performances, and the *kant*-like style would have been known at court in the mid-1670s.

52. "Depuis qu'ils sont revenu du peur que les Turqs les faisoit la plus grande occupation de ce primier Ministre [Matveev] est, à faire jouer des commoedies, jusques à s'eposer au theatre, pour faire tenir ordre aux enfants qui juoent." Mons Giøe to Conrad Bierman, Moscow 19 November 1672, Tyske kancelli, udenrigske afdeling, Rusland B 38, Rigsarkivet, Copenhagen; many thanks to Martha Lahana for providing the text of this source, and to Ben Albritton for his advice on the translation. The passage is also quoted in Forsten, "Datskie diplomaty pri moskovskom dvore," *ZhMNP* 9 (1904): 119, n. 3, and in Bushkovitch, "Cultural Change among the Russian Boyars," 99 (on which the present translation is based). On Giøe's connections and role in Muscovy, see Ellersieck, "Russia under Aleksei Mikhailovich," esp. 30–33 (and, on Staden's ambiguous career, p. 37 and n. 113); the Danish envoy Giøe was close to Matveev at this time and had every reason to be informed about the theatrical activities taking place. Lahana, "Breaking the Rules," traces the uneasy relationship between Giøe and Matveev, and see also Bushkovitch, 96–100. The task of keeping order at rehearsals may have been a difficult one. Bogoiavlenskii, "Moskovskii teatr," xi and 46, recounts the destructive power of the young actors on their surroundings.

53. Bogoiavlenskii, "Moskovskii teatr," iv and 1.

54. "2 chel. trubachei samykh dobrykh i uchenykh, 2 chel., kotorye-b umeli vsiakie komedii stroit' " (ibid., 1).

55. Ibid., 8.

56. "ia nashol 2 chelovek, kotorye nedavno izuchilis', a umeiut roznye musikiiskie pesni trubit' i mogut eshche nauchiti i inykh, a polnye trubachei nikogo ne uchat" (ibid., 3). The music guilds in Latvia are discussed in Braun, "National Interrelationships and Conflicts," and in his "Aspects of Early Latvian Professional Musicianship." Bogoiavlenskii, "Moskovskii teatr," 17, lists Johann Waldonn (Ivashko Valdov), who was hired later, as a "polnoi trubach." Findeizen, *History*, 1:395, n. 383, suggests that the term "polnoi" may be a misprint for "polevoi" (field trumpeter).

57. This point is also made, for example, in *IRM* 1:194–95, and in Roizman, *Organ*, e.g. p. 81.

58. Bogoiavlenskii, "Moskovskii teatr," iv, notes that Staden exceeded his original assignment; the references to the trumpeters are on pp. 3–4.

59. "[T]ri cheloveka molodykh, kotorye na vsiakikh igrakh igraiut, chto nikogda prezh sego na Moskve ne slykhano" (ibid., 5).

60. Ibid., 6 (the 1672 summary) and 18–19 (the contracts).

61. Ibid., 18–19; their nationalities are given in the 3 December summary on p. 6. The spelling of the names varies; spelling here is according to Bogoiavlenskii's transcription of the German-language contract.

62. Ibid., 6–7 and 18; p. 27 reports a reduced salary.

63. "Der Herr Obriste [Staden] hat auch Melthung gethan, dass mir unss um einen gueten Sänger und Laudenisten umthun sollten; dahin bemühen wir unss täglich" (ibid., 21). Paulsen's letter, dated 4 April 1673, indicates that she and Staden had been in contact earlier. She apologizes for her late reply, saying that she had just received his letter of invitation and that the troupe had wanted to go to Moscow from Riga the previous spring but had not been able to get permission from the Danish king.

64. The 3 December summary says that the *muzykanty* brought seven various instruments (ibid., 6); their contracts list eight instruments, including the organ, that they knew how to play (p. 19).

65. Ibid., 76. Roizman, *Organ*, 85, suggests that Hasenkruch waited to petition until Tsar Aleksei was dead and Matveev out of power, fearing he would not get much sympathy for his request otherwise. This seems to be the same strategy Repskii followed in his own petition.

66. See chapter 4. Roizman, *Organ*, 89–90, discusses Hasenkruch's organ, suggesting that he might have procured it in Arkhangel'sk in his capacity as a trader.

67. Bogoiavlenskii, "Moskovskii teatr," 17–19 (a request for payment, with the contracts entered as proof of agreement); p. 40 (the departure of Waldonn in 1674); and pp. 47–48 (from 1675 on the runaway *muzykanty*). These documents are also cited in Findeizen, *History*, 1:394–95, n. 383.

68. Roizman, *Organ*, 75–76.

69. Hasenkruch is mentioned throughout Bogoiavlenskii, "Moskovskii teatr," indicating that he had a continuing role in theatrical activities, especially concerning costumes, which may reflect his activities as a merchant. In Bogoiavlenskii, 39, Hasenkruch is listed among the players (*igretsy*), with the *muzykanty* forming a different group, and "Simon arganist" and his students yet another group; on p. 30, the *muzykanty* are listed as one group, and Timofei Gazenkrukh and his associates as a separate group (the word

igretsy is not used). The term *igrets* has been the subject of some discussion. Kudriavtsev, 'Artakserksovo deistvo'—*Pervaia p'esa russkogo teatra*, 25, n. 72, suggests that *igrets*, used to describe Hasenkruch's activities, indicated a musician, and Keldysh, *IRM* 1:197, appears to support this interpretation. Roizman, *Organ*, 90, however, leans toward an interpretation of the term as signifying an actor rather than a musician. In the performance described in Helmfelt's "Extract," Hasenkruch was clearly an actor, although the role he played, as Pickleherring, had musical associations.

70. *DR* 3: col. 1058; see also *DR* 3: cols. 1059–60.

71. *DR* 3: col. 1081, from October 1674.

72. *DR* 3: cols. 1131–32. These documents are entered between items from 8–9 December 1672 and are preceded by a brief description, apparently lacking some text, of a production of *Judith* (*DR* 3: col. 1131); Kholodov, "K istorii," 149–50, suggests that these references describe theatrical performances from November 9–13 of that year. As noted above in chapter 4, Roizman, "Iz istorii," 596–97, suggests that *stramenty* were some sort of mechanical, self-playing instruments in which wires were plucked to produce a tone and which were played along with other, conventional instruments. Keldysh, in *IRM* 1:196, suggests that such instruments were unlikely to have been used in the context of the theater but adds that the term was also used to indicate a mixed group of instruments, as appears to be the case in this document.

73. The Menzies mission is described in Dukes, "Paul Menzies and His Mission from Muscovy to Rome," where the trumpeters are mentioned on p. 91. The documents requesting the trumpeters are in *PDS* 4: col. 800, where the first request appears to come at the end of a long series of instructions for the mission, dated 11 October, following the signature of the clerk who drew up the documents (the instructions begin on col. 769). The request is repeated in the same column, clearly under the date 17 October, and it appears again on cols. 801–802, from 18 October. The request for the trumpeters is cited in Charykov, *Posol'stvo v Rim*, 28 (citing *PDS* 4:800), where it is placed clearly in the context of the theater. See also the reference in Protopopov, "Neizvestnoe posobie po teorii muzyki," 294.

74. Rinhuber, *Relation du voyage en Russie*, 29; his account is in a dispatch dated March 1673. Translation based on Stone, "The Pastor and the Tzar," 229, n. 59, and Brikner, "Lavrentii Ringuber," 401. Many thanks to Robert Fradkin for his advice on the translation of this text.

75. Important work on the meanings and contexts of the court theater appears in many sources; see the valuable introductory articles to *RRD* 1:7–98 (by O. A. Derzhavina, A. S. Demin, and A. N. Robinson) and discussions of individual plays in *RRD* 1 and 2 and *SKK*, and the extensive bibliography cited in all these sources; see also Robinson's expanded version of his essay in *Bor'ba idei*, chap. 2; and his "Pervyi russkii teatr." In this last essay, Robinson makes the important point that before the court theater was conceived, Simeon Polotskii had invoked the image of Esther to describe the situation of the new tsaritsa, Natal'ia (p. 13)—the relevance of the subject was thus certainly not lost on the audience at the opening production. Demin, "Russkie p'esy 1670-kh godov i pridvornaia kul'tura," surveys the themes of the court productions as a whole, and see also the observations in Crummey, "Court Spectacles in Seventeenth-Century Russia," esp. 139–40. Berkov, "Iz istorii russkoi teatral'noi terminologii," discusses the various terms used to describe the plays.

76. On the musical implications of the court plays, see, for example, Findeizen,

History, 1:251–57; Livanova, *Ocherki i materialy,* 1:177–89; Keldysh in *IRM* 1:196–202; and Günther, "Neue deutsche Quellen," 669–72. Other references are summarized in Jensen, "Music for the Tsar," 387–88. For a director's approach to the work, see [Muratova], "Irina Muratova: Debiut rossiiskogo muzykal'nogo."

77. The Vologda source (RGB, Vologodskoe sobr., No. 208) was discovered by I. M. Kudriavtsev and published in his *"Artakserksovo deistvo": Pervaia p'esa russkogo teatra.* This is the text published in *RRD* 1, cited throughout the present study. The Lyon copy (Bibliothèque de la Ville de Lyon, No. 1346) preserves the play's text in German and Slavic; it was published in Mazon and Cocron, *"La Comédie d'Artaxerxès."* This source lacks act 2, which is supplied in the Weimar fragment, published in Günther, "Das Weimarer Bruchstück," a (largely) bilingual version of act 2, scenes 1–6.

78. A summary sheet (Mazon and Cocron, *"La Comédie d'Artaxerxès,"* 54) also includes an act 7, scene 4 (described as "Mardoch. in solio, cum Judaeis"), apparently following the fourth *interscenium;* no text for such a scene survives in any copy of the play and it would, indeed, have been quite an anticlimax after the rousing choral finale of scene 3 and the wrapping up of the comic action in the final *interscenium.*

79. *RRD* 1:103–105, where the final word, *nemtsy,* can refer to Germans specifically or to foreigners in general; translation from Louria, "Comedy," 147 (spellings from this and all subsequent citations from her translation have been modified to fit the transliteration system used in the present volume). In the version of the play published in *RRD* 1:101, the character who delivers the prologue and epilogue is given the stage name Mamurza; no such name appears in the summary listing of characters in Mazon and Cocron, *"La Comédie d'Artaxerxès,"* 55. Rinhuber, in his description of the premiere, says that the tsar particularly enjoyed Blumentrost's performance (Blumentrost also played the role of Mordecai): "Indeed, following the performance of the play, the great Tsar expressed his thanks and approbation both to the author, Master M. Gregorii, and [to] Master Blumentrost's son, who had surpassed the other children by acting excellently in one of the principal roles" (translation from Stone, "The Pastor and the Tzar," 248, n. 105, citing Rinhuber, *Relation du voyage en Russie,* 30).

80. The language Gregorii assigns to Astin' and her attendants in act 1, scene 2 is extraordinary, beginning with her opening statement: "Let me say what I have in mind. I really think that the laws of nature should be changed.... Is it not because of custom that the male sex wants to be above us, although we women are the more beautifully endowed? It is an injustice" (Louria, "Comedy," 149, where the character is labeled by her biblical name, Vashti; *RRD* 1:108). Stone, "The Pastor and the Tzar," 235–37, sees Astin'/ Vashti as a fully characterized comic figure "in a play which has more comedy than is generally recognized," including, primarily, the role of Haman. For a different approach to analyzing the play's overall structure, see Sofronova, "O strukture dramaticheskogo siuzheta."

81. Louria, "Comedy," 198; *RRD* 1:227.

82. Stone, "The Pastor and the Tzar," 240 (where the dog terminology is described in n. 78). Many thanks to Robert Fradkin for his advice on the *interscenia* titles. The *interscenia* characters are listed in the summary sheet of the Lyon copy in Mazon and Cocron, *"La Comédie d'Artaxerxès,"* 54–55, and in the Vologda copy in *RRD* 1:102.

83. Mazon and Cocron, *"La Comédie d'Artaxerxès,"* 54 and 89; translation from Stone, "The Pastor and the Tzar," 240 and n. 79.

84. Mazon and Cocron, *"La Comédie d'Artaxerxès,"* 54, with the lament text begin-

ning on 86, and *RRD* 1:120. A female attendant, Naomi, makes her appearance known by speaking in the brief dialogue that concludes the scene—it is not clear if she remains on stage throughout or enters at the end of the soliloquy.

85. In the first of the three segments, the Russian text has only three lines in the series of exclamations (*RRD* 1:120, and Mazon and Cocron, *"La Comédie d'Artaxerxès,"* 87); the German text has four (Mazon and Cocron, 86). In the following two segments, the Russian text has four lines.

86. *RRD* 1:135–37 (Vologda text); translation from Louria, "Comedy," 160. The listing of the "aria" in the Cyrillic text of the Weimar copy is in Günther, "Das Weimarer Bruchstück," 159. The summary list is in Mazon and Cocron, *"La Comédie d'Artaxerxès,"* 54, although this act is not preserved in the Lyon copy.

87. *RRD* 1:146; Louria, "Comedy," 164.

88. Louria, "Comedy," 180; *RRD* 1:185.

89. The Latin, German, and Slavic texts are quoted from Mazon and Cocron, *"La Comédie d'Artaxerxès,"* 155–57, where the psalm texts are identified in the notes; the non-psalm portions of the English translation are from Louria, "Comedy," 182; *RRD* 1:188.

90. Mazon and Cocron, *"La Comédie d'Artaxerxès,"* 154–55 (where the incomplete German transliteration from Hebrew begins: "Anna Jehovah hoschiah na"), and Louria, "Comedy," 182; *RRD* 1:187–88.

91. Polotskii, *Izbrannye sochineniia,* 213 (second foreword to the translation).

92. Günther, "Neue deutsche Quellen," 670, comes to the same conclusion.

93. Texts in this passage from the Lyon manuscript (Mazon and Cocron, *"La Comédie d'Artaxerxès,"* 172–81); English translation (except the psalm texts) from Louria, "Comedy," 186–89; *RRD* 1:198.

94. Mazon and Cocron, *"La Comédie d'Artaxerxès,"* 240–45; translation in Louria, "Comedy," 205–206; *RRD* 1:244–46.

95. The direction "Mox conjungenda cum Musica" (They then join together in music) appears in the German text only, just before the song text is cued in (Mazon and Cocron, *"La Comédie d'Artaxerxès,"* 258; see *RRD* 1:256); the text in this scene also alludes to psalms and other biblical passages (Mazon and Cocron, 263, n. 3). The scene is translated in Louria, "Comedy," 209–10.

96. Rinhuber, *Relation du voyage en Russie,* 154.

97. Early writing exploring the connection between musical laments and gender are by Ellen Rosand, Susan McClary, and Suzanne Cusick—their work has stimulated a great deal of later writing on the subject. Bochkarev, *Russkaia istoricheskaia dramaturgiia,* 26–27, mentions the prominence of female roles in the earliest plays and, in a separate passage, notes the presence of the laments (pp. 65–66). Many visitors remarked upon the strong link in Russia between funeral lamentation and gender. See for example, "The Voyage, wherein Osep Napea the Moscovite Ambassadour returned home into his countrey," 435 and 437 (from 1557–58), which mentions both wedding and funeral laments by women, as well as Paul of Aleppo's remarks, describing the relatively restrained lamenting (as compared to the Middle Eastern traditions with which he was accustomed) by women during the plague (Paul of Aleppo, in Belfour 1:333–34 and Murkos 4 [1897]: 173, in the town of Kolomna).

98. The story is translated in Zenkovsky, *Medieval Russia's Epics, Chronicles, and Tales,* 490–501 (which includes some references to singing and song); *RRD* 2:28 points out the presence of the Adam and Eve story in the Tale of Misery-Luckless-Plight ("Povest' o Gore-Zlochastii"). Diletskii's reference is in RGB 107, p. 12.

99. M. D. Kagan, in *SKK XVII v.*, pt. 2:178–79, notes the importance of the subjects of the three earliest plays—Esther, Judith, and Tobit—in the views of Martin Luther. According to *RRD* 1 and 2 and *SKK*, the titles and approximate dates are as follows: *Artakserksovo deistvo* (October 1672); *Iudif'* (Judith; February 1673); *Komediia o Tovii mladshem* (The Comedy of Tobit the Younger; November 1673, lost); *O Navkhodonosore tsare, o tele zlate i o triekh otrotsekh, v peshchi ne sozhzhennykh* (King Nebuchadnezzar, the Golden Idol, and the Three Boys Who Were Not Burned in the Furnace; copy bound in February 1674); *Temir-Aksakovo deistvo* (The Play of Tamerlane; February 1675); *Komediia o chude sviatogo Georgiia* (The Comedy of the Miracle of St. George; fall 1673 or 1675, lost); *Zhalobnaia komediia ob Adame i Eve* (The Mournful Comedy of Adam and Eve; 1675); *Malaia prokhladnaia komediia ob Iosife* (The Small and Refreshing Comedy of Joseph; November 1675, partially preserved); a play on the story of David and Goliath (January 1676, lost); a play on the story of Bacchus and Venus (January 1676, lost). Polotskii's *Komidiia pritchi o bludnem syne* (The Parable of the Prodigal Son) was written between 1673 and 1678; see below on the complex dating of this work. Kholodov, *Teatr i zriteli*, esp. 78–80, has a slightly different calendar of events.

100. Similarly, the play on the story of Joseph is only partially preserved; as it stands, the role of his wife, Vilga, is fairly prominent, and although it does not seem to include any extended musical elements, we cannot know how it might have been developed in the complete work. Baiazet's wife, Mikla, makes a very brief appearance at the end of the Tamerlane play, with a single exclamation of lament (*RRD* 2:88–91).

101. The authorship of the play is discussed in *SKK XVII v.*, pt. 1:320–22, and the following discussion is based on the text in *RRD* 2:115–37.

102. After the earliest performances, the theatrical planners recruited another group of young actors, in addition to the youths from the Foreign Quarter. This new group is identified as the *meshchanskie* children, from the non-Russian families of the newly settled suburb made up of merchants and artisans from Belarus and Poland (see Bogoiavlenskii, "Moskovskii teatr," xii, and Lahana, "Novaia nemetskaia sloboda," 87 and 125). Hesse probably referred to these two groups when he mentioned comedies staged by Polish and German youngsters; see n. 32 above. It is not clear which group performed the play about Adam and Eve.

103. German text in Spengler, *Schriften*, 1:401, modernized according to Günther, "Neue deutsche Quellen," 671 (where he also identifies the hymn as a source for the text in the play); translation from http://www.bach-cantatas.com/Texts/Chorale045-Eng3.htm (English translation by Francis Browne, November 2005). The Slavic and German texts are not identical, particularly in the final lines, in which the Slavic version refers to *kazn'* (literally, death, execution) visited upon all, as opposed to the German version, which specifies God's wrath visited upon Eve. Could this reflect doctrinal differences between the Eastern and Western churches over the nature of sin? In the Orthodox Church, humankind inherited the consequences of Adam's and Eve's transgression—death—but sin itself is not transferrable. Many thanks to Valerie Kivelson for pointing out the differences in these texts; although far beyond the bounds of this study, this is surely an issue worthy of further consideration. "Durch Adams fall" was among a long series of Lutheran hymn texts translated in the first decade of the eighteenth century by Pastor Ernst Glück, in connection with the academy he established in St. Petersburg (see Günther, 671, citing the texts published in Peretts, *Iz istorii razvitiia russkoi poezii*, where "Durch Adams fall" is on pp. 56–59 of the appendix); although the translation is rather free (Peretts, 106), a comparison might be revealing. Although it certainly would not have

taken much prodding for a German pastor to alight on the idea of translating a series of hymn texts for his new school, one might also suggest that here too, the popularity in Russia in the early decades of the eighteenth century of the hymn-like *kant* style might have provided an additional spur. Strophic part singing is not the only similarity; both types share a general affinity for an AAB-type poetic and musical layout as well.

104. Eleonskaia, " 'Plach Adama' v tvorchestve russkikh pisatelei XVII v.," 25–26, places the play's lament text in the context of the long Russian tradition, and see also chapter 3 above.

105. The dating and source transmission of *The Prodigal Son* is complex; it is preserved, in a source that also includes Polotskii's setting of the Nebuchadnezzar tale, in a manuscript compiled in 1678. In addition to its relatively widespread transmission in manuscript sources, this play is also preserved in an early and controversial published edition carrying the date 1685—scholars now believe that the publication is actually from a later date (see *RRD* 2:313–24). Illustrations from this publication are widely reproduced (for example in Polotskii, *Izbrannye sochineniia,* following p. 160, and Findeizen, *History,* 1:256). Nikolaev, "Russkie intermedii XVII v.," suggests that texts preserved in a Viennese collection (Österreichische Nationalbibliothek, Cod. slav. 174), dating from the 1690s, may contain *intermedia*-like material, including singing and *musikiia,* associated with Polotskii's plays; see also Sazonova, *Literaturnaia kul'tura Rossii,* 333.

106. On the theatrical context of Polotskii's declamations, see, for example, Vsevolodskii-Gerngross, *Istoriia russkogo dramaticheskogo teatra,* 1:56–57, where he also points out (as noted above in chapter 2) that the declamations were, in some cases, treated as private entertainments, on occasion performed in private homes. One wonders why Polotskii was not involved in the theater from the very beginning. Perhaps he was cooling his heels, waiting to see whether or not the enterprise would be successful, for he certainly had no hesitation about jumping in after the initial favorable response.

107. This discussion is based on the text of the play in *RRD* 2:161–71.

108. The stage directions say: "And they begin to play the horns (trumpets) and to pipe" ("I nachnut trubiti i piskati"); *RRD* 2:165.

109. Velimirović, "Liturgical Drama in Byzantium and Russia," 367. The text in the liturgical drama is first spoken by the archdeacon and then sung by the children, and this layout—speaking the lines and then singing them—is duplicated in Polotskii's rendition.

110. The text is in the *Oxford Annotated Bible with the Apocrypha,* 94–95 (Judith 16), and compare to *RRD* 1:456–58.

111. *RRD* 1:398–99. The text assigned to Amarfal in the *mezhdosenie* is one of two texts supplied with music in the early eighteenth-century source described in Shliapkin, *Tsarevna Natal'ia Alekseevna,* v–vi; see n. 51 above. The monophonic musical setting for this text, described in Shliapkin, v, as a transcription from "old notes" ("starye noty"—thus apparently transcribed from staff notation rather than from neumes) is quite problematic, but there is some sense that the musical line follows roughly the strophic arrangement of the text (although it is not laid out clearly in the transcription).

112. The fox tail scene is in *RRD* 1:441. Findeizen, *History,* 1:398, n. 389, calls attention to this sequence, as does Derzhavina, "Zhanrovaia priroda pervykh russkikh p'es," 67ff. According to Stříbrný, *Shakespeare and Eastern Europe,* 18, in an illustration published in 1621, Pickleherring wears a cap "decorated with a fox brush as a sign of his cunning"—one must admit, however, that cunning is a trait quite absent from the Susakim character in the Muscovite play.

113. *RRD* 3 covers early eighteenth-century school drama in Moscow, and see the

brief discussion and bibliography on the school dramas in Belarus and Ukraine, for example, in Kotliarchuk, *Prazdnichnaia kul'tura,* 68–70; Petrov, "O slovesnykh naukakh," *TKDA* nos. 11 and 12 (1866); Karlinsky, *Russian Drama from Its Beginnings,* 14–33; Lewin, "The Ukrainian School Theater"; and the same author's "The Staging of Plays at the Kiev Mohyla Academy" (although it is not clear why she suggests [p. 321] that the court theater may have sent theatrical equipment to Kiev).

114. The *balety* mentioned above also seem to belong to the enhancements of the later plays, whether they were integrated into the main dramatic action, formed part of the *interscenia,* or were used in some different fashion. These *balety* seem to culminate in the planned performances of *David and Goliath* and *Bacchus and Venus,* for which the rehearsal records list dancers, actors portraying musicians on stage, elaborate costumes, a special person in charge of the dancing, etc. Documents are in Bogoiavlenskii, "Moskovskii teatr," 67–75, from early 1676.

115. This discussion is based on Sazonova, "Teatral'naia programma." The text of the play is in Tikhonravov, *Russkie dramaticheskie proizvedeniia,* 1:3–75.

116. The wedding scene with the call for instruments is in Tikhonravov, *Russkie dramaticheskie proizvedeniia,* 1:26–35, and see also the term *intermedium* in Sazonova, "Teatral'naia programma," 147.

117. The directions for this second *intermedium* are in Sazonova, "Teatral'naia programma," 147 ("Vlokh priidet do kozakov zaporozskykh, kotorye z vlokha kozaka nariadiat"; thanks to Elena Dubinets and Barbara Henry for their advice on this text). Lewin, "Polish-Ukrainian-Russian Literary Relations," 266–67, emphasizes the improvisatory aspect in Ukrainian *intermedia.* Sazonova, 135–37, outlines Trubetskoi's career and experiences.

118. Tikhonravov, *Russkie dramaticheskie proizvedeniia,* 1:55, and see the discussion in Sazonova, "Teatral'naia programma," 145.

119. See the passage for Aleksei's bride in Tikhonravov, *Russkie dramaticheskie proizvedeniia,* 1:55–57.

120. According to Sazonova, "Teatral'naia programma," 136, Trubetskoi achieved the rank of boyar in 1671. Crummey, *Aristocrats and Servitors,* 197–98, dates this event in November 1672, that is, after the court theater's opening.

121. [Lyseck], *Relatio,* 118–19; a Russian translation is in [Lyseck], "Skazanie Adol'fa Lizeka," 391–92. Paul Menzies, who had departed Moscow at the premiere of the first court play, had returned by spring 1674; he was not yet a general, however, at this time (Dukes, "Paul Menzies and His Mission from Muscovy to Rome," 93). This passage indicates a certain flexibility in the court plays, which (in this case at least) appear to have incorporated such comedic elements (and actors) as available.

122. Schlafly, "Filippo Balatri in Peter the Great's Russia," 195, and in his "A Muscovite *Boiarynia,*" 264–65. The description of the Judith drama is Schlafly's summary of Balatri (appearing in both articles), not a direct quotation from Balatri's diary.

123. [Tolstoi], *The Travel Diary of Peter Tolstoi,* 154. This passage begins in the context of Tolstoi's breathless description of Venetian theater: "impossible to describe adequately, and nowhere in the whole world are there such marvelous operas and comedies" (p. 153). For Tolstoi, everything was impressive: the theaters themselves, the costumes, the "marvelous music." Yet even here, Tolstoi notes the tradition of masks (and of women appearing in public) with some unease: "Many people come to these operas in *mashkarakh . . .* in Slavic, in masks, so that no one will recognize them if they are at the opera, because many come with their wives, and visiting foreigners also come with girls;

and because of this men and women put on masks and strange clothes, so that they are not recognized together." He then continues with his description of hand-holding on the square which, as editor Max Okenfuss notes (n. 69), strongly suggests some personal knowledge of the behavior of visiting foreigners.

124. *RRD* 1:88–89, and in Robinson, *Bor'ba idei*, 156ff.

125. Quoted and translated in Bushkovitch, "Cultural Change among the Russian Boyars," 99.

126. Schleussing's comments are in Lapteva, "Rasskaz ochevidtsa o zhizni Moskovii," 112; translation from Hughes, *Sophia*, 174, where she mentions the possible contact with Rinhuber (citing *Relation du voyage en Russie*, 229). Such contacts with visiting foreigners were important in transmitting the texts of the initial group of plays. For example, texts of *The Prodigal Son, Adam and Eve,* and *Joseph* were preserved in a late seventeenth-century manuscript compiled by Johan Sparwenfeld, the lexicographer who studied in Moscow in the mid-1680s. Sparwenfeld was close to foreigners there, including "Old Doctor Blumentrost," step-father to Pastor Gregorii and father of the young Blumentrost who performed in the court theater; he was also acquainted with the Golitsyn family, and worked on his language studies with personnel from the Diplomatic Chancellery. Sparwenfeld was an avid manuscript collector, he wrote poetry in Slavic, and he compiled the large dictionary cited many times above. See [Sparwenfeld], *J. G. Sparwenfeld's Diary*, 231 (Sparwenfeld's listing of his friends in Russia), and 13ff. (his activities as a collector), and *SKK XVII v.*, pt. 3:489–90. Descriptions of the Sparwenfeld manuscript in which the Muscovite plays were preserved are in *RRD* 2:296–97, and in Cherepnin, "Materialy po istorii russkoi kul'tury," 470–76. This manuscript is discussed at length in Dahl, *Codex Ad 10*.

127. "Chetyre knigi v dest', pismennyia: O stroenii Kamedii" (*Rozysknyia dela o Fedore Shaklovitom*, 4: col. 33); see also the reference in, for example, Berkov, "Iz istorii russkoi teatral'noi terminologii," 283. Hughes, *Sophia*, 175, reviews the lack of evidence for the regent's participation in theatrical productions or performances (within the larger context of her reported activities as an author), and see also Karlinsky, *Russian Drama from Its Beginnings*, 51, n. 22, and Shliapkin, *Tsarevna Natal'ia Alekseevna*, xi–xii. Thyrêt, *Between God and Tsar*, chap. 5, considers the many images used to bolster Sofiia's position as regent and ruler, including a reliance on Old Testament heroines, many of whom had appeared on stage during her father's last years, and both Thyrêt and Hughes discuss the performed recitations and texts written for Sofiia.

128. There are several studies of Natal'ia's theater: *SKK XVII v.*, pt. 3:278–89; Shliapkin, *Tsarevna Natal'ia Alekseevna; RRD* 4; Lebedeva, "Biblioteka Tsarevny Natalii Alekseevny" (an inventory of Natal'ia's extensive library, which also included a sizable collection of *kontserty*); and a series of important works by archivist L. M. Starikova, especially "Russkii teatr petrovskogo vremeni" and her *Teatr v Rossii XVIII veka*, chap. 1. See also Hughes, "Between Two Worlds," 30, and Bushkovitch, "Cultural Change among the Russian Boyars," 109–10. On Tsaritsa Praskov'ia, see the bibliography listed in *RRD* 4:14 and 641 (including the important references to contemporary accounts).

Epilogue

1. Kivelson and Greene, *Orthodox Russia*, 14.

2. For general background on Peter's abolition of the patriarchate and subsequent establishment of the Synod, see Hughes, *Russia in the Age of Peter the Great*, chap. 10. On the singers in the court (*pridvornyi*) choir (which supplanted the *gosudarevy pevchie*

d'iaki) and the new Synodal choir, see the articles by Chudinova in *MP* 2:456–78 and 3:96–100; *IRM* 2:57–64; Protopopov, *Muzyka na Poltavskuiu pobedu;* Butskaia, "Stefan Ivanovich Beliaev"; and Morosan, *Choral Performance,* 57–73. Bergholz's somewhat qualified praise of the singers is quoted above in chapter 2.

3. The writings of the Viatka observers are described in Waugh [Uo], *Istoriia odnoi knigi,* 106, 108, and 308; see also his "'Anatolii's Miscellany,'" 752. Other references to Peter's singing abilities are in Butskaia, "Stefan Ivanovich Beliaev," 154, and Dolskaya, "Choral Music in the Petrine Era," 177.

4. Important studies of *kant* and art song are in Findeizen, *History,* vol. 2; Livanova, *Russkaia muzykal'naia kul'tura,* vol. 1; *IRM* 2; and Dolskaya, "From Titov to Teplov." The legacy of the *kant* extends even to Glinka, who invoked the style in the famous "Slav'sia" chorus at the end of *A Life for the Tsar* (Brown and Mazo, *A Collection of Russian Folksongs,* 13, n. 46, citing Livanova, *Russkaia muzykal'naia kul'tura,* 1:466–67, n. 1; and see also Taruskin, *Defining Russia Musically,* 36).

5. On the assemblies and dancing in this period, see Sander, *Social Dancing,* and on instrumental ensembles, see Saverkina and Semenov, "Orkestr i khor A. D. Menshikova," and Porfir'eva, "Legenda o kapelle gertsoga golshtinskogo." Even the Spiritual Regulation suggested that seminarians might be entertained by instrumental music on important holidays, noting that this would not be difficult, "for only one musician in the beginning need be hired. Those interested seminarians who have learned from him shall be obliged also to teach the others without charge" (Muller, *The Spiritual Regulation of Peter the Great,* 42).

6. Bibliographical information on the eighteenth-century publications is in Vol'man, *Russkie pechatnye noty;* Findeizen, *History,* especially 2: chap. 19 (with extensive updated bibliography); Livanova, *Russkaia muzykal'naia kul'tura* (vol. 2 includes many excerpts); and *MP.* Texts are available in the microfilmed series of the items in *Svodnyi katalog.* Many of the theoretical works were issued by Khristian Ludvig Vever (Wewer), head of the Moscow University Press, which purchased a music typeface from Breitkopf in 1772. The first of Vever's initial batch of offerings was *Metodicheskii opyt, kakim obrazom mozhno vyuchit' detei chitat' muzyku stol' zhe legko, kak i obyknovennoe pis'mo* (1773), a translation of an anonymous French work from about a decade earlier: *Essai méthodique pour apprendre aux enfans à lire aussi aisément la musique, qu'on leur apprend à lire l'écriture ordinaire* (Liège: F. J. Desoer, ca. 1763, with a second edition from ca. 1768). Georg Simon Löhlein's *Clavier-Schule* (Leipzig and Züllichau, 1765, with several later editions) appeared as *Klavikordnaia shkola* in two volumes from 1773–74. David Kellner's *Treulicher Unterricht im General-Bass* (Hamburg, 1732, with many subsequent editions) was issued as *Vernoe nastavlenie v sochinenii general-basa* (1791). In 1764 Vever had offered Jean-Henri-Samuel Formey's popular *Abrégé de toutes les sciences* in a Russian translation. Ten years later, shortly after he acquired his Breitkopf type, he issued a second edition, which included a section on music. The various Russian editions of Formey are listed in *Svodnyi katalog* 3: Nos. 7867–74, and Mel'nikova, *Izdaniia, napechatannye v tipografii Moskovskogo universiteta,* Nos. 247–50 and 725–27.

7. See Poe, "*A People Born to Slavery,*" esp. chap. 4; the bibliography in the same author's *Foreign Descriptions of Muscovy,* 61–65; and Leitsch, "Herberstein's Impact."

8. This listing is drawn from Berry, *The English Works of Giles Fletcher,* 149–50 (cited also in Palmer, *Writing Russia in the Age of Shakespeare,* 153).

9. Olearius, *The Travels of Olearius,* vii–ix, and Poe, *Foreign Descriptions of Muscovy,* 159–60.

10. Anderson, "English Views of Russia in the 17th Century," summarizes these

images, and on p. 144 cites Sidney's verse, from sonnet 2 of his *Astrophel and Stella* (1591); see also the discussion of this sonnet (with a slightly different view) in Palmer, *Writing Russia in the Age of Shakespeare*, 78–79. Poe, *"A People Born to Slavery,"* traces the origins of these images in Western European narrative accounts, and other references to Muscovites in English literature of the period are in Draper, "Shakespeare and Muscovy," and Ruffmann, *Das Russlandbild im England Shakespeares*, esp. chap. 3.

11. The Barents account (1596) is discussed in Palmer, *Writing Russia in the Age of Shakespeare*, 167ff., in the context of *Measure for Measure*. On images of the north in the Western imagination, see Bedford, "Milton's Journeys North"; both sources include important bibliography. The European fascination with the Muscovite cold is discussed in Loewenson, "The Works of Robert Boyle."

12. Quoted from [Hall], *Hall's Chronicle*, 513 (from the editions of 1548 and 1550); see also Dillon, *Performance and Spectacle in Hall's "Chronicle,"* 9 (where the author notes that this court revel set the stage for similar performances for more than a decade), and 32. The reprint of Hall's *Chronicle* and its possible impact on Shakespeare's play is discussed in Sorensen, " 'The Masque of the Muscovites,' " and see also Palmer, *Writing Russia in the Age of Shakespeare*, 83ff. It is probably not a coincidence that the Russians in Henry's masquerade were yoked with the Turks, the other perennial Other in Western culture; see below.

13. A survey of early eighteenth-century Western writings about Russian music, which draws similar conclusions, is in Voznesenskii, "Khorovoe iskusstvo petrovskoi epokhi."

14. Stählin's "Nachrichten von der Musik in Russland" was published in *M. Johann Joseph Haigold's Beylagen zum neuveränderten Russland* (Riga, 1769–70), vol. 1. Biographical information and a Russian translation of his work is in Stählin [Shtelin], *Muzyka i balet v Rossii XVIII veka*, and see also Findeizen, *History*, vol. 2, passim.

15. The tune in *Essai sur la littérature russe*, 75, appears in Stählin's work in Stählin [Shtelin], *Muzyka i balet v Rossii*, 66.

16. On Guthrie, see Papmehl, "An Eighteenth-Century English Translation," and the additional bibliography cited there. Many of Guthrie's illustrations are reproduced in Findeizen, *History*. Cross, "Early British Acquaintance with Russian Popular Song and Music," includes information on individual Russian songs published in England and refers to the review of Guthrie's book in the *Monthly Review* (December 1795). On the various editions of the Prach collection, see Brown and Mazo, *A Collection of Russian Folk Songs*, xi.

17. Pepys, *The Diary of Samuel Pepys*, 1: part 2 (April 1661–December 1662, paginated separately), p. 377 (27 November 1662) and p. 402 (29 December 1662). Pepys's diary is also cited in Konovalov, "England and Russia: Three Embassies," 60–61.

18. The "Gawdy spectators" are in *Occasional Reflections upon Several Subjects*, 388 (Reflection 5). John Evelyn noted similarly that in Potemkin's 1681 party, "nothing was so splendid & exotick, as the Ambassador" himself ([Evelyn], *The Diary of John Evelyn*, 4:262). Anderson, "English Views of Russia in the 17th Century," 153, calls attention to the gifts themselves as indicating the Russians' alien status. There are two portraits of Potemkin dating from his 1681–82 trip. One is a full-length painting by Juan Carreño de Miranda, now in the Prado Museum; see *Museo del Prado*, 1:516. Color reproductions are in Lorente, *The Prado*, 2:100, and in *Rossiia i Ispaniia*, 1: following p. 256. Another portrait, a three-quarters view, was painted in England by Sir Godfrey Kneller; see Dukelskaya and Renne, *The Hermitage Catalogue of Western European Painting*, 13:91–92.

A copy of this painting is in the Armory of the Moscow Kremlin. Two engravings were made from Kneller's portrait: one ascribed to Abraham Blooteling (Dukelskaya and Renne, 13:91, and Stewart, *Sir Godfrey Kneller*, 124, No. 585); and another by Robert White. A reproduction of White's engraving is in Vinogradoff, "Russian Missions to London," following p. 52; and see also Cracraft, *The Petrine Revolution in Russian Imagery*, 162–63 and fig. 35.

19. Cross, *The Russian Theme*, 5, suggests the connection between Mikulin and Heywood; the ambassador appears in [Heywood], *The Dramatic Works of Thomas Heywood*, 2:115–20 (act 1, scene 1; plays in the volume paginated separately). *The Travels of the Three English Brothers* was written by John Day, William Rowley, and George Wilkins and acted in 1607; see the edition by Parr, *Three Renaissance Travel Plays*, 84–87 (scenes 4 and 5) and the introductory remarks on 7–20, as well as the discussions in Chew, *The Crescent and the Rose*, 504–509, and chaps. 6 and 7 passim.

20. Jensen and Powell, " 'A Mess of Russians,' " 137–38. Palmer, *Writing Russia in the Age of Shakespeare*, 192–95, discusses bear imagery, with emphasis on Shakespeare. John Chamberlain, for example, compared Ambassador Mikulin to a "dauncing beare" (*The Letters of John Chamberlain*, 1:123). Samuel Collins made his own contribution to this imagery in a little poem: "if you you [*sic*] have heard the Musick of the Sphears / Pray stay and hear the Musick of the Bears. / Which do at pleasure force both smiles and tears." (*The Present State of Russia*, 31).

21. Translation by John Powell in Jensen and Powell, " 'A Mess of Russians,' " 140, n. 20; French verse original on p. 134.

22. Ibid., 141, n. 23; French text on p. 134.

23. The play is summarized in ibid., 141, n. 22.

24. Depping, "Une ambassade russe à Paris en 1654," 145; see Jensen and Powell, " 'A Mess of Russians,' " 135.

25. Vinogradoff, "Russian Missions to London," 54, and see further Jensen and Powell, " 'A Mess of Russians,' " 136.

26. Translation by John Powell in Jensen and Powell, " 'A Mess of Russians,' " 142–43, n. 41; French text on p. 136.

27. Ibid., 137, and see also p. 143, n. 47 on the "Cérémonie turque" in *Le bourgeois gentilhomme* and its similar origins in diplomatic *faux pas*. Depping, "Une ambassade russe à Paris en 1654," 143, notes the similarity, from the French point of view, of the Muscovites and the Turks, and see above on the appearance of both in Henry VIII's masquerade; other links between Muscovites and Turks in the early sixteenth century are noted in Poe, *"A People Born to Slavery,"* 19ff. John Evelyn echoed the connection in describing the Russian ambassador's speech in a 1667 visit: "halfe of it consisted in repetition of the Zarrs titles which were very haughty & oriental" (*The Diary of John Evelyn*, 3:494). Cross, *The Russian Theme*, 3–4, calls attention to a more explicit line in a poem by George Turbervile (in Russia in the late 1560s): "The maners are so Turkie like" (from "To Parker," in Hakluyt, *The Principal Navigations*, 2:107).

28. Quoted in Vinogradoff, "Russian Missions to London," 61. Potemkin's theatrical schedule is quoted in *The Calendar of State Papers Domestic Series* (1682), 24; see also van Lennep, *The London Stage 1660–1800*, 304 and 308 (where the plays are identified as Shadwell's, performed on 11 January 1682, and Crowne's, on 13 January).

29. Potemkin's 1681 visit to Paris is described briefly in Isherwood, *Music in the Service of the King*, 302–303, and contemporary documents are published in "Donoseniia frantsuzskikh poslannikov . . ." 1–10.

30. Stubbs, "Johann Mattheson," 286 and 289. The score has been published as Mattheson, *Boris Goudenow*.

31. Stubbs, "Johann Mattheson," 286ff., sets out this background in diplomatic and military history. A brief survey of Peter's Grand Embassy is in Hughes, *Russia in the Age of Peter the Great,* 22–26; Peter's transparent incognito status is noted, for example, in Anderson, "English Views of Russia in the Age of Peter the Great," 200.

32. Stubbs, "Johann Mattheson," 286.

33. Ibid., 292, n. 19; he also proposes Erasmus Francisci, *Acerra exoticorum. Oder historisches Rauchfass* (Frankfurt, 1674), as one of Mattheson's sources; this work was unavailable for the present study. On Petreius, see G. Edward Orchard's brief biography in *MERSH* 28:18–19, and Poe, *Foreign Descriptions of Muscovy,* 152–53. Both sources indicate that the latest edition of Petreius's work was the German translation from Leipzig, 1620, so further investigation of Mattheson's (and the Wich family's) library holdings might be in order. This edition is available in Russian translation by Shemiakin in [Petreius], "Istoriia o velikom kniazhestve Moskovskom."

34. *MERSH* 28:18. On the complex history of the various recensions and attributions of Bussow's text, see his *The Disturbed State of the Russian Realm,* xxxi–xxxvii (where editor G. Edward Orchard also notes the work's role as a source for the great nineteenth-century Russian treatments by Pushkin and Musorgskii). The passing of the scepter is on p. 9.

35. Anderson, "English Views of Russia in the 17th Century," 148. Poe, "*A People Born to Slavery,*" traces the origins of this imagery back to the anti-Muscovite pamphlet literature of the 1560s, documenting Ivan's war with Livonia; see pp. 128ff., complete with gruesome contemporary illustrations of Muscovite cruelties. An example is the work by Matthias Schaum, *Tragoedia Demetrio-Moscovitica* (1614), which, in describing the famines in Russia in the early seventeenth century, nonchalantly mentions the pervasive cannibalism that took place there. A Russian translation is in Obolenskii, *Inostrannye sochineniia i akty,* where the cannibalism is in pt. 1:3.

36. Poe, "*A People Born to Slavery,*" 96–97, emphasizes the use of the Dmitrii story as a narrative foundation for many Westerners writing about Russia; as he remarks, the Western writers "had the material for a good story, and one that was important to their audience."

37. *Sir Thomas Smithes Voiage and Entertainment in Rushia* (1605), K[1], and Henry Brereton, *Newes of the Present Miseries of Rushia* (1614), published in Howe, *The False Dmitri,* 72. These passages are singled out in Palmer, *Writing Russia in the Age of Shakespeare,* 215.

38. Lope de Vega's work, although motivated by the political turmoils of the Dmitrii era, also used an earlier traveler's account, by Antonio Possevino, which had been published in the 1580s and which served for many years as an authoritative source on Russia. A much fuller treatment of Lope de Vega's play and its possible sources is in Brody, *The Demetrius Legend*; see also Alekseev, *Ocherki istorii ispano-russkikh literaturnykh otnoshenii,* 11–13, and Balashov, "Renessansnaia problematika ispanskoi dramy XVII v." Possevino's account is available in English translation in Possevino, *The Moscovia of Antonio Possevino.*

39. Anderson, "English Views of Russia in the 17th Century," 148–49. See Brody, *The Demetrius Legend,* 131–32, on the play *El príncipe perseguido. Infeliz Juan Basilio* (1650) by the Spanish playwrights Luis de Belmonte, Augustin Moreto, and Antonio Martines, also discussed in Kennedy, *The Dramatic Art of Moreto,* where a synopsis of the play is on pp. 191–93. Brody, 132, also suggests other works inspired by Lope's play.

40. Three works by Shakespeare with Russian imagery or characters—*Love's Labour's Lost, Measure for Measure,* and *The Winter's Tale*—form the center of Palmer's *Writing Russia in the Age of Shakespeare.*

41. Brody, *The Demetrius Legend,* chap. 3, views the work through the prism of the Time of Troubles and discusses the complex relationships between Fletcher's treatment of the Dmitrii theme and his possible sources; see also the review of Brody's book by Jack V. Haney on Brody's treatment of Jerome Horsey's account as a source for Fletcher. On the playwright, see *DLB* 58, s.v. "Francis Beaumont and John Fletcher," by Cyrus Hoy. Palmer, *Writing Russia in the Age of Shakespeare,* chap. 8, proposes a different interpretation of the work. In addition to the discussions in Brody's work, especially chap. 4, on German and Russian settings of the Dmitrii theme from the eighteenth and nineteenth centuries, see the summaries in Jensen and Powell, "'A Mess of Russians,'" esp. 138, as well as the preliminary listing of Dmitrii plays in Barbour, *Dimitry Called the Pretender,* 375–76. Emerson, *Boris Godunov,* focuses on the nineteenth century, with a vivid analysis of the subject's sources and historiography.

42. Pix's play is cited in Avery, *The London Stage 1660–1800,* 8, and see also Alekseev, "Boris Godunov i Dmitrii Samozvanets v zapadnoevropeiskoi drame"; Anderson, "English Views of Russia in the 17th Century," 149, n. 73; and Cross, *The Russian Theme,* 8–9. Theodoli's work is cited in Anderson, 149, n. 73, and in Alekseev, 97; it has not been possible to establish if the other Italian work cited by Anderson and Alekseev, Bianco Bianchi's *Il Demetrio* (Lucca, 1645), is actually on a Russian theme. Alekseev, 98 (citing Gottschall, "Dramaturgische Parallelen," 100), mentions a *commedia dell'arte* presentation of the Dmitrii theme by Boccabadati (Boccabodatti?), popular in a French translation in the early eighteenth century. Although Alekseev and Gottschall are at times unreliable (for example, the Aubry play they mention is not on the Russian Dmitrii theme), one might note that there was a *commedia* character with a Slavic background. See Clubb, *Italian Drama in Shakespeare's Time,* 262, where she notes the probable Dalmatian provenance of one of Francesco Andreini's *commedia* roles.

43. See the publications listed in Poe, *Foreign Descriptions of Muscovy,* 174–75 and 181–82.

44. Both editions of Manley's history were published in London, printed by J. C. for Thomas Basset in 1674 and 1677. Manley's authorship and his sources are discussed in Loewenson, "Sir Roger Manley's History of Muscovy," where, on p. 239, Loewenson characterizes Manley's work as "one of the earliest learned histories of Russia" written in England, comparing it to the similar approach in Milton's *A Brief History of Moscovia,* also based on research using earlier accounts; neither author was ever in Russia. Milton's work is also discussed in Bedford, "Milton's Journeys North." One wonders if there is any particular influence of Manley's book on Mattheson, given the composer's close contact with the English diplomatic world.

45. Mary Pix's *The Tsar of Muscovy,* like Mattheson's opera, appears to be another example of a Russian Dmitrii-themed work written in the wake of Peter's visits to the West. According to Cross, *The Russian Theme,* 8, the first Russian play to be translated into English was Sumarokov's *Dimitrii samozvanets* (Dmitrii the Pretender, 1771, translated in 1807). Some elements of this Western image of Muscovy are traced into the nineteenth century, for example, in Hartley, "England 'Enjoys the Spectacle of a Northern Barbarian,'" and in Cross, "Petrus Britannicus."

46. Translation of all titles in this passage from Karlinsky, *Russian Drama from Its Beginnings,* 48. These plays were part of the repertoire of the short-lived public theater headed by the foreigners Johann Kunst and Otto Fürst between 1702 and 1706; see

Starikova, "Russkii teatr petrovskogo vremeni," 137–38, and Vsevolodskii-Gerngross, *Istoriia russkogo dramaticheskogo teatra,* 1:90–96. Primary source materials for this period are published in Bogoiavlenskii, "Moskovskii teatr," and see also Kholodov, "K istorii starinnogo russkogo teatra," 161–69. Bibliography on Natal'ia Alekseevna's theatrical enterprise is listed in chapter 6 above.

47. Karlinsky, *Russian Drama from Its Beginnings,* 47, where the author notes that Jodelet was a famous comedian in Molière's time.

Bibliography

Manuscripts Cited

[Only musical sources in Russian and Ukrainian collections are listed here. Manuscripts transmitting Diletskii's *Grammatika* are listed separately below.]

KIEV
NBU Natsional'na biblioteka Ukrainy [Ukrainian National Library]
Sof. 127/381 (Korenev 1671 text)

KOSTROMA
Gosudarstvennyi arkhiv Kostromskoi oblasti
[State Archive of the Kostroma Province]
f. 558, op. 2, No. 583 (Korenev excerpts; see below under Diletskii sources)
f. 670, No. 44 (Korenev, Tikhon, other excerpts)

L'VIV
Natsional'nyi muzei [National Museum]

MOSCOW
GIM Gosudarstvennyi istoricheskii muzei [State Historical Museum]
Muz. sobr., No. 1743 (*kant* ms; late 17th century)
Muz. sobr., No. 1938 (*kant* ms; 1680s; published in Dolskaya, *Spiritual Songs*)
Muz. sobr., No. 2469 (*kant* ms; late 17th century)
Muz. sobr., No. 4072 (Korenev; see below under Diletskii sources)
NDM 122 and 123/457 (liturgical mss copied at Novodevichii Convent, mid-17th century)
Otd. ruk., No. 2473 (*kant* ms; second quarter 18th century; partially published in Livanova, *Sbornik kantov*)
Sin. pev. sobr., No. 486 (Diletskii four-part *kant;* late 17th century)
Sin. pev. sobr., No. 712 (*kontserty* part-books; excerpts published in PRMI 7 and Dylets'kyi, *Khorovi tvory*)
Sin. pev. sobr., No. 757 (Diletskii four-part *kant;* late 17th century)

Sin. pev. sobr., No. 777 (Korenev; see below under Diletskii sources)

Sin. pev. sobr., No. 927 (*kant* ms; ca. 1700)

Sobr. Barsova, No. 1340 (Korenev; see below under Diletskii sources)

Sobr. Barsova, No. 1382 (Tikhon, other excerpts; late 18th century; see below under Diletskii sources)

Sobr. Khludova, No. 126d (*kant* ms; 1680s–early 1690s)

Sobr. Shchukina, No. 61 (*kant* ms; early 18th century)

Sobr. Uvarova, No. 760 (Polotskii-Titov Psalter; late 17th–early 18th century)

Glinka Museum Gosudarstvennyi tsentral'nyi muzei muzykal'noi kul'tury im. M. I. Glinki
[M. I. Glinka State Central Museum of Musical Culture]

MGK Moskovskaia gosudarstvennaia konservatoriia [Moscow State Conservatory]

V 68 (*Nauka*, Tikhon, other excerpts; 1740s–70s; see below under Diletskii sources)

RGADA Rossiiskii arkhiv drevnikh aktov
[Russian Archive of Ancient Acts; formerly TsGADA]

f. 381, No. 1195 (theory treatises, second half 18th century)

f. 381, No. 1474 (theory treatises, second half 18th century)

f. 381, No. 1590 (ms original of *Opyt irmoloinago peniia*)

RGB Rossiiskaia gosudarstvennaia biblioteka
[Russian State Library; formerly GBL]

f. 173, No. 116 (Korenev; ca. 1700; see below under Diletskii sources)

f. 178, No. 10944 (*kant* texts only; dated 1675)

f. 187, No. 9498 (*kant* ms; early 18th century)

f. 205, No. 146 (Korenev; late 17th–early 18th century; see below under Diletskii sources)

f. 272, No. 429 (*dvoznamennik;* last quarter 17th century; excerpts in Shabalin, *Pevcheskie azbuki,* 1:236ff.)

f. 310, No. 899 (some Polotskii-Titov settings)

f. 379, No. 3 (Tikhon and *dvoznamennik;* late 17th century)

f. 379, No. 4 (*dvoznamennik;* last quarter 17th century; excerpts in Shabalin, *Pevcheskie azbuki,* 1:261ff.)

Muz. sobr., No. 3893 (Tikhon and *Nauka;* late 17th century)

ST. PETERSBURG
BAN Biblioteka Akademii nauk [Library of the Academy of Sciences]

Sobr. Petra I A 66 [16.15.11] (Polotskii-Titov Psalter, presentation copy to Sofiia)

Sobr. Petra I B 117 [16.15.9] (Polotskii-Titov Psalter; late 17th–early 18th century)

Sobr. Pliushkina, No. 263 (Korenev; second half 18th century; see below under Diletskii sources)

Institut istorii (Rossiiskaia akademiia nauk)
[St. Petersburg Historical Institute, Russian Academy of Sciences]

RGIA Rossiiskii gosudarstvennyi istoricheskii arkhiv
[Russian State Historical Archive; formerly TsGIA]

f. 834, op. 3, ed. khr. 3764 (mixed ms, includes some *kanty;* late 17th century)

RNB Rossiiskaia natsional'naia biblioteka [Russian National Library; formerly GPB]

F.I.244 (Korenev 1671 text)

Q.I.1101 (Korenev 1671 text; third quarter 17th century; excerpts in Shabalin, *Pevcheskie azbuki,* 1:350ff.)

Q.XII.1 (*Nauka* and Tikhon texts, *azbuka;* 1680s; excerpts in Shabalin, *Pevcheskie azbuki,* 1:364ff.)

Q.XIV.25 (*kant* ms; 1690s)

Q.XIV.41 (Polotskii-Titov Psalter, dedicated to co-tsars Ivan and Peter)

Q.XIV.141 (*kant* ms; 18th century)

Sobr. Pogodina, No. 426 (*kant* ms; 1680s)

Sobr. Pogodina, No. 1974 (*kant* ms; early 1680s)

Sobr. Titova, No. 4172 (*kant* ms; 1690s)

Sobr. Viazemskogo, O.57 (*Mudrost' chetvertaia Musikia;* published in OLDP Izdaniia 6)

Sobr. Viazemskogo, Q.215 (musical hands; late 17th–early 18th century; published in *Znameniia osmoglasnago peniia*)

Sol. sobr., 647/619 (*dvoznamennik*)

Sol. sobr., No. 800/692 (Polotskii-Titov Psalter, associated with Solovetskii Monastery)

TVER'
Gosudarstvennyi arkhiv Tverskoi oblasti
[State Archive of the Tver' Province; formerly Kalinin]

f. 103, No. 651a (Korenev; see below under Diletskii sources)

Sources Transmitting Diletskii's *Grammatika*

[This is an informational listing; not all sources listed here were discussed in the text. Sources marked with an asterisk were available for this study. More detailed descriptions are in Protopopov, PRMI 7:454–92, and Jensen, "Nikolai Diletskii's *Grammatika,*" appendix 3. See abbreviations above for collections. Protopopov, PRMI 7:481, does not classify RGB, f. 210, No. 5, which was not available for this study. The source dates from the second quarter of the eighteenth century. Aravin, "U istokov," 108, notes that GIM, sobr. Barsova, No. 1382 (late 18th century) includes excerpts from the *Grammatika* (as well as other theoretical works from the late 17th century).]

SMOLENSK 1677 VERSION

*RGADA, f. 181, No. 541	mid-late 1690s
*L'viv, otd. ruk. 87/510804	dated by scribe 1723 (facsimile published in Dylets'kyi, *Hramatyka muzykal'na.*)
*Tver', f. 103, No. 553	1750s
Institut istorii, f. 238, op. 1, No. 256	last quarter of the 18th century
*Sakharov manuscript	lost; known in published fragments
Kiev, St. Sophia library	lost; apparently transmitted the Smolensk version

MOSCOW 1679 VERSION

*RGB, f. 173, No. 107	late 1670s (published in facsimile in PRMI 7)
*RNB, Q.XII.4	late 17th–early 18th century (one gathering published in facsimile in PRMI 7)
RGB, f. 35, No. 5.41	late 17th–early 18th century
RGB, f. 310, No. 177	early 18th century
*GIM, Sin. pev. sobr., No. 777	also includes Korenev excerpts; 1705–11
RGB, f. 218, No. 347/1	gathering XVIII from GIM 777
*Tver', f. 103, No. 651a	also includes Korenev excerpts; early-mid 18th century

RGB, f. 7, No. 57	second quarter of the 18th century
*GIM, sobr. Zabelina, No. 168	1730s–40s
RGB, f. 218, No. 14	mid-18th century
Glinka Museum, f. 283, No. 8126	mid-18th century

MOSCOW 1679–81 VERSION

*GIM, sobr. Barsova, No. 1340	also includes Korenev; late 1670s
*RGB, f. 205, No. 146	late 17th–early 18th century (published transcription in *Musikiiskaia grammatika Nikolaia Diletskogo*)
RGB, f. 173, No. 116	late 17th–early 18th century
RNB, sobr. Titova, No. 3753	late 17th–early 18th century
*GIM, Sin. pev. sobr., No. 184	late 17th–early 18th century
GIM, Muz. sobr., No. 4072	early 18th century
MGK V 68	also includes Korenev excerpts; 1740s–70s
BAN, sobr. Pliushkina, No. 263	also includes Korenev; second half 18th century
Kostroma, f. 558, op. 2, No. 583	also includes Korenev excerpts; second half 18th century
RGB, f. 37, No. 101	1760s–80s

Published Works Cited

Abramowicz, Ludwik. *Cztery wieki drukarstwa w Wilnie*. Wilno: L. Chominski, 1925.

Adrianova-Peretts, V. P., ed. *Russkaia sillabicheskaia poeziia XVII–XVIII vv.* Leningrad: Sovetskii pisatel', 1970.

Akty istoricheskie, sobrannye i izdannye Arkheograficheskoi komissiei. 5 vols. St. Petersburg: V Tip. II-go otdeleniia Sobstvennoi E. I. V. kantseliarii, 1841–42.

Alekseev, M. P. "Boris Godunov i Dmitrii Samozvanets v zapadnoevropeiskoi drame." In *"Boris Godunov" A. S. Pushkina*, edited by K. N. Derzhavin, 79–124. Leningrad: Gos. akademicheskii teatr dramy, 1936.

———. *Ocherki istorii ispano-russkikh literaturnykh otnoshenii XVI–XIX vv.* Leningrad: Izdatel'stvo Leningradskogo universiteta, 1964.

Alekseevna, O. B., and others, eds. *Istoricheskie pesni XVII veka.* Pamiatniki russkogo fol'klora. Moscow: Nauka, 1966.

Amburger, Erik. "Die Mitwirkenden bei der Moskauer Aufführung des 'Artaxerxes' am 17. Oktober 1672." *Zeitschrift für Slawische Philologie* 25 (1956): 304–309.

Anderson, Matthew S. "English Views of Russia in the Age of Peter the Great." *American SEER* 13, no. 2 (1954): 200–14.

———. "English Views of Russia in the 17th Century." *SEER* 33, no. 80 (1954): 140–60.

Annushkin, V. I. *Pervaia russkaia "Ritorika" XVII veka: Tekst. Perevod. Issledovanie.* Moscow: "Dobrosvet," "CheRo," 1999.

Aravin, N. "U istokov russkogo mnogogolosiia." *SM*, no. 1 (1978): 107–14.

Arkheograficheskii sbornik dokumentov, otnosiashchikhsia k istorii severo-zapadnoi Rusi. Vol. 9. Vilnius: Vilenskii uchebnyi okrug Ministerstva narodnogo prosveshcheniia, 1870.

Arkhiv iugo-zapadnoi Rossii. Pt. 1, 12 vols. Kiev: Komissiia dlia razbora drevnikh aktov, 1859–1904.

Arsenii Elassonskii. *Memuary iz russkoi istorii.* In *Khroniki smutnogo vremeni*, edited by

A. Liberman, B. Morozov, and S. Shokarev, 163–210. Istoriia Rossii i doma Romanovykh v memuarakh sovremennikov XVII–XX vv. Moscow: Fond Sergeia Dubova, 1998.

Aumayr, Manfred. *Historische Untersuchungen an Bezeichnungen von Musikinstrumenten in der russischen Sprache.* Dissertationen der Universität Wien 169. Vienna: VWGÖ, 1985.

Avery, Emmett, ed. *The London Stage 1660–1800.* Part 2, *1700–1729.* Carbondale, Illinois: Southern Illinois University Press, 1960.

Balashov, N. I. "Renessansnaia problematika ispanskoi dramy XVII v. na vostochnoslavianskie temy." In *Slavianskie literatury: Doklady sovetskoi delegatsii. V Mezhdunarodnyi s"ezd slavistov,* 89–124. Moscow: Izdatel'stvo Akademii nauk, 1963.

Balatri, Filippo. *Frutti del Mondo, autobiografia di Filippo Balatri da Pisa.* Edited by Karl Vossler. [Palermo]: R. Sandron, 1924.

Baranova, T. B. "Muzykal'naia estetika." In *Khudozhestvenno-esteticheskaia kul'tura drevnei Rusi XI–XVII veka,* edited by V. V. Bychkov, 358–74. Moscow: Nauchno-izdatel'skii tsentr "Ladomir," 1996.

Barbour, Philip. *Dimitry Called the Pretender: Tsar and Great Prince of All Russia, 1605–1606.* Boston: Houghton Mifflin and Cambridge, Mass.: Riverside Press, 1966.

Baronius, Cesare. *Annales Ecclesiastici, auctore Caesare Baronio.* Edited and with commentary by A. Pagi. 34 vols. Lucca: Leonardo Venturini, 1738–56.

Barsov, E. V., comp. "Rospis' vsiakim veshcham, den'gam i zapasam, chto ostalos' po smerti boiarina Nikity Ivanovicha Romanova i dachi po nem na pomin dushi." *ChOIDR* 3 (1887), pt. 1:1–128.

Bedford, R. D. "Milton's Journeys North: *A Brief History of Moscovia* and *Paradise Lost.*" *Renaissance Studies* 7, no. 1 (1993): 71–85.

Belkin, A. A. *Russkie skomorokhi.* Moscow: Nauka, 1975.

Belobrova, O. A. "Allegorii nauk v litsevykh spiskakh 'Knigi izbranoi vkrattse . . .' Nikolaia Spafariia." *TODRL* 32 (1977): 107–20.

———. "K izucheniiu 'Knigi izbranoi vkrattse o deviatikh musakh i o sedmikh svobodnykh khudozhestvakh' Nikolaia Spafariia." *TODRL* 30 (1976): 307–17.

———, ed. *Nikolai Spafarii: Esteticheskie traktaty.* Leningrad: Nauka, 1978.

———. "Ob istochnikakh miniatiur k sochineniiam Nikolaia Spafariia 1670-kh gg." *TODRL* 45 (1992): 414–34.

Belokurov, S. A. "Deianie moskovskogo tserkovnogo sobora 1649 goda (vopros ob edinoglasii v 1649–1651 gg.)." *ChOIDR* 4 (1894), pt. 3:29–52.

———. "Iurii Krizhanich v Rossii." *ChOIDR* 2 (1903), pt. 3:1–210.

Belonenko, A. S. "Pokazaniia arkhiereiskikh pevchikh XVII veka." *TODRL* 36 (1981): 320–28.

Bergholz, Friedrich von. *Dnevnik kamer-iunkera Fridrikha-Vil'gel'ma Berkhgol'tsa, 1721–1725 (okonchanie).* In *Iunost' derzhavy,* edited by V. Naumov, 9–324. Istoriia Rossii i doma Romanovykh v memuarakh sovremennikov XVII–XX vv. Moscow: Fond Sergeia Dubova, 2000.

Berkov, P. N. "Iz istorii russkoi teatral'noi terminologii XVII–XVIII vekov ("Komediia," "intermediia," "dialog," "igrishche" i dr.)." *TODRL* 11 (1955): 280–99.

Berry, Lloyd E., ed. *The English Works of Giles Fletcher, the Elder.* Madison: University of Wisconsin Press, 1964.

———, and Robert O. Crummey, eds. *Rude and Barbarous Kingdom: Russia in the Accounts of Sixteenth-Century English Voyagers.* Madison: University of Wisconsin Press, 1968.

Berynda, Pamvo. *Leksykon slovenoros'kyi Pamvy Beryndy.* Pam'iatky ukrains'koi movy XVII st. Edited by V. V. Nimchuk. Kiev: AN URSR, 1961.

Bestuzhev-Riumin, K. N., ed. *Pamiatniki diplomaticheskikh snoshenii moskovskogo gosu-darstva s Anglii.* Vol. 2 of *Pamiatniki diplomaticheskikh snoshenii drevnei Rossii s derzhavami inostrannymi.* Sbornik Imperatorskogo russkogo istoricheskogo obshchestva 38. St. Petersburg: Tip. V. S. Balasheva, 1883.

Bezsonov, P. *Kaleki perekhozhie. Sbornik stikhov i issledovanie,* 6 vols. Moscow: A. Semen, 1861–64. Reprint of vol. 1, with a new introduction by Sergei Hackel. Farnborough: Gregg International, 1970.

Biblioteka literatury drevnei Rusi. Vol. 6, *XIV–seredina XV veka.* St. Petersburg: Nauka, 1999.

Bobrova, E. I. *Biblioteka Petra I: Ukazatel'-spravochnik.* Leningrad: Biblioteka AN SSSR, 1978.

Bochkarev, V. A. *Russkaia istoricheskaia dramaturgiia XVII–XVIII vv.* Moscow: Prosveshchenie, 1988.

Bogoiavlenskii, S. K. "Moskovskaia Nemetskaia sloboda." *Izvestiia Akademii nauk SSSR. Seriia istorii i filosofii* 3 (1947): 220–32.

——. "Moskovskii teatr pri Tsariakh Aleksee i Petre." *ChOIDR* 2 (1914): pt. 1:i–xxi, 1–192.

Bond, Edward, ed. "Russia at the Close of the sixteenth century, Comprising the Treatise 'Of the Russe Common Wealth,' by Dr. Giles Fletcher; and the Travels of Sir Jerome Horsey, Knt." *The Hakluyt Society* 20 (1856; entire volume).

Brailovskii, S. M., ed. *Pis'ma Sil'vestra Medvedeva.* OLDP Pamiatniki 144. St. Petersburg, 1901.

Braun, Joachim. "Aspects of Early Latvian Professional Musicianship." *Journal of Baltic Studies* 16, no. 2 (1985): 95–110.

——. "National Interrelationships and Conflicts in the Musical Life of 17th and 18th Century Riga." *Journal of Baltic Studies* 11, no. 1 (1980): 62–70.

Brazhnikov, M. V. *Drevnerusskaia teoriia muzyki po rukopisnym materialam XV–XVIII vekov.* Leningrad: Muzyka, 1972.

Brereton, Henry. *Newes of the Present Miseries of Rushia* (London, 1614). In *The False Dmitri: A Russian Romance and Tragedy Described by British Eye-Witnesses, 1604–1612,* edited by Sonia E. Howe, 69–150. London: Williams and Norgate, 1916.

Brikner, A. "Lavrentii Ringuber." Review of *Relation du voyage en Russie fait en 1684 par Laurent Rinhuber,* by Laurent Rinhuber. *ZhMNP* (Feb. 1884): 396–421.

Brody, Ervin C. *The Demetrius Legend and Its Literary Treatment in the Age of the Baroque.* Rutherford, N.J.: Fairleigh Dickinson University Press, 1972.

Brown, Malcolm. "Native Song and National Consciousness in Nineteenth-Century Russian Music." In *Art and Culture in Nineteenth-Century Russia,* edited by Theofanis George Stavrou, 57–84. Bloomington: Indiana University Press, 1983.

——, ed., and Margarita Mazo, intro. *A Collection of Russian Folk Songs by Nikolai Lvov and Ivan Prach.* Russian Music Studies 13, edited by Malcolm Brown. Ann Arbor: UMI Research Press, 1987.

Brown, William Edward. *A History of Seventeenth-Century Russian Literature.* Ann Arbor: Ardis, 1980.

Browne, Francis, trans., and Aryeh Oron, webmaster. "Bach Cantatas Website," available at http://www.bach-cantatas.com/Texts/Chorale045-Eng3.htm ("Durch Adams Fall") (accessed January 2007).

Bubnov, N. Iu. " 'Deianiia tserkovnye i grazhdanskie' Tsezaria Baroniia v russkoi publitsistike 3-i chetverti XVIII [*sic:* XVII] v." In *Rukopisnye i redkie pechatnye knigi v fondakh Biblioteki AN SSSR*, 99–109. Leningrad: BAN SSSR, 1976.

——, and N. S. Demkova. "Vnov' naidennoe poslanie iz Moskvy v Pustozersk 'Vozveshchenie ot syna dukhovnago ko ottsu dukhovnomu' i otvet protopopa Avvakuma (1676 g.)." *TODRL* 36 (1981): 127–50.

——, and others, comps. *Opisanie Rukopisnogo otdela Biblioteki Akademii nauk SSSR*. Vol. 3, vyp. 3. *Istoricheskie sborniki XVIII–XIX vv.* Leningrad: Nauka, 1971.

Buelow, George. *A History of Baroque Music*. Bloomington: Indiana University Press, 2004.

Buganov, V. I., and M. P. Lukichev, eds. *Posol'skaia kniga po sviaziam Rossii s Gretsiei (pravoslavnymi ierarkhami i monastyriami). 1588–1594 gg.* Moscow: AN SSSR, 1988.

Burilina, E. L. "Chin 'za prilivok o zdravii gosudaria.' " In *Drevnerusskaia literatura: Istochnikovedenie*, 204–14. Leningrad: Nauka, 1984.

Bushkovitch, Paul. "Cultural Change among the Russian Boyars 1650–1680: New Sources and Old Problems." *Forschungen zur osteuropäischen Geschichte* 56 (2000): 91–111.

——. "The Epiphany Ceremony of the Russian Court in the Sixteenth and Seventeenth Centuries." *Russian Review* 49, no. 1 (1990): 1–17.

——. *Religion and Society in Russia: The Sixteenth and Seventeenth Centuries.* New York: Oxford University Press, 1992.

Bussow, Conrad. *The Disturbed State of the Russian Realm.* Translated and edited by G. Edward Orchard. Montreal: McGill-Queen's University Press, 1994.

[Bussow, Conrad]. *Moskovskaia khronika* [*Die Moskauer Chronik*], *1584–1613.* Translated and edited by I. I. Smirnov. Moscow and Leningrad: Izd. Akademii nauk SSSR, 1961.

Butskaia, S. B. "Printsipy obrazovaniia mnogogolosiia v partesnykh garmonizatsiiakh vtoroi poloviny XVII–nachala XVIII vv." In *Iz istorii dukhovnoi muzyki*, 52–63. Rostov: Izd. Rostovskogo gos. pedagogicheskogo instituta, 1992.

——. "Stefan Ivanovich Beliaev—gosudarev pevchii d'iak." *PKNO 1992* (1993): 151–56.

Buturlin, M. D. *Bumagi florentinskogo tsentral'nogo arkhiva kasaiushchiiasia do Rossii / Documenti che si conservano nel R. Archivio di Stato in Firenze, Sezione Medicea, riguardanti l'antica Moscovia (Russia).* Moscow: Tip. Gracheva, 1871.

Bykova, T. A., and M. M. Gurevich. *Opisanie izdanii, napechatannykh kirillitsei: 1689–ianvar' 1725 g.* Vol. 2 of *Opisanie izdanii, napechatannykh pri Petre I.* Moscow: AN SSSR, 1958.

Bylinin, V. K., and A. L. Pososhenko. "Tsar' Aleksei Mikhailovich kak master raspeva." *PKNO 1987* (1988): 131–37.

The Calendar of State Papers Domestic Series, Jan. 1st to Dec. 31st, 1682. Edited by F. H. Blackburne Daniell. London: Longman, Green, Longman, and Roberts, 1932.

[Chamberlain, John]. *The Letters of John Chamberlain.* Edited by Norman Egbert McClure. 2 vols. Philadelphia: American Philosophical Society, 1939.

Charykov, N. V. *Posol'stvo v Rim i sluzhba v Moskve Pavla Meneziia (1637–1694).* St. Petersburg: Tip. A. S. Suvorina, 1906.

Cherepnin, L. V. "Materialy po istorii russkoi kul'tury i russko-shvedskikh kul'turnykh sviazei XVII v. v arkhivakh Shvetsii." *TODRL* 17 (1961): 454–81.

Chew, Samuel C. *The Crescent and the Rose: Islam and England during the Renaissance.* New York: Oxford University Press, 1937.

Chistiakova, M. V. *Monakhini "s Beloi Rosi" v Novodevich'em monastyre.* Trudy Gosudarstvennogo istoricheskogo muzeia 116. Moscow: Gos. istoricheskii muzei, 2000.

Clubb, Louise George. *Italian Drama in Shakespeare's Time.* New Haven: Yale University Press, 1989.

Cohen, Albert. "*Musique* in the *Dictionnaire mathématique* (1691) of Jacques Ozanam." *Music Review* 36, no. 2 (1975): 85–91.

Collins, Samuel. *The Present State of Russia, In a Letter to a Friend at London; Written by an Eminent Person residing at the Great Czars Court at Mosco for the space of nine years.* London: Printed by John Winter, 1671.

Cracraft, James. *The Petrine Revolution in Russian Imagery.* Chicago: University of Chicago Press, 1997.

Cross, Anthony G. "Early British Acquaintance with Russian Popular Song and Music (The Letters and Journals of the Wilmot Sisters)." *SEER* 66 (1988): 21–30.

——. "Petrus Britannicus: The Image of Peter the Great in Eighteenth-Century Britain." In *A Window on Russia: Papers from the V International Conference of the Study Group on Eighteenth-Century Russia, Gargnano, 1994,* 3–9. Rome: La Fenice, 1996.

——. *The Russian Theme in English Literature: From the Sixteenth Century to 1980. An Introductory Survey and a Bibliography.* Oxford: Willem A. Meeuws, 1985.

Crummey, Robert O. *Aristocrats and Servitors: The Boyar Elite in Russia, 1613–1689.* Princeton: Princeton University Press, 1983.

——. "Court Spectacles in Seventeenth-Century Russia: Illusion and Reality." In *Essays in Honor of A. A. Zimin,* edited by Daniel Clarke Waugh, 130–46. Columbus, Ohio: Slavica, 1985.

Dahl, Staffan. *Codex Ad 10 der Västeråser Gymnasial-Bibliothek.* Publications de l'Institut slave d'Upsal 2. Uppsala: Almqvist & Wiksell, 1949.

Danilov, V. V. "Sborniki pesen XVII stoletiia—Richarda Dzhemsa i P. A. Kvashnina." *TODRL* 2 (1935): 165–80.

Deianiia moskovskikh soborov 1666 i 1667 godov. 1893. Reprint, edited by C. H. van Schooneveld. The Hague: Slavistic Printings and Reprintings 190, 1968.

Demetrakopoulos, Photios A. *Arsénios Elassónos (1550–1626). Bíos kaí Ergo: Symbolē stē melétē tôn metabyzantinôn logíōn tês Anatolês* [Arsenios of Elasson (1550–1626). Life and Work: Contribution to the Study of Post-Byzantine Literati of the East]. Athens: Imago, 1984.

—— [Demetracopoulos]. "On Arsenios, Archbishop of Elasson." *Byzantinoslavica* 42, fasc. 2 (1981): 145–53.

Demin, A. S. "Russkie p'esy 1670-kh godov i pridvornaia kul'tura." *TODRL* 27 (1972): 273–83.

——. "'Zhezl pravleniia' i aforistika Simeona Polotskogo." In *Simeon Polotskii i ego knigoizdatel'skaia deiatel'nost',* edited by A. N. Robinson, 60–92. Moscow: Nauka, 1982.

Depping, G.-B. "Une ambassade russe à Paris en 1654." *Revue de Paris* (1 July 1853): 140–47.

Derzhavina, O. A. "Simeon Polotskii v rabote nad 'Psaltyr'iu rifmotvornoi.'" In *Simeon Polotskii i ego knigoizdatel'skaia deiatel'nost',* edited by A. N. Robinson, 116–33. Moscow: Nauka, 1982.

——. "Zhanrovaia priroda pervykh russkikh p'es." In *Novye cherty v russkoi literature i iskusstve (XVII–nachalo XVIII v.),* edited by A. N. Robinson, 62–72. Moscow: Nauka, 1976.

Diletskii, Nikolai. See also under Dylets'kyi, Mykola.

Diletskii, Nikolai. *Idea grammatiki musikiiskoi.* Translated, edited, and with commentary by V. V. Protopopov. PRMI 7. Moscow: Muzyka, 1979.

[——]. *Musikiiskaia grammatika Nikolaia Diletskogo.* Edited by S. V. Smolenskii. OLDP Izdaniia 128. [St. Petersburg]: Tip. M. A. Aleksandrova, 1910.

Dillon, Janette. *Performance and Spectacle in Hall's "Chronicle."* London: The Society for Theatre Research, 2002.

Dingley, J. Review of *Hramatyka muzykal'na,* by Mykola Dylets'kyi, edited by O. S. Tsalai-Iakymenko. *Journal of Byelorussian Studies* 2, no. 3 (1971): 323–24.

Di Salvo [Di Sal'vo], M. "Kastrat Petra Velikogo: Filippo Balatri v Moskovii (1699–1701)." In *Inozemtsy v Rossii v XV–XVII vekakh: Sbornik materialov konferentsii 2002–2004 gg.,* 430–39. Moscow: "Drevlekhranilishche," 2006.

Dmitriev, Iu. "Teoriia iskusstva i vzgliady na iskusstvo v pis'mennosti drevnei Rusi." *TODRL* 9 (1953): 97–116.

Dmitrievskii, A. *Arkhiepiskop elassonskii Arsenii i memuary ego iz russkoi istorii.* Kiev: Tip. Imp. universiteta sv. Vladimira, 1899.

Dnevnik Mariny Mnishek. Edited by D. M. Bulanin, translated by V. N. Kozliakov, commentary by A. A. Sevast'ianova. St. Petersburg: Dmitrii Bulanin, 1995.

Dolskaya, Olga. "Choral Music in the Petrine Era." In *Russia in the Reign of Peter the Great: Old and New Perspectives,* part 2, edited by Anthony Cross, 173–85. Cambridge: Study Group on Eighteenth-Century Russia, 1998.

——. "From Titov to Teplov: The Origins of the Russian Art Song." In *A Window on Russia: Papers from the V International Conference of the Study Group on Eighteenth-Century Russia, Gargnano, 1994,* 197–213. Rome: La Fenice, 1996.

——, ed. *Spiritual Songs in Seventeenth-Century Russia.* Bausteine zur Slavischen Philologie und Kulturgeschichte, Reihe B: Editionen, Neue Folge Band 4. Series editor Hans Rothe. Cologne: Böhlau Verlag, 1996.

Dolskaya-Ackerly, Olga. "The Early Kant in Seventeenth-Century Russian Music." Ph.D. diss., University of Kansas, 1983.

——. "German Voskresenskij: A Seventeenth-Century Poet-Musician." *Slavic and East European Arts* 8, no. 1 (1993): 6–17.

——. "Vasilii Titov and the 'Moscow' Baroque." *Journal of the Royal Musical Association* 118, no. 2 (1993): 203–22.

"Donoseniia frantsuzskikh poslannikov . . ." *Sbornik Imperatorskogo russkogo istoricheskogo obshchestva* 34 (1881), section 1:i–xlvii, 1–123.

Draper, J. W. "Shakespeare and Muscovy." *SEER* 33, no. 80 (1954): 217–21.

Dukelskaya, Larissa A., and Elizaveta P. Renne. *The Hermitage Catalogue of Western European Painting.* Vol. 13, *British Painting: Sixteenth to Nineteenth Centuries.* Moscow and Florence: Giunti, 1990.

Dukes, Paul. "Paul Menzies and His Mission from Muscovy to Rome, 1672–1674." *The Innes Review* 35, no. 2 (1984): 88–95.

Dunning, Chester. *Russia's First Civil War: The Time of Troubles and the Founding of the Romanov Dynasty.* University Park: Pennsylvania State University Press, 2001.

Dylets'kyi, Mykola. See also Diletskii, Nikolai.

——. *Hramatyka muzykal'na. Fotokopiia rukopysu 1723 roku.* Edited by O. S. Tsalai-Iakymenko. Kiev: Muzychna Ukraina, 1970.

——. *Khorovi tvory.* Edited by N. O. Herasymova-Persyds'ka. Kiev: Muzychna Ukraina, 1981.

Eingorn, Vitalii. "O snosheniiakh malorossiiskogo dukhovenstva s moskovskim pravitel'stvom v tsarstvovanie Alekseia Mikhailovicha." *ChOIDR* 2 (1893), pt. 4:i–xiv, 1–370.

Eleonskaia, A. S. " 'Plach Adama' v tvorchestve russkikh pisatelei XVII v." *Germenevtika drevnerusskoi literatury* 4 (1992): 5–27.

———. *Russkaia oratorskaia proza v literaturnom protsesse XVII veka.* Moscow: Nauka, 1990.

Ellersieck, Heinz. "Russia under Aleksei Mikhailovich and Feodor Alekseevich, 1645–1682: The Scandinavian Sources." Ph.D. diss., University of California, Los Angeles, 1955.

Emchenko, E. B., ed. *Stoglav: Issledovanie i tekst.* Moscow: Indrik, 2000.

Emerson, Caryl. *Boris Godunov: Transpositions of a Russian Theme.* Bloomington: Indiana University Press, 1986.

Encyclopedia Lituanica. 6 vols. Edited by Simas Sužiėdelis. Boston: J. Kapočius, 1970–78.

Eremin, I. P. " 'Deklamatsiia' Simeona Polotskogo." *TODRL* 8 (1951): 354–61.

———. "Poeticheskii stil' Simeona Polotskogo." *TODRL* 6 (1948): 125–53.

Essai sur la littérature russe. Livorno: [n.p.], 1774.

Estreicher, Karol. *Bibliografia polska.* 1870–1939. Reprint, in 33 vols. Warsaw: Wydawnictwa Artystyczne i Filmowe, 1977.

Evans, N. E. "The Meeting of the Russian and Scottish Ambassadors in London in 1601." *SEER* 55, no. 4 (1977): 517–28.

[Evelyn, John]. *The Diary of John Evelyn.* Edited by E. S. de Beer. 6 vols. Oxford: Clarendon Press, 1955.

Evgen'eva, A. P., and B. N. Putilov, eds. *Drevnie rossiiskie stikhotvoreniia sobrannye Kirsheiu Danilovym.* 1958. 2nd, enlarged ed. Moscow: Nauka, 1977.

Farrell, Allan P. *The Jesuit Code of Liberal Education: Development and Scope of the Ratio Studiorum.* Milwaukee: Bruce, 1938.

Fedotov, G. P. *The Russian Religious Mind.* 2 vols. Cambridge: Harvard University Press, 1946 and 1966.

Fennell, J. L. I. *The Correspondence between Prince A. M. Kurbsky and Tsar Ivan IV of Russia, 1564–1579.* Cambridge: Cambridge University Press, 1955.

Findeizen, N. F. *History of Music in Russia from Antiquity to 1800.* 2 vols. Edited and annotated by Miloš Velimirović and Claudia R. Jensen. Bloomington: Indiana University Press, 2008. Originally published as *Ocherki po istorii muzyki v Rossii.* 2 vols. Moscow: Gos. izdatel'stvo Muzsektor, 1928.

———. "Petrovskie kanty." *Izvestiia AN SSSR,* VI seriia, no. 7–8 (1927): 667–90.

Flier, Michael S. "Breaking the Code: The Image of the Tsar in the Muscovite Palm Sunday Ritual." In *Medieval Russian Culture* 2, edited by Michael S. Flier and Daniel Rowland. Special issue, *California Slavic Studies* 19 (1994): 213–42.

———. "Court Ceremony in an Age of Reform: Patriarch Nikon and the Palm Sunday Ritual." In *Religion and Culture in Early Modern Russia and Ukraine,* edited by Samuel Baron and Nancy Shields Kollmann, 73–95. DeKalb: Northern Illinois University Press, 1997.

———. "The Iconology of Royal Ritual in Sixteenth-Century Muscovy." In *Byzantine Studies: Essays on the Slavic World and the Eleventh Century,* edited by Speros Vryonis, 53–76. New Rochelle, N.Y.: Aristide D. Caratzas, 1992.

Fonkich, B. L. *Grechesko-russkie kul'turnye sviazi v XV–XVII vv.* Moscow: Nauka, 1977.

———. "Meletii Grek." *Rossiia i khristianskii vostok* 1 (1997): 159(–78.

Forsten, G. "Datskie diplomaty pri moskovskom dvore vo vtoroi polovine XVII veka." *ZhMNP* 9 (1904): 110–81; 11 (1904): 67–101; and 12 (1904): 291–374.

Frick, David. "The Bells of Vilnius: Keeping Time in a City of Many Calendars." In *Making Contact: Maps, Identity, and Travel*, edited by Glenn Burger and others, 23–59. Edmonton: University of Alberta Press, 2003.

Galitzin, A. P., ed. "Une ambassade russe à la cour de Louis XIV." *Bibliothèque russe*, nouvelle série 3. Paris: Librairie A. Franck, 1860.

Gardner, Ivan [Johann von]. *Bogosluzhebnoe penie russkoi pravoslavnoi tserkvi.* 2 vols. Jordanville, N.Y.: Holy Trinity Russian Orthodox Monastery, 1978.

Gardner, J. von [Ivan]. *Russian Church Singing.* Vol. 1, *Orthodox Worship and Hymnography.* Vol. 2, *History from the Origins to the Mid-Seventeenth Century.* Translation and edition of *Bogosluzhebnoe penie russkoi pravoslavnoi tserkvi*, by Vladimir Morosan. Crestwood, N.Y.: St. Vladimir's Seminary Press, 1980 and 2000.

Gardner, J. von, and E. Koschmieder. *Ein handschriftliches Lehrbuch der altrussischen Neumenschrift.* Bayerische Akademie der Wissenschaften, Abhandlungen NF, H. 57. Munich: Verlag der Bayerischen Akademie der Wissenschaften, 1963.

Gerasimova, Iu. I. "Vospominaniia Filippo Balatri—Novyi inostrannyi istochnik po istorii petrovskoi Rossii (1698–1701)." *Zapiski Otdela rukopisei* 27 (1965): 164–90.

Gerasimova-Persidskaia, N. A. See also Herasymova-Persyds'ka, N. O.

Gerasimova-Persidskaia, N. A. "Partesnoe mnogogolosie i formirovanie stilevykh napravlenii v muzyke XVII–pervoi poloviny XVIII v." *TODRL* 32 (1977): 121–32.

——. *Partesnyi kontsert v istorii muzykal'noi kul'tury.* Moscow: Muzyka, 1983.

——. *Russkaia muzyka XVII veka. Vstrecha dvukh epokh.* Moscow: Muzyka, 1994.

——. "Srednevekovye stikhi v partesnoi interpretatsii." *PKNO 1978* (1979): 205–10.

Gol'dberg, A. L., and others. "Traktat o muzyke Iuriia Krizhanicha." *TODRL* 38 (1985): 356–410.

Gołos, Jerzy. "Manuscript Sources of Eastern Chant before 1700 in Polish Libraries." *Studies in Eastern Chant* 3 (1973): 74–80.

——. "A New Source of Old-Polish Secular Music." *The Polish Review* 18, no. 3 (1973): 58–64.

——, and Jan Stęszewski, with Zofia Stęszewska, eds. *Muzyczne Silva Rerum z XVII wieku: Rękopis 127/56 Biblioteki Jagiellońskiej.* Warsaw: Polskie Wydawnictwo Muzyczne, 1970.

Golubtsov, A. "Chinovnik Novgorodskogo Sofiiskogo sobora." *ChOIDR* 2 (1899), pt. 1:i–xx, 1–272.

Gorczyn, Jan Aleksander. *Tabulatura muzyki, abo zaprawa muzykalna.* Cracow: Walerian Piątkowski, 1647. Reprinted in Monumenta musicae in Polonia, Series D, Bibliotheca Antiqua 16. Edited by Jerzy Morawski. Cracow: Polskie Wydawnictwo Muzyczne, 1990.

Gordon, Patrick. *Passages from the Diary of General Patrick Gordon of Auchleuchries in the Years 1635–1699.* 1859. Reprint, New York: Da Capo Press, 1968.

Gorelov, A. A. "Kem byl avtor sbornika 'Drevnie rossiiskie stikhotvoreniia.'" *Russkii fol'klor* 7 (1962): 293–312.

Goshovskii, V., and I. Durnev. "K sporu o Diletskom." *SM* no. 9 (1967): 137–46.

Gottschall, Rudolf von. "Dramaturgische Parallelen: 3. Die Demetriusdramen." In *Studien zur neuen deutschen Litteratur.* Berlin: Allgemeiner Verein für Deutsche Litteratur, 1892.

"Gramota konstantinopol'skogo patriarkha Paisiia I k moskovskomu patriarkhu Nikonu." *Khristianskoe chtenie* no. 3–4 (March–April 1881): 303–53 and no. 5–6 (May–June 1881): 539–95.

Gudziak, Borys. *Crisis and Reform: The Kyivan Metropolitanate, the Patriarchate of Constantinople, and the Genesis of the Union of Brest.* Cambridge, Mass.: Distributed by Harvard University Press for the Ukrainian Research Institute, Harvard University, 1998.

——. "The Sixteenth-Century Muscovite Church and Patriarch Jeremiah II's Journey to Muscovy, 1588–1589: Some Comments Concerning the Historiography and Sources." *Harvard Ukrainian Studies* 19 (1995): 200–25.

Günther, K. "Neue deutsche Quellen zum ersten russischen Theater." *Zeitschrift für Slawistik* 8, no. 5 (1963): 664–75.

——. "Das Weimarer Bruchstück des ersten russischen Dramas 'Artaxerxovo dejstvo' (1672)." *Studien zur Geschichte der russischen Literatur des 18. Jahrhunderts* 3:120–78. Veröffentlichungen des Instituts für Slawistik 28. Berlin: Akademie-Verlag, 1968.

Gurliand, I. Ia. *Ivan Gebdon: Kommissarius i rezident (Materialy po istorii administratsii Moskovskogo gosudarstva vtoroi poloviny XVII veka).* Iaroslavl': Tip. gubernskogo pravleniia, 1903.

Gushee, Lawrence. "Questions of Genre in Medieval Treatises on Music." In *Gattungen der Musik in Einzeldarstellungen: Gedenkschrift Leo Schrade,* edited by Wulf Arlt, Ernst Lichtenhahn, and Hans Oesch, 365–433. Bern: Francke Verlag, 1973.

Guthrie, Matthew. *Dissertations sur les antiquités de Russie.* St. Petersburg, 1795. Reviewed anonymously in *Monthly Review* 18 (appendix) (December 1795): 560–64.

[Hall, Edward]. *Hall's Chronicle; Containing the History of England, during the Reign of Henry the Fourth, and the Succeeding Monarchs, to the End of the Reign of Henry the Eighth . . . Carefully Collated with the Editions of 1548 and 1550.* London: Printed for J. Johnson et al., 1809.

Halperin, Charles J. "Friend and Foe in Paul of Aleppo's *Travels of Patriarch Macarios.*" *Modern Greek Studies Yearbook* 14–15 (1998–99): 97–114.

——. "In the Eye of the Beholder: Two Views of Seventeenth-Century Muscovy." *Russian History / Histoire Russe* 24, no. 4 (1997): 409–23.

Haney, Jack V. Review of *The Demetrius Legend and Its Literary Treatment in the Age of the Baroque,* by Ervin C. Brody. *Slavic and East European Journal* 17, no. 4 (1973): 454–55.

Hartley, Janet M. "England 'Enjoys the Spectacle of a Northern Barbarian': The Reception of Peter I and Alexander I." In *A Window on Russia: Papers from the V International Conference of the Study Group on Eighteenth-Century Russia, Gargnano, 1994,* 11–18. Rome: La Fenice, 1996.

Heinichen, Johann. *Der General-bass in der Komposition.* Dresden, 1728. Reprint, Hildesheim: G. Olms, 1969.

——. *Neu erfundene und gründliche Anweisung . . . zu vollkommener Erlernung des General-Basses.* Hamburg, 1711. Reprint, Documenta Musicologica Erste Reihe: Druckschriften-Faksimiles 40. Kassel: Bärenreiter, 2000.

Hellie, Richard. *The Economy and Material Culture of Russia: 1600–1725.* Chicago: University of Chicago Press, 1999.

Herasymova-Persyds'ka, N. O. See also Gerasimova-Persidskaia, N. A.

Herasymova-Persyds'ka, N. O. *Khorovyi kontsert na Ukraini v XVII–XVIII st.* Kiev: Muzychna Ukraina, 1978.

——. *Ukrains'ki partesni motety pochatku XVIII stolittia z Iuhoslavs'kykh zibran'.* Kiev: Muzychna Ukraina, 1991.

Herberstein, Sigismund von. *Notes Upon Russia: Being a Translation of the Earliest Account of that Country, entitled Rerum Moscoviticarum Commentarii.* Translated and edited by R. H. Major. 2 vols. 1851–52. Reprint, New York: Burt Franklin, 1963?

[Heywood, Thomas]. *The Dramatic Works of Thomas Heywood.* Vol. 2. Edited by J. Payne Collier. London: Printed for the Shakespeare Society, 1853.

Hippisley, Anthony. *The Poetic Style of Simeon Polotsky.* Birmingham Slavonic Monographs 16. Birmingham: Dept. of Russian Language and Literature, University of Birmingham, 1985.

——. "Simeon Polotsky's Library." *Oxford Slavonic Papers* n.s. 16 (1983): 52–61.

Hirsch, Ferdinand, ed. "Brandenburg und Russland 1673–1679." *Urkunden und Actenstücke zur Geschichte des Kurfürsten Friedrich Wilhelm von Brandenburg.* Vol. 19, *Politische Verhandlungen,* 12. Band, sect. 2:247–330. Berlin: Georg Reimer, 1906.

Hoffmann von Fallersleben, A. H. "August Buchner." *Weimarisches Jahrbuch für deutsche Sprache, Litteratur und Kunst* 2 (1855): 1–39.

Hotson, Leslie. *The First Night of "Twelfth Night."* New York: Macmillan, 1954.

Howe, Sonia E., ed. *The False Dmitri: A Russian Romance and Tragedy Described by British Eye-Witnesses, 1604–1612.* London: Williams and Norgate, 1916.

Hughes, Lindsey. "Between Two Worlds: Tsarevna Natal'ia Alekseevna and the 'Emancipation' of Petrine Women." In *A Window on Russia: Papers from the V International Conference of the Study Group on Eighteenth-Century Russia, Gargnano, 1994,* 29–36. Rome: La Fenice, 1996.

——. "The Moscow Armoury and Innovations in Seventeenth-Century Muscovite Art." *Canadian-American Slavic Studies* 13, nos. 1–2 (1979): 204–23.

——. *Russia in the Age of Peter the Great.* New Haven: Yale University Press, 1998.

——. "Secularization and Westernization Revisited: Art and Architecture in Seventeenth-Century Russia." In *Modernizing Muscovy: Reform and Social Change in Seventeenth-Century Russia,* edited by Jarmo Kotilaine and Marshall Poe, 343–62. London: RoutledgeCurzon, 2004.

——. *Sophia Regent of Russia: 1657–1704.* New Haven: Yale University Press, 1990.

Iavorskii, Stefan. *Ritoricheskaia ruka, sochinenie Stefana Iavorskogo, perevod s latinskogo Feodora Polikarpova.* OLDP 20. St. Petersburg, 1878.

Igoshev, L. A. "Proiskhozhdenie grecheskogo rospeva (opyt analiza)." *PKNO 1992* (1993): 147–50.

Isaievych, Ia. D. *Voluntary Brotherhood: Confraternities of Laymen in Early Modern Ukraine.* Edmonton: Canadian Institute of Ukrainian Studies Press, 2006. This is an expanded translation of *Bratstva ta ikh rol' v rozvytku ukrains'koi kul'tury XVI–XVIII st.* Kiev: Naukova dumka, 1966.

Isherwood, Robert M. *Music in the Service of the King: France in the Seventeenth Century.* Ithaca, N.Y.: Cornell University Press, 1973.

Istomin, Karion. *Bukvar' sostavlen Karionom Istominym, gravirovan Leontiem Buninym, otpechatan v 1694 godu v Moskve.* Edited by V. I. Luk'ianenko and M. A. Alekseeva. Leningrad: Avrora, 1981.

Iusim, M. A. "Knigi iz biblioteki Simeona Polotskogo-Sil'vestra Medvedeva." *TODRL* 47 (1993): 312–27.

Janowka, Thomas. *Clavis ad thesaurum magnae artis musicae.* Prague, 1701. Reprint, Amsterdam: F. Knuf, 1973.

Jansson, Maija, and Nikolai Rogozhin, eds. *England and the North: The Russian Embassy of 1613–1614*. Translated by Paul Bushkovitch. Philadelphia: American Philosophical Society, 1994.

Jensen, Claudia R. "Music for the Tsar: A Preliminary Study of the Music of the Muscovite Court Theater." *Musical Quarterly* 79, no. 2 (1995): 368–401.

———. "Nikolai Diletskii's *Grammatika* (Grammar) and the Musical Culture of Seventeenth-Century Muscovy." Ph.D. diss., Princeton University, 1987.

———. "Orpheus in Muscovy: On the Early History of the Muscovite Court Theater." *Gimnologiia* 4 (2003): 281–300.

———, and John Powell. "'A Mess of Russians left us but of late': Diplomatic Blunder, Literary Satire, and the Muscovite Ambassador's 1668 Visit to Paris Theatres." *Theatre Research International* 24, no. 2 (1999): 131–44.

Kaiser, Daniel H. "Symbol and Ritual in the Marriages of Ivan IV." *Russian History / Histoire Russe* 14 (1987): 247–62.

[Kakash, Stefan, and Georgii Tektander]. "Puteshestvie v Persiiu cherez Moskoviiu 1602–1603 gg." Translated by A. Stankevich. *ChOIDR* 2 (1896), pt. 3:1–54.

Kalaidovich, K., and P. Stroev. *Obstoiatel'noe opisanie slaviano-rossiiskikh rukopisei, khraniashchikhsia v Moskve v biblioteke . . . grafa Fedora Andreevicha Tolstogo*. Moscow: V Tip. Selivanovskogo, 1825.

Kapterev, N. F. "Snosheniia ierusalimskikh patriarkhov s russkim pravitel'stvom s poloviny XVI do kontsa XVIII stoletiia." *Pravoslavnyi palestinskii sbornik* 15, vypusk 1 (1895; entire volume).

Karlinsky, Simon. *Russian Drama from Its Beginnings to the Age of Pushkin*. Berkeley: University of California Press, 1985.

Karpiak, Robert. "Culture of the Keyboard in 18th-Century Russia." *Continuo* (December 1998): 5–8.

Kazanskii, P. S. "Ispravlenie tserkovno-bogosluzhebnykh knig pri Patriarkhe Filarete." *ChOIDR* 8 (1848), pt. 1:1–26.

———. *Selo Novospaskoe, Dedenovo tozh i rodoslovnaia Golovinykh, vladel'tsev onogo*. Moscow: S. Selivanovskii, 1847.

Keenan, Edward L. *The Kurbskii-Groznyi Apocrypha: The Seventeenth-Century Genesis of the "Correspondence" Attributed to Prince A. M. Kurbskii and Tsar Ivan IV*. Cambridge, Mass.: Harvard University Press, 1971.

Keep, J. L. H. "The Régime of Filaret, 1619–1633." *SEER* 38 (1959–60): 334–60.

Keldysh, G. V., and others, eds. *Muzykal'nyi entsiklopedicheskii slovar'*. Moscow: Sovetskaia entsiklopediia, 1990.

Keldysh, Iu. V. "Rannii russkii kant." In *Ocherki i issledovaniia po istorii russkoi muzyki*, 64–91. Moscow: Sovetskii kompozitor, 1978. An earlier version published as "Ob istoricheskikh korniakh kanta." *Musica antiqua Europae orientalis* 2 (1969): 437–62.

Kennedy, Ruth. *The Dramatic Art of Moreto*. Philadelphia: Banta, 1932. Reprint from the *Smith College Studies in Modern Languages* 13, nos. 1–4.

Kharlampovich, K. V. *Malorossiiskoe vliianie na velikorusskuiu tserkovnuiu zhizn'*. 1914. Reprint, edited by C. H. van Schooneveld. The Hague: Slavistic Printings and Reprintings No. 119, 1968.

———. *Zapadnorusskie pravoslavnye shkoly XVI i nachala XVII veka*. Kazan': Tipo-lit. Imperatorskogo universiteta, 1898.

Kholodov, E. G. "K istorii starinnogo russkogo teatra (neskol'ko utochnenii)." *PKNO 1981* (1983): 149–70.

———. *Teatr i zriteli. Stranitsy istorii russkoi teatral'noi publiki.* Moscow: Gos. institut iskusstvoznaniia, 2000.

Kivelson, Valerie A., and Robert H. Greene, eds. *Orthodox Russia: Belief and Practice under the Tsars.* University Park: Pennsylvania State University Press, 2003.

Klenk, Koenraad van. *Posol'stvo Kunraada fan-Klenka k tsariam Alekseiu Mikhailovichu i Feodoru Alekseevichu / Historisch verhael, of Beschryving van de Voyagie, Gedaen onder de suite van den Heere Koenraad van Klenk.* St. Petersburg: Tip. Glavnogo upravleniia udelov, 1900.

Kliuchevskii, V. *Kurs russkoi istorii.* 5 vols. Moscow: Gos. sotsial'no-ekonomicheskoe izdatel'stvo, 1937.

Kniga nazyvaemaia Novyi letopisets. In *Khroniki smutnogo vremeni,* edited by A. Liberman, B. Morozov, and S. Shokarev, 263–410. Istoriia Rossii i doma Romanovykh v memuarakh sovremennikov XVII–XX vv. Moscow: Fond Sergeia Dubova, 1998.

Knös, Börje. "Une version grecque de l'histoire du Faux Démétrius, Tzar de la Russie." *Deltíon tês Historikês kaí Ethnologikês Hetaireías tês Helládos* 16 (1962): 223–66.

Koch, Ernst. "Die Sachsenkirche in Moskau und das erste Theater in Russland." *Neues Archiv für Sächsische Geschichte und Altertumskunde* 32 (1911): 270–316.

Kolesov, V. V., and V. V. Rozhdestvenskaia, eds. *Domostroi.* St. Petersburg: Nauka, 2000.

Kollmann, Nancy S. "Pilgrimage, Procession and Symbolic Space in Sixteenth-Century Russian Politics." In *Medieval Russian Culture* 2, edited by Michael S. Flier and Daniel Rowland. Special issue, *California Slavic Studies* 19 (1994): 163–81.

Kononenko, Natalie. *Ukrainian Minstrels: And the Blind Shall Sing.* Armonk, N.Y.: M. E. Sharpe, 1998.

Kononovich, S. S. "Epifanii Slavinetskii i 'Grazhdanstvo obychaev detskikh.'" *Sovetskaia pedagogika* 10 (1970): 107–13.

Konotop, A. V. "K voprosu rasshifrovki pevcheskikh notolineinykh pamiatnikov XVII veka." *SM* no. 7 (1973): 78–85.

———. "Struktura Suprasl'skogo irmologiona 1598–1601 gg.: Drevneinego pamiatnika ukrainskogo notolinienogo pis'ma." *Musica antiqua Europae orientalis* 4 (1975): 521–33.

———. "Suprasl'skii irmologii 1638–1639 gg." *PKNO 1980* (1981): 233–40.

———. "Suprasl'skii irmologion." *SM* no. 2 (1972): 117–21.

Konovalov, S. "England and Russia: Three Embassies, 1662–5." *Oxford Slavonic Papers* 10 (1962): 60–85.

Korableva, K. Iu. "Pokaiannye stikhi kak zhanr drevnerusskogo pevcheskogo iskusstva." Avtoreferat dissertatsii, Vsesoiuznyi nauchno-issledovatel'skii institut iskusstvoznaniia, 1979.

[Korb, Johann Georg]. "Korbs *Diarium itineris in Moscoviam* und Quellen, die es ergänzen." Edited by Friedrich Dukmeyer. *Historische Studien* 70 and 80 (1909 and 1910). Reprint, Vaduz, Liechtenstein: Kraus Reprint Ltd., 1965; complete volumes.

Koshelev, V. V. "Ispol'zovanie Pistsovykh knig v istoricheskikh issledovaniiakh." In *Referaty dokladov i soobshchenii VI Vserossiiskogo nauchno-prakticheskogo soveshchaniia po izucheniiu i izdaniiu pistsovykh knig i drugikh istoriko-geograficheskikh istochnikov,* 62–67. St. Petersburg: Rossiiskaia Akademiia nauk, 1993.

———. *Skomorokhi: Annotirovannyi bibliograficheskii ukazatel' 1790–1994 gg.* St. Petersburg: "Liki Rossii," 1994.

———. "Skomorokhi novgorodskoi zemli v XV–XVII stoletiiakh." In *Proshloe Novgoroda i novgorodskoi zemli: tezisy, dokladov i soobshchenii nauchnoi konferentsii 10–12 noia-bria 1992 g.*, 113–15. Novgorod: Izd. NGPI, 1992.

——, ed. *Skomorokhi: Problemy i perspektivy izucheniia (K 140-letiiu so dnia vykhoda pervoi raboty o skomorokhakh).* St. Petersburg: Rossiiskii institut istorii iskusstv, 1994.

——. " 'V tserkvi—obraza, a v kel'e—gudochnik.' " In *Iazychestvo vostochnykh slavian,* edited by I. V. Dubov, 88–97. Leningrad: Gos. ordena Druzhby narodov Muzei etnografii narodov SSSR, 1990.

Kostiukovets, L. F. *Kantovaia kul'tura v Belorussii.* Minsk: Vysheishaia shkola, 1975.

Kotkov, S. I., A. S. Oreshnikov, and I. S. Filippova, eds. *Moskovskaia delovaia i bytovaia pis'mennost' XVII veka.* Moscow: Nauka, 1968.

Kotliarchuk, A. S. *Prazdnichnaia kul'tura v gorodakh Rossii i Belorussii XVII veka: ofi-tsial'nye tseremonii i krest'ianskaia obriadnost'.* St. Petersburg: Peterburgskoe Vosto-kovedenie, 2001.

Kotoshikhin, Grigorii. *O Rossii v tsarstvovanie Alekseia Mikhailovicha.* In *Moskoviia i Evropa,* edited by A. Liberman and S. Shokarev, 9–146. Istoriia Rossii i doma Ro-manovykh v memuarakh sovremennikov XVII–XX vv. Moscow: Fond Sergeia Du-bova, 2000.

Kovrigina, V. A. *Nemetskaia sloboda Moskvy i ee zhiteli v kontse XVII–pervoi chetverti XVIII vv.* Moscow: Arkheograficheskii tsentr, 1998.

Krajcar, Jan, S.J. "Religious Conditions in Smolensk 1611–1654." *Orientalia christiana periodica* 33, fasc. 2 (1967): 404–56.

Kubilius, J., ed. *A Short History of Vilnius University.* Vilnius: Mokslas, 1979.

Kudriavtsev, I. M., ed. *'Artakserksovo deistvo'—Pervaia p'esa russkogo teatra XVII v.* Mos-cow: Izd. Akademii nauk SSSR, 1957.

——. "Dve liricheskie pesni, zapisannye v XVII veke." *TODRL* 9 (1953): 380–86.

——, ed. *Sobraniia D. V. Razumovskogo i V. F. Odoevskogo. Arkhiv D. V. Razumovskogo. Opisaniia.* Moscow: Tip. Biblioteki imeni V. I. Lenina, 1960.

Labyntsev, Iu. A. "Neizvestnyi pamiatnik notnoi pechati." *SM* no. 3 (1983): 76–78.

Lahana, Martha. "Breaking the Rules in Muscovy: The Example of A. S. Matveev." Un-published article.

——. "Novaia Nemetskaia Sloboda: Seventeenth Century Moscow's Foreign Suburb." Ph.D. diss., University of North Carolina at Chapel Hill, 1983.

Lapteva, L. P. "Rasskaz ochevidtsa o zhizni Moskovii kontsa XVII veka." *Voprosy istorii* 1 (1970): 103–26.

Larin, B. A. *Tri inostrannykh istochnika po razgovornoi rechi Moskovskoi Rusi XVI–XVII vekov.* St. Petersburg: Izdatel'stvo S.-Peterburgskogo universiteta, 2002.

Lauxmin, Sigismund [Žygimantas Liauksminas]. *Ars et praxis musica.* 1667. Edited by Vytautas Jurkštas and others. Vilnius: Vaga, 1977.

Lebedeva, I. N. "Biblioteka Tsarevny Natalii Alekseevny, russkoi obrazovannoi zhen-shchiny nachala XVIII v." In *Materialy i soobshcheniia po fondam Otdela rukopisnoi i redkoi knigi Biblioteki Rossiiskoi Akademii nauk,* edited by L. I. Kiseleva, 240–53. St. Petersburg: Biblioteka Rossiiskoi Akademii nauk, 1994.

La Légende de la vie et de la mort de Demétrius. Amsterdam, 1606. Published in *Histoire des guerres de la Moscovie,* edited by A. van der Linde, 1:287–310. Brussels: Fr. J. Olivier, 1866.

Lehmann, Dieter. "Dilezki und die grosse Wandlung der russischen Musik." *Studia Musi-cologica Academiae Scientiarum Hungaricae* 9 (1967): 343–69.

——. "Mikołaj Dylecki a muzyka polska w XVII wieku." *Muzyka* 10, no. 3 (1965): 38–51.

——. "Nikolai Dilezki und seine 'Musikalische Grammatik' in ihrer Bedeutung für die Geschichte der russischen Musik." Habilitationsschrift, Humboldt University, 1962.

Leitsch, Walter. "Herberstein's Impact on the Reports about Muscovy in the 16th and 17th Centuries: Some Observations on the Technique of Borrowing." *Forschungen zur osteuropäischen Geschichte* 24 (1978): 163–77.

Leonard, Richard Anthony. *A History of Russian Music.* New York: Macmillan, 1968.

Leonid, Archimandrite. "Istoricheskoe opisanie stavropigial'nogo Voskresenskogo Novyi Ierusalim imenuemogo monastyria." *ChOIDR* 3 (1874), pt. 1:i–iv, 1–124; 4 (1874): pt. 1:125–366; 1 (1875), pt. 1:367–464; 2 (1875), pt. 1:465–543; 3 (1875), pt. 1:545–767.

——. *Sistematicheskoe opisanie slaviano-rossiiskikh rukopisei sobraniia Grafa A. S. Uvarova.* Moscow: Tip. Mamontova, 1893.

——. "Svedenie o slavianskikh pergamennykh rukopisiakh, postupivshikh iz knigokhranilishcha Sviato-Troitskoi Sergievoi Lavry v biblioteku Troitskoi Dukhovnoi seminarii v 1747." *ChOIDR* 2 (1883), pt. 2:81–167. (This is part 2 of a long continuing series.)

Lester, Joel. *Between Modes and Keys: German Theory 1592–1802.* Harmonologia Series 3. Stuyvesant, N.Y.: Pendragon Press, 1989.

——. "Major-Minor Concepts and Modal Theory in Germany: 1592–1680." *JAMS* 30, no. 2 (1977): 208–53.

——. "The Recognition of Major and Minor Keys in German Theory: 1680–1730." *Journal of Music Theory* 22, no. 1 (1978): 65–103.

Letiche, John M., and Basil Dmytryshyn, eds. *Russian Statecraft: The "Politika" of Iurii Krizhanich.* Oxford: Basil Blackwell, 1985.

Lewin, Paulina. "Jan Kochanowski: The Model Poet in Eastern Slavic Lectures on Poetics of the Seventeenth and Eighteenth Centuries." In *The Polish Renaissance in Its European Context,* edited by Samuel Fiszman, 429–43. Bloomington: Indiana University Press, 1988.

——. "Polish-Ukrainian-Russian Literary Relations of the Sixteenth–Eighteenth Centuries: New Approaches." *Slavic and Eastern European Journal* 24, no. 1 (1980): 256–69.

——, intro. *Seventeenth-Century Writings on the Kievan Caves Monastery.* Vol. 4, *Harvard Library of Early Ukrainian Literature. Texts.* Cambridge, Mass.: Distributed by the Harvard University Press for the Ukrainian Research Institute of Harvard University, 1987.

——. "The Staging of Plays at the Kiev Mohyla Academy in the Seventeenth and Eighteenth Centuries." *Harvard Ukrainian Studies* 5, no. 3 (1981): 320–34.

——. "The Ukrainian School Theater in the Seventeenth and Eighteenth Centuries: An Expression of the Baroque." *Harvard Ukrainian Studies* 5, no. 1 (1981): 54–65.

Likhachev, D. S., ed. *Puteshestviia russkikh poslov XVI–XVII vv.: Stateinye spiski.* Moscow: AN SSSR, 1954.

——, A. M. Panchenko, and N. V. Ponyrko. *Smekh v drevnei Rusi.* Leningrad: Nauka, 1984. First edition by D. S. Likhachev and A. M. Panchenko. *"Smekhovoi mir" drevnei Rusi.* Leningrad: Nauka, 1976.

Livanova, T. N. *Ocherki i materialy po istorii russkoi muzykal'noi kul'tury.* Moscow: Iskusstvo, 1938.

——. *Russkaia muzykal'naia kul'tura XVIII veka.* 2 vols. Moscow: Gos. muzykal'noe izdatel'stvo, 1952–53. Includes a separately published transcription of *kanty,* as *Sbornik kantov XVIII veka.* Moscow: Gos. muzykal'noe izdatel'stvo, 1952.

Loewenson, Leo. "Sir Roger Manley's History of Muscovy, *The Russian Impostor* (1674)." *SEER* 31, no. 76 (1952): 232–40.

———. "The Works of Robert Boyle and 'The Present State of Russia' by Samuel Collins (1671)." *SEER* 33 (1954–55): 470–85.

Longworth, Philip. *Alexis, Tsar of All the Russias.* New York: Franklin Watts, 1984.

Lorente, Manuel. *The Prado: Madrid.* 2 vols. New York: Appleton-Century, 1965.

Louria, Yvette, trans. "The Comedy of Artaxerxes (1672)." *Bulletin of the New York Public Library* 72, no. 3 (1968): 139–210.

Lunden, Siri Sverdrup. *The Trondheim Russian-German MS Vocabulary: A Contribution to 17th-Century Russian Lexicography.* Oslo: Universitetsforlaget, 1972.

[Lyseck, Adolf]. "Posol'stvo Battoni ot Avstriiskogo Imperatora Leopol'da k Tsariu Alekseiu Mikhailovichu v 1675 godu, opisannoe Adol'fom Lizekkom, sekretarem posol'stva." *Otechestvennye zapiski* 33 (Jan. 1828): 290–316; 35 (Sept. 1828): 280–96 and 301–32.

[———]. *Relatio eorum, quae circa Sacrae Caesareae Maiestatis ad Magnum Moscorum Czarum Ablegatos Annibalem Franciscum de Bottoni.* Salzburg: J. B. Mayr, 1676.

[———]. "Skazanie Adol'fa Lizeka o posol'stve ot Imperatora rimskogo Leopol'da k velikomu tsariu moskovskomu Aleksiiu Mikhailovichu, v 1675 godu." Translated by I. Tarnav-Borichevskii. *ZhMNP* 16 (1837): section 2: 327–94.

Magnitskii, Leontii. *Arifmetika, sirech' Nauka chislitel'naia.* Moscow: Sinodal'naia tip., 1703.

Maiasova, N. A. "Literaturnyi obraz Ksenii Godunovoi i pripisyvaemye ei proizvedeniia shit'ia (K voprosu o vzaimootnoshenii literatury, iskusstva i deistvitel'nosti)." *TODRL* 22 (1966): 294–310.

Maier, Ingrid. "Newspaper Translations in Seventeenth-Century Muscovy: About the Sources, Topics and Periodicity of *Kuranty* 'Made in Stockholm' (1649)." In *Explorare necesse est. Hyllningsskrift till Barbro Nilsson,* 181–90. Acta Universitatis Stockholmiensis. Stockholm: Universitet Stockholms, 2002.

———, and Wouter Pilger. "Second-hand Translation for Tsar Aleksej Mixajlovič—A Glimpse into the 'Newspaper Workshop' at *Posol'skij Prikaz* (1648)." *Russian Linguistics* 25, no. 2 (2001): 209–42.

Makarii, Metropolitan of Moscow. *Istoriia russkoi tserkvi.* Vols. 10–11 (2nd ed.) and 12 (1st ed.). St. Petersburg: Pechatnia R. Golike, 1883 and 1902–1903.

Malyshev, V. I. "Stikhotvornaia parallel' k 'Povesti o Gore i Zlochastii' (Stikh 'pokaianny' o p'ianstve)." *TODRL* 5 (1947): 142–48.

———. "Stikh 'pokaianny' o 'liute' vremeni i 'poganykh' nashestvii." *TODRL* 15 (1958): 371–74.

———. "Zametka o rukopisnykh spiskakh Zhitiia protopopa Avvakuma (Materialy dlia bibliografii)." *TODRL* 8 (1951): 379–91.

Manley, Roger. *The Russian Impostor: or, the History of Muskovy, under the Usurpation of Boris and the Imposture of Demetrius, Late Emperours of Muskovy.* London: Thomas Bassett, 1674; 2nd ed., with An Appendix, being the Amours of Demetrius and Dorenski, 1677.

Margeret, Jacques. *The Russian Empire and Grand Duchy of Muscovy: A 17th-Century French Account.* Translated and edited by Chester S. L. Dunning. Pittsburgh: University of Pittsburgh Press, 1983.

Markelov, G. V., and S. V. Frolov. "Stroganovskie rukopisi v Pushkinskom dome." *PKNO* 1975 (1976): 70–72.

Markov, A. V. *Belomorskie stariny i dukhovnye stikhi.* Edited by S. N. Azbelev and Iu. I. Marchenko. St. Petersburg: Dmitrii Bulanin, 2002.

Martin, Russell E. "Archival Sleuths and Documentary Transpositions: Notes on the Typology and Textology of Muscovite Royal Wedding Descriptions." *Russian History / Histoire Russe* 30, no. 3 (2003): 253–300.

———. "Choreographing the 'Tsar's Happy Occasion': Tradition, Change, and Dynastic Legitimacy in the Weddings of Tsar Mikhail Romanov." *Slavic Review* 63, no. 4 (2004): 794–817.

Massa, Isaac. *Een cort verhael van begin en oorspronck deser tegenwoordighe oorloogen en troeblen in Moscouia totten jare 1610.* Published in *Histoire des guerres de la Moscovie (1601–1610),* edited by A. van der Linde, 1:1–219. Brussels: Fr. J. Olivier, 1866.

———. *A Short History of the Beginnings and Origins of These Present Wars in Moscow under the Reign of Various Sovereigns down to the Year 1610.* Translated and with an introduction by G. Edward Orchard. Toronto: University of Toronto Press, 1982.

Massie, Robert K. *Peter the Great: His Life and World.* New York: Ballantine Books, 1981.

Massie, Suzanne. *Land of the Firebird: The Beauty of Old Russia.* Blue Hill, Maine: Heart Tree Press, 1980.

Mattheson, Johann. *Boris Goudenow.* Edited by Jörg Jacobi, Paul O'Dette, and Stephen Stubbs. [Cambridge, Mass.]: Boston Early Music Festival, [2004].

Mazon, André, and Frédéric Cocron, eds. *"La Comédie d'Artaxerxès" (Artakserksovo deistvo) présentée en 1672 au Tsar Alexis par Gregorii le Pasteur.* Paris: Institut d'Études slaves de l'Université de Paris, 1954.

Meierberg, Avgustin. *Puteshestvie v Moskoviiu barona Avgustina Meierberga,* in *Utverzhdenie dinastii,* edited by A. Liberman, 43–184. Istoriia Rossii i doma Romanovykh v memuarakh sovremennikov XVII–XX vv. Moscow: Fond Sergeia Dubova, 1997.

Mel'nikova, N. N. *Izdaniia, napechatannye v tipografii Moskovskogo universiteta XVIII v.* Edited by P. N. Berkov. Moscow: Izdatel'stvo Moskovskogo universiteta, 1966.

Metallov, V. M. *Ocherk istorii pravoslavnogo tserkovnogo peniia v Rossii.* Moscow: Tip. A. I. Snegirevoi, 1915.

———. "Starinnyi traktat po teorii muzyki, 1679 goda, sostavlennyi kievlianinom Nikolaem Diletskim." *Russkaia muzykal'naia gazeta* no. 12 (1897): 1728–62.

Meyendorff, Paul. *Russia, Ritual, and Reform: The Liturgical Reforms of Nikon in the 17th Century.* Crestwood, N.Y.: St. Vladimir's Seminary Press, 1991.

[Mezenets, Aleksandr]. *Aleksandr Mezenets i prochie, Izveshchenie . . . zhelaiushchim uchitsia peniiu, 1670 g.* Edited by Zivar Guseinova and Nikolai Parfent'ev. Cheliabinsk: Kniga, 1996.

———. *Azbuka znamennogo peniia (Izveshchenie o soglasneishikh pometakh) startsa Aleksandra Mezentsa (1668-go goda).* Edited by S. V. Smolenskii. Kazan': Tip. Imp. universiteta, 1888.

[Miege, Guy]. *A Relation of Three Embassies from his sacred Majestie Charles II to the Great Duke of Muscovie, the King of Sweden, and the King of Denmark. Performed by the Right Ho-ble the Earle of Carlisle in the years 1663 and 1664.* London: Printed for John Starkey, 1669.

Mikulin, N. B. "Kommentarii k naznacheniiu rossiiskogo poslannika v Angliiu Grigoriia Ivanovicha Mikulina i ego prebyvaniiu v Londone v 1600–1601 gg." *Vspomogatel'nye istoricheskie distsipliny* 27 (2000): 32–38.

Moleva, N. M. "Kaftany dlia khaldeev." *Znanie-sila* 9 (1970): 36–38.

———. "Muzyka i zrelishcha v Rossii XVII stoletiia." *Voprosy istorii* (November 1971): 143–54.

Morosan, Vladimir. *Choral Performance in Pre-Revolutionary Russia*. Russian Music Studies 17. Ann Arbor: UMI Research Press, 1986.

——, ed. *One Thousand Years of Russian Church Music / Tysiacha let russkoi tserkovnoi muzyki*. Monuments of Russian Sacred Music series 1, vol. 1. Washington, D.C.: Musica Russica, 1991.

——. "*Penie* and *Musikiia*: Aesthetic Changes in Russian Liturgical Singing during the Seventeenth Century." *St. Vladimir's Theological Quarterly* 23, nos. 3–4 (1979): 149–79.

Mudrost' chetvertaia Musikia. OLDP Izdaniia 6. [St. Petersburg], 1877.

Muller, Alexander V., trans. and ed. *The Spiritual Regulation of Peter the Great*. Seattle: University of Washington Press, 1972.

[Mundy, Peter]. *The Travels of Peter Mundy in Europe and Asia, 1608–1667*. Edited by Sir Richard Carnac Temple. Vol. 4. Works issued by the Hakluyt Society, second series, no. 55. London: Printed for the Hakluyt Society, 1925.

[Muratova, Irina]. "Irina Muratova: Debiut rossiiskogo muzykal'nogo." Interview by E. Pol'diaeva. *Muzykal'naia akademiia* 2 (1992): 119–20.

Murphy, Declan C. "Cicero and the Icon Painters: The Transformation of Byzantine Image Theory in Medieval Muscovy." In *The Byzantine Legacy in Eastern Europe*, edited by Lowell Clucas, 149–64. New York: Distributed by Columbia University Press, 1988.

Museo del Prado: Inventario general de pinturas. Vol. 1, *La colección real*. Madrid: Museo del Prado, 1990.

Niemojewski, Stanisław. *Pamiętnik Stanisława Niemojewskiego*. Edited by Aleksander Hirschberg. Lwów: Nakładem zakładu N. im. Ossolińskich, 1899.

[——]. "Zapiski Stanislava Nemoevskogo (1606–1608)." Translated by A. A. Titov. *Rukopisi slavianskie i russkie, prinadlezhashchie I. A. Vakhrameevu*. Vol. 6, section 2 (unnumbered but with new pagination): i–xii, 1–292. Moscow: Tip. A. I. Snegirevoi, 1907.

Nikolaev, S. I. "Russkie intermedii XVII v.: novye materialy." *TODRL* 55 (2004): 423–26.

Nikolaevskii, Pavel. "Uchrezhdenie patriarshestva v Rossii." *Khristianskoe chtenie* 7–8 (1879): 3–40; 9–10 (1879): 369–406; 11–12 (1879): 552–81; and 1–2 (1880): 128–58 (under the title "Snosheniia russkikh s Vostokom ob ierarkhicheskoi stepeni moskovskogo patriarkha").

Nowak-Dłużewski, J., and others, eds. *Kolędy polskie: średniowiecze i wiek XVI*. 2 vols. Warsaw: Instytut Wydawniczy Pax, 1966.

Obolenskii, M. *Inostrannye sochineniia i akty, otnosiashchiesia do Rossii*. Part 4. Moscow: Universitetskaia tip., 1848.

Occasional Reflections upon Several Subjects, Whereto is premis'd a Discourse about such kind of Thoughts. 2nd edition. London: Printed for Henry Herringman, 1669.

Odoevskii, V. F. "Mirskaia pesnia napisannaia na vosem' glasov kriukami s kinovarnymi pometami." *Trudy I-go arkheologicheskogo s"ezda v Moskve, 1869 g.* (1871), 2:484–91.

Okenfuss, Max J. *The Discovery of Childhood in Russia: The Evidence of the Slavic Primer*. Newtonville, Mass.: Oriental Research Partners, 1980.

——. "Education in Russia in the First Half of the Eighteenth Century." Ph.D. diss., Harvard University, 1970.

——. "The Jesuit Origins of Petrine Education." In *The Eighteenth Century in Russia*, edited by John G. Garrard, 106–30. Oxford: Clarendon, 1973.

——. *The Rise and Fall of Latin Humanism in Early-Modern Russia: Pagan Authors, Ukrainians, and the Resiliency of Muscovy.* Leiden: E. J. Brill, 1995.

Olearius, Adam. *Offt begehrte Beschreibung der Newen Orientalischen Reyse.* Schleswig: Bey Jacob zur Glocken, 1647. Available in the series Bibliothek der deutschen Literatur, fiche 9454–9456.

——. *The Travels of Olearius in Seventeenth-Century Russia.* Translated and edited by Samuel Baron. Stanford: Stanford University Press, 1967.

——. *Vermehrte Newe Beschreibung Der Muscowitischen vnd Persischen Reyse (Schleswig 1656).* Edited by Dieter Lohmeier. Tübingen: Max Niemeyer Verlag, 1971.

Opyt irmoloinago peniia, v kratkikh pravilakh v Belogorodskoi dukhovnoi seminarii dlia legchaishago onomu izucheniia napisannyi. Moscow: Sinodal'naia tip., 1798.

Orlov, A. "Chashi gosudarevy." *ChOIDR* 4 (1913), pt. 2:1–69.

Ornithoparchus, Andreas. *Musicae actiue micrologus.* Leipzig: Valentin Schumann, 1517.

Oxford Annotated Bible with the Apocrypha. Edited by Herbert G. May and Bruce M. Metzger. Oxford: Oxford University Press, 1965.

Ozanam, Jacques. *Dictionnaire mathématique, ou Idée general des mathématiques.* Paris: Estienne Michallet, 1691.

Palmer, Daryl W. *Writing Russia in the Age of Shakespeare.* Aldershot, Hampshire: Ashgate, 2004.

Palmer, William. *The Patriarch and the Tsar.* 6 vols. London: Trübner and Co., 1871–76.

Pamuła, Maria. "*Tabulatura muzyki* Jana Aleksandra Gorczyna." *Muzyka* 2 (1977): 65–78.

Panchenko, A. M. "Deklamatsiia Sil'vestra Medvedeva na temu strastei Khristovykh." In *Rukopisnoe nasledie drevnei Rusi po materialam Pushkinskogo doma,* 115–35. Leningrad: Nauka, 1972.

——. "Pridvornye virshi 80-kh godov XVII stoletiia." *TODRL* 21 (1965): 65–73.

——. *Russkaia stikhotvornaia kul'tura XVII veka.* Leningrad: Nauka, 1973.

Papadopoulos, Chrysostomos. *Hoi patriárchai Hierosolýmōn hōs pneumatikoí cheiragōgoí tês Rosías katá tón IZ′ aiôna* [The Patriarchs of Jerusalem as Spiritual Leaders of Russia during the 17th Century]. Jerusalem: Typois hierou koinou tou Panagiou Taphou, 1907.

Papadopoulos, George-Julius, and Claudia Jensen. " 'A Confusion of Glory': Orthodox Visitors as Sources for Muscovite Musical Practice (Late 16th–mid 17th Century)." *Intersections: Canadian Journal of Music* 26, no. 1 (2005): 3–33.

Papmehl, K. A. "An Eighteenth-Century English Translation of a Ukrainian Folk Song." *Canadian Slavonic Papers* 24 (1982): 175–80.

Parfent'ev, N. P. "Avtografy vydaiushchegosia russkogo muzykal'nogo teoretika XVII v. Aleksandra Mezentsa (Stremoukhova)." *PKNO 1990* (1992): 173–85.

——. *Drevnerusskoe pevcheskoe iskusstvo v dukhovnoi kul'ture Rossiiskogo gosudarstva XVI–XVII vv.: Shkoly. Tsentry. Mastera.* Sverdlovsk: Izdatel'stvo Ural'skogo universiteta, 1991.

——. "Prikaznye dokumenty o stroganovskikh 'spevakakh.' " In *Issledovaniia po istorii obshchestvennogo soznaniia epokhi feodalizma v Rossii,* 213–23. Novosibirsk: Nauka, 1984.

——. *Professional'nye muzykanty Rossiiskogo gosudarstva XVI–XVII vekov.* Cheliabinsk: Izdatel'stvo Cheliabinskogo poligr. ob"edineniia "Kniga," 1991.

——. "Usol'skaia shkola v drevnerusskom pevcheskom iskusstve XVI–XVII vv. i proizvedeniia ee masterov v pamiatnikakh pis'mennosti." In *Pamiatniki literatury i obshchestvennoi mysli epokhi feodalizma,* edited by E. K. Romodanovskaia, 52–69. Novosibirsk: Nauka, 1985.

——, and N. V. Parfent'eva. *Usol'skaia (Stroganovskaia) shkola v russkoi muzyke XVI– XVII vekov.* Cheliabinsk: Izdatel'stvo Cheliabinskogo poligr. ob"edineniia "Kniga," 1993.

Parr, Anthony, ed. *Three Renaissance Travel Plays.* Manchester: Manchester University Press, 1995.

Paul of Aleppo. "Puteshestvie antiokhiiskogo patriarkha Makariia v Rossiiu v polovine XVII v., opisannoe ego synom, arkhidiakonom Pavlom Aleppskim." Translated by G. A. Murkos. *ChOIDR* 4 (1896), pt. 2:i–x, 1–156; 4 (1897), pt. 3:i–viii, 1–202; 3 (1898), pt. 3:i–iv, 1–208; 4 (1898), pt. 2:i–ix, 1–195; and 2 (1900), pt. 3:i–v, 1–246.

——. *The Travels of Macarius.* Translated by F. C. Belfour. 2 vols. London: Printed for the Oriental Translation Committee, 1829–36.

——. "Voyage du Patriarche Macaire d'Antioche: Text arab et traduction française." Translated by Basile Radu. *Patrologia Orientalis* 22, fasc. 1 (1930): 1–200; 24, fasc. 4 (1933): 443–604 (with continuous pagination in square brackets as [203–364]); and 26, fasc. 5 (1949): 603–720 [367–484]).

Pekarskii, P. *Nauka i literatura v Rossii pri Petre Velikom.* 2 vols. St. Petersburg: Obshchest-vennaia pol'za, 1862.

Pepys, Samuel. *The Diary of Samuel Pepys.* Edited, with additions, by Henry B. Wheatley. 3 vols. London: G. Bell and Sons, and New York: Harcourt, Brace and Co., 1924.

Perepisnaia kniga goroda Moskvy 1638 goda. Moscow: Tip. M. P. Shchepkina, 1881.

Perepisnye knigi goroda Moskvy 1665–76 gg. Moscow: Gorodskaia tip., 1886.

Peretts, V. N. *Iz istorii razvitiia russkoi poezii XVIII v.* Vol. 3 of *Istoriko-literaturnye issledovaniia i materialy.* St. Petersburg: Tip. F. Vaisberga i P. Gershunina, 1902.

——. *Iz istorii russkoi pesni.* Vol. 1 of *Istoriko-literaturnye issledovaniia i materialy.* St. Petersburg: Tip. F. Vaisberga i P. Gershunina, 1900.

——. "K istorii drevne-russkoi liriki ('Stikhi umilennye')." *Slavia. Časopis pro slovanskou filologii* 11, no. 3–4 (1932): 474–79.

Perrie, Maureen. *Pretenders and Popular Monarchism in Early Modern Russia: The False Tsars of the Time of Troubles.* Cambridge: Cambridge University Press, 1995.

[Petreius, Peter]. "Istoriia o velikom kniazhestve Moskovskom." Translated by A. N. Shemiakin. *ChOIDR* 4 (1865), pt. 4:i–xii, 1–88; 1 (1866), pt. 4:89–184; 2 (1866), pt. 4:185–280; 3 (1866), pt. 4:281–341; and 2 (1867), pt. 4:343–454.

Petrov, N. I. "Kievskaia Akademiia vo vtoroi polovine XVII veka." *TKDA* no. 8 (Aug. 1895): 586–622; no. 9 (Sept. 1895): 36–56; no. 10 (Oct. 1895): 201–56; and no. 12 (Dec. 1895): 574–632.

——. "O slovesnykh naukakh i literaturnykh zaniatiiakh v Kievskoi Akademii ot nachala ee do preobrazovaniia v 1819 godu." *TKDA* no. 7 (1866): 305–30; no. 11 (1866): 343– 88; no. 12 (1866): 552–69; no. 1 (1867): 82–118; and no. 3 (1868): 465–525.

Petrova, L. A., and N. S. Seregina. *Ranniaia russkaia lirika.* Leningrad: Biblioteka Akademii nauk, 1988.

Petrovskaia, I. "Ob izuchenii russkoi muzykal'noi kul'tury vtoroi poloviny XVII—pervoi chetverti XVIII veka." *Kritika i muzykoznanie: sbornik statei* 2: 232–41. Leningrad: Muzyka, 1980.

Petukhov, V. I. "Svedeniia o skomorokhakh v pistsovykh, perepisnykh i tamozhennykh knigakh XVI–XVII vv." *Trudy Moskovskogo gos. istoriko-arkhivnogo instituta* 16 (1961): 409–19.

Phipps, Geraldine. "Britons in Seventeenth-Century Russia: A Study in the Origins of Modernization." Ph.D. diss., University of Pennsylvania, 1971.

——. "The Russian Embassy to London of 1645–46 and the Abrogation of the Muscovy Company's Charter." *SEER* 68, no. 2 (1990): 257–76.

Pichura, H. "The Podobny Texts and Chants of the Suprasl Irmologion of 1601." *Journal of Byelorussian Studies* 2 (1970): 192–221.

Pis'ma i bumagi Imperatora Petra Velikogo. Vol. 1. St. Petersburg: Gosudarstvennaia tip., 1887.

Pitirim, Bishop of Volokolamsk. "Arsenii, Arkhiepiskop elassonskii: Opisanie puteshestviia, predpriniatogo Ieremiei vtorym, Patriarkhom konstantinopol'skim, v Moskoviiu, i uchrezhdeniia moskovskogo patriarshestva." *Bogoslovskie trudy* 4 (1968): 251–79.

Platonov, S. F. *The Time of Troubles.* Translated by John T. Alexander. Lawrence: University Press of Kansas, 1970.

Poe, Marshall T. *Foreign Descriptions of Muscovy: An Analytic Bibliography of Primary and Secondary Sources.* Columbus, Ohio: Slavica, 1995.

——. *"A People Born to Slavery": Russia in Early Modern European Ethnography, 1476–1748.* Ithaca, N.Y.: Cornell University Press, 2000.

Polotskii, Simeon. *Izbrannye sochineniia.* Edited by I. P. Eremin. 1953. Reprint, St. Petersburg: Nauka, 2004.

——. *Orel rossiiskii: Tvorenie Simeona Polotskogo.* Edited by N. A. Smirnov. OLDP Izdaniia 133. [St. Petersburg]: Tip. M. A. Aleksandrova, 1915.

——. *Virshi.* Minsk: Mastatskaia litaratura, 1990.

—— [Symeon Polockij]. *Zezl pravlenija (Moskva 1753).* Bibliotheca Slavica 2. Zug: Inter Documentation Co. [1967].

Ponyrko, N. V. "Avtor stikhov pokaiannykh i raspevshchik iurodivyi Stefan." *TODRL* 54 (2003): 220–30.

——. "Stikhi pokaiannye galitskogo iurodivogo XVII v. Stefana." *TODRL* 56 (2004): 596–600.

Pope, Richard W. F. "Fools and Folly in Old Russia." Review of *"Smekhovoi mir" drevnei Rusi,* by D. S. Likhachev and A. M. Panchenko. *Slavic Review* 39, no. 3 (1980): 476–81.

Popov, N. P. "1685 g. O poezdke v Smolensk k mitrop. Simeonu 'dlia velikikh dukhovnykh del.'" *ChOIDR* 2 (1907), pt. 5:38–44.

Porfir'eva, A. L. "Legenda o kapelle gertsoga golshtinskogo i podlinnaia istoriia pridvornogo orkestra v 1702–1728 gg." *PKNO 1996* (1998): 168–85.

Possevino, Antonio. *The Moscovia of Antonio Possevino, S. J.* Translated by Hugh F. Graham. Pittsburgh: University Center for International Studies, 1977.

Pouncy, Carolyn, trans. *The Domostroi: Rules for Russian Households in the Time of Ivan the Terrible.* Ithaca, N.Y.: Cornell University Press, 1994.

Pozdneev, A. V. "Die geistlichen Lieder des Epifanij Slavineckij." *Die Welt der Slaven* 5, H. 3–4 (1960): 356–85.

——. "Knizhnye pesni XVII veka o vossoedinenii Ukrainy s Rossiei." *Slavia: Časopis pro slovanskou filologii* 27, no. 2 (1958): 226–40.

——. "Nikonovskaia shkola pesennoi poezii." *TODRL* 17 (1961): 419–28.

——. "Pesni-akrostikhi Germana." *TODRL* 14 (1958): 364–70.

——. "Poet XVII veka German (master akrostikha)." *Československá rusistika* 14, no. 4 (1969): 150–58.

——. "Pol'skii element v russkikh rukopisnykh pesennikakh XVII v." *TODRL* 23 (1968): 335–38.

——. "Rukopisnye pesenniki XVII–XVIII vekov (Iz istorii pesennoi sillabicheskoi poezii)." *Uchenye zapiski Moskovskogo gosudarstvennogo zaochnogo pedagogicheskogo instituta* 1 (1958): 5–112.

——. *Rukopisnye pesenniki XVII–XVIII vv. Iz istorii pesennoi sillabicheskoi poezii.* Moscow: Nauka, 1996.

——. "Svetskie pol'skie pesni v russkikh rukopisnykh pesennikakh XVII v." In *Pol'sko-Russkie literaturnye sviazi,* 56–70. Moscow: Nauka, 1970.

Prashkovich, N. I. "Iz rannikh deklamatsii Simeona Polotskogo ('Metry' i 'Dialog kratkii')." *TODRL* 21 (1965): 29–38.

Preobrazhenskii, A. "Iz pervykh let partesnogo peniia v Moskve." *Muzykal'nyi sovremennik* 3 (1915): 33–41.

——. *Kul'tovaia muzyka v Rossii.* Leningrad: "Academia," 1924.

Proehl, Friedrich-Karl. "Eine Beschreibung Moskaus durch den Kurländer Jakob Reutenfels." *Zeitschrift für Ostforschung. Länder und Völker im östlichen Mitteleuropa* 3 (1962): 455–75.

Prosnak, Jan. "Z dziejów staropolskiego szkolnictwa muzycznego." *Muzyka* 6, no. 9–10 (1955): 11–23.

Protopopov, V. V. "Chetyrekhgolosnaia khorovaia kompozitsiia tsaria Alekseia Mikhailovicha." *PKNO 1991* (1997): 107–10.

——. " 'Musikiia' Ioannikiia Koreneva." *Starinnaia muzyka* 3 (1999): 12–15.

——. *Muzyka na Poltavskuiu pobedu.* PRMI 2. Moscow: Muzyka, 1973.

——. "Neizvestnoe posobie po teorii muzyki XVIII v." *PKNO 1974* (1975): 294–302.

——. "Nikolai Diletskii i ego russkie sovremenniki." *SM* no. 12 (1973): 82–93.

——. "Notnaia biblioteka tsaria Fedora Alekseevicha." *PKNO 1976* (1977): 119–33.

——. "Panegiricheskii kant 1690 g." *PKNO 1980* (1981): 241–44.

——. *Russkaia mysl' o muzyke v XVII veke.* Moscow: Muzyka, 1989.

——. "Tvoreniia Vasiliia Titova—Vydaiushchegosia russkogo kompozitora vtoroi poloviny XVII–nachala XVIII veka." *Musica antiqua Europae orientalis* 3 (1972): 847–65.

Przywecka-Samecka, Maria. *Dzieje drukarstwa muzycznego w Polsce do końca XVIII wieku.* Wrocław: Wydawnictwo Uniwersytetu Wrocławskiego, 1993.

Rabinovich, M. G. "The Wedding in the Sixteenth-Century Russian City." *Soviet Anthropology and Archeology* 18, no. 4 (1980): 32–54, and 20, no. 1 (1981): 55–72. Originally published as "Svad'ba v russkom gorode v XVI v." In *Russkii narodnyi svadebnyi obriad: Issledovaniia i materialy,* edited by K. V. Chistova and T. A. Bernshtam, 7–31. Leningrad: Nauka, 1978.

Radziwiłł, Albrycht Stanisław. *Memoriale rerum gestarum in Polonia: 1632–1656.* Edited by Adam Przyboś and Roman Żelewski. 5 vols. Wrocław: Polska akademia nauk, 1968–75.

——. *Pamiętnik o dziejach w Polsce.* Edited by Adam Przyboś and Roman Żelewski. 3 vols. Warsaw: Państwowy Instytut Wydawniczy, 1980.

Ramazanova, N. V. *Moskovskoe tsarstvo v tserkovno-pevcheskom iskusstve.* St. Petersburg: Dmitrii Bulanin, 2004.

Razumovskii, D. V. "Gosudarevy pevchie d'iaki XVII veka." *Obshchestvo drevne-russkogo iskusstva na 1873 g.* (1873): 153–81.

——. *Patriarshie pevchie diaki i poddiaki i gosudarevy pevchie diaki.* St. Petersburg: Izd. N. F. Findeizena, 1895.

———. *Tserkovnoe penie v Rossii.* Moscow: Tip. T. Ris, 1867–68.

Reitenfel's. See also Reutenfels.

Reitenfel's, Iakov. *Skazaniia svetleishemu gertsogu toskanskomu Koz'me tret'emu o Mos-kovii.* In *Utverzhdenie dinastii,* edited by A. Liberman, 231–406. Istoriia Rossii i doma Romanovykh v memuarakh sovremennikov XVII–XX vv. Moscow: Fond Sergeia Dubova, 1997. This is a reprint of the translation by A. Stankevich originally appearing in *ChOIDR* 3 (1905), pt. 2:i–x, 1–128, and 3 (1906), pt. 3:129–228.

Relazione della segnalata, e come miracolosa conquista del Paterno Imperio, conseguita dal Serenissimo Giovine Demetrio Gran Duca di Moscovia. Venice, 1605. A Russian trans-lation is published in M. Obolenskii, *Inostrannye sochineniia i akty, otnosiashchiesia do Rossii.* Part 4. Moscow: Universitetskaia tip., 1848.

Reporte of a Bloudie and Terrible Massacre in the Citty of Mosco. London: Printed by Val. Sims for S. Macham and M. Cooke, 1607. Published in *The False Dmitri: A Russian Romance and Tragedy Described by British Eye-Witnesses, 1604–1612,* edited by Sonia E. Howe, 27–62. London: Williams and Norgate, 1916.

Reutenfels. See also Reitenfel's.

Reutenfels, Jacob. *De rebus Moschoviticis ad Serenissimum Magnum Hetruriae Ducem Cosmum Tertium.* Padua: Typis Petri Mariae Frambotti, 1680.

Reynolds, Stephen. Review of *Hramatyka muzykal'na,* by Mykola Dylets'kyi, edited by O. S. Tsalai-Iakymenko. *Recenzija* 5, no. 2 (1975): 27–33.

Rinhuber, Laurent. *Relation du voyage en Russie fait en 1684 par Laurent Rinhuber.* Berlin: Albert Cohn, 1883.

Robinson, A. N. *Bor'ba idei v russkoi literature XVII veka.* Moscow: Nauka, 1974.

———. "Pervyi russkii teatr kak iavlenie evropeiskoi kul'tury." In *Novye cherty v russkoi literature i iskusstve (XVII–nachalo XVIII v.),* edited by A. N. Robinson, 8–27. Mos-cow: Nauka, 1976.

Rode, Andrei. *Opisanie vtorogo posol'stva v Rossiiu datskogo poslannika Gansa Ol'delanda v 1659 godu, sostavlennoe posol'skim sekretarem Andreem Rode.* In *Utverzhdenie di-nastii,* edited by A. Liberman and S. Shokarev, 9–42. Istoriia Rossii i doma Ro-manovykh v memuarakh sovremennikov XVII–XX vv. Moscow: Fond Sergeia Du-bova, 1997.

Rogov, A. I., comp. *Muzykal'naia estetika Rossii XI–XVIII vekov.* Moscow: Muzyka, 1973.

———. "Suprasl' kak odin iz tsentrov kul'turnykh sviazei Belorussii s drugimi slavianskimi stranami." In *Slaviane v epokhu feodalizma: k stoletiiu akademika V. I. Pichety,* 321–34. Moscow: Nauka, 1978.

Roizman, L. I. "Iz istorii organnoi kul'tury v Rossii (vtoraia polovina XVII veka)." *Vo-prosy muzykoznaniia* 3 (1960): 565–97.

———. *Organ v istorii russkoi muzykal'noi kul'tury.* Moscow: Muzyka, 1979.

Rossiia i Ispaniia: Dokumenty i materialy. Vol. 1, 1667–1799. Moscow: Mezhdunarodnye otnosheniia, 1991.

Rothe, Hans, ed., and Franz Schäfer and Joachim Bruss, comps. *Verse und Lieder bei den Ostslaven, 1650–1720, Incipitarium.* Vol. 1, *Anonyme Texte.* Bausteine zur Geschichte der Literatur bei den Slaven, Band 23, no. 1. Cologne: Böhlau Verlag, 1984.

Rozhdestvenskii, N. V. "K istorii bor'by s tserkovnymi bezporiadkami, otgoloskami iazychestva i porokami v russkom bytu XVII v." *ChOIDR* 2 (1902), pt. 4:1–31.

Rozysknye dela o Fedore Shaklovitom i ego soobshchnikakh. 4 vols. St. Petersburg: Obshchestvennaia pol'za, 1884–93.

Ruffmann, Karl Heinz. *Das Russlandbild im England Shakespeares.* Göttinger Bausteine zur Geschichtswissenschaft 6. Göttingen: Musterschmidt, 1952.

Rumiantseva, V. S. "Andreevskii uchilishchnyi monastyr' v Moskve v XVII v." In *Kul'tura srednevekovoi Moskvy XVII vek,* 292–304. Moscow: Nauka, 1999.

Sajkowski, Alojzy, and Władysław Czapliński, eds. *Pamiętniki Samuela i Bogusława Kazimierza Maskiewiczów.* Wrocław: Zakład narodowy im. Ossolińskikh, 1961.

Sakharov, I. "Issledovaniia o russkom tserkovnom pesnopenii." *ZhMNP* 61 (1849), pt. 2:147–96, 263–84.

Samodelova, E. A. "Opisaniia drevnerusskoi svad'by kak pervoistochnik nauchnykh znanii o russkom svadebnom obriade." *Germenevtika drevnerusskoi literatury* 12 (2005): 797–816.

Sander, Elizabeth. *Social Dancing in Peter the Great's Russia.* Hildesheim: Georg Olms Verlag, 2007.

Sathas, K. N. *Biographikón Schedíasma perí toû Patriárchou Hieremíou B' (1572–1594)* [Biographical Sketch of Patriarch Hieremias II (1572–1594)]. 1870. Reprint, Thessaloniki: Pan. S. Pournaras Editions, 1979.

Savel'eva, O. A. " 'Plach Adama.' Krug istochnikov i literaturnaia sem'ia pamiatnika." In *Pamiatniki literatury i obshchestvennoi mysli epokhi feodalizma,* 164–82. Novosibirsk: Nauka, 1985.

———. "Strukturnye osobennosti kratkoi i prostrannoi redaktsii 'Placha Adama.' " In *Issledovaniia po istorii obshchestvennogo soznaniia epokhi feodalizma v Rossii,* 152–65. Novosibirsk: Nauka, 1984.

Saverkina, I. V., and Iu. N. Semenov. "Orkestr i khor A. D. Menshikova (K istorii russkoi muzykal'noi kul'tury)." *PKNO 1989* (1990): 160–66.

Sazonova, L. I. *Literaturnaia kul'tura Rossii: Rannee Novoe vremia.* Moscow: Iazyki slavianskikh kul'tur, 2006.

———. "Teatral'naia programma XVII v. 'Aleksei chelovek bozhii.' " *PKNO 1978* (1979): 131–49.

Schaum, Matthias. *Tragoedia Demetrio-Moscovitica.* Rostock: J. Fuesz, 1614. Russian translation published in M. Obolenskii, *Inostrannye sochineniia i akty, otnosiashchiesia do Rossii.* Part 1:1–26. Moscow: Universitetskaia tip., 1847.

Scheliha, Wolfram von. "The Orthodox Universal Church and the Emergence of Intellectual Life in Muscovite Russia." *Forschungen zur osteuropäischen Geschichte* 56 (2000): 273–89.

Schidlovsky, Nicolas. "Sources of Russian Chant Theory." In *Russian Theoretical Thought in Music,* edited by Gordon McQuere, 83–108. Ann Arbor: UMI Research Press, 1983.

Schlafly, Daniel L. "Filippo Balatri in Peter the Great's Russia." *Jahrbücher für Geschichte Osteuropas* 45, no. 2 (1997): 181–98.

———. "A Muscovite *Boiarynia* Faces Peter the Great's Reforms: Dar'ia Golitsyna Between Two Worlds." *Canadian-American Slavic Studies* 31, no. 3 (1997): 249–68.

Schrickx, Willem. " 'Pickleherring' and English Actors in Germany." *Shakespeare Survey* 36 (1983): 135–47.

Seaman, Gerald. *History of Russian Music.* Oxford: Blackwell, 1967.

Sebes, Joseph, S.J., ed. *The Jesuits and the Sino-Russian Treaty of Nerchinsk (1689): The Diary of Thomas Pereira, S.J.* Bibliotheca Instituti Historici S.I. 18. Rome: Institutum Historicum S. I., 1961.

Semenov, V. "K istorii snoshenii so Shvetsiei. Otryvki shvedskogo dnevnika vremen tsaria Alekseia Mikhailovicha." *ChOIDR* 1 (1912), pt. 3:1–28.

Senyk, Sophia. *Women's Monasteries in Ukraine and Belorussia to the Period of Suppressions.* Orientalia Christiana Analecta 222. Rome: Pont. Institutum Studiorum Orientalium, 1983.

Seregina, N. S. "Muzykal'naia letopis' Rossii." *SM* no. 1 (1984): 87–90.

———. "Pevcheskie rukopisi iz knigopisnoi masterskoi Stroganovykh kontsa XVI–pervoi poloviny XVII v." *PKNO 1986* (1987): 202–209.

Sergeev, V. N. "Dukhovnyi stikh 'Plach Adama' na ikone." *TODRL* 31 (1971): 278–86.

Serman, I. Z. "'Psaltyr' rifmotvornaia' Simeona Polotskogo i russkaia poeziia XVIII v." *TODRL* 18 (1962): 214–32.

Shabalin, D. S. *Pevcheskie azbuki Drevnei Rusi.* 2 vols. Krasnodar: Sovetskaia Kuban', 2003–2004.

Shcheglova, S. A. "Deklamatsiia Simeona Polotskogo." In *Sbornik statei v chest' Akademika Alekseia Ivanovicha Sobolevskogo,* edited by V. N. Peretts, 5–9. Leningrad: AN SSSR, 1928.

Sheptaev, L. S. "Russkoe skomoroshestvo v XVII v." *Uchenye zapiski Ural'skogo universiteta* 6 (Filologicheskii) (1949): 47–68.

———. "Zametki o pesniakh, zapisannykh dlia Richarda Dzhemsa." *TODRL* 14 (1958): 304–308.

Sheremetev, S. D., ed. *Opisanie rukopisei kniazia Pavla Petrovicha Viazemskogo.* OLDP Izdaniia 119. [St. Petersburg]: Tip. Glavnogo upravleniia udelov, 1902.

Shliapkin, I. A. *Tsarevna Natal'ia Alekseevna i teatr ee vremeni.* Pamiatniki drevnei pis'mennosti 128. [St. Petersburg]: V. Balashev, 1898.

Shreer-Tkachenko, A., E. Maiburovaia, and T. Bulat. "Za nauchnuiu ob"ektivnost' i printsipal'nost'." *SM* no. 8 (1968): 139–43.

Shusherin, I. K. *Izvestie o rozhdenii i vospitanii i o zhitii sviateishego Nikona Patriarkha Moskovskogo i vseia Rossii.* Moscow: Universitetskaia tip., 1871.

Shvedova, M. M. "Tsaritsy-inokini Novodevich'ego monastyria." In *Novodevichii monastyr' v russkoi kul'ture: Materialy nauchnoi konferentsii 1995 g.,* edited by V. L. Egorov, 73–93. Trudy Gosudarstvennogo istoricheskogo muzeia 99. Moscow: Gos. istoricheskii muzei, 1998.

Simoni, P. K. *Velikorusskie pesni, zapisannye v 1619–20 gg. dlia Richarda Dzhemsa na krainem severe moskovskogo tsarstva.* In Pamiatniki starinnogo russkogo iazyka i slovesnosti XV–XVIII stoletii, vyp. 2, pt. 1. St. Petersburg: Tip. Imperatorskoi Akademii nauk, 1907.

Sir Thomas Smithes Voiage and Entertainment in Rushia. London: Printed for Nathanyell Butter, 1605.

Słownik polszczyzny XVI wieku. Wrocław: Zaklad Narodowy im. Ossolińskich, 1966–.

Smirnova, Engelina S. "Simon Ushakov—'Historicism' and 'Byzantinism': On the Interpretation of Russian Painting from the Second Half of the Seventeenth Century." In *Religion and Culture in Early Modern Russia and Ukraine,* edited by Samuel H. Baron and Nancy Shields Kollmann, 169–83. DeKalb: Northern Illinois University Press, 1997.

Smith, G. S. "A. V. Pozdneev and the Russian 'Literary Song.' " *Journal of European Studies* 5, no. 2 (1975): 177–89.

Smith, R. E. F., and David Christian. *Bread and Salt: A Social and Economic History of Food and Drink in Russia.* Cambridge: Cambridge University Press, 1984.

Smotritskii, Meletii. *Grammatika.* Moscow, 1648.

Sobranie pisem tsaria Alekseia Mikhailovicha. Moscow: Tip. V. Got'e, 1856.

Sofronova, L. A. "O strukture dramaticheskogo siuzheta ('Artakserksovo deistvo')." In

Novye cherty v russkoi literature i iskusstve (XVII–nachalo XVIII v.), edited by A. N. Robinson, 88–118. Moscow: Nauka, 1976.

Solov'ev, S. M. *Istoriia Rossii s drevneishikh vremen v piatnadtsati knigakh.* Vol. 5, books 9–10 and vol. 6, books 11–12. Moscow: Mysl', 1990–91.

Soloviev, Sergei. *The First Romanov, Tsar Michael, 1613–1634.* Vol. 16 of *History of Russia.* Translated by G. Edward Orchard. Gulf Breeze, Fla.: Academic International Press, 1991.

———. *Michael Romanov, The Last Years, 1634–1645.* Vol. 17 of *History of Russia.* Translated by G. Edward Orchard. Gulf Breeze, Fla.: Academic International Press, 1996.

———. *Tsar Alexis. A Reign Ends.* Vol. 23 of *History of Russia.* Translated by Martha L. Lahana. Gulf Breeze, Fla.: Academic International Press, 1998.

Sorensen, Fred. " 'The Masque of the Muscovites' in *Love's Labour's Lost.*" *Modern Language Notes* 50, no. 8 (1935): 499–501.

Spangenberg, Johann. *Quaestiones musicae in usum scholae Northusianae.* Cologne: Petrus Horst, 1563.

[Sparwenfeld, Johan]. *J. G. Sparwenfeld's Diary of a Journey to Russia 1684–87.* Edited by Ulla Birgegård. Slavica Suecana, Series A: Publications, Vol. 1. Stockholm: Kungl. Vitterhets Historie och Antikvitets Akademien, 2002.

———. *Lexicon Slavonicum.* Edited by Ulla Birgegård. 5 vols. Acta Bibliothecae R. Universitatis Upsaliensis 24. Uppsala: Distributed by Almqvist and Wiksell, 1987–92.

Spengler, Lazarus. *Schriften.* Vol. 1, *Schriften der Jahre 1509 bis Juni 1525.* Edited by Berndt Hamm and Wolfgang Huber. Quellen und Forschungen zur Reformationsgeschichte 61. Gütersloh: Gütersloher Verlagshaus, 1995.

Spitsyn, A. A. "Peshchnoe deistvo i khaldeiskaia peshch." *Zapiski Imperatorskogo russkogo arkheologicheskogo obshchestva* 12 (1901): 95–131.

Sreznevskii, I. I. *Materialy dlia slovaria drevnerusskogo iazyka.* 3 vols. 1893–1903. Reprint, Moscow: Gos. izdatel'stvo inostrannykh i natsional'nykh slovarei, 1958.

[Stadnicki, Martyn]. "Istoriia Dimitriia Tsaria moskovskogo i Mariny Mnishek, docheri sendomirskogo voevody." Translated by A. Titov. *Russkii arkhiv* 2 (1906): 129–74.

Stählin, Jacob [Shtelin, Ia.]. *Muzyka i balet v Rossii XVIII veka.* Edited by B. I. Zagurskii. St. Petersburg: Soiuz khudozhnikov, 2002.

Stählin, Jacob. "Nachrichten von der Musik in Russland." In *M. Johann Joseph Haigold's Beylagen zum neuveränderten Russland.* Vol. 1. Riga: J. F. Hartknoch, 1769–70. An abridged translation published in *Sanktpeterburgskii vestnik,* 1779, part 4.

Starikova, L. M. "K istorii domashnikh krepostnykh teatrov i orkestrov v Rossii kontsa XVII–XVIII vv." *PKNO 1991* (1997): 53–65.

———. "Russkii teatr petrovskogo vremeni, komedial'naia khramina i domashnie komedii tsarevny Natal'i Alekseevny." *PKNO 1990* (1992): 137–56.

———. *Teatr v Rossii XVIII veka: Opyt dokumental'nogo issledovaniia.* Moscow: GTsTM im. A. A. Bakhrushina, 1997.

Starowolski, Szymon. *Musices practicae erotemata.* Cracow: Ex Officina Francisci Caesarii, 1650.

Stewart, J. Douglas. *Sir Godfrey Kneller and the English Baroque Portrait.* Oxford: Clarendon Press, 1983.

Stone, Gerald, ed. *A Dictionarie of the Vulgar Russe Tongue Attributed to Mark Ridley.* Bausteine zur Slavischen Philologie und Kulturgeschichte, Reihe B, Neue Folge Band 8. Cologne: Böhlau, 1996.

Stone, John A. "The Pastor and the Tzar: A Comment on *The Comedy of Artaxerxes.*" *Bulletin of the New York Public Library* 72, no. 4 (1968): 215–51.

Stratii, Ia. M., V. D. Litvinov, and V. A. Andrushko. *Opisanie kursov filosofii i ritoriki professorov Kievo-Mogilianskoi Akademii.* Kiev: Naukova dumka, 1982.

Stříbrný, Zdeněk. *Shakespeare and Eastern Europe.* Oxford: Oxford University Press, 2000.

Stubbs, Stephen. "Johann Mattheson—the Russian Connection: The Rediscovery of *Boris Goudenow* and His Other Lost Operas." *Early Music* 33, no. 2 (2005): 283–92.

Subbotin, N., ed. *Materialy dlia istorii raskola.* Vol. 1. Moscow: Tip. T. Ris, 1875.

Svodnyi katalog russkoi knigi grazhdanskoi pechati XVIII veka, 1725–1800. Edited by E. I. Katsprzhak and others. 5 vols. Moscow: Izd. Gos. Biblioteki SSSR im V. I. Lenina, 1962–65.

Swoboda, Marina. "*The Furnace Play* and the Development of Liturgical Drama in Russia." *Russian Review* 61 (2002): 220–34.

Sydorenko, Alexander. *The Kievan Academy in the Seventeenth Century.* University of Ottawa Ukrainian Studies 1. Ottawa: University of Ottawa Press, 1977.

Sysyn, Frank E. "Peter Mohyla and the Kiev Academy in Recent Western Works: Divergent Views on Seventeenth-Century Ukrainian Culture." *Harvard Ukrainian Studies* 8, no. 1–2 (1984): 155–87.

Tanner, Bernard. *Legatio Polono-Lithuanica in Moscoviam.* Nuremberg: Johannis Ziegerl, 1689.

[———]. "Opisanie puteshestviia pol'skogo posol'stva v Moskvu v 1678 godu." Translated by I. Ivakin. *ChOIDR* 3 (1891), pt. 3:iii–xi, 1–202.

Taruskin, Richard. *Defining Russia Musically.* Princeton: Princeton University Press, 1997.

———. "Musorgsky versus Musorgsky: The Versions of *Boris Godunov.*" In *Musorgsky: Eight Essays and an Epilogue,* 201–90. Princeton: Princeton University Press, 1993.

Teletova, N. K. "Pervyi russkii liricheskii poet P. A. Kvashnin-Samarin." *TODRL* 47 (1993): 293–307.

Thyrêt, Isolde. *Between God and Tsar: Religious Symbolism and the Royal Women of Muscovite Russia.* DeKalb: Northern Illinois University Press, 2001.

Tikhonravov, Nikolai. *Russkie dramaticheskie proizvedeniia 1672–1725 godov.* Vol. 1. St. Petersburg: Izdanie D. E. Kozhanchikova, 1874.

Titov, A. A. *Rukopisi slavianskie i russkie, prinadlezhashchie I. A. Vakhrameevu.* Vol. 2 (1892). Moscow: Tip. A. I. Snegirevoi, 1892.

Titov, Vasilii. *Vasilii Titov i russkoe barokko: Izbrannye khorovye proizvedeniia / Vasily Titov and the Russian Baroque: Selected Choral Works.* Edited by Olga Dolskaya. Madison, Connecticut: Musica Russica, 1995.

[Tolstoi, P. A.]. "Puteshestvie stol'nika P. A. Tolstogo." *Russkii arkhiv* (1888): no. 2:161–204; no. 3:321–68; no. 4:505–52; no. 5:5–62; no. 6:113–56; no. 7:225–64; no. 8:369–400.

———. *The Travel Diary of Peter Tolstoi: A Muscovite in Early Modern Europe.* Translated and edited by Max J. Okenfuss. DeKalb: Northern Illinois University Press, 1987.

Tragoedia Moscovitica. Cologne, 1608. Published in a dual Latin-Russian edition as *Moskovskaia tragediia ili rasskaz o zhizni i smerti Dimitriia.* Translated by A. Braudo and I. Rostsius. St. Petersburg: Balashev, 1901.

Trilupaitene, Iu. S. "Muzykal'nye rukopisi XVI v. vil'niusskogo bernardinskogo monastyria." *PKNO 1986* (1987): 196–201.

——— [Trilupaitiené, Júraté]. "Vilnius als Musikzentrum des Grossfürstentums Litauen."

In *Musica Baltica: Interregionale musikkulturelle Beziehungen im Ostseeraum,* 144–50. Frankfurt: P. Lang, 1997.

—— [Trilupaitiene, Jurate]. "Zygmunt Lauksmin w życiu muzycznym Akademii Wileńskiej." *Muzyka* 1 (1991): 101–15.

Trutneva, N. F., and M. M. Shvedova. *Novodevichii monastyr' / The Novodevichy Convent.* Moscow: Sovetskaia Rossiia, 1988.

Tsalai-Iakimenko, A. S. "Muzykal'no-teoreticheskaia mysl' na Ukraine v X[V]III stoletii i trudy Nikolaia Diletskogo." *Musica antiqua Europae orientalis* 2 (1969): 347–63.

Tsalai-Iakymenko, O. S. *Kyivs'ka shkola muzyky XVII stolittia.* Kiev and L'viv: Naukove tovarystvo imeni T. Shevchenka, 2002.

——, and O. Zelins'kyi. " 'More neprebrannoe . . .' (novoznaidenyi avtohraf tvoru Mykoly Dilets'koho)." *Zhovten'* 7 (1966): 109–16.

Tschižewskij, D. "Akrostikhi Germana i starorusskie akrostikhi." *Československá rusistika* 15, no. 3 (1970): 102–104.

Turbervile, George. "To Parker." In Richard Hakluyt, *The Principal Navigations Voyages Traffiques and Discoveries of the English Nation,* 2:104–108. London: J. M. Dent and New York: E. P. Dutton, 1927.

Turilova, S. L. "Memuary russkogo raznochintsa pervoi poloviny XVIII v. ("Skaski" perevodchika i arkhivariusa Kollegii inostrannykh del Moiseia Arsen'eva)." *PKNO 1989* (1990): 10–15.

Uspenskii, A. I. *Tsarskie ikonopistsy i zhivopistsy XVII v.* 4 vols. Moscow: Pechatnia A. I. Snegirevoi, 1910–16.

Uspenskii [Uspensky], B. A. "The Attitude to Grammar and Rhetoric in Old Russia of the 16th and 17th Centuries." In *The Legacy of Saints Cyril and Methodius to Kiev and Moscow,* edited by Anthony-Emil N. Tachiaos, 485–97. Thessaloniki: Hellenic Association for Slavic Studies, 1992.

—— [Uspensky]. "Schism and Cultural Conflict in the Seventeenth Century." In *Seeking God: The Recovery of Religious Identity in Orthodox Russia, Ukraine, and Georgia,* edited by Stephen K. Batalden, 106–43. DeKalb: Northern Illinois University Press, 1993.

——. "Svad'ba Lzhedmitriia." *TODRL* 50 (1997): 404–25.

—— [Uspenskij]. "Tsar and Pretender: *Samozvančestvo* or Royal Imposture in Russia as a Cultural-Historical Phenomenon." In Ju. M. Lotman and B. A. Uspenskij, *The Semiotics of Russian Culture,* edited by Ann Shukman, 259–92. Michigan Slavic Contributions 11. Ann Arbor: University of Michigan, 1984.

Ustrialov, N., ed. and trans. *Dnevnik Mariny Mnishek i poslov pol'skikh.* Part 4 of *Skazaniia sovremennikov o Dimitrii Samozvantse.* St. Petersburg: V Tip. Imper. Rossiiskoi akademii, 1834.

——. *Zapiski Maskevicha.* Part 5 of *Skazaniia sovremennikov o Dimitrii Samozvantse.* St. Petersburg: V Tip. Imper. Rossiiskoi akademii, 1834.

van der Linde, A., ed. *Histoire des guerres de la Moscovie (1601–1610).* 2 vols. Brussels: Fr. J. Olivier, 1866.

van Lennep, William, ed. *The London Stage 1660–1800.* Part 1, *1660–1700.* Carbondale: Southern Illinois University Press, 1965.

Vasil'eva, E. E. "Tri Voskresnykh gimna arkhimandrita Germana." In *Nikonovskie chteniia v muzee "Novyi Ierusalim,"* edited by G. M. Zelenskaia, 253–62. Moscow: Severnyi palomnik, 2002.

Velimirović, Miloš. "The First Organ Builder in Russia." In *Literary and Musical Notes: A Festschrift for Wm. A. Little,* edited by G. C. Orth, 219–28. Bern: Peter Lang, 1995.

———. "Liturgical Drama in Byzantium and Russia." *Dumbarton Oaks Papers* 16 (1962): 351–85.

———. "Russian Musical *Azbuki:* A Turning Point in the History of Slavonic Chant." In *The Study of Medieval Chant: Paths and Bridges, East and West—In Honor of Kenneth Levy,* edited by Peter Jeffery, 257–68. Woodbridge: Boydell & Brewer, 2001.

———. "An Unusual Russian 'Spiritual Verse.'" *Studies in Eastern Chant* 2 (1971): 166–72.

———. "Warsaw, Moscow and St. Petersburg." In *The Late Baroque Era: From the 1680s to 1740,* edited by George Buelow, 435–65. London: Macmillan, 1993.

Vidaković, Albe, ed. *Yury Krizanitch's "Asserta Musicalia" (1656) and His Other Musical Works.* Zagreb: Yugoslav Academy of Sciences and Arts, 1967.

Videneeva, A. E. *Rostovskii arkhiereiskii dom i sistema eparkhial'nogo upravleniia v Rossii XVIII veka.* Moscow: Nauka, 2004.

Viktorov, A. *Opisanie zapisnykh knig i bumag starinnykh dvortsovykh prikazov 1584–1725 g.* 2 vols. Moscow: S. P. Arkhipov and M. P. Shchepkin, 1877 and 1883.

Vinogradoff, Igor. "Russian Missions to London, 1569–1687: Seven Accounts by the Masters of the Ceremonies." *Oxford Slavonic Papers* n.s. 14 (1981): 36–72.

Vladyshevskaia, T. F. "K voprosu o sviazi narodnogo i professional'nogo drevnerusskogo pevcheskogo iskusstva." *Muzykal'naia fol'kloristika* 2 (1978): 315–36.

———. "Stanovlenie stilia barokko i istoriia mnogogolos'ia Rossii." *Filevskie chteniia* 1 (1993): 21–32.

Vol'man, B. "O nachale notopechataniia v Rossii." *SM* no. 5 (1953): 79–82.

———. *Russkie pechatnye noty XVIII veka.* Leningrad: Gos. muzykal'noe izdatel'stvo, 1957.

Vomperskii, V. P. *Ritoriki v Rossii XVII–XVIII vv.* Moscow: Nauka, 1988.

"The Voyage, wherein Osep Napea the Moscovite Ambassadour returned home into his countrey." In Richard Hakluyt, *The Principal Navigations Voyages Traffiques and Discoveries of the English Nation,* 1:418–38. London: J. M. Dent and New York: E. P. Dutton, 1927.

Voznesenskii, M. V. "Khorovoe iskusstvo petrovskoi epokhi (po materialam dnevnikov i vospominanii)." In *Drevnerusskaia pevcheskaia kul'tura i knizhnost',* 140–63. Leningrad: Leningradskii gos. institut teatra, muzyki i kinematografii, 1990.

Vsevolodskii-Gerngross, V. N. *Istoriia russkogo dramaticheskogo teatra: Ot istokov do kontsa XVIII veka.* Vol. 1 of *Istoriia russkogo dramaticheskogo teatra v semi tomakh.* Edited by E. G. Kholodov and others. Moscow: Iskusstvo, 1977.

Vvedenskii, Andrei. "Biblioteka i arkhiv u Stroganovykh v XVI–XVII v." *Sever* 3–4 (1923): 69–115.

Waugh, Daniel Clarke. "'Anatolii's Miscellany': Its Origins and Migration." *Harvard Ukrainian Studies* 19 (1995 [1997]): 747–55.

——— [Uo, D. K.]. *Istoriia odnoi knigi.* St. Petersburg: Dmitrii Bulanin, 2003.

———. "The Library of Aleksei Mikhailovich." *Forschungen zur osteuropäischen Geschichte* 38 (1986): 299–324.

———. "The Publication of Muscovite *Kuranty.*" *Kritika: A Review of Current Soviet Books on Russian History* 9, no. 3 (1973): 104–20.

Weiner, Jack. "The Death of Philip IV of Spain and the Early Russian Theatrical Repertoire." *Theatre Research / Recherches Théâtrales* 10, no. 3 (1970): 179–85.

———. *Mantillas in Muscovy: The Spanish Golden Age Theater in Tsarist Russia, 1672–1917.*

University of Kansas Humanistic Studies 41. Lawrence: University of Kansas Publications, 1970.

Werckmeister, Andreas. *Hypomnemata musica.* 1697. Reprint, Hildesheim: G. Olms, 1970.

Yurchyshyn-Smith, Oksana. "The Antimension (1620) of Theophanes, Patriarch of Jerusalem." *Oriens Christianus* 88 (2004): 93–110.

Zabelin, Ivan. *Domashnii byt russkikh tsarei v XVI i XVII st.* Vol. 1, pts. 1 and 2 of *Domashnii byt russkogo naroda v XVI i XVII st.* Reprint, from 1918 and 1915 editions. Moscow: Iazyki russkoi kul'tury, 2000–2003.

——. *Domashnii byt russkikh tsarits v XVI i XVII st.* Vol. 2 of *Domashnii byt russkogo naroda v XVI i XVII st.* Reprint, from 1901 edition (3rd ed., with additions). Moscow: Iazyki russkoi kul'tury, 2001.

——. "Dopolneniia k Dvortsovym razriadam." *ChOIDR* 1 (1882), pt. 2:i–xv, 1–287; 3 (1882), pt. 1:289–640; 2 (1883): pt. 1:641–800; 4 (1883), pt. 1:801–912.

——. *Materialy* [accompanying *Domashnii byt russkikh tsarei v XVI i XVII st.* and *Domashnii byt russkikh tsarits v XVI i XVII st.*]. Reprint, from various editions, with overlapping pagination. Moscow: Iazyki russkoi kul'tury, 2003.

——. *Materialy dlia istorii, arkheologii i statistiki goroda Moskvy.* 2 vols. Moscow: Moskovskaia gorodskaia tip., 1884 and 1891.

——. *Opyty izucheniia russkikh drevnostei i istorii. Issledovaniia, opisaniia i kriticheskie stat'i.* 2 vols. Moscow: Tip. Gracheva, 1872.

Zabolotnaia, N. V. "Barochnye formy muzykal'noi kul'tury." In *Khudozhestvenno-esteticheskaia kul'tura drevnei Rusi XI–XVII veka,* edited by V. V. Bychkov, 505–17. Moscow: Nauchno-izdatel'skii tsentr "Ladomir," 1996.

Zakharova, O. "Ritoricheskaia traditsiia v russkoi muzyke vtoroi poloviny XVII veka." *Filevskie chteniia* 2 (1993): 11–18.

——. *Ritorika i zapadnoevropeiskaia muzyka XVII–pervoi poloviny XVIII veka: printsipy, priemy.* Moscow: Muzyka, 1983.

Zenkovsky, Serge A. *Medieval Russia's Epics, Chronicles, and Tales.* Rev. and enlarged ed. New York: E. P. Dutton, 1974.

Zguta, Russell. *Russian Minstrels: A History of the Skomorokhi.* [Philadelphia]: University of Pennsylvania Press, 1978.

Zhivov, V. M. "Religious Reform and the Emergence of the Individual in Russian Seventeenth-Century Literature." In *Religion and Culture in Early Modern Russia and Ukraine,* edited by Samuel H. Baron and Nancy Shields Kollmann, 184–98. DeKalb: Northern Illinois University Press, 1997.

Znameniia osmoglasnago peniia s liternymi pometami i lineinymi notami. OLDP Izdaniia 51. [St. Petersburg], 1880.

Zvereva, S. G. "Gosudarevy pevchie d'iaki posle 'Smuty' (1613–1649 gg.)." *Germenevtika drevnerusskoi literatury* 2 (1989): 355–82.

——. "Muzykal'nye chernoviki khora gosudarevykh pevchikh d'iakov nachala XVII v." *PKNO 1991* (1997): 102–106.

——. "O khore gosudarevykh pevchikh d'iakov v XVI v." *PKNO 1987* (1988): 125–30.

Index

Page numbers in italics refer to illustrations.

Abbas I (Persian Shah), 265n50
Abbas II (Persian Shah), 91, 92, 184
Adam's Lament ("Plach Adama"), 59, 164,
  198, 202, 252n8. *See also* Muscovite
  Court Theater, Music: laments, Penitential Verses
Aiuk (Kalmyk Khan), 103, 270n91
Aleksei Alekseevich (Tsarevich), 45, 90,
  125
Aleksei Mikhailovich (Tsar), 5, 45, 90, 126;
  addressed in texts of plays, 187, 188–89;
  fanfares and processional music for, 41,
  83, 84, 261n25; interest in liturgical and
  religious singing, 30, 47–48, 49, 57,
  249n80; interest in theater and performances, 54–55, 163–66, 169, 171, 173,
  176–80, 184–85, 206–207, 214, 223–24,
  299n79; period of marriage to Mariia
  Miloslavskaia, 38–39, 44, 57, 77–79, 87–
  88, 91, 101, 260n8; period of marriage to
  Natal'ia Naryshkina, 101, 164, 179,
  269n85; weddings, 44, 77–79, 87–88,
  192, 101–102, 259n3, 267n66
Aleksei Petrovich (Tsarevich), 254n22,
  256n41
Alvarez, Emmanuel (author of Latin
  grammar text), 125, 278n61

Anna Ivanovna (Empress), 214
Anonymous untitled music theory
  treatise (RGADA, f. 381, No. 1195), 160–
  61
Arkhangel'sk, 26, 234n17, 239n2, 297n66
Arsen'ev, Moisei (copyist of Diletskii
  source), 271n6
Arsenios of Elasson (archbishop), 4,
  229n1; installation of Patriarch Iov, 1–2,
  40, 229n1; wedding of Dmitrii and
  Marina, 13–14, 18, 235n27, 236n32,
  239n59
Ascension, Feast of, 17, 86
Avvakum (archpriest), 53–54, 75, 171,
  250n89, 271n3
Azbuka nachalnago ucheniia (An Elemen-
  tary Alphabet), 160–61, *160*
Azbuki (listings of neumes). *See under*
  Music Notation
Azov, 73, 256n41

Balatri, Filippo (singer), 102–104, 209,
  269n89, 270nn90–92
Ballet Royal de l'Impatience (1661), 217
Banquets, 44, 45, 51, 185, 244n44, 249n80,
  257n43, 265n53; for installation of
  Patriarch Iov, 2, 229n2, 230n4; in Paul
  of Aleppo's account, 40, 45, 48, 244n43,
  257n43; in plays at Muscovite court the-

Banquets (*continued*)
ater, 189, 190, 196, 202, 208; for wedding of Aleksei Mikhailovich, 78, 101; for wedding of Dmitrii and Marina, 14, 12, 18, 19, 235n27; in Western diplomatic ceremony, 166, 167, 220, 290n6, 291n9

Baronius, Cesare (historian), 155, 288n162

Bears: associated with *maslenitsa*, 165, 174, 176, 263n36; associated with *skomorokhi*, 17, 86, 259n7; imagery in Western accounts, 217, 307n20

Belarusian Singers. *See* Singers (liturgical): *vspevaki*

Belobotskii, Andrei (author of rhetoric treatise), 145, 283n128

Benedict VIII (Pope), 155

Bergholz, Friedrich Wilhelm von (Holstein diplomat), 49, 213, 267n68

Besov, Tomila (*tsynbal'nik*), 91, 265n52

"Beznevestnaia Devo" (Titov), *36–37*, 38

Blumentrost (Saxon physician), 179, 295n50, 304n126

Blumentrost, Laurentius (actor in court theater), 188–89, 299n79

Boethius, 111, 154–55

Boris Goudenow (Mattheson, opera). *See under* Mattheson, Johann

Boris Godunov (Musorgskii, opera). *See under* Musorgskii, Modest

Brass Instruments, 84, 93, 98, 101, 168–69, 170–71, 185, 186; defined in foreign glossaries, 81–82, 260n17; in Muscovite court theater, 181–82, 197 (*see also* Muscovite Court Theater, Music, Muscovite Court Theater, Plays: *Artaxerxes*). *See also* Fanfare and Processional Music, Weddings: instrumental fanfare associated with

Buchner, August (librettist), 173, 178–79

Burmistrov, Lavrii (Lavrentii) Kuz'min (singer), 46, 247n66

Bussow, Conrad (German chronicler), 221, 232n7, 308n34; descriptions of music, 12, 13, 18, 82; uprising and deaths of Dmitrii and Polish musicians, 20–21, 23, 236n33, 237nn39,42,43, 238n53

Carlisle. *See* Howard, Charles, Earl of Carlisle, Miege, Guy

Caroling and Carols, 39, 49, 62, 69, 244n41

Catherine I (Empress), 296n51

Catheux, Sieur de (French official), 169–70, 293n20

Catholics, Eastern Rite. *See* Uniate Church

Chaldeans. *See* Play of the Furnace (liturgical drama): roles of Chaldeans

Chamberlain, John (English writer), 307n20

Chant. *See* Singing (liturgical)

Chant Books. *See* Singing (liturgical): chant books and collections

Charles II (King of Spain), 169

Charles XI (King of Sweden), 174

Charles XII (King of Sweden), 221

Chashi. See Toasts (*chashi*)

Cherkasskaia, Avdot'ia Ivanovna (princess), 74

Chernitsyn, Pavel (composer), 38

Cherubic Hymn, 31, *32*, 133, *133*, 255n29

Church Councils (1666–67), 29, 49–53, 241n15

Churches and Cathedrals: Cathedral of the Annunciation (Moscow), 83; Cathedral of the Dormition (L'viv), 229n1; Cathedral of the Dormition (Uspenskii Cathedral, Moscow), 2, 13, 64; Church of St. John the Apostle (Moscow), 50; Church of St. Nicholas (Ukraine), 99; Presentation (Sretenskii) Cathedral (Moscow), 152; St. Sophia Cathedral (Kiev), 265n50; St. Sophia Cathedral (Novgorod), 242n27

Circles of Fifths (Western), 141–44. *See also under* Diletskii, Nikolai, *Grammatika* (music-theoretical contents): musical circles

Clement VII (pope), 245n46

Collins, Samuel (English physician), 49, 58, 248n75, 269n87, 307n20

Commedia dell'arte, 170, 190, 309n42

Commissions on Church Singing. *See* Singing (liturgical): reforms and codifications

Concha (Kievan rhetoric treatise, 1698), 128, 278n60, 280n79

Confraternities, 100, 146, 229n1, 278n62

Convents: Convent of the Ascension (Moscow), 12, 22, 254n21; Convent of the Divine Ascension (Ukraine), 48; Convent of St. Savva, 241n18; Novodevichii (New Maiden) Convent, 29–30, 241nn15,18, 242nn20,22

Corpus Christi, Feast of, 100

Cosimo III (Duke of Florence), 103, 175, 269n89

Council of Florence, 222, 245n51

Courland (Duchy of), 172, 181–83, 186, 293n25

Court Theater. *See* Muscovite Court Theater

Cracow, 12, 99, 115, 150, 157, 235n30, 273n14, 286n148

Damaskin (*ierodiakon*), 64, 68

Dance and Dancing: associated with Dmitrii and Marina, 17, 19–21, 23, 88, 235n30, 236nn35–36, 237n38; associated with *skomorokhi*, 4, 15, 17, 21–22, 86, 87–88; Muscovite, 74, 87, 95–96, 267nn66,68, 278n57; in Muscovite court theater, 102, 164–65, 173–74, 175, 185–86, 196, 203, 206, 294n33, 303n114; in Old Believer sources, 53, 75–76; at Petrine assemblies, 96, 214, 267n68; Western, 98, 99, 168, 171, 217, 218, 291n9. *See also* Weddings

David (biblical King), 93, 194, 253n16

Declamations, 44–47, 55, 70, 71, 100, 171, 250n89, 302n106; associated with singers, 46, 247n66. *See also under* Polotskii, Simeon

Denmark, 93, 166

Diletskii, Nikolai (composer, music theorist): as "akademik," 107–109, 272nn9,13; biography, 106–110, 147, 272n13, 273nn14,16; compositions, 109, 111, 128, 129, 143, 146–47; general views of music, 55–56, 106, 111, 118; *kontserty*, 38, 111, 118, 128, 132, 137, *138*, 146, 154 (*see also Kontserty*); and Korenev, 106, 110, 148–50, 152–53, 271nn3–4, 274n17,

285n144, 286n151, 287nn155–56; and Stroganov family, 29, 110, 111; *Toga złota*, 107–108, 124, 157, 272nn8,13

Diletskii, Nikolai, *Grammatika* (general): composers and works cited, 59, 111, 119, *119*, 198, 273n14; *kanty* cited, 65, 66–67, 99–100, 146–47; liturgical texts and books cited, 109, 118, 128, 129, 133, *133*, 146, 149–50; organs and musical instruments cited, 111, 116–17, 121, 123, 130, 131, 136, 137–39, *138*, 144, 276n42; sources and versions of treatise (overview), 106–107, 109–110, 152–53, 271nn3,5,6, 280n76, 285n144, 287n156

Diletskii, Nikolai, *Grammatika* (music-theoretical contents), 214; cadences, 134–36, *136*, 281n100; circles of fifths, *see* Circles of Fifths, Diletskii, Nikolai, *Grammatika* (music-theoretical contents): musical circles; clefs, 117, *118*, 275n32, 276n38; compositional rules, 61, 70, 111, 118–21, *119–20*, 127–29, 137–38; and contemporary Muscovite theory, 146–50, 152–55, 157, 287n155 (*see also* Korenev, Ioannikii, Music Theory, Muscovite and Russian); and contemporary Western theory, 123–24, 141–46, 157–58, *158* (*see also* Music Theory, Western); contrary rule (*pravilo protivnoe*), 119, 132–34, *133–35*; figured bass, 99, 137, *138*; happy and sad music, 112–13, *112–13*, 116, 118–19, 121, 131–36, *133–35*, 139, *141–42*, 149, 275n32; hexachordal syllables and solmization, 113–18, *114*, *118*, 131–32, 136–41, *138*, *141–42*, 148–49, 154–55, 276n37, 281n91, 286n151; *kliuch* (key), 113–16, *115*, 121, 132, 136, 139–41, *141*, 157, 275nn29–32; major and minor keys, 131–36, 281nn90–91,100; musical circles (circles of fifths), 120, 136–43, *140–42* (*see also* Circles of Fifths); musical hand, 121, 155–62, *156*, 288nn164–65; text setting, 119, 127–29, 130, 137

Diletskii, Nikolai, *Grammatika* (non-musical models): artistic models, 111, 123, 145, 277n54; Classical references, 123–24, 125, 178; dedication to Stroganov, 29, 110, 111, 122, 123–24, 125, 127,

Diletskii, Nikolai (*continued*)
149, 277n56; drawings and diagrams,
140, 141, 144–45, *156*, 157, 158–59,
283n125, 284n138 (*see also under* Diletskii, Nikolai, *Grammatika* (music-
theoretical contents)); liberal arts, 55–
56, 109, 123–27, 128, 272n13, 277nn50–51,
278n64; Muscovite traditions, 125–27,
130, 145; non-Muscovite sources, 125,
127, 157–59, 278n60; rhetorical and linguistic models (general), 55–56, 111, 113,
121–24, 129–30, 137–38, 159; rhetorical
terms (specific), 120, 122–23, 124, 127–
28, 137, 139, 159, 277n56, 280nn75–76
Dionysios (Greek singer), 29, 51, 241n15
Diplomatic Chancellery (*Posol'skii prikaz*), 85, 126, 178; and Muscovite court
theater, 164, 166, 171–72, 178, 294n28,
304n126
Dmitrii (infant, Tsarevich), 231n3
Dmitrii (Pretender, Tsar), 10–13, 22, 72–
73, 238n50; Polish musicians associated
with and their deaths, 11, 15–18, 22–24,
79, 80, 88, 238n54; *skomorokh* imagery
associated with, 21–22, 88, 237nn42–43,
238n49; uprising and death of, 11, 12,
20–22, 236n37, 238nn47,49; wedding to
Marina Mniszech, 17–20, 78, 94,
235n30; Western dramatic works
depicting, 221–23, 309nn41–42. *See also*
Marina Mniszech, Time of Troubles
Dnevnik Mariny Mnishek (anonymous
diary), 14, 15–16, 19, 20, 232n4, 234n22,
236nn32,36
Dolgorukii Family, 96–97
Domostroi, 78
Dresden, 173, 179, 295n50
"Durch Adams fall" (Lutheran hymn
text), 201–202, 301n103. *See also* Adam's
Lament, Muscovite Court Theater,
Music: strophic singing

Easter: musical performances associated
with, 97, 98, 143, 244n41; Palm Sunday
procession, 41, 245n48, 257n44
Education: "akademik," 107–109,
272nn9,13; classical grammar school
curriculum, 45, 108, 121–25, 277n51,

278n61; Greek-Latin-Slavonic Academy,
71, 271n6; Kievan College, 125, 127, 139,
145, 158–59, 177, 206–207, 278nn60–61;
Muscovite traditions of liberal arts, 55,
123–27, 130, 145, 178, 278n64, 286n148;
non-Muscovite Orthodox curricula
and schools, 45, 70, 108, 125, 278n61;
theatrical presentations in non-
Muscovite curricula, 55, 108, 205–207,
250n89; Vilnius (Jesuit) College, 108–
109, 125, 127, 272n13, 282n121. *See also*
Diletskii, Nikolai, *Grammatika* (non-
musical models), Rhetoric and Rhetoric Treatises
ektsellentovyi bass (ornamented bass line),
61
Elizabeth I (Queen of England), 14, 166,
217
Engels, Peter (artist), 172, 293n26
Entertainers at Muscovite Court (non-
musical), 4, 74, 89, 92, 207–208, 264n43,
266n59, 267nn64,66. *See also* Dmitrii
(Pretender, Tsar), Masks and Masking
Entertainment Hall (*Poteshnaia palata*),
91, 265n49
Epiphany (Blessing of the Waters), 40, 43,
245n46. *See also* Lesser Blessing of the
Waters
Esther (biblical Queen), 298n75. *See also*
Muscovite Court Theater, Plays: *Artax-
erxes*, Muscovite Court Theater: themes
and plots
Evdokiia Streshneva (Tsaritsa, wife of Tsar
Mikhail), 264n48
Evelyn, John (English diarist), 306n18,
307n27
Evfrosin (monk), 3–4

Fanfare and Processional Music, 4, 71–72,
185–86; associated with Aleksei
Mikhailovich, 41, 83, 84, 185–86, 261n25;
defined in foreign glossaries, 81–82;
descriptions of, 12–13, 80, 82–85, 170,
233n9, 261n22, 262n27; owned by Muscovite elite, 84; performers recruited
from abroad (excluding theater), 84,
168–69, 181, 261n21, 262n29; Petrine era,
71, 83, 89–90, 213–14, 256n41; played by

Muscovite musicians abroad, 84–85, 262n32; weddings, *see* Weddings: instrumental fanfare associated with. *See also* Brass Instruments

Faux Moscovites, Les (Poisson, 1668), 218–20, 222

Fedor Alekseevich (Tsar), 30, 38, 63, 71, 90, 250n89; closing of court theater, 163, 183, 210

Fedor Ivanovich (Tsar), 2, 89, 221, 231n3, 264n43

Figured Bass. *See under* Music Notation

Filaret (Patriarch of Russia), 4, 72, 230n10, 246n56

Findeizen, Nikolai, 24, 93, 173

Fletcher, Giles (English representative in Muscovy), 4, 42, 43, 89, 95, 215, 222, 240n12

Fletcher, John (playwright), 215, 222, 309n41

Flier, Michael, 41, 245n48

Florence, 102, 103, 167–69, 170, 175, 292nn13,17, 295n39

Folk Texts, 73–74, 198, 216, 258n52, 259n7, 270n92, 306n16. *See also Kanty* and Psalm Settings: historical elements

Foreign Quarter (*Nemetskaia sloboda*, Moscow), 103; Muscovite court theater and, 93, 164, 181, 197, 295n50; musical practices associated with, 96–97, 181, 197

Froberger, Johann (composer, organist), 144

Funerals and Memorial Services, 5, 28, 38–39, 58, 71–72, 113, 231n16, 242n20, 244n39, 300n97

Gabriel (Polish organist), 14, 23

Galiatovskii, Ioannikii (author of rhetoric treatise), 278n60

Gazenkrukh, Timofei. *See* Hasenkruch, Timofei

German (composer, poet at New Jerusalem Monastery), 64, 65, 66–71, 75, 93, 125, 145, 256n33. *See also Kanty* and Psalm Settings

Germogen (Patriarch of Russia), 15, 234n19

Giøe, Mons (Danish diplomat), 180, 210, 296n52

Glossaries, 24, 26, 80–82, 90. *See also under individual musical instrument families*

Glück, Ernst (Lutheran pastor in St. Petersburg), 301n103

Godunov, Boris (Tsar), 12, 14, 23, 231n3

Golitsyn, Petr Alekseevich (prince, Muscovite diplomat), 102–103, 209

Golitsyn, Vasilii Vasil'evich (prince, boyar), 84, 92, 210, 262n28, 266n57

Golitsyna, Dar'ia (princess), 104, 209, 267n68

Gorczyn, Jan Aleksander (music theorist), 157–58, *158*

Gosiewski, Alexander (Polish diplomat), 23, 235n27, 239n55

Gosudarevy pevchie d'iaki. See Singers (liturgical): sovereign's ensembles

Grammatika musikiiskago peniia. See Diletskii, Nikolai, *Grammatika*

Gregorii, Johann (pastor in Foreign Quarter, playwright), 179, 181, 187, 200, 295n50, 299n79, 304n126. *See also* Muscovite Court Theater, Muscovite Court Theater, Plays

Guido of Arezzo (music theorist), 155

Guidonian Hand, 157. *See also* Diletskii, Nikolai, *Grammatika* (music-theoretical contents): musical hand, Music Theory, Muscovite and Russian: musical hand, Music Theory, Western

Gusli. See under Stringed Instruments

Gutovskii, Simeon (organist, craftsman), 91–92, 94, 266n56, 269n82; and Muscovite court theater, 184, 297n69

Hall, Edward (author of *Chronicle*, 1548), 216, 217, 306n12

Hasenkruch, Timofei (participant in Orpheus and Muscovite court theater), 97, 173, 176–77, 183–84, 297nn65,69

Hebdon, John (English agent for Muscovy), 84, 168–69, 181

Heinichen, Johann (music theorist), 142–143, 144

Helmfelt, Simon Grundel (Swedish agent in Muscovy), 174–77, 178, 180, 295n42

Henry VIII (King of England), 216, 307n27

Herberstein, Sigismund von (Imperial diplomat), 75–76, 215, 257n43

Herbinius, Johannes (Western cleric in Kiev), 248n69, 289n168

Hesse, Hermann Dietrich (Prussian diplomat), 173–74, 294n32, 301n102

Heywood, Thomas (English playwright), 217, 307n19

Hieremias (Patriarch of Constantinople), 1–2, 229n1

Horn, Bengt (Swedish official), 174

Horsey, Jerome (English representative in Muscovy), 4, 16, 82, 95, 97, 234n23, 264n43, 309n41

Howard, Charles, Earl of Carlisle (English ambassador), 43–44, 82–84, 98, 170–71. *See also* Miege, Guy

Iavorskii, Stefan (teacher, author of rhetoric treatise), 158–59

Icons, 54, 56, 123, 253n16, 277n54, 286n153

Imperial Russia (eighteenth century): musical life, 213–15, 216; theaters, 210–211, 214, 223–24, 309n46; works issued by Synodal Press, 160–62, *160–61*. *See also* Music Theory, Muscovite and Russian, Music Theory, Western, Peter (the Great, Tsar)

Instrumental Music. *See* Musical Instruments (general), and *see under individual musical instrument families*

Ioakim (Patriarch of Russia), 254n17

Iosaf (Patriarch of Russia), 17

Iosif (Patriarch of Russia), 175

Iov (Patriarch of Russia), 1–3, 4, 229n1

Irina Fedorovna (Tsaritsa, wife of Fedor Ivanovich), 3, 16

Irina Mikhailovna (Tsarevna, daughter of Mikhail Fedorovich), 90

Istomin, Karion (poet, writer), 46, 93, *94–95*, 266n62

Ivan III (Grand Prince), 245n51

Ivan IV (the Terrible, Tsar), 230n13; as composer, 30, 256n39; depicted in Western writings, 215, 221, 308n35; and singers and singing, 3, 5, 27, 40, 59, 252n7; and *skomorokhi*, 4–5, 21; and

Time of Troubles, 10, 21, 59, 231n3. *See also* Time of Troubles, Western Views of Muscovy

Ivan Alekseevich (co-Tsar, with Peter), 63

James (Duke of Courland), 182

James, Richard (English representative in Muscovy), 26, 40, 239n2, 257n43; glossary written by, 26, 80–81, 82, 86–87, 260n10; song texts written for, 72–73, 198

Janowka, Thomas (music theorist), 142, 282n116

Jenkinson, Anthony (English representative in Muscovy), 5

Kalenda (Kolenda; composer), 111, 130

Kanty and Psalm Settings: concordances and variants, 61–62, 64–68, 99–100, 255n30; defined, 60–61, *61*, 253n14; Diletskii's citation of, 65, 66–67, 99–100, 146–47; German (at New Jerusalem Monastery), 64, *65*, 66–71, 75, 93, 125, 145, 256n33; historical elements in, 70–74, 256nn39,41, 296n51; Kochanowski Psalter, 63, 67, 68, 100–101, 254n17; monastic connections of, 64, 68–70, 75, 254n21; musical influences on, 62, 74–75, 99–101, 256n35; non-Russian linguistic elements in, 62–63, 66, 67–68, 74, 99–100; Polotskii-Titov Psalter settings, 63–64, 66, 67–70, 74, 93, 101, 197, 253n16, 254nn17,22; popularity and longevity of, 62, 63, 64–67, 69–70, 93, 147, 197, 208, 214, 296n51, 301n103, 305n4; Rostovskii texts, 67, 227; Skrzolotowicz collection, 62–63, 64–66, 68, 97, 101, 147; Slavinetskii texts, 61, *61*, 64, 228; text sources for, 60, 62, 63–64, 147

Kanty and Psalm Settings, Works, 146–47; "A sarocca, biela bocca" ("A soroki-beloboki"), 270n92 (*see also* Balatri, Filippo); "Angel pastyrem movil," 255n24; "Bozhe laskavyi," 225–26; "Dai nam Khriste vspomozhene," 255n24; "Dayci Boze dobranoc," 100, 268n80; "Ditiatko sia narodilo," 64–65, 255n24; "Dzieciątko sie narodziło," 226, 255n24;

"Est' prelest v svete," 226; "Ezu Khriste pane milyi," 65, 99, 255n24; "Jesu Christe, Panie mily," 99, 268n80; "Kako vozmozhem dostoino khvaliti" (attributed to Slavinetskii), *61;* "Khristos razhdaetsia" (German), 64, *65;* "Khristos z mertvykh vstal est'," 255n24; "Mesiash prished," 65, 255n24; "Mesiia pride vo mir istinnyi," 226–27, 255n24; "Nakłon o Ewropo," 227; "Nasventsha panno i matko bozha," 255n24; "Nasventsha panno slichna Mariia," 255n24; "Nekh monarhove," 227; "Pokhvalu prinesu," 227; "Raduisia radost' tvoiu vospevaiu," 228

Kellner, David (music theorist), 214, 305n6

Keyboard Instruments. *See* Organs and Keyboard Instruments

Kholmogory, 26, 40, 81, 239n2, 260n14

Khrest'ianin, Fedor (singer), 235n29

Kiev, 26, 28, 206–207, 230n10, 231n16, 265n50; Diletskii and, 66, 106–107, 121, 152, 271n3 (*see also* Diletskii, Nikolai: biography); musical styles associated with, 33, 50, 99, 109, 243n31, 250n84, 256n33; Repskii and, 46, 247n67. *See also* Education, Rhetoric and Rhetoric Treatises

Kievan Notation, 33, 153, 284n136. *See also* Music Notation

Kircher, Athanasius (music theorist), 144, 282n121

Klenk, Koenraad van (Dutch diplomat), 62–63, 83, 97, 98

Kliros, 27, 29, 249n80

Kliuch razumeniia. See Tikhon Makar'evskii

Kochanowski, Jan (poet), 63, 67, 68, 100–101, 254n17

Kolenda (composer). *See* Kalenda

Koletzides, Matthaios (Greek cleric), 233n9

Konstantinov, Fedor (singer), 240n10, 242n26

Kontserty, 33–38, *34–35,* 59, 153, 154, 240n11, 243n32, 288n158, 304n128; and Diletskii, 38, 111, 118, 128, 132, 137, *138,* 146, 154; and Titov, *36–37,* 38, 64, 71, 129, 146. *See also Partesnoe penie*

Korenev, Ioannikii (music theorist), 126, 129, 269n87; and Diletskii, 106, 110, 150, 152–53, 271nn3–4, 274n17, 285n144, 287n155; general views of music, 55–56, 101–102, 150; hexachordal theory in, 148–49, 150–52, *151,* 286nn151–52; linguistic and non-musical models for, 55–56, 122, 127; *O penii bozhestvennom* (On Sacred Singing) by, 150–53, *151,* 178; sources for, 150, 152, 153, 285nn144–45, 287nn155–56. *See also* Diletskii, Nikolai, *Grammatika* (music-theoretical contents): and contemporary Muscovite theory

Koshirska (Polish princess), 19, 236n35

Kotoshikhin, Grigorii Karpovich (Muscovite official), 58, 78, 95, 252n4, 258n52, 259n5, 267n66

Kratkosobrannaia mussikiia (A Brief Resume of Music), 154–55, 288nn158–59

Krestovye d'iaki. See Singers (liturgical): *krestovye d'iaki*

Križanić, Juraj (Iurii Krizhanich, Croatian cleric and scholar), 260n17, 261n21, 279n70

Kseniia Borisovna (Tsarevna), 58, 72–73, 198

Kuhnau, Johann (music theorist, composer), 144

Kuranty (vesti-kuranty), 85, 166, 179, 217

Kurbskii, Andrei (prince), 5, 230n13

Kvashnin-Samarin, Petr Andreevich (poet, court servitor), 73–74

"Kyrie eleison," 33, *34–35*

Ladoga, 74, 87

Laments, 72–73. *See also* Muscovite Court Theater, Music: laments, Weddings: laments, Women

Lauxmin, Sigismund (teacher at Vilnius College), 108

Légende de la vie et de la mort de Démetrius, La (1606), 232n8

Lesser Blessing of the Waters, 40–41. *See also* Epiphany (Blessing of the Waters)

Lester, Joel, 144, 282n116

Ligarides, Paisios (Greek cleric), 241n15, 249n80

Likhachev, Vasilii (Muscovite ambassador), 167–69, 291n9, 292nn10,17

Likhud (brothers, educators), 271n6

Liturgical Drama. *See* Play of the Furnace

Liturgical Reforms. *See* Nikon, Singing (liturgical): reforms and codifications

Litvinov, Timofei Dementianovich (dedicatee of Diletskii's *Grammatika*) 109–110

Login (singer), 249n77

Löhlein, Georg Simon (music theorist), 214, 305n6

Lope, Felix de Vega Carpio (Spanish playwright), 222, 308nn38–39

Louis XIV (King of France), 218, 220, 269n89, 270n91

Luhn, Johann and Melchior (Melchert) (Dutch organists), 91, 94, 97, 260n8

L'viv, 146, 229n1, 278n62. *See also* Diletskii, Nikolai, *Grammatika* (general): sources and versions

Lyon. *See* Muscovite Court Theater: sources (archival)

Lyseck, Adolf (chronicler of Imperial embassy), 83, 207–208, 248n73, 261n22

Magnitskii, Leontii (author of mathematics treatise), 125, 278n59

Major-Minor Tonality. *See* Circles of Fifths (Western), Diletskii, Nikolai, *Grammatika* (music-theoretical contents): musical circles

Makar'evskii, Tikhon. *See* Tikhon Makar'evskii

Makarii (Metropolitan of Novgorod, author of rhetoric treatise), 127, 279n73, 280n76

Makarios (Patriarch of Antioch), 29, 41, 51–53. *See also* Church Councils (1666–67), Paul of Aleppo

Manley, Roger (English historian), 223, 309n44

Marais (theatrical company, Paris), 169, 218

Margeret, Jacques (military officer in Muscovy), 235n27

Mariia Alekseevna (Tsarevna), 45

Mariia Miloslavskaia (Tsaritsa, first wife of Aleksei Mikhailovich), 38–39, 77, 260n8. *See also* Aleksei Mikhailovich: period of marriage to Mariia Miloslavskaia

Marina Mniszech (Tsaritsa, wife of Dmitrii): coronation/wedding of, 11, 12, 13–14, 17–20, 234n18, 235n30, 236n35; entry into Moscow, 12, 13, 80, 233n9; Polish musicians associated with and their deaths, 11, 15, 17–18, 22–24, 238n54; trip to Moscow, 12, 14–15, 97–98, 233nn9,14; uprising and death of Dmitrii, 20, 23–24, 209. *See also* Dmitrii (Pretender, Tsar), Time of Troubles

Markov, Aleksei, 59, 252n8

Maskiewicz, Samuel (Polish diplomat), 95–96, 269n87

Masks and Masking, 43, 102, 174; and Dmitrii, 11, 15, 20, 21–22, 88, 95, 237nn38,43, 238n46; and *skomorokhi*, 15, 17–18, 21–22, 86, 88, 95–96; in West, 104, 209–210, 216, 303n123

Maslenitsa (Carnival, Shrovetide), 263n36; association with Muscovite court theater and Orpheus, 165, 173, 174–76, 179

Massa, Isaac (Dutch merchant, writer), 13, 17–18, 19, 20, 232n8; uprising and deaths of Dmitrii and Polish musicians, 23, 233n11, 237nn39,43, 238n51

Mattheson, Johann (composer, music theorist), 308n33, 309n44; *Boris Goudenow* (opera, 1710), 220–21, 223

Matveev, Artemon (head of Diplomatic Chancellery), 47, 92, 293n23, 294n28, 297n65; and Muscovite court theater, 102, 164, 171–73, 180–81, 183–86; and Orpheus entertainment, 174, 176–78, 180, 295n43

Medvedev, Sil'vestr (monk, poet), 46–47, 110, 247n66, 250n89, 293n24

Meierberg (Meyerberg), Augustin (Imperial diplomat), 248n73, 261n22

Meletios (Greek singer), 28–29, 51, 241n15

Menzies, Paul (envoy from Muscovy), 84, 175, 186, 208, 295n39, 303n121

Mercury (mythological character), 177, 178–79

Meshchanskaia sloboda (merchant or artisan quarter, Moscow), 294n28

Mezenets, Aleksandr (singer, music theorist), 55, 105–106, 149, 243n30, 287nn154,156. *See also* Singing (liturgical): reforms and codifications

Miege, Guy (chronicler of Carlisle embassy), 5, 82–84, 170–71, 217, 224. *See also* Howard, Charles, Earl of Carlisle

Mielczewski, Marcin (composer), 167, 243n32, 273n14; cited by Diletskii, 111, 119, *119*, 157

Mikhail Fedorovich (Tsar), 42, 74, 87, 90; weddings of, 77–78, 87–89, 94–95, 258nn1–2, 263n42, 267n64

Mikulin, Grigorii Ivanovich (Muscovite diplomat), 14, 166, 217, 234n17, 307nn19–20

Milescu, Nikolai Spafarii. *See* Spafarii, Nikolai

Miloslavskii Family, 293n23, 295n41

Miloslavskii, I. D. (boyar), 84

Milton, John, 215, 309n44

Minevskii (composer), 243n32

Misery-Luckless-Plight (*Povest' o Gore-Zlochastii*, secular narrative poem), 198, 300n98

Mniszech, Marina. *See* Marina Mniszech

Mniszech, Stanisław (brother of Marina Mniszech), 15, 17, 23, 88, 238n54

Mnogoglasie, 50, 52, 248n76. *See also* Singing (liturgical): abuses

Mnogoletie (Many Years, acclamation). *See under* Singing (liturgical)

Mode (ancient Greek), 126

Mohilev, 100

Molière, 169–70, 218, 219, 223, 310n47

Monasteries: Andreevskii Monastery, 241n13; Annunciation (Blagoveshchenskii) Monastery (Supraśl), 100–101; Chudov (Miracles) Monastery, 64, 68, 254n17; Epiphany (Bogoiavlenskii) Monastery (Polotsk), 45, 100; Iverskii Monastery, 33, 45, 100, 243n32; Kievan Caves (Kievo-Pecherskii) Monastery, 100, 289n168; Pafnut'ev (St. Paphnu-

tius) Monastery, 75, 254n22; Resurrection-New Jerusalem (Voskresenskii Novoierusalimskii) Monastery, 33, 64, 66, 68, 70, 75, 100, 241n15, 243n32 (*see also Kanty* and Psalm Settings: German); St. Macarius Yellow Lake (Makar'ev-Zheltovodskii) Monastery (Nizhnii Novgorod), 149; St. Savva Monastery, 30, 47, 149; Solovetskii Monastery, 254n21; Trinity-St. Sergius Monastery, 3, 83

Mons, Anna (foreign resident of Moscow), 103, 270n92

Morozov, Boris Ivanovich (boyar), 84

Mosal'skii, Vasilii Mikhailovich (prince), 19, 236n35

Mudrost' chetvertaia Musikia (The Fourth Art: Music), 126–27, 287n156

Mundy, Peter (English traveler), 261n21

Muscovite Court Theater: actors and participants, 169, 171–73, 181, 183–84, 187, 188–89, 201, 297n69, 299n79, 303n114; actors and participants (students from Foreign Quarter), 55, 93, 174, 294n32, 296n52, 301n102; *Aleksei, Man of God* (*Aleksei chelovek bozhii*), 206–207; audience (viewing arrangements), 163, 176; dance in, 173–74, 185–86, 203, 206, 294n33, 303n114; imagery associated with, 54–55, 165, 250n89; influences from diplomatic exchange, 166–71, 180, 196, 208, 291n8, 292n10; influences from Muscovite performance traditions, 164, 179, 290n1; *interscenia* (*intermedia*), 188–90, 196, 203–207, 208, 302n105; opposition to, 102, 171; Orpheus, 173–80, 183–84, 186, 188, 205, 206, 207, 223–24 (*see also* Orpheus (Muscovite court entertainment)); performance dates, 163, 175, 185, 187, 199, 200, 202, 298n72, 301n99, 302n105; Reutenfels, 164–65, 209; sources (archival), 188, 190, 191, 194, 195, 299nn77–78, 302n105, 304n126; themes and plots, 164, 181, 187, 188–90, 202, 206–207, 301n99; venues, 172, 180, 183–84, 185, 211, 294n28, 295n41

Muscovite Court Theater, Music, 187–88, 296n51; Hebrew psalm texts, 192–95,

Muscovite Court Theater (*continued*)
198–99, 208; influences from Muscovite
musical traditions, 164, 184–86, 197–98,
202, 208; instrumental ensemble assembled for, 16, 172, 181–86, 190, 196, 203,
298n72; instrumental music used in,
190, 191–92, 196–97, 200, 202–204, 208–
209, 303n114; *interscenia* (*intermedia*),
196, 203–207, 208, 302n105; laments,
189, 191–95, 196, 197–99, 200–202, 204–
205, 207, 208–209, 300n97; organ, 97,
172, 182, 183–86, 197; strophic singing,
190–91, 194–97, 200–202, 204–205, 207,
208, 302n111; structure created by
music, 188, 190, 192, 199, 200, 203–204,
208–209, 299n80

Muscovite Court Theater, Plays: *Adam
and Eve, The Mournful Comedy of
(Zhalobnaia komediia ob Adame i Eve)*,
200–202, 208, 250n89, 301n99, 304n126;
Aleksei, Man of God, see under Muscovite Court Theater; *Artaxerxes
(Artaksertsovo deistvo)*, 174, 181, 186–87,
188–99, 202, 204, 206, 207, 208–209,
296n51, 301n99; *Bacchus and Venus*
(lost), 200, 301n99, 303n114; *David and
Goliath* (lost), 301n99, 303n114; *Joseph,
The Small and Refreshing Comedy of
(Malaia prokhladnaia komediia ob
Iosife)*, 301nn99–100, 304n126; *Judith
(Iudif')*, 174, 199–200, 204–206, 208,
296n51, 298n72, 301n99, 302n111;
*Nebuchadnezzar, King (O Navkhodono-
sore tsare*, Polotskii), 44, 200, 202–204
206–207, 301n99, 302nn105,109;
Orpheus, see Muscovite Court Theater:
Orpheus, Orpheus (Muscovite court
entertainment); *Prodigal Son, The Para-
ble of the (Komidiia pritchi o bludnem
syne,* Polotskii), 200, 202–203, 205–206,
208–209, 301n99, 302n105, 304n126; *St.
George, Comedy of the Miracle of
(Komediia o chude sviatogo Georgiia,*
lost), 301n99; *Tamerlane, Play of
(Temir-Aksakovo deistvo)*, 202, 205, 207,
295n42, 301nn99–100; *Tobit the
Younger, Comedy of (Komediia o Tovii
mladshem,* lost), 199, 301n99

Muscovy Company. *See* Russia (Muscovy)
Company

Muscovy, Western Views of. *See* Western
Views of Muscovy

Music Notation: *azbuki* (listings of
neumes), 3, 106, 148, 284n134;
dvoznamenniki, 106, 148–49, 157,
284n136; figured bass, 99, 137, *138;*
Kievan notation, 33, 153, 284n136;
Mezenets and commission, 55, 105–106,
249n78 (*see also* Mezenets, Aleksandr,
Singing (liturgical): reforms and codifications); neumed notation, 3, 31, 59,
145, 147, 240n10, 258n54, 284nn134,136;
staff notation (Muscovite sources), 30,
31–33, 46, 70, 93, *95,* 148–49, 240n10,
249n78, 284n136; staff notation (non-
Muscovite sources), 49, 99, 100,
286n153. *See also* Music Printing, Music
Scribes, Music Theory, Muscovite and
Russian

Music Printing, 100, 160–61, 214, 266n56,
269n82, 289nn174–75, 305n6

Music Scribes, 27, 30, 58, 240nn10–11,
242n22

Music Theory, Muscovite and Russian:
chant theory, 145, 147–50, 157,
284nn132,138; eighteenth-century Russian sources, 159–62, *160–61,* 214;
Kratkosobrannaia mussikiia (A Brief
Resume of Music), 154–55, 288nn158–
59; musical hand, 121, 155–62, *156, 160–
61; Nauka vseia musikii* (The Complete
Science of Music), 153, 287nn154–55;
soglasiia, 147–48, 157, 284n135; Tikhon
Makar'evskii, 149–50, 153, 284n136,
285n140, 287nn154,156. *See also* Diletskii, Nikolai, *Grammatika* (music-
theoretical contents), Korenev,
Ioannikii

Music Theory, Western, 141–44, 147–48,
150–52, *151,* 157–58, *158,* 284n135; in
eighteenth-century Russia, 214, 305n6.
See also under Diletskii, Nikolai, *Grammatika* (music-theoretical contents

Musical Circles. *See* Circles of Fifths, Diletskii, Nikolai, *Grammatika* (music-
theoretical contents): musical circles

Musical Hand. *See* Diletskii, Nikolai, *Grammatika* (music-theoretical contents): musical hand, Music Theory, Muscovite and Russian

Musical Instruments, 11; belonging to royal children, 89–90, 92, 264n48, 266n55; court use and performers, 85–96, 96–97, 98, 101–102, 184–86, 213–14, 291n9; defined in foreign glossaries, 80–82, 258n55; "*musikiia*" (and variants) as descriptive term, 24, 104, 112, 259n5, 302n105; played by foreign musicians in Muscovy (general), 15–16, 17–18, 62, 96–98, 101, 170–71, 177, 261n21; prohibited in Russian Orthodox church, 3, 4, 14–15, 18, 48, 74–76, 79, 231n16, 248n73, 260n8; *stramenty*, 185, 265n53, 298n72; Ukrainian and Belorusian influences, 93, 95, 98–101, 266n62; used in West, 14, 85, 98–101, 167. *See also* Fanfare and Processional Music, Muscovite Court Theater, Music, *Skomorokhi*, Weddings, *and under individual musical instrument families*

Musikiia (as term). *See under* Musical Instruments (general)

Musin-Pushkin, I. A. (boyar), 240n10

Musorgskii, Modest, 308n34; *Boris Godunov* (opera), 10, 11

Natal'ia Alekseevna (Tsarevna, daughter of Aleksei Mikhailovich), 210–211, 296n51, 304n128

Natal'ia Naryshkina (Tsaritsa, second wife of Aleksei Mikhailovich), 163, 179, 298n75. *See also* Aleksei Mikhailovich: period of marriage to Natal'ia Naryshkina

Nauka vseia musikii (The Complete Science of Music), 153, 287nn154–55

Nemetskaia sloboda. *See* Foreign Quarter (*Nemetskaia sloboda*, Moscow)

Neronov, Ioann (priest), 259nn3,7

Niemojewski, Stanisław (Polish merchant), 233nn13–14; uprising and deaths of Dmitrii and Polish musicians, 23, 238nn46,54; wedding of Dmitrii and Marina, 14, 19–20, 88, 235n31, 236n36, 237n38

Nikon (Patriarch of Russia), 45, 241n15; musical interests of, 28, 33, 40, 47–48, 49, 55, 64, 66, 243nn31–32, 250n84; reforms of, 4, 49–52, 56, 245n48, 246n58, 248n76

Nizhnii Novgorod, 86, 149. *See also* Ascension, Feast of

Novgorod, 261n22; liturgical singing traditions, 2–3, 5, 31, 33, 55, 242n27, 248n70; *skomorokhi*, 5, 15, 21

O penii bozhestvennom. *See* Korenev, Ioannikii

Okenfuss, Max, 53, 70, 178

Old Believers, 52–55, 75–76, 250n84, 252n8. *See also* Avvakum

Olearius, Adam (Holstein diplomat), 43, 84, 97, 215, 246n57, 257n43; burning of instruments, 79, 86, 96, 97, 213, 259n6; illustrations of instruments, 81, *87;* Russian singing, 74, *87; skomorokhi*, 79, 81, 86–87, *87;* wedding practices, 78, 231n16, 267n66

Oleśnicki, Mikołaj (Castellan of Małogość, Polish diplomat), 20, 23, 235n27, 236n36, 239n55

Ontsyforov, Kharka (played role of Chaldean), 246n55

Opyt irmoloinago peniia (A Method of Irmologii Singing, 1798), 161–62, *161,* 289n176

Organs and Keyboard Instruments, *94,* 103; associated with Dmitrii and Marina, 14, 23, 80; associated with Muscovite court theater, 97, 172, 182, 183–86; associated with Western circles of fifths, 143–44; court use and performers, 78, 88, 90–93, *94,* 96–98, 101, 183–86, 260n8, 265nn50–51,53; defined in foreign glossaries, 81–82, 265n51; in Diletskii, 111, 116–17, 121, 123, 130, 131, 136, 137–39, *138,* 144; Horsey's delivery of, 4, 16, 82, 95, 97, 234n23; imagery associated with, 53–55, 91, 251n90, 265n54; owned by Muscovite elite, 92, 96, 184; *tsynbaly* and players, 88, 90–92, 96–97, 263n40, 265n51; Uniate influence, 98–101, 269n87; used in West, 14, 167, 291n9. *See also* Weddings

Ornithoparchus, Andreas (music theorist), 152

Orpheus (mythological figure), 103, 124, 125, 152, 177–79, 278n63

Orpheus (Muscovite court entertainment), 173–80, 207, 223–24, 295n41; music, 177, 186, 188; participants and roles, 176–77, 178–79, 183–84, 205, 206; Reutenfels, 173–76, 295n38; sources describing, 174–77

Ovid, 177, 178

Ozanam, Jacques (music theorist), 142, 144, 283n124

Paisios (Metropolitan of Gaza), 75

Paisios (Patriarch of Alexandria), 51–53. *See also* Church Councils (1666–67)

Paisios (Patriarch of Constantinople), 51–52, 213

Paleologue, Zoe (Sofiia) (married to Grand Prince Ivan III), 245n51, 265n50

Palm Sunday Procession, 41, 245n48, 257n44. *See also* Easter

Panchenko, Aleksandr, 44–45

Paris, 169–70, 215, 218–20, 223–24, 260n14, 293n20

Partesnoe penie, 33, 70, 100, 240nn9,11, 249n78, 250n84, 256nn33,38, 276n41, 284n132; discussed at Church Councils (1666–67), 50–52; in theoretical writings, 106, 149, 154, 287n156. *See also Kontserty*

Paschales (singer), 2, 229n3

Patriarchal Singers. *See* Singers (liturgical): patriarchal ensembles

Patriarchate (Russian), 1–3, 28, 71. *See also* Iov (Patriarch of Russia)

Patriarchs. *See individual names of patriarchs*

Patriarshie pevchie d'iaki. See Singers (liturgical): patriarchal ensembles

Paul of Aleppo (Syrian cleric), 29, 30, 39–40, 43, 246n58, 257n43, 261n25; convents, 29, 241n18, 242n20; organs, 99; religious processions and readings, 40–41, 45, 72, 244nn41,43, 257n46; singing styles, 47–49, 248nn69–70, 300n97

Paulsen, Anna (director of theatrical troupe), 93, 182–83, 297n63

Pazukhin, Semen Ivanovich (poet, court servitor), 258n52

Penitential Verses (*pokaiannye stikhi*), 58–60, 62, 69–70, 73, 164, 198, 252nn7–8, 253n12. *See also* Adam's Lament

Pepys, Samuel, 217

Percussion Instruments (general), 81–82, 89–90, 93, 98, 101, 185, 263n42; associated with *skomorokhi*, 15, 17, 22, 86. *See also* Fanfare and Processional Music

Pereira, Thomas (Portuguese Jesuit), 85, 263n34

Persia, 91; and organs, 92, 183, 184, 265n50. *See also* Muscovite Court Theater, Plays: *Artaxerxes,* Muscovite Court Theater: themes and plots

Peter (the Great, Tsar), 24, 63, 92, 102–103, 163, 209, 210, 220–21, 309n45; assemblies, 96, 214, 267n68; music in victory celebrations, 64, 71, 83, 213, 256n41 (*see also* Fanfare and Processional Music: Petrine era); musical activities in childhood, 89–90, 93, 264n46; musical talents of, 30, 103, 213

Petreius, Peter (Swedish diplomat), 221, 223, 308n33

Philip IV (King of Spain), 169

Pickleherring (stock comic character), 176–77, 179, 183, 205, 223–24, 295n42, 297n69, 302n112

Pix, Mary (playwright), 222, 309n45

Play of the Furnace (liturgical drama), 41–44, 187–88, 203, 245n51, 247n59, 302n109; non-liturgical actors, 42–43; origins, 42, 245nn50–51; roles of Chaldeans, 42–43, 246nn54–55,57–58

Poisson, Raymond (French actor, playwright), 218–20, 222

Poland: diplomatic exchanges with, 166–67, 169, 172, 224. *See also* Diletskii, Nikolai: biography, Dmitrii (Pretender, Tsar), Marina Mniszech

Polikarpov, Fedor (translator of rhetoric treatise), 159

Polish Musicians. *See under* Dmitrii (Pretender, Tsar), Marina Mniszech

Polotsk, 45, 100, 247n63, 268n81

Polotskii, Simeon (monk, poet, teacher), 56, 70, 177–79, 271n3, 272n8, 273n16; declamations, 45–46, 100, 171, 179, 203; library of, 177–79, 288n162; plays for court theater, 44, 200, 202–204, 205–207, 208–209, 293n24, 298n75, 301n99, 302nn105–106,109 (*see also* Muscovite Court Theater, Plays); Psalter translation and musical setting by Titov, 63–64, 66, 67–70, 74, 101, 193–94, 197, 253n16, 254nn17,22; teaching activities, 46–47, 63, 110, 172, 293n24; writing (poetry, art), 56, 125, 145, 177, 210, 251n96, 278n64, 298n75

Poltava (military victory, 1709), 71, 213, 220–21

Ponyrko, Natal'ia, 60, 253n12

Posol'skii prikaz. Se e Diplomatic Chancellery

Potemkin, Petr Ivanovich (Muscovite ambassador), 84–85, 169–70, 217, 262n32, 293n20, 306n18; attendance at London theaters, 84–85, 220; attendance at Paris theaters, 169–70, 218–20, 223

Poteshnaia palata (Entertainment Hall), 91, 265n49

Povest' o Gore-Zlochastii (Misery-Luckless-Plight, secular narrative poem), 198, 300n98

Praskov'ia Fedorovna (Tsaritsa, wife of Ivan Alekseevich), 74, 210–211

Preobrazhenskoe, 183, 185, 211

Processional Music. *See* Fanfare and Processional Music

Proskurovskii, Iurii (organist, *tsynbal'nik*), 91, 267n64

Protopopov, Vladimir, 71, 109–110, 154–55, 281nn90,100, 287n155

Prussia, 174, 181, 182

Pskov, 181, 182

Pythagoras, 126, 152, 279n70

Relazione della segnalata (1605), 234n18

Reporte of a Bloudie and Terrible Massacre in the Citty of Moscow, The (1607), 20, 21, 22, 23, 232n8

Repskii, Vasilii (singer, instrumentalist), 46–47, 171–73, 184, 186, 247n67, 293nn23–24, 297n65

Reutenfels, Jacob (Courlander at Muscovite court), 43, 260n8, 267n66, 295n39; description of Muscovite theatrical presentations, 164–65, 170, 173–76, 177, 179, 187, 209, 295n38

Rhetoric and Rhetoric Treatises, 113, 125, 130, 139, 145; Belobotskii, 145, 283n128; circulation in Muscovy, 126–27, 130, 145, 278n58, 279n73; *Concha,* 128, 278n60, 280n79; Diletskii, *see* Diletskii, Nikolai: *Grammatika* (non-musical models); Galiatovskii, 278n60; Iavorskii, 158–59; Makarii, 127, 279n73, 280n76; Usachev, 130, 278n58, 281n87. *See also* Education

Riati, Antonio (Italian jester), 88, 263n41

Ridley, Mark (English physician, compiler of glossary), 82, 265n51

Riga, 181, 297n63

Rinhuber, Laurent (Saxon physician), 163, 175–76, 179, 186–87, 197, 210, 295n39, 299n79

Robinet, Charles (Parisian gazetteer), 170, 218

Rode, Andrei (chronicler of Danish embassy), 97

Roizman, Leonid, 90, 91, 96–97

Romanov, Nikita Ivanovich (boyar), 84, 92, 96, 97

Rome, 84, 155, 175, 186, 208, 279n70, 295n39

Rosenberg (Rosenburg; participant in Orpheus entertainment), 176, 295n42

Rostov, 86, 274n24

Rostovskii, Dimitrii (Metropolitan of Rostov), 67, 227

Różycki, Jacek (composer), 111, 157, 273n14

Russia (Muscovy) Company, 5, 26, 222

Russian Far North, 26, 82, 86, 215. *See also* Kholmogory, Arkhangel'sk

St. Nicholas, Feast of, 19

St. Petersburg, 107, 211, 273n16, 301n103

Sandomierz, Voevoda of (father of Marina Mniszech), 19, 20, 23–24

Sauvage, Jean (French trader, compiler of glossary), 81, 265n51, 276n42

Schaum, Matthias (writer), 308n35

Schleussing (Schleussinger), Georg Adam (Saxon in Muscovy), 210, 217, 248n73, 267n66

School Drama. *See* Education: theatrical presentations in non-Muscovite curricula

Schütz, Heinrich (composer), 173, 178–79

Shaidur, Ivan (singer), 31

Shakespeare, William, 215, 216, 220, 222, 290n6, 306n12, 309n40

Shuiskii, Vasilii (Tsar), 20, 234n19, 238n47

Sidney, Philip (poet), 215

Simeon (archbishop of Vologda and Belozersk), 31

Simeon (Metropolitan of Smolensk), 38, 109, 244n35

Singers (liturgical): Belarusian, *see* Singers (liturgical): *vspevaki;* duties (liturgical), 26, 27, 28, 38–39, 40–44, 51, 244n39; duties (non-liturgical), 30, 39–41, 49, 58, 71, 77–79, 244nn40–41,43, 256n41, 261n25 (*see also* Play of the Furnace); eighteenth century, 49, 213, 304n2; Greek, 2, 3, 28–29, 51, 229n3, 230n10, 241n15; *krestovye d'iaki*, 28, 38–39, 57, 58, 240n12; nuns, 29–30, 48, 241n18, 242nn21–22 (*see also* Women: convents); origins, 26–27; patriarchal ensembles (*patriarshie pevchie d'iaki*), 2–3, 27, 49, 51; regional ensembles, 2, 3, 27, 31, 38, 39, 51; size of ensembles, 3, 18, 27; sovereign's ensembles (*gosudarevy pevchie d'iaki*), 2–3, 27, 51, 63, 64, 77–79, 254n21; *stanista* system, 2, 3, 27, 31, 39, 58, 240n6, 254n20; Ukrainian, *see* Singers (liturgical): *vspevaki; vspevaki*, 28, 31–33, 46, 47, 50, 64, 66, 68, 171, 241n14, 243n31, 271n6; wages and payment, 27, 38–39, 245n51. *See also* Music Scribes, Singing (liturgical), *and names of individual singers*

Singing (liturgical): abuses, 3–4, 50, 52, 55, 248n76, 249n77; Adam's Lament ("Plach Adama"), 59, 164, 198, 202, 252n8 (*see also* Muscovite Court The-ater, Music: laments, Penitential Verses); chant books and collections, 30, 46, 59, 78, 100, 161, 242nn22,27, 259n3, 289n174 (*see also* Diletskii, Nikolai: liturgical texts and books cited); chant types and styles, 3, 31, *32*, 39, 71, 77–79, 100, 275n32 [*see also* Sing-ing (liturgical): *troestrochnoe*]; in Greek, 2, 4, 51, 230n5, 241n15, 244n43, 245n46, 249n80; historical elements in, 71–72, 256nn39,41; *mnogoglasie*, 50, 52, 248n76 [*see also* Singing (liturgical): abuses]; *mnogoletie* (Many Years, acclamation), 2, 3, 77, 203, 230n5, 249n80, 256n41, 258n1; penitential verses (*pokaiannye stikhi*), 58–60, 62, 69–70, 73, 164, 198, 252nn7–8, 253n12 (*see also* Adam's Lament); reforms and codifications, 31, 49–52, 55, 105–106, 243n30, 248n76, 273n16; *troestrochnoe* (*strochnoe*), 31, *32*, 51, 78–79, 249n81, 275n32, 277n54; Uniate Church, 98–101. *See also* Kontserty, Novgorod: liturgical singing traditions, *Partesnoe penie*

Singing (non-liturgical and secular), 4, 249n80, 263n36; Adam's Lament ("Plach Adama"), 59, 164, 198, 202, 252n8 (*see also* Muscovite Court The-ater, Music: laments, Penitential Verses); at banquets, *see* Banquets; *bogomol'tsy*, 57–60, 68–69, 92, 253n11; caroling and carols, 39, 49, 62, 69, 244n41; domestic, 60, 62, 63, 73–74, 253n16 (*see also* Balatri, Filippo, *Kanty and Psalm Settings*, Women); *iurodivyi/iurodstvo* (Holy Fool), 60, 68–69, 253n11; mendicant singers, 49, 58–60, 68–69, 251n2; penitential verses (*pokaiannye stikhi*), 58–60, 62, 69–70, 73, 164, 198, 252nn7–8, 253n12 (*see also* Adam's Lament). *See also Kanty and Psalm Settings*, Works, *Skomorokhi*

Skazanie o sedmi svobodnykh mudrostekh (A History of the Seven Liberal Arts), 126–27, 286n148

Skomorokhi: associations with Dmitrii, 21–22, 88, 237nn42–43, 238n49; associa-tions with Play of the Furnace, 42–43,

246n54 (*see also* Play of the Furnace); bears, 17, 86, 259n7 (*see also* Bears); dance, 4, 15, 17, 21–22, 86, 87–88; defined and depicted in foreign accounts and glossaries, 80–82, *87,* 259n7, 260n10; denunciations and prohibitions, 4–5, 17, 44, 79–80, 86–87, 96, 253n16; musical instruments and performances associated with, 4–5, 11, 15, 17, 21–24, 53, 79–82, 85–89, *87,* 93–96, 263nn36,42; Novgorodian associations, 5, 15, 21; singing associated with, 4–5, 15, 17, 86, 101, 263n36; wedding associations, 5, 17, 87–89, 95–96, 101–102

Skopin-Shuiskii, M. V. (military leader), 72

Skrzolotowicz, Petr (compiler of *kant* texts), 62–63, 64–66, 68, 97, 101, 147

Slavinetskii, Epifanii (monk, teacher), 53–54, 241n13, 250n86, 285n144; *kanty*, 61, *61,* 64, 228

Slavynets'kyi. *See* Slavinetskii, Epifanii

Smith, Thomas (English agent in Muscovy), 222

Smolensk, 41, 91, 184, 268n81; Diletskii and, 106, 107, 109, 147, 274n17; Marina Mniszech in, 14, 233nn9,14; musical styles associated with, 14, 38, 109, 244n35. *See also* Diletskii, Nikolai, *Grammatika* (general): sources and versions

Smotritskii, Meletii (monk, writer), 122, 278n64, 286n148

Smotryts'kiy. *See* Smotritskii, Meletii

Sofiia Alekseevna (Tsarevna, regent), 30, 63, 74, 210, 242n22, 304n127

Songs. *See under Kanty* and Psalm Settings, Works, Singing (non-liturgical and secular), Singing (liturgical)

Sovereign's singers. *See* Singers (liturgical): sovereign's ensembles

Spafarii, Nikolai (Moldovan scholar, writer), 126, 178, 286nn148–49

Spangenberg, Johann (music theorist), 152, 286n148

Sparwenfeld, Johan (Swedish representative in Muscovy), 33, 261n22, 304n126; glossary, 258n55, 259n7

Spiritual Regulation (Peter the Great), 242n21, 251n2, 305n5

Staden, Nicholas von (agent for Muscovy), 180–84

Stadnicki, Martyn (head of Marina Mniszech's court), 20, 233n14, 234n22, 236n32, 237n39

Starowolski, Szymon (music theorist), *114, 115,* 150–52, 286n148, 287n155, 289n168

Stefan (*iurodivyi*), 60, 68–69

Stepanov, Meletii (Melentii, *tsynbal'nik*), 91, 263n40

Stockholm, 181, 182

Stoglav Council, 4, 17, 87

Storytellers. *See* Entertainers at Muscovite Court

Stramenty, 185, 265n53, 298n72

Stringed Instruments, 74, 75, 80–82, 87–88, *87, 95;* associated with foreigners, 96–98, 177; associated with Muscovite court theater, 172, 182–83, 185; court use and performers, 85–90, 92–94, *95,* 186, 264n44; defined in foreign glossaries, 80–82, 258n55; in Diletskii, 130; *gusli,* 15, 17, 56, 75–76, 80–82, 85–89, *87,* 93, *95,* 130, 178, 186, 264n44, 267n65, 274n24; *liutnia,* 75, 93, 258n55; in Olearius, 74, 87, *87;* owned by Muscovite elite, 92; played by *skomorokhi,* 15, 17, 86–89, *87,* 95–96, 263n42

Stroganov, Grigorii Dmitrievich, 29, 110, 111. *See also* Diletskii, Nikolai, *Grammatika* (non-musical models): dedication to Stroganov

Stroganov Family, 29, 59–60, 110, 111, 241n16

Supraśl, 100–101

Surna. See Fanfare and Processional Music

Sweden, 172, 181, 182, 213, 220–21

Synodal Choir, 160, 213, 304n2

Synodal Press, 160–161, *160–61,* 289n174

Tanner, Bernard (chronicler of Polish embassy), 98, 262n27

Tectander, Georg (Imperial diplomat), 265n50

Terem, 28, 74, 89, 103

Theater. *See* Muscovite Court Theater

Theodoli, Giuseppi (playwright), 222

Theophanes (Patriarch of Jerusalem), 4, 5, 230n10, 231n16

Tikhon Makar'evskii (music theorist), 149–50, 153, 284n136, 285n140, 287nn154,156

Time of Troubles: events of, 10–11, 15, 220, 221, 231n3, 234n19; music and musical imagery associated with, 11, 15, 21–22, 59, 72–73, 257n48; Western dramatic works depicting, 221–23, 309nn41–42. *See also* Dmitrii (Pretender, Tsar), Ivan IV, Marina Mniszech, Western Views of Muscovy

Titov, Vasilii (singer, composer): *kontserty, 36–37,* 38, 64, 71, 129, 146; setting of Polotskii Psalter translation, 63–64, 74, 93, 101, 197, 254nn20,22 (*see also under* Polotskii, Simeon)

Toasts (*chashi*), 2–3, 71–72, 257nn43–44

Tobol'sk, 31, 53, 279n70

Tolstoi, Petr (Muscovite official), 209–210, 293n26, 303n123

Tonality. *See* Circles of Fifths (Western), Diletskii, Nikolai, *Grammatika* (music-theoretical contents): musical circles

Tragoedia Moscovitica (1608), 13, 21, 232n8

Trondheim Vocabulary (glossary), 81, 260n17

Trubetskoi, Iu. P. (boyar), 206–207

Tsars. *See individual names of tsars*

Turbervile, George (English traveler), 307n27

Turks, Turkey, 180, 186, 207, 261n21, 306n12, 307n27; depicted in Western dramatic works, 218, 219–20. *See also* Western Views of Muscovy

Ukrainian Singers. *See* Singers (liturgical): *vspevaki*

Uniate Church (Eastern Rite Catholics), 272n8, 279n70; musical influences from, 98–101

Usachev, Mikhail (author of rhetoric treatise), 130, 278n58, 281n87

Ushakov, Simon (icon painter), 56, 123, 251n96, 253n16, 278n64

Uspenskii, Boris, 21–22, 56

"Ut queant laxis," 154–55, 284n135, 288n161. *See also* Diletskii, Nikolai, *Grammatika* (music-theoretical contents): hexachordal syllables and solmization

Vasil'ev, Sava (treasury employee, played role of Chaldean), 43, 246n55

Vasilii III (Grand Prince), 245n46

Venice, 102, 209–210, 303n123

Veselye (merry-makers, merry folk), 43, 88, 263n42. *See also Skomorokhi*

Vesti-kuranty. See Kuranty

Vienna, 102–104, 208, 209, 295n39

Vilnius, 272n8; Diletskii and, 66, 106, 107–109, 123–24, 147, 157, 272n8; Franciscan Press, 107, 108–109. *See also under* Diletskii, Nikolai: biography

Vilnius (Jesuit) College, 108–109, 125, 127, 272n13, 282n121

Vivaty, 71. *See also* Fanfare and Processional Music: Petrine era, Peter (the Great, Tsar): music in victory celebrations

Vladimirov, Iosif (icon painter), 56

Vlas'ev, Afanasii Ivanovich (Muscovite diplomat), 12, 19, 236n35

Vologda, 31, 44, 98, 170–71, 242n27, 247n59. *See also* Muscovite Court Theater: sources (archival)

Vorob'ev, Evgenii, 271n3, 285n140, 289n176

Vorotynskii Family, 92, 96–97

Waldemar (Danish King), 85

Warachtige ende eygentlijcke Beschryvinghe (1606), 232n8

Warsaw, 167, 273n14

Weddings, 5, 38, 92, 101–102, 231n16, 259n3, 269n87; Aleksei Mikhailovich, 44, 77–79, 87–88, 192, 101–102, 259n3, 267n66; dancing associated with, 95–96, 267nn66,68; instrumental fanfare associated with, 18, 77–78, 86, 101, 235n31, 258n2, 259n5; instrumental music associated with, 78, 87–89, 101, 267n66; laments, 73, 300n97; Mikhail Fedorovich, 77–78, 87–89, 94–95,

258nn1–2, 263n42, 267n64; *skomorokhi,*
5, 17, 87–89, 95–96, 101–102. *See also
under* Dmitrii (Pretender, Tsar),
Marina Mniszech
Weimar. *See* Muscovite Court Theater:
sources (archival)
Werckmeister, Andreas, 142, 143–44
Western Views of Muscovy, 215–16, 220–
23, 308nn35–36, 309nn42,45; *Boris
Goudenow* (Mattheson, 1710), 220–21,
223; *Faux Moscovites, Les* (Poisson,
1668), 218–20, 222; influences from visiting Muscovite diplomats, 216–18, 219,
309n45; plays and poetry reflecting,
215–16, 217, 309nn41,45. *See also under*
Dmitrii (Pretender, Tsar), Ivan IV,
Time of Troubles
Wich, John and Cyrill (English diplomats), 221, 308n33
Wind Instruments, 92, 93, 95, 98, 101,

261n21; associated with Muscovite court
theater, 182; defined in foreign glossaries, 81–82, 276n42; played by
skomorokhi, 5, 15, 17, 22, 86. *See also*
Fanfare and Processional Music
Women, 171, 293n20; convents, 29–30, 48,
241n18, 242nn20–22, 300n97; and music
making, 28, 72–73, 74, 89, 92–93, 103,
266n60, 300n97; spiritual qualities of,
58, 252n4. *See also* Balatri, Filippo,
Dancing, Muscovite Court Theater,
Music: laments, Singing (liturgical):
nuns, Singing (non-liturgical): domestic, *Terem*

Zamarevich (composer), 111
Zaval'skii, Fedor (organist), 91, 94
Zheliabuzhskii, Ivan (Muscovite ambas-
sador), 292n13
Ziuska (composer), 111

CLAUDIA R. JENSEN has published articles on
Russian music in *The Musical Quarterly* and *Journal of the
American Musicological Society.* She co-edited Nikolai Findeizen's
History of Music in Russia from Antiquity to 1800
(Indiana University Press, 2008).